Criminological Theory: Past to Present

Essential Readings

Francis T. Cullen
University of Cincinnati

Robert Agnew
Emory University

Roxbury Publishing Company
Los Angeles, California

Library of Congress Cataloging-in-Publication Data

Cullen, Francis T.
Criminological Theory: Past to Present/ by Francis T. Cullen, Robert Agnew
p. cm.
Includes bibliographical references and index.
ISBN 0-935732-91-8 (acid-free paper)
1. Criminology. I. Agnew, Robert, 1953- . II. Title
HV6025.C85 1999
364—dc21   97-33460
                                                                        CIP

Criminological Theory: Past to Present *(Essential Readings)*

Publisher and Editor: Claude Teweles
Editor: Sacha Howells
Assistant Editor: Dawn VanDercreek
Production Assistants: Carla Max-Ryan and David Massengill
Typography: Synergistic Data Systems
Cover Design: Marnie Deacon Kenney

Printed on acid-free paper in the United States of America. This paper meets the standards for recycling of the Environmental Protection Agency.

ISBN 0-935732-91-8

ROXBURY PUBLISHING COMPANY
P.O. Box 491044
Los Angeles, California 90049-9044
Tel: (213) 653-1068 • Fax: (213) 653-4140
Email: roxbury@crl.com

Table of Contents

Preface

Criminology is a field rich in theoretical imagination. To an extent, this diversity of theorizing reflects the discipline's immaturity—its inability as of yet to develop a single paradigm that is so empirically superior to its competitors that it earns the allegiance of most scholars. But criminology's richness also is a manifestation of the complexity of its subject matter. Like much social behavior, crime is multifaceted and potentially shaped by a range of factors that operate inside and outside individuals, that exist on the macro level and the micro level, and that have effects across various points in the life cycle. Illuminating what causes crime is thus a daunting task that benefits from efforts to view its origins from many angles and through different colored lenses.

This volume attempts to capture the diversity of thinking on crime causation that now prevails within criminology. As we surveyed the large and growing body of theoretical criminology, it became apparent that a surplus of worthy contributions was available; this reader easily could have doubled in size. The practicalities of editing a single volume of manageable length and appropriate for classroom use, however, required that we make tough choices as to what to include and what, regrettably, to omit. In doing so, two principles guided our decision making.

First, we attempted to select the most essential readings—that is, works that have had or are now having the largest impact on criminological theory and research. These writings either were instrumental in creating a theoretical tradition or subsequently extended an existing perspective in noteworthy ways.

Second, we included contributions that illuminated the development of theories—works that, when taken together, showed the continuity and growth of ideas within theoretical perspectives from past to present. Criminological theory is dynamic, not static. Studying the past—the classic works—is needed both to understand the history of the discipline and to learn in detail how a scholar or scholars first set forth a distinct way of viewing crime causation. But classic works, while due their respect, should not be enshrined as having conveyed sacred truths that are beyond criticism and revision. Knowledge grows, and as this process unfolds new ideas develop that extend earlier statements of a theory. As Robert K. Merton observed, however far-sighted the "giants" in the field have been, those who stand "on the shoulders of giants" can see even farther.

In short, our goal was to select works that were essential readings and that revealed the development of criminological theory from past to present. One by-product of this approach is that this volume includes a good deal of material on contemporary criminological theories. Readers thus will become acquainted with the theoretical ideas that are most influential in the field of criminology today. At the same time, understanding the present requires understanding the past to see how classic statements inform and evolve into current theorizing. Accordingly, each part of the reader begins with an excerpt from one or more classic theoretical works that laid the foundation for a perspective, which then are followed by selections detailing contemporary versions of the theory.

The book is divided into 10 parts, each representing a distinct theoretical approach to the explanation of crime. To guide readers on their adventure across time (from past to present) and across theories, each of the volume's parts is preceded by a general introduction that places its readings in their scholarly context. For a given section, the introduction conveys the central thrust of a perspective; that is, it addresses what makes the theory unique or different from other explanations of crime. It also attempts to show how specific readings "fit into" the theoretical paradigm covered in that part of the book. Furthermore, we have written separate introductions for each of the 38 selections in the reader (which are arranged as chapters in this volume). These introductions should make the excerpts more understandable by pointing out the key issues that readers should attend to as they study each selection.

Although the contents of this reader ultimately are our responsibility, we were fortunate to be guided in our efforts to design this volume by a number of scholars who generously reviewed and provided advice on preliminary tables of contents. When their recommendations were compiled, we faced an embarrassment of riches; as noted there were just too many interesting and informative works to include in a single volume. We regret not following all of the wise guidance offered, but wish to thank all those who assisted us. With apologies to anyone inadvertently omitted, we appreciate the time and effort of Joanne Belknap, Robert Bohm, James Bonta, Meda Chesney-Lind, Kathleen Daly, Edna Erez, David Farrington, Diana Fishbein, Paul Gendreau, Mark Hamm, Stuart Henry, Nancy Jurik, Michael Lynch, Doris MacKenzie, Joan McDermott, Terrie Moffitt, Martin Schwartz, Sally Simpson, Mary Stohr, and Patricia Van Voorhis. We also benefitted from the insights of scholars who were commissioned by the publisher to review our prospectus: Ronald Akers, Gregg Barak (who provided additional advice to us at our request), Thomas Bernard, Dean Champion, Chris Eskridge, Gary LaFree, Steven Messner, Frank Scarpitti, Kip Schlegel, and Richard A. Wright.

We are grateful, of course, to the staff at Roxbury Publishing Company for their faith in the project and for their tolerance of our delays and idiosyncracies. Claude Teweles deserves our special praise not only for approving the project for publication but also for helping us to develop a collection of essays that would be accessible to and advance the learning of readers about to take their first trip across the landscape of criminological theory. We must recognize as well the expert assistance given to the project at Roxbury of Dawn VanDercreek, Carla Max-Ryan, Renee Burkhammer, Jim Ballinger, and David Massengill.

We also wish to thank for their support our respective academic units: the Division of Criminal Justice at the University of Cincinnati and the Department of Sociology at Emory University. Our colleagues and students have contributed in many ways to us personally and professionally. We must single out for credit Sharon Levrant, Jeff Maas, Deborah Schaefer, Jody Sundt, and Michael Turner, who provided invaluable assistance in various stages of the project.

Finally, we are most indebted to our families: Paula Dubeck and Jordan Cullen, and Mary, Willie, and Jenny Agnew. For their continuing love and presence, which give meaning and joy to our lives, we dedicate this book to them. ◆

Part I

Biological and Psychological Theories of Crime

Sociological theories of crime have dominated the discipline of criminology since at least the middle part of this century. This fact is reflected in this volume: most of the theories we present are sociological in nature, arguing that crime is a function of the individual's social environment, including family, school, peer group, workplace, community, and society. Before the rise of sociological theories, however, biological and psychological theories dominated the scientific literature.

It is important to study such theories for two reasons. First, they had an important effect on certain of the sociological theories which now dominate the literature. In some cases, sociological theories were developed partly in reaction to psychological theories. Merton (1938) begins his classic article "Social Structure and Anomie," for example, by attacking a core assumption of psychoanalytic theory: that crime results when people's biological drives are not properly controlled by social institutions (see Chapter 13 in Part IV). More commonly, however, sociological theories have drawn heavily on psychological theories. Certain versions of learning theory draw heavily on behavioral and social learning theory in psychology (see Part III), certain versions of strain theory draw on frustration-aggression and social learning theory

(see Part IV), and the assumptions which underlie control theories were popularized by psychoanalytic theory (see Part V). Many sociological theories, in fact, are built on a psychological base: they draw on many of the arguments and assumptions of psychological theories in their efforts to explain how the social environment fosters crime.

There is also a second and more important reason for studying biological and psychological theories. An understanding of these theories is necessary if we are to fully understand the causes of crime. Sociological theories focus on the effect of the social environment on crime; they specify which features of the social environment are important and how the social environment leads to crime. Certain psychological theories focus on the *processes by which individuals learn to behave.* Behavioral theory, for example, states that our behavior is a function of the reinforcements and punishments we receive: we repeat those behaviors which are reinforced and avoid those which are punished (see the Bandura and Akers articles in this volume for a fuller discussion). These learning theories help us understand *how* the social environment affects the individual (e.g., some families are more likely to produce delinquent children because they reinforce delinquency

1

more often and punish it less often than other families). Other psychological theories focus primarily on *individual traits*, such as intelligence, activity level, and emotional disposition. These traits are a function of environmental (e.g., family environment) and biological factors (e.g., genetic inheritance, brain injury). Such traits influence *how* individuals respond to their environment. Even though the social environment has an important influence on crime, we know that individuals often respond to the same environment in different ways. This difference in response may be due to differences in the above types of traits. A hyperactive child, for example, may be more likely to rebel against school authorities than a calm child. Individual traits may also influence the individual's environment. For example, individuals with irritable dispositions may call forth a different set of responses from family members and teachers than individuals with more agreeable dispositions. Irritable individuals may also end up sorting themselves into negative environments, like delinquent peer groups, bad marriages, and low-paying jobs (see the Moffitt article in this section).

A complete understanding of crime, then, requires a consideration of biological, psychological, and sociological factors. And some of the most recent theories of crime assign a central role to all three sets of factors (see the Wilson and Herrnstein and the Moffitt chapters). At the same time, however, it should be noted that there is still much debate over the importance that should be attributed to biological and psychological factors (as well as sociological factors). Many sociologists continue to discount the importance of biological and psychological factors (see the discussion in Andrews and Bonta, 1994; Andrews and Wormith, 1989; also see Gottfredson and Hirschi, 1990; Katz and Chambliss, 1995; and Vold and Bernard, 1986 for recent critiques of biological and/or psychological theories). Our reading of the evidence, however, leads us to believe that biological and psychological factors play at least some role in the generation of some crime— and that such factors *may* be especially important in understanding the behavior of chronic offenders (Raine, 1993, provides a comprehensive overview of much of this evidence).

Biological Theories

Biological theories were the dominant theories of crime around the turn of the century, and Lombroso's (1911) theory was the leading one (see Chapter 1 in this Part). These early theories were heavily influenced by Darwin's theory of evolution, as witnessed in Lombroso's argument that many criminals are "genetic throwbacks," primitive people in the midst of modern society. Lombroso was a physician working in the Italian penal system, and his examinations of convicts led him to develop a list of traits that could be used to determine if a person was one of these genetic throwbacks or "born criminals" (e.g., traits like large jaw and cheekbones, swollen or protruding lips, arm span greater than the individual's height, excessive wrinkling, prehensile foot). If you imagine what someone with these traits looks like, the image you get is that of the stereotypical "caveman." It should be noted that Lombroso increasingly came to recognize that environmental factors also play an important role in the explanation of crime, and he later argued that there were several different types of criminals, with the "born criminals" making up about one-third of all criminals.

Lombroso's theory and other early biological theories were rather simplistic in nature: they pointed to rather gross biological features that were said to distinguish criminals from noncriminals and they argued that biological factors often lead directly to crime. These theories were rigorously evaluated during the early to middle part of this century, with researchers comparing the traits of criminals to those of carefully matched samples of noncriminals (samples similar in age, class, race, etc. to the criminals being studied). Such comparisons provided little support for the early biological theories. This fact, along with a concern for the policy implications of these theories (e.g., selective breeding and sterilization, justification for racist policies), led to the decline of biological theories of crime (see Brennan et al., 1995; Raine, 1993; see Vold and Bernard, 1986 for an excellent overview of early biological theories).

There has, however, been a recent resurgence of interest in biological theories of crime. The newest biological theories differ from the early theories in several important ways. First, such theories focus on a broad range of biological factors, including genetic inheritance and environmental factors like head injuries, diet, exposure to toxins such as lead, and pregnancy and birth complications. These factors are said to affect individuals' nervous systems and thereby their behavior. A variety of studies have explored the different ways in which these factors might impact the nervous system, including numerous studies on brain structure and functioning. It is difficult to summarize these studies in a few sentences, but excellent treatments can be found in Brennan et al. (1995), Fishbein (1996), and Raine (1993). Second, these theories do not argue that biological factors lead directly to crime; for example, no one argues that there is a gene that leads inevitably to crime. Rather, the theories suggest that biological factors influence crime by affecting the processes by which individuals learn to behave and by affecting the development of traits conducive to crime. Biological factors, for example, may influence individuals' ability to learn from punishment or may increase the likelihood that individuals will develop traits like irritability and sensation seeking. Third, most biological theories now recognize that the impact of biological factors is influenced by the social environment. The social environment influences whether biological factors lead to the development of certain traits and whether these traits lead to crime. Birth complications, for example, may be more likely to result in crime among children in disrupted family environments. Modern biological theories, then, recognize the importance of psychological and sociological variables (see the Wilson and Herrnstein and the Moffitt selections for discussions of the interaction between biological, psychological, and sociological variables; see Brennan and Raine, forthcoming, for an excellent overview of the research on the interaction between biological and social factors).

Again, however, it should be recognized that some researchers remain skeptical of biological theories of crime (see the references cited above). And even the leading biological theorists are careful to note that the evidence only *suggests* that some biological factors partially account for some crime in some types of offenders, most often chronic offenders (who account for a majority of all serious crime).

Psychological Theories

Psychological theories became popular early in this century, but—like biological theories—they were soon overshadowed by sociological theories of crime. Psychological theories of crime, however, have also experienced a recent resurgence in interest. Freud's psychoanalytic theory was the leading psychological theory of crime early in this century, although it is no longer popular today. Many of the ideas underlying the theory, however, had an important effect on subsequent psychological and sociological theories (for overviews of psychoanalytic theory and its effect on contemporary theories, see Andrews and Bonta, 1994; Redl and Toch, 1979). Other psychological theories, like frustration-aggression theory, also experienced periods of popularity (see Berkowitz, 1989 for a discussion of the contemporary status of frustration-aggression theory). Today, however, two general categories of psychological theory are dominant: those that focus on individual traits and those that focus on the processes by which individuals learn to behave (with recent theories emphasizing both learning processes and individual differences). For recent overviews see Andrews and Bonta (1994), Blackburn (1993), Farrington (1994), Feldman (1993), Hollin (1989; 1992), and Shoham and Seis (1993).

Trait theories argue that individuals with certain traits are more likely to engage in crime in a given environment, are more likely to elicit negative responses from others (which may foster crime), and are more likely to sort themselves into negative environments (which may foster crime). For example, irritable individuals may be more likely to (1) respond to mild slights with aggression,

(2) provoke insults and challenges from others, and (3) associate with other criminals and have poor employment histories.

The selection by Glueck and Glueck (1950) describes some of the individual traits which may be related to crime. In their classic study, Glueck and Glueck compared 500 delinquents with 500 nondelinquents. They did not employ any one particular theoretical approach in their study, but very deliberately drew on a wide range of approaches. Nevertheless, their study attracted much attention because it challenged many of the dominant sociological theories of the time. Glueck and Glueck argued that individuals often respond to the same environment in different ways. Some individuals in disorganized neighborhoods, for example, become criminals while others do not. Glueck and Glueck argued that one must consider individual traits to understand why this is so (and to fully explain crime).

Based on their comparison of delinquents and nondelinquents, they list several individual traits which they believe are conducive to crime. Their list has much in common with the traits listed by contemporary psychologists. Psychologists, in particular, have argued that the following sorts of traits predispose individuals to crime and delinquency: hyperactivity, impulsivity, attention deficit, sensation seeking, low verbal intelligence, reduced ability to learn from punishment, low empathy, irritability, immature moral reasoning, and poor social and problem-solving skills (see Caspi et al., 1994; Farrington, 1994; Feldman, 1993). The selections by Wilson and Herrnstein and by Moffitt also list individual traits that are said to predispose individuals to crime. It is typically argued that these traits are a function of both biological factors and the social environment, especially the family environment.

Psychologists who focus on learning processes argue that individuals learn to engage in crime in the same way that they learn to engage in any other behavior. Such theorists then describe the processes by which individuals learn to behave, including the ways they learn to engage in aggression or criminal behavior. Bandura's (1973) social learning theory, described in Chapter 3 of this volume, is the dominant learning theory in psychology. The theory incorporates the arguments of certain other theories, most notably behavioral theory. Social learning theory, however, significantly extends behavioral theory by focusing both on the thought processes of individuals and on the external reinforcements and punishments received by individuals. Bandura argues that we initially learn behavior in several ways, with the observation of others being the most significant. Individuals often learn how to perform aggressive acts by observing others engage in aggression. He then argues that aggressive acts may be instigated by several factors, including exposure to aggressive models, aversive treatment by others, and imagining the positive consequences that may result from aggression. Whether individuals continue to commit aggressive acts is said to be dependent on the extent to which their aggression is reinforced and punished—with Bandura arguing that individuals may engage in self-reinforcement and experience vicarious reinforcement. The selections by Wilson and Herrnstein and by Moffitt also draw on social learning theory.

Contemporary psychological theories, then, are distinguished by their focus on the learning process and individual differences. It is important to note, however, that virtually all psychological theories also recognize the importance of the social environment. The social environment influences the development of traits conducive to crime and provides the context in which crime is learned. Psychologists have devoted much research to the influence of the social environment on crime—and it is here where we find much overlap between psychological and sociological research. This attention to the social environment is evident in the selections by Glueck and Glueck, Bandura, Wilson and Herrnstein, and Moffitt (also see the overviews in the psychology and crime texts cited above).

The final selections, by Wilson and Herrnstein and by Moffitt, represent leading examples of contemporary psychological theories of crime. As indicated, these theories draw on and integrate much previous psychological research, including research on individual traits, learning processes, and the social environment. Wilson and Herrnstein's (1985) theory is built around a fundamental argument derived from social learning theory: people choose to engage in crime when they believe that the rewards of crime will outweigh the costs. Individuals' perceptions of the rewards and costs of crime are influenced by both individual traits and the social environment. A central individual trait is the degree to which individuals are concerned about the future consequences of their behavior. Certain individuals have little concern for future consequences, which increases the likelihood of crime because the rewards of crime are usually immediate while the costs are often distant. This trait, in turn, is influenced by traits like intelligence and impulsivity. Wilson and Herrnstein's theory generated much controversy when it was first published, particularly over the central role assigned to biological factors and individual traits. Nevertheless, their theory led mainstream criminologists to pay greater attention to individual differences and to the possible origins of such differences.

The selection by Moffitt attempts to explain trends in crime over the life course. Moffitt (1993) argues that most individuals experience an increase in offending during the adolescent years, but substantially reduce their level of offending when they become adults. Other individuals, however, engage in high rates of offending (or analogous behaviors) over most of their lives. Moffitt develops two theories to account for these patterns: a theory of "adolescent-limited" offending and a theory of "life-course persistent" offending.

The theory of life-course persistent offending is of special interest. It begins with a discussion of individual traits that are conducive to crime, with such traits being said to be partly a function of biological factors. The focus of the theory, however, is on the interaction between such traits and the social environment. Negative environments often exacerbate traits conducive to offending, while such traits often increase individuals' exposure to negative environments. The ultimate result is a persistent pattern of offending. The Moffitt article represents one of the best descriptions of the different ways in which individual traits and the social environment may interact with one another to produce crime. This article, we believe, will serve as a prototype for future efforts to integrate biopsychological and sociological theories of crime.

In sum, biological and psychological theories of crime complement sociological theories in several fundamental ways. They help us understand the mechanisms by which the social environment leads individuals to engage in crime, the reasons why some individuals respond to a given environment with crime and others do not, and the reasons why some individuals are more likely to be in environments that are conducive to crime. While the precise importance of biological and psychological (as well as sociological) factors is yet to be determined, we believe that the existing evidence strongly suggests that such factors will play a central role in the explanation of crime.

References

Andrews, D. A. and James Bonta. 1994. *The Psychology of Criminal Conduct*. Cincinnati: Anderson.

Andrews, D. A. and J. Stephen Wormith. 1989. "Personality and Crime: Knowledge Destruction and Construction in Criminology." *Justice Quarterly* 6: 289-309.

Bandura, Albert. 1973. *Aggression: A Social Learning Analysis*. Englewood Cliffs, NJ: Prentice Hall.

Berkowitz, Leonard. 1989. "Frustration-Aggression Hypothesis: Examination and Reformulations." *Psychological Bulletin* 106: 59-73.

Blackburn, Ronald. 1993. *The Psychology of Criminal Conduct*. Chichester, England: John Wiley and Sons.

Brennan, Patricia A., Sarnoff A. Mednick, and Jan Volavka. 1995. "Biomedical Factors in Crime." Pp. 65-90 in *Crime*, edited by James Q. Wilson and Joan Petersilia. San Francisco: ICS Press.

Brennan, Patricia A. and Adrian Raine. forthcoming. "Biosocial Bases of Antisocial Behavior: Psychophysiological, Neurological and Cognitive Factors." *Clinical Psychology Review*.

Caspi, Avshalom, Terrie E. Moffitt, Phil A. Silva, Magda Stouthamer-Loeber, Robert F. Krueger, and Pamela S. Schmutte. 1994. "Are Some People Crime-Prone: The Personality-Crime Relationship Across Countries, Genders, Races and Methods." *Criminology* 32: 163-195.

Farrington, David P., ed. 1994. *Psychological Explanations of Crime*. Aldershot, England: Dartmonth.

Feldman, Philip. 1993. *The Psychology of Crime*. Cambridge: Cambridge University Press.

Fishbein, Diana H. 1996. "The Biology of Antisocial Behavior." Pp. 26-38 in *New Perspectives in Criminology*, edited by John E. Conklin. Boston: Allyn and Bacon.

Gottfredson, Michael R. and Travis Hirschi. 1990. *A General Theory of Crime*. Stanford: Stanford University Press.

Glueck, Sheldon and Eleanor Glueck. 1950. *Unraveling Juvenile Delinquency*. New York: Commonwealth Fund.

Hollin, Clive. 1989. *Psychology and Crime*. London: Routledge.

——. 1992. *Criminal Behaviour: A Psychological Approach to Explanation and Prevention*. London: Falmer Press.

Katz, Janet and William J. Chambliss. 1995. "Biology and Crime." Pp. 275-303 in *Criminology: A Contemporary Handbook*, 2nd edition, edited by Joseph F. Sheley. Belmont, CA: Wadsworth.

Lombroso, Cesare. 1911. *Criminal Man*, summarized by Gina Lombroso Ferrero. New York: G.P. Putman's Sons.

Merton, Robert K. 1938. "Social Structure and Anomie." *American Sociological Review* 3: 672-682.

Moffitt, Terrie E. 1993. "Adolescent-Limited and Life-Course Persistent Antisocial Behavior: A Developmental Taxonomy." *Psychological Review* 100: 674-701.

Raine, Adrian. 1993. *The Psychopathology of Crime*. San Diego: Academic Press.

Redl, Fritz and Hans Toch. 1979. "The Psychoanalytic Perspective." Pp. 183-197 in *Psychology of Crime and Criminal Justice*, edited by Hans Toch. New York: Holt, Rinehart and Winston.

Shoham, S. Giora and Mark Seis. 1993. *A Primer in the Psychology of Crime*. New York: Harrow and Heston.

Vold, George B. and Thomas J. Bernard. 1986. *Theoretical Criminology*, 3rd edition. New York: Oxford University Press.

Wilson, James Q. and Richard J. Herrnstein. 1985. *Crime and Human Nature*. New York: Touchstone. ✦

1

The Criminal Man

Cesare Lombroso

As Summarized by Gina Lombroso Ferrero

Lombroso's theory is the most prominent of the early biological theories of crime. In fact, it was perhaps the dominant theory of crime around the turn of the century. The theory was first presented in 1876 and was then revised and expanded several times over the next three and a half decades. The following selection describes the key features of his theory, as summarized by his daughter.

Lombroso's theory stands in marked contrast to the classical school of criminology, which dominated crime theory during the late 1700s and much of the 1800s. Classical theory argued that individuals freely chose to engage in crime, in an effort to maximize their pleasure and minimize their pain. Lombroso, by contrast, argued that crime was due to biological differences between criminals and "normal individuals." Drawing on Darwin's evolutionary theory, he claimed that criminals were not as evolved as other individuals: they were savages in the midst of modern society (Lombroso described such people as "atavistic"), and it was their savage or primitive state that caused their criminal behavior. As indicated in the following selection, Lombroso came to this conclusion while working as a physician in the Italian penal system. His examinations of criminals convinced him of their biological inferiority, and through such examinations he developed a list of traits that could be used to distinguish "born criminals" from others. Many of these traits are listed in the selection (for an excellent overview of both classical the-

ory and Lombroso's work, see Vold and Bernard, 1986).

Lombroso's later research convinced him that environmental factors also play an important role in crime. Further, he came to the conclusion that there were actually several different types of criminals. "Born criminals," the genetic throwbacks that he first described, were said to make up only about one-third of all criminals—but the savagery of their crimes made them an especially important class of criminals. Subsequent research, however, discredited Lombroso's arguments regarding biology. Most of the traits listed by Lombroso failed to distinguish criminals from carefully matched samples of noncriminals (see Vold and Bernard, 1986).

Lombroso's research, however, was important because it helped to establish what is known as the "positive school" of criminology. The positive school is distinguished by its search for the causes of crime, be those causes biological, psychological, or sociological. Positivists reject the classical view that crime is entirely the result of free choice or free will. Positivism is also distinguished by its reliance on the scientific method: the theories we develop must be tested against our observations of the world. Positivists such as Lombroso attacked the "armchair theorizing" of classical criminals and, although their methods were sometimes flawed, positivists relied heavily on empirical observation in developing and testing their own theories. Lombroso is sometimes called the "father" of modern criminology for the role he played in the positive school.

Reference

Vold, George and Thomas J. Bernard. 1986. *Theoretical Criminology*, 3rd edition. New York: Oxford.

... The Classical School based its doctrines on the assumption that all criminals, except in a few extreme cases, are endowed with intelligence and feelings like normal individuals, and that they commit misdeeds consciously, being prompted thereto by their unrestrained desire for evil. The offence alone was considered, and on it the whole existing penal system has been founded, the severity of the sentence meted out to the offender being regulated by the gravity of his misdeed.

The Modern, or Positive, School of Penal Jurisprudence, on the contrary, maintains that the anti-social tendencies of criminals are the result of their physical and psychic organisation, which differs essentially from that of normal individuals; and it aims at studying the morphology and various functional phenomena of the criminal with the object of curing, instead of punishing him. . . .

If we examine a number of criminals, we shall find that they exhibit numerous anomalies in the face, skeleton, and various psychic and sensitive functions, so that they strongly resemble primitive races. It was these anomalies that first drew my father's attention to the close relationship between the criminal and the savage and made him suspect that criminal tendencies are of atavistic origin.

When a young doctor at the Asylum in Pavia, he was requested to make a post-mortem examination on a criminal named Vilella, an Italian Jack the Ripper, who by atrocious crimes had spread terror in the Province of Lombardy. . . . "At the sight of that skull," says my father, "I seemed to see all at once, standing out clearly illumined as in a vast plain under a flaming sky, the problem of the nature of the criminal, who reproduces in civilised times characteristics, not only of primitive savages, but of still lower types as far back as the carnivora."

Thus was explained the origin of the enormous jaws, strong canines, prominent zygomae, and strongly developed orbital arches which he had so frequently remarked in criminals, for these peculiarities are common to carnivores and savages, who tear and devour raw flesh. Thus also it was easy to understand why the span of the arms in criminals so often exceeds the height, for this is a characteristic of apes, whose fore-limbs are used in walking and climbing. The other anomalies exhibited by criminals—the scanty beard as opposed to the general hairiness of the body, prehensile foot, diminished number of lines in the palm of the hand, cheek-pouches, enormous development of the middle incisors and frequent absence of the lateral ones, flattened nose and angular

or sugar-loaf form of the skull, common to criminals and apes; the excessive size of the orbits, which, combined with hooked nose, so often imparts to criminals the aspect of birds of prey, the projection of the lower part of the face and jaws (prognathism) found in negroes and animals, and supernumerary teeth (amounting in some cases to a double row as in snakes) and cranial bones (epactal bone as in the Peruvian Indians): all these characteristics pointed to one conclusion, the atavistic origin of the criminal, who reproduces physical, psychic, and functional qualities of remote ancestors.

Subsequent research on the part of my father and his disciples showed that other factors besides atavism come into play in determining the criminal type. These are: disease and environment. Later on, the study of innumerable offenders led them to the conclusion that all law-breakers cannot be classed in a single species, for their ranks include very diversified types, who differ not only in their bent towards a particular form of crime, but also in the degree of tenacity and intensity displayed by them in their perverse propensities, so that, in reality, they form a graduated scale leading from the born criminal to the normal individual.

Born criminals form about one third of the mass of offenders, but, though inferior in numbers, they constitute the most important part of the whole criminal army, partly because they are constantly appearing before the public and also because the crimes committed by them are of a peculiarly monstrous character; the other two thirds are composed of criminaloids (minor offenders), occasional and habitual criminals, etc., who do not show such a marked degree of diversity from normal persons. . . .

Discussion Questions

1. The Positive School of Criminology, which Lombroso helped found, argues that crime is not the result of free will; rather, it is due to factors over which the individual often has little or no con-

trol. As such, this school focuses less on the punishment of the offender and more on "curing" the offending. To what extent do you think crime is the result of free will versus forces beyond the individual's control?

2. What policy recommendations might an adherent of Lombroso's theory make for controlling crime? (A consideration of these recommendations will help you understand one of the reasons why the theory was later attacked).

3. List those factors said to distinguish "born criminals" from others. How would one go about providing a good test of Lombroso's theory? ✦

2

Unraveling Juvenile Delinquency

Sheldon Glueck
Eleanor Glueck

The Gluecks begin their 1950 book Unraveling Juvenile Delinquency *by arguing that no one theoretical approach or disciplinary perspective is sufficient for studying the causes of delinquency. A full explanation of delinquency requires that factors from all disciplines be considered, including biological, psychological, and sociological factors. This "multi-factor" approach guided their analysis in* Unraveling Juvenile Delinquency *and is one of the distinguishing features of their work. In particular, their list of causal factors includes variables from all domains—ranging from physique to temperamental traits to family factors. The reader may wonder, then, why their article is included in the section on biological and psychological theories.*

Part of the response is that their study was published at a time when sociological theories were coming to dominate the discipline of criminology. While the Gluecks' study focuses on factors from all domains, it assigns special importance to biological and psychological factors; the study stood out for this reason. With the exception of the family, the importance of social factors is discounted or not considered. For example, they argue that while delinquency is associated with school factors (e.g., low achievement, dislike of school) and association with delinquent peers, such factors do not have a causal effect on delinquency. Rather, they are simply another reflection of the individual traits and early family problems that cause delinquency.

The selection that follows summarizes the major findings from a study that the Gluecks began in 1939. The Gluecks compared 500 institutionalized delinquent boys in Massachusetts to a matched sample of 500 nondelinquent boys from the Boston area. The delinquents and nondelinquents were matched by age, race/ethnicity, neighborhood characteristics, and intelligence (the matching procedure helped ensure that the two groups were similar on these traits). They then collected a wide range of data on these boys from several sources, and Unraveling Juvenile Delinquency *describes the results of their comparisons. They conclude that delinquency results from the interplay between somatic (physique), temperamental, intellectual, and sociocultural (especially family) forces. They do not describe the interactions between these factors in any detail, however (see the Wilson and Herrnstein and Moffitt selections).*

Their study has been critiqued on a number of points and Sampson and Laub (1993) recently reanalyzed the Gluecks' data, partly in an effort to overcome many of these criticisms. Nevertheless, many of their findings have stood the test of time. Other findings, however, have been challenged. Certain data suggest that school factors and association with delinquent peers do have some causal impact on delinquency (see Akers, 1997; Vold and Bernard, 1986; also see Wilson and Herrnstein, 1985).

References

Akers, Ronald. 1997. *Criminological Theories: Introduction and Evaluation*, 2nd edition. Los Angeles: Roxbury.

Sampson, Robert J. and John H. Laub. 1993. *Crime in the Making.* Cambridge, MA: Harvard University Press.

Vold, George B. and Thomas J. Bernard. 1986. *Theoretical Criminology*, 3rd edition. New York: Oxford University Press.

Wilson, James Q. and Richard J. Herrnstein. 1985. *Crime and Human Nature.* New York: Touchstone.

. . . By and large, examination of existing researches in juvenile delinquency discloses a tendency to emphasize a particular approach or explanation. Proponents of various theories of causation still too often insist that the truth is to be found only in their own special fields of study, and that, *ex hypothesi*, researches made by those working in other disciplines can contribute very little to the understanding and management of the crime problem. Like the blind men and the elephant of the fable, each builds the entire subject in the image of that piece of it which he happens to have touched.

Yet it stands to reason that since so little is as yet known about the intricacies of normal human behavior, it is the better part of wisdom not to be overawed by any branch of science or methodology to the neglect of other promising leads in the study of aberrant behavior. When, therefore, research into the causes of delinquency emphasizes the sociologic, or ecologic, or cultural, or psychiatric, or psychoanalytic, or anthropologic approach, relegating the others to a remote position, if not totally ignoring them, we must immediately be on guard. The problems of human motivation and behavior involve the study of man as well as society, of nature as well as nurture, of segments or mechanisms of human nature as well as the total personality, of patterns of intimate social activity as well as larger areas of social process or masses of culture. They involve, therefore, the participation of several disciplines. Without recognition of such factors, bias must weaken the validity of both method and interpretation.

For example, a weakness or an incompleteness of much sociologic reasoning on the causal process in crime is the assumption that the mass social stimulus to behavior, as reflected in the particular culture of a region, is alone, or primarily, the significant causal force. This presupposition ignores two undeniable facts: first, that in every society— whether largely rural or largely urban, whether agricultural or industrial, whether composed essentially of one ethnic group or of many or of a consistent culture or several clashing ones, whether existing at one historic period or another—there have been individuals who would not or could not conform to the taboos and laws prohibiting particular forms of behavior; second, and relatedly, that differences exist in the responses of various individuals or classes of persons to many of the elements in the culture-complex of a region.

As an illustration of the mass-culture approach to crime causation we may cite the studies of human ecology, the relation of neighborhood to human behavior, especially to delinquency. The numerous area-studies have revealed certain crude correlations between the gross physical make-up and composite culture of different zones of a city, on the one hand, and the incidence of delinquency and other aspects of social pathology, on the other. The most frequently quoted finding of these sociologic contributions is that there is a typical patterning of delinquency rates in different urban regions, the general trend of variation being from the highest rate in core-areas around central parts of cities and business districts to a lesser and lesser incidence in zones farther removed from the central section. The area of highest incidence of delinquency is also one of deterioration, in the sense that from a physical standpoint it is likely to be adjacent to industry and commerce and to be a neighborhood of dilapidated houses, dirty alleys, low rents, much poverty and dependency, and inadequate recreational facilities. From a cultural standpoint it is a place where the neighborhood has ceased to be an integrated and integrative agency of sentiments, values, behavior standards, and social control; has drawn in peoples of differing and more or less conflicting mores, morals, and standards of behavior; has to some extent developed a tradition of delinquency; and has largely failed to furnish unifying and edifying substitutes for the crumbling traditional patterns of behavior and authority.

This kind of approach to the problem of delinquency, although of much aid in studying the phenomenon in the mass, is of relatively little help in exploring the mechanisms of causation. These mechanisms are operative, not in the external area or culture, but in the mental life of the individual, and in detail as well as en masse. The area-studies establish that a region of economic and cultural disorganization tends to have a criminogenic effect on people residing therein; but the studies fail to emphasize that this influence affects only a selected group comprising a relatively small proportion of all residents. They do not reveal why the deleterious influences of even the most extreme delinquency area fail to turn the great majority of its boys into persistent delinquents. They do not disclose whether the children who do not succumb to the evil and disruptive neighborhood influence differ from those who become delinquents and if so, in what respects. Until they take this factor into account, they cannot penetratingly describe even the culture of the delinquency area. For to say that certain bacteria have a fatal effect on some individuals but no such effect on the majority without describing the differently reacting persons or explaining the differential influences, is to describe that infective agent inadequately.

The true significance of the factors dealt with by the area sociologist can be determined only through close study of the points of impact of social forces upon individuals and classes of varying biologic make-up and childhood conditioning. The varieties of the physical, mental, and social history of different persons must determine, in large measure, the way in which they will be influenced by social disorganization, culture conflict, and the growing-pains of the city. To overemphasize the neighborhood matrix as a coherent whole and underemphasize or virtually ignore the biologic make-up and developmental history of the different human beings who themselves contribute to the modification of that matrix is to overlook many of the factors that account for variations in the effect of the culture on the human beings and thereby to distort reality with reference not only to the casual problem but even to the nature of the culture in question.

After presenting a great many studies showing the regional distribution of delinquency and stressing the influence of the disintegrating culture of the delinquency area on the behavior of its inhabitants, the ecologic sociologists are compelled to resort to psychologic insights when they come to grapple realistically with causal influences in the individual case. For example, Shaw's work, *The Natural History of a Delinquent Career*, begins with the familiar sociologic analysis of "A Delinquency Area." But it ends,

significantly, with an analysis by a prominent ecologic sociologist employing such specific and individualized psychologic-psychiatric concepts as the precocious personality, the inferiority complex, and the difficult personality problem. The conclusion implied is that the delinquency area is after all not the major villain to be unmasked and coped with, but rather that the "personality type, as revealed in his [the individual boy's] autobiography, would require, if reformation is to be achieved, individualized treatment by a skilled and sympathetic person.

The same enthusiastic emphasis on a single approach to crime causation—this time involving the economic factor of poverty—is to be found in many European studies of crime and it has proved equally sterile and distorted without psychologic adjuncts. Since poverty operates differently on various types of persons, it should have been obvious that something more than the sociologic-economic datum of poverty (or unemployment, or the fluctuations in the price of some standard commodity, or the vicissitudes of the business cycle) had to be examined before the role of poverty in the genesis of delinquency or crime could be understood.

Unilateral study of the causes of delinquency and criminalism is not confined to some sociologists and economists. Such an approach has also existed on the part of proponents of various biologic theories. Lombroso's belated recognition of the operation of sociologic factors was submerged in his persistent enthusiasm for the theory that crime is often the natural activity of persons destined from birth, by virtue of atavism (hereditary reversion or throw-back to some remote ancestry), to become criminal. More recently, some enthusiastic endocrinologists have also made claims for the exclusiveness or primacy of glandular dysfunction as the causal agency in delinquency, without recognizing that any unilateral approach is a distortion of reality. Psychoanalytic explanations of delinquency are also inclined to an overemphasis of a single point of view; but the general acceptance of the role of early environmental conditioning upon the development of personality and character tends to make psychoanalysts recognize the importance of both biologic and cultural forces and of the interchanging influences of endowment and nurture in the genesis of maladapted behavior.

Other illustrations could be given of the tendency toward one-sided study of the causes of delinquency which springs from specialization in some particular science or method. But enough has been said to indicate that this is a pitfall which we have made every effort to avoid in the planning and execution of a research designed to throw light on the complexities of the causal process in delinquency.

Need for Eclectic Approach to Study of Crime Causation

At the present stage of knowledge an eclectic approach to the study of the causal process in human motivation and behavior is obviously necessary. It is clear that such an inquiry should be designed to reveal meaningful integrations of diverse data from several levels of inquiry. There is need for a systematic approach that will not ignore any promising leads to crime causation, covering as many fields and utilizing as many of the most reliable and relevant techniques of investigation and measurement as are necessary for a fair sampling of the various aspects of a complex biosocial problem. Ideally, the focus in such a study should be upon the selectivity that occurs when environment and organism interact. The searchlight should be played upon the point of contact between specific social and biologic processes as they coalesce, accommodate, or conflict in individuals. . . .

Dynamic Pattern of Delinquency

In the foregoing chapters we have unraveled and laid out the separate strands of the tangled skein of causation. Here we shall see if we can reweave them into a meaningful pattern without leaving too many loose ends. If we are to isolate the probable causal factors, we must focus attention on the ones that differentiate the delinquents and non-delinquents and that were operative before delinquency became evident. Factors that come

into play after persistent antisocial behavior is established can hardly be regarded as relevant to the original etiology of maladaptation, except as they may reflect deep-rooted forces which do not make themselves felt in a tendency to dissocial behavior until puberty or adolescence is reached. . . .

Factors with Probable Causal Significance

We are now ready to focus attention on those factors that may have causal significance. It should be emphasized that in examining the tapestry of delinquency it is difficult to differentiate the warp of hereditary (genetic) factors from the woof of conditioned (environmental, cultural) factors. It is as yet too early to arrive at unassailable conclusions regarding the relative degrees of participation of biological and social factors in human behavior in general; and criminology, being a dependent discipline, must await the evidence of other sciences.

It is well nigh impossible to differentiate with assurance the completely innate from the completely acquired in the etiology of antisocial behavior. Birth injuries or anomalies of embryologic development may be confused with inherited conditions. Social inheritance may be mistaken for biologic. Certain inherited physical or mental traits may be confused with a "criminal instinct." The mechanisms of human heredity are as yet far from clear, especially where mental abnormalities are involved.

Nevertheless, our data do permit of a rough division. There are, on the one hand, factors that are closer to the genetic than to the environmental end of the biosocial scale, and, on the other, those that are closer to the "conditioned," cultural end of the scale.

Physique. The data closest to the genetic are those dealing with the bodily morphology—the physique—of the two groups of boys under study. The most striking finding in the anthropologic analysis is the very high incidence of mesomorphic (muscular, solid) dominance in the body structure of the delinquents. Among the non-delinquents, on the other hand, there is a considerable incidence of ectomorphic (linear, thin) dominance.

This basic difference in bodily morphology (the more subtle ones we are not at present bringing into the discussion) may reasonably be regarded as fundamentally related to differences in natural energy-tendencies. . . .

Thus, the delinquents, as a group, tend toward the outline of a solid, closely-knit, muscular type, one in which there is a relative predominance of muscle, bone, and connective tissue. There may be contradictory, dysplastic components in individual instances, but the general tendency is mesomorphic.

To the outlines of this solidly-structured, muscular, anatomical pattern derived by anthropologic analysis should now be added the evidence obtained from other sources, independently arrived at by other means. For example, a much higher proportion of the delinquents than of the non-delinquents are reported to have been extremely restless as young children in terms of energy output, and a considerably higher proportion of them were persistent enuretics. The health examination disclosed, by way of contrast, that neurologic handicaps and dermographia are less prevalent among the delinquents than among the control group.

Temperamental Traits and Emotional Dynamics. No direct statistical linkage between physique types and psychologic factors has been attempted here. It may be that when somatotypes are interrelated with temperament-types and character-types, meaningful associations will emerge. In the meantime, a general review of the traits of temperament and the emotional dynamics of the two groups permits us to make a rough association between the two orders of data.

Let us consider, first, the dynamics of personality as disclosed by the Rorschach Test, which projects essentially subconscious materials. Such dynamics involve both the impulsive tendencies and desires and the inhibiting apparatus. The delinquents have been found to be considerably more extroversive in their trends of action, more vivacious, more emotionally labile or impulsive (as opposed to stability of emotional expression), more destructive and sadistic, more aggressive and adventurous. Accompanying these more excessive dynamic emotional tendencies is the lesser self-control of the delinquents.

Reviewing next what may be called emotional attitudes in contrast to dynamisms, it will be recalled that the delinquents have been found by the Rorschach Test to be more hostile, defiant, resentful, and suspicious than the non-delinquents. The delinquent group, further, contains a higher proportion of socially assertive boys; of boys who have a feeling of not being recognized or appreciated; and of boys characterized by oral trends (unconsciously motivated by a desire to be looked after without effort) and by narcissistic trends (reflecting a strong need for status, power, and superiority). They are also less conventional (as disclosed by both the Rorschach Test and the psychiatric interview), less cooperative, less inclined to meet the expectations of others, less dependent upon others, and far less submissive to authority or more ambivalent to it.

To these traits can now be added others obtained through the psychiatric interview, which tend to support some of the findings from the deeper layers tapped by the Rorschach Test: The delinquents, as a group, are more stubborn and egocentric, less critical of themselves, and more sensual than the non-delinquents. They are far less conscientious, less practical and realistic, less aesthetic, and less "adequate."

The psychiatric examination has also revealed that twice as many delinquents as non-delinquents evidence conflicts resulting from all sorts of environmental stresses. . . . In respect to feelings of physical or mental inferiority (largely the latter), in sexual identification, in the relationship between boy and father and between boy and mother, and in stress growing out of companionship, a consistently greater proportion of conflicts was found among the delinquents than among the non-delinquents.

It is, however, in the manner in which they typically resolve such conflicts that the distinction between the two groups under comparison weaves most meaningfully into the general pattern. More than twice as many delinquents tend to resolve mental conflicts by extroversion of action and/or feeling (largely the former); while, by way of contrast, eight times as many non-delinquents as delinquents tend to resolve their conflicts by introversion. . . .

On the whole, the delinquents are more extroverted, vivacious, impulsive, and less self-controlled than the non-delinquents. They are more hostile, resentful, defiant, suspicious, and destructive. They are less fearful of failure or defeat than the non-delinquents. They are less concerned about meeting conventional expectations, and are more ambivalent toward or far less submissive to authority. They are, as a group, more socially assertive. To a greater extent than the control group, they express feelings of not being recognized or appreciated.

Intellectual Traits. The instruments of adaptive behavior are not only physiologic and affective but also intellectual. The findings in this area must therefore be woven into the total dynamic pattern. General intelligence in the two groups under comparison is of course similar, by virtue of the manner in which the boys were originally selected and matched. Still, certain differences in the constituents of intelligence have been found which, though separately not large, show quite a definite trend.

First, the delinquents, as a group, are distinguished from the non-delinquents in having a lesser capacity to approach problems methodically. Such a trait possibly bears on the capacity to reflect on contemplated behavior and to assess its consequences.

The delinquents have less verbal intelligence, scoring lower than the control group on the Vocabulary, Information, Comprehension, and Digit Symbol subtests of the Wechsler-Bellevue Scale. On the other hand, they attained a somewhat higher score on two out of five of the performance subtests, namely, Block Design and Object Assembly. . . .

These findings seem to indicate that the delinquent group is made up of a somewhat greater variety of intelligence than the non-delinquent, despite the fact that the two groups were originally matched by intelligence quotient. Greater variability is also evident among the delinquents as individuals in their responses to the verbal series of intelligence tests and their scores on the achievement tests in reading and arithmetic. This greater scatter may reflect greater emotional disharmony, which, in turn, affects intellectual tasks.

The delinquents tend to express themselves intellectually in a direct, immediate, and concrete manner rather than through the use of intermediate symbols or abstractions. There seems also to be a somewhat greater emotional disharmony connected with their performance of intellectual tasks.

Behavior Reflecting Significant Traits

Certain forms of behavior, in and out of school, are in a sense not fundamentally etiologic. But since they reflect, at least partially, temperamental tendencies and character traits that have their roots in early childhood, they may be included in the general pattern. These forms of behavior are school attainment, school misbehavior, general misbehavior tendencies, use of leisure, and type of companions.

School Attainment. Although school attainment itself cannot be regarded as a causal factor, it nevertheless may reflect either temperamental and intellectual differences or variations in early environment and training. The school accomplishment of the delinquents was definitely inferior to that of the control group. (The reader is reminded that the boys were matched by age, and that they were of like age upon school entrance). . . .

The poorer school achievement of the delinquent boys is reflected in their attitude toward schooling. Far more of them than of the non-delinquents markedly disliked school, and far fewer expressed any desire for education beyond grade school. To a much greater extent than the non-delinquents, they revealed themselves as misfits in the school situation. As a group, they were less interested in academic tasks, less attentive in class, more often tardy, less reliable, more careless in their work, lazier, more restless, less truthful, and they sought harder to attract attention to themselves.

Here again, we have strands of the delinquent pattern, namely, evidences of restless energy with accompanying difficulties in social adaptation and conformity to a regime of rules and discipline involving distasteful intellectual tasks.

School Misbehavior. Probably bound up with somatic and temperamental traits, as well as with their home background, are the manifestations of maladaptive behavior displayed by the delinquents in school in marked excel over the non-delinquents. (School misbehavior characterized almost all the delinquents, compared with less than a fifth of the control group.) The average age of the delinquents at first school misbehavior was nine and a half—fully three years younger than the mean age of the small number of non-delinquents when they showed the first evidences of any maladaptive behavior in school. At the time the delinquents were, on the average, in the fourth grade, and the non-delinquents in the seventh.

As to the nature of their misconduct, there is manifest, first, a very marked attempt on the part of the delinquents to escape from the burdensome restraints of the school regime by persistent truancy. Other kinds of school misconduct in which the delinquents greatly exceeded the non-delinquents (disobedience, disorderliness, stubbornness, sullenness, impertinence, defiance, and impudence) are to be expected in the light of the predominance of traits already noted. Although still other types of misconduct (quarrelsomeness, cruelty, domineering attitude, and destruction of school materials) involve relatively small numbers of boys, the delinquents considerably exceeded the non-delinquents in all of them.

Some manifestations of school misconduct may, of course, be essentially reactive; others seem to reflect root traits and fundamental drives. They all fit consistently, however, into the temperamental segment of the general pattern that has been inductively achieved.

General Misbehavior Tendencies. As for the misbehavior tendencies of the two sets of boys outside of school, the delinquents, far more than the control group, were in the habit of stealing rides or hopping trucks, committing acts of destructive mischief, setting fires, sneaking into theatres without paying, running away from home, bunking out, and keeping late hours. In marked excel over the non-delinquents, they also gambled and begged, and a far greater proportion of them began to smoke or drink at a very early age.

In their general misbehavior tendencies, there is further evidence of a driving, uninhibited energy and thirst for adventure on the part of the delinquents.

Leisure Time and Companions. Passing in review the findings regarding the leisure-time activities of the boys, we again see marked differences, which take their place significantly in the general pattern. Less than half as many of the delinquents as of the non-delinquents spent some of their leisure time at home. This may have resulted from the fact that far fewer of the delinquents' families indulged in family group recreations and also from the reluctance of the parents to entertain the boys' friends at home. The delinquents, far more than the non-delinquents, preferred to play in distant neighborhoods and to hang around street corners, vacant lots, waterfronts, railroad yards, and poolrooms. They expressed a much greater preference for adventurous activities. Perhaps that is why they gravitated toward the more exciting street trades in seeking after-school jobs. Apart from concrete outlets for restless energy, many more of them sought vicarious adventure through the movies.

As might be expected from the foregoing, the delinquents were less inclined to supervised recreational activities than the non-delinquents, and were also far less willing to spend any of their leisure hours in the circumscribed areas of playgrounds. This dislike of controlled environments may also be partially reflected in the far higher proportion of them who were neglectful of their church duties.

In their choice of companions, also, they differed greatly from the control group. Almost all of them, in contrast to very few of the non-delinquents, preferred to chum with other delinquents. More than half of them, compared with less than one percent of the non-delinquents, were members of gangs. In far higher measure than the control group, their companions were older boys—possibly indicating a search for temperamentally congenial "ego-ideals."

In their recreational activities and companionship, the delinquents further evidence a craving for adventure and for opportunities to express aggressive energy-output, with the added need of supportive companionship in such activities.

Thus far it seems clear that the physical, temperamental, intellectual, and behavioral segments of the inquiry tend to interweave into a meaningful pattern: The delinquents, far more than the non-delinquents, are of the essentially mesomorphic, energetic type, with tendencies to restless and uninhibited expression of instinctual-affective energy and to direct and concrete, rather than symbolic and abstract, intellectual expression. It is evidently difficult for them to develop the high degree of flexibility of adaptation, self-management, self-control, and sublimation of primitive tendencies and self-centered desires demanded by the complex and confused culture of the times. Nevertheless, there are some delinquents who do not fit into this pattern, either on a somatic or a temperamental level; and there are some non-delinquents who do.

Socio-Cultural Factors. An examination of socio-cultural factors should shed some light on the reasons for these difficulties of adaptation. Character is the result of training as well as of natural equipment. Mechanisms of sublimation and of constructive or harmless energy-canalization, as well as "knowledge of right and wrong," are part of the apparatus of character expression. However, a boy does not express himself in a vacuum, but in a cultural milieu ranging from the intimate, emotion-laden atmosphere of the home to that of the school, the neighborhood, and general society. Primitive tendencies are morally and legally neutral. It is the existence of laws and taboos that qualifies their expression in certain ways as delinquent, or criminal, or otherwise dissocial or anti-social from the point of view of the particular society and culture in question. Adaptation to the demands and prohibitions of any specific social organization requires certain physical, temperamental, and intellectual capacities dependent upon the values protected by that society through law and custom and characteristics of the cultural matrix.

Modern culture, especially in crowded urban centers, is highly complex, and it is ill-defined because of conflicting values. The demands upon the growing human organism by every vehicle of today's culture are numerous, often subtle, and sometimes inconsistent. This is true of the home, the school, the neighborhood, and the general, all-pervasive culture of the times. Against insistence that he be honest, nonaggressive, self-controlled, and the like, the child soon finds vivid contradicting attitudes, values, and behavior all about him in an environment that in large measure rewards selfishness, aggression, a predatory attitude, and success by any means. Thus, the demands made upon the growing child at every level at which he is called upon to adapt his natural inclinations to the taboos, laws, and other prohibitions are neither simple nor well defined. They require a great deal of adaptive power, self-control, and self-management, the ability to choose among alternative values and to postpone immediate satisfactions for future ones—all this in a cultural milieu in which fixed points are increasingly difficult to discern and to hold to. This means that during the earliest years, when the difficult task of internalization of ideals and symbols of authority is in process, desirable attitudes and behavior standards are not clearly enough defined, or are inconsistent, leaving a confused residue in the delicate structure of personality and character.

While responses to the complex modern culture differ with the varying constitution and temperament of each person subjected to it, the basic desires of growing child, especially as he emerges into adolescence, are similar and imperative. Clinical experience has shown that among these are the striving for happiness and for expression of a desire for freedom from restraint; the thirst for new experience and for the satisfaction of curiosity; the need for an assured feeling of security and affectional warmth from parents, other adults whom the child admires, and companions; the desire to achieve a feeling of success and status.

How did the home conditions of the delinquents and non-delinquents in this study tend to facilitate or hamper the process of internalization of authority, the taming and sublimation of primitive impulses, and the definition of standards of good and bad?

To answer this significant question requires, first, a review of the findings concerning the background of the parents of the boys; for the parents are not only the products of the biologic and cultural systems in which they were born and reared, but also the transmitters of that biosocial heritage to their children. We found that while the divergencies between the delinquents and non-delinquents were sometimes not as marked as those found in other aspects of the research, *the biosocial legacy of the parents of the delinquents was consistently poorer than that of the non-delinquents.* There was a greater incidence of emotional disturbances, mental retardation, alcoholism, and criminalism among the families of the mothers of the delinquents. These differences existed despite the fact that the economic condition of the homes in which the mothers of the delinquent boys had been reared was not very different from that of the homes in which the mothers of the non-delinquents grew up. In the families of the fathers of the delinquents, also, there was more emotional disturbance and criminalism than among the families of the fathers of the non-delinquents.

Thus, to the extent that the parents of the boys communicated the standards and ideals of their own rearing to that of their children, it is evident that the social—and perhaps, partially also, biologic—legacy of the delinquents was worse than that of the non-delinquents.

As for the parents themselves, their biosocial handicaps should be considered as at least partly influencing their capacity to rear their children properly. A higher proportion of the parents of the delinquents suffered from serious physical ailments, were mentally retarded, emotionally disturbed, alcoholic, and—most significant—many more of them had a history of delinquency.

The generally poorer hygienic and moral climate in which the delinquents were reared is further emphasized in the greater burden among their brothers and sisters of serious physical ailments, mental retardation, emotional disturbances, excessive drinking, and delinquency.

These are not the only ways in which the familial background of the delinquents was less adequate than that of the non-delinquents. There are other aspects of family life in which the delinquents were more deprived, often markedly so. For example: A somewhat higher proportion of their parents than of the parents of the non-delinquents came to the responsibilities of marriage with no more than grade-school education. A far higher proportion of the marriages proved to be unhappy. (More of the homes of the delinquents were broken by desertion, separation, divorce, or death of one or both parents, many of the breaches occurring during the early childhood of the boys. Because of this, many more delinquents than non-delinquents have had substitute parents, and more of them were shifted about from one household to another during their formative years. Further, there has been less of an effort among the families of the delinquent group to set up decent standards of conduct—less ambition, less self-respect, and less planning for the future.

As for the economic status of the two groups of families, a finding has emerged which is particularly significant in view of the fact that the boys were matched at the outset on the basis of residence in underprivileged areas, namely, that sporadic or chronic dependency has been markedly more prevalent among the families of the delinquents. This is attributable, at least in part, to the far poorer work habits of the fathers, and in part also to less planful management of the family income.

These differences between the families of the delinquents and the families of the non-delinquents do not so much pertain to the obvious issue of the relationship of dependence or poverty to crime (the vast majority of both groups of families are of the underprivileged class); they are important, rather, as reflecting the differences in the quality of the adults in the families and therefore the variance in influence on the children.

The greater inadequacy of the parents of the delinquents is also reflected in the extremes of laxity and harshness with which they attempted to meet the disciplinary problems of their children and in the greater carelessness of their supervision of the children, amounting often to outright neglect.

It is, however, within the family emotional setting—the family drama—that the most deep-rooted and persistent character and personality traits and distortions of the growing child are developed.

We may at once dispose of the claim often made that being the only or the first-born, or the youngest child has special implications for delinquency. The fact is that, in our study, a *lower* proportion of the delinquents than of the non-delinquents were so placed in order of birth.

In interpersonal family relationships, however, we found an exceedingly marked difference between the two groups under comparison. A much higher proportion of the families of the delinquents were disorganized (not cohesive). Family disorganization, with its attendant lack of warmth and of respect for the integrity of each member, can have serious consequences for the growing child. It may prevent the development of both an adequate sense of responsibility and an effective mechanism for the inhibition of conduct that might disgrace the family name. Since the family is the first and foremost vehicle for the transmission of the values of a culture to the young child, non-cohesiveness of the family may leave him without ethical moorings or convey to him a confused and inconsistent cultural pattern.

Apart from the lesser cohesiveness of the families in which the delinquents grew up, many more of their fathers, mothers, brothers, and sisters have been indifferent or frankly hostile to the boys. A far *lower* proportion of the delinquents than of the non-delinquents have been affectionately attached to their parents; and considerably more of them have felt that their parents have not been concerned about their welfare. Finally, twice as many of the delinquents do not look upon their fathers as acceptable symbols for emulation.

These far-spread and marked differences cannot be attributable only to cultural inequalities in the two groups. Culture does not originate or operate in a vacuum. It is made, modified, and transmitted by human beings. The greater criminalism of the antecedents of the delinquent group, for example, cannot be attributed to a cultural tradition of lawlessness in these families, but must have sprung from individuals whose physical and psychologic equipment inclined them to select the antisocial culture as opposed to the conventional, or who found the former more congenial to their biologic tendencies.

In the light of the obvious inferiority of the families of the delinquents as sources of sound personality development and character formation, it is not surprising that these boys were never adequately socialized, and that they developed persistent antisocial tendencies, even apart from the fundamental somatic and temperamental differentiations between them and the non-delinquents.

Without attempting a psychoanalytic discussion of interpersonal emotional dynamics, we may point out that the development of a mentally hygienic and properly oriented superego (conscience) must have been greatly hampered by the kind of parental ideals, attitudes, temperaments, and behavior found to play such a major role on the family stage of the delinquents.

The Causal Complex

It will be observed that in drawing together the more significant threads of each area explored, we have not resorted to a theoretical explanation from the standpoint, exclusively, of any one discipline. It has seemed to us, at least at the present stage of our reflections upon the materials, that it is premature and misleading to give exclusive or even primary significance to any one of the avenues of interpretation. On the contrary, the evidence seems to point to the participation of forces from several areas and levels in channeling the persistent tendency to socially unacceptable behavior. The foregoing summation of the major resemblances and dissimilarities between the two groups included in the present inquiry indicates that the separate findings, independently gathered, integrate into a dynamic pattern which is neither exclusively biologic nor exclusively socio-cultural, but which derives from an interplay of somatic, temperamental, intellectual, and socio-cultural forces.

We are impelled to such a multidimensional interpretation because, without it, serious gaps appear. If we resort to an explanation exclusively in terms of somatic constitution, we leave unexplained why most persons of mesomorphic tendency do *not* commit crimes; and we further leave unexplained how bodily structure affects behavior. If we limit ourselves to a socio-cultural explanation, we cannot ignore the fact that socio-cultural forces are selective; even in underprivileged areas most boys do *not* become delinquent and many boys from such areas do not develop into persistent offenders. And, finally, if we limit our explanation to psychoanalytic theory, we fail to account for the fact that the great majority of non-delinquents, as well as of delinquents, who traits usually deemed unfavorable to sound character development, such as vague feelings of insecurity and feelings of not being wanted; the fact that many boys who live under conditions in which there is a dearth of parental warmth and understanding nevertheless remain non-delinquent; and the fact that some boys, under conditions unfavorable to the development of a wholesome superego, do not become delinquents, but do become neurotics.

If, however, we take into account the dynamic interplay of these various levels and channels of influence, a tentative causal formula or law emerges, which tends to accommodate these puzzling divergencies so far as the great mass of delinquents is concerned:

The delinquents as a group are distinguishable from the non-delinquents: (1) physically, in being essentially mesomorphic in constitution (solid, closely knit, muscular); (2) temperamentally, in being restlessly energetic, impulsive, extroverted, aggressive, destructive (often sadistic)—traits which may be related more or less to the erratic growth pattern and its physiologic correlates or consequences; (3) in attitude, by being hostile, defiant, resentful, suspicious, stubborn, socially assertive, adventurous, unconventional, non-submissive to authority; (4) psychologically, in tending to direct and concrete, rather than symbolic, intellectual expression, and in being less methodical in their approach in problems, (5) socio-culturally, in having been reared to a far greater extent than the control group in homes of little understanding, affection, stability, or

moral fibre by parents usually unfit to be effective guides and protectors, or, according to psychoanalytic theory, desirable sources for emulation and the construction of a consistent, well-balanced, and socially normal superego during the early stages of character development. While in individual cases the stresses contributed by any one of the above pressure-areas of dissocial-behavior tendency may adequately account for persistence in delinquency, in general the high probability of delinquency is dependent upon the interplay of the conditions and forces from all these areas.

In the exciting, stimulating, but little-controlled and culturally inconsistent environment of the underprivileged area, such boys readily give expression to their untamed impulses and their self-centered desires by means of various forms of delinquent behavior. Their tendencies toward uninhibited energy-expression are deeply anchored in soma and psyche and in the malformations of character during the first few years of life. . . .

Reprinted from Sheldon and Eleanor Glueck, *Unraveling Juvenile Delinquency.* Copyright ©1950 by Commonwealth Fund. Reprinted by permission of the Commonwealth Fund.

Discussion Questions

1. Many of the theories described in this reader argue that crime and delinquency are caused by the social environment—by one's family and friends, social class position, neighborhood characteristics, etc. Why would the Gluecks criticize such approaches (be as specific as you can in your response)?

2. Drawing on the Gluecks, describe the individual traits and social environment that characterized the delinquents in their sample.

3. Even though delinquents are more likely than nondelinquents to do poorly at school and experience other school problems, the Gluecks argue that school factors do not cause delinquency. Why do they make this argument? ✦

3

Social Learning and Aggression

Albert Bandura

While certain psychological theories focus on individual traits and their impact on crime, others focus on the processes by which behavior—including crime and aggression—are learned. Bandura's social learning theory of aggression is the leading learning theory in psychology and one of the leading theories of crime. It does not deny the importance of individual traits or biological factors; they may influence the rate of learning and one's response to environmental stimuli. They may also set limits on what can be learned. Aggressive behavior, however, is said to be primarily a function of social learning.

Bandura's social learning theory draws heavily on behavioral theory, which was the dominant learning theory in the middle part of this century. Behavioral theory argues that we learn from the consequences of our behavior. We repeat those behaviors which have been reinforced, especially when we are in situations where the behavior was previously reinforced. We avoid those behaviors which have been punished. Our behavior, then, is shaped by the external consequences that follow it. Individuals engage in crime because they are in environments where crime is differentially reinforced over conformity. Bandura acknowledges the importance of learning through direct experience, but breaks from behavioral theory in that he also argues that the cognitive or thought processes of individuals play a central role in learning.

For example, while we sometimes learn to perform a behavior through direct experience (i.e., trial-and-error learning shaped by its consequences), we most often learn by observing the behavior of others and the consequences they experience. We then draw on our observa-tions and use them as a guide for our own ac-tion. Likewise, aggressive responses may be in-stigated by the anticipation of positive conse-quences. Further, aggressive behavior may be maintained through self-reinforcement, as well as the experience of external reinforce-ment.

In the following selection, Bandura draws on both behavioral theory and cognitive psy-chology in discussing the methods by which aggressive behavior is acquired, instigated, and maintained. He also mentions certain of the voluminous research that stems from or is compatible with social learning theory, such as the research on the effects of TV violence. Ban-dura's theory has not only inspired much re-search, but has also had an important impact on Akers's Social learning theory in sociol-ogy—another leading theory of crime (see Ak-ers's Chapter 10 in Part III).

. . . A complete theory of aggression must explain how aggressive patterns are devel-oped, what provokes people to behave ag-gressively, and what sustains such actions af-ter they have been initiated. Figure 3.1 sum-marizes the determinants of these three as-pects of aggression within the framework of social learning theory.

Acquisition Mechanisms

People are not born with preformed reper-toires of aggressive behavior. They must learn them. Some of the elementary forms of ag-gression can be perfected with minimal guid-ance, but most aggressive activities—whether they be dueling with switchblade knives, sparring with opponents, military combat, or vengeful ridicule—entail intricate skills that require extensive learning.

Observational Learning

. . . Psychological theories have tradition-ally assumed that learning can occur only by performing responses and experiencing their consequences. In fact, virtually all learning phenomena resulting from direct experience can occur on a vicarious basis by observing the behavior of others and its consequences for them. The capacity to learn by observa-tion enables individuals to acquire large, in-

Figure 3.1
Social Learning Analysis of Behavior

Origins of Aggression	Instigators of Aggression	Regulators of Aggression

Observational learning
 	
Reinforced performance
 	
Structural determinants
	Modeling influences
	  disinhibitory
	  facilitative
	  arousing
	  stimulus enhancing
	Aversive treatment
	  physical assaults
	  verbal threats and insults
	  adverse reductions in reinforcement
	  thwarting
	Incentive inducements
	Instructional control
	Bizarre symbolic control
		External reinforcement
		  tangible rewards
		  social and status rewards
		  expressions of injury
		  alleviation of aversive treatment
		Punishment
		  inhibitory
		  informative
		Vicarious reinforcement
		  observed reward
		  observed punishment
		Self-reinforcement
		  self-reward
		  self-punishment
		  neutralization of self-punishment
		    moral justification
		    palliative comparison
		    euphemistic labeling
		    displacement of responsibility
		    diffusion of responsibility
		    dehumanization of victims
		    attribution of blame to victims
		    misrepresentation of
		      consequences

tegrated patterns of behavior without having to form them gradually by tedious trial and error. . . .

In a modern society, aggressive styles of behavior can be adopted from three principal sources. One prominent origin is the aggression modeled and reinforced by family members. Studies of familial determinants of aggression show that parents who favor aggressive solutions to problems have children who tend to use similar aggressive tactics in dealing with others (Bandura and Walters, 1959; Hoffman, 1960). That familial violence breeds violent styles of conduct is further shown by similarities in child abuse practices across several generations (Silver, Dublin, and Lourie, 1969).

Although familial influences play a major role in setting the direction of social development, the family is embedded in a network of other social systems. The subculture in which people reside, and with which they have re-peated contact, provides a second important source of aggression. Not surprisingly, the highest incidence of aggression is found in communities in which aggressive models abound and fighting prowess is regarded as a valued attribute (Short, 1968; Wolfgang and Ferracuti, 1967).

The third source of aggressive conduct is the abundant symbolic modeling provided by the mass media. The advent of television has greatly expanded the range of models available to a growing child. Whereas their predecessors rarely, if ever, observed brutal aggression in their everyday life, both children and adults today have unlimited opportunities to learn the whole gamut of violent conduct from televised modeling within the comfort of their homes.

A considerable amount of research has been conducted in recent years on the effects of televised influences on social behavior. The findings show that exposure to televised violence can have at least four different effects on viewers: (1) It teaches aggressive styles of conduct; (2) it alters restraints over aggressive behavior; (3) it desensitizes and habituates people to violence; and (4) it shapes people's images of reality upon which they base many of their actions. . . .

Learning by Direct Experience

People rarely teach social behaviors that are never exemplified by anyone in their environment. Therefore, in behavior acquired under natural conditions it is often difficult to determine whether reinforcing experiences create the new responses or activate what was already partly learned by observation. Although modeling influences are universally present, patterns of behavior can be shaped through a more rudimentary form of learning relying on the consequences of trial-and-error performance.

Until recently, learning by reinforcement was portrayed as a mechanistic process in which responses are shaped automatically by their immediate consequences. In more recent theoretical analyses, learning from response consequences is conceived of largely as a cognitive process, especially in humans. Consequences serve as an unarticulated way of informing performers what they must do to gain beneficial outcomes and to avoid punishing ones. By observing the differential effects of their actions, individuals discern which responses are appropriate in which settings, and behave accordingly. Although the empirical issue is not yet fully resolved, evidence that human behavior is not much affected by consequences until the point at which the contingencies are discerned, raises serious questions concerning the automaticity of reinforcement. . . .

Modeling and reinforcement influences operate jointly in the social learning of aggression in everyday life. Styles of aggression are largely learned through observation, and refined through reinforced practice. The effects of these two determinants on the form and incidence of aggression are graphically revealed in ethnographic reports of societies that pursue a warlike way of life and those that follow a pacific style. In cultures lacking aggressive models and devaluing injurious

conduct, people live peaceably (Alland, 1972; Dentan, 1968; Levy, 1969; Mead, 1935; Turnbull, 1961). In other societies that provide extensive training in aggression, attach prestige to it, and make its use functional, people spend a great deal of time threatening, fighting, maiming, and killing each other (Bateson, 1936; Chagnon, 1968; Gardner and Heider, 1969; Whiting, 1941).

Instigation Mechanisms

A theory must explain not only how aggressive patterns are acquired but also how they are activated and channeled. Social learning theory distinguishes between two broad classes of motivators of behavior. First, there are the biologically based motivators. These include internal aversive stimulation arising from tissue deficits and external sources of aversive stimulation that activate behavior through their painful effects. The second major source of response inducement involves cognitively based motivators. The capacity to represent future consequences in thought provides one cognitively based source of motivation. Through cognitive representation of future outcomes, individuals can generate current motivators of behavior. The outcome expectations may be material (e.g., consummatory, physically painful), sensory (e.g., novel, enjoyable, or unpleasant sensory stimulation), or social (e.g., positive and negative evaluative reactions). Another cognitively based source of motivation operates through the intervening influences of goal setting and self-evaluative reactions. Self-motivation involves standards against which to evaluate performances. By making positive self-evaluation conditional on attaining a certain level of behavior, individuals create self-inducements to persist in their efforts until their performances match self-prescribed standards.

As we shall show shortly, some aggressive acts are motivated by painful stimulation. However, most of the events that lead people to aggress, such as insults, verbal challenges, status threats, and unjust treatment, gain this activating capacity through learning experiences. People learn to dislike and to attack certain types of individuals either through direct unpleasant encounters with them, or on the basis of symbolic and vicarious experiences that conjure up hatreds. Because of regularities in environmental events, antecedent cues come to signify events to come and the outcomes particular actions are likely to produce. Such uniformities create expectations about what leads to what. When aggressive behavior produces different results depending on the times, places, or persons toward whom it is directed, people use cues predictive of probable consequences in regulating their behavior. They tend to aggress toward persons and in contexts where it is relatively safe and rewarding to do so, but they are disinclined to act aggressively when aggression carries high risk of punishment. The different forms that aggression elicitors take are discussed separately in the sections that follow.

Aversive Instigators

. . . In social learning theory, rather than frustration generating an aggressive drive that is reducible only by injurious behavior, aversive stimulation produces a general state of emotional arousal that can facilitate any number of responses. The type of behavior elicited will depend on how the source of arousal is cognitively appraised, the modes of response learned for coping with stress, and their relative effectiveness. When distressed, some people seek help and support; others increase achievement efforts; others display withdrawal and resignation; some aggress; others experience heightened somatic reactivity; still others anesthetize themselves against a miserable existence with drugs or alcohol; and most, intensify constructive efforts to overcome the source of distress. . . .

Frustration or anger arousal is a facilitative, rather than a necessary, condition for aggression. Frustration tends to provoke aggression mainly in people who have learned to respond to aversive experiences with aggressive attitudes and conduct. Thus, after being frustrated, aggressively trained children behave more aggressively, whereas cooperatively trained children behave more cooperatively (Davitz, 1952).

There exists a large body of evidence that painful treatment, deprivation or delay of re-

wards, personal insults, failure experiences, and obstructions, all of which are aversive, do not have uniform behavioral effects (Bandura, 1969). Some of these aversive antecedents convey injurious intent more clearly than others and therefore have greater aggression-provoking potential.

Physical Assaults. If one wished to provoke aggression, one way to do so would be simply to hit another person, who is likely to oblige with a counterattack. To the extent that counteraggression discourages further assaults it is reinforced by pain reduction and thereby assumes high functional value in social interactions . . .

Nonsocial sources of pain rarely lead people to attack bystanders. Whether or not humans counteraggress in the face of physical assaults depends upon their combat skill and the power of their assailant. Those who possess fighting prowess escalate counterattacks to subdue assailants (Edward, 1968; Peterson, 1971). Given other alternatives, low aggressors are easily dissuaded from counterattacks under retaliative threats.

Verbal Threats and Insults. Social interchanges are typically escalated into physical aggression by verbal threats and insults. In analyzing dyadic interchanges of assault-prone individuals, Toch (1969) found that humiliating affronts and threats to reputation and manly status emerged as major precipitants of violence. High sensitivity to devaluation was usually combined with deficient verbal skills for resolving disputes and to restore self-esteem without having to dispose of antagonists physically. The counterattacks evoked by physical assaults are probably instigated more by humiliation than by physical pain. Indeed, it is not uncommon for individuals, groups, and even nations, to pay heavy injury costs in efforts to "save face" by combat victory.

Insult alone is less effective in provoking attack in those who eschew aggression, but it does heighten their aggressiveness, given hostile modeling and other disinhibitory influences (Hartmann, 1969; Wheeler and Caggiula, 1966). In subcultures in which social ranking is determined by fighting prowess, status threats from challengers within the group or rival outsiders are quick to provoke defensive aggression (Short, 1968).

The most plausible explanation of how insults acquire aggression-eliciting potential is in terms of foreseen consequences. Affronts that are not counteracted can have far-reaching effects for victims. Not only do they fear being targets for further victimization, but they are apt to forfeit the rewards and privileges that go with social standing. To the extent that punishment of insults reduces the likelihood of future maltreatment, the insult-aggression reaction becomes well established.

Adverse Reductions in Conditions of Life. Aversive changes in the conditions of life can also provoke people to aggressive action. Explanations of collective aggression usually invoke impoverishment and discontent arising from privations as principal causal factors. However, since most impoverished people do not aggress, the view that discontent breeds violence requires qualification. This issue is well illustrated in interpretations of urban riots in ghetto areas. Despite condemnation of their degrading and exploitive conditions of life, comparatively few of the disadvantaged take active measures to force warranted changes. Even in cities that experienced civil disturbances, only a small percent of ghetto residents actively participated in the aggressive activities (Lieberson and Silverman, 1965; McCord and Howard, 1968; Sears and McConahay, 1969). . . .

More recent explanations of violent protest emphasize relative deprivation rather than the actual level of aversive conditions as the instigator of collective aggression. In an analysis of conditions preceding major revolutions, Davies (1969) reports that revolutions are most likely to occur when a period of social and economic advances that instills rising expectations is followed by a sharp reversal. People judge their present gains not only in relation to those they secured in the past; they also compare their lot in life with the benefits accruing to others (Bandura, 1977a). Inequities between observed and experienced outcomes tend to create discontent, whereas individuals may be satisfied with limited rewards so long as these are as good as those others are receiving. . . .

Although aggression is more likely to be provoked by relative than by absolute privation, clarification of the role of relative deprivation requires greater consideration of the multifaceted bases of comparative evaluation. People judge their life circumstances in relation to their aspirations, to their past conditions, and to the life situations of others, whom they select for social comparison. Discontent created by raised aspirations, by reduction of rewards and privileges from accustomed levels, and by deceleration in the rate of improvement compared to others, undoubtedly has variant effects. Different sources of inequity (social, economic, political) may have differential aggression-activating potential. Response to inequitable deprivation is further influenced by mollifying social justifications and promise of social reforms. Considering the complex interplay of influences, it is hardly surprising that level of deprivation alone, whether defined in absolute or in relative terms, is a weak predictor of collective aggression (McPhail, 1971).

Thwarting of Goal-Oriented Behavior. Proponents of the frustration-aggression theory define frustrations in terms of interference or blocking of goal-seeking activities. In this view, people are provoked to aggression when obstructed, delayed, or otherwise thwarted from getting what they want. Research bearing on this issue shows that thwarting can lead people to intensify their efforts, which, if sufficiently vigorous, may be construed as aggressive. However, thwarting fails to provoke forceful action in people who have not experienced sufficient success to develop reward expectations, and in those who are blocked far enough from the goal that it appears unattainable (Bandura and Walters, 1963; Longstreth, 1966).

When thwarting provokes aggression it is probably attributable more to personal affront than to blocking of ongoing behavior. Consistent with this interpretation, people report more aggression to thwartings that appear unwarranted or suggest hostile intent than to those for which excusable reasons exist, even though both involve identical blocking of goal-directed behavior (Cohen, 1955; Pastore, 1952).

The overall evidence regarding the different forms of aversive instigators supports the conclusion that aversive antecedents, though they vary in their activating potential, are facilitative rather than necessary or sufficient conditions for aggression.

Incentive Instigators

The preceding discussion was concerned solely with aversive instigators of aggression, which traditionally occupied a central role in psychological theorizing, often to the neglect of more important determinants. The cognitive capacity of humans to represent future consequences enables them to guide their behavior by outcomes extended forward in time. A great deal of human aggression, in fact, is prompted by anticipated positive consequences. Here, the instigator is the pull of expected benefits, rather than the push of painful treatment.

The consequences that people anticipate for their actions are derived from, and therefore usually correspond to, prevailing conditions of reinforcement. The anticipatory activation and incentive regulation of aggression receive detailed consideration below. Expectation and actuality do not always coincide because anticipated consequences are also partly inferred from the observed outcomes of others, from what one reads or is told, and from other indicators of likely consequences. Because judgments are fallible, aggressive actions are sometimes prompted and temporarily sustained by erroneous anticipated consequences. Habitual offenders, for example, often err by overestimating the chances of success for transgressive behavior (Claster, 1967). In social interchanges and collective protest, coercive actions are partly sustained, even in the face of punishing consequences, by expectations that continued pressure may eventually produce desired results.

Modeling Instigators

Of the numerous antecedent cues that influence human behavior at any given moment, none is more common than the actions of others. Therefore, a reliable way to prompt people to aggress is to have others do it. Indeed, both children and adults are more likely to behave aggressively and with greater intensity if they have seen others act aggressively than if they have not been exposed to aggressive models (Bandura, 1973; Liebert et al.,1973). The activation potential of modeling influences is enhanced if observers are angered (Berkowitz, 1965; Hartmann, 1969; Wheeler, 1966), the modeled aggression is socially justified (Berkowitz, 1965; Meyer, 1972), or is shown to be successful in securing rewards (Bandura, Ross, and Ross, 1963), and the victim invites attack through prior association with aggression (Berkowitz, 1970). . . .

Instructional Instigators

During the process of socialization, people are trained to obey orders. By rewarding compliance and punishing disobedience, directives issued in the form of authoritative commands elicit obedient aggression. After this form of social control is established, legitimate authorities can secure obedient aggression from others, especially if the actions are presented as justified and necessary, and the issuers possess strong coercive power. As Snow (1961) has perceptively observed, "When you think of the long and gloomy history of man, you will find more hideous crimes have been committed in the name of obedience than in the name of rebellion" (p. 24). . . .

Delusional Instigators

In addition to responding to external instigators, aggressive behavior can be prompted by bizarre beliefs. Every so often tragic episodes occur in which individuals are led by delusional belief to commit acts of violence. Some follow divine inner voices commanding them to murder. There are those who resort to self-protective attacks on paranoid suspicions that others are conspiring to harm them (Reich and Hepps, 1972). Others kill for deranged sacrificial purposes. And still others are prompted by grandiose convictions that it is their heroic responsibility to eliminate evil individuals in positions of influence. . . .

Maintaining Mechanisms

So far we have discussed how aggressive behavior is learned and activated. The third major feature of the social learning formulation concerns the conditions that *sustain* aggressive responding. It is amply documented in psychological research that behavior is extensively regulated by its consequences. This principle applies equally to aggression. Injurious modes of response, like other forms of social behavior, can be increased, eliminated, and reinstated by altering the effects they produce.

People aggress for many different reasons. Similar aggressive actions may thus have markedly different functional value for different individuals and for the same individual on different occasions. Traditional behavior theories conceptualize reinforcement influences almost exclusively in terms of the effects of external outcomes impinging directly upon performers. But external consequences, as influential as they often are, are not the only kind of outcomes that regulate human behavior. People partly guide their actions on the basis of consequences they observe, and by consequences they create for themselves. These three forms of outcomes—external, vicarious, and self-produced—not only serve as separate sources of influence, but they interact in ways that weaken or enhance their effects on behavior (Bandura, 1977a).

External Reinforcement

As we have previously noted, consequences exert effects on behavior largely through their informative and incentive functions. For the most part, response consequences influence behavior antecedently by creating expectations of similar outcomes on future occasions. The likelihood of particular actions is increased by anticipated benefits and reduced by anticipated punishment.

Aggression is strongly influenced by its consequences. Extrinsic rewards assume special importance in interpersonal aggression because such behavior, by its very nature, usually produces some costs among its diverse effects. People who get into fights, for example, will suffer pain and injury even though they eventually triumph over their opponents. Under noncoercive conditions, positive incentives are needed to overcome inhibitions arising from the aversive concomitants of aggression. The positive incentives take a variety of forms.

Tangible Rewards. Aggression is often used by those lacking better alternatives because it is an effective means of securing desired tangible rewards. Ordinarily docile animals will fight when aggressive attacks produce food or drink (Azrin and Hutchinson, 1967; Ulrich, Johnston, Richardson, and Wolff, 1963). Observation of children's interactions reveals that most of the assaultive actions of aggressors produce rewarding outcomes for them (Patterson et al., 1967). Given this high level of positive reinforcement of aggressive behavior, there is no need to invoke an aggressive drive to explain the prevalence of such actions. Aggressive behavior is especially persistent when it is reinforced only intermittently, which is usually the case under the variable conditions of everyday life (Walters and Brown, 1963).

There are other forms of aggression that are sustained by their material consequences though, for obvious reasons, they are not easily subject to systematic analysis. Delinquents and adult transgressors can support themselves on income derived from aggressive pursuits; protesters can secure, through forceful collective response, social reforms that affect their lives materially; governments that rule by force are rewarded in using punitive control by the personal gains it brings to those in power and to supporters who benefit from the existing social arrangements; and nations are sometimes able to gain control over prized territories by military force.

Social and Status Rewards. Aggressive styles of behavior are often adopted because they win approval and status rewards. When people are commended for behaving punitively they become progressively more aggressive, whereas they display a relatively low level of aggression when it is not treated as praiseworthy (Geen and Stonner, 1971; Staples and Walters, 1964). Approval not only increases the specific aggressive responses that are socially reinforced but it tends to enhance other forms of aggression as well (Geen and Pigg, 1970; Loew, 1967; Slaby, 1974).

Analyses of social reinforcement of aggressive behavior in natural settings are in general agreement with results of laboratory studies. Parents of assaultive children are generally nonpermissive for aggressive behavior in the home, but condone, actively encourage, and reinforce provocative and aggressive actions toward others in the community (Bandura, 1960; Bandura and Walters, 1959).

In aggressive gangs, members not only gain approval but achieve social status through their skills in fighting (Short, 1968). In status rewards, performance of valued behavior gains one a social rank that carries with it multiple benefits as long as the position is occupied. A rank-contingent system of reward is more powerful than one in which specific responses are socially rewarded. If failure to behave aggressively deprives one of a specific reward, the negative consequence is limited and of no great importance. A demotion in rank, however, results in forfeiture of all the social and material benefits that go with it. The pressure for aggressive accomplishments is especially strong when status positions are limited and there are many eager competitors for them. . . .

Reduction of Aversive Treatment. People are often treated aversively by others, from which treatment they seek relief. Coercive action that is not unduly hazardous is the most direct and quickest means of alleviating maltreatment, if only temporarily. Defensive forms of aggression are frequently reinforced by their capacity to terminate humiliating and painful treatment. Reinforcement through pain reduction is well documented in studies cited earlier, which show that children who are victimized but can end the abuse by successful counteraggression eventually become highly aggressive in their behavior (Patterson et al., 1967). . . .

In the social learning analysis, defensive aggression is sustained to a greater extent by anticipated consequences than by its instantaneous effects. People will endure the pain of reprisals on expectations that their aggressive efforts will eventually remove deleterious conditions. Aggressive actions may also be partly maintained in the face of painful counterattack by anticipated costs of timidity. In aggression-oriented circles, failure to fight back can arouse fear of future victimization and humiliation. A physical pummeling may, therefore, be far less distressing than repeated social derision or increased likelihood of future abuse. In other words, humans do not behave like unthinking servomechanisms directed solely by immediate response feedback. Under aversive conditions of life, people will persist, at least for a time, in aggressive behavior that produces immediate pain but prospective relief from misery.

Expressions of Injury. In the view of drive theorists, the purpose of aggression is infliction of injury. Just as eating relieves hunger, hurting others presumably discharges the aggressive drive. It has therefore been widely assumed that aggressive behavior is reinforced by signs of suffering in the victim. . . .

From the standpoint of social learning theory, suffering of one's enemies is most apt to augment aggression when hurting them lessens maltreatment or benefits aggressors in other ways. When aggressors suffer reprisals or self-contempt for harming others, signs of suffering function as negative reinforcers that deter injurious attacks. . . .

Punishing Consequences

Restraints over injurious behavior arise from two different sources. *Social restraints* are rooted in threats of external punishment. *Personal restraints* operate through anticipatory self-condemning reactions toward one's own conduct. In developmental theories these two sources of restraint are traditionally characterized as fear control and guilt control, respectively. Punishing consequences that are observed or experienced directly convey information about the circumstances under which aggressive behavior is safe and when it is hazardous. Aggressive actions are therefore partly regulated on the basis of anticipated negative consequences. Since the behavior is under cognitive and situational control, restraints arising from external threats vary in durability and in how widely they generalize beyond the prohibitive situations.

The effectiveness of punishment in controlling behavior is determined by a number of factors (Bandura, 1969; Campbell and Church, 1969). Of special importance are the benefits derived through aggressive actions and the availability of alternative means of securing goals. Other determinants of the suppressive power of punishment include the likelihood that aggression will be punished, the nature, severity, timing, and duration of aversive consequences. In addition, the level of instigation to aggression and the characteristics of the prohibitive agents influence how aggressors will respond under threat of punishment.

When alternative means are available for people to get what they seek, aggressive modes of behavior that carry high risk of punishment are rapidly discarded. Aggression control through punishment becomes more problematic when aggressive actions are socially or tangibly rewarded, and alternative means of securing desired outcomes are either unavailable, less effective in producing results, or not within the capabilities of the aggressors. Here, punishment must be applied with considerable force and consistency to outweigh the benefits of aggression. Even then it achieves, at best, temporary selective control in the threatening situation. Functional aggression is reinstated when threats are removed, and readily performed in settings in which the chance of punishment is low (Bandura and Walters, 1959). Punishment is not only precarious as an external inhibitor of intermittently rewarded behavior, but its frequent use can inadvertently promote aggression by modeling punitive modes of control (Hoffman, 1960).

Punishment, whether direct or observed, is informative as well as inhibitory. People can profit from witnessing the failures of others or from their own mistakes. Given strong instigation to aggression and limited options, threats lead people to adopt safer forms of aggression or to refine the prohibited behavior to improve its chances of success. For this reason, antisocial aggression is best prevented by combining deterrents with the cultivation of more functional alternatives. Most law-abiding behavior relies more on deter-rence through preferable prosocial options than on threats of legal sanctions.

There are certain conditions under which aggression is escalated through punishment, at least in the short run. Individuals who repeatedly engage in aggressive behavior have experienced some success in controlling others through force. In interpersonal encounters, they respond to counterattacks with progressively more punitive reactions to force acquiescence (Edwards, 1968; Patterson, 1977; Toch, 1969). The use of punishment as a control technique also carries risks of escalating collective aggression when grievances are justifiable and challengers possess substantial coercive power (Bandura, 1973; Gurr, 1970). Under these circumstances, continued aggressive behavior eventually succeeds in changing social practices that lack sufficient justification to withstand concerted protest.

Vicarious Reinforcement

In the course of everyday life there are numerous opportunities to observe the actions of others and the circumstances under which they are rewarded, ignored, or punished. Observed outcomes influence behavior in much the same way as directly experienced consequences. People can profit from the successes and mistakes of others as well as from their own experiences. As a general rule, seeing aggression rewarded in others increases, and seeing it punished decreases, the tendency to behave in similar ways (Bandura, 1965; Bandura et al., 1963). The more consistent the observed response consequences, the greater are the facilitators and inhibitory effects on viewers (Rosekrans and Hartup, 1967). . . .

Self-Regulatory Mechanisms

The discussion thus far has analyzed how behavior is regulated by external consequences that are either observed or experienced firsthand. People are not simply reactors to external influences. Through self-generated inducements and self-produced consequences they can exercise some influence over their own behavior. In this self-regulatory process, people adopt through tuition and modeling certain standards of behavior and respond to their own actions in self-rewarding or self-punishing ways. An act therefore includes among its determinants self-produced influences. . . .

Self-regulated incentives are conceptualized as motivational devices rather than as automatic strengtheners of preceding responses. By making self-reward and self-punishment contingent on designated performances, people motivate themselves to expend the effort needed to attain performances that give them self-satisfaction and they refrain from behaving in ways that result in self-censure. Because of self-reactive tendencies, aggressors must contend with themselves as well as with others when they behave in an injurious manner.

Self-Reward for Aggression. One can distinguish several ways in which self-generated consequences enter into the self-regulation of aggressive behavior. At one extreme are persons who have adopted behavioral standards and codes that make aggressive feats a source of personal pride. Such individuals readily engage in aggressive activities and derive enhanced feelings of self-worth from physical conquests (Bandura and Walters, 1959; Toch, 1969; Yablonsky, 1962). Lacking self-reprimands for hurtful conduct, they are deterred from cruel acts mainly by reprisal threats. Idiosyncratic self-systems of morality are not confined to individuals or fighting gangs. In aggressive cultures where prestige is closely tied to fighting prowess, members take considerable pride in aggressive exploits.

Self-Punishment for Aggression. After ethical and moral standards of conduct are adopted, anticipatory self-condemning reactions for violating personal standards ordinarily serve as self-deterrents against reprehensible acts. . . .

Disengagement of Internal Control. Theories of internalization generally portray incorporated entities in the form of a conscience, superego, and moral codes as continuous internal overseers of conduct. Such theories encounter difficulties in explaining the variable operation of internal control and the perpetration of gross inhumanities by otherwise humane, compassionate people. Such concepts as "superego lacunae. . . .islands of superego," and various "mental defense mechanisms" have been proposed as the explanatory factors.

In the social learning analysis, moral people perform culpable acts through processes that disengage evaluative self-reactions from such conduct rather than through defects in the development or the structure of their superegos (Bandura, 1973). Acquisition of self-regulatory capabilities does not create an invariant control mechanism within a person. Self-evaluative influences do not operate unless activated, and many situational dynamics influence their selective activation.

Self-deterring consequences are likely to be activated most strongly when the causal connection between conduct and the detrimental effects it produces is unambiguous. There are various means, however, by which self-evaluative consequences can be dissociated from censurable behavior.

One set of disengagement practices operates at the level of the behavior. People do not ordinarily engage in reprehensible conduct until they have justified to themselves the morality of their actions. What is culpable can be made honorable through cognitive restructuring. In this process, reprehensible conduct is made personally and socially acceptable by portraying it in the service of moral ends. Over the years, much destructive and reprehensible conduct has been perpetrated by decent, moral people in the name of religious principles and righteous ideologies. Acting on moral or ideological imperative reflects not an unconscious defense mechanism, but a conscious offense mechanism.

Self-deplored acts can also be made righteous by contrasting them with flagrant inhumanities. The more outrageous the comparison practices, the more likely are one's reprehensible acts to appear trifling or even benevolent. Euphemistic language provides an additional convenient device for disguising reprehensible activities and according them a respectable status. Through convoluted verbiage pernicious conduct is made benign and those who engage in it are relieved of a sense of personal agency (Gambino, 1973). Moral justifications and palliative characterizations are especially effective disinhibitors because they not only eliminate self-generated deterrents, but engage self-reward in the service of injurious behavior. What was morally unacceptable becomes a source of self-pride.

Another set of dissociative practices operates by obscuring or distorting the relationship between actions and the effects they cause. People will behave in highly punitive ways they normally repudiate if a legitimate authority acknowledges responsibility for the consequences of the conduct (Diener, Dineen, Endresen, Beaman, and Fraser, 1975; Milgram, 1974). By displacing responsibility people do not see themselves as personally accountable for their actions and are thus spared self-prohibiting reactions. Nor is self-censure activated when the link between conduct and its consequences is obscured by diffusing responsibility. Through division of labor, diffusion of decision making, and collective action people can behave injuriously without anyone feeling personally responsible for culpable behavior. They therefore act more aggressively when responsibility is obscured by a collective instrumentality (Bandura, Underwood, and Fromson, 1975).

Additional ways of weakening self-deterring reactions operate by disregarding or obscuring the consequences of actions. When people embark on a self-disapproved course of action for personal gain, or because of other inducements, they avoid facing the harm they cause. Self-censuring reactions are unlikely to be activated as long as the detrimental effects of conduct are disregarded, minimized, or misjudged (Brock and Buss, 1962, 1964).

The final set of disengagement practices operate at the level of the recipients of injurious effects. The strength of self-evaluative reactions partly depends on how the people toward whom actions are directed are viewed. Maltreatment of individuals who are regarded as subhuman or debased is less apt to arouse self-reproof than if they are seen as human beings with dignifying qualities (Bandura et al., 1975; Zimbardo, 1969). Analysis of the cognitive concomitants of injurious behavior reveals that dehumanization fosters a variety of self-exonerating maneuvers (Bandura et al., 1975). People strongly disapprove of cruel behavior and rarely excuse its use when they interact with humanized individuals. By contrast, people seldom condemn punitive conduct and generate self-disinhibiting justifications for it when they direct their behavior toward individuals divested of humanness.

Many conditions of contemporary life are conducive to dehumanization. Bureaucratization, automation, urbanization, and high social mobility lead people to relate to each other in anonymous, impersonal ways. In addition, social practices that divide people into in-group and out-group members produce human estrangement that fosters dehumanization. Strangers can be more easily cast as unfeeling beings than can personal acquaintances.

Psychological research tends to focus on the disinhibiting effects of social practices that divest people of human qualities. This emphasis is understandable considering the prevalence and the serious consequences of people's inhumanities toward each other. Of equal theoretical and social significance is the power of humanization to counteract injurious conduct. Studies examining this process reveal that, even under conditions that ordinarily weaken self-deterrents, it is difficult for people to behave cruelly towards others when others are characterized in ways that personalize and humanize them (Bandura et al., 1975).

Attributing blame to one's victims is still another expedient that can serve self-exonerative purposes. Detrimental interactions usually involve a series of reciprocally escalative actions in which the victims are rarely faultless. One can always select from the chain of events an instance of defensive behavior by the adversary and view it as the original instigation. Victims then get blamed for bringing suffering on themselves, or extraordinary circumstances are invoked to vindicate irresponsible conduct. By blaming others, one's own actions are excusable. People are socially aided in dehumanizing and blaming groups held in disfavor by pejorative stereotyping and indoctrination.

Gradualism and Disinhibition. The aforementioned practices will not instantaneously transform a gentle person into a brutal aggressor. Rather, the change is usually achieved through a gradual desensitization process in which participants may not fully recognize the marked changes they are undergoing. Initially, individuals are prompted to perform aggressive acts they can tolerate without excessive self-censure. After their discomfort and self-reproof are diminished through repeated performance, the level of aggression is progressively increased in this manner until eventually gruesome deeds, originally regarded as abhorrent, can be performed without much distress.

As is evident from the preceding discussion, the development of self-regulatory functions does not create a mechanical servocontrol system wherein behavioral output is accurately monitored, compared against an internal standard and, if judged deviant, is promptly brought in line with the referent standard. Nor do situational influences exercise mechanical control. Personal judgments operating at each subfunction preclude the automaticity of the process. There is leeway in judging whether a given behavioral standard is applicable. Because of the complexity and inherent ambiguity of most events, there is even greater leeway in the judgment of behavior and its effects. To add further to the variability of the self-control process, most activities are performed under collective arrangements that obscure responsibility, thus permitting leeway in judging the degree of personal agency in the effects that are socially produced. In short, there exists considerable latitude for personal judgmental factors to affect whether or not self-regulatory influences will be engaged in any given activity.

Discussion Questions

1. According to Bandura and others, we often learn to behave aggressively within our families. Drawing on Bandura's theory, describe the different ways in which families might foster aggression.

2. Bandura's theory emphasizes the important role that cognitive or thought processes play in aggressive behavior (as opposed, for example, to the role of direct experience). Describe the different ways in which cognitive processes are implicated in aggression.

3. Imagine you are a therapist trying to determine why one of your patients behaves in an aggressive manner. Drawing on Bandura's theory, what questions might you ask your patient?

4. Drawing on Bandura's theory, list the steps that you would take to reduce crime in the United States. ✦

4

Crime and Human Nature

James Q. Wilson
Richard J. Herrnstein

Wilson and Herrnstein present a contemporary theory of crime that draws on biological, psychological, and sociological research. The core of the theory is built around an assumption derived from behavioral and social learning theory in psychology: individuals choose to engage in crime when they believe that the net rewards of crime outweigh the net rewards of "noncrime." The rewards of crime include material gain and "intangible benefits, such as obtaining emotional or sexual gratification, receiving the approval of peers, satisfying an old score against an enemy, or enhancing one's sense of justice." The judgements that individuals make about the rewards of crime and noncrime depend on both individual traits (many of which are largely a function of biological factors) and the social environment.

Wilson and Herrnstein point out that the rewards of crime (e.g., money) are usually more immediate than the rewards of noncrime (e.g., the good opinion of family and friends). As a result, traits that increase the individual's tendency to discount the future are especially conducive to crime. Such traits include low intelligence and a range of personality traits, like impulsiveness, sensation seeking, the inability to learn from punishment, and low anxiety (which are said to characterize psychopathic personalties). The individual's social environment, especially family environment, is also important. Families may contribute to the development of traits that foster crime, fail to instill a desire for the approval of others, fail to instill a conscience, and reinforce or at least fail to effectively sanction deviance. Individuals from such families are obviously more likely to conclude that the rewards of crime

outweigh those of noncrime. Wilson and Herrnstein also discuss the ways in which the school, peer group, community, and other aspects of the social environment may contribute to crime. They argue, however, that crime is largely a result of individual traits and the family environment. They point out, for example, that most serious offenders begin offending at an early age and that their behavior shows much continuity over time.

Wilson and Herrnstein's theory generated much controversy when it first appeared, with sociologists claiming that they assigned too much importance to biological factors and the individual's traits resulting from such factors and not enough importance to the social environment. In particular, much of the evidence cited by Wilson and Herrnstein in support of their theory was challenged—including their argument that offenders are much more likely to discount the future than nonoffenders (for example, see Gottfredson and Hirschi, 1990; Kamin, 1986). The debate over the importance of biological and psychological factors (as well as social factors) continues, but at a minimum Wilson and Herrnstein's theory forced mainstream criminologists to give serious attention to biological and psychological factors.

References

Gottfredson, Michael R. and Travis Hirschi. 1990. *A General Theory of Crime*. Stanford: Stanford University Press.

Kamin, L. J. 1986. "Is Crime in the Genes? The Answer Depends on Who Chooses What Evidence." *Scientific American* 254 (February): 22-27.

... Our theory rests on the assumption that people, when faced with a choice, choose the preferred course of action. This assumption is quite weak; it says nothing more than that whatever people choose to do, they choose it because they prefer it. In fact, it is more than weak; without further clarification, it is a tautology. When we say people "choose," we do not necessarily mean that they consciously deliberate about what to do. All we mean is that their behavior is determined by its consequences. A person will do that thing the consequences of which are perceived by him or her to be preferable to the consequences of doing something else. What can save such a statement from being a tautology is how plausibly we describe the gains and losses associated with alternative courses of action and the standards by which a person evaluates those gains and losses.

These assumptions are commonplace in philosophy and social science. Philosophers speak of hedonism or utilitarianism, economists of value or utility, and psychologists of reinforcement or reward. We will use the language of psychology, but it should not be hard to translate our terminology into that of other disciplines. Though social scientists differ as to how much behavior can reasonably be described as the result of a choice, all agree that at least some behavior is guided, or even precisely controlled, by things variously termed pleasure, pain, happiness, sorrow, desirability, or the like. Our object is to show how this simple and widely used idea can be used to explain behavior.

At any given moment, a person can choose between committing a crime and not committing it (all these alternatives to crime we lump together as "noncrime"). The consequences of committing the crime consist of rewards (what psychologists call "reinforcers") and punishments; the consequences of not committing the crime (i.e., engaging in noncrime) also entail gains and losses. The larger the ratio of the net rewards of crime to the net rewards of noncrime, the greater the tendency to commit the crime. The net rewards of crime include, obviously, the likely material gains from the crime, but they also include intangible benefits, such as obtaining emotional or sexual gratification, receiving the approval of peers, satisfying an old score against an enemy, or enhancing one's sense of justice. One must deduct from these rewards of crime any losses that accrue immediately—that are, so to speak, contemporaneous with the crime. They include the pangs of conscience, the disapproval of onlookers, and the retaliation of the victim.

The value of noncrime lies all in the future. It includes the benefits to the individual of avoiding the risk of being caught and punished and, in addition, the benefits of avoiding penalties not controlled by the criminal justice system, such as the loss of reputation or the sense of shame afflicting a person later discovered to have broken the law and the possibility that, being known as a criminal, one cannot get or keep a job.

The value of any reward or punishment associated with either crime or noncrime is, to some degree, uncertain. A would-be burglar can rarely know exactly how much loot he will take away or what its cash value will prove to be. The assaulter or rapist may exaggerate the satisfaction he thinks will follow the assault or the rape. Many people do not know how sharp the bite of conscience will be until they have done something that makes them feel the bite. The anticipated approval of one's buddies may or may not be forthcoming. Similarly, the benefits of noncrime are uncertain. One cannot know with confidence whether one will be caught, convicted, and punished, or whether one's friends will learn about the crime and as a result withhold valued esteem, or whether one will be able to find or hold a job.

Compounding these uncertainties is time. The opportunity to commit a crime may be ready at hand (an open, unattended cash register in a store) or well in the future (a bank that, with planning and preparation, can be robbed). And the rewards associated with noncrime are almost invariably more distant than those connected with crime, perhaps many weeks or months distant. The strength of reinforcers tends to decay over time at rates that differ among individuals. As a result, the extent to which people take into account distant possibilities—a crime that can be committed only tomorrow, or punishment that will be inflicted only in a year—will affect whether they choose crime or noncrime. . . .

The Theory as a Whole

The larger the ratio of the rewards (material and nonmaterial) of noncrime to the rewards (material and nonmaterial) of crime, the weaker the tendency to commit crimes. The bite of conscience, the approval of peers, and any sense of inequity will increase or decrease the total value of crime; the opinions of family, friends, and employers are important benefits of noncrime, as is the desire to avoid the penalties that can be imposed by the criminal justice system. The strength of any reward declines with time, but people differ in the rate at which they discount the future. The strength of a given reward is also affected by the total supply of reinforcers. . . .

Constitutional Factors

The average offender tends to be constitutionally distinctive, though not extremely or abnormally so. The biological factors whose traces we see in faces, physiques, and correlations with the behavior of parents and siblings are predispositions toward crime that are expressed as psychological traits and activated by circumstances. It is likely that the psychological traits involve intelligence and personality, and that the activating events include certain experiences within the family, in school, and in the community at large, all large topics in their own right and dealt with in chapters of their own.

The existence of biological predispositions means that circumstances that activate criminal behavior in one person will not do so in another, that social forces cannot deter criminal behavior in 100 percent of a population, and that the distributions of crime within and across societies may, to some extent, reflect underlying distributions of constitutional factors. Perhaps the simplest thing to say at this point is that crime cannot be understood without taking into account individual predispositions and their biological roots. . . .

Dimensions of Personality

Instead of a sharply defined entity, psychopathy is made up of deviations along some of the common dimensions of personality. In a medical metaphor, it is more like anemia than like a broken bone. Everyone has a red blood count; the anemic's is just too low. Likewise, everyone has a rate of discounting future events; the psychopath's is relatively high. Everyone has some level of internal arousal or emotionality and a susceptibility to the conditioning of internalized prohibitions; the psychopath's are relatively weak.

Everyone has his or her own habitual level of internal speech; the psychopath's level tends to be minimal. People who deviate toward psychopathy, but not as much as the full-blown psychopath, will suffer a smaller risk of asocial behavior, but still more than average. People who deviate in the other direction—toward more gradual time discounting, greater verbal mediation, a richer inner life, and a more deeply ingrained set of standards for behavior—should be less susceptible to the temptations of ordinary crime.

The symptoms of psychopathy affect two elements in our theory . . . specifically the rewards for noncrime and the internalized decrements ("conscience") in the rewards for crime. Legal punishment deters psychopaths less than it does others because it is delayed and aversive, and aversive stimuli are especially ineffective for psychopaths if they are delayed. At the same time, crime is more attractive for psychopaths because it is not so much weakened by internalized prohibitions. However, the choice between crime and noncrime may vary with individual differences along dimensions besides those of psychopathy. There are other atypicalities that increase the relative strength of crime. . . .

To say that someone has a criminogenically deviant characteristic is to say that in settings in which more ordinary people would not offend, he or she would. A dark city street may strike one person as tempting and another as frightening. The difference may depend on many variables, some already considered and others to be taken up in the next section. Age, sex, physique, a history of academic or socioeconomic success or failure, impulsiveness, fearfulness, cruelty, momentary need, and longstanding habits and values are among the factors that may distinguish the potential offender from his victim. The offender offends not just because of immediate needs and circumstances but also because of enduring personal characteristics, some of whose traces can be found in his behavior from early childhood on, as this chapter, and succeeding ones, show.

Consistencies in behavior can arise either from inherited predispositions or from consistencies in the environment, or both. As an approximate guideline, this part of the book has leaned toward the inherited sources and the next part leans toward the environmental. But the guideline cannot avoid being approximate, for many of the ordinary variables of behavioral analysis combine the effects of both genes and environment.

Personality, intelligence, and psychopathologies of various sorts each involve some genetic inheritance. This may seem controversial to some readers, but it is the clear consensus of those most intimately acquainted with the data. The details of inheritance are complex and incompletely understood, but it would be hard to find a serious contemporary student of these topics who denies a genetic contribution, and, in many cases, a substantial one. Current estimates place the heritability of intelligence between 50 and 80 percent, and the heritability of most common dimensions of personality perhaps 20 percent lower, on the average. If the predictors of criminal behavior are genetic to some degree, it follows that crime should be too.

. . . Criminal behavior runs in families because variation along its controlling dimensions have both genetic and environmental origins. The genes may express their influence at any point in the model of criminal behavior, just as the environment may. The strengths of various reinforcers, the time-discounting rates, the opportunity costs of legal punishment, the likelihood of success in crime or noncrime, the social consequences of a certain physique or face-all of these potentially criminogenic variables are rooted in individual characteristics shaped by both inheritance and experience. . . .

Families

There are strong reasons for believing that the interaction between constitutional and familial factors has a powerful effect on later misconduct, especially physical aggression. We have suggested that most of this effect can be explained in behavioral terms—that is, as the result of patterns of reinforcement. To say this, however, is not to say that only external consequences (or material ones) control behavior, for what is learned by the early association between activities and responses is not merely how best to achieve rewards controlled by others but also the extent to which one rewards oneself (by the averted pang of conscience) and how far in the future it is reasonable to value consequences. Moreover, people not only learn what behavior will affect the approval of others but also how valuable (i.e., how reinforcing) that approval is.

Neither the studies that observe childhood aggression directly nor those that follow it, using official data or self-reports, over time provide us with direct measures of the growth of either conscience or a distant time horizon. But everything they do tell us is consistent with the findings of research that describe the subjective states of offenders. For example, offenders are much more likely than nonoffenders to prefer an immediate small reward to a delayed larger one. And among offenders, recidivists are more likely to be impulsive than nonrecidivists. Moreover, impulsiveness is strongly associated with other kinds of behavior-aggressiveness, hyperactivity, and having problems in school—that are, in turn, often precursors of criminality.

Most children who have conduct disorders are also hyperactive, and vice versa. Among delinquents, the hyperactive ones tend to be the most antisocial. Though there is some disagreement about how distinctive hyperkinesis is, Michael Rutter and Henri Giller, in their review of the evidence, conclude that it is a recognizable disorder consisting of inattentiveness and extreme impulsiveness that appears before the age of three.

Being impulsive is to some degree a characteristic of all young children, but especially of less bright ones; in a sense, the child who remains impulsive as he grows older suffers from a kind of arrested development, such that he approaches the larger world with a temperament more appropriate to the nursery school. As Mischel puts it in his summary of research on this subject, "It is difficult to conceive of socialization (or, indeed, of civilization) without such self-imposed delays." A predisposition to impulsiveness . . . when combined with a family setting in which rewards and penalties are not systematically made contingent on behavior, leads to inadequate socialization and a strain on civilization.

After taking these factors into account, it is not entirely clear how much of the individual differences in criminality remains to be explained. Some offenders are late bloomers who have no record of youthful misconduct, and many delinquents are casual offenders who stop breaking the law before they reach adulthood. It is easier to explain why misconduct stops in these later years than why it should begin then. . . . [A]s a person grows older he becomes subject to a larger and more various array of reinforcers, and this is sufficient, for most casual offenders, to induce them to alter their behavior in approved ways. Behavior that was useful in winning a schoolyard fight or stealing a neighbor's bicycle becomes much less useful—indeed, downright disadvantageous—when one wants to find a wife, get a regular job, or enlarge one's circle of friends. The explanation for late bloomers is harder to devise, but probably has much to do with later experiences—in school, the neighborhood, or the world at large—that reinforce responses that had not previously been rewarded.

But these late bloomers are only a small minority of adult criminals. Most important, they are rarely the serious, repeat offenders. The chronic recidivists begin their misdeeds at a very early age. This means that constitutional and familial factors are most important in explaining the behavior of the most serious offenders. Later experiences, especially among peers and in schools, will have some effect on the behavior of this group, but probably a second-order effect. . . .

Schooling

The full story of the effects, if any, of schooling on crime cannot be told; the studies we have, informative as they are, leave many questions unanswered. But the evidence from the best of these studies is consistent with the view that individual differences affect crime rates both directly (the common-cause model) and indirectly (the intervening-variable model), the latter occurring as personal attributes interact with school processes. Boys with below-normal verbal intelligence will commit more crimes, on the average, than boys with higher verbal skills, whether or not they attend a good school, but if they attend a good one, their probability of committing a crime—and the probability of their brighter friends committing a crime—will drop. Perhaps the same relationship between schools and behavior exists with respect to other personal traits, such as temperament and attitudes. A "good school" seems to be one that, regardless of its socioeconomic composition, is not swamped with low-aptitude students and provides a firm but nurturant social environment in its classrooms. In the United States, such an environment appears to be more readily attained in private and Catholic schools than in public ones.

Boys who attend a poor or mediocre school are likely to find that the personal deficits with which they begin their schooling are unaffected or made worse. Success in schools comes to students with good verbal skills; boys without those skills are likely to seek other rewards, such as those that accrue to physical prowess. The benefits of schooling lie in the future; boys who are impulsive are likely to discount those future rewards heavily and allow their actions to be governed by more immediate consequences. Teachers expect their students to conform to rules and to defer to their authority; boys from cold families with inconsistent disciplinary practices are likely to attach little value to such teacher expectations and, if the teacher attempts to enforce those expectations in the same cold and inconsistent manner as the parents, the boys may well rebel even more. In this way, deficits that had a constitutional or familial origin accumulate and, possibly, worsen.

The accumulation of deficits can be moderated or reversed, but only with difficulty and then chiefly for the less serious offenders. The chronic, major offenders, as we have seen in study after study, begin their delinquent careers very early in life, well before schools make any very difficult demands. Special programs designed for the most troublesome youth, such as those in Columbus and Kansas City, are not likely to have much effect, even though the boys themselves like them. There is some evidence—but as yet not much—that preschool programs aimed at preventing the emergence of high-rate offending may have some value.

Schools may also affect criminality in ways that are largely independent of what teachers do. A school, after all, brings together a large number of young persons. If the school is in a high-crime neighborhood, boys attending it will be more likely to meet high-rate offenders than if the school were in a low-crime area. Thus, the school may contribute to criminality because of the peer groups that form there. These peer and community influences are the subject of the next chapter. . . .

Community

Aspects of community life—friends on the street corner, the boundaries of the neighborhood, the density of opportunities, the informal processes of social control—affect individual crime rates to some degree, but the magnitude of that effect is hard to estimate. Moreover, we do not know whether community factors chiefly affect the prevalence of crime (i.e., what proportion of a group of young persons ever commits a crime) or the incidence of offending (i.e., the number of crimes a given offender commits per year). In our view, most of the variation among individuals in criminality can be accounted for by personal traits, family socialization, and (perhaps) school experiences, and this is especially true for variations in incidence. The evidence of previous chapters strongly suggests that high-rate offenders begin offending very early in their lives, well before communal factors—whether peers who are "rotten apples" or neighborhood social processes that set boundaries, supply targets, or provide surveillance—could play much of a role. We speculate that neighborhood conditions affect prevalence more than incidence, especially to the extent that those conditions create threats to personal safety that are met by reciprocal violence or provide dense criminal opportunities. There is some evidence from self-report studies of young persons in an upper-middle-class suburb that peer effects may be greatest on delinquency rates among affluent children for whom offending is more a

form of "play," and thus more likely to require shared experiences to be enjoyable, than a quest for material gains. And even among lower-status youth, peer effects may be greater for those offenses, such as drug use and vandalism, that derive their reinforcement from the group setting than for rapes and robberies that supply individual rewards.

The search for the mechanism by which aspects of community life affect criminality has involved the use of some rather vague, hard-to-grasp concepts—anonymity, mobility, territoriality—that might better be stated as sources of reinforcement and punishment. Peers and gangs can affect the value a person assigns to the rewards of crime (by adding the approval of colleagues to the perceived value of the loot or the direct gratification of the act); the social boundaries of the neighborhood can affect the value he assigns to the rewards of noncrime (by narrowing the range of persons whose good opinion is valued and widening the range of persons who are thought to be undeserving of consideration); the density of human settlement can affect the frequency with which one encounters opportunities for crime (by presenting a chance to steal a purse or a car when one is to the right of his "crossover point"—that is, when the rewards of crime appear stronger than the delayed rewards of not committing the crime); and the extent of natural surveillance of the streets, provided it is carried out by persons willing to act on the basis of what they see, may affect the probability of being caught and punished.

Human Nature and the Political Order

. . . The argument of this [chapter] is that there *is* a human nature that develops in intimate settings out of a complex interaction of constitutional and social factors, and that this nature affects how people choose between the consequences of crime and its alternatives. Young men are everywhere more likely than females or older persons to commit common street crimes, because of the way nature and nurture combine to make male children more impulsive and aggressive and less concerned with the well-being of others than are females or adults. Most male children outgrow such behavior, but whenever the socializing processes of family and community are insufficient to extend the time horizon or enlarge the sympathies of young boys, the incidence of crime among them will tend to remain high. Even when the conditions of family and community life are favorable, a few young persons (especially those displaying psychopathic personalities) may persist in criminality. Among the many who experiment with crime and the few who persist in it, the contingencies of reinforcements and punishments will have an effect on the rate at which they offend, but it may often be less than the effect obtained by the presence or absence of internalized restraints on crime, notably conscience and a desire for the good opinion of others. Society, by the institutions it designs and the values it sustains, affects the extent to which families and communities are able and willing to lengthen the time horizon, inculcate a conscience, and instill a concern for others among the young in ways that make an orderly society possible.

Though there is much we have yet to learn and though controversies abound over how best to interpret what we do know, the facts summarized in the preceding chapters rivet our attention on the earliest stages of the life cycle. There are high-rate offenders who are late bloomers, there are mass murderers who first kill in middle age, there are serious delinquents who enter the path of righteousness when they reach their early twenties. But these cases account for the minority of all those persons who frequently commit serious crimes. We have seen that what happens in school has some effect on criminality, that television and the mass media may have a small impact, and that experiences in the community and the labor market no doubt make some difference; but after all is said and done, the most serious offenders are those boys who begin their delinquent careers at a very early age. The correlation between early age of onset and a high rate of offending is one of the best-established generalizations in all of criminology. As the twig is bent. . . .

That is not a counsel of despair or an argument for the inevitability of crime among certain kinds of persons. Society's discovery that some young persons enter school with a serious learning disability was not greeted with a sense of hopelessness or scornfully rejected as the misguided conclusion of social Darwinism; instead, it was hailed as a good reason for abandoning educational methods that punished slow learners and as a new opportunity for finding better ways to identify and help those youngsters most at risk.

We are aware that criminality is not quite the same as a learning disability, though we remind our readers that until recently many people thought they were the same ("he won't learn because he's a rotten kid"). When we explain such a disability, or when we give an account of many other forms of behavior—for example, anxiety, extroversion, athletic prowess, or school achievement—there is rarely much dispute about the conclusion that both constitutional factors and social circumstances, especially those occurring at an early age, are properly part of the explanation. But explaining criminality arouses our moral and political sensibilities, and as a result many persons are more inclined to accept one set of explanations for crime over another almost without regard to the facts.

To some extent, that is understandable. Crime brings a person into conflict with society; having violated its rules, he risks shame and punishment. It is the mark of a decent and compassionate instinct for people to fear any explanation of crime that could be interpreted as suggesting that some individuals are destined, beyond hope, to experience those penalties.

We offer no such theory of predestination. If one asks whether criminals are born or made, the answer, in one sense, is that they are both and, in a more important sense, that the question is badly phrased. The words "born or made" imply that some part of criminality may be assigned, categorically and permanently, to constitutional (including genetic) factors and the other part, categorically and permanently, to social factors. Such an effort at partitioning variations in criminality between two types of causes neglects, obviously, the complex interactions that exist between those causes.

This partitioning, properly done, may make sense when the trait to be explained is relatively stable and easily measured. For example, it may make perfectly good sense to say that differences among persons in their allergy to ragweed is "largely" (or 80 percent, or whatever) attributable to their genetic makeup. An allergic reaction can be reliably, repeatedly, and measurably induced in a subject by means of a double-blind patch test. Though some people may be allergic to ragweed for psychological reasons having nothing to do with constitutional factors, such persons can be identified and sorted out. It also may make some sense to speak of the degree to which schizophrenia is heritable. Schizophrenia is a mental condition that can often (but not always) be diagnosed by independent observers, that is much more common (i.e., concordant), especially in its more severe forms, among identical than among fraternal twins, and that is better treated with drugs than with verbal therapy. But how much of the variation among persons in their tendency (and it is only a tendency) to display schizophrenic symptoms is genetic is hard to say, because the chemicals in the blood that are associated with the condition may be produced, to unknown degrees, by both genetic factors and environmental stress. Among the sources of that stress is the behavior of other family members, some of whom may themselves be constitutionally predisposed to schizophrenia.

Criminality is an even more difficult problem because it is harder to measure its incidence and prevalence (schizophrenics do not usually conceal their aberrant behavior; criminals usually do), because we do not have any good clues as to what biochemical agents may be responsible for putting individuals at risk, and because we know of no drugs that constitute an effective treatment for it.

Nevertheless, the evidence . . . leaves little doubt, we think, that constitutional factors are implicated, to an unknown but not trivial degree, in the prevalence of high-rate offending. The problem is to acquire a better understanding of how those factors interact with familial and other social experiences. . . .

Discussion Questions

1. Describe the potential rewards and costs of both crime and noncrime. What do Wilson and Herrnstein mean when they state that "the value of noncrime lies all in the future"?

2. Describe the traits and the environment of a person who is likely to conclude that the rewards of crime outweigh the rewards of noncrime.

3. Why do Wilson and Herrnstein conclude that aspects of the social environment like the school and community only have a secondary effect on crime? ✦

5

Pathways in the Life Course to Crime

Terrie E. Moffitt

Moffitt begins her article by arguing that there are two major types of antisocial persons: a small group of persons who engage in antisocial behavior at a high rate over much of their life ("life course-persistent" offenders), and a much larger group of those who limit their antisocial behavior to the adolescent years ("adolescent-limited" offenders). She then develops a theory of antisocial behavior for each group. The theory designed to explain life course-persistent antisocial behavior is most relevant to this section. It represents one of the best attempts to integrate biological, psychological, and sociological variables in the recent literature.

At the heart of the theory is the assertion that persistent antisocial behavior is a product of the interaction between individual traits and the social environment. Moffitt begins by describing certain traits that predispose one to antisocial behavior, and she argues that such traits are a function of biological factors and the early family environment. She then describes the various ways in which individual traits and the social environment mutually influence one another. In certain cases, an escalating process occurs: negative environments exacerbate negative traits and negative traits increase the likelihood of exposure to negative environments. By late adolescence, those traits conducive to antisocial behavior may be so entrenched that changing the person's behavior becomes extremely difficult. A pattern of persistent antisocial behavior has been established. Adolescent-limited antisocial behavior, however, is not fueled by individual traits and,

for reasons indicated in the selection, such behavior is abandoned in early adulthood.

Moffitt's theory is distinguished by its description of the various ways in which individual traits and the social environment may interact with one another to produce persistent antisocial behavior. It is also one of a group of recent theories that attempts to explain patterns in antisocial behavior over the life course (other examples of developmental theories in this volume are provided in the Sampson and Laub and the Thornberry selections). As Moffitt points out, most crime theories focus on the explanation of adolescent crime: they do not attempt to explain patterns of offending over time. Moffitt's theory is compatible with much data on antisocial behavior, and key portions of her theory have received qualified empirical support (see Bartusch et al., 1997; Moffitt, 1997; Paternoster and Brame, 1997).

References

Bartusch, Dawn R. Jeglum, Donal R. Lynam, Terrie E. Moffitt, and Phil A. Silva. 1997. "Is Age Important? Testing a General Versus a Developmental Theory of Antisocial Behavior." *Criminology* 35: 13-48.

Moffitt, Terrie E. 1997. "Adolescent-Limited and life course Persistent Offending: A Complementary Pair of Developmental Theories." Pp. 11-54 in *Developmental Theories of Crime and Delinquency, Advances in Criminological Theory, Volume 7*, edited by Terence P. Thornberry. New Brunswick, NJ: Transaction.

Paternoster, Raymond and Robert Brame. 1997. "Multiple Routes to Delinquency? A Test of Developmental and General Theories of Crime." *Criminology* 35: 49-84.

There are marked individual differences in the stability of antisocial behavior. Many people behave antisocially, but their antisocial behavior is temporary and situational. In contrast, the antisocial behavior of some people is very stable and persistent. Temporary, situational antisocial behavior is quite common in the population, especially among adolescents. Persistent, stable antisocial behavior is found among a relatively small number of males whose behavior problems are also quite extreme. The central tenet of this article is that temporary versus persistent antisocial persons constitute two qualitatively distinct types of persons. In particular, I suggest that juvenile delinquency conceals two qualitatively distinct categories of individuals, each in need of its own distinct theoretical explanation. . . .

For delinquents whose criminal activity is confined to the adolescent years, the causal factors may be proximal, specific to the period of adolescent development, and theory must account for the discontinuity in their lives. In contrast, for persons whose adolescent delinquency is merely one inflection in a continuous lifelong antisocial course, a theory of antisocial behavior must locate its causal factors early in their childhoods and must explain the continuity in their troubled lives. . . .

Figure 5.1
Hypothetical Illustration of the Changing Prevalence of Participation in Antisocial Behavior Across the Life Course (The solid line represents the known curve of crime over age. The arrows represent the duration of participation in antisocial behavior by individuals.)

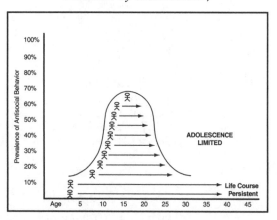

Figure 5.1 depicts the typological thesis to be argued here. A small group of persons is shown engaging in antisocial behavior of one sort or another at every stage of life. I have labeled these persons *life course-persistent* to reflect the continuous course of their antisocial behavior. A larger group of persons fills out the age-crime curve with crime careers of shorter duration. I have labeled these persons

adolescence-limited to reflect their more temporary involvement in antisocial behavior. Thus, timing and duration of the course of antisocial involvement are the defining features in the natural histories of the two proposed types of offenders. . . .

Life Course Persistent Antiscocial Behavior

Continuity of Antisocial Behavior Defined

As implied by the label, continuity is the hallmark of the small group of life course-persistent antisocial persons. Across the life course, these individuals exhibit changing manifestations of antisocial behavior: biting and hitting at age 4, shoplifting and truancy at age 10, selling drugs and stealing cars at age 16, robbery and rape at age 22, and fraud and child abuse at age 30; the underlying disposition remains the same, but its expression changes form as new social opportunities arise at different points in development. This pattern of continuity across age is matched also by cross-situational consistency: life course-persistent antisocial persons lie at home, steal from shops, cheat at school, fight in bars, and embezzle at work (Farrington, 1991; Loeber, 1982; Loeber and Baicker-McKee, 1989; Robins, 1966, 1978; White et al., 1990). . . .

Beginnings: Neuropsychological Risk for Difficult Temperament and Behavioral Problems

If some individuals' antisocial behavior is stable from preschool to adulthood as the data imply, then investigators are compelled to look for its roots early in life, in factors that are present before or soon after birth. It is possible that the etiological chain begins with some factor capable of producing individual differences in the neuropsychological functions of the infant nervous system. Factors that influence infant neural development are myriad, and many of them have been empirically linked to antisocial outcomes.

One possible source of neuropsychological variation that is linked to problem behavior is disruption in the ontogenesis of the fetal brain. Minor physical anomalies, which are thought to be observable markers for hidden anomalies in neural development, have been found at elevated rates among violent offenders and subjects with antisocial personality traits (Fogel, Mednick, and Michelson. 1985; E. Kandel, Brennan, and Mednick. 1989; Paulhus and Martin, 1986). Neural development may be disrupted by maternal drug abuse, poor prenatal nutrition, or pre or postnatal exposure to toxic agents (Needleman and Beringer, 1981; Rodning, Beckwith, and Howard, 1989; Stewart, 1983). Even brain insult suffered because of complications during delivery has been empirically linked to later violence and antisocial behavior in carefully designed longitudinal studies (E. Kandel and Mednick, 1991; Szatmari, Reitsma-Street, and Offord, 1986). In addition, some individual differences in neuropsychological health are heritable in origin (Borecki and Ashton, 1984; Martin, Jardine, and Eaves, 1984; Plomin, Nitz, and Rowe, 1990; Tambs, Sundet, and Magnus, 1984; Vandenberg, 1969). Just as parents and children share facial resemblances, they share some structural and functional similarities within their nervous systems. After birth, neural development may be disrupted by neonatal deprivation of nutrition, stimulation, and even affection (Cravioto and Arrieta, 1983; Kraemer, 1988; Meany, Aitken, van Berkel, Bhatnagar, and Sapolsky, 1988). Some studies have pointed to child abuse and neglect as possible sources of brain injury in the histories of delinquents with neuropsychological impairment (Lewis, Shanok, Pincus, and Glaser. 1979; Milner and McCanne, 1991; Tarter. Hegedus, Winsten, and Alterman, 1984).

There is good evidence that children who ultimately become persistently antisocial do suffer from deficits in neuropsychological abilities. I have elsewhere reviewed the available empirical and theoretical literatures: the link between neuropsychological impairment and antisocial outcomes is one of the most robust effects in the study of antisocial behavior (Moffitt, 1990b; Moffitt and Henry, 1991; see also Hirschi and Hindelang, 1977). Two sorts of neuropsychological deficits are empirically associated with antisocial behavior: verbal and "executive" functions. The verbal deficits of antisocial children are pervasive, affecting receptive listening and reading, problem solving, expressive speech and writing, and memory. In addition, executive deficits produce what is sometimes referred to as a compartmental learning disability (Price, Daffner, Stowe, and Mesulam, 1990), including symptoms such as inattention and impulsivity. These cognitive deficits and antisocial behavior share variance that is independent of social class, race, test motivation, and academic attainment (Moffitt, 1990b; Lynam, Moffitt, and Stouthamer Loeber, 1993). In addition, the relation is not an artifact of slow witted delinquents' greater susceptibility to detection by police; undetected delinquents have weak cognitive skills too (Moffitt and Silva, 1988a).

The evidence is strong that neuropsychological deficits are linked to the kind of antisocial behavior that begins in childhood and is sustained for lengthy periods. In a series of articles (Moffitt, 1990a; Moffitt and Henry, 1989; Moffitt and Silva, 1988b), I have shown that poor verbal and executive functions are associated with antisocial behavior, if it is extreme and persistent. In these studies, adolescent New Zealand boys who exhibited symptoms of both conduct disorder and attention-deficit disorder with hyperactivity (ADDH) scored very poorly on neuropsychological tests of verbal and executive functions and had histories of extreme antisocial behavior that persisted from age 3 to age 15. Apparently, their neuropsychological deficits were as long standing as their antisocial behavior; at ages 3 and 5 these boys had scored more than a standard deviation below the age norm for boys on the Baviev and McCarthy tests of motor coordination and on the Stanford-Binet test of cognitive performance. Contrast groups of boys with single diagnoses of either conduct disorder or ADDH did not have neuropsychological deficits or cognitive-motor delays, but neither were their behavior problems stable over time.

In a study designed to improve on measurement of executive functions (White, Moffitt, Caspi, Jeglum, Needles, and Stouthamer-Loeber, in press), we gathered data on self-control and impulsivity for 430 Pittsburgh youths. Twelve measures were taken from multiple sources (mother, teacher, self, and observer) by using multiple methods (rating scales, performance tests, computer games, Q sorts, and videotaped observations). A linear composite of the impulsivity measures was strongly related to the 3-year longevity of antisocial behavior, even after controlling for IQ, race, and social class. Boys who were very delinquent from ages 10 to 13 scored significantly higher on impulsivity than both their nondelinquent and temporarily delinquent age-mates. Taken together, the New Zealand and Pittsburgh longitudinal studies suggest that neuropsychological dysfunctions that manifest themselves as poor scores on tests of language and self-control—and as the inattentive, overactive, and impulsive symptoms of ADDH—are linked with the early childhood emergence of aggressive antisocial behavior and with its subsequent persistence.

Neuropsychological Variation and the "Difficult" Infant. Before describing how neuropsychological variation might constitute risk for antisocial behavior, it is useful to define what is meant here by neuropsychological. By combining neuro with psychological, I refer broadly to the extent to which anatomical structures and physiological processes within the nervous system influence psychological characteristics such as temperament, behavioral development, cognitive abilities, or all three. For example, individual variation in brain function may engender differences between children in activity level, emotional reactivity, or self-regulation (temperament); speech, motor coordination, or impulse control (behavioral development); and attention, language, learning, memory, or reasoning (cognitive abilities).

Children with neurological difficulties severe enough to constitute autism, severe physical handicap, or profound mental retardation are usually identified and specially treated by parents and professionals. However, other infants have subclinical levels of problems that affect the difficulty of rearing them, variously referred to as difficult temperament, language or motor delays, or mild cognitive deficits. Compromised neuropsychological functions are associated with a variety of consequences for infants' cognitive and motor development as well as for their personality development (Rothbart and Der-

ryberry, 1981). Toddlers with subtle neuropsychological deficits may be clumsy and awkward, overactive, inattentive, irritable, impulsive, hard to keep on schedule, delayed in reaching developmental milestones, poor at verbal comprehension, deficient at expressing themselves, or slow at learning new things (Rutter, 1977, 1983; Thomas and Chess, 1977, Wender; 1971).

Hertzig (1983) has described an empirical test of the proposed relationship between neurological damage and difficult behavior in infancy. She studied a sample of 66 low-birth-weight infants from intact middle-class families. Symptoms of brain dysfunction detected during neurological examinations were significantly related to an index of difficult temperament taken at ages 1, 2 and 3 (Thomas and Chess, 1977; the index comprised rhythmicity, adaptability, approach-withdrawal, intensity, and mood). The parents of the children with neurological impairment and difficult temperament more often sought help from child psychiatrists as their children grew up, and the most frequent presenting complaints were immaturity, overactivity, temper tantrums, poor attention, and poor school performance. Each of these childhood problems has been linked by research to later antisocial outcomes (cf. Moffitt, 1990a, 1990b). Importantly, the impairments of the children with neural damage were not massive; their mean IQ score was 96 (only 4 points below the population mean). Hertzig's study showed that even subtle neurological deficits can influence an infant's temperament and behavior, the difficulty of rearing the infant, and behavioral problems in later childhood.

Child-Environment Covariation in Nature: A Source of Interactional Continuity. Up to this point, I have emphasized in this article the characteristics of the developing child as if environments were held constant. Unfortunately, children with cognitive and temperamental disadvantages are not generally born into supportive environments, nor do they even get a fair chance of being randomly assigned to good or bad environments. Unlike the aforementioned infants in Hertzig's (1983) study of temperament and neurological symptoms, most low-birthweight infants are not born into intact, middle-class families. Vulnerable infants are disproportionately found in environments that will not be ameliorative because many sources of neural maldevelopment co-occur with family disadvantage or deviance.

Indeed, because some characteristics of parents and children tend to be correlated, parents of children who are at risk for antisocial behavior often inadvertently provide their children with criminogenic environments (Sameroff and Chandler, 1975). The intergenerational transmission of severe antisocial behavior has been carefully documented in a study of three generations (Huesmann et al., 1984). In that study of 600 subjects, the stability of individuals' aggressive behavior from age 8 to age 30 was exceeded by the stability of aggression across the generations: from grandparent to parent to child. Thus, with regard to risk for antisocial behavior, nature does not follow a 2 x 2 design with equal cell sizes.

Parents and children resemble each other on temperament and personality. Thus, parents of children who are difficult to manage often lack the necessary psychological and physical resources to cope constructively with a difficult child (Scarr and McCartney, 1983; Snyder and Patterson, 1987). For example, temperamental traits such as activity level and irritability are known to be partly heritable (Plomin, Chipuer, and Loehlin, 1990). This suggests that children whose hyperactivity and angry outbursts might be curbed by firm discipline will tend to have parents who are inconsistent disciplinarians; the parents tend to be impatient and irritable too. The converse is also true: Empirical evidence has been found for a relationship between variations in parents' warmth and infants' easiness (Plomin, Chipuer, and Loehlin, 1990).

Parents and children also resemble each other on cognitive ability. The known heritability of measured intelligence (Plomin, 1990; Loehlin, 1989) implies that children who are most in need of remedial cognitive stimulation will have parents who may be least able to provide it. Moreover, parents' cognitive abilities set limits on their own educational and occupational attainment (Barrett and Depinet, 1991). As one consequence, families whose members have below-average cognitive capacities will often be least able financially to obtain professional interventions or optimal remedial schooling for their at-risk children.

Even the social and structural aspects of the environment may be stacked against children who enter the world at risk. Plomin and Bergeman (1990) have shown that there are genetic components to measures that are commonly used by developmental psychologists to assess socialization environments. For example, the Home Observation for Measurement of the Environment scale, the Moos Family Environment scales, and the Holmes and Rahe scales of stressful life events all revealed the influence of heritable factors when they were examined with behavior genetic research designs (Plomin and Bergeman, 1990). Vulnerable children are often subject to adverse homes and neighborhoods because their parents are vulnerable to problems too (cf. Lahev et al., 1990).

Importantly, although examples from behavior genetics research have been cited in the previous three paragraphs, the perverse compounding of children's vulnerabilities with their families' imperfections does not require that the child's neuropsychological risk arise from any genetic disposition. In fact, for my purposes, it is immaterial whether parent-child similarities arise from shared genes or shared homes. A home environment wherein prenatal care is haphazard, drugs are used during pregnancy, and infants' nutritional needs are neglected is a setting where sources of children's neuropsychological dysfunction that are clearly environmental coexist with a criminogenic social environment.

Problem Child–Problem Parent Interactions and the Emergence of Antisocial Behaviors. I believe that the juxtaposition of a vulnerable and difficult infant with an adverse rearing context initiates risk for the life course-persistent pattern of antisocial behavior. The ensuing process is a transactional one in which the challenge of coping with a difficult child evokes a chain of failed parent-child encounters (Sameroff and Chandler, 1975). The assertion that children exert important effects on their social environments is useful in understanding this hypothetical process (Bell and Chapman, 1986). It is now widely acknowledged that personality and behavior are shaped in large measure by interactions between the person and the environment (cf. Buss, 1987; Plomin, DeFries, and Loehlin, 1977; Scarr and McCartney, 1983). One form of interaction may play a particularly important role both in promoting an antisocial style and in maintaining its continuity across the life course: *Evocative* interaction occurs when a child's behavior evokes distinctive responses from others (Caspi et al., 1987).

Children with neuropsychological problems evoke a challenge to even the most resourceful, loving, and patient families. For example, Tinsley and Parke (1983) have reviewed literature showing that low-birthweight, premature infants negatively influence the behavior of their caretakers; they arrive before parents are prepared, their crying patterns are rated as more disturbing and irritating, and parents report that they are less satisfying to feed, less pleasant to hold, and more demanding to care for than healthy babies. Many parents of preterm infants hold unrealistic expectations about their children's attainment of developmental milestones, and these may contribute to later dysfunctional parent-child relationships (Tinsley and Parke, 1983). More disturbing, an infant's neurological health status has been shown to be related to risk for maltreatment and neglect (Friedrich and Boriskin, 1976; Frodi et al., 1978; Hunter, Kilstrom, Kraybill, and Loda, 1978; Milowe and Lowrie, 1964; Sandgrund, Gaines, and Green, 1974).

Numerous studies have shown that a toddler's problem behaviors may affect the parents' disciplinary strategies as well as subsequent interactions with adults and peers (Bell and Chapman, 1986; Chess and Thomas, 1987). For example, children characterized by a difficult temperament in infancy are more likely to resist their mothers' efforts to control them in early childhood (Lee and Bates, 1985). Similarly, mothers of difficult boys experience more problems in their efforts to socialize their children. Maccoby and Jacklin (1983) showed that over

time these mothers reduce their efforts to actively guide and direct their children's behavior and become increasingly less involved in the teaching process. In a study of unrelated mothers and children, K. E. Anderson, Lytton, and Romney (1986) observed conduct-disordered and nonproblem boys interacting with mothers of conduct-disordered and nonproblem sons in unrelated pairs. The conduct-disordered boys evoked more negative reactions from both types of mothers than did normal boys, but the two types of mothers did not differ from each other in their negative reactions. It may well be that early behavioral difficulties contribute to the development of persistent antisocial behavior by evoking responses from the interpersonal social environment, responses that exacerbate the child's tendencies (Goldsmith, Bradshaw, and Rieser-Danner, 1986; Lytton, 1990). "The child acts; the environment reacts; and the child reacts back in mutually interlocking evocative interaction" (Caspi et al., 1987, p. 308).

Such a sequence of interactions would be most likely to produce lasting antisocial behavior problems if caretaker reactions were more likely to exacerbate than to ameliorate children's problem behavior. To my knowledge, students of child effects have not yet tested for interactions between child behavior and parental deviance or poor parenting, perhaps because very disadvantaged families are seldom studied with such designs. Nonetheless, some data suggest that children's predispositions toward antisocial behavior may be exacerbated under deviant rearing conditions. In the New Zealand longitudinal study, there was a significant interaction effect between children's neuropsychological deficit and family adversity on one type of delinquent act: aggressive confrontation with a victim or adversary. Among the 536 boys in the sample, the 75 boys who had both low neuropsychological test scores and adverse home environments earned a mean aggression score more than four times greater than that of boys with either neuropsychological problems or adverse homes (Moffitt, 1990b). The index of family adversity included parental characteristics such as poor mental health and low intelligence as well as socioeconomic status. Behavior-genetic adoption studies of antisocial behavior often report a similar pattern of findings, wherein the highest rates of criminal outcomes are found for adoptees whose foster parents, as well as their biological parents, were deviant (e.g. Mednick, Gabrielli, and Hutchings, 1984). Thus, children's predispositions may evoke exacerbating responses from the environment and may also render them more vulnerable to criminogenic environments.

If the child who "steps off on the wrong foot" remains on an ill-starred path, subsequent stepping-stone experiences may culminate in life course-persistent antisocial behavior. For lifecourse-persistent antisocial individuals, deviant behavior patterns later in life may thus reflect early individual differences that are perpetuated or exacerbated by interactions with the social environment: first at home, and later at school. Quay (1987) summarized this as "this youth is likely to be at odds with everyone in the environment, and most particularly with those who must interact with him on a daily basis to raise, educate, or otherwise control him. . . . This pattern is the most troublesome to society, seems least amenable to change, and has the most pessimistic prognosis for adult adjustment" (p. 121).

However, inauspicious beginnings do not complete the story. In the New Zealand study, for example, a combination of preschool measures of antisocial behavior and cognitive ability was able to predict 70% of the cases of conduct disorder at age 11 but at the cost of a high false-positive rate (White et al., 1990). The next section explores the specific interactional processes that nourish and augment the life course-persistent antisocial style beyond childhood.

Maintenance and Elaboration Over the Life Course: Cumulative Continuity, Contemporary Continuity, and Narrowing Options for Change

In the previous section, the concept of evocative person-environment interaction was called on to describe how children's difficult behaviors might affect encounters with their parents. Two additional types of interaction may help to explain how the life

course-persistent individual's problem behavior, once initiated, might promote its own continuity and pervasiveness. *Reactive* interaction occurs when different youngsters exposed to the same environment experience it, interpret it, and react to it in accordance with their particular style. For example, in interpersonal situations where cues are ambiguous, aggressive children are likely to mistakenly attribute harmful intent to others and then act accordingly (Dodge and Frame, 1982). *Proactive* interaction occurs when people select or create environments that support their styles. For example, antisocial individuals appear to be likely to affiliate selectively with antisocial others, even when selecting a mate. Some evidence points to nonrandom mating along personality traits related to antisocial behavior (Buss, 1984), and there are significant spouse correlations on conviction for crimes (e.g., Baker, Mack, Moffitt, and Mednick, 1989).

The three types of person-environment interactions can produce two kinds of consequences in the life course: *cumulative consequences* and *contemporary consequences* (Caspi and Bem, 1990). Early individual differences may set in motion a downhill snowball of cumulative continuities. In addition, individual differences may themselves persist from infancy to adulthood, continuing to influence adolescent and adult behavior in a proximal contemporary fashion. Contemporary continuity arises if the life course-persistent person continues to carry into adulthood the same underlying constellation of traits that got him into trouble as a child, such as high activity level, irritability, poor self-control, and low cognitive ability.

The roles of cumulative and contemporary continuities in antisocial behavior have been explored by Caspi, Bem, and Elder (1989; Caspi et al., 1987), using data from the longitudinal Berkeley Guidance Study. They identified men who had a history of temper tantrums during late childhood (when tantrums are not developmentally normative). Then they traced the continuities and consequences of this personality style across the subsequent 30 years of the subjects' lives and into multiple diverse life domains: education, employment, and marriage. A major finding was that hot-tempered boys who came from middle-class homes suffered a progressive deterioration of socioeconomic status as they moved through the life course. By age 40, their occupational status was indistinguishable from that of men born into the working class. A majority of them held jobs of lower occupational status than those held by their fathers at a comparable age. Did these men fail occupationally because their earlier ill-temperedness started them down a particular path (cumulative consequences) or because their current ill-temperedness handicapped them in the world of work (contemporary consequences)?

Cumulative consequences were implied by the effect of childhood temper on occupational status at midlife: Tantrums predicted lower educational attainment, and educational attainment, in turn, predicted lower occupational status. Contemporary consequences were implied by the strong direct link between ill-temperedness and occupational stability. Men with childhood tantrums continued to be hot-tempered in adulthood, where it got them into trouble in the world of work. They had more erratic work lives, changing jobs more frequently and experiencing more unemployment between ages 18 and 40. Ill-temperedness also had a contemporary effect on marital stability. Almost half (46%) of the men with histories of childhood tantrums had divorced by age 40 compared with only 22% of other men.

Elsewhere, I describe in detail some of the patterns of interaction between persons and their social environments that may promote antisocial continuity across time and across life domains (Caspi and Moffitt, in press-b). Two sources of continuity deserve emphasis here because they narrow the options for change. These processes are (a) failing to learn conventional prosocial alternatives to antisocial behavior and (b) becoming ensnared in a deviant life-style by crime's consequences. These concepts have special implications for the questions of why life course-persistent individuals fail to desist from delinquency as young adults and why they are so impervious to intervention.

A Restricted Behavioral Repertoire. This theory of life course-persistent antisocial behavior asserts that the causal sequence begins very early and the formative years are dominated by chains of cumulative and contemporary continuity. As a consequence, little opportunity is afforded for the life course-persistent antisocial individual to learn a behavioral repertoire of prosocial alternatives. Thus, one overlooked and pernicious source of continuity in antisocial behavior is simply a lack of recourse to any other options. In keeping with this prediction, Vitaro, Gagnon, and Tremblay (1990) have shown that aggressive children whose behavioral repertoires consist almost solely of antisocial behaviors are less likely to change over years than are aggressive children whose repertoires comprise some prosocial behaviors as well.

Life course-persistent persons miss out on opportunities to acquire and practice prosocial alternatives at each stage of development. Children with poor self-control and aggressive behavior are often rejected by peers and adults (Coie, Belding, and Underwood, 1988; Dodge, Coie, and Brakke, 1982; Vitaro et al., 1990). In turn, children who have learned to expect rejection are likely in later settings to withdraw or strike out preemptively, precluding opportunities to affiliate with prosocial peers (Dodge and Newman, 1981; Dodge and Frame, 1982; LaFrenier and Sroufe, 1985; Nasby, Hayden, and DePaulo, 1980). Such children are robbed of chances to practice conventional social skills. Alternatively, consider this sequence of narrowing options: Behavior problems at school and failure to attain basic math and reading skills place a limit on the variety of job skills that can be acquired and thereby cut off options to pursue legitimate employment as an alternative to the underground economy (Farrington, Gallagher, Morley, Ledger, and West, 1986; Maughan, Gray, and Rutter, 1985; Moffitt, 1990a). Simply put, if social and academic skills are not mastered in childhood, it is very difficult to later recover lost opportunities.

Becoming Ensnared by Consequences of Antisocial Behavior. Personal characteristics such as poor self-control, impulsivity, and inability to delay gratification increase the risk that antisocial youngsters will make irrevocable decisions that close the doors of opportunity. Teenaged parenthood, addiction to drugs or alcohol, school dropout, disabling or disfiguring injuries, patchy work histories, and time spent incarcerated are *snares* that diminish the probabilities of later success by eliminating opportunities for breaking the chain of cumulative continuity (Cairns and Cairns, 1991; J. Q. Wilson and Hernstein, 1985). Similarly, labels accrued early in life can foreclose later opportunities; an early arrest record or a "bad" reputation may rule out lucrative jobs, higher education, or an advantageous marriage (Farrington, 1977; Klein, 1986; West, 1982). In short, the behavior of life course-persistent antisocial persons is increasingly maintained and supported by narrowing options for conventional behavior.

Interventions with life course-persistent persons have met with dismal results (Lipton, Martinson, and Wilks, 1975; Palmer, 1984; Sechrest, White, and Brown, 1979). This is not surprising, considering that most interventions are begun relatively late in the chain of cumulative continuity. The forces of continuity are formidable foes (Caspi and Moffitt, in press-a). After a protracted deficient learning history, and after options for change have been eliminated, efforts to suppress antisocial behavior will not automatically bring prosocial behavior to the surface in its place. Now-classic research on learning shows conclusively that efforts to extinguish undesirable behavior will fail unless alternative behaviors are available that will attract reinforcement (Azrin and Holz, 1966). My analysis of increasingly restricted behavioral options suggests the hypothesis that opportunities for change will often be actively transformed by life course-persistents into opportunities for continuity: Residential treatment programs provide a chance to learn from criminal peers, a new job furnishes the chance to steal, and new romance provides a partner for abuse. This analysis of life course-persistent antisocial behavior anticipates disappointing outcomes when such antisocial persons are thrust into new situations that purportedly offer the chance "to turn over a new leaf."

The Reason for Persistence: Traits, Environments, and Developmental Processes

According to some accounts of behavioral continuity, an ever present underlying trait generates antisocial outcomes at every point in the life span (e.g., Gottfredson and Hirschi, 1990). By other accounts, antisocial behavior is sustained by environmental barriers to change (e.g., Bandura, 1979, pp. 217-224). In this theory of life course-persistent antisocial behavior, neither traits nor environments account for continuity.

True, the theory begins with a trait: variation between individuals in neuropsychological health. The trait is truly underlying in that it seldom comes to anyone' attention unless an infant is challenged by formal examinations; it is manifested behaviorally as variability in infant temperament, developmental milestones, and cognitive abilities.

Next, the theory brings environments into play. Parents and other people respond to children's difficult temperaments and developmental deficits. In nurturing environments, toddlers' problems are often corrected. However, in disadvantaged homes, schools, and neighborhoods, the responses are more likely to exacerbate than amend. Under such detrimental circumstances, difficult behavior is gradually elaborated into conduct problems and a dearth of prosocial skills. Thus, over the years, an antisocial personality is slowly and insidiously constructed. Likewise, deficits in language and reasoning are incrementally elaborated into academic failure and a dearth of job skills. Over time, accumulating consequences of the youngster's personality problems and academic problems prune away the options for change.

This theory of life course-persistent antisocial behavior emphasizes the constant process of reciprocal interaction between personal traits and environmental reactions to them. The original attribute is thus elaborated on during development, to become a syndrome that remains conceptually consistent, but that gains new behavioral components (Caspi and Bem, 1990). Through that process, relatively subtle childhood variations in neuropsychological health can be transformed into an antisocial style that pervades all domains of adolescent and adult behavior. It is this infiltration of the antisocial disposition into the multiple domains of a life that diminishes the likelihood of change.

When in the life course does the potential for change dwindle to nil? How many person-environment interactions must accumulate before the life course-persistent pattern becomes set? I have argued that a person-environment interaction process is needed to predict emerging antisocial behavior, but after some age will the "person" main effect predict adult outcomes alone? An answer to these questions is critical for prevention efforts. The well-documented resistance of antisocial personality disorder to treatments of all kinds seems to suggest that the life course-persistent style is fixed sometime before age 18 (Suedfeld and Landon, 1978). Studies of crime careers reveal that it is very unusual for males to first initiate crime after adolescence, suggesting that if an adult is going to be antisocial, the pattern must be established by late adolescence (Elliott, Huizinga, and Menard, 1989).[1] At the same time, efforts to predict antisocial outcomes from childhood conduct problems yield many errors (e.g., White et al., 1990). These errors seem to suggest that antisocial styles become set sometime after childhood. . . .

Adolescence-Limited Antisocial Behavior

Discontinuity: The Most Common Course of Antisocial Behavior

As implied by the proffered label, discontinuity is the hallmark of teenaged delinquents who have no notable history of antisocial behavior in childhood and little future for such behavior in adulthood. However, the brief tenure of their delinquency should not obscure their prevalence in the population or the gravity of their crimes. In contrast with the rare life course-persistent type, adolescence-limited delinquency is ubiquitous. Several studies have shown that about one third of males are arrested during their lifetime for a serious criminal offense, whereas

fully four fifths of males have police contact for some minor infringement (Farrington, Ohlin, and Wilson, 1986). Most of these police contacts are made during the adolescent years. Indeed, numerous rigorous self-report studies have now documented that it is statistically aberrant to refrain from crime during adolescence (Elliott et al., 1983; Hirschi, 1969; Moffitt and Silva, 1988c).

Compared with the life course-persistent type, adolescence-limited delinquents show relatively little continuity in their antisocial behavior. Across age, change in delinquent involvement is often abrupt, especially during the periods of onset and desistence. For example, in my aforementioned longitudinal study of a representative sample of boys, 12% of the youngsters were classified as new delinquents at age 13; they had no prior history of antisocial behavior from age 5 to age 11. Between age 11 and age 13, they changed from below the sample average to 1.5 standard deviations above average on self-reported delinquency (Moffitt, 1990a). By age 15, another 20% of this sample of boys had joined the newcomers to delinquency despite having no prior history of antisocial behavior (Moffitt, 1991). Barely into mid-adolescence, the prevalence rate of markedly antisocial boys had swollen from 5% at age 11 to 32% at age 15. When interviewed at age 18, only 7% of the boys denied all delinquent activities. By their mid-20s, at least three fourths of these new offenders are expected to cease all offending (Farrington, 1986).

Adolescence-limited delinquents may also have sporadic, crime-free periods in the midst of their brief crime "careers." Also, in contrast with the life course-persistent type, they lack consistency in their antisocial behavior across situations. For example, they may shoplift in stores and use drugs with friends but continue to obey the rules at school. Because of the chimeric nature of their delinquency, different reporters (such as self, parent, and teacher) are less likely to agree about their behavior problems when asked to complete rating scales or clinical interviews (Loeber, Green, Lahey, and Stouthamer-Loeber, 1990; Loeber and Schmaling, 1985).

These observations about temporal instability and cross-situational *in*consistency are more than merely descriptive. They have implications for a theory of the etiology of adolescence-limited delinquency. Indeed, the flexibility of most delinquents' behavior suggests that their engagement in deviant lifestyles may be under the control of reinforcement and punishment contingencies.

Unlike their life course-persistent peers, whose behavior was described as inflexible and refractory to changing circumstances, adolescence-limited delinquents are likely to engage in antisocial behavior in situations where such responses seem profitable to them, but they are also able to abandon antisocial behavior when prosocial styles are more rewarding. They maintain control over their antisocial responses and use antisocial behavior only in situations where it may serve an instrumental function. Thus, principles of learning theory will be important for this theory of the cause of adolescence-limited delinquency.

A theory of adolescence-limited delinquency must account for several empirical observations: modal onset in early adolescence, recovery by young adulthood, widespread prevalence, and lack of continuity. Why do youngsters with no history of behavior problems in childhood suddenly become antisocial in adolescence? Why do they develop antisocial problems rather than other difficulties? Why is delinquency so common among teens? How are they able to spontaneously recover from an antisocial life-style within a few short years?

Just as the childhood onset of life course-persistent persons compelled me to look for causal factors early in their lives, the coincidence of puberty with the rise in the prevalence of delinquent behavior compels me to look for clues in adolescent development. Critical features of this developmental period are variability in biological age, the increasing importance of peer relationships, and the budding of teenagers' self-conscious values, attitudes, and aspirations. These developmental tasks form the building blocks for a theory of adolescence-limited delinquency.

Beginnings: Motivation, Mimicry, and Reinforcement

Why do adolescence-limited delinquents begin delinquency? The answer advanced here is that their delinquency is "social mimicry" of the antisocial style of life course-persistent youths. The concept of social mimicry is borrowed from ethology. Social mimicry occurs when two animal species share a single niche and one of the species has cornered the market on a resource that is needed to promote fitness (Moynihan, 1968). In such circumstances, the "mimic" species adopts the social behavior of the more successful species to obtain access to the valuable resource. For example, cowbird chicks, who are left by their mothers to be reared in the nests of unsuspecting parent birds, learn to behave like the parent birds' own true chicks and thus stimulate the parents to drop food their way. Social mimicry may also allow some species to safely pass among a more successful group and thus share access to desired resources. For example, some monkey species have learned to mimic bird calls. One such species of monkeys, rufous-naped tamarins, is able to share the delights of ripe fruit after a tree has been located by tyrant flycatchers, whose superior avian capacities in flight and distance vision better equip them to discover bearing trees. Similarly, zebras are sensitive to the social signals of impalas and gazelles and thus benefit from the latter species' superior sensitivity to approaching predators (E. O. Wilson, 1975).

If social mimicry is to explain why adolescence-limited delinquents begin to mimic the antisocial behavior of their lifecourse-persistent peers, then, logically, delinquency must be a social behavior that allows access to some desirable resource. I suggest that the resource is mature status, with its consequent power and privilege.

Before modernization, biological maturity came at a later age, social adult status arrived at an earlier age, and rites of passage more clearly delineated the point at which youths assumed new roles and responsibilities. In the past century, improved nutrition and health care have decreased the age of biological maturity at the rate of three tenths of a year per decade (Tanner, 1978; Wyshak and Frisch, 1982). Simultaneously, modernization of work has delayed the age of laborforce participation to ever later points in development (Empey, 1978; Horan and Hargis, 1991; Panel on Youth of the President's Science Advisory Committee, 1974). Thus, secular changes in health and work have lengthened the duration of adolescence. The ensuing gap leaves modern teenagers in a 5- to 10-year role vacuum (Erikson, 1960). They are biologically capable and compelled to be sexual beings, yet they are asked to delay most of the positive aspects of adult life (see Buchanan, Eccles, and Becker, 1992, for a review of studies of the compelling influence of pubertal hormones on teens' behavior and personality). In most American states, teens are not allowed to work or get a driver's license before age 16, marry or vote before age 18, or buy alcohol before age 21, and they are admonished to delay having children and establishing their own private dwellings until their education is completed at age 22, sometimes more than 10 years after they attain sexual maturity. They remain financially and socially dependent on their families of origin and are allowed few decisions of any real import. Yet they want desperately to establish intimate bonds with the opposite sex, to accrue material belongings, to make their own decisions, and to be regarded as consequential by adults (Csikszentmihalyi and Larson, 1984). Contemporary adolescents are thus trapped in a *maturity gap*, chronological hostages of a time warp between biological age and social age.

This emergent phenomenology begins to color the world for most teens in the first years of adolescence. Steinberg has shown that, between ages 10 and 15, a dramatic shift in youngsters' self-perceptions of autonomy and self-reliance takes place. Moreover, the timing of the shift for individuals is connected with their pubertal maturation (Steinberg, 1987; Steinberg and Silverberg, 1986; Udry, 1988). At the time of biological maturity, salient pubertal changes make the remoteness of ascribed social maturity painfully apparent to teens. This new awareness coincides with their promotion into a high school society that is numerically dominated by older youth. Thus, just as teens begin to feel the discomfort of the maturity gap, they enter a social reference group that has endured the gap for 3 to 4 years and has already perfected some delinquent ways of coping with it. Indeed, several researchers have noted that this life course transition into high school society may place teens at risk for antisocial behavior. In particular, exposure to peer models, when coupled with puberty, is an important determinant of adolescence-onset cases of delinquency (Caspi, Lynam, Moffitt, and Silva, 1993; Magnusson, 1988; Simmons and Blyth, 1987).

Life course-persistent youngsters are the vanguard of this transition. Healthy adolescents are capable of noticing that the few life course-persistent youths in their midst do not seem to suffer much from the maturity gap. (At a prevalence rate of about 5%, one or two such experienced delinquents in every classroom might be expected.) Already adept at deviance, life course-persistent youths are able to obtain possessions by theft or vice that are otherwise inaccessible to teens who have no independent incomes (e.g., cars, clothes, drugs, or entry into adults-only leisure settings). life course-persistent boys are more sexually experienced and have already initiated relationships with the opposite sex. life course-persistent boys appear relatively free of their families of origin; they seem to go their own way, making their own rules. As evidence that they make their own decisions, they take risks and do dangerous things that parents could not possibly endorse. As evidence that they have social consequence in the adult world, they have personal attorneys, social workers, and probation officers; they operate small businesses in the underground economy; and they have fathered children (Weiher, Huizinga, Lizotte, and Van Kammen, 1991). Viewed from within contemporary adolescent culture, the antisocial precocity of life course-persistent youths becomes a coveted social asset (cf. Finnegan, 1990a, 1990b; Jessor and Jessor, 1977; Silbereisen and Noack, 1988). Like the aforementioned bird calls that were mimicked by hungry tamarin monkeys, antisocial behavior becomes a valuable technique that is demonstrated by life course-persistents and imitated carefully by adolescence-limiteds. The effect of peer delinquency on the onset of delinquency is among the most robust facts in criminology research (Elliott and Menard, in press; Jessor and Jessor, 1977; Reiss, 1986; Sarnecki, 1986). However, is there evidence consistent with a social mimicry interpretation? I describe the evidence in the next section.

Social Mimicry and the Relationships Between Life Course-Persistent and Adolescence-Limited Delinquents. One hypothesized by-product of the maturity gap is a shift during early adolescence by persistent antisocial youth from peripheral to more influential positions in the peer social structure. This shift should occur as aspects of the antisocial style become more interesting to other teens. In terms of its epidemiology, delinquent participation shifts from being primarily an individual psychopathology in childhood to a normative group social behavior during adolescence and then back to psychopathology in adulthood. Consider that the behavior problems of the few pioneering antisocial children in an age cohort must develop on an individual basis; such early childhood pioneers lack the influence of delinquent peers (excepting family members). However, near adolescence, a few boys join the life course-persistent ones, then a few more, until a critical mass is reached when almost all adolescents are involved in some delinquency with age peers. Elliott and Menard (in press) have analyzed change in peer group membership from age 11 to age 24 in a national probability sample. Their data show a gradual population drift from membership in nondelinquent peer groups to membership in delinquent peer groups up to age 17; the trend reverses thereafter. For example, 78% of 11-year-olds reported no or minimal delinquency among their friends. In contrast, 66% of 17-year-olds reported substantial delinquency on the part of the friends in their group.

The word *friends* in the previous sentence seems to imply a personal relationship between life course-persistents and adolescence-limiteds that is implausible. Much evidence suggests that, before adolescence, life course-persistent antisocial children are ignored and rejected by other children because of their unpredictable, aggressive behavior (Coie et al., 1988; Dodge et al., 1982). After adolescence has passed, life course-persistent adults are often described as lacking the capacity for loyalty or friendship (Cleckley, 1976; Robins, 1985). At first, these observations may seem contrary to my assertion that life course-persistents assume social influence over youths who admire and emulate their style during adolescence. However, it is important to recall that social mimicry required no exchange of affection between the successful birds and their monkey mimics. In this theory, adolescents who wish to prove their maturity need only notice that the style of life course-persistents resembles adulthood more than it resembles childhood. Then they need only observe antisocial behavior closely enough and long enough to imitate it successfully. What is contended is that adolescence-limited youths should regard life course-persistent youths as models, and life course-persistent teens should regard themselves as magnets for other teens. Neither perception need involve reciprocal liking between individuals.

A modeling role would imply that measures of exposure to delinquent peers (e.g., knowledge of their delinquent behavior or time spent in proximity to them) should be better predictors of self-delinquency than measures of relationship quality (e.g., shared attitudes or attachment to delinquent peers). Few studies have parsed peer-delinquency effects into separate components, but two findings consistent with this prediction have been reported from the National Youth Survey, a representative sample of more than 500 teens. Agnew (1991) examined relationship characteristics in interaction with levels of peer delinquency. He argued that attachment to peers should encourage deviance if peers are delinquent but discourage it if they are not. Agnew's results showed that such interaction terms were good predictors. However, the results also showed that time spent with delinquent peers was a stronger unique predictor of self-delinquency than the interaction between peer attachment and peer crime. Warr and Stafford (1991) found that the knowledge of friends' delinquent behavior was 2.5 to 5 times more important for self-

delinquency than friends' attitudes about delinquency. (This pattern has been replicated
in another sample by Nagin and Paternoster,
1991.) Moreover, the effect of peer delinquency was direct; it was not mediated by influencing the respondents' attitudes to be
more like those of deviant peers. These findings are not consistent with the notion that
teens take up delinquency after pro-delin-
quency attitudes are transferred in the context of intimate social relations. Rather, Warr
and Stafford concluded that the data on peer
effects are best interpreted in terms of imitation or vicarious reinforcement.

A magnet role would imply that children
who were rejected and ignored by others
should experience newfound "popularity" as
teens, relative to their former rejected status.
That is, life course-persistent youth should
encounter more contacts with peers during
adolescence when other adolescents draw
near so as to imitate their life-style. Some research is consistent with this interpretation.
For example, in a study of 450 students in
middle school, aggressive youths who were
rejected by their peers reported that they did
not feel lonely, whereas submissive rejected
youths did feel lonely (Parkhurst and Asher,
1992). Similarly, aggressive seventh-graders
in the Carolina Longitudinal Study were
rated as popular as often as nonaggressive
youths by both teachers and themselves and
were as likely as other youths to be nuclear
members of peer groups (Cairns, Cairns,
Neckerman, Gest, and Gariepy, 1988). In
their review of peer-relationship studies,
Coie, Dodge, and Kupersmidt (1990) noted
that the relationship between overt aggression and peer rejection is weaker or absent in
adolescent samples compared with child
samples. Findings such as these suggest that
aggressive teens experience regular contacts
with peers, however short-lived. Similarly, in
the Oregon Youth Study, rejection by peers at
age 10 was prognostic of greater involvement
with delinquent peers 2 years later (Dishion,
Patterson, Stoolmiller, and Skinner, 1991).
Although the Oregon researchers interpreted
their results as suggesting that aggressive
children seek delinquent friends, their data
are equally consistent with my interpretation
that aggressive youths begin to serve as a

magnet for novice delinquents during early
adolescence. Definitive sociometric research
must follow up aggressive-rejected children
to test whether they develop networks in adolescence that include late-onset delinquents
of the adolescence-limited type.

Researchers from the Carolina Longitudinal Study have carefully documented that
boys with an aggressive history do participate
in peer networks in adolescence but that the
networks are not very stable (Cairns et al.,
1988). Consistent with a social mimicry hypothesis, delinquent groups have frequent
membership turnover. In addition, the interchanges between network members are characterized by much reciprocal antisocial behavior (Cairns et al., 1988). Reiss and Farrington (1991) have shown that the most experienced high-rate young offenders tend to
recruit different co-offenders for each offense.

Life course-persistents serve as core members of revolving networks, by virtue of being
role models or trainers for new recruits
(Reiss, 1986). They exploit peers as drug customers, as fences, as lookouts, or as sexual
partners. Such interactions among life
course-persistent and adolescence-limited
delinquents may represent a symbiosis of
mutual exploitation. Alternatively, life course-
persistent offenders need not even be aware
of all of the adolescence-limited youngsters
who imitate their style. Unlike adolescence-
limited offenders, who appear to need peer
support for crime, life course-persistent offenders are willing to offend alone (Knight
and West, 1975). The point is that the phenomena of "delinquent peer networks" and
"co-offending" during the adolescent period
do not necessarily connote supportive friendships that are based on intimacy, trust, and
loyalty, as is sometimes assumed. Social
mimicry of delinquency can take place if experienced offenders actively educate new recruits. However, it can also take place if motivated learners merely observe antisocial
models from afar.

***Reinforcement of Delinquency by Its
"Negative" Consequences.*** For teens who become adolescence-limited delinquents, antisocial behavior is an effective means of knif-
ing-off childhood apron strings and of prov-

ing that they can act independently to conquer new challenges (Erikson, 1960). Hypothetical reinforcers for delinquency include damaging the quality of intimacy and communication with parents, provoking responses from adults in positions of authority, finding ways to look older (such as by smoking cigarettes, being tattooed, playing the big spender with ill-gotten gains), and tempting fate (risking pregnancy, driving while intoxicated, or shoplifting under the noses of clerks). None of these putative reinforcers may seem very pleasurable to the middle-aged academic, but each of the aforementioned consequences is a precious resource to the teenager and can serve to reinforce delinquency. Bloch and Niederhoffer (1958) have offered an anthropological perspective: "It is almost as if the contemporary young person, in the absence of puberty rituals and ordeals, is moved to exclaim: If you don't care to test us, then we will test ourselves!" (p. 28).

I suggest that every curfew violated, car stolen, drug taken, and baby conceived is a statement of personal independence and thus a reinforcer for delinquent involvement. Ethnographic interviews with delinquents reveal that proving maturity and autonomy are strong personal motives for offending (e.g., Goldstein, 1990). Such hypothetical reinforcing properties have not been systematically tested for most types of delinquent acts. However, epidemiological studies have confirmed that adolescent initiation of tobacco, alcohol, and drug abuse are reinforced because they symbolize independence and maturity to youth (D. Kandel, 1980; Mausner and Platt, 1971).

In summary, in this narrative account of the etiology of adolescent-onset delinquency I have emphasized three conditions: motivation, mimicry, and reinforcement. I have suggested that a secular change in the duration of adolescence has generated an age-dependent motivational state. In addition, life course-persistent antisocial models must be available so that their delinquent behaviors can be imitated. Finally, adolescents' fledgling attempts to mimic antisocial styles will continue if they are socially reinforced by the "negative consequences" of crime.

Why Doesn't Every Teenager Become Delinquent?

The proffered theory of adolescence-limited delinquency regards this sort of delinquency as an adaptive response to contextual circumstances. As a consequence, the theory seems to predict that every teen will engage in delinquency. Data from epidemiological studies using the self-report method suggest that almost all adolescents do commit some illegal acts (Elliott et al., 1983). In addition, even studies using official records of arrest by police find surprisingly high prevalence rates (for a review see Farrington, Ohlin, and Wilson, 1986). Nevertheless, some youths commit less delinquency than others, and a small minority abstains completely. Unfortunately, almost no research sheds light on the characteristics of teens who abstain from antisocial behavior altogether. Speculations are thus ill-informed by empirical observations. However, some predictions may be derived from the present theory of adolescence-limited delinquency. The predictions center on two theoretical prerequisites for adolescent-onset delinquency: the motivating maturity gap and antisocial role models. Some youths may skip the maturity gap because of late puberty or early initiation into adult roles. Others may find few opportunities for mimicking life course-persistent delinquent models.

Some youths who refrain from antisocial behavior may, for some reason, not sense the maturity gap and therefore lack the hypothesized motivation for experimenting with crime. Perhaps such teens experience very late puberty so that the gap between biological and social adulthood is not signaled to them early in adolescence. For example, Caspi and Moffitt (1991) have shown that girls who do not menstruate by age 15 tend not to become involved in delinquency; in fact they evidence fewer than normal behavior problems as teens. Perhaps other abstainers belong to cultural or religious subgroups in which adolescents are given legitimate access to adult privileges and accountability. In his vivid ethnographic account of "old heads" and teenaged boys in a poor black neighborhood, Anderson (1990) described how mature community leaders drew certain boys into their own work and social lives, deliberately and publicly initiating the boys into manhood (and preventing delinquent involvement).

Some nondelinquent teens may lack structural opportunities for modeling antisocial peers. Adolescent crime rates are generally lower in rural areas than in inner-city areas (Skogan, 1979, 1990). Teens in urban areas are surrounded by a greater density of age peers (and have readier unsupervised access to them through public transportation and meeting venues such as parks and shopping malls) than are teens in relatively isolated rural areas. For instance, Sampson and Groves (1989) determined that the strongest community-level correlate of local rates of robbery and violence was the presence of "unsupervised groups of teenagers hanging out and making a nuisance" (p. 789). In that study, more traditional community correlates of crime, such as socioeconomic status, residential mobility, and ethnicity, were mediated by the teenaged social scene. School structures may also constrain or facilitate access to life course-persistent models. Caspi et al. (1993) found that early puberty was associated with delinquency in girls but only if they had access to boys through attending coed high schools. Girls who were enrolled in girls' schools did not engage in delinquency. In that study, the difference in delinquent involvement between coed and single-sex school settings could not be explained by any personal or family characteristics that may have influenced how the girls came to be enrolled in their schools; access to delinquent role models was clearly the best explanation for the girls' behavior problems.

Youths may also be excluded from opportunities to mimic antisocial peers because of some personal characteristics that make them unattractive to other teens or that leave them reluctant to seek entry to newly popular delinquent groups. Shedler and Block (1990) found such an effect on the use of illegal drugs. They compared the personality styles of three adolescent groups: teens who abstained from trying any drug, teens who experimented with drugs, and teens who were frequent heavy drug users. Adolescents who experimented were the best adjusted teens in the sample. As expected, frequent users were troubled teens, who were alienated and antisocial. However, the abstainers were also problem teens: They were "relatively tense, overcontrolled, emotionally constricted... somewhat socially isolated and lacking in interpersonal skills" (p. 618). This personality style was not a consequence of failing to try drugs. Rather, it was an enduring personality configuration. At age 7, these abstainers had been prospectively described by raters as "overcontrolled, timid, fearful and morose ... they were not warm and responsive, not curious and open to new experience, not active, not vital, and not cheerful" (pp. 619-620). Similarly, Farrington and West (1990) reported that boys from criminogenic circumstances who did not become delinquent seemed nervous and withdrawn and had few or no friends. These provocative findings remind us that deviance is defined in relationship to its normative context. During adolescence, when delinquent behavior becomes the norm, nondelinquents warrant our scientific scrutiny.

In summary, this theory of adolescence-limited delinquency suggests that adolescents who commit no antisocial behavior at all have either (a) delayed puberty, (b) access to roles that are respected by adults, (c) environments that limit opportunities for learning about delinquency, (d) personal characteristics that exclude them from antisocial peer networks, or (e) all four. Research is needed to determine whether or not abstaining from delinquency is necessarily a sign of good adolescent adjustment. . . .

Desistence From Crime: Adolescence-Limiteds Are Responsive to Shifting Reinforcement Contingencies

By definition, adolescence-limited delinquents generally do not maintain their delinquent behavior into adulthood. The account of life course-persistent persons I made earlier in this article required an analysis of maintenance factors. In contrast, this account of adolescence-limited delinquents demands an analysis of desistence: Why do adolescence-limited delinquents desist from delinquency? This theory's answer: Healthy youths respond adaptively to changing contingencies. If motivational and learning mechanisms initiate and maintain their delinquency, then, likewise, changing contingencies can extinguish it. . . .

With the inevitable progression of chronological age, more legitimate and tangible adult roles become available to teens. Adolescence-limited delinquents gradually experience a loss of motivation for delinquency as they exit the maturity gap. Moreover, when aging delinquents attain some of the privileges they coveted as teens, the consequences of illegal behavior shift from rewarding to punishing, *in their perception.* An adult arrest record will limit their job opportunities, drug abuse keeps them from getting to work on time, drunk driving is costly, and bar fights lead to accusations of unfit parenthood. Adolescence-limited delinquents have something to lose by persisting in their antisocial behavior beyond the teen years.

There is some evidence that many young adult offenders weigh the relative rewards from illegal and conventional activities when they contemplate future offending. In a study of three samples, the effect of age on criminal participation was mediated by young men's expectations about whether illegal earnings would exceed earnings from a straight job (Piliavin, Thornton, Gartner, and Matsueda, 1986). Important for this theory, research shows that "commitment costs" are among the factors weighed by young adults when they decide to discontinue offending. In the criminological subfield of perceptual deterrence research, commitment costs are defined as a person's judgment that past accomplishments will be jeopardized or that future goals will be foreclosed (Williams and Hawkins, 1986). Criminal behavior incurs commitment costs if it risks informal sanctions (disapproval by family, community, or employer) as well as formal sanctions (arrest or conviction penalty). Given that very few delinquent acts culminate in formal sanctions, perceptual deterrence theories consider informal sanctions as keys to deterrence. Paternoster and colleagues have tested the proposed effects of commitment costs and informal sanctions in a follow-up study of 300 young adults. They found that criminal offending 1 year later was best predicted by prospective indexes of commitment costs ($r = -.23$) and informal sanctions ($r = -.40$). Those variables outdid gender, perceived risk of arrest, grade point average, and peer attachment (Paternoster, Saltzman, Waldo, and Chiricos, 1983).

Options for change. Consistent with this motivational analysis, the antisocial behavior of many delinquent teens has been found to decline after they leave high school (Elliott and Voss, 1974), join the army (Eider, 1986; Mattick, 1960), marry a prosocial spouse (Sampson and Laub, 1990), move away from the old neighborhood (West, 1982), or get a full-time job (Sampson and Laub, 1990). As these citations show, links between the assumption of adult roles and criminal desistence have been observed before. The issue left unaddressed by theory is why are some delinquents able to desist when others are not? What enables adolescence-limited delinquents to make these (often abrupt) transitions away from crime? Why do adolescence-limited delinquents come to realize that they have something to lose, whereas life course-persistent delinquents remain undeterred? Here, two positions are advanced: Unlike their life course-persistent counterparts, adolescence-limited delinquents are relatively exempt from the forces of (a) cumulative and (b) contemporary continuity.

First, without a lifelong history of antisocial behavior, the forces of cumulative continuity have had fewer years in which to gather the momentum of a downhill snowball. Before taking up delinquency, adolescence-limited offenders had ample years to develop an accomplished repertoire of prosocial behaviors and basic academic skills. These social skills and academic achievements make them eligible for postsecondary education, good marriages, and desirable jobs.

The availability of alternatives to crime may explain why some adolescence-limited delinquents desist later than others. (As shown in Figure 5.1, the desistence portion of the age-crime curve slopes more gradually than the abrupt criminal initiation portion.) Although the forces of cumulative continuity build up less momentum over the course of their relatively short crime careers, many adolescence-limited youths will fall prey to many of the same snares that maintain continuity among life course-persistent persons. Those whose teen forays into delinquency inadvertently attracted damaging consequences may have more difficulty desisting. A drug habit, an incarceration, interrupted education, or a teen pregnancy are snares that require extra effort and time from which to escape. Thus, this theory predicts that variability in age at desistance from crime should be accounted for by the cumulative number and type of ensnaring life events that entangle persons in a deviant life-style.

Second, in stark contrast with the earlier account of life course-persistent offenders, personality disorder and cognitive deficits play no part in the delinquency of adolescence-limited offenders. As a result, they are exempt from the sources of contemporary continuity that plague their life course-persistent counterparts. In general, these young adults have adequate social skills, they have a record of average or better academic achievement, their mental health is sturdy, they still possess the capacity to forge close attachment relationships, and then, retain the good intelligence they had when they entered adolescence. One study of girls who grew up in institutional care has illustrated that individual differences influence which adolescents are able to attain prosocial outcomes in young adulthood (Quinton and Rutter, 1988). In that study, some girls reared in institutions were able to escape adversity for advantage through marriage to a supportive husband, but a constellation of individual psychological attributes determined which girls were able to marry well.

At the crossroads of young adulthood, adolescence-limited and life course-persistent delinquents go different ways. This happens because the developmental histories and personal traits of adolescence-limiteds allow them the option of exploring new life pathways. The histories and traits of life course-persistents have foreclosed their options, entrenching them in the antisocial path. To test this hypothesis, research must examine conditional effects of individual histories on opportunities for desistence from crime. . . .

Note

1. Between 9% and 22% of males not arrested as juveniles are arrested as adults, suggesting that adult-onset offenders constitute between 5% and 15% of all males (for a review see Farrington, Ohlin, & Wilson, 1986). However, estimates that are based on such official data are too high because most offenders engage in crime for some time before they are first arrested. Longitudinal studies of self-report delinquency show that only 1% to 4% of males commit their first criminal offense after age 17 (Elliott, Huizinga, & Menard, 1989). Adult-onset crime is not only very unusual, but it tends to be low rate, nonviolent (Blumstein & Cohen, 1987), and generally not accompanied by the many complications that attend a persistent and pervasive antisocial lifestyle (Farrington, Loeber, Elliott, et al., 1990).

Discussion Questions

1. Describe the different ways in which individual traits and environmental factors interact with (or influence) one another to produce persistent antisocial behavior.

2. What types of individual traits foster antisocial behavior, according to Moffitt? *Why* do these traits increase the likelihood of antisocial behavior? How is Moffitt's theory similar to and different from Wilson and Herrnstein's theory in these areas?

3. Describe Moffitt's theory of adolescent-limited antisocial behavior. Why is it that individuals in the "adolescent-limited" group are able to desist from crime in early adulthood while individuals in the "adolescent-persistent" group are not?

4. Why does Moffitt state that adolescent-limited antisocial behavior is *not pathological* while adolescent-persistent antisocial behavior is *pathological*? ✦

Part II

The Chicago School: The City, Social Disorganization, and Crime

As the United States proceeded into the 20th century, individualistic theories of crime enjoyed substantial popularity (Gould, 1981). Cesare Lombroso's biological theory, for example, was widely read and accepted (Lindesmith and Levin, 1937). In 1939, Harvard anthropologist E. A. Hooton not only claimed boldly that "criminals are organically inferior," but also proposed that "the elimination of crime can be effected only by the extirpation of the physically, mentally, and morally unfit; or by their complete segregation in a social aseptic environment" (quoted in Vold and Bernard, 1986: 6). Hooton's work may have been extreme, even for its time (see Merton and Montagu, 1940), but it represented a way of thinking that persists six decades later: the seeds of crime lie within people and the only way to protect public safety is to incapacitate this dangerous class (see Herrnstein and Murray, 1994; compare with Cullen et al., 1997 and Gordon, 1994).

Other social observers in the early part of the century, however, criticized these individualistic theories for their myopia. While criminal anthropologists like Lombroso and Hooton focused their attention on discerning whether criminals had larger foreheads or more tattoos than non-criminals, they ignored the larger changes in society that were occurring around them. The United States was rapidly moving into the modern era, transforming itself from a land sprinkled with small, stable farming communities into a land dominated by crowded cities that were centered around booming industries and whose residents were constantly in flux. For these social observers, it defied common sense not to see how these vast changes were intimately implicated in the cause of crime. In fact, they claimed that our understanding of the origins and prevention of criminal conduct depended on a careful study of how the forces *outside* individuals prompted their willingness to break the law.

Social Disorganization in the City

Perhaps nowhere was social change more rapid and more dramatic than in the city of Chicago. When first incorporated in 1833, Chicago had a population of just over 4,000. By 1890, this number had climbed to 1 million, and in just 20 years, the population had doubled to 2 million (Palen, 1981). Sheer numbers, however, capture only part of the changes that were taking place. Like other large cities, Chicago was the settling place for virtually every racial and ethnic group, as African Americans traveled to the North in search of a better life and immigrants from Europe ended their journey in the "windy city" that butted up against Lake Michigan. These urban newcomers typically secured work at and settled in the shadows of factories erected in the center of the city. Their lives were hard—they worked long hours in the factories and lived in overcrowded tenements dirtied by industrial pollution. Upton Sinclair captured the social reality of these inner-city neighborhoods in the title of his book, *The Jungle* (1905).

In this context, it may not be surprising that scholars at the University of Chicago believed that the key to understanding crime lay not in studying the traits of individuals but in studying the traits of neighborhoods. Did it make a difference, they asked, if a child grew up in an inner-city community that was characterized by poverty, a mixing together of diverse peoples (i.e., "heterogeneity"), and by people constantly moving in and, when able, moving out (i.e., "transiency")? And if so, might not the solution to crime lay more in changing neighborhoods than in changing people?

This line of inquiry was developed most clearly by Clifford Shaw and Henry McKay (1942 [Chapter 6 in this volume]), who worked at the Institute for Social Research in Chicago and who were deeply influenced by the thinking of sociologists at the University of Chicago. To explain how cities such as Chicago develop, Ernest Burgess (1967 [1925]) had theorized that urban areas grow through a process of continual expansion from their inner core toward outer areas. As this growth process matures, we find cities that have a central business or industrial area. Just outside this area is the "zone in transition." It is here that impoverished newcomers settle, attracted by factory jobs and inexpensive housing. In a series of concentric circles, three more zones exist outside the inner city; Burgess called these the "zone of workingmen's homes," the "residential zone," and the "commuters' zone." These areas are settled by people who have adjusted to city life and have accumulated the resources to leave the zone in transition.

Shaw and McKay believed that Burgess's theory of the city might help direct their in-

vestigations of juvenile delinquency. If Burgess was correct, then rates of delinquency should be higher in the inner-city areas. In these locations, the intersection of persistent poverty, rapid population growth, heterogeneity, and transiency combined to disrupt the core social institutions of society such as the family; that is, these conditions caused *social disorganization*. They hypothesized that delinquency would be higher in these communities and lower in neighborhoods that were more affluent and stable (i.e., "organized").

But how would they test these ideas? In an innovative and enormous effort in data collection, whose results were published in *Juvenile Delinquency and Urban Areas* (1942), Shaw and McKay analyzed how measures of crime—such as youths referred to the juvenile court, truancy, and recidivism—were distributed in the zones of the city. By hand, they mapped the addresses of each delinquent, which they then compiled to compute rates of delinquency by census track and then by city zone. They discovered that over time, rates of crime by *area* remained relatively the same—regardless, that is, of which ethnic group resided there. This finding suggested that characteristics of the area, not of the individuals living in the area, regulated levels of delinquency. They also learned, as their theory predicted, that crime rates were pronounced in the zone of transition and became progressively lower as one moved away from the inner city toward the outer zones. This finding supported their contention that social disorganization was a major cause of delinquency (Bursik and Grasmick, 1993: 30-31).

Just how did social disorganization cause delinquency? Unfortunately, Shaw and McKay did not supply a refined discussion of this concept in which they systematically explored the dimensions of disorganization and how each one was criminogenic (Bursik and Grasmick, 1993). Even so, they broadly suggested that social disorganization referred to the breakdown of the social institutions in a community. In the inner city, then, families would be disrupted, schools would be marked by disorder, adult-run activities for youths would be sparse, churches would be poorly attended, and political groups would be ineffectual. When such a pervasive breakdown occurred, adults would be unable to control youths or to stop competing forms of criminal organization from emerging (e.g., gangs, vice activities). This combination was highly criminogenic. Freed from adult control, youths roamed the streets, where they came into contact with older juveniles who transmitted to them criminal values and skills (see also, Thrasher, 1927).

Shaw and McKay gained many of their insights on the process by which youths become embedded in delinquency from in-depth interviews—"life histories"—that they conducted with wayward adolescents (see, e.g., Shaw, 1966 [1930]). In *The Natural History of a Delinquent Career* (1976 [1931]), for example, Shaw compiled the story of Sidney Blotzman, who by age 16 had engaged in numerous crimes, including robbery and sexual assault. Shaw recorded that Sidney had begun his "career in delinquency" by age 7, a career that persisted and grew more serious as he matured (see Moffitt, Chapter 5 in Part I). Referring to Sidney's story, Shaw noted that due to his associations with older delinquents and adult criminals, the boy "began to identify himself with the criminal world and to embody in his own philosophy of life the moral values which prevailed in the criminal groups with which he had contact" (p. 228).

But why was Sidney exposed to these criminogenic influences? Here, Shaw reminds the reader that Sidney "lived in one of the most deteriorated and disorganized sections of the city" (p. 229). In these communities, continued Shaw, "the conventional traditions, neighborhood institutions, and public opinion, through which neighborhoods usually effect a control over the behavior [of the] child, were largely disintegrated" (p. 229). The community, however, "was not only disorganized and thus ineffective as a unit of control"; in addition, "various forms of stealing and many organized delinquent and criminal gangs were prevalent in the area" (p. 229). These criminal groups competed for the lives, in effect, of the area's children. "These groups," observed Shaw, "exercised a powerful influence and tended to create a community spirit which not only tolerated but actually fostered delinquent and criminal practices" (p. 229).

In Parts III and V, we will discuss two theoretical traditions whose roots extend to the work of Shaw and McKay: differential association/social learning theory and control theory. Thus, the work of Edwin Sutherland (Chapter 8) draws directly on Shaw and McKay's contentions that social areas have different mixes of criminal and conventional influences, and that the exposure to and learning of criminal values, mainly by associating with others in the same neighborhood, is a key source of crime. Sutherland captures these ideas in his "theory of differential association," which is an effort to systematize the insights of Shaw and McKay and of other Chicago School theorists (see, e.g., Thrasher's 1927 work, *The Gang*). Similarly, early statements of control theory, such as that by Reckless (1961) and that by Reiss (1951)—both of whom studied at the University of Chicago—build directly from Shaw and McKay's observations and helped to lay the foundation for today's control theories.

It is ironic that in contemporary criminology, these two traditions, which branched off from Shaw and McKay, now are seen as rival theories of crime (compare Akers, 1997 and Matsueda, 1988, with Gottfredson and Hirschi, 1990 and Kornhauser, 1978). Although some efforts have been made to *integrate* these two perspectives (see Part VI), most often advocates of learning and control theories see themselves as advancing incompatible perspectives, only one of which can be correct.

Revitalizing Social Disorganization Theory

Although Shaw and McKay's work was read by subsequent generations of criminologists, by the 1960s their theory of social disorganization had lost its appeal and its ability to direct research. Instead, other theories, advocating new ways of thinking and identifying new questions to be answered, ascended and captured scholars' attention (see Cole, 1975; Pfohl, 1985). Beginning in the 1980s, however, Shaw and McKay's disorganization perspective earned renewed interest—an interest that has remained until this day.

In part, criminologists reconsidered the value of disorganization theory because of a more general interest in the "ecology" of crime. This approach analyzes how crime rates vary by *ecological units*, such as neighborhoods, cities, counties, states, or nations. (Recall that Shaw and McKay examined how delinquency rates varied by zones of the city.) This approach is often seen as being on the "macro-level." In *micro*-level theories, the concern is with identifying how characteristics of *individuals* (e.g., personality, how much strain a person feels) are related to their involvement in criminal behavior. In *macro*-level theories, however, individuals and their traits are not studied; the concern is only with how the characteristics of geographical areas, such as whether they are disorganized, influence crime rates.

In 1982, Judith and Peter Blau published an article that captured the attention of criminologists. Examining 125 of the largest metropolitan areas in the United States, they found that violence was more pronounced in urban areas marked by socioeconomic inequality, especially by a wide gap in riches between African Americans and whites. Indeed, "high rates of criminal violence," concluded the Blaus, "are apparently the price of racial and economic inequalities" (p. 126). This analysis showed the important insights that a macro-level study could uncover. It also was a reminder that governmental policies that increased inequality—such as those embraced in the administration of President Reagan—might make our streets less safe (see also, Currie 1985). At a time when individualistic theories were gaining in prominence (recall that Wilson and Herrnstein's *Crime and Human Nature* was published in 1985), the Blaus' research spoke to the continuing relevance of community characteristics in understanding the roots of crime in America.

Beyond the general interest in ecological research (see Bursik and Grasmick, 1993; Byrne and Sampson, 1986; Reiss and Tonry, 1986), Robert Sampson was most responsible for specifically showing the relevance of using Shaw and McKay's theory to illuminate crime in today's society (see also, Bursik 1988). Sampson (1986) argued that crime was high in inner cities because the residents had lost the capacity to exercise "informal social control." Especially in neighborhoods where most families were "broken," the adult resources needed to supervise youths and involve them in wholesome activities were depleted. Coming from a broken home per se was not the key issue, said Sampson. Rather, it was living in a neighborhood where a high proportion of families were headed by a single parent that created a context in which control could not be exercised effectively. Like Shaw and McKay, Sampson stressed that independent of the traits of individuals, communities varied in their capacity to regulate conduct and suppress criminal behavior.

With W. Byron Groves, Sampson (1989 [Chapter 7 in this volume]) extended this research. Using data from the British Crime Survey, the authors tested Shaw and McKay's idea that in communities marked by poverty, heterogeneity, and residential transiency, informal relations and controls would be weakened and, as a result, crime would be high. Their data largely supported the conclusion that social disorganization was a strong predictor of community rates of crime (see also Bursik and Grasmick, 1993; Sampson and Lauritsen, 1994).

Recently, Sampson has continued this line of inquiry. In an important essay coauthored with William Julius Wilson, he extends social disorganization theory by placing it within the realities of contemporary America. Sampson and Wilson (1995) accept the basic thesis of disorganization theory that a breakdown of community controls, rooted in structural conditions, is criminogenic. They argue, however, that the Chicago school was incorrect in seeing social disorganization as a "natural" part of the process by which cities grow. Instead, variations in disorganization across communities are intimately linked to *racial inequality* (see Blau and Blau, 1982; Currie, 1985; Pfohl, 1985).

Independent of their individual socioeconomic status, African Amercans are much more likely to reside in neighborhoods where there is a *concentration* of severe poverty and widespread family disruption ("broken homes")—conditions that spawn disorganization. Why is this so? According to Sampson and Wilson, "macrostructural factors"—some economic, some conscious political decisions—are responsible for disproportionately consigning African Americans to these inner-city neighborhoods. These factors include, for example, the loss of jobs due to the deindustrialization of the American economy; the departure of middle-class blacks—who provided the social glue that helped to hold neighborhoods together—to more affluent areas; policies that channeled blacks into dense, high-rise public housing; the lack of investment in keeping up the housing stock in inner-city neighborhoods; and urban renewal that displaced African Americans from their homes and disrupted their communities (see Wilson, 1987, 1996).

Sampson and Wilson also rekindle the cultural side of social disorganization theory. Although their argument differs somewhat from Shaw and McKay's, they follow these early Chicago theorists in proposing that structural conditions affect the content of the culture in communities. For Sampson and Wilson, the near apartheid conditions in which many African Americans live (see Massey and Denton, 1993) create intense "social isolation—defined as the lack of contact or of sustained interaction with individuals and institutions that represent mainstream society" (1995: 51). In response, cultural values emerge that do not so much approve of violence and crime but rather define such actions as an unavoidable part of life in the ghetto (see Anderson, Chapter 12 in Part III).

In the end, state Sampson and Wilson (1995: 53), the "intersection of race, place, and poverty goes to the heart of our theoretical concerns with society and community organization." The result is that race-based inequality in urban areas fosters the breakdown of the conventional institutions and cultural values needed to restrain criminal conduct. The cost of this inequality is borne most fully by African Americans, who must live in communities where one in 21 black males will be murdered in his lifetime (the rate for white males is 1 in 131) (Sampson and Wilson, 1995: 36).

Sampson et al. (1997) provide further support for the disorganization approach in a study that examines rates of violence across 343 Chicago neighborhoods. They show that "concentrated disadvantage"—a combined measure of a community's poverty, race and age composition, and family disruption—is related to neighborhood rates of violence, even controlling for the characteristics of the people surveyed. Importantly, they reveal that the effects of concentrated disadvantage are largely mediated by the degree of "collective efficacy" in the neighborhood. Collective efficacy is a concept that includes the willingness of community residents both to exercise informal control (e.g., telling youths to quiet down) and to trust and help one another. These findings again point to the essential truth of Shaw and McKay's observation that strong communities can act to quell disorder while communities weakened by structural problems will be fertile soil for the growth of crime.

References

Akers, Ronald L. 1997. *Criminological Theories: Introduction and Evaluation*, 2nd edition. Los Angeles: Roxbury.

Blau, Judith R. and Peter M. Blau. 1982. "The Cost of Inequality: Metropolitan Structure and Violent Crime." *American Sociological Review* 47: 114-129.

Burgess, Ernest W. 1967 [originally published in 1925]. "The Growth of the City: An Introduction to a Research Project." Pp. 47-62 in *The City*, edited by Robert E. Park and Ernest W. Burgess. Chicago: University of Chicago Press.

Bursik, Robert J., Jr. 1988. "Social Disorganization and Theories of Crime and Delinquency." *Criminology* 26: 519-551.

Bursik, Robert J., Jr. and Harold G. Grasmick. 1993. *Neighborhoods and Crime: The Dimensions of Effective Community Control*. New York: Lexington.

Byrne, James M. and Robert J. Sampson, eds. 1986. *The Social Ecology of Crime*. New York: Springer-Verlag.

Cole, Stephen. 1975. "The Growth of Scientific Knowledge: Theories of Crime as a Case Study." Pp. 175-220 in *The Idea of Social Structure: Papers in Honor of Robert K. Merton*, edited by Lewis A. Coser. New York: Harcourt Brace Jovanovich.

Cullen, Francis T., Paul Gendreau, G. Roger Jarjoura, and John Paul Wright. 1997. "Crime and the Bell Curve: Lessons from Intelligent Criminology." *Crime and Delinquency* 43:387-411.

Currie, Elliott. 1985. *Confronting Crime: An American Challenge*. New York: Pantheon.

Gordon, Diana R. 1994. *The Return of the Dangerous Classes: Drug Prohibition and Policy Politics*. New York: Norton.

Gottfredson, Michael G. and Travis Hirschi. 1990. *A General Theory of Crime*. Stanford, CA: Stanford University Press.

Gould, Stephen Jay. 1981. *The Mismeasure of Man*. New York: Norton.

Herrnstein, Richard J. and Charles Murray. 1994. *The Bell Curve: Intelligence and Class Structure in American Life*. New York: The Free Press.

Kornhauser, Ruth Rosner. 1978. *Social Sources of Delinquency: An Appraisal of Analytic Models*. Chicago: University of Chicago Press.

Lindesmith, Alfred and Yale Levin. 1937. "The Lombrosian Myth in Criminology." *American Journal of Sociology* 42:653-671.

Pfohl, Stephen J. 1985. *Images of Deviance and Social Control: A Sociological History*. New York: McGraw-Hill.

Massey, Douglas S. and Nancy A. Denton. 1993. *American Apartheid: Segregation and the Making of the Underclass*. Cambridge, MA: Harvard University Press.

Matsueda, Ross L. 1988. "The Current State of Differential Association Theory." *Crime and Delinquency* 34: 277-306.

Merton, Robert K. and M. F. Ashley Montagu. 1940. "Crime and the Anthropologist." *American Anthropologist* 42: 384-408.

Palen, John J. 1981. *The Urban World*, 3rd edition. New York: McGraw-Hill.

Reckless, Walter C. 1961. *The Crime Problem*, 3rd edition. New York: Appleton-Century-Crofts.

Reiss, Albert J., Jr. 1951. "Delinquency as the Failure of Personal and Social Controls." *American Sociological Review* 16:196-207.

Reiss, Albert J., Jr. and Michael Tonry, eds. 1986. *Communities and Crime*. Chicago: University of Chicago Press.

Sampson, Robert J. 1986. "Crime in Cities: The Effects of Formal and Informal Social Control." Pp. 271-311 in *Communities and Crime*, edited by Albert J. Reiss, Jr. and Michael Tonry. Chicago: University of Chicago Press.

Sampson, Robert J. and W. Byron Groves. 1989. "Community Structure and Crime: Testing Social-Disorganization Theory." *American Journal of Sociology* 94: 774-802.

Sampson, Robert J. and Janet Lauritsen. 1994. "Violent Victimization and Offending: Individual, Situational, and Community-Level Risk Factors." Pp. 1-114 in *Understanding and Preventing Violence: Social Influences*, Vol. 3, edited by Albert J. Reiss, Jr., and Jeffrey A. Roth. Washington, DC: National Academy Press.

Sampson, Robert J., Stephen W. Raudenbush, and Felton Earls. 1997. "Neighborhoods and Violent Crime: A Multilevel Study of Collective Efficacy." *Science* 277 (August 15): 918-924.

Sampson, Robert J. and William Julius Wilson. 1995. "Toward a Theory of Race, Crime, and Urban Inequality." Pp. 36-54 in *Crime and Inequality*, edited by John Hagan and Ruth D. Peterson. Stanford, CA: Stanford University Press.

Shaw, Clifford R. 1966 [originally published in 1930]. *The Jack-Roller: A Delinquent Boy's Own Story*. Chicago: University of Chicago Press.

Shaw, Clifford R., with Maurice E. Moore. 1976 [originally published in 1931]. *The Natural History of a Delinquent Career*. Chicago: University of Chicago Press.

Shaw, Clifford R. and Henry D. McKay. 1942. *Juvenile Delinquency and Urban Areas*. Chicago: University of Chicago Press.

Sinclair, Upton. 1905. *The Jungle*. New York: Signet.

Thrasher, Frederic M. 1927. *The Gang: A Study of 1,313 Gangs in Chicago*. Chicago: University of Chicago Press.

Vold, George B. and Thomas J. Bernard. 1986. *Theoretical Criminology*, 3rd edition. New York: Oxford University Press.

Wilson, William Julius. 1987. *The Truly Disadvantaged: The Inner City, the Underclass, and Public Policy*. Chicago: University of Chicago Press.

——. 1996. *When Work Disappears: The World of the New Urban Poor*. New York: Alfred A. Knopf. ✦

6

Juvenile Delinquency and Urban Areas

Clifford R. Shaw
Henry D. McKay

"*Delinquency,*" *observed Shaw and McKay in their classic book* Juvenile Delinquency in Urban Areas, "*has its roots in the dynamic life of the community*" *(1942: 435). Theories that focus only on personality or biological traits ignore that youths are surrounded by a community that they interact with over many years. These daily experiences, claimed Shaw and McKay, shape patterns of behavior.*

Not all communities, however, are the same. Surveying the urban landscape, Shaw and McKay noted that in more affluent communities, "the similarity of attitudes and values as to social control is expressed in institutions and voluntary associations designed to perpetuate and protect these values" (p. 165). But in areas wracked by poverty and constant social change, the conventional institutions become weak and a value system supportive of crime is nurtured. Shaw and McKay recognized that even in disorganized inner-city communities, parents and other adults try to inculcate children with moral values. However, they must compete against a range of criminal influences—gangs, adult criminals, ongoing illegal enterprises—that simply are not present in organized communities. Further, these influences are difficult to uproot; once delinquent traditions take hold, they are transmitted from one generation to the next, typically through interactions in neighborhood peer groups.

One criticism of Shaw and McKay's theory is that it paints too rosy a picture of communities outside the inner city. Although serious predatory crimes are more pronounced in ghetto areas, delinquency is commonplace among youths in all communities. It is possible that social disorganization and cultural values supportive of crime are more evenly spread across communities than Shaw and McKay anticipated.

Finally, Shaw and McKay's perspective has important policy implications: if community disorganization is the main source of delinquency, then the solution to crime is to organize communities. Toward this end, in the early 1930s Shaw took steps to put theory into practice by initiating the Chicago Area Project, called the "first systematic challenge to the dominance of psychology and psychiatry in public and private programs for the prevention and treatment of juvenile delinquency" (Schlossman et al., 1984). The Project involved such activities as creating recreational programs, sprucing up the physical appearances of the neighborhood so as to reduce signs of disorder, working with school or criminal justice officials to see how problem youths might be helped, and using community residents to counsel the neighborhood's youngsters. The precise effectiveness of the Chicago Area Project is not known, although some evidence exists that it helped to reduce delinquency (Schlossman et al., 1984). Regardless, the Project illuminates an insight that has relevance to today: interventions—whether by the police or by correctional officials—that ignore community dynamics will be limited in their ability to prevent the onset of criminal conduct.

Reference

Schlossman, Steven, Gail Zellman, and Richard Shavelson, with Michael Sedlak and Jane Cobb. 1984. *Delinquency Prevention in South Chicago: A Fifty-Year Assessment of the Chicago Area Project.* Santa Monica, CA: RAND.

...It is clear from the data included in this volume that there is a direct relationship between conditions existing in local communities of American cities and differential rates of delinquents and criminals. Communities with high rates have social and economic characteristics which differentiate them from communities with low rates. Delinquency—particularly group delinquency, which constitutes a preponderance of all officially recorded offenses committed by boys and young men—has its roots in the dynamic life of the community.

. . . It may be observed, in the first instance, that the variations in rates of officially recorded delinquents in communities of the city correspond very closely with variations in economic status. The communities with the highest rates of delinquents are occupied by those segments of the population whose position is most disadvantageous in relation to the distribution of economic, social, and cultural values. Of all the communities in the city, these have the fewest facilities for acquiring the economic goods indicative of status and success in our conventional culture. Residence in the community is in itself an indication of inferior status, from the standpoint of persons residing in the more prosperous areas. It is a handicap in securing employment and in making satisfactory advancement in industry and the professions. Fewer opportunities are provided for securing the training, education, and contacts which facilitate advancement in the fields of business, industry, and the professions.

The communities with the lowest rates of delinquents, on the other hand, occupy a relatively high position in relation to the economic and social hierarchy of the city. Here the residents are relatively much more secure; and adequate provision is offered to young people for securing the material possessions symbolic of success and the education, training, and personal contacts which facilitate their advancement in the conventional careers they may pursue. . . .

Differential Systems of Values

In general, the more subtle differences between types of communities in Chicago may be encompassed within the general proposition that in the areas of low rates of delinquents there is more or less uniformity, consistency, and universality of conventional values and attitudes with respect to child care, conformity to law, and related matters; whereas in the high-rate areas systems of competing and conflicting moral values have developed. Even though in the latter situation conventional traditions and institutions are dominant, delinquency has developed as a powerful competing way of life. It derives its impelling force in the boy's life from the fact that it provides a means of securing economic gain, prestige, and other human satisfactions and is embodied in delinquent groups and criminal organizations, many of which have great influence, power, and prestige.

In the areas of high economic status where the rates of delinquents are low there is, in general, a similarity in the attitudes of the residents with reference to conventional values, as has been said, especially those related to the welfare of children. This is illustrated by the practical unanimity of opinion as to the desirability of education and constructive leisure-time activities and of the need for a general health program. It is shown, too, in the subtle, yet easily recognizable, pressure exerted upon children to keep them engaged in conventional activities, and in the resistance offered by the community to behavior which threatens the conventional values. It does not follow that all the activities participated in by members of the community are lawful; but, since any unlawful pursuits are likely to be carried out in other parts of the city, children living in the low-rate communities are, on the whole, insulated from direct contact with these deviant forms of adult behavior.

In the middle-class areas and the areas of high economic status, moreover, the similarity of attitudes and values as to social control is expressed in institutions and voluntary associations designed to perpetuate and protect these values. Among these may be included such organizations as the parent-teachers associations, women's clubs, service clubs, churches, neighborhood centers, and the like. Where these institutions represent dominant values, the child is exposed to, and participates in a significant way in one mode of life only. While he may have knowledge of alternatives, they are not integral parts of the system in which he participates.

In contrast, the areas of low economic status, where the rates of delinquents are high, are characterized by wide diversity in norms and standards of behavior. The moral values range from those that are strictly conventional to those in direct opposition to conventionality as symbolized by the family, the church, and other institutions common to our general society. The deviant values are symbolized by groups and institutions ranging from adult criminal gangs engaged in theft and the marketing of stolen goods, on the one hand, to quasi-legitimate businesses and the rackets through which partial or complete control of legitimate business is sometimes exercised, on the other. Thus, within the same community, theft may be defined as right and proper in some groups and as immoral, improper, and undesirable in others. In some groups wealth and prestige are secured through acts of skill and courage in the delinquent or criminal world, while in neighboring groups any attempt to achieve distinction in this manner would result in extreme disapprobation. Two conflicting systems of economic activity here present roughly equivalent opportunities for employment and for promotion. Evidence of success in the criminal world is indicated by the presence of adult criminals whose clothes and automobiles indicate unmistakably that they have prospered in their chosen fields. The values missed and the greater risks incurred are not so clearly apparent to the young.

Children living in such communities are exposed to a variety of contradictory standards and forms of behavior rather than to a relatively consistent and conventional pattern. More than one type of moral institution and education are available to them. A boy may be familiar with, or exposed to, either the system of conventional activities or the system of criminal activities, or both. Similarly, he may participate in the activities of groups which engage mainly in delinquent activities, those concerned with conventional pursuits, or those which alternate between the two worlds. His attitudes and habits will be formed largely in accordance with the extent to which he participates in and becomes identified with one or the other of these several types of groups.

Conflicts of values necessarily arise when boys are brought in contact with so many forms of conduct not reconcilable with conventional morality as expressed in church and school. A boy may be found guilty of delinquency in the court, which represents the values of the larger society, for an act which has had at least tacit approval in the community in which he lives. It is perhaps common knowledge in the neighborhood that public funds are embezzled and that favors and special consideration can be received from some public officials through the payment of stipulated sums; the boys assume that all officials can be influenced in this way. They are familiar with the location of illegal institutions in the community and with the procedures through which such institutions are opened and kept in operation; they know where stolen goods can be sold and the kinds of merchandise for which there is a ready market; they know what the rackets are; and they see in fine clothes, expensive cars, and other lavish expenditures the evidences of wealth among those who openly engage in illegal activities. All boys in the city have some knowledge of these activities; but in the inner-city areas they are known intimately, in terms of personal relationships, while in other sections they enter the child's experience through more impersonal forms of communication, such as motion pictures, the newspaper, and the radio.

Other types of evidence tending to support the existence of diverse systems of values in various areas are to be found in the data on delinquency and crime. In the previous chapter, variations by local areas in the number and rates of adult offenders were presented. When translated into its significance for children, the presence of a large number of adult criminals in certain areas means that children there are in contact with crime as a career and with the criminal way of life, symbolized by organized crime. In this type of organization can be seen the delegation of authority, the division of labor, the specialization of function, and all the other characteristics common to well-organized business institutions wherever found.

Similarly, the delinquency data presented graphically on spot maps and rate maps in the preceding pages give plausibility to the existence of a coherent system of values supporting delinquent acts. In making these interpretations it should be remembered that delinquency is essentially group behavior. A study of boys brought into the Juvenile Court of Cook County during the year 1928 revealed that 81.8 per cent of these boys committed the offenses for which they were brought to court as members of groups. And when the offenses were limited to stealing, it was found that 89 per cent of all offenders were taken to court as group or gang members. In many additional cases where the boy actually committed his offense alone, the influence of companions was, nevertheless, apparent. This point is illustrated in certain cases of boys charged with stealing from members of their own families, where the theft clearly reflects the influence and instigation of companions, and in instances where the problems of the boy charged with incorrigibility reveal conflicting values, those of the family competing with those of the delinquent group for his allegiance.

The heavy concentration of delinquency in certain areas means, therefore, that boys living in these areas are in contact not only with individuals who engage in proscribed activity but also with groups which sanction such behavior and exert pressure upon their members to conform to group standards. Examination of the distribution map reveals that, in contrast with the areas of concentration of delinquents, there are many other communities where the cases are so widely dispersed that the chances of a boy's having intimate contact with other delinquents or with delinquent groups are comparatively slight.

The importance of the concentration of delinquents is seen most clearly when the effect is viewed in a temporal perspective. The maps representing distribution of delinquents at successive periods indicate that, year after year, decade after decade, the same areas have been characterized by these concentrations. This means that delinquent boys in these areas have contact not only with other delinquents who are their contemporaries but also with older offenders, who in turn had contact with delinquents preceding them, and so on back to the earliest history of the neighborhood. This contact means that the traditions of delinquency can be and are transmitted down through successive generations of boys, in much the same way that language and other social forms are transmitted. . . .

The way in which boys are inducted into unconventional behavior has been revealed by large numbers of case studies of youths living in areas where the rates of delinquents are high. Through the boy's own life-story the wide range of contacts with other boys has been revealed. These stories indicate how at early ages the boys took part with older boys in delinquent activities, and how, as they themselves acquired experience, they initiated others into the same pursuits. These cases reveal also the steps through which members are incorporated into the delinquent group organization. Often at early ages boys engage in malicious mischief and simple acts of stealing. As their careers develop, they become involved in more serious offenses, and finally become skilled workmen or specialists in some particular field of criminal activity. In each of these phases the boy is supported by the sanction and the approbation of the delinquent group to which he belongs. . . .

Taken together, these studies indicate that most delinquent acts are committed by boys in groups, that delinquent boys have frequent contact with other delinquents, that the techniques for specific offenses are transmitted through delinquent group organization, and that in his officially proscribed activity the boy is supported and sustained by the delinquent group to which he belongs.

Differential Social Organization

Other subtle differences among communities are to be found in the character of their local institutions, especially those specifically related to the problem of social control. The family, in areas of high rates of delinquents, is affected by the conflicting systems of values and the problems of survival and conformity with which it is confronted. Family organization in high-rate areas is affected in several different ways by the divergent systems of values encountered. In the first place, it may be made practically impotent by the existing interrelationships between the two systems. Ordinarily, the family is thought of as representing conventional values and opposed to deviant forms of behavior. Opposition from families within the area to illegal practices and institutions is lessened, however, by the fact that each system may be contributing in certain ways to the economic well-being of many large family groups. Thus, even if a family represents conventional values, some member, relative, or friend may be gaining a livelihood through illegal or quasi-legal institutions—a fact tending to neutralize the family's opposition to the criminal system.

Another reason for the frequent ineffectiveness of the family in directing the boys' activities along conventional lines is doubtless the allegiance which the boys may feel they owe to delinquent groups. A boy is often so fully incorporated into the group that it exercises more control than does the family. This is especially true in those neighborhoods where most of the parents are European-born. There the parents' attitudes and interests reflect an Old World background, while their children are more fully Americanized and more sophisticated, assuming in many cases the role of interpreter. In this situation the parental control is weakened, and the family may be ineffective in competing with play groups and organized gangs in which life, though it may be insecure, is undeniably colorful, stimulating, and enticing.

A third possible reason for ineffectiveness of the family is that many problems with which it is confronted in delinquency areas are new problems, for which there is no traditional solution. An example is the use of leisure time by children. This is not a problem in the Old World or in rural American communities, where children start to work at an early age and have a recognized part in the system of production. Hence, there are no time-honored solutions for difficulties which arise out of the fact that children in the city go to work at a later age and have much more leisure at their disposal. In the absence of any accepted solution for this problem, harsh punishment may be administered; but this is often ineffective, serving only to alienate the children still more from family and home.

Other differences between high-rate and low-rate areas in Chicago are to be seen in the nature of the existing community organization. Thomas and Znaniecki have analyzed the effectively organized community in terms of the presence of social opinion with regard to problems of common interest, identical or at least consistent attitudes with reference to these problems, the ability to reach approximate unanimity on the question of how a problem should be dealt with, and the ability to carry this solution into action through harmonious co-operation.

Such practical unanimity of opinion and action does exist, on many questions, in areas where the rates of delinquents are low. But, in the high-rate areas, the very presence of conflicting systems of values operates against such unanimity. Other factors hindering the development of consistently effective attitudes with reference to these problems of public welfare are the poverty of these high-rate areas, the wide diversity of cultural backgrounds represented there, and the fact that the outward movement of population in a city like Chicago has resulted in the organization of life in terms of ultimate residence. Even though frustrated in his attempts to achieve economic security and to move into other areas, the immigrant, living in areas of first settlement, often has defined his goals in terms of the better residential community into which he hopes some day to move. Accordingly, the immediate problems of his present neighborhood may not be of great concern to him. . . .

Briefly summarized, it is assumed that the differentiation of areas and the segregation of population within the city have resulted in wide variation of opportunities in the struggle for position within our social order. The groups in the areas of lowest economic status find themselves at a disadvantage in the struggle to achieve the goals idealized in our civilization. These differences are translated into conduct through the general struggle for those economic symbols which signify a desirable position in the larger social order. Those persons who occupy a disadvantageous position are involved in a conflict between the goals assumed to be attainable in a free society and those actually attainable for a large proportion of the population. It is understandable, then, that the economic position of persons living in the areas of least opportunity should be translated at times into unconventional conduct, in an effort to reconcile the idealized status and their practical prospects of attaining this status. Since, in our culture, status is determined largely in economic terms, the differences between contrasted areas in terms of economic status become the most important differences. Similarly, as might be expected, crimes against property are most numerous.

The physical, economic, and social conditions associated with high rates of delinquents in local communities occupied by white population exist in exaggerated form in most of the Negro areas. Of all the population groups in the city, the Negro people occupy the most disadvantageous position in relation to the distribution of economic and social values. Their efforts to achieve a more satisfactory and advantageous position in the economic and social life of the city are seriously thwarted by many restrictions with respect to residence, employment, education, and social and cultural pursuits. These restrictions have contributed to the development of conditions within the local community conducive to an unusually large volume of delinquency. . . .

The development of divergent systems of values requires a type of situation in which traditional conventional control is either weak or nonexistent. It is a well-known fact that the growth of cities and the increase in devices for transportation and communication have so accelerated the rate of change in our society that the traditional means of social control, effective in primitive society and in isolated rural communities, have been weakened everywhere and rendered especially ineffective in large cities. Moreover, the city, with its anonymity, its emphasis on economic rather than personal values, and its freedom and tolerance, furnishes a favorable situation of the development of devices to improve one's status, outside of the conventionally accepted and approved methods. This tendency is stimulated by the fact that the wide range of secondary social contacts in modern life operates to multiply the wishes of individuals. The automobile, motion picture, magazine and newspaper advertising, the radio, and other means of communication flaunt luxury standards before all, creating or helping to create desires which often cannot be satisfied with the meager facilities available to families in areas of low economic status. The urge to satisfy the wishes and desires so created has helped to bring into existence and to perpetuate the existing system of criminal activities.

It is recognized that in a free society the struggle to improve one's status in terms of accepted values is common to all persons in all social strata. And it is a well-known fact that attempts are made by some persons in all economic classes to improve their positions by violating the rules and laws designed to regulate economic activity. However, it is assumed that these violations with reference to property are most frequent where the prospect of thus enhancing one's social status outweighs the chances for loss of position and prestige in the competitive struggle. It is in this connection that the existence of a system of values supporting criminal behavior becomes important as a factor in shaping individual life-patterns, since it is only where such a system exists that the person through criminal activity may acquire the material goods so essential to status in our society and at the same time increase, rather than lose, his prestige in the smaller group system of which he has become an integral part.

Reprinted from Clifford R. Shaw and Henry D. McKay, *Juvenile Delinquency in Urban Areas.* Copyright © 1942 by the University of Chicago Press. Reprinted by permission of the University of Chicago Press.

Discussion Questions

1. What does it mean to say that a community is socially "disorganized"? Why is crime less likely to occur in an organized community?

2. Why do Shaw and McKay take special pains to point out that delinquency usually occurs in groups? How do they believe that peer groups in the inner city contribute to the causation of crime?

3. Although written several decades ago, how might Shaw and McKay's theory help to explain the occurrence of street violence in today's inner-city communities?

4. Would Shaw and McKay favor efforts to fight crime by "getting tough" and locking up more offenders, including juveniles, in prison? ✦

7

Community Social Disorganization and Crime

Robert J. Sampson
W. Byron Groves

Most control theories argue that crime is restrained either by people exercising internal (or self-) control or by the bonds individuals have established with their parents, teachers, friends, and the like (see Part V). Building on Shaw and McKay, Sampson and Groves shift the focus away from individuals and toward communities. They argue that a key to understanding variations in crime across ecological areas is to realize that communities differ in the collective capacity of residents to control one another (see also Sampson et al., 1997).

A noteworthy contribution of Shaw and McKay's theory is that it provided clues as to why communities vary in their ability to exercise social control. Sampson and Groves note that Shaw and McKay had focused on the structural conditions that weaken community organization, such as persistent poverty, ethnic heterogeneity, and residential mobility. To this, the authors add urbanization and family disruption.

Many studies testing social disorganization theory have only measured whether these structural conditions are related to crime rates (e.g., do communities with more residential mobility have higher crime rates?). Although valuable, this research does not demonstrate that these conditions actually affect the exercise of social control in the community. What is needed is to identify the components of informal social control, and then to see if these components (1) are influenced by structural conditions and (2) serve as the conduit through which these structural conditions influence crime.

Sampson and Groves thus identify the "intervening dimensions of social disorganization" that Shaw and McKay's theory would predict mediate the effects of structural conditions on crime. Three main factors are highlighted: "the ability of a community to supervise and control teenage peer groups (e.g., gangs)"; the strength of "local friendship networks"; and the "rate of local participation in formal and voluntary organizations" (1989: 778-779). Crime rates, they theorize, will be lower when people know and interact with one another, have a stake in the neighborhood, and are willing to bind together to stop teenagers from congregating in and disrupting the peace of public spaces.

Although not shown in the selection reprinted here, Sampson and Groves (1989) tested this theory by using data from the British Crime Survey to assess crime rates across 238 localities in England and Wales. In large part, the analysis revealed strong support for their theoretical prediction that components of informal social control mediate the effects of structural conditions on community crime rates. This empirical investigation also is important because it shows that a theory developed many years before in the United States by Shaw, and McKay can help to explain crime in today's world and in another country. Thus, it appears that social disorganization theory can be generalized both across time and space.

References

Sampson, Robert J. and W. Byron Groves. 1989. "Community Structure and Crime: Testing Social-Disorganization Theory." *American Journal of Sociology* 94: 774-802.

Sampson, Robert J., Stephen W. Raudenbush, and Felton Earls. 1997. "Neighborhood and Violent Crime: A Multilevel Study of Collective Efficacy." *Science* 277 (August 15): 918-924.

One of the most fundamental sociological approaches to the study of crime and delinquency emanates from the Chicago-school research of Shaw and McKay. As Bursik

(1984) and others (see, e.g., Morris 1970; Short 1969) have argued, few works in criminology have had more influence than *Juvenile Delinquency and Urban Areas* (1942, 1969). In this classic work, Shaw and McKay argued that three structural factors—low economic status, ethnic heterogeneity, and residential mobility—led to the disruption of community social organization, which, in turn, accounted for variations in crime and delinquency (see also Shaw et al. 1929). . . .

A Community-Level Theory of Social Disorganization

In general terms, social disorganization refers to the inability of a community structure to realize the common values of its residents and maintain effective social controls (Kornhauser 1978, p. 120; Bursik 1984, p. 12). Empirically, the structural dimensions of community social disorganization can be measured in terms of the prevalence and interdependence of social networks in a community—both informal (e.g., friendship ties) and formal (e.g., organizational participation)—and in the span of collective supervision that the community directs toward local problems (Thomas and Znaniecki 1920; Shaw and McKay 1942; Kornhauser 1978). This approach is grounded in what Kasarda and Janowitz (1974, p. 329) term the *systemic model*, in which the local community is viewed as a complex system of friendship and kinship networks and formal and informal associational ties rooted in family life and ongoing socialization processes (see also Sampson 1988). As Bursik (1984, p. 31) notes, the correspondence of the systemic model with Shaw and McKay's social-disorganization model lies in their shared assumption that structural barriers impede development of the formal and informal ties that promote the ability to solve common problems. Social organization and social *dis*organization are thus seen as different ends of the same continuum with respect to systemic networks of community social control. When formulated in such a way, the notion of social disorganization is clearly separable not only from the processes that may lead to it (e.g., poverty and mobility), but also from the degree of de-

linquent behavior that may result from it (see Bursik 1984, p. 14).

Intervening Dimensions of Social Disorganization

The first and most important intervening construct in Shaw and McKay's disorganization model was the *ability of a community to supervise and control teenage peer groups* (e.g., gangs). It has been well documented that delinquency is primarily a group phenomenon (Thrasher 1963; Shaw and McKay 1942; Short and Strodtbeck 1965; Reiss 1986b), and hence, according to Shaw and McKay, the capacity of the community to control group-level dynamics is a key mechanism linking community characteristics with delinquency. Indeed, a central fact underlying Shaw and McKay's research was that most gangs developed from unsupervised, spontaneous play groups (Thrasher 1963, p. 25; Bordua 1961, p. 120). Shaw and McKay (1969) thus argued that residents of cohesive communities were better able to control the teenage behaviors that set the context for group-related delinquency (Thrasher 1963, pp. 26-27; Short 1963, p. xxiv; Short and Strodtbeck 1965). Examples of such controls include supervision of leisure-time youth activities, intervention in street-corner congregating (Thrasher 1963, p. 339; Maccoby et al. 1958; Shaw and McKay 1969, pp. 176-85; Bordua 1961), and challenging youth "who seem to be up to no good" (Skogan 1986, p. 217). Theoretically, then, the suggestion is that communities that are unable to control street-corner teenage groups will experience higher rates of delinquency than those in which peer groups are held in check through collective social control.

Socially disorganized communities with extensive street-corner peer groups are also expected to have higher rates of adult crime, especially among younger adults who still have ties to youth gangs. As Thrasher (1963, p. 281) argued: "There is no hard and fast dividing line between predatory gangs of boys and criminal groups of younger and older adults. They merge into each other by imperceptible gradations, and the latter have their real explanation, for the most part, in the former." Similarly, Shaw and McKay pointed to the link between juvenile delinquency and adult criminality, reporting a correlation of .90 between delinquency rates of juveniles aged 10-16 and referral rates of young adults aged 17-20 (1969, p. 95). They further noted the "striking" fact that over 70% of the juveniles in high-gang-delinquency areas were arrested as adults (Shaw and McKay 1969, p. 134). Therefore, the general hypothesis derived from the basic Shaw and McKay model is that street-corner teenage peer groups will have a positive effect on both crime and delinquency rates.

A second dimension of community social organization is formal *local friendship networks*. Systemic theory holds that locality-based networks constitute the core social fabric of human ecological communities (Hunter 1974; Kasarda and Janowitz 1974). When residents form local social ties, their capacity for community social control is increased because they are better able to recognize strangers and more apt to engage in guardianship behavior against victimization (Skogan 1986, p. 216).

Relatedly, Krohn (1986) and Freudenberg (1986) point out, the network density of acquaintances and friendships has been largely ignored in past research. To correct for this, we conceptualize local friendship networks as a community-level structural characteristic. On the basis of systemic theory, we expect that local friendship networks will (*a*) increase the capacity of community residents to recognize strangers, thereby enabling them to engage in guardianship behavior against predatory victimization and (*b*) exert structural constraints on the deviant behavior of residents within the community. Hence, local friendship networks are hypothesized to reduce both predatory victimization rates and local crime and delinquency offender rates.

A third component of social organization is the rate of *local participation in formal and voluntary organizations*. Community organizations reflect the structural embodiment of local community solidarity (Hunter 1974, p. 191), and, with this in mind, Kornhauser (1978, p. 79) argues that institutional instability and the isolation of community institutions are key factors underlying the structural dimension of social disorganization. Her argument, in short, is that when links between community institutions are weak, the capacity of a community to defend its local interests is weakened. Shaw and McKay (1969, pp. 184-85), and more recently Simcha-Fagan and Schwartz (1986, p. 688), have also argued that a weak community organizational base serves to attenuate local social-control functions regarding youth.

Taken together, these theorists suggest that efforts to solve common problems (e.g., predatory victimization) and socialize youth against delinquency are to a large degree dependent on a community's organizational base. The key to the success of these efforts hinges on the community's ability to encourage high rates of participation in both formal groups and voluntary associations (Shaw and McKay 1969, pp. 322-26; Kornhauser 1978, p. 81; Simcha-Fagan and Schwartz 1986, p. 688). Consequently, we hypothesize that communities with high rates of participation in committees, clubs, local institutions, and other organizations will have lower rates of victimization and delinquency than communities in which such participation is low.

Exogenous Sources of Social Disorganization

According to Kornhauser's (1978, p. 83) theoretical interpretation of Shaw and McKay, "economic level, mobility, and heterogeneity are, in that order, the variables assumed to account for variations in the capacity of subcommunities within a city to generate an effective system of controls." *Socioeconomic status* (SES) has long been a mainstay ecological correlate of crime and delinquency (Kornhauser 1978; Bursik 1984; Byrne and Sampson 1986), and Shaw and McKay placed a heavy emphasis on how community social disorganization mediated the effects of SES on delinquency. By definition, they argued, communities of low economic status lack adequate money and resources. In conjunction with the well-established positive correlation between SES and participation in formal and voluntary organizations (Tomeh 1973, p. 97), the model suggests that low-socioeconomic-status communities will suffer from a weaker organizational base than higher-status communities. The effects of SES on crime and delinquency rates are thus hypothesized to operate primarily through formal and informal controls as reflected in organizational participation and community supervision of local youth. Most previous ecological research has attempted to establish direct effects of SES on crime (see Kornhauser 1978; Byrne and Sampson 1986) and has consequently failed to measure the hypothesized mediating links necessary to corroborate social-disorganization theory.

In Shaw and McKay's (1942) original model, *residential mobility* was hypothesized to disrupt a community's network of social relations (Kornhauser 1978). In a similar vein, Kasarda and Janowitz (1974, p. 330) argue that, since assimilation of newcomers into the social fabric of local communities is necessarily a temporal process, residential mobility operates as a barrier to the development of extensive friendship networks, kinship bonds, and local associational ties. In this study, we examine a macrosocial conceptualization of systemic theory by focusing on the consequences of residential stability for community organization. The specific hypothesis is that community residential stability has direct positive effects on local friendship networks, which, in turn, reduce crime.

The third source of social disorganization in the Shaw and McKay model was racial and ethnic *heterogeneity*, which was thought to thwart the ability of slum residents to achieve consensus. In Suttles's (1968) account, fear and mistrust accompany heterogeneity, pushing residents into associations selected on the basis of personalistic criteria (e.g., age and sex). As a result of these defensive associations, the social order of the slum becomes segmented, provincial, and personalistic. Hence, while various ethnic groups may share conventional values (e.g., reducing crime), heterogeneity impedes communication and patterns of interaction.

Again, like mobility and SES, heterogeneity has usually been assessed only in terms of its direct effects on crime. In contrast, we test the basic disorganization postulate by hypothesizing that variations in ethnic heterogeneity will also increase delinquency by weakening the mediating components of social organization—especially control of disorderly peer groups.

Family Disruption. In a recent contribution to this *Journal*, Sampson (1987) argued that marital and family disruption may decrease informal social controls at the community level. The basic thesis was that two-parent households provide increased supervision and guardianship not only for their own children and household property (Cohen and Felson 1979), but also for general activities in the community. From this perspective, the supervision of peer-group and gang activity is not simply dependent on one child's family, but on a network of collective family control (Thrasher 1963, pp. 26, 65, 339; Reiss 1986a). In support of this theoretical model, Sampson (1987) showed that macro-level family disruption had large direct effects on rates of juvenile crime by both whites and blacks. However, the analysis was based on city-level rather than local community data, and empirical measures of hypothesized intervening constructs (e.g., informal community supervision of peer groups) were not available. Sampson (1987, p. 376) thus emphasized that "definitive resolution of the mechanisms linking family disruption with crime rates must await further research."

The present study addresses this limitation by examining the mediating effects of community social organization on crime. In particular, we hypothesize that community-level family disruption has a direct positive effect on the prevalence of street-corner teenage peer groups, which, in turn, increases rates of crime and delinquency.

Urbanization. The fifth and final exogenous variable to be examined is level of urbanization. Although Shaw and McKay (1942) were primarily concerned with intra-city patterns of delinquency, their theoretical framework is consistent with the idea that urban communities have a decreased capacity for social control, compared with suburban and rural areas. In particular, urbanization may weaken local kinship and friendship networks and impede social participation in local affairs (see, e.g., Fischer 1982). To provide a strict test of our hypothesized effects of community structure on crime, we thus control for between-community variations in urbanization.

In sum, our extended model of Shaw and McKay relies on the theoretical explication of Kornhauser (1978), recent contributions of systemic and social-network theory (Kasarda and Janowitz 1974; Krohn 1986), and a macrosocial conceptualization of family disruption and crime (Sampson 1987). . . .

Discussion Questions

1. Why do Sampson and Groves call their perspective a *community-level* theory?

2. What kinds of communities would be least likely to be able to exercise social control?

3. Why is controlling the conduct of teenagers in public a key to reducing crime?

4. Crime at times occurs on college campuses. How would you use social disorganization theory to explain why crime might be higher in some residence halls and lower in others? ✦

Part III

Learning to Be a Criminal: Differential Association, Subcultural, and Social Learning Theories

The theories in this section argue that people *learn* to engage in criminal behavior, in much the same way that they learn to engage in other sorts of behavior. Certain learning theories are at the micro or individual level: they attempt to explain how individuals learn to engage in crime. Others are at the macro or group level: they attempt to explain why certain groups, like Southerners or young people, have higher rates of certain types of crime.

Micro-Level Learning Theories

While learning theories of crime have been advanced by many theorists over the years, Sutherland's theory of differential association was the first and most prominent formal statement of micro-level learning theory (see Chapter 8 in this Part). Sutherland first provided a complete statement of the theory in the 1939 edition of his criminology textbook, and presented the final version of the theory in the 1947 edition. The theory is presented in the form of nine propositions. In brief, it states that criminal behavior is learned in interaction with others, particularly intimate others like friends and family. Through such interaction, we learn techniques of committing crime and "definitions" (motives, drives, rationalizations, attitudes) favorable and unfavorable toward violation of the law. An individual becomes criminal "because of an excess of definitions favorable to violation of law over definitions unfavorable to violation of law." Individuals are most likely to engage in crime if they are exposed to definitions favorable to law violation (1) early in life, (2) on a relatively frequent basis, (3) over a long period of time, and (4) from sources they like and respect. Recent versions of Sutherland's textbook address some common misconceptions about and criticisms of the theory (see Sutherland, Cressey, and Luckenbill, 1992; also see Akers, 1997, and Matsueda, 1988).

One major criticism of the theory is that Sutherland does not present a good description of definitions favorable and unfavorable to crime. Several theorists have tried to more precisely define the nature of these definitions. In certain cases, it has been said that individuals hold values that unconditionally approve of crime. In other cases, it has been claimed that individuals hold values that do not directly approve of crime, but are conducive to crime: values such as excitement or

77

thrills, toughness, and the desire for quick, easy success (see Agnew, 1995 for a discussion; Matza and Sykes, 1961). More commonly, however, it is argued that individuals hold beliefs that approve of or justify crime *in certain situations* (see Agnew, 1995; Akers, 1997).

Sykes and Matza (1957) have written the key article in this area (see Chapter 9 in this Part). They begin their article by attacking those who claim that delinquents unconditionally approve of crime (they especially attack Cohen, whose theory of the origin of delinquent subcultures is described in the next Part). They then present five "techniques of neutralization" that delinquents commonly use to justify their delinquency. While these techniques may be used as after-the-fact rationalizations, Sykes and Matza claim that they are also used before crime occurs and that they make crime possible by neutralizing one's belief that crime is bad. The individual essentially says that while crime in general is bad, it is justifiable in their particular case because the victim has it coming, the behavior will not really hurt anyone, etc.

A second criticism of differential association theory is that it fails to fully describe the process by which crime is learned. The theory simply says we learn definitions favorable (or unfavorable) to crime through our association with others. Burgess and Akers (1966) and Akers (1985, 1997) drew on behavioral and social learning theory in psychology to more fully describe the process by which individuals learn to engage in crime (see the Bandura selection on social learning theory in Part I). In brief, Akers argues that crime is learned through three processes (see Chapter 10 in this Part). First, individuals learn beliefs that define crime as desirable or justified in certain situations. This portion of the theory is very compatible with the emphasis of Sutherland on definitions, although Akers more precisely describes the beliefs that lead to crime. Second, individuals engage in crime because they are differentially reinforced for criminal behavior. This reinforcement may be positive, such as when one receives rewards for engaging in crime (e.g., the social approval of friends, money from a robbery); it may also be negative, such as when the commission of a crime allows one to avoid or escape from unpleasant stimuli (e.g., friends stop taunting you after you use the illicit drugs they offer). Third, individuals engage in crime because they imitate the criminal behavior of others, especially valued others whose own criminal behavior is reinforced (e.g., imitating the successful drug dealers in one's neighborhood).

Differential association theory was first tested by examining the relationship between delinquency and association with delinquent peers. While one may learn definitions favorable to law violation from both criminals and conventional people, it was felt that delinquent friends were a major source of such definitions. Much data indicate that individuals with delinquent friends are more likely to engage in delinquency. In fact, association with delinquent friends emerges as the strongest correlate of delinquency in most studies. Some people have questioned the meaning of this correlation. They claim that it is due to fact that delinquents pick other delinquents as friends ("birds of a feather flock together"), rather than to the fact that associating with delinquents *causes* one to engage in delinquency. Several recent studies which have examined adolescents *over time* suggest that association with delinquent friends does have a causal effect on delinquency (see Agnew, 1995; Akers, 1997; Thornberry et al., 1993).

The above data are usually taken as support for differential association theory, since it is assumed that associating with delinquent friends leads one to adopt definitions or attitudes favorable to delinquency. Several recent studies, however, have tried to determine *why* associating with delinquent friends increases the likelihood of delinquency. The data from these studies are somewhat mixed, but they tend to suggest that the effect of delinquent friends on delinquency is only *partly* explained by delinquent attitudes. Part of the effect of delinquent friends is also due to the fact that these friends reinforce delinquency and provide the individual with delinquent models (see Agnew, 1995; Akers, 1997). Such studies provide support for Akers's social learning theory.

A number of studies have also examined the nature of definitions favorable to delinquency. These studies suggest that very few people unconditionally approve of crime (with the exception of a few rather minor forms of crime, like marijuana use and gambling). At most, some individuals are close to amoral in their view of crime. That is, they neither approve of nor condemn crime. This amoral orientation is probably best explained in terms of social control theory, which argues that some individuals are not properly socialized (see Part V). Data do suggest, however, that some individuals hold values conducive to crime (thrills or excitement, toughness, quick or easy success) and that some individuals approve of or justify crime *under certain conditions*. Such individuals are more likely to engage in crime (see Agnew, 1994; 1995; Akers, 1997). These studies provide support for Sykes and Matza's arguments regarding the techniques of neutralization.

In sum, micro-level learning theories such as those of Sutherland and Akers have had a major impact on crime research and now constitute the leading theories of crime.

Macro-Level Learning Theories

The macro-level versions of learning theory argue that there are certain groups in the United States with values that are conducive to crime or that approve of or justify crime in certain circumstances. Such values explain the higher rates of crime in these groups.

Some theorists have argued that members of the lower class or that certain segments of the lower class hold such values. Miller (1958), for example, proposes that there is a lower-class culture whose members sometimes emphasize values like trouble, toughness, smartness (the ability to outsmart or con others), and excitement. Such values are said to explain the allegedly higher rate of crime in the lower class (see Tittle and Meier, 1990). The "subculture of violence" thesis developed by Wolfgang and Ferracuti has its origins in an attempt to explain the high rate of homicide among young African-American males in the inner city. They assert that in this group violence is seen as an appropriate, even expected response to a wide range of insults and provocations. They state, for example, that "a male is expected to defend the name and honor of his mother, the virtue of womanhood . . . and to accept no derogation about his race (even from a member of his own race), his age, or his masculinity" (1967: 153). The selection from Wolfgang and Ferracuti in Chapter 11 in this volume presents a general statement of their thesis. The following selection in Chapter 12 by Anderson provides a contemporary account of the subculture of violence thesis. Anderson (1994) describes the "code of the streets," and argues that this code pressures African American youth in the inner city to respond to shows of disrespect with violence. (The theories of Cohen [1955] and Cloward and Ohlin [1960], described in Part IV, also argue that certain segments of the lower class have values conducive to crime.)

Other theorists have argued that young people constitute a deviant subculture. In particular, young people are said to approve of certain minor forms of crime, like gambling and underage drinking, and to hold values that are conducive to crime—like an emphasis on thrills and excitement (this "youth subculture" is a popular subject for movies and TV shows). Still other theorists have argued that Southerners hold values that are conducive to the use of lethal violence. Such values have been used to explain the higher rate of homicide in the South. Finally, it has been argued that executives in certain corporations approve of select forms of crime, like price fixing and consumer fraud (see Agnew, 1995; Vold and Bernard, 1986, for brief overviews of these theories).

The origin of these deviant subcultures has been explained in several ways (see Agnew, 1995). The most common explanation draws on strain theory, which is described in the next part of this book. According to one version of this theory, individuals who are unable to achieve valued goals through legitimate channels may attempt to achieve them through illegitimate channels. In the process, they may come to justify or approve of their illegal behavior. Individuals who cannot achieve monetary success through conventional means, for example, may come to justify illegitimate means of goal achievement like theft and drug selling. A second version of strain theory argues that when individuals cannot achieve conventional goals through legitimate channels, they may substitute alternative goals which they are capable of achieving in their place. These alternative goals may sometimes involve crime. For example, individuals who cannot achieve middle-class status may reject this goal, and instead define status in terms of how good a fighter one is. Wolfgang and Ferracuti do not discuss the origin of the subculture of violence in their article (although see Curtis, 1975), but elements of these strain explanations can be found in the Anderson article (also see the Cohen and Cloward and Ohlin selections in Part IV).

Surprisingly, there has not been much research on macro-level learning theories. The few studies that have been done suggest that all groups—regardless of income, age, race, gender, or area of residence—condemn crime. There may, however, be differences in the degree to which crime is condemned. Also, it is unclear whether groups differ in the extent to which they hold values conducive to crime (e.g., toughness, excitement or thrills) and in the extent to which they approve of or justify crime under varying conditions. While several studies have been conducted in this area, their findings are often suspect due to various methodological problems—like the use of questionable measures of values. Recent evidence from observational studies and survey research, however, suggests that socioeconomic differences in violence may be at least partly explained by differences in values conducive to violence and beliefs justifying violence (see the Anderson selection; Heimer, 1997). For summaries of the literature in this area, see Agnew (1995), Cao et al. (1997), Heimer (1997), Luckenbill and Doyle (1989), and Messner (1988).

Macro-level learning theories, then, have less support than micro-level theories. While it is clear that individuals and small groups differ in their values regarding crime and the extent to which they reinforce crime, it is less clear whether this is the case for larger groups.

References

Agnew, Robert. 1994. "The Techniques of Neutralization and Violence." *Criminology* 32: 555-580.

——. 1995. "Strain and Subcultural Theories of Criminality." Pp. 305-327 in *Criminology: A Contemporary Handbook*, 2nd edition, edited by Joseph F. Sheley. Belmont: Wadsworth.

Akers, Ronald L. 1985. *Deviant Behavior: A Social Learning Approach*. Belmont: Wadsworth.

——. 1997. *Criminological Theories: Introduction and Evaluation*, 2nd edition. Los Angeles: Roxbury.

Anderson, Elijah. 1994. "The Code of the Streets." *Atlantic Monthly* 273 (May): 81-94.

Burgess, Robert L. and Ronald L. Akers. 1966. "A Differential Association-Reinforcement Theory of Criminal Behavior." *Social Problems* 14: 128-147.

Cao, Liqun, Anthony Adams, and Vickie J. Jensen. 1997. "A Test of the Black Subculture of Violence Thesis: A Research Note." *Criminology* 35: 367-379.

Cloward, Richard A. and Lloyd Ohlin. 1960. *Delinquency and Opportunity*. New York: Free Press.

Cohen, Albert K. 1955. *Delinquent Boys: The Culture of the Gang*. New York: Free Press.

Curtis, Lynn A. 1975. *Violence, Race, and Culture*. Lexington, MA: Heath.

Heimer, Karen. 1997. "Socioeconomic Status, Subcultural Definitions, and Violent Delinquency." *Social Forces* 75: 799-833.

Luckenbill, David F. and Daniel P. Doyle. 1989. "Structural Position and Violence: Developing a Cultural Explanation." *Criminology* 27: 419-436.

Matsueda, Ross L. 1988. "The Current State of Differential Association Theory." *Crime and Delinquency* 34: 277-306.

Matza, David and Gresham M. Sykes. 1961. "Juvenile Delinquency and Subterranean Values." *American Sociological Review* 26: 712-719.

Messner, Steven F. 1988. "Research on Criminal and Socioeconomic Factors in Criminal Violence." *The Psychiatric Clinics of North America* 11: 511-525.

Miller, Walter B. 1958. "Lower Class Culture as a Generating Milieu of Gang Delinquency." *Journal of Social Issues* 14: 5-19.

Sutherland, Edwin H., Donald R. Cressey, and David F. Luckenbill. 1992. *Principles of Criminology*. Dix Hills, NY: General Hall.

Sykes, Gresham M. and David Matza. 1957. "Techniques of Neutralization." *American Sociological Review* 22: 664-670.

Thornberry, Terence P., Marvin D. Krohn, Alan J. Lizotte, and Deborah Chard-Wierschem. 1993. "The Role of Juvenile Gangs in Facilitating Delinquent Behavior." *Journal of Research in Crime and Delinquency* 30: 55-87.

Tittle, Charles R. and Robert F. Meier. 1990. "Specifying the SES/Delinquency Relationship." *Criminology* 28: 271-299.

Vold, George B. and Thomas J. Bernard. 1986. *Theoretical Criminology*, 3rd edition. New York: Oxford.

Wolfgang, Marvin E. and Franco Ferracuti. 1982. *The Subculture of Violence: Towards an Integrated Theory in Criminology*. Beverly Hills: Sage. ✦

8

A Theory of Differential Association

Edwin H. Sutherland
Donald R. Cressey

Before Sutherland developed his theory, crime was usually explained in terms of multiple factors—like social class, broken homes, age, race, urban or rural location, and mental disorder. Sutherland developed his theory of differential association in an effort to explain why these various factors were related to crime. In doing so, he hoped to organize and integrate the research on crime up to that point, as well as to guide future research. Sutherland's theory is stated in the form of nine propositions. He argues that criminal behavior is learned by interacting with others, especially intimate others. Criminals learn both the techniques of committing crime and definitions favorable to crime from these others. The sixth proposition, which forms the heart of the theory, states that "a person becomes delinquent because of an excess of definitions favorable to law violation over definitions unfavorable to violation of law." According to Sutherland, factors such as social class, race, and broken homes influence crime because they affect the likelihood that individuals will associate with others who present definitions favorable to crime.

Sutherland's theory has had a tremendous influence on crime research and it remains one of the dominant theories of crime. Studies on the causes of crime routinely attempt to determine whether individuals are associating with delinquent or criminal others. While one can learn definitions favorable to crime from law-abiding individuals, one is most likely to learn such definitions from delinquent friends or criminal family members. These studies typically find that association with delinquent others is the best predictor of crime, and that these delinquent others partly influence crime by leading the individual to adopt beliefs conducive to crime (see Agnew, 1995; Akers, 1997 for summaries of such studies).

Sutherland's theory has also inspired much additional theorizing in criminology. Theorists have attempted to better describe the nature of those definitions favorable to violation of the law (see the next selection in Chapter 9 by Sykes and Matza). They have attempted to better describe the processes by which we learn criminal behavior from others (see the description of social learning theory by Akers in Chapter 10). And they have drawn on Sutherland in an effort to explain group differences in crime rates (see the Wolfgang and Ferracuti and Anderson selections in this Part). Sutherland's theory of differential association, then, is one of the enduring classics in criminology (for an excellent discussion of the current state of differential association theory, see Matsueda, 1988).

References

Agnew, Robert. 1995. "Strain and Subcultural Theories of Criminality." Pp. 305-327 in *Criminology: A Contemporary Handbook*, 2nd edition, edited by Joseph F. Sheley. Belmont: Wadsworth.

Akers, Ronald L. 1997. *Criminological Theories: Introduction and Evaluation*, 2nd edition. Los Angeles: Roxbury.

Matsueda, Ross L. 1988. "The Current State of Differential Association Theory." *Crime and Delinquency* 34: 277-306.

. . . The following statement refers to the process by which a particular person comes to engage in criminal behavior.

1. *Criminal behavior is learned.* Negatively, this means that criminal behavior is not inherited, as such; also, the person who is not already trained in crime does not invent criminal behavior, just as a person does not make mechanical inventions unless he has had training in mechanics.

2. *Criminal behavior is learned in interaction with other persons in a process of communication.* This communication is verbal in

many respects but includes also "the communication of gestures."

3. *The principal part of the learning of criminal behavior occurs within intimate personal groups*. Negatively, this means that the impersonal agencies of communication, such as movies and newspapers, play a relatively unimportant part in the genesis of criminal behavior.

4. *When criminal behavior is learned, the learning includes (a) techniques of committing the crime, which are sometimes very complicated, sometimes very simple; (b) the specific direction of motives, drives, rationalizations, and attitudes.*

5. *The specific direction of motives and drives is learned from definitions of the legal codes as favorable or unfavorable.* In some societies an individual is surrounded by persons who invariably define the legal codes as rules to be observed, while in others he is surrounded by persons whose definitions are favorable to the violation of the legal codes. In our American society these definitions are almost always mixed, with the consequence that we have culture conflict in relation to the legal codes.

6. *A person becomes delinquent because of an excess of definitions favorable to violation of law over definitions unfavorable to violation of law.* This is the principle of differential association. It refers to both criminal and anticriminal associations and has to do with counteracting forces. When persons become criminal, they do so because of contacts with criminal patterns and also because of isolation from anti-criminal patterns. Any person inevitably assimilates the surrounding culture unless other patterns are in conflict; a Southerner does not pronounce "r" because other Southerners do not pronounce "r." Negatively, this proposition of differential association means that associations which are neutral so far as crime is concerned have little or no effect on the genesis of criminal behavior. Much of the experience of a person is neutral in this sense, e.g., learning to brush one's teeth. This behavior has no negative or positive effect on criminal behavior except as it may be related to associations which are concerned with the legal codes. This neutral behavior is important especially as an occupier

of the time of a child so that he is not in contact with criminal behavior during the time he is so engaged in the neutral behavior.

7. *Differential associations may vary in frequency, duration, priority, and intensity.* This means that associations with criminal behavior and also associations with anti-criminal behavior vary in those respects. "Frequency" and "duration" as modalities of associations are obvious and need no explanation. "Priority" is assumed to be important in the sense that lawful behavior developed in early childhood may persist throughout life, and also that delinquent behavior developed in early childhood may persist throughout life. This tendency, however, has not been adequately demonstrated, and priority seems to be important principally through its selective influence. "Intensity" is not precisely defined but it has to do with such things as the prestige of the source of a criminal or anti-criminal pattern and with emotional reactions related to the associations. In a precise description of the criminal behavior of a person these modalities would be stated in quantitative form and a mathematical ratio be reached. A formula in this sense has not been developed, and the development of such a formula would be extremely difficult.

8. *The process of learning criminal behavior by association with criminal and anti-criminal patterns involves all of the mechanisms that are involved in any other learning.* Negatively, this means that the learning of criminal behavior is not restricted to the process of imitation. A person who is seduced, for instance, learns criminal behavior by association, but this process would not ordinarily be described as imitation.

9. *While criminal behavior is an expression of general needs and values, it is not explained by those general needs and values since noncriminal behavior is an expression of the same needs and values.* Thieves generally steal in order to secure money, but likewise honest laborers work in order to secure money. The attempts by many scholars to explain criminal behavior by general drives and values, such as the happiness principle, striving for social status, the money motive, or frustration, have been and must continue to be futile since they explain lawful behavior as com-

pletely as they explain criminal behavior. They are similar to respiration, which is necessary for any behavior but which does not differentiate criminal from non-criminal behavior.

It is not necessary, at this level of explanation, to explain why a person has the associations which he has; this certainly involves a complex of many things. In an area where the delinquency rate is high, a boy who is sociable, gregarious, active, and athletic is very likely to come in contact with the other boys in the neighborhood, learn delinquent behavior from them, and become a gangster; in the same neighborhood the psychopathic boy who is isolated, introverted, and inert may remain at home, not become acquainted with the other boys in the neighborhood, and not become delinquent. In another situation, the sociable, athletic, aggressive boy may become a member of a scout troop and not become involved in delinquent behavior. The person's associations are determined in a general context of social organization. A child is ordinarily reared in a family; the place of residence of the family is determined largely by family income; and the delinquency rate is in many respects related to the rental value of the houses. Many other aspects of social organization affect the kinds of associations a person has.

The preceding explanation of criminal behavior purports to explain the criminal and non-criminal behavior of individual persons. As indicated earlier, it is possible to state sociological theories of criminal behavior which explain the criminality of a community, nation, or other group. The problem, when thus stated, is to account for variations in crime rates and involves a comparison of the crime rates of various groups or the crime rates of a particular group at different times. The explanation of a crime rate must be consistent with the explanation of the criminal behavior of the person, since the crime rate is a summary statement of the number of persons in the group who commit crimes and the frequency with which they commit crimes. One of the best explanations of crime rates from this point of view is that a high crime rate is due to social disorganization. The term "social disorganization" is not entirely satisfactory and it seems preferable to substitute for it the term "differential social organization." The postulate on which this theory is based, regardless of the name, is that crime is rooted in the social organization and is an expression of that social organization. A group may be organized for criminal behavior or organized against criminal behavior. Most communities are organized both for criminal and anti-criminal behavior and in that sense the crime rate is an expression of the differential group organization. Differential group organization as an explanation of variations in crime rates is consistent with the differential association theory of the processes by which persons become criminals.

Reprinted from Edwin H. Sutherland and Donald R. Cressey, "A Theory of Differential Association" in *Principles of Criminology*, 6th edition. Copyright © 1960 by Elaine S. Cressey. Reprinted by permission of Elaine S. Cressey.

Discussion Questions

1. What does Sutherland mean by "definitions favorable to violation of law"? Give examples of such definitions.

2. According to Sutherland, our associations do not carry equal weight; some are more influential than others. What types of associations carry the greatest weight in influencing our behavior?

3. Strain theorists, described in the next section, argue that frustration is a major cause of crime. How would Sutherland respond to this argument?

4. What policy recommendations might Sutherland make for controlling crime? ✦

9

Techniques of Neutralization

Gresham M. Sykes
David Matza

Sykes and Matza, like Sutherland, feel that criminal behavior is learned. And like Sutherland, they feel that part of that learning involves "motives, drives, rationalizations, and attitudes favorable to violation of law." They state, however, that the specific content of these rationalizations, attitudes, etc. has not received much attention. When they wrote their article in 1957, the dominant view was that delinquents held values which were the opposite of middle-class values. Delinquents, in particular, were said to generally approve of acts like theft and fighting. This position, represented in the work of Albert Cohen (see Chapter 14 in Part IV), is attacked by Sykes and Matza (also see Matza, 1964).

The first part of their article presents evidence suggesting that delinquents do not generally approve of delinquency. The second part of their article presents an alternative formulation, in which they contend that delinquents are able to engage in delinquency by employing certain "techniques of neutralization." While delinquents believe that delinquency is generally bad, they claim that their delinquent acts are justified for anyone of several reasons (e.g., the victim had it coming, they didn't really hurt anybody). These justifications are said to be used before the delinquent act, and they make the delinquent act possible by neutralizing the individual's belief that it is bad.

Data indicate that individuals differ in the extent to which they accept the neutralization techniques listed by Sykes and Matza (as well as additional techniques described by others). Those individuals who accept more neutralization techniques are generally more likely to engage in crime, although the effect of neutrali-

zation on crime is influenced by several variables (see Agnew, 1994 for an overview). Neutralization, for example, is more likely to lead to crime among individuals who associate with delinquent peers (perhaps because these individuals have more opportunities for delinquency and are more predisposed to respond to troublesome situations with delinquency). The data, then, do suggest that the techniques of neutralization may well be a "crucial component" of Sutherland's "definitions favorable to violation of law."

References

Agnew, Robert. 1994. "The Techniques of Neutralization and Violence." *Criminology* 32: 555-580.

Matza, David. 1964. *Delinquency and Drift.* New York: Wiley.

In attempting to uncover the roots of juvenile delinquency, the social scientist has long since ceased to search for devils in the mind or stigma of the body. It is now largely agreed that delinquent behavior, like most social behavior, is learned and that it is learned in the process of social interaction.

The classic statement of this position is found in Sutherland's theory of differential association, which asserts that criminal or delinquent behavior involves the learning of (a) techniques of committing crimes and (b) motives, drives, rationalizations, and attitudes favorable to the violation of law. Unfortunately, the specific content of what is learned—as opposed to the process by which it is learned—has received relatively little attention in either theory or research. Perhaps the single strongest school of thought on the nature of this content has centered on the idea of a delinquent sub-culture. The basic characteristic of the delinquent sub-culture, it is argued, is a system of values that represents an inversion of the values held by respectable, law-abiding society. The world of the delinquent is the world of the law-abiding turned upside down and its norms constitute a countervailing force directed against the conforming social order. Cohen sees the process of developing a delinquent sub-culture as a matter of building, maintaining, and re-inforcing a code for behavior which exists by opposition, which stands in point by point contradiction to dominant values, particularly those of the middle class. Cohen's portrayal of delinquency is executed with a good deal of sophistication, and he carefully avoids overly simple explanations such as those based on the principle of "follow the leader" or easy generalizations about "emotional disturbances." Furthermore, he does not accept the delinquent sub-culture as something given, but instead systematically examines the function of delinquent values as a viable solution to the lower-class, male child's problems in the area of social status. Yet in spite of its virtues, this image of juvenile delinquency as a form of behavior based on competing or countervailing values and norms appears to suffer from a number of serious defects. It is the nature of these defects and a possible alternative or modified explanation for a large portion of juvenile delinquency with which this paper is concerned.

The difficulties in viewing delinquent behavior as springing from a set of deviant values and norms—as arising, that is to say, from a situation in which the delinquent defines his delinquency as "right"—are both empirical and theoretical. In the first place, if there existed in fact a delinquent sub-culture such that the delinquent viewed his illegal behavior as morally correct, we could reasonably suppose that he would exhibit no feelings of guilt or shame at detection or confinement. Instead, the major reaction would tend in the direction of indignation or a sense of martyrdom. It is true that some delinquents do react in the latter fashion, although the sense of martyrdom often seems to be based on the fact that others "get away with it" and indignation appears to be directed against the chance events or lack of skill that led to apprehension. More important, however, is the fact that there is a good deal of evidence suggesting that many delinquents *do* experience a sense of guilt or shame, and its outward expression is not to be dismissed as a purely manipulative gesture to appease those in authority. Much of this evidence is, to be sure, of a clinical nature or in the form of impressionistic judgments of those who must deal first hand with the youthful offender. Assigning a weight to such evidence calls for caution, but it cannot be ignored if we are to avoid the gross stereotype of the juvenile delinquent as a hardened gangster in miniature.

In the second place, observers have noted that the juvenile delinquent frequently accords admiration and respect to law-abiding persons. The "really honest" is often revered, and if the delinquent is sometimes overly keen to detect hypocrisy in those who conform, unquestioned probity is likely to win his approval. A fierce attachment to a humble, pious mother or a forgiving, upright priest (the former, according to many observers, is often encountered in both juvenile delinquents and adult criminals) might be dismissed as rank sentimentality, but at least it is clear that the delinquent does not necessarily regard those who abide by the legal rules as immoral. In a similar vein, it can be noted that the juvenile delinquent may exhibit great resentment if illegal behavior is imputed to "significant others" in his immediate social environment or to heroes in the world of sport and entertainment. In other words, if the delinquent does hold to a set of values and norms that stand in complete opposition to those of respectable society, his norm-holding is, of a peculiar sort. While supposedly thoroughly committed to the deviant system of the delinquent sub-culture, he would appear to recognize the moral validity of the dominant normative system in many instances.

In the third place, there is much evidence that juvenile delinquents often draw a sharp line between those who can be victimized and those who cannot. Certain social groups are not to be viewed as "fair game" in the performance of supposedly approved delinquent acts while others warrant a variety of attacks. In general, the potentiality for victimization would seem to be a function of the social distance between the juvenile delinquent and others and thus we find implicit maxims in the world of the delinquent such as "don't steal from friends" or "don't commit vandalism against a church of your own faith." This is all rather obvious, but the implications have not received sufficient attention. The fact that supposedly valued behavior tends to be directed against disvalued social groups hints that the "wrongfulness" of such delinquent behavior is more widely recognized by delinquents than the literature has indicated. When the pool of victims is limited by considerations of kinship, friendship, ethnic group, social class, age, sex, etc., we have reason to suspect that the virtue of delinquency is far from unquestioned.

In the fourth place, it is doubtful if many juvenile delinquents are totally immune from the demands for conformity made by the dominant social order. There is a strong likelihood that the family of the delinquent will agree with respectable society that delinquency is wrong, even though the family may be engaged in a variety of illegal activities. That is, the parental posture conducive to delinquency is not apt to be a positive prodding. Whatever may be the influence of parental example, what might be called the "Fagin" pattern of socialization into delinquency is probably rare. Furthermore, as Redl has indicated, the idea that certain neighborhoods are completely delinquent, offering the child a model for delinquent behavior without reservations, is simply not supported by the data.

The fact that a child is punished by parents, school officials, and agencies of the legal system for his delinquency may, as a number of observers have cynically noted, suggest to the child that he should be more careful not to get caught. There is an equal or greater probability, however, that the child will internalize the demands for conformity. This is not to say that demands for conformity cannot be counteracted. In fact, as we shall see shortly, an understanding of how internal and external demands for conformity are neutralized may be crucial for understanding delinquent behavior. But it is to say that a complete denial of the validity of demands for conformity and the substitution of a new normative system is improbable, in light of the child's or adolescent's dependency on adults and encirclement by adults inherent in his status in the social structure. No matter how deeply enmeshed in patterns of delinquency he may be and no matter how much this involvement may outweigh his associations with the law-abiding, he cannot escape the condemnation of his deviance. Somehow the demands for conformity must be met and answered; they cannot be ignored as part of an alien system of values and norms.

In short, the theoretical viewpoint that sees juvenile delinquency as a form of behavior based on the values and norms of a deviant sub-culture in precisely the same way as law-abiding behavior is based on the values and norms of the larger society is open to serious doubt. The fact that the world of the delinquent is embedded in the larger world of those who conform cannot be overlooked nor can the delinquent be equated with an adult thoroughly socialized into an alternative way of life. Instead, the juvenile delinquent would appear to be at least partially committed to the dominant social order in that he frequently exhibits guilt or shame when he violates its proscriptions, accords approval to certain conforming figures, and distinguishes between appropriate and inappropriate targets for his deviance. It is to an explanation for the apparent paradoxical fact of his delinquency that we now turn.

As Morris Cohen once said, one of the most fascinating problems about human behavior is why men violate the laws in which they believe. This is the problem that confronts us when we attempt to explain why delinquency occurs despite a greater or lesser commitment to the usages of conformity. A basic clue is offered by the fact that social rules or norms calling for valued behavior seldom if ever take the form of categorical imperatives. Rather, values or norms appear as *qualified* guides for action, limited in their applicability in terms of time, place, persons, and social circumstances. The moral injunction against killing, for example, does not apply to the enemy during combat in time of war, although a captured enemy comes once again under the prohibition. Similarly, the taking and distributing of scarce goods in a time of acute social need is felt by many to be right, although under other circumstances private property is held inviolable. The normative system of a society, then, is marked by what Williams has termed *flexibility*; it does not consist of a body of rules held to be binding under all conditions.

This flexibility is, in fact, an integral part of the criminal law in that measures for "defenses to crimes" are provided in pleas such as nonage, necessity, insanity, drunkenness, compulsion, self-defense, and so on. The individual can avoid moral culpability for his criminal action—and thus avoid the negative sanctions of society—if he can prove that criminal intent was lacking.

It is our argument that much delinquency is based on what is essentially an unrecognized extension of defenses to crimes, in the form of justifications for deviance that are see as valid by the delinquent but not by the legal system or society at large.

These justifications are commonly described as rationalizations. They are viewed as following deviant behavior and as protecting the individual from self-blame and the blame of others after the act. But there is also reason to believe that they precede deviant behavior and make deviant behavior possible. It is this possibility that Sutherland mentioned only in passing and that other writers have failed to exploit from the viewpoint of sociological theory. Disapproval flowing from internalized norms and conforming others in the social environment is neutralized, turned back, or deflected in advance. Social controls that serve to check or inhibit deviant motivational patterns are rendered inoperative, and the individual is freed to engage in delinquency without serious damage to his self image. In this sense, the delinquent both has his cake and eats it too, for he remains committed to the dominant normative system and yet so qualifies its imperatives that violations are "acceptable" if not "right." Thus the delinquent represents not a radical opposition to law-abiding society but something more like an apologetic failure, often more sinned against than sinning in his own eyes. We call these justifications of deviant behavior techniques of neutralization; and we believe these techniques make up a crucial component of Sutherland's "definitions favorable to the violation of law." It is by learning these techniques that the juvenile becomes delinquent, rather than by learning moral imperatives, values or attitudes standing in direct contradiction to those of the dominant society. In analyzing these techniques, we have found it convenient to divide them into five major types.

The Denial of Responsibility

In so far as the delinquent can define himself as lacking responsibility for his deviant actions, the disapproval of self or others is sharply reduced in effectiveness as a restraining influence. As Justice Holmes has said, even a dog distinguishes between being stumbled over and being kicked, and modern society is no less careful to draw a line between injuries that are unintentional, i.e., where responsibility is lacking, and those that are intentional. As a technique of neutralization, however, the denial of responsibility extends much further than the claim that deviant acts are an "accident" or some similar negation of personal accountability. It may also be asserted that delinquent acts are due to forces outside of the individual and beyond his control such as unloving parents, bad companions, or a slum neighborhood. In effect, the delinquent approaches a "billiard ball" conception of himself in which he sees himself as helplessly propelled into new situations. From a psychodynamic viewpoint, this orientation toward one's own actions may represent a profound alienation from self, but it is important to stress the fact that interpretations of responsibility are cultural constructs and not merely idiosyncratic beliefs. The similarity between this mode of justifying illegal behavior assumed by the delinquent and the implications of a "sociological" frame of reference or a "humane" jurisprudence is readily apparent. It is not the validity of this orientation that concerns us here, but its function of deflecting blame attached to violations of social norms and its relative independence of a particular personality structure. By learning to view himself as more acted upon than acting, the delinquent prepares the way for deviance from the dominant normative system without the necessity of a frontal assault on the norms themselves.

The Denial of Injury

A second major technique of neutralization centers on the injury or harm involved in the delinquent act. The criminal law has long made a distinction between crimes which are *mala in se* and *mala prohibita*—that is between acts that are wrong in themselves and acts that are illegal but not immoral—and the delinquent can make the same kind of distinction in evaluating the wrongfulness of his behavior. For the delinquent, however, wrongfulness may turn on the question of whether or not anyone has clearly been hurt by his deviance, and this matter is open to a variety of interpretations. Vandalism, for example, may be defined by the delinquent simply as "mischief"—after all, it may be claimed, the persons whose property has been destroyed can well afford it. Similarly, auto theft may be viewed as "borrowing," and gang fighting may be seen as a private quarrel, an agreed upon duel between two willing parties, and thus of no concern to the community at large. We are not suggesting that this technique of neutralization, labelled the denial of injury, involves an explicit dialectic, rather, we are arguing that the delinquent frequently, and in a hazy fashion, feels that his behavior does not really cause any great harm despite the fact that it runs counter to law. Just as the link between the individual and his acts may be broken by the denial of responsibility, so may the link between acts and their consequences be broken by the denial of injury. Since society sometimes agrees with the delinquent, e.g., in matters such as truancy, "pranks," and so on, it merely reaffirms the idea that the delinquent's neutralization of social controls by means of qualifying the norms is an extension of common practice rather than a gesture of complete opposition.

The Denial of Victim

Even if the delinquent accepts the responsibility for his deviant actions and is willing to admit that his deviant actions involve an injury or hurt, the moral indignation of self and others may be neutralized by an insistence that the injury is not wrong in light of the circumstances. The injury, it may be claimed, is not really an injury; rather, it is a form of rightful retaliation or punishment. By a subtle alchemy the delinquent moves himself into the position of an avenger and the victim is transformed into a wrong-doer. Assaults on homosexuals or suspected homosexuals, attacks on members of minority groups who are said to have gotten "out of place," vandalism as revenge on an unfair teacher or school official, thefts from a "crooked" store owner—all may be hurts inflicted on a transgressor, in the eyes of the delinquent. As Orwell has pointed out, the type of criminal admired by the general public has probably changed over the course of years and Raffles no longer serves as a hero; but Robin Hood, and his latter day derivatives such as the tough detective seeking justice outside the law, still capture the popular imagination, and the delinquent may view his acts as part of a similar role. To deny the existence of the victim, then, by transforming him into a person deserving injury is an extreme form of a phenomenon we have mentioned before, namely, the delinquent's recognition of appropriate and inappropriate targets for his delinquent acts. In addition, however, the existence of the victim may be denied for the delinquent, in a somewhat different sense, by the circumstances of the delinquent act itself. Insofar as the victim is physically absent, unknown, or a vague abstraction (as is often the case in delinquent acts committed against property), the awareness of the victim's existence is weakened. Internalized norms and anticipations of the reactions of others must somehow be activated, if they are to serve as guides for behavior; and it is possible that a diminished awareness of the victim plays an important part in determining whether or not this process is set in motion.

The Condemnation of the Condemners

A fourth technique of neutralization would appear to involve a condemnation of the condemners or, as McCorkle and Korn have phrased it, a rejection of the rejectors. The delinquent shifts the focus of attention from his own deviant acts to the motives and behavior of those who disapprove of his violations. His condemners, he may claim, are hypocrites, deviants in disguise, or impelled by personal spite. This orientation toward the conforming world may be of particular importance when it hardens into a bitter cynicism directed against those assigned the task of enforcing or expressing the norms of the dominant society. Police, it may be said, are corrupt, stupid, and brutal. Teachers always show favoritism and parents always "take it out" on their children. By a slight extension, the rewards of conformity—such as material success—become a matter of pull or luck, thus decreasing still further the stature of those who stand on the side of the law-abiding. The validity of this jaundiced viewpoint is not so important as its function in turning back or deflecting the negative sanctions attached to violations of the norms. The delinquent, in effect, has changed the subject of the conversation in the dialogue between his own deviant impulses and the reactions of others; and by attacking others, the wrongfulness of his own behavior is more easily repressed or lost to view.

The Appeal to Higher Loyalties

Fifth, and last, internal and external social controls may be neutralized by sacrificing the demands of the larger society for the demands of the smaller social groups to which the delinquent belongs such as the sibling pair, the gang, or the friendship clique. It is important to note that the delinquent does not necessarily repudiate the imperatives of the dominant normative system, despite his failure to follow them. Rather, the delinquent may see himself as caught up in a dilemma that must be resolved, unfortunately, at the cost of violating the law. One aspect of this situation has been studied by Stouffer and Toby in their research on the conflict between particularistic and universalistic demands, between the claims of friendship and general social obligations, and their results suggest that "it is possible to classify people according to a predisposition to select one or the other horn of a dilemma in role conflict." For our purposes, however, the most important point is that deviation from certain norms may occur not because the norms are rejected but because other norms, held to be more pressing or involving a higher loyalty,

are accorded precedence. Indeed, it is the fact that both sets of norms are believed in that gives meaning to our concepts of dilemma and role conflict.

The conflict between the claims of friendship and the claims of law, or a similar dilemma, has of course long been recognized by the social scientist (and the novelist) as a common human problem. If the juvenile delinquent frequently resolves his dilemma by insisting that he must "always help a buddy" or "never squeal on a friend," even when it throws him into serious difficulties with the dominant social order, his choice remains familiar to the supposedly law-abiding. The delinquent is unusual, perhaps, in the extent to which he is able to see the fact that he acts in behalf of the smaller social groups to which he belongs as a justification for violations of society's norms, but it is a matter of degree rather than of kind. "I didn't mean it." "I didn't really hurt anybody." "They had it coming to them." "Everybody's picking on me." "I didn't do it for myself." These slogans or their variants, we hypothesize, prepare the juvenile for delinquent acts. These "definitions of the situation" represent tangential or glancing blows at the dominant normative system rather than the creation of an opposing ideology; and they are extensions of patterns of thought prevalent in society rather than something created *de novo*.

Techniques of neutralization may not be powerful enough to fully shield the individual from the force of his own internalized values and the reactions of conforming others, for as we have pointed out, juvenile delinquents often appear to suffer from feelings of guilt and shame when called into account for their deviant behavior. And some delinquents may be so isolated from the world of conformity that techniques of neutralization need not be called into play. Nonetheless, we would argue that techniques of neutralization are critical in lessening the effectiveness of social controls and that they lie behind a large share of delinquent behavior. Empirical research in this area is scattered and fragmentary at the present time, but the work of Redl, Cressy, and others has supplied a body of significant data that has done much to clarify the theoretical issues and enlarge the fund of supporting evidence. Two lines of investigation seem to be critical at this stage. First, there is need for more knowledge concerning the differential distribution of techniques of neutralization, as operative patterns of thought, by age, sex, social class, ethnic group, etc. On *a priori* grounds it might be assumed that these justifications for deviance will be more readily seized by segments of society for whom a discrepancy between common social ideals and social practice is most apparent. It is also possible however, that the habit of "bending" the dominant normative system—if not "breaking" it—cuts across our cruder social categories and is to be traced primarily to patterns of social interaction within the familial circle. Second, there is need for a greater understanding of the internal structure of techniques of neutralization, as a system of beliefs and attitudes, and its relationship to various types of delinquent behavior. Certain techniques of neutralization would appear to be better adapted to particular deviant acts than to others, as we have suggested, for example, in the case of offenses against property and the denial of the victim. But the issue remains far from clear and stands in need of more information.

In any case, techniques of neutralization appear to offer a promising line of research in enlarging and systematizing the theoretical grasp of juvenile delinquency. As more information is uncovered concerning techniques of neutralization, their origins, and their consequences, both juvenile delinquency in particular, and deviation from normative systems in general may be illuminated.

Reprinted from Gresham M. Sykes and David Matza, "Techniques of Neutralization: A Theory of Delinquency" in the *American Sociological Review* 22. Copyright © 1957.

Discussion Questions

1. In their article, Sykes and Matza paraphrase Morris Cohen: "one of the most fascinating problems about human behavior is why men violate the laws in which they believe." What solution do Sykes and Matza offer to this problem?

2. Most students disapprove of cheating on exams, but many nevertheless cheat. List possible justifications such students might give for their cheating behavior. Which techniques of neutralization do these justifications illustrate?

3. Sykes and Matza argue that the techniques of neutralization are learned from others. They do not, however, describe those groups or types of individuals that are most likely to employ the techniques of neutralization. What groups or categories of individuals do you think are most likely to employ the techniques of neutralization (and why)? ✦

10

A Social Learning Theory of Crime

Ronald L. Akers

As *Akers points out in this selection, his social learning theory is a reformulation and extension of Sutherland's differential association theory. Differential association theory argues that criminal behavior is learned in interaction with others, but it does not specify the mechanisms by which such behavior is learned. Burgess and Akers (1966) and Akers (1985) draw on several theories of learning, particularly behavioral theory and social learning theory in psychology, to more precisely describe how crime is learned.*

Akers's theory is compatible with Sutherland's theory. Like Sutherland, Akers argues that we learn to engage in crime through exposure to and the adoption of definitions favorable to crime. Akers, however, more fully describes the nature of such definitions. In doing so, he draws heavily on Sykes and Matza's description of the techniques of neutralization— although he also argues that the definitions favorable to crime include more than neutralization techniques (i.e., he argues that there are both positive and neutralizing definitions favorable to crime).

At the same time, Akers extends differential association theory. He argues that crime may also be learned through imitation and differential reinforcement. Akers's theory, then, is much broader than that of Sutherland. In fact, Akers (1985) has argued that his theory is capable of subsuming most of the major sociological theories of crime. As Akers points out in this selection, his theory has received much empirical support. Social learning theory is now perhaps the leading theory of crime.

References

Akers, Ronald L. 1985. *Deviant Behavior: A Social Learning Approach*. Belmont, CA: Wadsworth.

Burgess, Robert L. and Ronald L. Akers. 1966. "A Differential Association-Reinforcement Theory of Criminal Behavior." *Social Problems* 14: 128-147.

Development of the Theory

Sutherland asserted in the eighth statement of his theory that all the mechanisms of learning are involved in criminal behavior. However, beyond a brief comment that more is involved than direct imitation (Tarde, 1912), he did not explain what the mechanisms of learning are. These learning mechanisms were specified by Burgess and Akers (1966b) in their "differential association-reinforcement" theory of criminal behavior. Burgess and Akers produced a full reformulation that retained the principles of differential association, combining them with, and restating them in terms of, the learning principles of operant and respondent conditioning that had been developed by behavioral psychologists. Akers has subsequently developed the differential association-reinforcement theory, most often labeling it "social learning" and applying it to criminal, delinquent, and deviant behavior in general (see Akers, 1973; 1977; 1985). He has modified the theory, devised specific measures of its key concepts, and tested its central propositions.

Social learning theory is not competitive with differential association theory. Instead, it is a broader theory that retains all the differential association processes in Sutherland's theory (albeit clarified and somewhat modified) and integrates it with differential reinforcement and other principles of behavioral acquisition, continuation, and cessation (Akers, 1985: 41). Thus, research findings supportive of differential association also support the integrated theory. But social learning theory explains criminal and delinquent behavior more thoroughly than does the original differential association theory (see, for instance, Akers et al., 1979; Warr and Stafford, 1991).

Burgess and Akers (1966b) explicitly identified the learning mechanisms as those found in modern behavioral theory. They retained the concepts of differential association and definitions from Sutherland's theory, but conceptualized them in more behavioral terms and added concepts from behavioral learning theory. These concepts include differential reinforcement, whereby "operant" behavior (the voluntary actions of the individual) is conditioned or shaped by rewards and punishments. They also contain classical or "respondent" conditioning (the conditioning of involuntary reflex behavior); discriminative stimuli (the environmental and internal stimuli that provides cues or signals for behavior), schedules of reinforcement (the rate and ratio in which rewards and punishments follow behavioral responses), and other principles of behavior modification.

Akers followed up his early work with Burgess with a fuller, more detailed presentation of the concepts and propositions of the theory in successive editions of *Deviant Behavior: A Social Learning Approach* (Akers, 1973; 1977; 1985). In this book, Akers shows how social learning theory relates to other theories of crime and deviance and gives a social learning explanation of drug and alcohol behavior, sexual deviance, white-collar crime, professional crime, organized crime, violent crime, suicide, and mental illness. Akers also retains Sutherland's and Cressey's concern with social structure and relates the social learning process to variations in the group rates of crime and deviance.

Social learning theory retains a strong element of the symbolic interactionism found in the concepts of differential association and definitions from Sutherland's theory (Akers, 1985:39-70). Symbolic interactionism is the theory that social interaction is mainly the exchange of meaning and symbols; individuals have the cognitive capacity to imagine themselves in the role of others and incorporate this into their conceptions of themselves (Ritzer, 1992). This, and the explicit inclusion of such concepts as imitation, anticipated reinforcement, and self-reinforcement, makes social learning "soft behaviorism" (Akers, 1985:65). As a result, the theory is closer to cognitive learning theories, such as Albert Bandura's (1973; 1977; 1986; Bandura and Walters, 1963), than to the radical or orthodox operant behaviorism of B. F. Skinner (1953; 1959) with which Burgess and Akers began.

The Central Concepts and Propositions of Social Learning Theory

Social learning theory offers an explanation of crime and deviance which embraces variables that operate both to motivate and control criminal behavior, both to promote and undermine conformity. The probability of criminal or conforming behavior occurring is a function of the balance of these influences on behavior.

> [T]he principal behavioral effects come from interaction in or under the influence of those groups with which one is in differential association and which control sources and patterns of reinforcement, provide normative definitions, and expose one to behavioral models . . . .
>
> Deviant behavior can be expected to the extent that it has been differentially reinforced over alternative behavior (conforming or other deviant behavior) and is defined as desirable or justified when the individual is in a situation discriminative for the behavior. (Akers, 1985:57-58)

While referring to all aspects of the learning process, Akers' development of the theory has focused on four major concepts: *differential association, definitions, differential reinforcement,* and *imitation* (Akers et al., 1979; Akers, 1985; Akers and Cochran, 1985; Akers, 1992a).

Differential Association. Differential association refers to the process whereby one is exposed to normative definitions favorable or unfavorable to illegal or law-abiding behavior. Differential association has both behavioral *interactional* and *normative* dimensions. The interactional dimension is the direct association and interaction with others who engage in certain kinds of behavior, as well as the indirect association and identification with more distant reference groups. The normative dimension is the different patterns of norms and values to which an individual is exposed through this association.

The groups with which one is in differential association provide the major social contexts in which all the mechanisms of social learning operate. They not only expose one to definitions, they also present them with models to imitate and with differential reinforcement (source, schedule, value, and amount) for criminal or conforming behavior. The most important of these groups are the primary ones of family and friends, though they may also be secondary and reference groups. Neighbors, churches, school teachers, physicians, the law and authority figures, and other individuals and groups in the community (as well as mass media and other more remote sources of attitudes and models) have varying degrees of effect on the individual's propensity to commit criminal and delinquent behavior. Those associations which occur first (priority), last longer (duration), occur more frequently (frequency), and involve others with whom one has the more important or closer relationships (intensity) will have the greater effect.

Definitions. Definitions are one's own attitudes or meanings that one attaches to given behavior. That is, they are orientations, rationaliza- tions, definitions of the situation, and other evaluative and moral attitudes that define the commission of an act as right or wrong, good or bad, desirable or undesirable, justified or unjustified.

In social learning theory, these definitions are both *general* and *specific*. General beliefs include religious, moral, and other conventional values and norms that are favorable to conforming behavior and unfavorable to committing any deviant or criminal acts. Specific definitions orient the person to particular acts or series of acts. Thus, one may believe that it is morally wrong to steal and that laws against theft should be obeyed, but at the same time one may see little wrong with smoking marijuana and rationalize that it is all right to violate laws against drug possession.

The greater the extent to which one holds attitudes that disapprove of certain acts, the less one is likely to engage in them. Conventional beliefs are *negative* toward criminal behavior. Conversely, the more one's own attitudes approve of a behavior, the greater the chances are that one will do it. Approving definitions favorable to the commission of criminal or deviant behavior are basically

positive or *neutralizing*. Positive definitions are beliefs or attitudes which make the behavior morally desirable or wholly permissible. Neutralizing definitions favor the commission of crime by justifying or excusing it. They view the act as something that is probably undesirable but, given the situation, is nonetheless all right, justified, excusable, necessary, or not really bad to do. The concept of neutralizing definitions in social learning theory incorporates the notions of verbalizations, rationalizations, techniques of neutralizations, accounts, and disclaimers (Cressey, 1953; Sykes and Matza, 1957; Lyman and Scott, 1970; Hewitt and Stokes, 1975). Neutralizing attitudes include such beliefs as, "Everybody has a racket," "I can't help myself, I was born this way," "I am not at fault," "I am not responsible," "I was drunk and didn't know what I was doing," "I just blew my top," "They can afford it," "He deserved it," and other excuses and justification for committing deviant acts and victimizing others. These definitions favorable and unfavorable to criminal and delinquent behavior are developed through imitation and differential reinforcement. Cognitively, they provide a mind-set that makes one more willing to commit the act when the opportunity occurs. Behaviorally, they affect the commission of deviant or criminal behavior by acting as internal discriminative stimuli. Discriminative stimuli operate as cues or signals to the individual as to what responses are appropriate or expected in a given situation.

Some of the definitions favorable to deviance are so intensely held that they almost "require" one to violate the law. For instance, the radical ideologies of revolutionary groups provide strong motivation for terrorist acts, just as the fervent moral stance of some anti-abortion groups justifies in their minds the need to engage in civil disobedience. For the most part, however, definitions favorable to crime and delinquency do not "require" or strongly motivate action in this sense. Rather, they are conventional beliefs so weakly held that they provide no restraint or are positive or neutralizing attitudes that facilitate law violation in the right set of circumstances.

Differential Reinforcement. Differential reinforcement refers to the balance of anticipated or actual rewards and punishments that follow or are consequences of behavior. Whether individuals will refrain from or commit a crime at any given time (and whether they will continue or desist from doing so in the future) depends on the past, present, and anticipated future rewards and punishments for their actions.

The probability that an act will be committed or repeated is increased by rewarding outcomes or reactions to it, e.g., obtaining approval, money, food, or pleasant feelings—positive reinforcement. The likelihood that an action will be taken is also enhanced when it allows the person to avoid or escape aversive or unpleasant events—negative reinforcement. Punishment may also be direct (positive), in which painful or unpleasant consequences are attached to a behavior; or indirect (negative), in which a reward or pleasant consequence is removed. Just as there are modalities of association, there are modalities of reinforcement—amount, frequency, and probability. The greater the value or amount of reinforcement for the person's behavior, the more frequently it is reinforced, and the higher the probability that it will be reinforced (as balanced against alternative behavior), the greater the likelihood that it will occur and be repeated. The reinforcement process does not operate in the social environment in a simple either/or fashion. Rather, it operates according to a "matching function" in which the occurrence of, and changes in, each of several different behaviors correlate with the probability and amount of, and changes in, the balance of reward and punishment attached to each behavior (Hamblin, 1979; Conger and Simons, 1995).

Reinforcers and punishers can be non-social; for example, the direct physical effects of drugs and alcohol. However, whether or not these effects are experienced positively or negatively is contingent upon previously learned expectations. Through social reinforcement, one learns to interpret the effects as pleasurable and enjoyable or as frightening and unpleasant. Individuals can learn without contact, directly or indirectly, with social reinforcers and punishers. There may be a physiological basis for the tendency of

some individuals (such as those prone to sensation-seeking) more than others to find certain forms of deviant behavior intrinsically rewarding (Wood et al., 1995). However, the theory proposes that most of the learning in criminal and deviant behavior is the result of social exchange in which the words, responses, presence, and behavior of other persons directly reinforce behavior, provide the setting for reinforcement (discriminative stimuli), or serve as the conduit through which other social rewards and punishers are delivered or made available.

The concept of social reinforcement (and punishment) goes beyond the direct reactions of others present while an act is committed. It also includes the whole range of actual and anticipated, tangible and intangible rewards valued in society or subgroups. Social rewards can be highly symbolic. Their reinforcing effects can come from their fulfilling ideological, religious, political, or other goals. Even those rewards which we consider to be very tangible, such as money and material possessions, gain their reinforcing value from the prestige and approval value they have in society. Non-social reinforcement, therefore, is more narrowly confined to unconditioned physiological and physical stimuli. In *self-reinforcement* the individual exercises self-control, reinforcing or punishing one's own behavior by taking the role of others, even when alone.

Imitation. Imitation refers to the engagement in behavior after the observation of similar behavior in others. Whether or not the behavior modeled by others will be imitated is affected by the characteristics of the models, the behavior observed, and the observed consequences of the behavior (Bandura, 1977). The observation of salient models in primary groups and in the media affects both pro-social and deviant behavior (Donnerstein and Linz, 1995). It is more important in the initial acquisition and performance of novel behavior than in the maintenance or cessation of behavioral patterns once established, but it continues to have some effect in maintaining behavior.

The Social Learning Process: Sequence and Feedback Effects

These social learning variables are all part of an underlying process that is operative in each individual's learning history and in the immediate situation in which an opportunity for a crime occurs. Akers stresses that social learning is a complex process with reciprocal and feedback effects. The reciprocal effects are not seen as equal, however. Akers hypothesizes a typical temporal sequence or process by which persons come to the point of violating the law or engaging in other deviant acts.

This process is one in which the balance of learned definitions, imitation of criminal or deviant models, and the anticipated balance of reinforcement produces the initial delinquent or deviant act. The facilitative effects of these variables continue in the repetition of acts, although imitation becomes less important than it was in the first commission of the act. After initiation, the actual social and non-social reinforcers and punishers affect whether or not the acts will be repeated and at what level of frequency. Not only the behavior itself, but also the definitions are affected by the consequences of the initial act. Whether a deviant act will be committed in a situation that presents the opportunity depends on the learning history of the individual and the set of reinforcement contingencies in that situation.

> The actual social sanctions and other effects of engaging in the behavior may be perceived differently, but to the extent that they are more rewarding than alternative behavior, then the deviant behavior will be repeated under similar circumstances. Progression into more frequent or sustained patterns of deviant behavior is promoted [to the extent] that reinforcement, exposure to deviant models, and definitions are not offset by negative formal and informal sanctions and definitions. (Akers, 1985:60; see also Akers, 1992a:87)

The theory does not hypothesize that definitions favorable to law violation only precede and are unaffected by the initiation of criminal acts. Acts in violation of the law can occur in the absence of any thought given to right and wrong. Furthermore, definitions may be applied by the individual retroactively to excuse or justify an act already committed. To the extent that such excuses successfully mitigate others' negative sanctions or one's self-punishment, however, they become cues for the repetition of deviant acts. At that point they precede the future commission of the acts.

Differential association with conforming and non-conforming others typically precedes the individual's committing the acts. Families are included in the differential association process, and it is obvious that association, reinforcement of conforming or deviant behavior, deviant or conforming modeling, and exposure to definitions favorable or unfavorable to deviance occurs within the family prior to the onset of delinquency. On the other hand, it can never be true that the onset of delinquency initiates interaction in the family (except in the unlikely case of the late-stage adoption of a child who is already delinquent who is drawn to and chosen by deviant parents). This is also hypothesized as the typical process within peer groups. While one may be attracted to deviant peer groups prior to becoming involved in delinquency, associations with peers and others are most often formed initially around attractions, friendships, and circumstances, such as neighborhood proximity, that have little to do directly with co-involvement in some deviant behavior. However, after the associations have been established and the reinforcing or punishing consequences of the deviant behavior are experienced, both the continuation of old and the seeking of new associations (over which one has any choice) will themselves be affected. One may choose further interaction with others based, in part, on whether they too are involved in similar deviant or criminal behavior. But the theory proposes that the sequence of events, in which deviant associations precede the onset of delinquent behavior, will occur more frequently than the sequence of events in which the onset of delinquency precedes the beginning of deviant associations.

Figure 10.1
Social Structure and Social Learning

Social Structure			Social Learning ──────►	Criminal Behavior / Conforming Behavior
Society	Age	Family	Differential Association	
Community	Sex	Peers	Differential Reinforcement	Individual
	Race	School	Definitions	Behavior
	Class	Others	Imitation	
			Other Learning Variables	

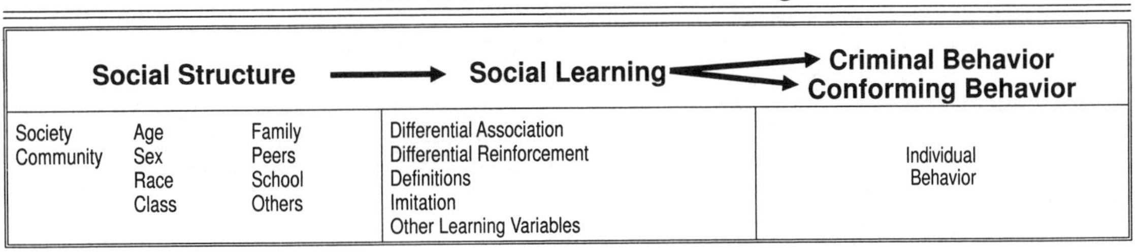

(Adapted from Akers, 1992:14)

Social Structure and Social Learning

Social learning theory has a broad scope in that it purports to be a general processual explanation of all criminal and delinquent behavior. Its scope, however, does not include a general explanation of laws, criminal justice, or the structural aspects of society that have an impact on crime. The theory is capable, however, of explaining how the social structure shapes individual behavior.

Sutherland (1947) and Cressey (1960) emphasized that the differential association process in individual criminality must be consistent with and related to differential social organization as an explanation of the structural distribution of crime rates. Akers (1973; 1985; 1989; 1992a) has reiterated this theme and shown the connection between social structure and the behavior of individuals.

The society and community, as well as class, race, gender, religion, and other structures in society, provide the general learning contexts for individuals. The family, peer groups, schools, churches, and other groups provide the more immediate contexts that promote or discourage the criminal or conforming behavior of the individual. Differences in the societal or group rates of criminal behavior are a function of the extent to which cultural traditions, norms, and social control systems provide socialization, learning environments, and immediate situations conducive to conformity or deviance.

Where individuals are situated in the social structure is indicated by age, sex, race, class, and other characteristics. These characteristics relate to the groups of which persons are likely to be members, with whom they interact, and how others around them are apt to respond to their behavior. These variables affect which behavioral models and normative patterns to which persons are exposed and the arrangements of reinforcement contingencies for conforming or law-violating behavior. This general model, in which social structure is hypothesized to have an effect on the individual's behavior through its effect on the social learning process, is diagrammed in Figure 10.1.

Akers argues that not only class, age, and other indicators of social location, but also the structural conditions identified in other theories (e.g., social disorganization, anomie, or conflict) can have an impact on one's exposure to criminal associations, models, definitions, and reinforcement. Social learning is hypothesized as the behavioral process by which the variables specified in macro-level theories induce or retard criminal actions in individuals. It is possible, therefore, to integrate these structural theories with social learning, though this has not yet been accomplished.

Empirical Validity of Social Learning Theory

Critiques and Research on Social Learning Variables

The social learning principles of association, imitation, definitions, reinforcement, and others (often in combination with guidelines from other theories) have become the basis for group counseling and self-help programs, positive peer counseling programs, gang interventions, family and school programs, teenage drug, alcohol, and delinquency prevention programs, and other private and public programs for delinquents and adult offenders in institutions and in the community. There is a broad range of behavior modification programs operating in correctional, treatment, and community facilities for juveniles and adults that follow learning principles (Bandura, 1969; Stumphauzer, 1986; Bynum and Thompson, 1992; Akers, 1992a; Lundman, 1993). These programs have had some successes, but, as is true for other theories, the validity of social learning theory can be judged only indirectly by its practical applications. It needs to be evaluated by the criteria of testability and empirical evidence.

The testability of the basic behavioral learning principles incorporated in social learning theory has been challenged because they may be tautological. The way in which the principle of reinforcement is often stated by behavioral psychologists makes the proposition true by definition. That is, they define reinforcement by stating that it occurs when behavior has been strengthened, that is, its rate of commission has been increased. If reinforcement is defined this way, then the statement "If behavior is reinforced, it will be strengthened" is tautological. If reinforcement means that behavior has been strengthened, then the hypothesis states simply, "If behavior is reinforced, it is reinforced." If the behavior is not strengthened, then by definition it has not been reinforced; therefore, no instance of behavior that is not being strengthened can be used to falsify the hypothesis.

Another criticism of social learning has to do with the temporal sequence of differential peer association and delinquency. Some have argued that youths become delinquent first then seek out other delinquent youths. Rather than delinquent associations causing delinquency, delinquency causes delinquent associations. If there is a relationship between one's own delinquency and one's association with delinquent peers, then it is simply a case of "birds of a feather flocking together" rather than a bird joining a flock and changing its feathers. Differential peer associations with delinquent friends is almost always a consequence rather than a cause of one's own behavior. Association with delinquent peers takes place only or mainly after peers have already independently established patterns of delinquent involvement. No deviance-relevant learning takes place in peer groups. From this point of view, any association with delinquent youths has no direct effect on an adolescent's delinquent behavior. Therefore, association with delinquent friends has an effect on neither the onset nor acceleration, the continuation nor cessation, of delinquent behavior (Hirschi, 1969; Gottfredson and Hirschi, 1990; Sampson and Laub, 1993).

These criticisms, however, may be off the mark. Burgess and Akers (1966a) identified this tautology problem and offered one solution to it. They separated the definitions of reinforcement and other behavioral concepts from non-tautological, testable propositions in social learning theory and proposed criteria for falsifying those propositions. Others as well have proposed somewhat different solutions (Liska, 1969; Chadwick-Jones, 1976). Moreover, the variables in the process of reinforcement are always measured separately (and hence non-tautologically) from measures of crime and deviance in research on social learning theory. The theory would be falsified if it is typically the case that positive social approval or other rewards for delinquency (that are not offset by punishment) more often reduce than increase its recurrence. Also, as shown above, feedback effects are built into the reinforcement concept with both prior and anticipated reward/punishment influencing present behavior.

Furthermore, the reciprocal relationship between one's own conduct and one's definitions and association with friends is clearly recognized in social learning theory. Therefore, the fact that delinquent behavior may precede the association with delinquent peers does not contradict this theory. "Social learning admits that birds of a feather do flock together, but it also admits that if the birds are humans, they also will influence one another's behavior, in both conforming and deviant directions" (Akers, 1991:210). It would contradict the theory if research demonstrated that the onset of delinquency always or most often predates interaction with peers who have engaged in delinquent acts and/or have adhered to delinquency-favorable definitions. It would not support the theory if the research evidence showed that whatever level of delinquent behavioral involvement preceded association with delinquent peers stayed the same or decreased rather than increased after the association. Research has not yet found this to be the case. Instead, the findings from several studies favor the process proposed by social learning theory, which recognizes both direct and reciprocal effects. That is, a youngster associates differentially with peers who are deviant or tolerant of deviance, learns definitions favorable to delinquent behavior, is exposed to deviant models that reinforce delinquency, then initiates or increases involvement in that behavior, which then is expected to influence further associations and definitions (Jessor et al., 1973; Krohn, 1974; Kandel, 1978; Andrews and Kandel, 1979; Krohn et al., 1985; Sellers and Winfree, 1990; Empey and Stafford, 1991; Elliott and Menard, 1991; Kandel and Davies, 1991; Warr, 1993b; Esbensen and Huizinga, 1993; Thornberry et al., 1994; Menard and Elliott, 1994; Akers and Lee, 1996).

Kandel and Davies (1991:442) note that "although assortive pairing plays a role in similarity among friends observed at a single point in time, longitudinal research that we and others have carried out clearly documents the etiological importance of peers in the initiation and persistence of substance use." Warr (1993b) also refers to the considerable amount of research evidence showing that peer associations precede the development of deviant patterns (or increase the frequency and seriousness of deviant behavior once it has begun) more often than involvement in deviant behavior precedes associations with deviant peers. The reverse sequence also occurs and Warr proposes that the process is ". . . a more complex, sequential, reciprocal process: Adolescents are commonly introduced to delinquency by their friends and subsequently become more selective in their choices of friends. The 'feathering' and 'flocking' . . . are not mutually exclusive and may instead be part of a unified process" (Warr, 1993b:39). This is, of course, completely consistent with the sequential and feedback effects in the social learning process spelled out above. Menard and Elliott (1990; 1994) also support the process as predicted by social learning theory. Reciprocal effects were found in their research, but:

> [I]n the typical sequence of initiation of delinquent bonding and illegal behavior, delinquent bonding (again, more specifically, association with delinquent friends) usually precedes illegal behavior for those individuals for whom one can ascertain the temporal order. . . . [S]imilarly . . . weakening of belief typically preceded the initiation of illegal behavior. (Menard and Elliott, 1994:174)

> Hirschi's hypothesis that illegal behavior influences Delinquent Bonding more than the reverse consistently fails to receive empirical support in the analysis. This finding, as well as the consistency with which the first hypothesis is confirmed, reinforces the conclusion [that] . . . Delinquent Bonding has a direct positive influence on illegal behavior. (Menard and Elliott, 1994:185)

Another criticism of the theory is that the strong relationship between self-reported delinquency and peer associations is entirely due to the fact that associations are often measured by the individual's report of the delinquency of his or her peers; they are the same thing measured twice. One is measuring the same underlying delinquent tendency, whether youngsters are asked about the delinquency of their friends or about their own delinquency. But research shows that the two are not the same and that the respondent's reports of friends' behavior is not simply a reflection of one's own delinquent behavior (Menard and Elliott, 1990; 1991; Agnew, 1991b; Warr, 1993b; Thornberry et al., 1994).

Almost all research conducted on social learning theory has found strong relationships in the theoretically expected direction between social learning variables and criminal, delinquent, and deviant behavior. When social learning theory is tested against other theories using the same data collected from the same samples, it is usually found to account for more variance in the dependent variables or have greater support than the theories with which it is being compared (for instance, see Akers and Cochran, 1985; Matsueda and Heimer, 1987; White et al., 1986; Kandel and Davies, 1991; McGee, 1992; Benda, 1994; Burton et al. 1994).

There is abundant evidence to show the significant impact on criminal and deviant behavior of differential association in primary groups such as family and peers. The role of the family is usually as a conventional socializer against delinquency and crime. It provides anti-criminal definitions, conforming models, and the reinforcement of conformity through parental discipline; it promotes the development of self-control. But deviant behavior may be the outcome of internal family interaction (McCord, 1991b). It is directly affected by deviant parental models, ineffective and erratic parental supervision and discipline in the use of positive and negative sanctions, and the endorsement of values and attitudes favorable to deviance. Patterson has shown that the operation of social learning mechanisms in parent-child interaction is a strong predictor of conforming/deviant behavior (Patterson, 1975; 1992; 1995; Snyder and Patterson, 1995). In some cases, parents directly train their children to commit deviant behavior (Adler and Adler, 1978). And in general, parental deviance and criminality is predictive of the children's future delinquency and crime (McCord, 1991). Moreover, youngsters with delinquent siblings in the family are more likely to be delinquent, even when parental and other family characteristics are taken into account (Rowe and Gulley, 1992; Lauritsen, 1993).

Delinquent tendencies learned in the family may be exacerbated by differential peer association (Simons et al., 1994; Lauritsen, 1993). Other than one's own prior deviant behavior, the best single predictor of the onset, continuance, or desistance of crime and delinquency is differential association with conforming or law-violating peers (Loeber and Dishion, 1987; Loeber and Stouthamer-Loeber, 1987). More frequent, longer-term, and closer association with peers who do not support deviant behavior is strongly correlated with conformity, while greater association with peers who commit and approve of delinquency is predictive of one's own delinquent behavior. It is in peer groups that the first availability and opportunity for delinquent acts are typically provided. Virtually every study that includes a peer association variable finds it to be significantly and usually most strongly related to delinquency, alcohol and drug use and abuse, adult crime, and other forms of deviant behavior. There is a sizable body of research literature that shows the importance of differential associations and definitions in explaining crime and delinquency.

Many studies using direct measures of one or more of the social learning variables of differential association, imitation, definitions, and differential reinforcement find that the theory's hypotheses are upheld (Winfree and Griffiths, 1983; Elliott et al., 1985; Dembo et al., 1986; White et al., 1986; Sellers and Winfree, 1990; McGee, 1992; Winfree et al., 1993; 1994). Research on expanded deterrence models, showing the strong effects of moral evaluations and actual or anticipated informal social sanctions on an individual's commission of crime or delinquency, also provides support for social learning theory (Grasmick and Green, 1980; Paternoster et al., 1983; Lanza-Kaduce, 1988; Stafford and Warr, 1993).

Akers' Research on Social Learning Theory

In addition to the consistently positive findings by other researchers, support for the theory comes from research conducted by Akers and his associates in which all of the key social learning variables are measured. These include tests of social learning theory by itself and tests that directly compare its empirical validity with other theories. The first of these, conducted with Marvin D. Krohn, Lonn Lanza-Kaduce, and Marcia J. Radosevich, was a self-report questionnaire survey of adolescent substance abuse involving 3000 students in grades 7 through 12 in eight communities in three Midwestern states (Akers et al., 1979; Krohn et al., 1982; Krohn et al., 1984; Lanza-Kaduce et al., 1984; Akers and Cochran, 1985). The second, conducted with Marvin Krohn, Ronald Lauer, James Massey, William Skinner, and Sherilyn Spear, was a five-year longitudinal study of smoking among 2000 students in junior and senior high school in one midwest community (Lauer et al., 1982; Krohn et al., 1985;

Spear and Akers, 1988; Akers, 1992a; Akers and Lee, 1996). The third project, conducted with Anthony La Greca, John Cochran, and Christine Sellers, was a four-year longitudinal study of conforming and deviant drinking among elderly populations (1400 respondents) in four communities in Florida and New Jersey (Akers et al., 1989; Akers and La Greca, 1991; Akers, 1992a). The fourth and fifth studies were the master's and doctoral research of Scot Boeringer, conducted under Akers' supervision, on rape and sexual coercion among samples of 200 and 500 college males (Boeringer et al., 1991; Boeringer, 1992; Boeringer and Akers, 1993). The dependent variables in these studies ranged from minor deviance to serious criminal behavior.

The findings in each of these studies demonstrated that the social learning variables of differential association, differential reinforcement, imitation, and definitions, singly and in combination, are strongly related to the various forms of deviant, delinquent, and criminal behavior studied. The social learning model produced high levels of explained variance, much more than other theoretical models with which it was compared.

The combined effects of the social learning variables on adolescent alcohol and drug use and abuse are very strong. High amounts (from 31% to 68%) of the variance in these variables are accounted for by the social learning variables. Social bonding models account for about 15% and anomie models account for less than 5% of the variance.

Similarly, adolescent cigarette smoking is highly correlated with the social learning variables. These variables also predict quite well the maintenance of smoking over a three-year period. They fare less well, however, when predicting which of the initially abstinent youngsters will begin smoking in that same period. The social learning variables do a slightly better job of predicting the onset of smoking over a five-year period. The sequencing and reciprocal effects of social learning variables and smoking behavior over the five-year period are as predicted by the theory. The onset, frequency, and quantity of elderly drinking is highly correlated with social learning, and the theory also successfully accounts for problem drinking among the elderly.

The social learning variables of association, reinforcement, definitions, and imitation explain the self-perceived likelihood of using force to gain sexual contact or committing rape by college men (55% explained variance). They also account for the actual use of drugs or alcohol, nonphysical coercion, and physical force by males to obtain sex (20% explained variance). Social bonding, self-control, and relative deprivation (strain) models account for less than 10% of the variance in these variables.

The research by Akers and others has also included some evidence on the hypothesized relationship between social structure and social learning. This research has found that the correlations of adolescent drug use and smoking, elderly alcohol abuse, and rape to socio-demographic variables of age, sex, race, and class are reduced toward zero when the social learning variables are taken into account. Also, differences in levels of marijuana and alcohol use among adolescents in four types of communities (farm, rural-nonfarm, suburban, and urban), and the differences in overall levels of drinking behavior among the elderly in four types of communities, are mediated by the social learning process. These findings show results that are predicted by social learning theory. However, at this time, there has not been enough research to confirm the relationship between social learning and the social structure expected by the theory.

Summary

Akers' social learning theory combines Sutherland's original differential association theory of criminal behavior with general behavioral learning principles. The theory proposes that criminal and delinquent behavior is acquired, repeated, and changed by the same process as conforming behavior. While referring to all parts of the learning process, Akers' social learning theory in criminology has focused on the four major concepts of differential association, definitions, differential reinforcement, and imitation. That process will more likely produce behavior that violates social and legal norms than conforming behavior when persons differentially associate with those who expose them to deviant patterns, when the deviant behavior is differentially reinforced over conforming behavior, when individuals are more exposed to deviant than conforming models, and when their own definitions favorably dispose them to commit deviant acts.

This social learning explanation of crime and delinquency has been strongly supported by the research evidence. Research conducted over many years, including that by Akers and associates, has consistently found that social learning is empirically supported as an explanation of individual differences in delinquent and criminal behavior. The hypothesis that social learning processes mediate the effects of sociodemographic and community variables on behavior has been infrequently studied, but the evidence so far suggests that it will also be upheld.

Discussion Questions

1. Much data indicate that associating with delinquents increases one's own level of delinquency. According to social learning theory, why might this be so?

2. Drawing on social learning theory, describe and give an example of the major types of "definitions" favorable to crime.

3. How does positive reinforcement differ from negative reinforcement?

4. Describe the social learning *process*—note how this process changes after the initiation into deviance and describe the feedback effects in this process.

5. How might Akers explain the fact that males have higher rates of crime than females? ✦

11

The Thesis of a Subculture of Violence

Marvin E. Wolfgang
Franco Ferracuti

Wolfgang and Ferracuti draw on Sutherland's differential association theory, as well as certain other theories, to explain why certain groups have higher rates of violence. Their "subculture of violence" thesis grew out of earlier work that Wolfgang (1958) conducted on homicide in Philadelphia. Wolfgang found that the homicide rate was highest among lower-class, young, African-American males. Many of the homicides he examined involved disputes between friends, relatives, and acquaintances over what seemed like trivial issues. Wolfgang explained these homicides in terms of the attitudes or "definitions" of the participants, claiming that they saw violence as an appropriate, even required response to a wide range of provocations and insults.

In the selection which follows, Wolfgang and Ferracuti present a more general version of the subculture of violence thesis. They make several key points in their list of the propositions constituting the thesis. Among other things, they note that the subculture of violence is not completely at odds with the larger culture, it does not unconditionally approve of violence, and it is not shared to the same extent by all members of the "subsociety." The subculture is most prominent among young adults, and it defines violence as an expected, even required response to a range of situations (a broader range than is recognized by the larger culture). Violence, then, is only required in certain situations. (This argument is similar to Sykes and Matza's techniques of neutralization—although Sykes and Matza argue that the

neutralizations simply allow or justify crime; they do not require it.) Drawing on Sutherland, Wolfgang and Ferracuti argue that the subculture is learned in interaction with others, although they note that personality variables may influence the extent to which the subcultural attitudes are assimilated. Individuals who assimilate the subculture of violence will interpret certain situations differently than others, such as taking serious offense at a verbal slight others would overlook, and will react differently to these situations. Wolfgang and Ferracuti do not describe the origins of this subculture, although Curtis (1975) provides an account that is compatible with strain theory (see Part IV; also see the Anderson article which follows in Chapter 12 and Bernard, 1990).

Wolfgang and Ferracuti's subculture of violence thesis has not only been used to explain the higher rate of violence among young, lower-class males, but also has been used to explain the higher rate of homicide in the South. Data on the theory are mixed, with several researchers arguing that the theory has not yet received an adequate test (Luckenbill and Doyle, 1989; Messner, 1988; Hawley and Messner, 1989). In particular, it is claimed that researchers have not properly measured the attitudes said to constitute the subculture of violence. Recent data, however, hold some promise for the theory. Observational studies of low-income communities have found evidence that certain community residents hold values conducive to violence (see the Anderson selection), and several recent quantitative studies provide qualified support for the theory (e.g., Cao et al., 1997; Felson et al., 1994; Heimer, 1997).

References

Bernard, Thomas. 1990. "Angry Aggression Among the 'Truly Disadvantaged.'" *Criminology* 28: 73-96.

Cao, Liqun, Anthony Adams, and Vickie J. Jensen. 1997. "A Test of the Black Subculture of Violence Thesis: A Research Note." *Criminology* 35: 367-379.

Curtis, Lynn. 1975. *Violence, Race, and Culture.* Lexington, MA: Heath.

Felson, Richard B., Allen E. Liska, Scott J. South, and Thomas L. McNulty. 1994. "The Subculture of Violence and Delinquency: Individual vs. School Context Effects." *Social Forces* 73:155-173.

Hawley, Frederick F. and Steven F. Messner. 1989. "The Southern Violence Construct: A Review of Arguments, Evidence, and the Normative Context." *Justice Quarterly* 6: 481-511.

Heimer, Karen. 1997. "Socioeconomic Status, Subcultural Definitions, and Violent Delinquency." *Social Forces* 75: 799-833.

Luckenbill, David F. and Daniel P. Doyle. 1989. "Structural Position and Violence: Developing a Cultural Explanation." *Criminology* 27: 419-436.

Messner, Steven F. 1988. "Research on Cultural and Socioeconomic Factors in Criminal Violence." *The Psychiatric Clinics of North America* 11: 511-525.

Wolfgang, Marvin E. 1958. *Patterns in Criminal Homicide.* Philadelphia: University of Pennsylvania Press.

T his [chapter] examines the proposition that there is a subculture of violence. . . . It should be remembered that the term itself—subculture—presupposes an already existing complex of norms, values, attitudes, material traits, etc. What the subculture-of-violence formulation further suggests is simply that there is a potent theme of violence current in the cluster of values that make up the lifestyle, the socialization process, the interpersonal relationships of individuals living in similar conditions. . . .

1. *No subculture can be totally different from or totally in conflict with the society of which it is a part*. A subculture of violence. . . is not entirely an expression of violence, for there must be interlocking value elements shared with the dominant culture. It should not be necessary to contend that violent aggression is the predominant mode of expression in order to show that the value system is set apart as subcultural. When violence occurs in the dominant culture, it is usually legitimized, but most often is vicarious and a part of phantasy. Moreover, subcultural variations, we have earlier suggested, may be viewed as quantitative and relative. The extent of difference from the larger culture and the degree of intensity, which violence as a subcultural theme may possess, are variables that could and should be measured by known socio-psychological techniques. At present, we are required to rely almost entirely upon expressions of violence in conduct of various forms—parent-child relationships, parental discipline, domestic quarrels, street fights, delinquent conflict gangs, criminal records of assaultive behavior, criminal homicides, etc.—but the number of psychometrically oriented studies in criminology is steadily increasing in both quantity and sophistication, and from them a reliable differential psychology of homicides should emerge to match current sociological research.

2. *To establish the existence of a subculture of violence does not require that the actors sharing in these basic value elements should express violence in all situations* The normative system designates that in some types of social interaction a violent and physically aggressive response is either expected or required of all members sharing in that system of values. That the actors' behavior expectations occur in more than one situation is obvious. There is a variety of circumstances in which homicide occurs, and the history of past aggressive crimes in high proportions, both in the victims and in the offenders, attests to the multisituational character of the use of violence and to its interpersonal characteristics. But, obviously, persons living in a subcultural milieu designated as a subculture of violence cannot and do not engage in violence continuously, otherwise normal social functioning would be virtually impossible. We are merely suggesting, for example, that ready access to weapons in this milieu may become essential for protection against others who respond in similarly violent ways in certain situations, and that the carrying of knives or other protective devices become a common symbol of willingness to participate in violence, to expect violence, and to be ready for its retaliation.

3. *The potential resort or willingness to resort to violence in a variety of situations emphasizes the penetrating and diffusive character of this culture theme*. The number and kinds of situations in which an individual uses violence may be viewed as an index of

the extent to which he has assimilated the values associated with violence. This index should also be reflected by quantitative differences in a variety of psychological dimensions, from differential perception of violent stimuli to different value expressions in questionnaire-type instruments. The range of violence from minor assault to fatal injury, or certainly the maximum of violence expected, is rarely made explicit for all situations to which an individual may be exposed. Overt violence may even occasionally be a chance result of events. But clearly this range and variability of behavioral expressions of aggression suggest the importance of psychological dimensions in measuring adherence to a subculture of violence.

4. *The subcultural ethos of violence may be shared by all ages in a subsociety, but this ethos is most prominent in a limited age group, ranging from late adolescence to middle age.* We are not suggesting that a particular ethnic, sex, or age group all share in common the use of potential threats of violence. We are contending merely that the known empirical distribution of conduct, which expresses the sharing of this violence theme, shows greatest localization, incidence, and frequency in limited subgroups and reflects differences in learning about violence as a problem solving mechanism.

5. *The counter-norm is nonviolence.* Violation of expected and required violence is most likely to result in ostracism from the group. Alienation of some kind, depending on the range of violence expectations that are unmet, seems to be a form of punitive action most feasible to this subculture. The juvenile who fails to live up to the conflict gang's requirements is pushed outside the group. The adult male who does not defend his honor or his female companion will be socially emasculated. The "coward" is forced to move out of the territory, to find new friends and make new alliances. Membership is lost in the subsociety sharing the cluster of attitudes positively associated with violence. If forced withdrawal or voluntary retreat are not acceptable modes of response to engaging in the counter-norm, then execution, as is reputed to occur in organized crime, may be the extreme punitive measure.

6. *The development of favorable attitudes toward, and the use of, violence in a subculture usually involve learned behavior and a process of differential learning, association, or identification.* Not all persons exposed—even equally exposed—to the presence of a subculture of violence absorb and share in the values in equal portions. Differential personality variables must be considered in an integrated social-psychological approach to an understanding of the subcultural aspects of violence. We have taken the position that aggression is a learned response, socially facilitated and integrated, as a habit, in more or less permanent form, among the personality characteristics of the aggressor. Aggression, from a psychological standpoint, has been defined by Buss as "the delivery of noxious stimuli in an interpersonal context." Aggression seems to possess two major classes of reinforcers: the pain and injury inflicted upon the victim and its extrinsic rewards. Both are present in a subculture of violence, and their mechanism of action is facilitated by the social support that the aggressor receives in his group. The relationship between aggression, anger, and hostility is complicated by the habit characteristics of the first, the drive state of the second, and the attitudinal interpretative nature of the third. Obviously, the immediacy and the short temporal sequence of anger with its autonomic components make it difficult to study a criminal population that is some distance removed from the anger-provoked event. Hostility, although amenable to easier assessment, does not give a clear indication or measure of physical attack because of its predominantly verbal aspects. However, it may dispose to or prepare for aggression.

Aggression, in its physical manifest form, remains the most criminologically relevant aspect in a study of violent assaultive behavior. If violent aggression is a habit and possesses permanent or quasi-permanent personality trait characteristics, it should be amenable to psychological assessment through appropriate diagnostic techniques. Among the several alternative diagnostic methodologies, those based on a perceptual approach seem to be able, according to the existing literature, to elicit sips and symptoms of behavioral aggression, demonstrating the existence of this "habit" and/or trait in the personality of the subject being tested. Obviously, the same set of techniques being used to diagnose the trait of aggression can be used to assess the presence of major psychopathology, which might, in a restricted number of cases, have caused "aggressive behavior" outside, or in spite of, any cultural or subcultural allegiance.

7. *The use of violence in a subculture is not necessarily viewed as illicit conduct and the users therefore do not have to deal with feelings of guilt about their aggression.* Violence can become a part of the life style, the theme of solving difficult problems or problem situations. It should be stressed that the problems and situations to which we refer arise mostly within the subculture, for violence is used mostly between persons and groups who themselves rely upon the same supportive values and norms. A carrier and user of violence will not be burdened by conscious guilt, then, because generally he is not attacking the representatives of the nonviolent culture, and because the recipient of this violence may be described by similar class status, occupational, residential, age, and other attribute categories which characterize the subuniverse of the collectivity sharing in the subculture of violence. Even law-abiding members of the local subculture area may not view various illegal expressions of vio-lence as menacing or immoral. Furthermore, when the attacked see their assaulters as agents of the same kind of aggression they themselves represent, violent retaliation is readily legitimized by a situationally specific rationale, as well as by the generally normative supports for violence.

Probably no single theory will ever explain the variety of observable violent behavior. However, the subculture-of-violence approach offers, we believe, the advantage of bringing together psychological and sociological constructs to aid in the explanation of the concentration of violence in specific socioeconomic groups and ecological areas. . . .

Discussion Questions

1. What types of questions might you ask someone to determine the extent to which they have assimilated the subculture of violence?

2. How might we explain the origin of the subculture of violence?

3. What alternative explanations might be given for the higher rate of homicide among young, lower-class African American males? Among Southerners? ✦

12

The Code of the Streets

Elijah Anderson

In this selection, Anderson provides a contemporary account of a "subculture of violence." Drawing on his field research in inner-city communities (e.g., Anderson, 1990), he argues that there exists a "code of the streets" in poor, inner-city African-American communities. While most people do not accept the values underlying this code, the code places all young African-American men under much pressure to respond to certain situations—shows of disrespect—with violence.

Anderson's account is perhaps the best description of a subculture of violence now available, and it is important because it makes us aware of the complexity of this subculture. While most people are opposed to the subculture, the subculture nevertheless shapes the behavior of most community residents. Further, the influence of the subculture is pervasive, affecting one's behavior in a wide range of situations and most especially affecting how one interprets and responds to challenges. Anderson's description of the socialization of "street kids"—those most immersed in the subculture—is especially compelling and sheds much light on the violent behavior of such youths. His discussion of the origins of the code of the streets makes us aware of the major task that is before us if we are to significantly reduce the level of violence in this country.

Anderson's research will hopefully prompt additional research into the code of the streets, which uses both survey research and field research of the type that Anderson employs.

Reference

Anderson, Elijah. 1990. *Streetwise*. Chicago: University of Chicago Press.

Of all the problems besetting the poor inner-city black community, none is more pressing than that of interpersonal violence and aggression. It wreaks havoc daily with the lives of community residents and increasingly spills over into downtown and residential middle-class areas. Muggings, burglaries, carjackings, and drug-related shootings, all of which may leave their victims or innocent bystanders dead, are now common enough to concern all urban and many suburban residents. The inclination to violence springs from the circumstances of life among the ghetto poor—the lack of jobs that pay a living wage, the stigma of race, the fallout from rampant drug use and drug trafficking, and the resulting alienation and lack of hope for the future.

Simply living in such an environment places young people at special risk of falling victim to aggressive behavior. Although there are often forces in the community which can counteract the negative influences, by far the most powerful being a strong, loving, "decent" (as inner-city residents put it) family committed to middle-class values, the despair is pervasive enough to have spawned an oppositional culture, that of "the streets," whose norms are often consciously opposed to those of mainstream society. These two orientations—decent and street—socially organize the community, and their coexistence has important consequences for residents, particularly children growing up in the inner city. Above all, this environment means that even youngsters whose home lives reflect mainstream values—and the majority of homes in the community do—must be able to handle themselves in a street-oriented environment.

This is because the street culture has evolved what may be called a code of the streets, which amounts to a set of informal rules governing interpersonal public behavior, including violence. The rules prescribe both a proper comportment and a proper way to respond if challenged. They regulate the use of violence and so allow those who are inclined to aggression to precipitate violent encounters in an approved way. The rules have been established and are enforced mainly by the street-oriented, but on the streets the distinction between street and decent is often irrelevant; everybody knows that if the rules are violated, there are penalties. Knowledge of the code is thus largely defensive; it is literally necessary for operating in public. Therefore, even though families with a decency orientation are usually opposed to the values of the code, they often reluctantly encourage their children's familiarity with it to enable them to negotiate the inner-city environment.

At the heart of the code is the issue of respect—loosely defined as being treated "right," or granted the deference one deserves. However, in the troublesome public environment of the inner city, as people increasingly feel buffeted by forces beyond their control, what one deserves in the way of respect becomes more and more problematic and uncertain. This in turn further opens the issue of respect to sometimes intense interpersonal negotiation. In the street culture, especially among young people, respect is viewed as almost an external entity that is hard-won but easily lost, and so must constantly be guarded. The rules of the code in fact provide a framework for negotiating respect. The person whose very appearance—including his clothing, demeanor, and way of moving—deters transgressions feels that he possesses, and may be considered by others to possess, a measure of respect. With the right amount of respect, for instance, he can avoid "being bothered" in public. If he is bothered, not only may he be in physical danger but he has been disgraced or "dissed" (disrespected). Many of the forms that dissing can take might seem petty to middle-class people (maintaining eye contact for too long, for example), but to those invested in the street code, these actions become serious indications of the other person's intentions. Consequently, such people become very sensitive to advances and slights, which could well serve as warnings of imminent physical confrontation.

This hard reality can be traced to the profound sense of alienation from mainstream society and its institutions felt by many poor inner-city black people, particularly the young. The code of the streets is actually a cultural adaptation to a profound lack of faith in the police and the judicial system. The police are most often seen as representing the dominant white society and not caring to protect inner-city residents. When called, they may not respond, which is one reason many residents feel they must be prepared to take extraordinary measures to defend themselves and their loved ones against those who are inclined to aggression. Lack of police accountability has in fact been incorporated into the status system: the person who is believed capable of "taking care of himself" is accorded a certain deference, which translates into a sense of physical and psychological control. Thus the street code emerges where the influence of the police ends and personal responsibility for one's safety is felt to begin. Exacerbated by the proliferation of drugs and easy access to guns, this volatile situation results in the ability of the street-oriented minority (or those who effectively "go for bad") to dominate the public spaces.

Decent and Street Families

Although almost everyone in poor inner-city neighborhoods is struggling financially and therefore feels a certain distance from the rest of America, the decent and the street family in a real sense represent two poles of value orientation, two contrasting conceptual categories. The labels "decent" and "street," which the residents themselves use, amount to evaluative judgments that confer status on local residents. The labeling is often the result of a social contest among individuals and families of the neighborhood. Individuals of the two orientations often coexist in the same extended family. Decent residents judge themselves to be so while judging others to be of the street, and street individuals often present themselves as decent, drawing distinctions between themselves and other people. In addition, there is quite a bit of circumstantial behavior—that is, one person may at different times exhibit both decent and street orientations, depending on the circumstances. Although these designations result from so much social jockeying, there do exist concrete features that define each conceptual category.

Generally, so-called decent families tend to accept mainstream values more fully and attempt to instill them in their children. Whether married couples with children or single-parent (usually female) households, they are generally "working poor" and so tend to be better off financially than their street-oriented neighbors. They value hard work and self-reliance and are willing to sacrifice for their children. Because they have a certain amount of faith in mainstream society, they harbor hopes for a better future for their children, if not for themselves. Many of them go to church and take a strong interest in their children's schooling. Rather than dwelling on the real hardships and inequities facing them, many such decent people, particularly the increasing number of grandmothers raising grandchildren, see their difficult situation as a test from God and derive great support from their faith and from the church community.

Extremely aware of the problematic and often dangerous environment in which they reside, decent parents tend to be strict in their child-rearing practices, encouraging children to respect authority and walk a straight moral line. They have an almost obsessive concern about trouble of any kind and remind their children to be on the lookout for people and situations that might lead to it. At the same time, they are themselves polite and considerate of others, and teach their children to be the same way. At home, at work, and in church, they strive hard to maintain a positive mental attitude and a spirit of cooperation.

So-called street parents, in contrast, often show a lack of consideration for other people and have a rather superficial sense of family and community. Though they may love their children, many of them are unable to cope with the physical and emotional demands of parenthood, and find it difficult to reconcile their needs with those of their children. These families, who are more fully invested in the code of the streets than the decent people are, may aggressively socialize their children into it in a normative way. They believe in the code and judge themselves and others according to its values.

In fact the overwhelming majority of families in the inner-city community try to approximate the decent-family model, but there are many others who clearly represent the worst fears of the decent family. Not only are their financial resources extremely limited, but what little they have may easily be misused. The lives of the street-oriented are often marked by disorganization. In the most desperate circumstances people frequently have a limited understanding of priorities and consequences, and so frustrations mount over bills, food, and at times, drink, cigarettes, and drugs. Some tend toward self-destructive behavior; many street-oriented women are crack-addicted ("on the pipe"), alcoholic, or involved in complicated relationships with men who abuse them. In addition, the seeming intractability of their situation, caused in large part by the lack of well-paying jobs and the persistence of racial discrimination, has engendered deep-seated bitterness and anger in many of the most desperate and poorest blacks, especially young people. The need both to exercise a measure of control and to lash out at somebody is often reflected in the adults' relations with their children. At the least, the frustrations of persistent poverty shorten the fuse in such people contributing to a lack of patience with anyone, child or adult, who imitates them.

In these circumstances a woman—or a man, although men are less consistently present in children's lives—can be quite aggressive with children, yelling at and striking them for the least little infraction of the rules she has set down. Often little if any serious explanation follows the verbal and physical punishment. This response teaches children a particular lesson. They learn that to solve any kind of interpersonal problem one must quickly resort to hitting or other violent behavior. Actual peace and quiet, and also the appearance of calm, respectful children conveyed to her neighbors and friends, are often what the young mother most desires, but at times she will be very aggressive in trying to get them. Thus she may be quick to beat her children, especially if they defy her law, not because she hates them but because this is the way she knows to control them. In fact, many street-oriented women love their children dearly. Many mothers in the community subscribe to the notion that there is a "devil in the boy" that must be beaten out of him or that socially "fast girls need to be whupped." Thus much of what borders on child abuse in the view of social authorities is acceptable parental punishment in the view of these mothers.

Many street-oriented women are sporadic mothers whose children learn to fend for themselves when necessary, foraging for food and money any way they can get it. The children are sometimes employed by drug dealers or become addicted themselves. These children of the street, growing up with little supervision, are said to "come up hard." They often learn to fight at an early age, sometimes using short-tempered adults around them as role models. The street-oriented home may be fraught with anger, verbal disputes, physical aggression, and even mayhem. The children observe these goings-on, learning the lesson that might makes right. They quickly learn to hit those who cross them, and the dog-eat-dog mentality prevails. In order to survive, to protect oneself, it is necessary to marshal inner resources and be ready to deal with adversity in a hands-on way. In these circumstances physical prowess takes on great significance.

In some of the most desperate cases, a street-oriented mother may simply leave her young children alone and unattended while she goes out. The most irresponsible women can be found at local bars and crack houses, getting high and socializing with other adults. Sometimes a troubled woman will leave very young children alone for days at a time. Reports of crack addicts abandoning their children have become common in drug-infested inner-city communities. Neighbors or relatives discover the abandoned children, often hungry and distraught over the absence of their mother. After repeated absences, a friend or relative, particularly a grandmother, will often step in to care for the young children, sometimes petitioning the authorities to send her, as guardian of the children, the mother's welfare check, if the mother gets one. By this time, however, the children may well have learned the first lesson of the streets: survival itself, let alone respect, can-

not be taken for granted; you have to fight for your place in the world.

Campaigning for Respect

These realities of inner-city life are largely absorbed on the streets. At an early age, often even before they start school, children from street-oriented homes gravitate to the streets, where they "hang"—socialize with their peers. Children from these generally permissive homes have a great deal of latitude and are allowed to "rip and run" up and down the street. They often come home from school, put their books down, and go right back out the door. On school nights eight- and nine-year-olds remain out until nine or ten o'clock (and teenagers typically come in whenever they want to). On the streets they play in groups that often become the source of their primary social bonds. Children from decent homes tend to be more carefully supervised and are thus likely to have curfews and to be taught how to stay out of trouble.

When decent and street kids come together, a kind of social shuffle occurs in which children have a chance to go either way. Tension builds as a child comes to realize that he must choose an orientation. The kind of home he comes from influences but does not determine the way he will ultimately turn out—although it is unlikely that a child from a thoroughly street-oriented family will easily absorb decent values on the streets. Youths who emerge from street-oriented families but develop a decency orientation almost always learn those values in another setting—in school, in a youth group, in church. Often it is the result of their involvement with a caring "old head" (adult role model).

In the street, through their play, children pour their individual life experiences into a common knowledge pool, affirming, confirming, and elaborating on what they have observed in the home and matching their skills against those of others. And they learn to fight. Even small children test one another, pushing and shoving, and are ready to hit other children over circumstances not to their liking. In turn, they are readily hit by other children, and the child who is toughest prevails. Thus the violent resolution of disputes, the hitting and cursing, gains social reinforcement. The child in effect is initiated into a system that is really a way of campaigning for respect.

In addition, younger children witness the disputes of older children, which are often resolved through cursing and abusive talk, if not aggression or outright violence. They see that one child succumbs to the greater physical and mental abilities of the other. They are also alert and attentive witnesses to the verbal and physical fights of adults, after which they compare notes and share their interpretations of the event. In almost every case the victor is the person who physically won the altercation, and this person often enjoys the esteem and respect of onlookers. These experiences reinforce the lessons the children have learned at home: might makes right, and toughness is a virtue, while humility is not. In effect they learn the social meaning of fighting. When it is left virtually unchallenged, this understanding becomes an ever more important part of the child's working conception of the world. Over time the code of the streets becomes refined.

Those street-oriented adults with whom children come in contact—including mothers, fathers, brothers, sisters, boyfriends, cousins, neighbors, and friends—help them along in forming this understanding by verbalizing the messages they are getting through experience: "Watch your back." "Protect yourself." "Don't punk out." "If somebody messes with you, you got to pay them back." "If someone disses you, you got to straighten them out." Many parents actually impose sanctions if a child is not sufficiently aggressive. For example, if a child loses a fight and comes home upset, the parent might respond, "Don't you come in here crying that somebody beat you up; you better get back out there and whup his ass. I didn't raise no punks! Get back out there and whup his ass. If you don't whup his ass, I'll whup your ass when you come home." Thus the child obtains reinforcement for being tough and showing nerve.

While fighting, some children cry as though they are doing something they are ambivalent about. The fight may be against their wishes, yet they may feel constrained to fight or face the consequences—not just from peers but also from caretakers or parents, who may administer another beating if they back down. Some adults recall receiving such lessons from their own parents and justify repeating them to their children as a way to toughen them up. Looking capable of taking care of oneself as a form of self-defense is a dominant theme among both street-oriented and decent adults who worry about the safety of their children. There is thus at times a convergence in their child-rearing practices, although the rationales behind them may differ.

Self-Image Based on 'Juice'

By the time they are teenagers, most youths have either internalized the code of the streets or at least learned the need to comport themselves in accordance with its rules, which chiefly have to do with interpersonal communication. The code revolves around the presentation of self. Its basic requirement is the display of a certain predisposition to violence. Accordingly, one's bearing must send the unmistakable if sometimes subtle message to "the next person" in public that one is capable of violence and mayhem when the situation requires it, that one can take care of oneself. The nature of this communication is largely determined by the demands of the circumstances but can include facial expressions, gait, and verbal expressions—all of which are geared mainly to deterring aggression. Physical appearance, including clothes, jewelry, and grooming, also plays an important part in how a person is viewed; to be respected, it is important to have the right look.

Even so, there are no guarantees against challenges, because there are always people around looking for a fight to increase their share of respect—or "juice," as it is sometimes called on the street. Moreover, if a person is assaulted, it is important, not only in the eyes of his opponent but also in the eyes of his "running buddies," for him to avenge himself. Otherwise he risks being "tried" (challenged) or "moved on" by any number of others. To maintain his honor he must show he is not someone to be "messed with" or "dissed." In general, the person must "keep himself straight" by managing his position of respect among others; this involves in part his self-image, which is shaped by what he thinks others are thinking of him in relation to his peers.

Objects play an important and complicated role in establishing self-image. Jackets, sneakers, gold jewelry, reflect not just a person's taste, which tends to be tightly regulated among adolescents of all social classes, but also a willingness to possess things that may require defending. A boy wearing a fashionable, expensive jacket, for example, is vulnerable to attack by another who covets the jacket and either cannot afford to buy one or wants the added satisfaction of depriving someone else of his. However, if the boy forgoes the desirable jacket and wears one that isn't "hip," he runs the risk of being teased and possibly even assaulted as an unworthy person. To be allowed to hang with certain prestigious crowds, a boy must wear a different set of expensive clothes—sneakers and athletic suit—every day. Not to be able to do so might make him appear socially deficient. The youth comes to covet such items especially when he sees easy prey wearing them.

In acquiring valued things, therefore, a person shores up his identity—but since it is an identity based on having things, it is highly precarious. This very precariousness gives a heightened sense of urgency to staying even with peers, with whom the person is actually competing. Young men and women who are able to command respect through their presentation of self—by allowing their possessions and their body language to speak for them—may not have to campaign for regard but may, rather, gain it by the force of their manner. Those who are unable to command respect in this way must actively campaign for it—and are thus particularly alive to slights.

One way of campaigning for status is by taking the possessions of others. In this context, seemingly ordinary objects can become trophies imbued with symbolic value that far exceeds their monetary worth. Possession of the trophy can symbolize the ability to violate somebody—to "get in his face," to take something of value from him, to "dis" him, and

thus to enhance one's own worth by stealing someone else's. The trophy does not have to be something material. It can be another person's sense of honor, snatched away with a derogatory remark. It can be the outcome of a fight. It can be the imposition of a certain standard, such as a girl's getting herself recognized as the most beautiful. Material things, however, fit easily into the pattern. Sneakers, a pistol, even somebody else's girlfriend, can become a trophy. When a person can take something from another and then flaunt it, he gains a certain regard by being the owner, or the controller, of that thing. But this display of ownership can then provoke other people to challenge him. This game of who controls what is thus constantly being played out on inner-city streets, and the trophy—extrinsic or intrinsic, tangible or intangible—identifies the current winner.

An important aspect of this often violent give-and-take is its zero-sum quality. That is, the extent to which one person can raise himself up depends on his ability to put another person down. This underscores the alienation that permeates the inner-city ghetto community. There is a generalized sense that very little respect is to be had, and therefore everyone competes to get what affirmation he can of the little that is available. The craving for respect that results gives people thin skins. Shows of deference by others can be highly soothing, contributing to a sense of security, comfort, self-confidence, and self-respect. Transgressions by others which go unanswered diminish these feelings and are believed to encourage further transgressions. Hence one must be ever vigilant against the transgressions of others or even *appearing* as if transgressions will be tolerated. Among young people, whose sense of self-esteem is particularly vulnerable, there is an especially heightened concern with being disrespected. Many inner-city young men in particular crave respect to such a degree that they will risk their lives to attain and maintain it.

The issue of respect is thus closely tied to whether a person has an inclination to be violent, even as a victim. In the wider society people may not feel required to retaliate physically after an attack, even though they are aware that they have been degraded or taken advantage of. They may feel a great need to defend themselves during an attack, or to behave in such a way as to deter aggression (middle-class people certainly can and do become victims of street-oriented youths), but they are much more likely than street-oriented people to feel that they can walk away from a possible altercation with their self-esteem intact. Some people may even have the strength of character to flee, without any thought that their self-respect or esteem will be diminished.

In impoverished inner-city black communities, however, particularly among young males and perhaps increasingly among females, such flight would be extremely difficult. To run away would likely leave one's self-esteem in tatters. Hence people often feel constrained not only to stand up and at least attempt to resist during an assault but also to "pay back"—to seek revenge—after a successful assault on their person. This may include going to get a weapon or even getting relatives involved. Their very identity and self-respect, their honor, is often intricately tied up with the way they perform on the streets during and after such encounters. This outlook reflects the circumscribed opportunities of the inner-city poor. Generally people outside the ghetto have other ways of gaining status and regard, and thus do not feel so dependent on such physical displays.

By Trial of Manhood

On the street, among males these concerns about things and identity have come to be expressed in the concept of "manhood." Manhood in the inner city means taking the prerogatives of men with respect to strangers, other men, and women—being distinguished as a man. It implies physicality and a certain ruthlessness. Regard and respect are associated with this concept in large part because of its practical application: if others have little or no regard for a person's manhood, his very life and those of his loved ones could be in jeopardy. But there is a chicken-and-egg aspect to this situation: one's physical safety is more likely to be jeopardized in public *because* manhood is associated with respect. In other words, an existential link has been cre-

ated between the idea of manhood and one's self-esteem, so that it has become hard to say which is primary. For many inner-city youths, manhood and respect are flip sides of the same coin; physical and psychological well-being are inseparable, and both require a sense of control, of being in charge.

The operating assumption is that a man, especially a real man, knows what other men know—the code of the streets. And if one is not a real man, one is somehow diminished as a person, and there are certain valued things one simply does not deserve. There is thus believed to be a certain justice to the code, since it is considered that everyone has the opportunity to know it. Implicit in this is that everybody is held responsible for being familiar with the code. If the victim of a mugging, for example, does not know the code and so responds "wrong," the perpetrator may feel justified even in killing him and may feel no remorse. He may think, "Too bad, but it's his fault. He should have known better."

So when a person ventures outside, he must adopt the code—a kind of shield, really—to prevent others from "messing with" him. In these circumstances it is easy for people to think they are being tried or tested by others even when this is not the case. For it is sensed that something extremely valuable is at stake in every interaction, and people are encouraged to rise to the occasion, particularly with strangers. For people who are unfamiliar with the code—generally people who live outside the inner city—the concern with respect in the most ordinary interactions can be frightening and incomprehensible. But for those who are invested in the code, the clear object of their demeanor is to discourage strangers from even thinking about testing their manhood. And the sense of power that attends the ability to deter others can be alluring even to those who know the code without being heavily invested in it—the decent inner-city youths. Thus a boy who has been leading a basically decent life can, in trying circumstances, suddenly resort to deadly force.

Central to the issue of manhood is the widespread belief that one of the most effective ways of gaining respect is to manifest "nerve." Nerve is shown when one takes another person's possessions (the more valuable the better), "messes with" someone's woman, throws the first punch, "gets in someone's face," or pulls a trigger. Its proper display helps on the spot to check others who would violate one's person and also helps to build a reputation that works to prevent future challenges. But since such a show of nerve is a forceful expression of disrespect toward the person on the receiving end, the victim may be greatly offended and seek to retaliate with equal or greater force. A display of nerve, therefore, can easily provoke a life-threatening response, and the background knowledge of that possibility has often been incorporated into the concept of nerve.

True nerve exposes a lack of fear of dying. Many feel that it is acceptable to risk dying over the principle of respect. In fact, among the hard-core street-oriented, the clear risk of violent death may be preferable to being "dissed" by another. The youths who have internalized this attitude and convincingly display it in their public bearing are among the most threatening people of all, for it is commonly assumed that they fear no man. As the people of the community say, "They are the baddest dudes on the street." They often lead an existential life that may acquire meaning only when they are faced with the possibility of imminent death. Not to be afraid to die is by implication to have few compunctions about taking another's life. Not to be afraid to die is the quid pro quo of being able to take somebody else's life—for the right reasons, if the situation demands it. When others believe this is one's position, it gives one a real sense of power on the streets. Such credibility is what many inner-city youths strive to achieve, whether they are decent or street-oriented, both because of its practical defensive value and because of the positive way it makes them feel about themselves. The difference between the decent and the street-oriented youth is often that the decent youth makes a conscious decision to appear tough and manly; in another setting—with teachers, say, or at his part-time job—he can be polite and deferential. The street-oriented youth, on the other hand, has made the concept of manhood a part of his very identity;

he has difficulty manipulating it—it often controls him.

Girls and Boys

Increasingly, teenage girls are mimicking the boys and trying to have their own version of "manhood." Their goal is the same—to get respect, to be recognized as capable of setting or maintaining a certain standard. They try to achieve this end in the ways that have been established by the boys, including posturing, abusive language, and the use of violence to resolve disputes, but the issues for the girls are different. Although conflicts over turf and status exist among the girls, the majority of disputes seem rooted in assessments of beauty (which girl in a group is "the cutest"), competition over boyfriends, and attempts to regulate other people's knowledge of and opinions about a girl's behavior or that of someone close to her, especially her mother.

A major cause of conflicts among girls is "he say, she say." This practice begins in the early school years and continues through high school. It occurs when "people," particularly girls, talk about others, thus putting their "business in the streets." Usually one girl will say something negative about another in the group, most often behind the person's back. The remark will then get back to the person talked about. She may retaliate or her friends may feel required to "take up for" her. In essence this is a form of group gossiping in which individuals are negatively assessed and evaluated. As with much gossip, the things said may or may not be true, but the point is that such imputations can cast aspersions on a person's good name. The accused is required to defend herself against the slander, which can result in arguments and fights, often over little of real substance. Here again is the problem of low self-esteem, which encourages youngsters to be highly sensitive to slights and to be vulnerable to feeling easily "dissed." To avenge the dissing, a fight is usually necessary.

Because boys are believed to control violence, girls tend to defer to them in situations of conflict. Often if a girl is attacked or feels slighted, she will get a brother, uncle, or cousin to do her fighting for her. Increasingly, however, girls are doing their own fighting and are even asking their male relatives to teach them how to fight. Some girls form groups that attack other girls or take things from them. A hard-core segment of inner-city girls inclined toward violence seems to be developing. As one thirteen-year-old girl in a detention center for youths who have committed violent acts told me, "To get people to leave you alone, you gotta fight. Talking don't always get you out of stuff." One major difference between girls and boys: girls rarely use guns. Their fights are therefore not life-or-death struggles. Girls are not often willing to put their lives on the line for "manhood." The ultimate form of respect on the male-dominated inner-city street is thus reserved for men.

'Going for Bad'

In the most fearsome youths such a cavalier attitude toward death grows out of a very limited view of life. Many are uncertain about how long they are going to live and believe they could die violently at any time. They accept this fate; they live on the edge. Their manner conveys the message that nothing intimidates them, whatever turn the encounter takes, they maintain their attack—rather like a pit bull, whose spirit many such boys admire. The demonstration of such tenacity "shows heart" and earns their respect.

This fearlessness has implications for law enforcement. Many street-oriented boys are much more concerned about the threat of "justice" at the hands of a peer than at the hands of the police. Moreover, many feel not only that they have little to lose by going to prison but that they have something to gain. The toughening-up one experiences in prison can actually enhance one's reputation on the streets. Hence the system loses influence over the hard core who are without jobs, with little perceptible stake in the system. If mainstream society has done nothing *for them*, they counter by making sure it can do nothing to them.

At the same time, however, a competing view maintains that true nerve consists in backing down, walking away from a fight, and going on with one's business. One fights only in self-defense. This view emerges from the decent philosophy that life is precious, and it is an important part of the socialization process common in decent homes. It discourages violence as the primary means of resolving disputes and encourages youngsters to accept nonviolence and talk as confrontational strategies. But "if the deal goes down," self-defense is greatly encouraged. When there is enough positive support for this orientation, either in the home or among one's peers, then nonviolence has a chance to prevail. But it prevails at the cost of relinquishing a claim to being bad and tough, and therefore sets a young person up as at the very least alienated from street-oriented peers and quite possibly a target of derision or even violence.

Although the nonviolent orientation rarely overcomes the impulse to strike back in an encounter, it does introduce a certain confusion and so can prompt a measure of soul-searching, or even profound ambivalence. Did the person back down with his respect intact or did he back down only to be judged a "punk"—a person lacking manhood? Should he or she have acted? Should he or she have hit the other person in the mouth? These questions beset many young men and women during public confrontations. What is the "right" thing to do? In the quest for honor, respect, and local status—which few young people are uninterested in—common sense most often prevails, which leads many to opt for the tough approach, enacting their own particular versions of the display of nerve. The presentation of oneself as rough and tough is very often quite acceptable until one is tested. And then that presentation may help the person pass the test, because it will cause fewer questions to be asked about what he did and why. It is hard for a person to explain why he lost the fight or why he backed down. Hence many will strive to appear to "go for bad," while hoping they will never be tested. But when they are tested, the outcome of the situation may quickly be out of their hands, as they become wrapped up in the circumstances of the moment.

An Oppositional Culture

The attitudes of the wider society are deeply implicated in the code of the streets. Most people in inner-city communities are not totally invested in the code, but the significant minority of hard-core street youths who are have to maintain the code in order to establish reputations, because they have—or feel they have—few other ways to assert themselves. For these young people the standards of the street code are the only game in town. The extent to which some children—particularly those who through upbringing have become most alienated and those lacking in strong and conventional social support—experience, feel, and internalize racist rejection and contempt from mainstream society may strongly encourage them to express contempt for the more conventional society in turn. In dealing with this contempt and rejection, some youngsters will consciously invest themselves and their considerable mental resources in what amounts to an oppositional culture to preserve themselves and their self-respect. Once they do, any respect they might be able to garner in the wider system pales in comparison with the respect available in the local system; thus they often lose interest in even attempting to negotiate the mainstream system.

At the same time, many less alienated young blacks have assumed a street-oriented demeanor as a way of expressing their blackness while really embracing a much more moderate way of life; they, too, want a nonviolent setting in which to live and raise a family. These decent people are trying hard to be part of the mainstream culture, but the racism, real and perceived, that they encounter helps to legitimate the oppositional culture. And so on occasion they adopt street behavior. In fact, depending on the demands of the situation, many people in the community slip back and forth between decent and street behavior.

A vicious cycle has thus been formed. The hopelessness and alienation many young inner-city black men and women feel, largely as a result of endemic joblessness and persistent racism, fuels the violence they engage in. This violence serves to confirm the negative feelings many whites and some middle-class blacks harbor toward the ghetto poor, further legitimating the oppositional culture and the code of the streets in the eyes of many poor young blacks. Unless this cycle is broken, attitudes on both sides will become increasingly entrenched, and the violence, which claims victims black and white, poor and affluent, will only escalate.

Reprinted from Elijah Anderson, "The Code of the Streets" in *The Code of the Streets*. Originally in *The Atlantic Monthly* 273, no. 5 (May 1994). Copyright © 1994 by Elijah Anderson. Reprinted with the permission of the author and W. W. Norton & Company, Inc.

Discussion Questions

1. Describe the central values and norms (or rules) that form the "code of the streets."

2. How does Anderson explain the origin of the code of the streets?

3. Describe the socialization of "street kids," noting how this socialization increases the likelihood that they will resort to violence in various situations. In your description, draw on both Sutherland's differential association and Akers's social learning theory.

4. Why do individuals who oppose the code of the streets nevertheless conform to its rules on occasion?

5. To what extent does the code of the streets affect the behavior of girls? ✦

Part IV

Anomie/Strain Theories of Crime

Anomie and strain theory are distinct but related theories of crime (see Agnew, 1987, 1997; Agnew and Passas, 1997; Bernard, 1987; Burton and Cullen, 1992; Messner, 1988 for discussions of the relationship between these theories). Contemporary versions of these theories trace their origins to the work of Merton (1938) and to the revisions in Merton's theory made by Cohen (1955) and Cloward and Ohlin (1960). Messner and Rosenfeld's (1997) institutional-anomie theory of crime now represents the leading version of anomie theory (also see Rosenfeld and Messner 1995), while Agnew's (1992) general strain theory represents the leading version of strain theory.

Anomie Theory

Anomie theory has focused on explaining why some societies, like the United States, have higher crime rates than others. According to Merton's (1938) version of the theory, the United States places a relatively strong emphasis on the goal of monetary success, but a weak emphasis on the legitimate norms for achieving this goal, like education and hard work. As a consequence, the goal-seeking behavior of individuals is subject to less regulation. Individuals are more likely to pursue monetary success using whatever means are necessary—including crime. Societies which fail to adequately regulate goal-seek-ing behavior are said to be characterized by a state of "anomie" or normlessness.

Merton's arguments in this area were largely neglected until the 1980s. Most attention, instead, focused on his version of strain theory (see below). During the 1980s and 1990s, however, several scholars called attention to Merton's anomie theory and began to suggest refinements to it (Bernard, 1987; Burton and Cullen, 1992; Cullen, 1984; Messner, 1988; Rosenfeld, 1989). Messner and Rosenfeld (1997) drew heavily on the theory when they developed their institutional-anomie theory of crime (see Chapter 16 in this Part). Like Merton, they attempt to explain why the United States has such a high crime rate (although, like Merton, their arguments are applicable to other societies). And they begin their explanation by drawing on Merton's argument that the higher crime rate in the United States stems from a cultural system that encourages everyone to strive for monetary success, but places little emphasis on the legitimate norms for achieving such success. This emphasis on the unrestrained pursuit of monetary success is what they refer to as the "American Dream."

Messner and Rosenfeld, however, go on to argue that the American Dream is only part of the explanation for the higher crime rate in the United States. In particular, they argue that the cultural emphasis on money is paralleled by an institutional structure that is dominated by the economy. The other major institutions in the United States—the family, school, and political system—are all subservient to economic institutions. Noneconomic functions and roles (e.g., parent, teacher) are devalued. Noneconomic institutions must accommodate themselves to the demands of the economy (e.g., parents struggle to arrange childcare so they can work). And economic norms have come to penetrate these other institutions (e.g., the school system, like the economic system, is based on the individualized competition for rewards). As a result, institutions like the family, school, and political system are less able to effectively socialize or train individuals and to effectively sanction deviant behavior.

The anomie theories of Merton and Messner and Rosenfeld have yet to receive a proper test (although see Chamlin and Cochran, 1995). Until recently, most researchers focused their attention on "micro-level" theories, which seek to explain the criminal behavior of individuals and groups within a society. Also, it is difficult to obtain good, comparable data on societal crime rates and on those factors believed to influence crime rates. Efforts are currently underway to test Messner and Rosenfeld's theory, however, and we should have a better idea of the support for this theory in the near future (see Chamlin and Cochran, 1995; Messner and Rosenfeld, 1997). For now, anomie theory remains an intriguing but largely untested explanation for societal differences in the rate of crime.

Strain Theory

Classic Strain Theory

Strain theory has focused on explaining why some individuals and groups *within* a society are more likely to engage in crime than others. According to the theory, individuals are pressured into crime. Most commonly, it has been argued that they are pressured into crime when they are prevented from achieving cultural goals like monetary success or middle-class status through legitimate channels. This is the central argument of the "classic" strain theories of Merton (1938), Cohen

(1955), and Cloward and Ohlin (1960) (see Chapters 13, 14, and 15 in this Part). These theorists argue that everyone is encouraged to pursue the goals of monetary success and/or middle class status. Lower-class individuals, however, are often prevented from achieving such goals through legitimate channels. Their parents do not equip them with the skills and values necessary to do well in school, they attend inferior schools and grow up in troubled neighborhoods, they cannot afford college, and they may face discrimination in the job market. Our society, then, encourages everyone to pursue certain goals, but then prevents large segments of the population from achieving these goals through legitimate channels. Individuals experiencing such goal blockage are under a great deal of strain or pressure, and they *may* respond by engaging in crime.

They may attempt to achieve their goals through illegitimate channels, like theft, drug-selling, and prostitution. They may reject the goals of monetary success and middle-class status and substitute new goals that they can achieve. Their hostility toward the society that frustrates them, among other things, may lead them to emphasize goals that are conducive to crime (e.g., being a good fighter). Or they may simply reject cultural goals and norms, retreating into drug use. Strain theorists are careful to emphasize that only some strained individuals turn to crime, and they have tried to specify the factors that determine whether strain leads to crime (see Agnew, 1995, 1997; Cullen, 1984). Cohen (1955) and Cloward and Ohlin (1960) argue that strained individuals are unlikely to engage in crime unless they first form or join a delinquent subculture whose values are conducive to crime. These theorists describe the conditions under which strained individuals are likely to form delinquent subcultures, and their accounts represent the dominant explanations for the origin of delinquent subcultures.

The classic strain theories dominated research on the causes of crime during the 1950s and 1960s, and had a major impact on public policy (see Burton and Cullen, 1992; Clinard, 1964; Cole, 1975; Empey and Stafford, 1991). Strain theory, in particular, was one of the inspirations for the "War on Poverty" that was launched during the 1960s. The War on Poverty was designed to increase opportunities for low-income and minority individuals to achieve success through legitimate channels. Many of the programs associated with the War on Poverty have since been dismantled, but some—like Project Headstart and Job Corps—remain.

Classic strain theory came under heavy attack during the late 1960s and 1970s, and it no longer dominates criminology as it once did (see Agnew and Passas, 1997; Akers, 1997; Bernard, 1984; Burton and Cullen, 1992; Cole, 1975; Rosenfeld, 1989). Among other things, a number of empirical studies failed to provide support for the theory (see Agnew, 1995; Akers, 1997; Hirschi, 1969; Jensen, 1995; Kornhauser, 1978). Classic strain theory was most commonly tested by examining the disjunction between aspirations (the goals one ideally would like to achieve) and expectations (the goals one realistically expects to achieve). If the theory is true, we would expect people with high aspirations and low expectations to be most delinquent (that is, people who say they ideally want a lot, but expect very little). The research, however, did not support this prediction. Crime is highest among those with both low aspirations and low expectations (a finding most commonly explained in terms of social control theory—see Part V). Further, a series of self-report studies during the 1960s and 1970s revealed that delinquency was not concentrated among lower-class individuals. Middle-class delinquency was quite common, perhaps as common as lower-class delinquency (see Akers, 1997; Tittle and Meier, 1990). This was taken as further evidence against classic strain theory (since the pressure for delinquency should be greatest in the lower classes).

Several researchers, however, have recently challenged the evidence against classic strain theory. Among other things, they argue that there are better ways to measure strain than by the disjunction between aspirations and expectations. Aspirations or ideal goals have something of the utopian in them, and so are not taken seriously. The failure to achieve such goals, then, is not an important

source of strain (see Agnew, 1992, 1995; Agnew and Passas, 1997; Bernard, 1984; Burton and Cullen, 1992; Burton and Dunaway, 1994; Burton et al., 1994; Cullen, 1984; 1988; Hoffman and Ireland, 1995; Menard, 1995; Messner, 1988; Passas and Agnew, 1997, for other criticisms). A few recent studies have attempted to provide better tests of classic strain theory (Agnew et al., 1996; Burton and Dunaway, 1994; Burton et al., 1994; Hagan and McCarthy, 1997; Menard, 1995, 1997). These studies tend to provide more support for the theory. Agnew et al. (1996), for example, attempt to directly measure strain by asking individuals how satisfied they are with their financial situation. This measure is related to crime, with the more dissatisfied being more criminal. Additional tests are needed before we can reach any definitive conclusions about classic strain theory, but the theory does seem to be experiencing a minor revival (see Adler and Laufer, 1995; Passas and Agnew, 1997).

Revisions in Classic Strain Theory

The criticisms against classic strain theory spurred several efforts to revise the theory (see Adler and Laufer, 1995; Agnew, 1995; Bernard, 1990; Burton and Cullen, 1992; Clinard, 1964; Cohen, 1964; Elliott et al., 1979; Greenberg, 1987; Merton, 1968; Passas and Agnew, 1997; Simon and Gagnon, 1976). Certain of the revisions attempt to apply the theory to the explanation of middle-class crime and delinquency. One major revision, for example, argues that strain is a function of *relative deprivation*. That is, one's level of strain or frustration is not dependent on the absolute amount of money one has, but is dependent on how much money one has *relative* to those in one's "reference group" (see Burton and Dunaway, 1994; Burton et al., 1994; Cohen, 1964, 1997; Passas, 1997). Wealthy individuals, as a consequence, may experience much strain if they compare themselves to even wealthier people around them. Limited data provide some support for this argument (Burton et al., 1994; Burton and Dunaway, 1994).

Another revision argues that adolescents pursue a variety of goals in addition to middle-class status and monetary success. Such goals include popularity with peers and potential romantic partners, athletic success, positive relations with parents and others, and good grades. The achievement of these goals is said to be a function of several factors in addition to social class—factors like intelligence, personality characteristics, and physical appearance and ability. As a result, middle-class adolescents may also experience strain quite frequently. This version of strain theory has not been well tested, although preliminary tests have not been encouraging (see Agnew, 1995 for an overview).

General Strain Theory

Most of the revisions in classic strain theory continue to argue that the major source of strain or frustration is the failure to achieve positively valued goals. They simply argue that goal achievement should be measured relative to others or they broaden the number of goals under consideration. Agnew's (1992) general strain theory, however, points to additional sources of strain.

According to Agnew (1992:50), strain results from negative relationships with others: "relationships in which others are not treating the individual as he or she would like to be treated." There are three major types of negative relations: relations where others 1) prevent or threaten to prevent the achievement of positively valued goals (e.g., monetary success, popularity with peers), 2) remove or threaten to remove positively valued stimuli (e.g., the loss of a romantic partner, the death of a parent), or 3) present or threaten to present negatively-valued stimuli (e.g., insults, physically assault, overwork). Such negative relationships increase the likelihood that individuals will experience anger or frustration. This anger/frustration creates pressure for corrective action, with crime being one possible response. Crime may be a method for alleviating strain (e.g., running away from home, assaulting those who insult) seeking revenge, or managing the anger/frustration that the individual experiences (e.g., through illicit drug use). Like previous theorists, Agnew argues that only some strained individuals turn to crime, and he discusses those factors that influence whether one reacts to strain with crime.

Agnew, then, significantly broadens the focus of strain theory. Preliminary tests provide tentative support for Agnew's general strain theory (Hagan and McCarthy, 1997; Hoffman and Su, forthcoming; Paternoster and Mazerolle, 1994). In one such test (Agnew and White, 1992), delinquency was found to be higher among individuals experiencing a variety of negative life events (e.g., assault, theft, parental divorce, parental unemployment) and various relational problems with teachers, parents, friends, and others (e.g., teachers talk down to and embarrass them, parents get angry over little things, classmates do not like them). Researchers, however, have only examined certain of the types of strain described by Agnew. Additional research is needed to determine which types of strain are most strongly related to delinquency. Research is also needed on those factors that influence whether individuals react to strain with crime. Here the data are less clearcut (Agnew and White, 1992; Paternoster and Mazerolle, 1994; Hoffman and Su, forthcoming). General strain theory, however, seems to hold some promise for explaining crime and delinquency.

Strain and anomie theory, then, no longer dominate the research on the causes of crime as they once did, but they remain among the more influential theories of crime. The readings which follow present the classic anomie and strain theories of Merton (1938), Cohen (1955) and Cloward and Ohlin (1960), as well as the new institutional-anomie theory of Messner and Rosenfeld (1995, 1997) and Agnew's (1992) general strain theory.

References

Adler, Freda and William S. Laufer. 1995. *Advances in Criminology Theory, Volume 6: The Legacy of Anomie.* New Brunswick, NJ: Transaction.

Agnew, Robert. 1992. "Foundation for a General Strain Theory of Crime and Delinquency." *Criminology* 30: 47-87.

——. 1995. "Strain and Subcultural Theories of Criminality." Pp. 305-327 in *Criminology: A Contemporary Handbook*, 2nd edition, edited by Joseph F. Sheley. Belmont: Wadsworth.

——. 1997. "The Nature and Determinants of Strain: Another Look at Durkheim and Merton," Pp. 27-51 in *The Future of Anomie Theory*, edited by Nikos Passas and Robert Agnew. Boston: Northeastern University Press.

Agnew, Robert, Francis T. Cullen, Velmer S. Burton, Jr., T. David Evans, and R. Gregory Dunaway. 1996. "A New Test of Classic Strain Theory." *Justice Quarterly* 13: 681-704.

Agnew, Robert and Nikos Passas. 1997. "Introduction." Pp. 1-26 in *The Future of Anomie Theory*, edited by Nikos Passas and Robert Agnew. Boston; Northeastern University Press.

Agnew, Robert and Helene Raskin White. 1992. "An Empirical Test of General Strain Theory." *Criminology* 30:475-499.=

Akers, Ronald L. 1997. *Criminological Theories: Introduction and Evaluation*, 2nd edition. Los Angeles: Roxbury.

Bernard, Thomas J. 1984. "Control Criticisms of Strain Theories: An Assessment of Theoretical and Empirical Adequacy." *Journal of Research in Crime and Delinquency* 21: 353-372.

——. 1987. "Testing Structural Strain Theories." *Journal of Research in Crime and Delinquency* 24: 262-280.

——. 1990. "Angry Aggression Among the 'Truly Disadvantaged.'" *Criminology* 28: 73-109.

Burton, Velmer S., Jr. and Francis T. Cullen. 1992. "The Empirical Status of Strain Theory." *Journal of Crime and Justice* 15: 1-30.

Burton, Velmer S., Jr., Francis T. Cullen, T. David Evans, and R. Gregory Dunaway. 1994. "Reconsidering Strain Theory: Operationalization, Rival Theories, and Adult Criminality." *Journal of Quantitative Criminology* 10: 213-239.

Burton, Velmer S., Jr. and R. Gregory Dunaway. 1994. "Strain, Relative Deprivation, and Middle-Class Delinquency." Pp. 79-95 in *Varieties of Criminology: Readings from a Dynamic Discipline*, edited by Greg Barak. Westport, Conn.: Praeger.

Chamlin, Mitchell B. and John K. Cochran. 1995. "Assessing Messner and Rosenfeld's Institutional Anomie Theory: A Partial Test." *Criminology* 33: 411-429.

Clinard, Marshall B. 1964. *Anomie and Deviant Behavior.* New York: Free Press.

Cloward, Richard A. and Lloyd Ohlin. 1960. *Delinquency and Opportunity: A Theory of Delinquent Gangs*. New York: Free Press.

Cohen, Albert K. 1955. *Delinquent Boys: The Culture of the Gang.* New York: Free Press.

——. 1965. "The Sociology of the Deviant Act: Anomie Theory and Beyond." *American Sociological Review* 30: 5-14.

——. 1997. "An Elaboration of Anomie Theory." Pp. 52–61 in *The Future of Anomie Theory*, edited by Nikos Passas and Robert Agnew. Boston: Northeastern University Press.

Cole, S. 1975. "The Growth of Scientific Knowledge: Theories of Deviance as a Case Study." Pp. 175-220 in *The Idea of Social Structure*, edited by Lewis A. Coser. New York: Harcourt Brace Javanovich.

Cullen, Francis T. 1984. *Rethinking Crime and Deviance: The Emergence of a Structuring Tradition.* Totowa, NJ: Rowman and Allanheld.

——. 1988. "Were Cloward and Ohlin Strain Theorists?: Delinquency and Opportunity Revisited." *Journal of Research in Crime and Delinquency* 25:214-241.

Elliott, Delbert S., Suzanne S. Ageton, and Rachelle Canter. 1979. "An Integrated Theoretical Perspective on Delinquent Behavior." *Journal of Research in Crime and Delinquency* 16: 3-27.

Empey, LaMar T. and Mark Stafford. 1991. *American Delinquency: Its Meaning and Construction.* Belmont, CA: Wadsworth.

Greenberg, David F. 1977. "Delinquency and the Age Structure of Society." *Contemporary Crises* 1: 189-223.

Hagan, John and Bill McCarthy. 1997. *Mean Streets.* New York: Cambridge University Press.

Hirschi, Travis. 1969. *Causes of Delinquency.* Berkeley: University of California Press.

Hoffman, John P. and Timothy Ireland. 1995. "Cloward and Ohlin's Strain Theory Reexamined: An Elaborated Theoretical Model," Pp. 247-270 in *Advances in Criminological Theory, Volume 6: The Legacy of Anomie*, edited by Freda Adler and William S. Laufer. New Brunswick, NJ: Transaction.

Hoffman, John P. and S. Susan Su. forthcoming. "The Conditional Effects of Negative Life Events on Delinquency and Drug Use: A Strain Theory Assessment of Gender Differences." *Journal of Research in Crime and Delinquency.*

Jensen, Gary F. 1995. "Salvaging Structure Through Strain: A Theoretical and Empirical Critique." Pp. 139-158 in *Advances in Criminological Theory, Volume 6: The Legacy of Anomie*, edited by Freda Adler and William S. Laufer. New Brunswick, NJ: Transaction.

Kornhauser, Ruth, 1978. *Social Sources of Delinquency.* Chicago: University of Chicago Press.

Menard, Scott. 1995. "A Developmental Test of Mertonian Anomie Theory." *Journal of Research in Crime and Delinquency* 32: 136-174.

———. 1997. "A Developmental Test of Cloward's Differential Opportunity Theory." Pp. 142-186 in *The Future of Anomie Theory,* edited by Nikos Passas and Robert Agnew. Boston: Northeastern University Press.

Messner, Steven F. 1988. "Merton's 'Social Structure and Anomie': The Road Not Taken." *Deviant Behavior* 9: 33-53.

Messner, Steven F. and Richard Rosenfeld. 1997. *Crime and the American Dream,* 2nd edition. Belmont, CA: Wadsworth.

Merton, Robert K. 1938. "Social Structure and Anomie." *American Sociological Review* 3:672-682.

———. 1968. *Social Theory and Social Structure.* New York: Free Press.

Passas, Nikos. 1997. "Anomie and Relative Deprivation." Pp. 62-94 in *The Future of Anomie Theory,* edited by Nikos Passas and Robert Agnew. Boston: Northeastern University Press.

Passas, Nikos and Robert Agnew. 1997. *The Future of Anomie Theory.* Boston: Northeastern University Press.

Paternoster, Raymond and Paul Mazerolle. 1994. "General Strain Theory and Delinquency: A Replication and Extension." *Journal of Research in Crime and Delinquency* 31: 235-263.

Rosenfeld, Richard. 1989. "Robert Merton's Contribution to the Sociology of Deviance." *Sociological Inquiry* 59: 453-466.

Rosenfeld, Richard and Steven F. Messner. 1995. "Crime and the American Dream: An Institutional Analysis." Pp. 159-181 in *Advances in Criminological Theory, Volume 6: The Legacy of Anomie,* edited by Freda Adler and William S. Laufer. New Brunswick, NJ: Transaction.

Simon, William and John H. Gagnon. 1976. "The Anomie of Affluence: A Post-Mertonian Conception." *American Journal of Sociology* 82: 356-378.

Tittle, Charles R. and Robert F. Meier. 1990. "Specifying the SES/Delinquency Relationship." *Criminology* 28: 271-299. ✦

13

Social Structure and Anomie

Robert K. Merton

I*t has been said that the following article by Merton, "Social Structure and Anomie," is the most widely read article in sociology (Cole, 1975). Merton opens the article by challenging psychoanalytic and related theories of crime. Such theories view crime as the result of "biological drives" which are not adequately restrained by society. Merton instead argues that the motivation for crime frequently derives from society. His theory is in two parts.*

The first part of the article presents what may be termed his "anomie" theory, which seeks to explain why some societies have higher rates of crime than others. This theory focuses on the relative emphasis placed on cultural goals and the institutionalized norms for achieving these goals. Societies that place a high relative emphasis on goals (like monetary success) and a low relative emphasis on the norms or rules for goal achievement have higher crime rates. Such societies are characterized by a state of anomie or normlessness, where the goal-seeking behavior of individuals is subject to little regulation. As a consequence, individuals employ the most expedient means—including crime—to achieve their goals. The United States is said be such a society, in which the goal of monetary success is stressed for everyone, but in which there is little emphasis on the norms regulating the achievement of this goal.

The second part of the article describes what may be termed Merton's "strain" theory. He argues that some individuals and groups within a society are subject to special pressure for crime. While everyone is urged to strive for monetary success, lower-class individuals are frequently prevented from achieving such success through legitimate channels. As a result,

they are under considerable strain or pressure. They may adapt to their strain in any one of the five ways listed by Merton. Certain of these adaptations involve crime, and Merton briefly discusses why some types of individuals are more likely to respond to strain with crime than others.

Merton's theory, particularly his strain theory, has been the subject of extensive commentary and research (for summaries, see Agnew, 1995; Akers, 1997; Burton and Cullen, 1992; Kornhauser, 1978). The evidence on his strain theory is mixed, although certain recent tests of this theory are promising (see Agnew and Passas, 1997, for a summary). Merton's anomie theory has never received an adequate test, although it is the direct inspiration for Messner and Rosenfeld's recent institutional-anomie theory, described shortly.

References

Agnew, Robert. 1995. "Strain and Subcultural Theories of Criminality." Pp. 305-327 in *Criminology: A Contemporary Handbook*, 2nd edition, edited by Joseph F. Sheley. Belmont: Wadsworth.

Agnew, Robert and Nikos Passas. 1997. "Introduction." Pp. 1-26 in *The Future of Anomie Theory*, edited by Nikos Passas and Robert Agnew. Boston: Northeastern University Press.

Akers, Ronald L. 1997. *Criminological Theories: Introduction and Evaluation*, 2nd edition. Los Angeles: Roxbury.

Burton, Velmer s. and Francis T. Cullen. 1992. "The Empirical Status of Strain Theory." *Journal of Crime and Justice* 15: 1-30.

Cole, S. 1975. "The Growth of Scientific Knowledge: Theories of Deviance as a Case Study." Pp. 175-220 in *The Idea of Social Structure*, edited by Lewis A. Coser. New York: Harcourt Brace Javanovich.

Kornhauser, Ruth. 1978. *Social Sources of Delinquency*. Chicago: University of Chicago Press.

There persists a notable tendency in sociological theory to attribute the malfunctioning of social structure primarily to those of man's imperious biological drives which are not adequately restrained by social control. In this view, the social order is solely a device for "impulse management" and the "social processing" of tensions. These impulses which break through social control, be it noted, are held to be biologically derived. Nonconformity is assumed to be rooted in original nature. Conformity is by implication the result of an utilitarian calculus or unreasoned conditioning. This point of view, whatever its other deficiencies, clearly begs one question. It provides no basis for determining the nonbiological conditions which induce deviations from prescribed patterns of conduct. In this paper, it will be suggested that certain phases of social structure generate the circumstances in which infringement of social codes constitutes a "normal" response.

The conceptual scheme to be outlined is designed to provide a coherent, systematic approach to the study of sociocultural sources of deviate behavior. Our primary aim lies in discovering how some social structures *exert a definite pressure* upon certain persons in the society to engage in nonconformist rather than conformist conduct. The many ramifications of the scheme cannot all be discussed; the problems mentioned outnumber those explicitly treated.

Among the elements of social and cultural structure, two are important for our purposes. These are analytically separable although they merge imperceptibly in concrete situations. The first consists of culturally defined goals, purposes, and interests. It comprises a frame of aspirational reference. These goals are more or less integrated and involve varying degrees of prestige and sentiment. They constitute a basic, but not the exclusive, component of what Linton aptly has called "designs for group living." Some of these cultural aspirations are related to the original drives of man, but they are not determined by them. The second phase of the social structure defines, regulates, and controls the acceptable modes of achieving these goals. Every social group invariably couples its scale of desired ends with moral or institutional regulation of permissible and required procedures for attaining these ends. These regulatory norms and moral imperatives do not necessarily coincide with technical or efficiency norms. Many procedures which from the standpoint of *particular individuals* would be most efficient in securing desired values, e.g., illicit oil-stock schemes, theft, fraud, are ruled out of the institutional area of permitted conduct. The choice of expedients is limited by the institutional norms.

To say that these two elements, culture goals and institutional norms, operate jointly is not to say that the ranges of alternative behaviors and aims bear some constant relation to one another. The emphasis upon certain goals may vary independently of the degree of emphasis upon institutional means. There may develop a disproportionate, at times, a virtually exclusive, stress upon the value of specific goals, involving relatively slight concern with the institutionally appropriate modes of attaining these goals. The limiting case in this direction is reached when the range of alternative procedures is limited only by technical rather than institutional considerations. Any and all devices which promise attainment of the all important goal would be permitted in this hypothetical polar case. This constitutes one type of cultural malintegration. A second polar type is found in groups where activities originally conceived as instrumental are transmuted into ends in themselves. The original purposes are forgotten and ritualistic adherence to institutionally prescribed conduct becomes virtually obsessive. Stability is largely ensured while change is flouted. The range of alternative behaviors is severely limited. There develops a tradition-bound, sacred society characterized by neophobia. The occupational psychosis of the bureaucrat may be cited as a case in point. Finally, there are the intermediate types of groups where a though changing, groups.

An effective equilibrium between the two phases of the social structure is maintained as long as satisfactions accrue to individuals who conform to both constraints, viz., satisfactions from the achievement of the goals and satisfactions emerging directly from the institutionally canalized modes of striving to attain these ends. Success, in such equilibrated cases, is twofold. Success is reckoned in terms of the product and in terms of the process, in terms of the outcome and in terms of activities. Continuing satisfactions must derive from sheer *participation* in a competitive order as well as from eclipsing one's competitors if the order itself is to be sustained. The occasional sacrifices involved in institutionalized conduct must be compensated by socialized rewards. The distribution of statuses and roles through competition must be so organized that positive incentives for conformity to roles and adherence to status obligations are provided *for every position* within the distributive order. Aberrant conduct, therefore, may be viewed as a symptom of dissociation between culturally defined aspirations and socially structured means.

Of the types of groups which result from the independent variation of the two phases of the social structure, we shall be primarily concerned with the first, namely, that involving a disproportionate accent on goals. This statement must be recast in a proper perspective. In no group is there an absence of regulatory codes governing conduct, yet groups do vary in the degree to which these folkways, mores, and institutional controls are effectively integrated with the more diffuse goals which are part of the culture matrix. Emotional convictions may cluster about the complex of socially acclaimed ends, meanwhile shifting their support from the culturally defined implementation of these ends. As we shall see, certain aspects of the social structure may generate countermores and antisocial behavior precisely because of differential emphases on goals and regulations. In the extreme case, the latter may be so vitiated by the goal-emphasis that the range of behavior is limited only by considerations of technical expediency. The sole significant question then becomes, which available means is most efficient in netting the socially approved value. The technically most feasible procedure, whether legitimate or not, is preferred to the institutionally prescribed conduct. As this process continues, the integration of the society becomes tenuous and anomie ensues.

Thus, in competitive athletics, when the aim of victory is shorn of its institutional trappings and success in contests becomes construed as "winning the game" rather than "winning through circumscribed modes of activity," a premium is implicitly set upon the use of illegitimate but technically efficient means. The star of the opposing football team is surreptitiously slugged; the wrestler furtively incapacitates his opponent through ingenious but illicit techniques; university alumni covertly subsidize "students" whose talents are largely confined to the athletic field. The emphasis on the goal has so attenuated the satisfactions deriving from sheer participation in the competitive activity that these satisfactions are virtually confined to a successful outcome. Through the same process, tension generated by the desire to win in a poker game is relieved by successfully dealing oneself four aces, or, when the cult of success has become completely dominant, by sagaciously shuffling the cards in a game of solitaire. The faint twinge of uneasiness in the last instance and the surreptitious nature of public delicts indicate clearly that the institutional rules of the game *are known* to those who evade them, but that the emotional supports of these rules are largely vitiated by cultural exaggeration of the success-goal. They are microcosmic images of the social macrocosm.

Of course, this process is not restricted to the realm of sport. The process whereby exaltation of the end generates a *literal demoralization*, i.e., a deinstitutionalization, of the means is one which characterizes many groups in which the two phases of the social structure are not highly integrated. The extreme emphasis upon the accumulation of wealth as a symbol of success in our own society militates against the completely effective control of institutionally regulated modes of acquiring a fortune. Fraud, corruption, vice, crime, in short, the entire catalogue of proscribed behavior, becomes increasingly common when the emphasis on the *culturally induced* success-goal becomes divorced from a coordinated institutional emphasis. This observation is of crucial theoretical importance in examining the doctrine that antisocial behavior most frequently derives from biological drives breaking through the restraints imposed by society. The difference is one between a strictly utilitarian interpretation which conceives man's ends as random and an analysis which finds these ends deriving from the basic values of the culture.

Our analysis can scarcely stop at this juncture. We must turn to other aspects of the social structure if we are to deal with the social genesis of the varying rates and types of deviate behavior characteristic of different societies. Thus far, we have sketched three ideal types of social orders constituted by distinctive patterns of relations between culture ends and means. Turning from these types of *culture patterning*, we find five logically possible, alternative modes of adjustment or adaptation *by individuals* within the culture-bearing society or group. These are schematically presented in the following table, where (+) signifies "acceptance," (-) signifies "elimination" and (+-) signifies "rejection and substitution of new goals and standards."

	Culture Goals	Institutionalized Means
I. Conformity	+	+
II. Innovation	+	-
III. Ritualism	-	+
IV. Retreatism	-	-
V. Rebellion	±	±

Our discussion of the relation between these alternative responses and other phases of the social structure must be prefaced by the observation that persons may shift from one alternative to another as they engage in different social activities. These categories refer to role adjustments in specific situations, not to personality *in toto*. To treat the development of this process in various spheres of conduct would introduce a complexity unmanageable within the confines of this paper. For this reason, we shall be concerned primarily with economic activity in the broad sense, "the production, exchange, distribution and consumption of goods and services" in our competitive society, wherein wealth has taken on a highly symbolic cast. Our task is to search out some of the factors which exert pressure upon individuals to engage in certain of these logically possible alternative responses. This choice, as we shall see, is far from random.

In every society, Adaptation I (conformity to both culture goals and means) is the most common and widely diffused. Were this not

so, the stability and continuity of the society could not be maintained. The mesh of expectancies which constitutes every social order is sustained by the modal behavior of its members falling within the first category. Conventional role behavior oriented toward the basic values of the group is the rule rather than the exception. It is this fact alone which permits us to speak of a human aggregate as comprising a group or society.

Conversely, Adaptation IV (rejection of goals and means) is the least common. Persons who "adjust" (or maladjust) in this fashion are, strictly speaking, in the society but not *of it*. Sociologically, these constitute the true "aliens." Not sharing the common frame of orientation, they can be included within the societal population merely in a fictional sense. In this category are *some* of the activities of psychotics, psychoneurotics, chronic autists, pariahs, outcasts, vagrants, vagabonds, tramps, chronic drunkards and drug addicts." These have relinquished, in certain spheres of activity, the culturally defined goals, involving complete aim-inhibition in the polar case, and their adjustments are not in accord with institutional norms. This is not to say that in some cases the source of their behavioral adjustments is not in part the very social structure which they have in effect repudiated nor that their very existence within a social area does not constitute a problem for the socialized population.

This mode of "adjustment" occurs, as far as structural sources are concerned, when both the culture goals and institutionalized procedures have been assimilated thoroughly by the individual and imbued with affect and high positive value, but where those institutionalized procedures which promise a measure of successful attainment of the goals are not available to the individual. In such instances, there results a twofold mental conflict insofar as the moral obligation for adopting institutional means conflicts with the pressure to resort to illegitimate means (which may attain the goal) and inasmuch as the individual is shut off from means which are both legitimate and effective. The competitive order is maintained, but the frustrated and handicapped individual who cannot cope with this order drops out. Defeatism, quietism and resignation are manifested in escape mechanisms which ultimately lead the individual to "escape" from the requirements of the society. It is an expedient which arises from continued failure to attain the goal by legitimate measures and from an inability to adopt the illegitimate route because of internalized prohibitions and institutionalized compulsives, *during which process the supreme value of the success-goal has as yet not been renounced.* The conflict is resolved by eliminating both precipitating elements, the goals and means. The escape is complete, the conflict is eliminated and the individual is socialized.

Be it noted that where frustration derives from the inaccessibility of effective institutional means for attaining economic or any other type of highly valued "success," that Adaptations II, III and V (innovation, ritualism and rebellion) are also possible. The result will be determined by the particular personality, and thus, the *particular* cultural background, involved. Inadequate socialization will result in the innovation response whereby the conflict and frustration are eliminated by relinquishing the institutional means and retaining the success-aspiration; an extreme assimilation of institutional demands will lead to ritualism wherein the goal is dropped as beyond one's reach but conformity to the mores persists; and rebellion occurs when emancipation from the reigning standards, due to frustration or to marginalist perspectives, leads to the attempt to introduce a "new social order."

Our major concern is with the illegitimacy adjustment. This involves the use of conventionally proscribed but frequently effective means of attaining at least the simulacrum of culturally defined success—wealth, power, and the like. As we have seen, this adjustment occurs when the individual has assimilated the cultural emphasis on success without equally internalizing the morally prescribed norms governing means for its attainment. The question arises, Which phases of our social structure predispose toward this mode of adjustment? We may examine a concrete instance, effectively analyzed by Lohman, which provides a clue to the answer. Lohman has shown that specialized areas of vice in the near north side of Chicago constitute a "normal" response to a situation where the cultural emphasis upon pecuniary success has been absorbed, but where there is little access to conventional and legitimate means for attaining such success. The conventional occupational opportunities of persons in this area are almost completely limited to manual labor. Given our cultural stigmatization of manual labor, and its correlate, the prestige of white collar work, it is clear that the result is a strain toward innovational practices. The limitation of opportunity to unskilled labor and the resultant low income can not compete *in terms of conventional standards of achievement* with the high income from organized vice.

For our purposes, this situation involves two important features. First, such antisocial behavior is in a sense "called forth" by certain conventional values of the culture and by the class structure involving differential access to the approved opportunities for legitimate, prestige-bearing pursuit of the culture goals. The lack of high integration between the means-and-end elements of the cultural pattern and the particular class structure combine to favor a heightened frequency of antisocial conduct in such groups. The second consideration is of equal significance. Recourse to the first of the alternative responses, legitimate effort, is limited by the fact that actual advance toward desired success-symbols through conventional channels is, despite our persisting open-class ideology, relatively rare and difficult for those handicapped by little formal education and few economic resources. The dominant pressure of group standards of success is, therefore, on the gradual attenuation of legitimate, but by and large ineffective, strivings and the increasing use of illegitimate, but more or less effective, expedients of vice and crime. The cultural demands made on persons in this situation are incompatible. On the one hand, they are asked to orient their conduct toward the prospect of accumulating wealth and on the other, they are largely denied effective opportunities to do so institutionally. The consequences of such structural inconsistency are psychopathological personality, and/or antisocial conduct, and/or revolutionary activities. The equilibrium between culturally designated means and ends becomes highly unstable with the progressive emphasis on attaining the prestige-laden ends by any means whatsoever. Within this context, Capone represents the triumph of amoral intelligence over morally prescribed "failure," when the channels of vertical mobility are closed or narrowed *in a society which places a high premium on economic affluence and social accent for all its members*.

This last qualification is of primary importance. It suggests that other phases of the social structure besides the extreme emphasis on pecuniary success, must be considered if we are to understand the social sources of antisocial behavior. A high frequency of deviate behavior is not generated simply by "lack of opportunity" or by this exaggerated pecuniary emphasis. A comparatively rigidified class structure, a feudalistic or caste order, may limit such opportunities far beyond the point which obtains in our society today. It is only when a system of cultural values extols, virtually above all else, certain *common* symbols of success *for a considerable part of the same population*, that antisocial behavior ensues on a considerable scale. In other words, our egalitarian ideology denies by implication the existence of noncompeting groups and individuals in the pursuit of pecuniary success. The same body of success-symbols is held to be desirable for all. These goals are held to *transcend class lines*, not to be bounded by them, yet the actual social organization is such that there exist class differentials in the accessibility of these *common* success-symbols. Frustration and thwarted aspiration lead to the search for avenues of escape from a culturally induced intolerable situation; or unrelieved ambition may eventuate in illicit attempts to acquire the dominant values. The American stress on pecuniary success and ambitiousness for all thus invites exaggerated anxieties, hostilities, neuroses and antisocial behavior.

This theoretical analysis may go far toward explaining the varying correlations between crime and poverty. Poverty is not an isolated variable. It is one in a complex of interdependent social and cultural variables. When viewed in such a context, it represents quite different states of affairs. Poverty as such, and consequent limitation of opportunity, are not sufficient to induce a conspicuously high rate of criminal behavior. Even the often mentioned "poverty in the midst of plenty" will not necessarily lead to this result. Only insofar as poverty and associated disadvantages in competition for the culture values approved for all members of the society is linked with the assimilation of a cultural emphasis on monetary accumulation as a symbol of success is antisocial conduct a "normal" outcome. Thus, poverty is less highly correlated with crime in southeastern Europe than in the United States. The possibilities of vertical mobility in these European areas would seem to be fewer than in this country, so that neither poverty *per se* nor its association with limited opportunity is sufficient to account for the varying correlations. It is only when the full configuration is considered, poverty, limited opportunity and a commonly shared system of success symbols, that we can explain the higher association between poverty and crime in our society than in others where rigidified class structure is coupled with *differential class symbols of achievement*.

In societies such as our own, then, the pressure of prestige-bearing success tends to eliminate the effective social constraint over means employed to this end. "The-end-justifies-the-means" doctrine becomes a guiding tenet for action when the cultural structure unduly exalts the end and the social organization unduly limits possible recourse to approved means. Otherwise put, this notion and associated behavior reflect a lack of cultural coordination. In international relations, the effects of this lack of integration are notoriously apparent. An emphasis upon national power is not readily coordinated with an inept organization of legitimate, i.e., internationally defined and accepted, means for attaining this goal. The result is a tendency toward the abrogation of international law, treaties become scraps of paper, "undeclared warefare" serves as a technical evasion, the bombing of civilian populations is rationalized, just as the same societal situation induces the same sway of illegitimacy among individuals.

The social order we have described necessarily produces this "strain toward dissolution." The pressure of such an order is upon outdoing one's competitors. The choice of means within the ambit of institutional control will persist as long as the sentiments supporting a competitive system, i.e., deriving from the possibility of outranking competitors and hence enjoying the favorable response of others, are distributed throughout the entire system of activities and are not confined merely to the final result. A stable social structure demands a balanced distribution of affect among its various segments. When there occurs a shift of emphasis from the satisfactions deriving from competition itself to almost exclusive concern with successful competition, the resultant stress leads to the breakdown of the regulatory structure. With the resulting attenuation of the institutional imperatives, there occurs an approximation of the situation erroneously held by utilitarians to be typical of society generally wherein calculations of advantage and fear of punishment are the sole regulating agencies. In such situations, as Hobbes observed, force and fraud come to constitute the sole virtues in view of their relative efficiency in attaining goals—which were for him, of course, not culturally derived.

It should be apparent that the foregoing discussion is not pitched on a moralistic plane. Whatever the sentiments of the writer or reader concerning the ethical desirability of coordinating the means-and-goals phases of the social structure, one must agree that lack of such coordination leads to anomie. Insofar as one of the most general functions of social organization is to provide a basis for calculability and regularity of behavior, it is increasingly limited in effectiveness as these elements of the structure become dissociated. At the extreme, predictability virtually disappears and what may be properly termed cultural chaos or anomie intervenes.

This statement, being brief, is also incomplete. It has not included an exhaustive treatment of the various structural elements which predispose toward one rather than another of the alternative responses open to individuals; it has neglected, but not denied the relevance of, the factors determining the specific incidence of these responses; it has not enumerated the various concrete responses which are constituted by combinations of specific values of the analytical variables; it has omitted, or included only by implication, any consideration of the social functions performed by illicit responses; it has not tested the full explanatory power of the analytical scheme by examining a large number of group variations in the frequency of deviate and conformist behavior; it has not adequately dealt with rebellious conduct which seeks to refashion the social framework radically; it has not examined the relevance of cultural conflict for an analysis of culture-goal and institutional-means malintegration. It is suggested that these and related problems may be profitably analyzed by this scheme.

Discussion Questions

1. Describe the "cultural goals" and "institutional norms" that exist at your school. Are these goals and norms in "balance"?

2. Describe the "adaptations" that individuals might employ when they cannot achieve the cultural goals emphasized at your school.

3. What factors determine whether individuals will chose adaptations that may involve crime, like innovation?

4. Would Merton argue that poverty, in and of itself, is a cause of crime?

5. What policy recommendations might Merton make for controlling crime? ◆

14

Delinquent Boys

Albert K. Cohen

Cohen was a student of both Robert Merton and Edwin Sutherland. Like Sutherland, Cohen was interested in delinquent subcultures, particularly the lower working-class urban gangs that were the subject of much attention during the 1950s. While a student of Sutherland, Cohen posed a question for which Sutherland did not have an adequate answer: how can we explain the origin and content of delinquent subcultures? Cohen drew heavily on Merton's strain theory to provide his own answer to this question, which is outlined in the following selection from his book: Delinquent Boys: The Culture of the Gang. *In the first part of the selection, Cohen provides a general explanation for the origin of deviant subcultures. In the second part of the selection, Cohen applies this theory to explain the origin and content of male, working-class urban gangs.*

In reading the selection, note the similarities and differences with Merton's strain theory. Like Merton, Cohen argues that delinquency is ultimately caused by goal blockage. Cohen, however, argues that lower-class and working-class boys are not simply concerned with the goal of monetary success. Rather, they want to achieve the broader goal of middle-class status, which involves respect from others as well as financial success. This difference in goals is crucial. One can achieve financial success through illegitimate channels like theft (Merton's adaptation of innovation). One cannot, however, achieve middle-class status through the same channels (one can't steal middle-class status). As a consequence, lower-class and working-class boys often adapt to their goal blockage by setting up an alternative status system in which they can achieve success (Merton's adaptation of rebellion, in which new goals and means are substituted for the old ones). The hostility of lower-class and working-class boys toward the middle class, among other things, leads them to set up a status system that values everything the middle class rejects. The middle class values private property and respect for the individual, for example, while the delinquent gang values the destruction and theft of property and aggression against others. Cohen thus explains the origin and content of the delinquent subculture.

Certain features of Cohen's theory have been criticized (see Akers, 1997). Theorists such as Cloward and Ohlin (Chapter 15) and Sykes and Matza (see Chapter 9) claim that the values of delinquents are not as opposed to conventional values as Cohen claims. The data tend to support this argument (see Agnew, 1995). Nevertheless, Cohen's use of strain theory to explain the origin of deviant subcultures is a fundamental contribution to the crime literature.

References

Agnew, Robert. 1995. "Strain and Subcultural Theories of Criminality." Pp. 305-327 in *Criminology: A Contemporary Handbook*, 2nd edition, edited by Joseph F. Sheley. Belmont: Wadsworth.

Akers, Ronald L. 1997. *Criminological Theories: Introduction and Evaluation*, 2nd edition. Los Angeles: Roxbury.

. . . When we speak of a delinquent subculture, we speak of a way of life that has somehow become traditional among certain groups in American society. These groups are the boys' gangs that flourish most conspicuously in the "delinquency neighborhoods" of our larger American cities. The members of these gangs grow up, some to become law-abiding citizens and others to graduate to more professional and adult forms of criminality, but the delinquent tradition is kept alive by the age-groups that succeed them. This book is an attempt to answer some important questions about this delinquent subculture. . . .

Why is there such a subculture? Why is it "there" to be "taken over"? Why does it have the particular content that it does and why is it distributed as it is within our social system? Why does it arise and persist, as it does, in such dependable fashion in certain neighborhoods of our American cities? Why does it not "diffuse" to other areas and to other classes of our population. . . .

Action Is Problem-Solving

Our point of departure is the "psychogenic" assumption that all human action—not delinquency alone—is an ongoing series of efforts to solve problems. By "problems" we do not only mean the worries and dilemmas that bring people to the psychiatrist and the psychological clinic. Whether or not to accept a proffered drink, which of two ties to buy, what to do about the unexpected guest or the "F" in algebra are problems too. They all involve, until they are resolved, a certain tension, a disequilibrium and a challenge. We hover between doing and not doing, doing this or doing that, doing it one way or doing it another. Each choice is an act, each act is a choice. Not every act is a *successful* solution, for our choice may leave us with unresolved tensions or generate new and unanticipated consequences which pose new problems, but is at least an attempt at a solution. On the other hand, not every problem need imply distress, anxiety, bedevilment. Most problems are familiar and recurrent and we have at hand for them ready solutions, habitual modes of action which we have found efficacious and acceptable both to ourselves and to our neighbors. Other problems, however, are not so readily resolved. They persist, they nag, and they press for novel solutions. . . .

We seek, if possible, solutions which will settle old problems and not create new ones. A first requirement, then, of a wholly acceptable solution is that it be acceptable to those on whose cooperation and good will we are dependent. This immediately imposes sharp limits on the range of creativity and innovation. Our dependence upon our social milieu provides us with a strong incentive to select our solutions from among those already established and known to be congenial to our fellows. . . .

We see then why, both on the levels of overt action and of the supporting frame of reference, there are powerful incentives not to deviate from the ways established in our groups. Should our problems be not capable of solution in ways acceptable to our groups and should they be sufficiently pressing, we are not so likely to strike out on our own as we are to shop around for a group with a different subculture, with a frame of reference we find more congenial. One fascinating aspect of the social process is the continual realignment of groups, the migration of individuals from one group to another in the unconscious quest for a social milieu favorable to the resolution of their problems of adjustment.

How Subcultural Solutions Arise

Now we confront a dilemma and a paradox. We have seen how difficult it is for the individual to cut loose from the culture models in his milieu, how his dependence upon his fellows compels him to seek conformity and to avoid innovation. But these models and precedents which we call the surrounding culture are ways in which other people think and other people act, and these other people are likewise constrained by models in *their* milieux. *These models themselves, however, continually change.* How is it possible for cultural innovations to emerge while each of the participants in the culture is so powerfully motivated to conform to what is already established? This is the central theoretical problem of this book.

The crucial condition for the emergence of new cultural forms is the existence, *in effective interaction with one another, of a number of actors with similar problems of adjustment.* These may be the entire membership of a group or only certain members, similarly circumstanced, within the group. Among the conceivable solutions to their problems may be one which is not yet embodied in action and which does not therefore exist as a cultural model. This solution, except for the fact that it does not already carry the social criteria of validity and promise the social rewards of consensus, might well answer more neatly to the problems of this group and appeal to its members more effectively than any of the solutions already institutionalized. For each participant, this solution would be adjustive and adequately motivated provided that he could anticipate a simultaneous and corresponding transformation in the frames of reference of his fellows. Each would welcome a sign from the others that a new departure in this direction would receive approval and support. But how does one *know* whether a gesture toward innovation will strike a responsive and sympathetic chord in others or whether it will elicit hostility, ridicule and punishment? *Potential* concurrence is always problematical and innovation or the impulse to innovate a stimulus for anxiety.

The paradox is resolved when the innovation is broached in such a manner as to elicit from others reactions suggesting their receptivity; and when, at the same time, the innovation occurs by increments so small, tentative and ambiguous as to permit the actor to retreat, if the signs be unfavorable, without having become identified with an unpopular position. Perhaps all social actions have, in addition to their instrumental, communicative and expressive functions, this quality of being *exploratory gestures*. For the actor with problems of adjustment which cannot be resolved within the frame of reference of the established culture, each response of the other to what the actor says and does is a clue to the directions in which change may proceed further in a way congenial to the other and to the direction in which change will lack social support. And if the probing gesture is motivated by tensions common to other participants it is likely to initiate a process of *mutual* exploration and *joint* elaboration of a new solution. My exploratory gesture functions as a cue to you; your exploratory gesture as a cue to me. . . .

The final product, to which we are jointly committed, is likely to be a compromise formation of all the participants to what we may call a cultural process, a formation perhaps unanticipated by any of them. . . .

Subcultural Solutions to Status Problems

One variant of this cultural process interests us especially because it provides the model for our explanation of the delinquent subculture. Status problems are problems of achieving respect in the eyes of one's fellows.

Our ability to achieve status depends upon the criteria of status applied by our fellows, that is, the standards or norms they go by in evaluating people. These criteria are an aspect of their cultural frames of reference. If we lack the characteristics or capacities which give status in terms of these criteria, we are beset by one of the most typical and yet distressing of human problems of adjustment. One solution is for individuals who share such problems to gravitate toward one another and jointly to establish new norms, new criteria of status which define as meritorious the characteristics they *do* possess, the kinds of conduct of which they *are* capable. It is clearly necessary for each participant, if the innovation is to solve his status problem, that these new criteria be shared with others, that the solution be a group and not a private solution. If he "goes it alone" he succeeds only in further estranging himself from his fellows. Such new status criteria would represent new subcultural values different from or even antithetical to those of the larger social system. . . .

Insofar as the new subculture represents a new status system sanctioning behavior tabooed or frowned upon by the larger society, the acquisition of status within the new group is accompanied by a loss of status outside the group. To the extent that the esteem of outsiders is a value to the members of the group, a new problem is engendered. To this problem the typical solution is to devalue the good will and respect of those whose good will and respect are forfeit anyway. The new subculture of the community of innovators comes to include hostile and contemptuous images of those groups whose enmity they have earned. Indeed, this repudiation of outsiders, necessary in order to protect oneself from feeling concerned about what they may think, may go so far as to make nonconformity with the expectations of the outsiders a positive criterion of status within the group. Certain kinds of conduct, that is, become reputable precisely because they are disreputable in the eyes of the "out-group. . . ."

In these chapters, in conformity with the model we have proposed, we shall try to demonstrate that certain problems of adjustment tend, in consequence of the structure of

American society, to occur most typically in those role sectors where the delinquent subculture is endemic. Then we shall try to show how the delinquent subculture provides a solution appropriate to those particular problems and to elaboration and perpetuation by social groups. . . .

Growing Up in a Class System

In summary, it may confidently be said that the working-class boy, particularly if his training and values be those we have here defined as working-class, is more likely than his middle-class peers to find himself at the bottom of the status hierarchy whenever he moves in a middle-class world, whether it be of adults or of children. To the degree to which he values middle-class status, either because he values the good opinion of middle-class persons or because he has to some degree internalized middle-class standards himself, he faces a problem of adjustment and is in the market for a "solution.

What the Delinquent Subculture Has to Offer

The delinquent subculture, we suggest, is a way of dealing with the problems of adjustment we have described. These problems are chiefly status problems: certain children are denied status in the respectable society because they cannot meet the criteria of the respectable status system. The delinquent subculture deals with these problems by providing criteria of status which these children *can* meet. . . .

The hallmark of the delinquent subculture is the explicit and wholesale repudiation of middle-class standards and the adoption of their very antithesis. . . .

It is precisely here, we suggest, in the refusal to temporize, that the appeal of the delinquent subculture lies. Let us recall that it is characteristically American, not specifically working-class or middle-class, to measure oneself against the widest possible status universe, to seek status against "all comers," to be "as good as" or "better than" anybody—anybody, that is, within one's own age and sex category. As long as the working-class corner-boy clings to a version, however attenuated and adulterated, of the middle-class culture, he must recognize his inferiority to working-class and middle-class college-boys. The delinquent subculture, on the other hand, permits no ambiguity of the status of the delinquent relative to that of anybody else. In terms of the norms of the delinquent subculture, defined by its negative polarity to the respectable status system, the delinquent's very nonconformity to middle-class standards sets him above the most exemplary college boy.

Another important function of the delinquent subculture is the legitimation of aggression. We surmise that a certain amount of hostility is generated among working-class children against middle-class persons, with their airs of superiority, disdain or condescension and against middle-class norms, which are, in a sense, the cause of their status-frustration. . . .

Discussion Questions

1. How is Cohen's use of strain theory similar to and different from Merton's version of strain theory?

2. Describe the conditions necessary for a deviant subculture to emerge.

3. Describe the major "problem of adjustment" faced by working-class boys.

4. How does the delinquent subculture solve the problem of adjustment described above? ✦

15

Delinquency and Opportunity

Richard A. Cloward
Lloyd E. Ohlin

Like Cohen, Cloward and Ohlin want to explain the origin and content of delinquent gangs or subcultures common among lower-class males in urban areas. They differ from Cohen, however, in arguing that there are three distinct types of delinquent subcultures: criminal subcultures oriented around theft, conflict subcultures oriented around fighting, and retreatist subcultures oriented around drug use. They draw on both Merton and Cohen in explaining the emergence of these subcultures. Drawing on Cohen, they claim that such subcultures represent solutions to "problems of adjustment." Drawing on Merton, they claim that the major problem of adjustment faced by lower-class boys is their inability to obtain monetary success through legitimate channels.

Cloward and Ohlin, however, extend the work of Cohen and Merton in a fundamental way. They argue that the inability to achieve monetary success makes one ripe for delinquency and, if conditions are right, strained individuals may form or join delinquent subcultures. These delinquent subcultures rationalize or justify the delinquency of their members, claiming that such delinquency is a "natural response to a trying situation" (1960: 132). So Cloward and Ohlin draw on strain theory to help explain the development of delinquent subcultures. The inability to achieve monetary success, however, does not determine the particular pattern of delinquency or type of subculture that results. Some individuals respond to strain with theft, others with fighting, and still others with drug use. In the final section of the selection which follows, Cloward and Ohlin describe the factors that influence the content of the delinquent subculture. This discussion focuses on the availability of what Cloward and Ohlin call "illegitimate means."

Cloward and Ohlin's theory has been criticized on a number of points (see Akers, 1997). In particular, data suggest that most gang members do not specialize in fighting or theft or drug use; rather they tend to engage in a broad range of delinquent behavior (although specialization may occur in certain cases—see Covey et al., 1992). At the same time, their work makes a major point regarding the explanation of crime: we must consider the availability of both legitimate and illegitimate opportunities if we want to fully explain crime. The lack of legitimate opportunities may create a general disposition for crime, but the availability of illegitimate opportunities or illegal means determines whether crime will occur and the form that it will take. This crucial point is discussed in detail by Cullen (1984).

References

Akers, Ronald L. 1997. *Criminological Theories: Introduction and Evaluation*, 2nd edition. Los Angeles: Roxbury.

Covey, Herbert C., Scott Menard, and Robert J. Franzese. 1992. *Juvenile Gangs*. Chicago: Thomas.

Cullen, Francis T. 1984. *Rethinking Crime and Deviance: The Emergence of a Structuring Tradition*. Totowa, NJ: Rowman and Allanheld.

This book is about delinquent gangs, or subcultures, as they are typically found among adolescent males in lower-class areas of large urban centers. It is devoted to an exposition of how delinquent subcultures arise, develop various law-violating ways of life, and persist or change. In particular, it is about three more or less distinctive kinds of delinquent subculture. One is what we call the "criminal subculture"—a type of gang which is devoted to theft, extortion, and other illegal means of securing income. A second is the "conflict subculture"—a type of gang in which the manipulation of violence predominates as a way of winning status. The third is the "retreatist subculture"—a type of gang in which the consumption of drugs is stressed. . . .

The Criminal Pattern

The most extensive documentation in the sociological literature of delinquent behavior patterns in lower-class culture describes a tradition which integrates youthful delinquency with adult criminality. In the central value orientation of youths participating in this tradition, delinquent and criminal behavior is accepted as a means of achieving success-goals. The dominant criteria of in-group evaluation stress achievement, the use of skill and knowledge to get results. In this culture, prestige is allocated to those who achieve material gain and power through avenues defined as illegitimate by the larger society. From the very young to the very old, the successful "haul"—which quickly transforms the penniless into a man of means—is an ever-present vision of the possible and desirable. Although one may also achieve material success through the routine practice of theft or fraud, the "big score" remains the symbolic image of quick success.

The Conflict Pattern

The role-model in the conflict pattern of lower-class culture is the "bopper" who swaggers with his gang, fights with weapons to win a wary respect from other gangs, and compels a fearful deference from the conventional adult world by his unpredictable and destructive assaults on persons and property. To other gang members, however, the key qualities of the bopper are those of the successful warrior. His performance must reveal a willingness to defend his personal integrity and the honor of the gang. He must do this with great courage and displays of fearlessness in the face of personal danger.

The immediate aim in the world of fighting gangs is to acquire a reputation for toughness and destructive violence. A "rep" assures not only respectful behavior from peers and threatened adults but also admiration for the physical strength and masculinity which it symbolizes. It represents a way of securing access to the scarce resources for adolescent pleasure and opportunity in underprivileged areas. . . .

The Retreatist Pattern

The dominant feature of the retreatist subculture of the "cat" lies in the continuous pursuit of the "kick." Every cat has a kick—alcohol, marijuana, addicting drugs, unusual sexual experiences, hot jazz, cool jazz, or any combination of these. Whatever its content, the kick is a search for ecstatic experiences. The retreatist strives for an intense awareness of living and a sense of pleasure that is "out of this world." In extreme form, he seeks an almost spiritual and mystical knowledge that is experienced when one comes to know "it" at the height of one's kick. The past and the future recede in the time perspective of the cat, since complete awareness in present experience is the essence of the kick.

The successful cat has a lucrative "hustle" which contrasts sharply with the routine and discipline required in the ordinary occupational tasks of conventional society. The many varieties of the hustle are characterized by a rejection of violence or force and a preference for manipulating, persuading, outwitting, or "conning" others to obtain resources for experiencing the kick. The cat begs, borrows, steals, or engages in some petty con-game. He caters to the illegitimate cravings of others by peddling drugs or working as a pimp. . . .

The Distribution and Evaluation of Delinquent Subcultures

Deviance ordinarily represents a search for solutions to problems of adjustment. . . .

Participation in a delinquent subculture ordinarily entails rather weighty personal and social costs. For an individual to shoulder these costs, he must be faced with a problem of adjustment that threatens activities and investments which are significant in his psychological and social economy. It is not enough, therefore, to show that the delinquent individual experiences a given problem of adjustment; we must also show that the problem has great significance for him.

A problem of adjustment may be more crucial if it is relatively permanent rather than transitory, and if it is so perceived by the actor. If the problem can be resolved by enduring adverse circumstances for a short time, it is probably not so likely to result in a delinquent solution. On the other hand, a problem to which there appears to be no legitimate solution may generate acute pressures for the emergence of a delinquent one. . . .

The pressures that lead to deviant patterns do not necessarily determine the particular pattern of deviance that results. A given problem of adjustment may result in any one of several solutions. In other words, we cannot predict the content of deviance simply from our knowledge of the problem of adjustment to which it is a response. In any situation, alternative responses are always possible. We must therefore explain each solution in its own right, identifying the new variables which arise to direct impulses toward deviance into one pattern rather than another and showing how these variables impinge upon actors in search of a solution to a problem of adjustment. Failure to recognize the need for this task is, as we have noted, a major weakness of many current theories of delinquency. All too often, a theory that explains the origin of a problem of adjustment is erroneously assumed to explain the resulting deviant adaptation as well. . . .

. . . What pressures lead the young to form or join delinquent subcultures? To what problem of adjustment is alienation from conventional styles of life a response? . . .

It is our view that pressures toward the formation of delinquent subcultures originate in marked discrepancies between culturally induced aspirations among lower-class youth and the possibilities of achieving them by legitimate means. . . .

Our hypothesis can be summarized as follows: The disparity between what lower-class youth are led to want and what is actually available to them is the source of a major problem of adjustment. Adolescents who form delinquent subcultures, we suggest, have internalized an emphasis upon conventional goals. Faced with limitations on legitimate avenues of access to these goals, and unable to revise their aspirations downward, they experience intense frustrations; the exploration of nonconformist alternatives may be the result. . . .

The results of several studies tend to confirm the hypothesis that most Americans, whatever their social position, are dissatisfied with their income. There are, however, social-class differences in the degree of dissatisfaction. In general, the poor desire a proportionately larger increase in income than do persons in higher strata. . . .

Thus we may conclude that persons in the lower reaches of society experience a relatively greater sense of position discontent despite the fact that their absolute aspirations are less lofty. . . .

Discrepancies between aspirations and legitimate avenues thus produce intense pressures for the use of illegitimate alternatives. Many lower-class persons, in short, are the victims of a contradiction between the goals toward which they have been led to orient themselves and socially structured means of striving for these goals. Under these conditions, there is an acute pressure to depart from institutional norms and to adopt illegitimate alternatives. . . .

Delinquent subcultures, we believe, represent specialized modes of adaptation to this problem of adjustment. Two of these subcultures—the criminal and the conflict—provide illegal avenues to success-goals. The retreatist subculture consists of a loosely structured group of persons who have withdrawn from competition in the larger society, who anticipate defeat and now seek escape from the burden of failure. We turn now to a discussion of the processes by which these subcultures evolve. . . .

The Process of Alienation

To understand the growth of delinquent subcultures, we must identify more explicitly the social conditions within which this alienation from established norms and acceptance of illegitimate models of behavior occurs. It seems evident that the members of a newly emerging delinquent subculture must pass through a complex process of change in attitudes toward themselves, other persons, and the established social order before such a major shift in allegiance can take place. First, they must be freed from commitment to and belief in the legitimacy of certain aspects of the existing organization of means. They must be led to question the validity of various conventional codes of conduct as an appropriate guide for their own actions before accepting a model of behavior involving forbidden acts. Secondly, they must join with others in seeking a solution to their adjustment problems rather than attempt to solve them alone. Thirdly, they must be provided with appropriate means for handling the problems of guilt and fear which new recruits to this subculture sometimes experience as a result of engaging in acts of deviance. Finally, they must face no obstacles to the possibility of joint problem-solving. . . .

It is our view that the most significant step in the withdrawal of sentiments supporting the legitimacy of conventional norms is the attribution of the cause of failure to the social order rather than to oneself, for the way in which a person explains his failure largely determines what he will do about it. . . .

When a person ascribes his failure to injustice in the social system, he may criticize that system, bend his efforts toward reforming it, or disassociate himself from it—in other words, he may become alienated from the established set of social norms. He may even be convinced that he is justified in evading these norms in his pursuit of success-goals. The individual who locates the source of his failure in his own inadequacy, on the other hand, feels pressure to change himself rather than the system. . . .

Techniques of Defense Against Guilt

A person who places blame for failure on the unjust organization of the established social order and who finds support from others for his withdrawal of legitimacy from official norms may be induced to resort to illegitimate means for achieving success-goals as a stable form of adaptation. Having withdrawn his acceptance of officially approved norms, he is psychologically protected against the guilt feelings that would otherwise result from violation of those norms. Successful communication and sharing of discontent with others who are similarly situated furnishes social support for and lends stability to whatever pattern of deviant conduct develops.

These steps are accompanied by the growth of a supporting structure of beliefs and values that provide advance justifications for deviant conduct. Those who regard the social order as unjust and evaluate themselves as the equal of persons who have been granted access to legitimate opportunities in effect rationalize their deviance before it occurs. Thus they take steps to preserve their sense of personal integrity as they change their allegiance from conforming to prohibited modes of conduct. The emerging deviant subculture acquires a set of beliefs and values which rationalize the shift in norms as a natural response to a trying situation. These beliefs are in the form of descriptions and evaluations of the social world of the delinquent which contradict those held by conforming persons. Armed with these new conceptions of his social situation, the delinquent is able to adhere to the norms of the delinquent subculture with less vulnerability to the invidious definitions of his actions by law-abiding persons. . . .

The Collective Problem-Solving Process

In addition to the motivation to seek support from others who feel alienated from the prevailing social norms, collective solutions require a set of conditions in which communication among alienated persons can take place. If there are serious barriers to communication among the disaffected, the chances for the development of a collective solution will be relatively slight. . . .

Given conditions favorable for the development of a delinquent subculture, there is still the problem of explaining why different types of delinquent subculture develop. We must identify a new set of variables to explain why certain beliefs, values, and prescriptions for action emerge rather than others. It is to this problem that we turn in the next chapter. . . .

Illegitimate Means and Delinquent Subcultures

Much of the criminological literature assumes, for example, that one may explain a criminal act simply by accounting for the individual's readiness to employ illegal alternatives of which his culture, though its norms, has already made him generally aware. Such explanations are quite unsatisfactory, however, for they ignore a host of questions regarding the *relative availability* of illegal alternatives to various potential criminals. The aspiration to be a physician is hardly enough to explain the fact of becoming a physician; there is much that transpires between the aspiration and the achievement. This is no less true of the person who wants to be a successful criminal. Having decided that he "can't make it legitimately," he cannot simply choose among an array of illegitimate means, all equally available to him. As we have noted earlier, it is assumed in the theory of anomie that access to conventional means is differentially distributed, that some individuals, because of their social class, enjoy certain advantages that are denied to those elsewhere in the class structure. For example, there are variations in the degree to which members of various classes are fully exposed to and us acquire the values, knowledge, and skills that facilitate upward mobility. It should not be startling, therefore, to suggest that there are socially structured variations in the availability of illegitimate means as well. In connection with delinquent subcultures, we shall be concerned principally with differentials in access to illegitimate means within the lower class. . . .

We can now look at the individual, not simply in relation to one or the other system of means, but in relation to both legitimate and illegitimate systems. This approach permits us to ask, for example, how the relative availability of illegitimate opportunities affects the resolution of adjustment problems leading to deviant behavior. We believe that the way in which these problems are resolved may depend upon the kind of support for one or another type of illegitimate activity that is given at different points in the social structure. If, in a given social location, illegal or criminal means are not readily available, then we should not expect a criminal subculture to develop among adolescents. By the same logic, we should expect the manipulation of violence to become a primary avenue to higher status only in areas where the means of violence are not denied to the

young. To give a third example, drug addiction and participation in subcultures organized around the consumption of drugs presuppose that persons can secure access to drugs and knowledge about how to use them. In some parts of the social structure, this would be very difficult; in others, very easy, In short, there are marked differences from one part of the social structure to another in the types of illegitimate adaptation that are available to persons in search of solutions to problems of adjustment arising from the restricted availability of legitimate means. In two opportunity structures—one legitimate, the other illegitimate. Given limited access to success-goals by legitimate means, the nature of the delinquent response that may result will vary according to the availability of various illegitimate means. . . .

Illegitimate Opportunities and the Social Structure of the Slum

When we say that the form of delinquency that is adopted is conditioned by the presence or absence of appropriate illegitimate means, we are actually referring to crucial differences in the social organization of various slum areas, for our hypothesis implies that the local milieu affects the delinquent's choice of a solution to his problems of adjustment. One of the principal ways in which slum areas vary is in the extent to which they provide the young with alternative (albeit illegitimate) routes to higher status. . . .

The Criminal Subculture

The criminal subculture, like the conflict and retreatist adaptations, requires a specialized environment if it is to flourish. Among the environmental supports of a criminal style of life are integration of offenders at various age-levels and close integration of the carriers of conventional and illegitimate values. . . .

Nowhere in the criminological literature is the concept of integration between different age-levels of offender made more explicit than in discussions of criminal learning. Most criminologists agree that criminal behavior presupposes patterned sets of relationships through which the requisite values and skills are communicated or transmitted from one age-level to another. . . .

Many accounts in the literature suggest that lower-class adults who have achieved success by illegitimate means not only are highly visible to young people in slum areas but often are willing to establish intimate relationships with these youth. . . .

Learning alone, as we have said, does not ensure that the individual can or will perform the role for which he has been prepared. The social structure must also support the actual performance of the role. . . .

Unless the carriers of criminal and conventional values are closely bound to one another, stable criminal roles cannot develop. The criminal, like the occupant of a conventional role, must establish relationships with other categories of persons, all of whom contribute in one way or another to the successful performance of criminal activity. As Tannenbaum says, "The development of the criminal career requires and finds in the immediate environment other supporting elements in addition to the active 'criminal gangs'; to development of the criminal career requires and finds in the immediate environment other supporting elements in addition to the active 'criminal gangs'; to develop the career requires the support of middlemen. These may be junk men, fences, lawyers, bondsmen, 'backers,' as they are called." The intricate systems of relationship between these legitimate and illegitimate persons constitute the type of environment in which the juvenile criminal subculture can come into being. . . .

The Conflict Subculture

But not all slums are integrated. Some lower-class urban neighborhoods lack unity and cohesiveness. Because the prerequisites for the emergence of stable systems of social relations are not present, a state of social disorganization prevails.

The many forces making for instability in the social organization of some slum areas include high rates of vertical and geographic mobility; massive housing projects in which "site tenants" are not accorded priority in occupancy, so that traditional residents are dispersed and "strangers" re-assembled; and

changing land use, as in the case of residential areas that are encroached upon by the expansion of adjacent commercial or industrial areas. Forces of this kind keep a community off balance, for tentative efforts to develop social organization are quickly checked. Transiency and instability become the overriding features of social life.

Transiency and instability, in combination, produce powerful pressures for violent behavior among the young in these areas. First, an unorganized community cannot provide access to legitimate channels to success-goals, and thus discontent among the young with their life-chances is heightened. Secondly, access to stable criminal opportunity systems is also restricted, for disorganized neighborhoods do not develop integration of different age-levels of offender or integration of carriers of criminal and conventional values. The young, in short, are relatively deprived of *both* conventional and criminal opportunity. Finally, social controls are weak in such communities. These conditions, we believe, lead to the emergence of conflict subcultures. . . .

The Retreatist Subculture

We have noted that there are differentials in access both to illegitimate and to legitimate means; not all of those who seek to attain success-goals by prohibited routes are permitted to proceed. There are probably many lower-class adolescents oriented toward success in the criminal world who fail; similarly, many who would like to acquire proficiency in the use of violence also fail. We might ask, therefore, what the response would be among those faced with failure in the use of *both* legitimate and illegitimate means. We suggest that persons who experience this "double failure" are likely to move into a retreatist pattern of behavior. That is, retreatist behavior may arise as a consequence of limitations on the use of illegitimate means, whether the limitations are internalized prohibitions or socially structured barriers. . . .

Our hypothesis states that adolescents who are double failures are more vulnerable than others to retreatist behavior; it does not imply that *all* double failures will subsequently become retreatists. Some will respond to failure by adopting a law-abiding lower-class style of life—the "corner boy" adaptation. It may be that those who become retreatists are incapable of revising their aspirations downward to correspond to reality. . . .

Discussion Questions

1. How is Cloward and Ohlin's use of strain theory similar to and different from that of Merton and Cohen?

2. What do Cloward and Ohlin mean when they talk about differentials in access both to illegitimate and legitimate means? Why are both legitimate and illegitimate means important in explaining crime?

3. What conditions must be satisfied before strained individuals will form or join a delinquent subculture?

4. What types of communities are most likely to produce criminal subcultures? What types are most likely to produce violent subcultures? What types of individuals are most likely to become involved in retreatist subcultures? ✦

16

Crime and the American Dream

Richard Rosenfeld
Steven F. Messner

Merton's (1938) theory of "Social Structure and Anomie" is in two parts: the first part tries to explain why the United States has such a high rate of crime and the second tries to explain why some groups within the United States are more likely to engage in crime. Until Messner and Rosenfeld (1997) developed their institutional-anomie theory of crime, researchers largely neglected the first part of Merton's theory. Like Merton, Messner and Rosenfeld seek to explain the high rate of crime in the U.S. They draw heavily on Merton's theory, arguing that our high crime rate stems partly from the fact that we encourage everyone to pursue the goal of monetary success, but place little emphasis on the legitimate norms for achieving such success (as they state, "it's not how you play the game; it's whether you win or lose").

They also extend Merton's theory in a fundamental way. They argue that the cultural emphasis on monetary success is paralleled by the fact that the economy dominates the major institutions in our society, including the family, school, and polity. As Rosenfeld and Messner indicate in the following selection, the domination of the economy interferes with the effective functioning of these other institutions. As a result, these institutions are not able to adequately socialize or train individuals and sanction deviance. This further contributes to our high crime rate.

Messner and Rosenfeld's theory is still in the process of being tested (Chamlin and Cochran, 1995), but it is important because it redirects our attention to the explanation of societal differences in crime rates. It also forces us to confront some very difficult issues: are the basic

values and organization of our society responsible for our high crime rate, and if so, what is to be done (see Messner and Rosenfeld, 1997, for a discussion of crime control strategies)?

References

Chamlin, Mitchell B. and John K. Cochran. 1995. "Assessing Messner and Rosenfeld's Institutional Anomie Theory: A Partial Test." *Criminology* 33: 411-429.

Messner, Steven F. and Richard Rosenfeld. 1997. *Crime and the American Dream*, 2nd edition. Belmont: Wadsworth.

... The obsession with crime in the United States cannot be dismissed as an irrational feature of the American character or as a peculiarly American penchant for inventing crime waves or using crime as a stage for enacting other social dramas. Rather, the American obsession with crime is rooted in an objective social reality. Levels of crime in the United States, and more specifically levels of serious crime, are in fact very high in comparative perspective. ...

We maintain that the comparatively high level of serious criminal behavior in the United States is one of the more important facts about crime to be explained by criminological theory (cf. Braithwaite 1989). Curiously, however, criminologists have devoted relatively little attention to this issue for at least two interrelated reasons: the dominance of individual-level perspectives in contemporary criminology and a corresponding deemphasis on serious forms of criminal behavior. Nonetheless, we propose that the foundations for an explanation of the distinctively high levels of crime in the United States can be found in the arguments advanced by Robert Merton in his classic essay "Social Structure and Anomie" (1938, 1968; hereafter SS&A).

Merton proposes that the sources of crime in the United States lie in the same cultural commitments and social arrangements that are conventionally regarded as part of the American success story. High rates of crime are thus not simply the "sick" outcome of individual pathologies, such as defective personalities or aberrant biological structures.

Nor are they the "evil consequence" of individual moral failings. Instead, crime in America derives in significant measure from highly prized cultural and social conditions—indeed, from the American Dream itself.

In this chapter, we offer an explanation of American crime rates that is based on an expanded version of Merton's theory. We amplify the theory in two ways. First, we restore the original macrolevel intent and orientation to SS&A that were removed in the conversion of "anomie theory" into "strain theory." We then extend anomie theory by considering the connections between core elements of the American Dream, which Merton discussed in some detail, and an aspect of social structure to which he devoted little attention: the interrelationships among social institutions. Our basic thesis is that the anomic tendencies inherent in the American Dream both produce and are reproduced by an *institutional balance of power* dominated by the economy. The result of the interplay between the basic cultural commitments of the American Dream and the companion institutional arrangements is widespread anomie, weak social controls, and high levels of crime. . . .

The Anomie Tendencies of the American Dream

In SS&A, Merton advances the provocative argument that there are inherent features of American culture, of the American Dream itself, that ultimately contribute to the high rates of crime and deviance observed in the United States. Although Merton does not provide a formal definition of "the American Dream," it is possible to formulate a reasonably concise characterization of this cultural orientation on the basis of his discussion of American culture in general and his scattered references to the American Dream. The American Dream refers to a commitment to the goal of material success, to be pursued by everyone in society, under conditions of open, individual competition.

Merton proposes that the American Dream has been highly functional for society in certain respects. This cultural ethos is particularly effective in satisfying motivational requirements because it encourages high levels of "ambition" (Merton 1968: 200). At the same time, there is a dark side to the American Dream. It tends to promote an anomic imbalance wherein the importance of using the legitimate means is de-emphasized relative to the importance of attaining the desired cultural goals.

Merton explains that this anomic tendency derives ultimately from the very same basic value commitments upon which the American Dream rests. One such commitment is a strong *achievement orientation*. In American society, personal worth tends to be evaluated on the basis of what people have achieved rather than who they are or how they relate to others in social networks. "Success" is to a large extent the ultimate measure of social worth. Quite understandably, then, there are pervasive cultural pressures to achieve at any cost. A strong achievement orientation, at the level of basic cultural values, thus cultivates and sustains a mentality that "it's not how you play the game; it's whether you win or lose."

A second basic value orientation that contributes to the anomic imbalance in American culture is *individualism*. In the pursuit of success, people are encouraged to "make it" on their own. Fellow members of society are thus competitors in the struggle for achievement and the ultimate validation of personal worth. This intense, individual competition to succeed further encourages a tendency to disregard normative restraints on behavior when these restraints interfere with the realization of goals. Andrew Hacker (1992: 29) offers a cogent description of this distinctive feature of American culture:

> America has always been the most competitive of societies. It poises its citizens against one another, with the warning that they must make it on their own. Hence the stress on moving past others, driven by a fear of failing behind. No other nation so rates its residents as winners or losers.

A third component of American culture that is conducive to anomic imbalance is its *universalism*. Everyone is encouraged to aspire to social ascent, and everyone is susceptible to evaluation on the basis of individual achievements. As a consequence, the pressures to "win" are pervasive; no one is exempt from the pursuit of success (Merton 1968: 200; Orru 1990: 234).

Finally, in American culture, success is signified in a special way: by the accumulation of *monetary rewards*. Merton is keenly aware of the high priority awarded to money in American culture. He observes that "in some large measure, money has been consecrated as a value in itself, over and above its expenditure for articles of consumption or its use for the enhancement of power" (1968: 190). Merton's key point is not that Americans are uniquely materialistic; a strong interest in material well-being can be found in most societies. Rather, the distinctive feature of American culture is the preeminent role of money as the "metric" of success. As Orru puts it, "money is literally, in this context, a *currency* for measuring achievement" (1990: 235).

Merton points to an important implication of the signification of achievement with reference to monetary rewards. Monetary success is inherently open-ended. Because it is always possible in principle to have more money, "in the American Dream there is no final stopping point" (1968: 190). Cultural prescriptions thus mandate "never-ending achievement" (Passas 1990: 159). Relentless pressures to accumulate money, in turn, encourage people to disregard normative restraints when they impede the pursuit of personal goals.

In sum, dominant value patterns of American culture, specifically its achievement orientation, its competitive individualism, its universalism in goal orientations and evaluative standards—when harnessed to the preeminent goal of monetary success—give rise to a distinctive cultural ethos: the American Dream. The American Dream, in turn, encourages members of society to pursue ends, in Merton's words, "limited only by considerations of technical expediency" (1968: 189). One consequence of this open, wide-spread competitive, and anomic quest for success by any means necessary is high levels of crime. . . .

Merton's cultural critique represents only a partial explanation of the high levels of crime in the United States considered in comparative perspective. A complete explanation requires identification of the social structural underpinnings of American culture and its associated strains toward anomie. Merton's analysis stops short of an explication of the ways in which specific features of the institutional structure—beyond the class system—interrelate to generate the anomic pressures that are held to be responsible for crime (cf. Cohen 1985: 233). As a consequence, the anomie perspective is best regarded a "work in progress." In Cohen's words, Merton "has laid the groundwork for an explanation of deviance [and crime] on the sociological level, but the task, for the most part, still lies ahead" (1985: 233).

The Institutional Dynamics of Crime

The Normal Functions of Social Institutions

Social institutions are the building blocks of whole societies. As such, they constitute the fundamental units of macrolevel analysis. Institutions are "relatively stable sets of norms and values, statuses and roles, and groups and organizations" that regulate human conduct to meet the basic needs of a society (Bassis, Gelles, and Levine 1991: 142). These social needs include the need to adapt to the environment, to mobilize and deploy resources for the achievement of collective goals, and to socialize members in the society's fundamental normative patterns.

Adaptation to the environment is the primary responsibility of economic institutions, which organize the production and distribution of goods and services to satisfy the basic material requirements for human existence. The political system, or "polity," mobilizes and distributes power to attain collective goals. One collective purpose of special importance is the maintenance of public safety. Political institutions are responsible for "protecting members of society from invasions from without, controlling crime and disorder within, and providing channels for resolving conflicts of interest" (Bassis, Gelles, and Levine 1991: 142).

The institution of the family has primary responsibility for the maintenance and replacement of members of society. These tasks involve setting the limits of legitimate sexual relations among adults; the physical care and nurturing of children; and the socialization of children into the values, goals, and beliefs of the dominant culture. In addition, a particularly important function of the family in modern societies is to provide emotional support for its members. To a significant degree, the family serves as a refuge from the tensions and stresses generated in other institutional domains. In this idea of the family as a "haven" from the rigors of the public world lies the implicit recognition of the need to counterbalance and temper the harsh, competitive conditions of public life (Lasch 1977).

The institution of education shares many of the socialization functions of the family. Like the family, schools are given responsibility for transmitting basic cultural standards to new generations. In modern industrial societies, schools are also oriented toward the specific task of preparing youth for the demands of adult occupational roles. In addition, education is intended to enhance personal adjustment, facilitate the development of individual human potential, and advance the general "knowledge base" of the culture.

These four social institutions—the economy, polity, family, and education—are the focus of our explanation of crime. They do not, of course, exhaust the institutional structure of modern societies, nor are they the only institutions with relevance to crime. However, the interconnections among these four institutions are central to an institutional analysis of crime in modern societies, in general, and of the exceptionally high levels of crime in the United States, in particular.

Social institutions are to some extent distinct with respect to the primary activities around which they are organized. At the same time, however, the functions of institutions are overlapping and interdependent. For example, the performance of the economy is dependent on the quality of the "human capital" (i.e., the motivations, knowledge, and skills) cultivated in the schools. The capacity of the schools to develop human capital is circumscribed by the individual backgrounds, what Pierre Bourdieu refers to as the "cultural capital," that students bring with them from their families (MacLeod 1987: 11-14). The effective functioning of all three of these institutions—the economy, education, and the family—presupposes an environment with at least a modicum of social order, for which the polity is largely responsible. Finally, the capacity of the polity to promote the collective good depends on the nature and quality of economic and human resources supplied by the other institutions.

The interdependence of major social institutions implies that some coordination and cooperation among institutions is required for societies to "work" at all. The requirements for the effective functioning of any given institution, however, may conflict with the requirements of another. This potential for conflict is illustrated by the particularly stark contrast between the dominant values embodied in two institutions: the economy and the family.

Economic life and family life are supposed to be governed by fundamentally different standards in modern industrial societies. Family relationships are expected to be regulated by the norm of particularism, and positions and roles in the family are allocated, in large measure, on the basis of ascribed characteristics. Each member is entitled to special considerations by virtue of his or her unique identity and position in the family. In contrast, economic relationships, such as transactions in the marketplace, are supposed to entail universalistic orientations, and economic positions are supposed to be filled according to achievement criteria. Persons who occupy the same or functionally equivalent statuses are to be treated similarly, and access to these statuses is supposed to be gained by demonstrating the capacity to successfully perform their duties and responsibilities. There is thus an inevitable tension between the kinds of normative orientations required for the effective functioning of the family and those required for the efficient operation of a market economy.

Any given society will therefore be characterized by a distinctive arrangement of social institutions that reflects a balancing of the sometimes competing claims and requisites of the different institutions, yielding a distinctive institutional balance of power. Further, the nature of the resulting configuration of institutions is itself intimately related to the larger culture. Indeed, our basic premise about social organization is that culture and the institutional balance of power are mutually reinforcing. On the one hand, culture influences the character of institutions and their positions relative to one another. Culture is in a sense "given life" in the institutional structure of society. On the other hand, the patterns of social relationships constituting institutions, which Parsons (1964: 239) terms the "backbone" of the social system, reproduce and sustain cultural commitments. This is, ultimately, where culture "comes from."

In the macrocriminological analysis of a concrete social system, then, the task is to describe the interpenetration of cultural and institutional patterns, to trace the resulting interconnections among institutions that constitute the institutional balance of power, and finally, to show how the institutional balance of power influences levels of crime. In the following sections, we apply this kind of analysis to the relationships among culture, institutional functioning, and crime in the United States.

The American Dream and the Institutional Balance of Power

. . .The core elements of the American Dream—a strong achievement orientation, a commitment to competitive individualism, universalism, and most important, the glorification of material success—have their institutional underpinnings in the economy. The most important feature of the economy of the United States is its capitalist nature. The defining characteristics of any capitalist economy are private ownership and control of property, and free market mechanisms for the production and distribution of goods and services.

These structural arrangements are conducive to, and presuppose, certain cultural orientations. For the economy to operate efficiently, the private owners of property must be profit-oriented and eager to invest, and workers must be willing to exchange their labor for wages. The motivational mechanism underlying these conditions is the promise of financial returns. The internal logic of a capitalist economy thus presumes that an attraction to monetary rewards as a result of achievement in the marketplace is widely diffused throughout the population (cf. Passas 1990: 159).

A capitalist economy is also highly competitive for all those involved, property owners and workers alike. Firms that are unable to adapt to shifting consumer demands or to fluctuations in the business cycle are likely to fail. Workers who are unable to keep up with changing skill requirements or who are unproductive in comparison with others are likely to be fired. This intense competition discourages economic actors from being wedded to conventional ways of doing things and instead encourages them to substitute new techniques for traditional ones if they offer advantages in meeting economic goals. In short, a capitalist economy naturally cultivates a competitive, innovative spirit.

These structural and cultural conditions are common to all capitalist societies. What is distinctive about the United States, however, is the *exaggerated* emphasis on monetary success and the *unrestrained* receptivity to innovation. The goal of monetary success overwhelms other goals and becomes the principal measuring rod for achievements. The resulting proclivity and pressures to innovate resist any regulation that is not justified by purely technical considerations. The obvious question that arises is why cultural orientations that express the inherent logic of capitalism have evolved to a particularly extreme degree in American society. The answer, we submit, lies in the inability of other social institutions to tame economic imperatives. In short, the institutional balance of power is tilted toward the economy. . . .

Capitalism developed in the United States without the institutional restraints found in other societies. As a consequence, the economy assumed an unusual dominance in the institutional structure of society from the very beginning of the nation's history. This economic dominance, we argue, has continued to the present and is manifested in three somewhat different ways: (1) in the *devalu-*

ation of noneconomic institutional functions and roles; (2) in the *accommodation* to economic requirements by other institutions; and (3) in the *penetration* of economic norms into other institutional domains.

Consider the relative devaluation of the distinctive functions of education and of the social roles that fulfill these functions. Education is regarded largely as a means to occupational attainment, which in turn is valued primarily insofar as it promises economic rewards. The acquisition of knowledge and learning for its own sake is not highly valued. Effective performance of the roles involved with education, accordingly, do not confer particularly high status. The "good student" is not looked up to by his or her peers; the "master teacher" receives meager financial rewards and public esteem in comparison with those to be gained by success in business.

Similar processes are observed in the context of the family, although the tendency toward devaluation is perhaps not as pronounced as in other institutional arenas. There is indeed a paradox here because "family values" are typically extolled in public rhetoric. Nevertheless, the lack of appreciation for tasks such as parenting, nurturing, and providing emotional support to others is manifested in actual social relationships. It is the home owner rather than the homemaker who is widely admired and envied—and whose image is reflected in the American Dream. Indeed, perhaps the most telling evidence of the relative devaluation of family functions is the inferior status in our society of those persons most extensively involved in these activities: women.

The relative devaluation of the family in comparison with the economy is not an inevitable consequence of the emergence of a modern, industrial society, whether capitalist or socialist. Adler (1983: 131) points to nations such as Bulgaria, the (then) German Democratic Republic, Japan, Saudi Arabia, and Switzerland to illustrate the possibilities for maintaining a strong commitment to the family despite the profound social changes that accompany the transformation from agriculturally based economies to industrial economies. Each of these countries has made extensive, and sometimes costly, efforts to preserve the vitality of the family. Furthermore, these are precisely the kinds of societies that exhibit low crime rates and are not, in Adler's words, "obsessed with crime."

The distinctive function of the polity, providing for the collective good, also tends to be devalued in comparison with economic functions. The general public has little regard for politics as an intrinsically valuable activity and confers little social honor on the role of the politician. Perhaps as a result, average citizens are not expected to be actively engaged in public service, which is left to the "career" politician. The contrast with economic activity is illuminating. The citizen who refuses to vote may experience mild social disapproval; the "able-bodied" adult who refuses to work is socially degraded. Economic participation is obligatory for most adults. In contrast, even the minimal form of political participation entailed in voting (which has more in common with shopping than with work) is considered discretionary, and useful primarily to the extent that it leads to tangible economic rewards (e.g., lower taxes).

Moreover, the very purpose of government tends to be conceptualized in terms of its capacity to facilitate the individual pursuit of economic prosperity. A good illustration is the advice given to the Democratic ticket in the 1992 presidential campaign by the conservative columnist, George Will. Will chastised liberal Democrats for allegedly becoming preoccupied with issues of rights based on ethnicity and sexuality and advised the Democratic presidential candidates to remember the following point that two popular presidents—Franklin Roosevelt and Ronald Reagan—understood very well: "Americans are happiest when pursuing happiness, happiness understood as material advancement, pursued with government's help but not as a government entitlement" (Will 1992: E5).

Will's advice to liberal Democrats is revealing, not only of the core content of the American Dream and its effect on popular views of government, but of a particular kind of collective "right" to which Americans *are* entitled: the right to consume (cf. Edsall 1992: 7). Both of the major political parties celebrate the right to acquire material possessions;

they differ mainly with respect to the proper degree of governmental involvement in expanding access to the means of consumption. No matter which party is in power, the function of government, at least in the domestic sphere, remains subsidiary to individual economic considerations.

Interestingly, one distinctive function of the polity does not appear to be generally devalued, namely, crime control. There is widespread agreement among the American public that government should undertake vigorous efforts to deal with the crime problem. If anything, Americans want government to do more to control crime. Yet, this apparent exception is quite compatible with the claim of economic dominance. Americans' "obsession" with crime is rooted in fears that crime threatens, according to political analyst Thomas Edsall (1992: 9) "their security, their values, their rights, and their livelihoods and the competitive prospects of their children." In other words, because crime control bears directly on the pursuit of the American Dream, this particular function of the polity receives high priority.

A second way in which the dominance of the economy is manifested is in the *accommodations* that emerge in those situations in which institutional claims are in competition. Economic conditions and requirements typically exert a much stronger influence on the operation of other institutions than vice versa. For example, family routines are dominated by the schedules, rewards, and penalties of the labor market. Consider the resistance of employers (and their representatives in government) to proposals for maternity leaves, flexible hours, or on-the-job child care. The contrast between the United States and another capitalist society with very low crime rates—Japan—is striking in this regard. In Japan, business enterprises are accommodated to the needs of the family, becoming in some respects a "surrogate family," with services ranging from child rearing to burial (Adler 1983: 132).

The most important way that family life is influenced by the economy, however, is through the necessity for paid employment to support a family. Joblessness makes it difficult for families to remain intact and to form in the first place. In the urban underclass, where rates of joblessness are chronically high, so too are rates of separation, divorce, single-parent households, and births to unmarried women (Wilson 1987).

Educational institutions are also more likely to accommodate to the demands of the economy than is the economy to respond to the requirements of education. The timing of schooling reflects occupational demands rather than intrinsic features of the learning process or personal interest in the pursuit of knowledge. People go to school largely to prepare for "good" jobs, and once in the labor market, there is little opportunity to pursue further education for its own sake. When workers do return to school, it is almost always to upgrade skills or credentials to keep pace with job demands, to seek higher paying jobs, or to "retool" during spells of unemployment. At the organizational level, schools are dependent on the economy for financial resources, and thus it becomes important for school officials to convince business leaders that education is suitably responsive to business needs.

The polity likewise is dependent on the economy for financial support. Governments must accordingly take care to cultivate and maintain an environment hospitable to investment. If they do not, they run the risk of being literally "downgraded" by financial markets, as happened to Detroit in 1992 when Moody's Investors Service dropped the city's credit rating to noninvestment grade. Cities have little choice but to accommodate to market demands in such situations. "A city proposes, Moody's disposes. There is no appeals court or court of last ratings resort" (*New York Times*, 1992: C1). The pursuit of the collective good is thus circumscribed by economic imperatives.

A final way in which the dominance of the economy in the institutional balance of power is manifested is in the *penetration* of economic norms into other institutional areas. Schools rely on grading as a system of extrinsic rewards, like wages, to insure compliance with goals. Learning takes place within the context of individualized competition for these external rewards, and teaching inevitably tends to become oriented toward testing. Economic terminology permeates the very language of education, as in the recent emphasis in higher education on "accountability" conceptualized in terms of the "value-added" to students in the educational production process.

Within the polity, a "bottom-line" mentality develops. Effective politicians are those who deliver the goods. Moreover, the notion that the government would work better if it were run more like a business continues to be an article of faith among large segments of the American public.

The family has probably been most resistant to the intrusion of economic norms. Yet even here, pressures toward penetration are apparent. Contributions to family life tend to be measured against the all-important "breadwinner" role, which has been extended to include women who work in the paid labor force. No corresponding movement of men into the role of "homemaker" has occurred, and a declining number of women desire or can afford to occupy this role on a full-time basis. Here again, shifts in popular terminology are instructive. Husbands and wives are "partners" who "manage" the household "division of labor." We can detect no comparable shifts in kin-based terminology, or primary group norms, from the family to the workplace.

In sum, the social organization of the United States is characterized by a striking dominance of the economy in the institutional balance of power. As a result of this economic dominance, the inherent tendencies of a capitalist economy to orient the members of society toward an unrestrained pursuit of economic achievements are developed to an extreme degree. These tendencies are expressed at the cultural level in the preeminence of monetary success as the overriding goal—the American Dream—and in the relative deemphasis placed on the importance of using normative means to reach this goal—anomie. The anomic nature of the American Dream and the institutional structure of American society are thus mutually supportive and reinforcing. The key remaining question is the impact of this type of social organization on crime.

Anomie, Weak Social Controls, and Crime

The American Dream contributes to high levels of crime in two important ways, one direct and the other indirect. It has a direct effect on crime through the creation of an anomic normative order, that is, an environment in which social norms are unable to exert a strong regulatory force on the members of society. It has an indirect effect on crime by contributing to an institutional balance of power that inhibits the development of strong mechanisms of external social control. The criminogenic tendencies of the American Dream are thus due in part to the distinctive content of the cultural values and beliefs that comprise it and in part to the institutional consequences of these values and beliefs.

One criminogenic aspect of the specific content of the American Dream is the expression of the primary success goal in monetary terms. Because monetary success is an inherently open-ended and elusive, the adequacy of the legitimate means for achieving this particular cultural goal is necessarily suspect. No matter how much money someone is able to make by staying within legal boundaries, illegal means will always offer further advantages in pursuit of the ultimate goal. There is thus a perpetual attractiveness associated with illegal activity that is an inevitable corollary of the goal of monetary success.

This culturally induced pressure to "innovate" by using illegitimate means is exacerbated by the dominance of the economy in the institutional balance of power. There are, of course, important noneconomic tasks carried out in other institutional arenas, tasks associated with goals that might in fact be readily attainable within the confines of the legal order. However, as we have suggested, roles effectively performed in the capacity of being a parent or spouse, a student or scholar, an engaged citizen or public servant are simply not the primary bases upon which success and failure are defined in American society. The dominance of the economy continuously erodes the structural supports for functional alternatives to the goal of economic success.

Nor does the ethos of the American Dream contain within it strong counterbalancing injunctions against substituting more effective illegitimate means for less effective legitimate means. To the contrary, the distinctive cultural "value" accompanying the monetary success goal in the American Dream is the *devaluation* of all but the most technically efficient means.

The American Dream does not completely subsume culture. There are other elements of culture that define socially acceptable modes of behavior and that affirm the legitimacy of social norms, including legal norms. In principle, these other cultural elements could counterbalance the anomic pressures that emanate from the American Dream. However, the very same institutional dynamics that contribute to the pressures to innovate in the pursuit of economic goals also make it less likely that the anomic pressures inherent in the American Dream will in fact be counterbalanced by other social forces.

As noneconomic institutions are relatively devalued, are forced to accommodate to economic needs, and are penetrated by economic standards, they are less able to fulfill their distinctive functions effectively. These functions include socialization into acceptance of the social norms. Weak families and poor schools are handicapped in their efforts to promote allegiance to social rules, including legal prohibitions. As a result, the pressures to disregard normative constraints in the pursuit of the goal of monetary success also tend to undermine social norms more generally. In the absence of the cultivation of strong commitments to social norms, the selection of the means for realizing goals *of any type* is guided mainly by instrumental considerations.

In addition, the relative impotence of noneconomic institutions is manifested in a reduced capacity to exert external social control. The government is constrained in its capacity to provide public goods that would make crime less attractive and in its efforts to mobilize collective resources—including moral resources—to effectively deter criminal choices. Single-parent families or those in which both parents have full-time jobs, all else equal, are less able to provide extensive supervision over children. All families must rely to some extent on other institutions, usually the schools, for assistance in social control. Yet poorly funded or crowded schools also find it difficult to exert effective supervision, especially when students see little or no connection between what is taught in the classroom and what is valued outside of it.

Finally, weak institutions invite challenge. Under conditions of extreme competitive individualism, people actively resist institutional control. They not only fall from the insecure grasp of powerless institutions, sometimes they deliberately, even proudly, push themselves away. The problem of "external" social control, then, is inseparable from the problem of the "internal" regulatory force of social norms, or anomie. Anomic societies will inevitably find it difficult and costly to exert social control over the behavior of people who feel free to use whatever means that prove most effective in reaching personal goals. Hence the very sociocultural dynamics that make American institutions weak also enable and entitle Americans to defy institutional controls. If Americans are exceptionally resistant to social control—and therefore exceptionally vulnerable to criminal temptations—it is because they live in a society that enshrines the unfettered pursuit of individual material success above all other values. In the United States, anomie is a virtue.

Conclusion

This reformulation of Merton's classic theory of social structure and anomie is intended to challenge criminologists and policymakers alike to think about crime in America as a macrolevel product of widely admired cultural and social structures with deep historical roots. Criminological theories that neglect the ironic interdependence between crime and the normal functioning of the American social system will be unable to explain the preoccupation with crime that so dramatically separates the United States from other developed societies. Significant reductions in crime will not result from reforms limited to the criminal justice system, which is itself shaped in important ways by the same cultural and social forces—the same desperate emphasis on ends over means—that produce high rates of crime. Nor will social reforms, whatever their other merits, that widen access to legitimate opportunities for persons "locked out" of the American Dream bring relief from the crimes of those who are "locked in" the American Dream, exposed to its limitless imperatives in the absence of moderating social forces. Reducing these crimes will require fundamental social transformations that few Americans desire, and a rethinking of a dream that is the envy of the world.

Reprinted from Richard Rosenfeld and Steven F. Messner, "Crime and the American Dream" in *The Legacy of Anomie Theory*, vol. 6. Copyright ©1995 by Transaction Publishers. Reprinted by permission of Transaction Publishers.

Discussion Questions

1. What are the core features of the American Dream? Do you agree with Rosenfeld and Messner's characterization of the American Dream?

2. Describe *how* the dominance of the economy interferes with the effective functioning of other institutions (family, school, polity) in the United States.

3. What policy recommendations would Rosenfeld and Messner make for controlling crime? Would they recommend increasing the opportunities for monetary success, as do many strain theorists?

4. Rosenfeld and Messner argue that the American Dream and the dominance of the economy promote crime by reducing social control (see Part V). Do you think that the American Dream and the dominance of the economy also promote the types of strain described by Merton and Agnew? ✦

17

A General Strain Theory of Crime and Delinquency

Robert Agnew

According to Merton (1938) and most subsequent strain theories, crime results from the inability to achieve monetary success or other positively valued goals through legitimate channels. This goal blockage creates strain or frustration in the individual, which increases the likelihood of a criminal response. Whether individuals respond to strain with crime is said to depend on several factors, such as the level of social control and whether the individual associates with criminal others. Evidence for this version of strain theory is mixed and, partly as a consequence, strain theory no longer occupies the dominant position that it once did (see Agnew, 1995; Akers, 1997; Burton and Cullen, 1992).

Agnew presents a new, much broader version of strain theory in the following selection. In the first part of the selection, Agnew argues that the failure to achieve positively valued goals is only one of several possible sources of strain or frustration/anger. Agnew then lists three major sources of strain, with the first type having several subtypes. In particular, Agnew tries to describe all those types of situations that may anger or frustrate individuals. In the second part of the selection, Agnew examines those factors that influence whether individuals respond to strain with crime. Like other strain theorists, Agnew recognizes that only some individuals respond to strain with crime. It is therefore important to describe those factors that influence the response to strain.

Agnew's strain theory, then, points to several sources of strain that have not been seriously considered in the crime literature and to a range of factors that may condition the reac-

tion to strain. The few tests of general strain theory that have been conducted are promising, although more research is needed to better determine (1) what types of strain are most strongly related to crime in different groups, and (2) what factors most strongly influence the response to strain (see Agnew and White, 1992; Hagan and McCarthy, 1997; Hoffman and Su, forthcoming; Paternoster and Mazerolle, 1994).

References

Agnew, Robert. 1995. "Strain and Subcultural Theories of Criminality." Pp. 305-327 in *Criminology: A Contemporary Handbook*, 2nd edition, edited by Joseph F. Sheley. Belmont: Wadsworth.

Agnew, Robert and Helene Raskin White. 1992. "An Empirical Test of General Strain Theory." *Criminology* 30:475-499.

Akers, Ronald L. 1997. *Criminological Theories: Introduction and Evaluation*, 2nd edition. Los Angeles: Roxbury.

Burton, Velmer S., Jr. and Francis T. Cullen. 1992. "The Empirical Status of Strain Theory." *Journal of Crime and Justice* 15: 1-30.

Hagan, John and Bill McCarthy. 1997. *Mean Streets*. New York: Cambridge University Press.

Hoffman, John P. and S. Susan Su. Forthcoming. "The Conditional Effects of Negative Life Events on Delinquency and Drug Use: A Strain Theory Assessment of Gender Differences." *Journal of Research in Crime and Delinquency*.

Paternoster, Raymond and Paul Mazerolle. 1994. "General Strain Theory and Delinquency: A Replication and Extension." *Journal of Research in Crime and Delinquency* 31: 235-263.

. . . Strain theory is distinguished by its focus on negative relationships with others and its insistence that such relationships lead to delinquency through the negative affect—especially anger—they sometimes engender. . . .

The Major Types of Strain

Negative relationships with others are, quite simply, relationships in which others are not treating the individual as he or she would like to be treated. The classic strain theories of Merton (1938), A. Cohen (1955), and Cloward and Ohlin (1960) focus on only one type of negative relationship: relationships in which others prevent the individual from achieving positively valued goals. In particular, they focus, on the goal blockage experienced by lower-class individuals trying to achieve monetary success or middle-class status. More recent versions of strain theory have argued that adolescents are not only concerned about the future goals of monetary success/middle-class status, but are also concerned about the achievement of more immediate goals such as good grades, popularity with the opposite sex, and doing well in athletics (Agnew, 1984; Elliott and Voss, 1974; Elliott et al., 1985; Empey, 1982; Greenberg, 1977; Quicker, 1974). The focus, however, is still on the achievement of positively valued goals. Most recently, Agnew (1985a) has argued that strain may result not only from the failure to achieve positively valued goals, but also from the inability to escape legally from painful situations. If one draws on the above theories—as well as the stress, equity/justice, and aggression literatures— one can begin to develop a more complete classification of the types of strain.

Three major types of strain are described—each referring to a different type of negative relationship with others. Other individuals may (1) prevent one from achieving positively valued goals, (2) remove or threaten to remove positively valued stimuli that one possesses, or (3) present or threaten to present one with noxious or negatively valued stimuli. These categories of strain are presented as ideal types. There is no expectation, for example, that a factor analysis of strainful events will reproduce these categories. These categories, rather, are presented so as to ensure that the full range of strainful events are considered in empirical research.

Strain as the Failure to Achieve Positively Valued Goals

At least three types of strain fall under this category. The first type encompasses most of the major strain theories in criminology, including the classic strain theories of Merton, A. Cohen, and Cloward and Ohlin, as well as those modern strain theories focusing on the achievement of immediate goals. The other two types of strain in this category are derived from the justice/equity literature and have not been examined in criminology.

Strain as the Disjunction Between Aspirations and Expectations/Actual Achievements. The classic strain theories of Merton, A. Cohen, and Cloward and Ohlin argue that the cultural system encourages everyone to pursue the ideal goals of monetary success and/or middle-class status. Lower-class individuals, however, are often prevented from achieving such goals through legitimate channels. In line with such theories, adolescent strain is typically measured in terms of the disjunction between *aspirations* (or ideal goals) and *expectations* (or expected levels of goal achievement). These theories, however, have been criticized for several reasons (see Agnew, 1986, 1991b; Clinard, 1964; Hirschi, 1969; Kornhauser, 1978; Liska, 1987; also see Bernard, 1984; Famworth and Leiber, 1989). Among other things, it has been charged that these theories (1) are unable to explain the extensive nature of middle-class delinquency, (2) neglect goals other than monetary success/middle-class status, (3) neglect barriers to goal achievement other than social class, and (4) do not fully specify why only some strained individuals turn to delinquency. The most damaging criticism, however, stems from the limited empirical support provided by studies focusing on the disjunction between aspirations and expectations (see Kornhauser, 1978, as well the arguments of Bernard, 1984;. Elliott et al., 1985; and Jensen, 1986).

As a consequence of these criticisms, several researchers have revised the above theories. The most popular revision argues that there is a youth subculture that emphasizes a variety of immediate goals. The achievement of these goals is further said to depend on a variety of factors besides social class: factors such as intelligence, physical attractiveness, personality, and athletic ability. As a result, many middle-class individuals find that they lack the traits or skills necessary to achieve their goals through legitimate channels. This version of strain theory, however, continues to argue that strain stems from the inability to achieve certain ideal goals emphasized by the (sub)cultural system. As a consequence, strain continues to be measured in terms of the disjunction between *aspirations* and actual achievements (since we are dealing with immediate rather than future goals, actual achievements rather than expected achievements may be examined).

It should be noted that empirical support for this revised version of strain theory is also weak (see Agnew, 1991b, for a summary). At a later point, several possible reasons for the weak empirical support of strain theories focusing on the disjunction between aspirations and expectations/achievements will be discussed. For now, the focus is on classifying the major types of strain.

Strain as the Disjunction Between Expectations and Actual Achievements. As indicated above, strain theories in criminology focus on the inability to achieve ideal goals derived from the cultural system. This approach stands in contrast to certain of the research on justice in social psychology. Here the focus is on the disjunction between *expectations* and *actual achievements* (rewards), and it is commonly argued that such expectations are existentially based. In particular, it has been argued that such expectations derive from the individual's past experience and/or from comparisons with referential (or generalized) others who are similar to the individual (see Berger et al., 1972, 1983; Blau, 1964; Homans, 1961; Jasso and Rossi, 1977; Mickelson, 1990; Ross et al., 1971; Thibaut and Kelley, 1959). Much of the research in this area has focused on income expectations, although the above theories apply to expectations regarding all manner of positive stimuli. The justice literature argues that the failure to achieve such expectations may lead to such emotions as anger, resentment, rage, dissatisfaction, disappointment, and unhappiness—that is, all the emotions customarily associated with strain in criminology. Further, it is argued that individuals will be strongly motivated to reduce the gap between expectations and achievements—with deviance being commonly mentioned as one possible option. This literature has not devoted much empirical research to deviance, although limited data suggest that the expecta-

tions-achievement gap is related to anger/hostility (Ross et al, 1971).

This alternative conception of strain has been largely neglected in criminology. This is unfortunate because it has the potential to overcome certain of the problems of current strain theories. First, one would expect the disjunction between expectations and actual achievements to be more emotionally distressing than that between aspirations and achievements. Aspirations, by definition, are *ideal* goals. They have something of the utopian in them, and for that reason, the failure to achieve aspirations may not be taken seriously. The failure to achieve expected goals, however, is likely to be taken seriously since such goals are rooted in reality—the individual has previously experienced such goals or has seen similar others experience such goals. Second, this alternative conception of strain assigns a central role to the social comparison process. As A. Cohen (1965) argued in a follow-up to his strain theory, the neglect of social comparison is a major shortcoming of strain theory. The above theories describe one way in which social comparison is important: Social comparison plays a central role in the formation of individual goals (expectations in this case; also see Suls, 1977). Third, the assumption that goals are culturally based has sometimes proved problematic for strain theory (see Kornhauser, 1978). Among other things, it makes it difficult to integrate strain theory with social control and cultural deviance theory (see Hirschi, 1979). These latter theories assume that the individual is weakly tied to the cultural system or tied to alternative/oppositional subcultures. The argument that goals are existentially based, however, paves the way for integrations involving strain theory.

Strain as the Disjunction Between Just/Fair Outcomes and Actual Outcomes. The above models of strain assume that individual goals focus on the achievement of specific outcomes. Individual goals, for example, focus on the achievement of a certain amount of money or a certain grade-point average. A third conception of strain, also derived from the justice/equity literature, makes a rather different argument. It claims that individuals do not necessarily enter interactions with specific outcomes in mind. Rather, they enter interactions expecting that certain distributive justice rules will be followed, rules specifying how resources should be allocated. The rule that has received the most attention in the literature is that of equity. An equitable relationship is one in which the outcome/input ratios of the actors involved in an exchange/allocation relationship are equivalent (see Adams, 1963, 1965; Cook and Hegtvedt, 1983; Walster et al., 1978). Outcomes encompass a broad range of positive and negative consequences, while inputs encompass the individual's positive and negative contributions to the exchange. Individuals in a relationship will compare the ratio of their outcomes and inputs to the ratio(s) of specific others in the relationship. If the ratios are equal to one another, they feel that the outcomes are fair or just. This is true, according to equity theorists, even if the outcomes are low. If outcome/input ratios are not equal, actors will feel that the outcomes are unjust and they will experience distress as a result. Such distress is especially likely when individuals feel they have been underrewarded rather than overrewarded (Hegtvedt, 1990).

The equity literature has described the possible reactions to this distress, some of which involve deviance (see Adams, 1963, 1965; Austin, 1977; Walster et al., 1973, 1978; see Stephenson and White, 1968, for an attempt to recast A. Cohen's strain theory in terms of equity theory). In particular, inequity may lead to delinquency for several reasons—all having to do with the restoration of equity. Individuals in inequitable relationships may engage in delinquency in order to (1) increase their outcomes (e.g., by theft); (2) lower their inputs (e.g., truancy from school); (3) lower the outcomes of others (e.g., vandalism, theft, assault); and/or (4) increase the inputs of others (e.g., by being incorrigible or disorderly). In highly inequitable situations, individuals may leave the field (e.g., run away from home) or force others to leave the field. There has not been any empirical research on the relationship between equity and delinquency, although much data suggest that inequity leads to anger and frustration. A few studies also suggest that insulting and vengeful behaviors may result from inequity (see Cook and Hegtvedt, 1991; Donnerstein and Hatfield, 1982; Hegtvedt, 1990; Mikula, 1986; Sprecher, 1986; Walster et al., 1973, 1978).

It is not difficult to measure equity. Walster et al. (1978:234-242) provide the most complete guide to measurement. Sprecher (1986) illustrates how equity may be measured in social surveys; respondents are asked who contributes more to a particular relationship and/or who "gets the best deal" out of a relationship. A still simpler strategy might be to ask respondents how fair or just their interactions with others, such as parents or teachers, are. One would then predict that those involved in unfair relations will be more likely to engage in current and future delinquency.

The literature on equity builds on the strain theory literature in criminology in several ways. First, all of the strain literature assumes that individuals are pursuing some specific outcome, such as a certain amount of money or prestige. The equity literature points out that individuals do not necessarily enter into interactions with specific outcomes in mind, but rather with the expectation that a particular distributive justice rule will be followed. Their goal is that the interaction conform to the justice principle. This perspective, then, points to a new source of strain not considered in the criminology literature. Second, the strain literature in criminology focuses largely on the individual's outcomes. Individuals are assumed to be pursuing a specific goal, and strain is judged in terms of the disjunction between the goal and the actual outcome. The equity literature suggests that this may be an oversimplified conception and that the individual's *inputs* may also have to be considered. In particular, an equity theorist would argue that inputs will condition the individual's evaluation of outcomes. That is, individuals who view their inputs as limited will be more likely to accept limited outcomes as fair. Third, the equity literature also highlights the importance of the social comparison process. In particular, the equity literature stresses that one's evaluation of outcomes is at least partly a function of the outcomes (and inputs) of those with whom one is involved in exchange/allocation relations. A given outcome, then, may be evaluated as fair or unfair depending on the outcomes (and inputs) of others in the exchange/allocation relation.

Summary: Strain as the Failure to Achieve Positively Valued Goals. Three types of strain in this category have been listed: strain as the disjunction between (1) aspirations and expectations/actual achievements, (2) expectations and actual achievements, and (3) just/fair outcomes and actual outcomes. Strain theory in criminology has focused on the first type of strain, arguing that it is most responsible for the delinquency in our society. Major research traditions in the justice/equity field, however, argue that anger and frustration derive primarily from the second two types of strain. To complicate matters further, one can list still additional types of strain in this category. Certain of the literature, for example, has talked of the disjunction between "satisfying outcomes" and reality, between "deserved" outcomes and reality, and between "tolerance levels" or minimally acceptable outcomes and reality. No study has examined all of these types of goals, but taken as a whole the data do suggest that there are often differences among aspirations (ideal outcomes), expectations (expected outcomes), "satisfying" outcomes, "deserved" outcomes, fair or just outcomes, and tolerance levels (Delia Fave, 1974; Delia Fave and Klobus, 1976; Martin, 1986; Martin and Murray, 1983; Messick and Sentis, 1983; Shepelak and Alwin, 1986). This paper has focused on the three types of strain listed above largely because they dominate the current literature.

Given these multiple sources of strain, one might ask which is the most relevant to the explanation of delinquency. This is a difficult question to answer given current research. The most fruitful strategy at the present time may be to assume that all of the above sources are relevant—that there are several sources of frustration. Alwin (1987), Austin (1977), Crosby and Gonzalez-Intal (1984), Hegtvedt (1991b), Messick and Sentis (1983), and Tomblum (1977) all argue or imply that people often employ a variety of standards to evaluate their situation. Strain theorists, then, might be best advised to employ measures that tap all of the above types of strain. One might, for example, focus on a broad range of positively valued goals and, for each goal, ask adolescents whether they are achieving their ideal outcomes (aspirations), expected outcomes, and just/fair outcomes. One would expect strain to be greatest when several standards were not being met, with perhaps greatest weight being given to expectations and just/fair outcomes.

Strain as the Removal of Positively Valued Stimuli From the Individual

The psychological literature on aggression and the stress literature suggest that strain may involve more than the pursuit of positively valued goals. Certain of the aggression literature, in fact, has come to de-emphasize the pursuit of positively valued goals, pointing out that the blockage of goal-seeking behavior is a relatively weak predictor of aggression, particularly when the goal has never been experienced before (Bandura, 1973; Zillman, 1979). The stress literature has largely neglected the pursuit of positively valued goals as a source of stress. Rather, if one looks at the stressful life events examined in this literature, one finds a focus on (1) events involving the loss of positively valued stimuli and (2) events involving the presentation of noxious or negative stimuli (see Pearlin, 1983, for other typologies of stressful life events/ conditions). So, for example, one recent study of adolescent stress employs a life-events list that focuses on such items as the loss of a boyfriend/girlfriend, the death or serious illness of a friend, moving to a new school district, the divorce/separation of one's parents, suspension from school, and the presence of a variety of adverse conditions at work (see Williams and Uchiyama, 1989, for an overview of life-events scales for adolescents; see Compas, 1987, and Compas and Phares, 1991, for overviews of research on adolescent stress).

Drawing on the stress literature, then, one may state that a second type of strain or negative relationship involves the actual or anticipated removal (loss) of positively valued stimuli from the individual. As indicated above, numerous examples of such loss can be found in the inventories of stressful life events. The actual or anticipated loss of positively valued stimuli may lead to delinquency as the individual tries to prevent the loss of the positive stimuli, retrieve the lost stimuli or obtain substitute stimuli, seek revenge against those responsible for the loss, or manage the negative affect caused by the loss by taking illicit drugs. While there are no data bearing directly on this type of strain, experimental data indicate that aggression often occurs when positive reinforcement previously administered to an individual is withheld or reduced (Bandura, 1973; Van Houten, 1983). And as discussed below, inventories of stressful life events, which include the loss of positive stimuli, are related to delinquency.

Strain as the Presentation of Negative Stimuli

The literature on stress and the recent psychological literature on aggression also focus on the actual or anticipated presentation of negative or noxious stimuli. Except for the work of Agnew (1985a), however, this category of strain has been neglected in criminology. And even Agnew does not focus on the presentation of noxious stimuli per se, but on the inability of adolescents to escape legally from noxious stimuli. Much data, however, suggest that the presentation of noxious stimuli may lead to aggression and other negative outcomes in certain conditions, even when legal escape from such stimuli is possible (Bandura, 1973; Zillman, 1979). Noxious stimuli may lead to delinquency as the adolescent tries to (1) escape from or avoid the negative stimuli; (2) terminate or alleviate the negative stimuli; (3) seek revenge against the source of the negative stimuli or related targets, although the evidence on displaced aggression is somewhat mixed (see Berkowitz, 1982; Bernard, 1990; Van Houten, 1983; Zillman, 1979); and/or (4) manage the resultant negative affect by taking illicit drugs.

A wide range of noxious stimuli have been examined in the literature, and experimental, survey, and participant observation studies have linked such stimuli to both general and specific measures of delinquency—with the experimental studies focusing on aggression. Delinquency/aggression, in particular, has been linked to such noxious stimuli as child abuse and neglect (Rivera and Widom, 1990), criminal victimization (Lauritsen et al., 1991), physical punishment (Straus, 1991), negative relations with parents (Healy and Bonner, 1969), negative relations with peers (Short and Strodtbeck, 1965), adverse or negative school experiences (Hawkins and Lishner, 1987), a wide range of stressful life events (Gersten et al., 1974; Kaplan et al., 1983; Linsky and Straus, 1986; Mawson, 1987; Novy and Donohue, 1985; Vaux and Ruggiero, 1983), verbal threats and insults, physical pain, unpleasant odors, disgusting scenes, noise, heat, air pollution, personal space violations, and high density (see Anderson and Anderson, 1984; Bandura, 1973, 1983; Berkowitz, 1982, 1986; Mueller, 1983). In one of the few studies in criminology to focus specifically on the presentation of negative stimuli, Agnew (1985a) found that delinquency was related to three scales measuring negative relations at home and school. The effect of the scales on delinquency was partially mediated through a measure of anger, and the effect held when measures of social control and deviant beliefs were controlled. And in a recent study employing longitudinal data, Agnew (1989) found evidence suggesting that the relationship between negative stimuli and delinquency was due to the *causal* effect of the negative stimuli on delinquency (rather than the effect of delinquency on the negative stimuli). Much evidence, then, suggests that the presentation of negative or noxious stimuli constitutes a third major source of strain.

Certain of the negative stimuli listed above, such as physical pain, heat, noise, and pollution, may be experienced as noxious largely for biological reasons (i.e., they may be unconditioned negative stimuli). Others may be conditioned negative stimuli, experienced as noxious largely because of their association with unconditioned negative stimuli (see Berkowitz, 1982). Whatever the case, it is assumed that such stimuli are experienced as noxious regardless of the goals that the individual is pursuing.

The Links Between Strain and Delinquency

Three sources of strain have been presented: strain as the actual or anticipated failure to achieve positively valued goals, strain as the actual or anticipated removal of positively valued stimuli, and strain as the actual or anticipated presentation of negative stimuli. While these types are theoretically distinct from one another, they may sometimes overlap in practice. So, for example, the insults of a teacher may be experienced as adverse because they (1) interfere with the adolescent's aspirations for academic success, (2) result in the violation of a distributive justice rule such as equity, and (3) are conditioned negative stimuli and so are experienced as noxious in and of themselves. Other examples of overlap can be given, and it may sometimes be difficult to disentangle the different types of strain in practice. Once again, however, these categories are ideal types and are presented only to ensure that all events with the potential for creating strain are considered in empirical research.

Each type of strain increases the likelihood that individuals will experience one or more of a range of negative emotions. Those emotions include disappointment, depression, and fear. Anger, however, is the most critical emotional reaction for the purposes of the general strain theory. Anger results when individuals blame their adversity on others, and anger is a key emotion because it increases the individual's level of felt injury, creates a desire for retaliation/revenge, energizes the individual for action, and lowers inhibitions, in part because individuals believe that others will feel their aggression is justified (see Averill, 1982; Berkowitz, 1982; Kemper, 1978; Kluegel and Smith, 1986: Ch. 10; Zillman, 1979). Anger, then, affects the individual in several ways that are conducive to delinquency. Anger is distinct from many of the other types of negative affect in this respect, and this is the reason that anger occupies a special place in the general strain theory. It is important to note, however, that delinquency may still occur in response to other types of negative affect—such as despair, although delinquency is less likely in such cases. The experience of negative affect, especially anger, typically creates a desire to take corrective steps, with delinquency being one possible response. Delinquency may be a method for alleviating strain, that is, for achieving positively valued goals, for protecting or retrieving positive stimuli, or for terminating or escaping from negative stimuli. Delinquency may be used to seek revenge; data suggest that vengeful behavior often occurs even when there is no possibility of eliminating the adversity that stimulated it (Berkowitz, 1982). And delinquency may occur as adolescents try to manage their negative affect through illicit drug use (see Newcomb and Harlow, 1986). The general strain theory, then, has the potential to explain a broad range of delinquency, including theft, aggression, and drug use.

Each type of strain may create a *predisposition* for delinquency or function as a *situational event* that instigates a particular delinquent act. In the words of Hirschi and Gottredson (1986), then, the strain theory presented in this paper is a theory of both "criminality" and "crime" (or to use the words of Clarke and Cornish [1985], it is a theory of both "criminal involvement" and "criminal events"). Strain creates a predisposition for delinquency in those cases in which it is chronic or repetitive. Examples include a continuing gap between expectations and achievements and a continuing pattern of ridicule and insults from teachers. Adolescents subject to such strain are predisposed to delinquency because (1) nondelinquent strategies for coping with strain are likely to be taxed; (2) the threshold for adversity may be lowered by chronic strains (see Averill, 1982:289); (3) repeated or chronic strain may lead to a hostile attitude—general dislike and suspicion of others and an associated tendency to respond in an aggressive manner (see Edmunds and Kendrick, 1980:21); and (4) chronic strains increase the likelihood that individuals will be high in negative affect/arousal at any given time (see Bandura, 1983; Bernard, 1990). A particular instance of strain may also function as the situational event that ignites a delinquent act, especially among adolescents predisposed to delinquency. Qualitative and survey data, in particular, suggest that particular instances of delinquency are often instigated by one of the three types of strain listed above (see Agnew, 1990; also see Averill, 1982, for data on the instigations to anger). . . .

Adaptations to (Coping Strategies for) Strain

The discussion thus far has focused on the types of strain that might promote delinquency. Virtually all strain theories, however, acknowledge that only *some* strained individuals turn to delinquency. Some effort has been made to identify those factors that determine whether one adapts to strain through delinquency. The most attention has been focused on the adolescent's commitment to legitimate means and association with other strained/ delinquent individuals (see Agnew, 1991b).

The following discussion builds on this effort and is in two parts. First, the major adaptations to strain are described. This discussion points to a number of cognitive, emotional, and behavioral coping strategies that have not been considered in the criminology literature. Second, those factors that influence whether one adapts to strain using delinquent or nondelinquent means are described. . . .

Constraints to Nondelinquent and Delinquent Coping

While there are many adaptations to objective strain, those adaptations are not equally available to everyone. Individuals are constrained in their choice of adaptation(s) by a variety of internal and external factors. The following is a partial list of such factors.

Initial Goals/Values/Identities of the Individual. If the objective strain affects goals/values/identities that are high in absolute and relative importance, and if the individual has few alternative goals/values/identities in which to seek refuge, it will be more difficult to relegate strain to an unimportant area of one's life (see Agnew, 1986; Thoits, 1991a). This is especially the case if the goals/values/identities receive strong social and cultural support (see below). As a result, strain will be more likely to lead to delinquency in such cases.

Individual Coping Resources. A wide range of traits can be listed in this area, including temperament, intelligence, creativity, problem-solving skills, interpersonal skills, self-efficacy, and self-esteem. These traits affect the selection of coping strategies by influencing the individual's sensitivity to objective strains and ability to engage in cognitive, emotional, and behavioral coping (Agnew, 1991a; Averill, 1982; Bernard, 1990; Compas, 1987; Edmunds and Kendrick, 1980; Slaby and Guerra, 1988; Tavris, 1984). Data, for example, suggest that individuals with high self-esteem are more resistant to stress (Averill, 1982; Compas, 1987; Kaplan, 1980; Pearlin and Schooler, 1978; Rosenberg, 1990; Thoits, 1983). Such individuals, therefore, should be less likely to respond to a given objective strain with delinquency. Individuals high in self-efficacy are more likely to feel that their strain can be alleviated by behavioral coping of a nondelinquent nature, and so they too should be less likely to respond to strain with delinquency (see Bandura, 1989, and Wang and Richarde, 1988, on self-efficacy; see Thoits, 1991b, on perceived control).

Conventional Social Support. Vaux (1988) provides an extended discussion of the different types of social support, their measurement, and their effect on outcome variables. Thoits (1984) argues that social support is important because it facilitates the major types of coping. The major types of social support, in fact, correspond to the major types of coping listed above. Thus, there is informational support, instrumental support, and emotional support (House, 1981). Adolescents with conventional social supports, then, should be better able to respond to objective strains in a nondelinquent manner.

Constraints to Delinquent Coping. The crime/delinquency literature has focused on certain variables that constrain delinquent coping. They include (1) the costs and benefits of engaging in delinquency in a particular situation (Clarke and Cornish, 1985), (2) the individual's level of social control (see Hirschi, 1969), and (3) the possession of those "illegitimate means" necessary for many delinquent acts (see Agnew, 1991a, for a full discussion).

Macro-Level Variables. The larger social environment may affect the probability of delinquent versus nondelinquent coping by affecting all of the above factors. First, the social environment may affect coping by influencing the importance attached to selected goals/values/identities. For example, certain ethnographic accounts suggest that there is a strong social and cultural emphasis on the goals of money/status among certain segments of the urban poor. Many poor individuals, in particular, are in a situation in which (1) they face strong economic/status demands, (2) people around them stress the importance of money/status on a regular basis, and (3) few alternative goals are given cultural support (Anderson, 1978; MacLeod, 1987; Sullivan, 1989). As such, these individuals should face more difficulty in cognitively minimizing the importance of money and status.

Second, the larger social environment may affect the individual's sensitivity to particular strains by influencing the individual's beliefs regarding what is and is not adverse. The subculture of violence thesis, for example, is predicated on the assumption that young black males in urban slums are taught that a wide range of provocations and insults are highly adverse. Third, the social environment may influence the individual's ability to minimize cognitively the severity of objective strain. Individuals in some environments are regularly provided with external information about their accomplishments and failings (see Faunce, 1989), and their attempts at cognitively distorting such information are quickly challenged. Such a situation may exist among many adolescents and among those who inhabit the "street-corner world" of the urban poor. Adolescents and those on the street corner live in a very "public world"; one's accomplishments and failings typically occur before a large audience or they quickly become known to such an audience. Further, accounts suggest that this audience regularly reminds individuals of their accomplishments and failings and challenges attempts at cognitive distortion.

Fourth, certain social environments may make it difficult to engage in behavioral coping of a nondelinquent nature. Agnew (1985a) has argued that adolescents often find it difficult to escape legally from negative stimuli, especially negative stimuli encountered in the school, family, and neighborhood. Also, adolescents often lack the resources to negotiate successfully with adults, such as parents and teachers (although see Agnew, 1991a). Similar arguments might be made for the urban underclass. They often lack the resources to negotiate successfully with many others, and they often find it difficult to escape legally from adverse environments—by, for example, quitting their job (if they have a job) or moving to another neighborhood.

The larger social environment, then, may affect individual coping in a variety of ways. And certain groups, such as adolescents and the urban underclass, may face special constraints that make nondelinquent coping more difficult. This may explain the higher rate of deviance among these groups.

Factors Affecting the Disposition to Delinquency

The selection of delinquent versus nondelinquent coping strategies is not only dependent on the constraints to coping, but also on the adolescent's disposition to engage in delinquent versus nondelinquent coping. This disposition is a function of (1) certain temperamental variables (see Tonry et al., 1991), (2) the prior learning history of the adolescent, particularly the extent to which delinquency was reinforced in the past (Bandura, 1973; Berkowitz, 1982), (3) the adolescent's beliefs, particularly the rules defining the appropriate response to provocations (Bernard's, 1990, "regulative rules"), and (4) the adolescent's attributions regarding the causes of his or her adversity. Adolescents who attribute their adversity to others are much more likely to become angry, and as argued earlier, that anger creates a strong predisposition to delinquency. Data and theory from several areas, in fact, suggest that the experience of adversity is most likely to result in deviance when the adversity is blamed on another. The attributions one makes are influenced by a variety of factors, as discussed in recent reviews by Averill (1982), Berwin (1988), R. Cohen (1982), Crittenden (1983, 1989), Kluegel and Smith (1986), and Utne and Kidd (1980). The possibility that there may be demographic and subgroup differences in the rules for assigning blame is of special interest (see Bernard, 1990; Crittenden, 1983, 1989).

A key variable affecting several of the above factors is association with delinquent peers. It has been argued that adolescents who associate with delinquent peers are more likely to be exposed to delinquent models and beliefs and to receive reinforcement for delinquency (see especially, Akers, 1985). It may also be the case that delinquent peers increase the likelihood that adolescents will attribute their adversity to others.

The individual's disposition to delinquency, then, may condition the impact of adversity on delinquency. At the same time, it is important to note that continued experience with adversity may create a disposition for delinquency. This argument has been made by Bernard (1990), Cloward and Ohlin (1960), A. Cohen (1955), Elliott et al. (1979), and others. In particular, it has been argued that under certain conditions the experience of adversity may lead to beliefs favorable to delinquency, lead adolescents to join or form delinquent peer groups, and lead adolescents to blame others for their misfortune.

Virtually all empirical research on strain theory in criminology has neglected the constraints to coping and the adolescent's disposition to delinquency. Researchers, in par-

ticular, have failed to examine whether the effect of adversity on delinquency is conditioned by factors such as self-efficacy and association with delinquent peers. This is likely a major reason for the weak empirical support for strain theory. . . .

Discussion Questions

1. Give examples of the types of questions you might ask to measure the three types of strain listed by Agnew.

2. *Why* might strained individuals turn to crime?

3. Drawing on Agnew, describe the type of person who would be *most likely* to respond to strain with crime.

4. Drawing on Agnew, why is it that many studies have failed to support the classic strain theories of Merton, Cohen, and Cloward and Ohlin?

5. What policy recommendation might Agnew make for controlling crime? ✦

Part V

Varieties of Control Theory

Sociological explanations of crime have been dominated by three main traditions: differential association/learning theory; anomie/strain theory; and control theory. Other theories have been set forth, but usually they have either integrated concepts from, or have been developed explicitly to challenge, these three dominant traditions. The enduring appeal of these traditions is in part due to the elegant way in which original statements of the theories conveyed powerful theses as to the origins of criminal conduct. Indeed, each perspective was authored by a scholar of enormous accomplishment: anomie/strain theory by Robert K. Merton; differential association theory by Edwin Sutherland; and control theory by Travis Hirschi.

Hirschi was not the first control theorist. As noted previously, Shaw and McKay (Chapter 6) tied delinquency to the attenuation of control in inner-city areas. Other theorists focused on how types of control—usually differentiating between those inside individuals (e.g., conscience) and those outside individuals (e.g., parental reactions)—were related to wayward behavior. Thus, Reckless (1961) focused on "inner and outer containment"; Reiss (1951) delineated "personal and social controls"; and Nye (1958) emphasized controls that were "internal," "direct," and "indirect." Sykes and Matza (Chapter 9) also are seen by some criminologists as control theorists (Akers, 1997; Lilly et al., 1995), because they examined how people become free to commit crime only when beliefs can be evoked to "neutralize" the restraint normative standards usually exert over them.

Despite these predecessors, it was Hirschi's "social bond theory" (Chapter 18 in this Part), published in *Causes of Delinquency* (1969), that emerged as the preeminent statement of control theory. In this work, Hirschi divided criminological theory into three main perspectives, which he identified by the terms "control theory," "strain theory," and "cultural deviance theory"—a term he used for differential association/learning approaches (see also, Kornhauser, 1978). He argued that these three perspectives were incompatible, and that they should be seen as rivals to be tested empirically against one another. Thus, in *Causes of Delinquency*, Hirschi not only set forth his social bond theory but also presented data showing the merits of his perspective and the comparative weaknesses of strain and cultural deviance perspectives.

Up until this time, most theoretical statements were just that—essays proposing a plausible explanation of crime. Hirschi, however, "upped the ante" by showing that theories could be tested and by claiming that empirical evidence should be the arbiter of which perspective deserved allegiance. In particular, Hirschi revealed the utility of us-

Where Is the Motivation?

The most disconcerting question the control theorist faces goes something like this: "Yes, but *why* do they do it?" In the good old days, the control theorist could simply strip away the "veneer of civilization" and expose man's "animal impulses" for all to see. These impulses appeared to him (and apparently to his audience) to provide a plausible account of the motivation to crime and delinquency. His argument was *not* that delinquents and criminals alone are animals, but that we are all animals, and thus all naturally capable of committing criminal acts. It took no great study to reveal that children, chickens, and dogs occasionally assault and steal from their fellow creatures; that children, chickens, and dogs also behave for relatively long periods in a perfectly moral manner. Of course the acts of chickens and dogs are not "assault" or "theft," and such behavior is not "moral"; it is simply the behavior of a chicken or a dog. The chicken stealing corn from his neighbor knows nothing of the moral law; he does not *want* to violate rules; he wants merely to eat corn. The dog maliciously destroying a pillow or feloniously assaulting another dog is the moral equal of the chicken. No motivation to deviance is required to explain his acts. So, too, no special motivation to crime within the human animal was required to explain his criminal acts.

Times changed. It was no longer fashionable (within sociology, at least) to refer to animal impulses. The control theorist tended more and more to deemphasize the motivational component of his theory. He might refer in the beginning to "universal human needs," or some such, but the driving force behind crime and delinquency was rarely alluded to. At the same time, his explanations of crime and delinquency left the reader uneasy. What, the reader asked, is the control theorist assuming? Albert K. Cohen and James F. Short answer the question this way:

> . . .it is important to point out one important limitation of both types of theory. They [culture conflict and social disorganization theories] are both *control* theories in the sense that they explain delinquency in terms of the *absence* of effec-

tive controls. They appear, therefore, to imply a model of motivation that assumes that the impulse to delinquency is an inherent characteristic of young people and does not itself need to be explained; it is something that erupts when the lid—i.e., internalized cultural restraints or external authority—is off.

There are several possible and I think reasonable reactions to this criticism. One reaction is simply to acknowledge the assumption, to grant that one is assuming what control theorists have always assumed about the motivation to crime—that it is constant across persons (at least within the system in question): "There is no reason to assume that only those who finally commit a deviant act usually have the impulse to do so. It is much more likely that most people experience deviant impulses frequently. At least in fantasy, people are much more deviant than they appear." There is certainly nothing wrong with *making* such an assumption. We are free to assume anything we wish to assume; the truth of our theory is presumably subject to empirical test.

A second reaction, involving perhaps something of a quibble, is to defend the logic of control theory and to deny the alleged assumption. We can say the fact that control theory suggests the absence of something causes delinquency is not a proper criticism, since negative relations have as much claim to scientific acceptability as do positive relations. We can also say that the present theory does not impute an inherent impulse to *delinquency* to anyone. That, on the contrary, it denies the necessity of such an imputation: "The desires, and other passions of man, are in themselves no sin. No more are the actions, that proceed from those passions, till they know a law that forbids them."

A third reaction is to accept the criticism as valid, to grant that a complete explanation of delinquency would provide the necessary impetus, and proceed to construct an explanation of motivation consistent with control theory. Briar and Piliavin provide situational motivation: "We assume these acts are prompted by short-term situationally induced desires experienced by all boys to obtain valued goods, to portray courage in the ing survey research to test theories. In this method, respondents—usually juveniles in a high school—would be given a questionnaire that contained *both* measures of theoretical concepts and a "self-report" scale of delinquency. In this way, it would be possible to see which theory, as operationalized by the measures on the questionnaire, could explain more or less involvement in delinquency. It is noteworthy that this approach is the chief way in which criminologists test micro-level theories of crime.

Social Bond Theory

Although often unstated, most theories of crime make assumptions about human nature and its potential influence on behavior. For strain and cultural deviance theories, humans are usually considered to be "blank slates" onto which society writes its script for the person's life. On occasion, scholars in these traditions will admit that humans have innate or universal drives, but they do not see these forces as inherently criminogenic. Take, for example, the ninth proposition of Sutherland's differential association theory (see Chapter 8), which states that, "while criminal behavior is an expression of general needs and values, it is not explained by those general needs and values since noncriminal behavior is an expression of the same needs and values" (Sutherland and Cressey, 1970: 76).

Once they have rejected the notion that humans are driven to break the law because of their "nature," strain and cultural deviance theorists must address the question: "Well, then, why do people commit crimes?" The theoretical challenge is to discern what social conditions *motivate* individuals to engage in illegal acts. For strain theory, the motivation is rooted in negative social relations and experiences that expose people to strain; crime is a way of relieving or otherwise responding to this strain. For cultural deviance or learning theories, the motivation is created by social relations or experiences in which individuals learn to positively value crime, at least under some circumstances. Just as youths learn to like going to baseball games, they can learn to like breaking windows, shoplifting from stores, and beating up others.

As Hirschi notes, control theorists start out with a different premise about human nature: people will "naturally" break the law. It is not necessary to show that humans have an "id," as psychoanalytic theory would suggest, or that they have unique "animal impulses" or are innately aggressive, as some biological theories contend. Rather, for control theorists, it is sufficient to observe that like other animals, humans seek gratification and that crime is often an easy means to secure such gratification (see also Gottfredson and Hirschi, 1990). People may vary in their need for gratification, but humans generally have enough desire to seek pleasure that they have ample motivation to commit crimes on a regular basis.

This assumption has important theoretical implications. If all humans have motivations for crime, then theories that set forth special explanations of criminal motivation—such as strain and cultural deviance theories—are not needed. They are explaining something that does not need explaining; they are addressing the wrong question. Thus, rather than asking, "why do they do it?", criminologists should be asking, "why don't they do it?" (Hirschi, 1969: 34). That is, if humans' natural pursuit of gratification makes crime attractive, what is it that stops them from acting on this impulse?

The answer, of course, is the *control* that society exerts over individuals. According to Hirschi (1969: 16), "control theories assume that delinquent acts result when an individual's bond to society is weak or broken." It follows that *variation in control*, not variation in motivation, explains why some people break the law more than others. The theoretical task thus is to uncover the nature of social control and how it constrains people from acting out their underlying wayward urges.

In *Causes of Delinquency* (1969), Hirschi set forth what remains, even to this day, the most influential variant of control theory, which he called "social bond" theory (see the selection in Chapter 18). This perspective is distinctly sociological, because Hirschi focused not on internal controls, such as a superego or inner containment, but rather on how an individuals *bond* to *society* influences decisions to break the law. He did not deny that internal controls exist—individual conduct is affected by what people think and anticipate will happen to them—but ultimately these controls originate with and are sustained by the person's bond to society.

Hirschi's theoretical genius is seen in his willingness to move beyond the general proposition that weak controls cause crime to specifying the four major elements of the social bond: attachment, commitment, involvement, and belief. In essence, Hirschi argued that delinquency would be low among youngsters who are attached to and care about the opinions of others—especially their parents, whose commitment to school gives them a strong investment in conformity that they do not wish to risk by getting into trouble, who are involved in conventional activities that occupy their time, and who believe they should obey rules. In contrast, youths who are not close to their parents, have few prospects for a successful future, are idle after school hours, and have no allegiance to conventional morality are prime candidates for delinquency.

Contemporary Control Theories

Self-Control Theory

Two decades after the publication of *Causes of Delinquency*, Travis Hirschi joined with Michael Gottfredson to author *A General Theory of Crime* (1990), a volume in which he set forth the premise that a lack of "self-control" was the chief source of criminal behavior (see Chapter 19 in this Part). In this book, Gottfredson and Hirschi did not explicitly try to reconcile social bond and self-control theories. It is clear, however, that Hirschi's thinking about crime had changed over time and that his latest work was a marked departure from his earlier theorizing. In particular, whereas Hirschi's social bond theory located control in a person's *relation to society*, self-control theory moved the locus of control *inside the individual*. To a large extent, Hirschi now saw crime as rooted not in social experiences but in individual differences that developed early in life and had effects across the life course (see Part I).

Gottfredson and Hirschi embraced the view that criminal behavior is gratifying; indeed, they observed that crime is an easy source of short-term pleasure because committing a crime requires few skills and opportunities to offend are readily available. Why, then, would people bypass the chance to gain easy gratification through crime? Why don't they do it? The answer to this classic control theory question, as in *Causes of Delinquency*, is that controls hold these impulses in check; but unlike before, Gottfredson and Hirschi asserted that self-control, not social bonds, is the chief source of resistance against criminal temptations.

Social bond theory was largely an explanation of *juvenile* delinquency, focusing on how adolescents attach to parents, commit to school, are involved in recreational activities, and the like. By 1990, however, research had revealed that many wayward youths do not suddenly become seriously delinquent in their teen years. Instead, they begin to manifest conduct problems in childhood—problems that evolve into delinquency (see Moffitt, Chapter 5). This continuity or stability in misconduct suggests that the roots of crime lie not in adolescence but in the first years of life. It would follow, of course, that criminologists should search for the causes of crime in childhood and not, as had previously been the case, in the experiences of juveniles in the teenage years.

The critical social milieu in childhood is the family, and the critical experiences children encounter are intimately shaped by their parents. What, then, distinguishes the children who can resist seeking immediate gratification from those who act on their impulses, engaging in such precursors of delinquency as stealing, bullying, and lying? For Gottfredson and Hirschi, the key differentiating factor is whether a child can exercise "self-control." They reject the idea that this self-control is caused by biological predispositions. Instead, here they remain sociologists in attributing the inculcation of self-control to how parents raise their children. In particular, they assert that parents who monitor their children, recognize deviant behavior when it occurs, and then correct this conduct will instill self-control. Conversely, say Gottfredson and Hirschi (1990: 97), "the major 'cause' of low self-control thus appears to be ineffective child-rearing."

Gottfredson and Hirschi contend that the level of self-control, once established in childhood, is an enduring propensity or individual difference that has *general* effects in a person's life. This explains why there is stability of offending across the life course. The continuing lack of self-control also explains why criminal offenders also engage in activities that are "analogous" to crime—that is, acts, such as smoking, drinking, skipping school, having unprotected sex, and driving fast, which, like crime, provide easy and immediate gratification. As Gottfredson and Hirschi note, traditional sociological theories of crime have not shown that they can account for these key empirical facts: the early emergence of conduct problems, the stability of offending, and the participation of criminals in wide-ranging forms of deviance.

Social Bond Theory Revisited

Although they share certain features because they are both control theories, self-control theory and social bond theory are incompatible in fundamental ways (compare Hirschi and Gottfredson, 1995 with Sampson and Laub, 1995). Social bond theory asserts that experiences beyond childhood can affect a person's ties to conventional society, and thus that as bonds strengthen or weaken, people's involvement in crime can ebb and flow. In contrast, self-control theory contends that criminal propensities are established in childhood, and thus that misconduct is stable across the life course. Even more provocatively, self-control theory claims that any apparent empirical relationship between social bonds (e.g., attachment to others, commitment to schooling) and crime is spurious. Self-control would account for both the bond and the level of crime. Thus, if being in a good marriage is associated with less crime, Gottfredson and Hirschi would argue that this is because people with high levels of self-control both are more likely to have good marriages and less likely to engage in crime.

Ironically, social bond theory received its most potent shot in the arm from two former students of Gottfredson and Hirschi, Robert Sampson and John Laub (1993 [Chapter 20

in this Part]). Sampson and Laub agree with their mentors that sociological theorists have largely neglected the "considerable evidence that antisocial behavior is relatively stable across stages of the life course" (1993: 11). But they take Gottfredson and Hirschi to task for committing what Elliott Currie (1985: 185) calls the "fallacy of intractability—the belief that because childhood problems often appear early in life they are therefore fundamentally irreversible, portents of criminality worsening into adulthood." While there is continuity in antisocial behavior, observe Sampson and Laub, there is also *change*. Some problem children grow up to be delinquents, but others do not; some delinquents become adult criminals, but others do not; some adult criminals persist in their offending, but others do not.

Individual difference theories, such as Gottfredson and Hirschi's self-control theory, are adept at explaining *continuity* in problem behavior. Once equipped with an enduring criminal propensity, people carry this trait from situation to situation and from one age to the next. These theories encounter difficulty, however, in explaining *change* in behavior. If, for example, a person has low self-control, why would he or she ever stop being criminal? Or why would a juvenile who had no record of childhood misconduct—and thus whose parents instilled self-control—start getting into trouble in the teenage years? (see Moffitt, Chapter 5).

Using a life-course perspective, Sampson and Laub suggest that people usually are on certain "trajectories" that result in continuity of behavior. Even so, people also experience "transitions," life-events that may serve as "turning points" that evoke behavioral change. Sampson and Laub propose that establishing *social bonds*, such as through schooling or marriage, is a salient reason why people are redirected away from crime and into conformity. Explaining change, in short, requires a consideration of sociological factors.

Although borrowing from Hirschi's social bond theory, Sampson and Laub do not simply rehash this perspective. First, while Hirschi focused on the juvenile years, Sampson and Laub examine the entire life course, from childhood to adulthood. Second, they develop an integrated theoretical perspective, accepting that individual differences and social bonds combine to explain the onset of and desistance from criminal behavior (see Part VI). Third, they argue that the key issue is not whether a social bond exists but whether the bond is of high *quality*. Quality relationships—such as a good marriage or a rewarding job—engender close attachment, growing commitment, and reciprocity. In turn, note Sampson and Laub (1990: 141), "relations characterized by an extensive set of obligations, expectations, and interdependent social networks are better able to facilitate social control."

Power-Control Theory

Traditionally, most control theories have recognized that the family is a major source of social control. Even so, these theories have typically failed to consider issues of gender as they pertain to relationships between husbands and wives or to relationships between parents and children. Writing in the advent of the rise of feminist criminology (see Part X), John Hagan attempts to rectify this omission with his "power-control theory" of delinquency (see Chapter 21).

Like other control theorists, Hagan portrays crime not as a grim adaptation to strain or as culturally mandated, but instead as being gratifying—that is, it is adventurous, exciting, and fun. Breaking the law, however, involves some daring; in fact, claims Hagan (1989: 153), "delinquency can be regarded as a form of risk taking." In turn, delinquency will be a more attractive behavioral choice to those who like to take risks.

Where do these "preferences for risk" come from? These preferences, contends Hagan, are not innate but rather are socially produced within the context of the family. Specifically, children that are exposed to strong controls—whether direct (or "instrumental") or indirect (or "relational")—will be constrained from entering situations where they are exposed to or can learn to enjoy risks. In short, control reduces risk preferences, which then makes delinquency less likely.

What determines, then, which children are more or less controlled? Hagan's answer to this question is both a weakness and a strength of his theory. Ideally, he would have considered a variety of factors that could influence the effective exercise of control, ranging from the personality traits of parents to the structural inequalities that break families apart (see, e.g., Currie, 1985; Gottfredson and Hirschi, 1990). By not doing so, his theory is limited in scope and is potentially misspecified. Despite this limitation, Hagan made a theoretical advance in offering an innovative insight into the basis of familial control: power relations between the father and mother determine the control exercised over the son and daughter.

To Hagan, gender is central to understanding delinquency. In traditional patriarchal families, where the working father commands and the housewife obeys, boys are exposed to fewer controls than girls, and thus they develop stronger risk preferences and have much higher involvement in crime. In more egalitarian families, where power differences between fathers and mothers are minimal, boys and girls are subjected to similar parental controls and thus have similar involvement in delinquency.

The empirical validity of Hagan's theory is still in dispute (Akers, 1997). How the theory would be applied to the study of families headed by a single parent is especially debatable. Further, Hagan suggests that his theory would best explain less serious or "common delinquent behavior," which leaves the important issue of violent, serious criminality outside the perspective's scope. Regardless, Hagan's work is critical in illuminating a neglected problem that warrants future research: how do gender-based power relations between parents affect the upbringing of boys and girls and, in turn, their propensity for crime?

References

Akers, Ronald L. 1997. *Criminological Theories: Introduction and Evaluation*, 2nd edition. Los Angeles: Roxbury.

Currie, Elliott. 1985. *Confronting Crime: An American Challenge*. New York: Pantheon.

Gottfredson, Michael R. and Travis Hirschi. 1990. *A General Theory of Crime*. Stanford, CA: Stanford University Press.

Hagan, John. 1989. *Structural Criminology*. New Brunswick, NJ: Rutgers University Press.

Hirschi, Travis. 1969. *Causes of Delinquency*. Berkeley: University of California Press.

Hirschi, Travis and Michael R. Gottfredson. 1995. "Control Theory and the Life-Course Perspective." *Studies on Crime and Crime Prevention* 4: 131-142.

Kornhauser, Ruth Rosner. 1978. *Social Sources of Delinquency: An Appraisal of Analytic Models*. Chicago: University of Chicago.

Lilly, J. Robert, Francis T. Cullen, and Richard A. Ball. 1995. *Criminological Theory: Context and Consequences*, 2nd edition. Thousand Oaks, CA: Sage.

Nye, F. Ivan. 1958. *Family Relationships and Delinquent Behavior*. New York: John Wiley.

Reckless, Walter C. 1961. *The Crime Problem*, 3rd edition. New York: Appleton-Century-Crofts.

Reiss, Albert J., Jr. 1951. "Delinquency as the Failure of Personal and Social Controls." *American Sociological Review* 16: 196-207.

Sampson, Robert J. and John H. Laub. 1993. *Crime in the Making: Pathways and Turning Points Through Life*. Cambridge, MA: Harvard University Press.

——. 1995. "Understanding Variability in Lives Through Time: Contributions of Life-Course Criminology." *Studies on Crime and Crime Prevention* 4: 143-158.

Sutherland, Edwin H. and Donald R. Cressey. 1970. *Principles of Criminology*, 8th edition. Philadelphia: Lippincott. ✦

18

Social Bond Theory

Travis Hirschi

Although Causes of Delinquency *is a complex book filled with intricate theoretical discussions and numerous statistical analyses, Hirschi's theory has an appealing quality: it can be simply stated and thus easily understood and studied by criminologists. Indeed, his theory can be reduced to two propositions. First, delinquency and social bonds are inversely related. Second, the concept of social bonds has four elements—attachment, commitment, involvement, and belief—which independently and in combination restrain criminal conduct.*

But how exactly do these bonds exert control over youngsters? Hirschi argued that youths could be attached to peers, teachers, and other adults, although relationships with parents are most crucial. Attachment involves an emotional connection to another person. When such a relationship exists, youths will be more likely to care what that other person thinks of them. In turn, when in a situation where the opportunity for trouble presents itself, they will be restrained from delinquency if they are concerned that such action will disappoint the other person or disrupt this relationship.

The importance of attachment is that during the teenage years, youths are frequently outside their parents' watchful eyes. In such instances, parents cannot exert "direct control"—that is, personally supervise their children and punish misconduct when it occurs. They can, however, exert "indirect control" if youths take into account their parents' preferences. When attachment is strong, observed Hirschi (1969:88), "the parent is psychologically present when temptation to commit a crime appears. If, in the situation of temptation, no thought is given to parental reaction, the child is to this extent free to commit the act."

Much like rational choice theory (see Part VII), Hirschi suggested that there is a "rational component" to conformity, which he calls "commitment." Juveniles who are doing well in school and have bright prospects ahead are less likely to engage in acts that will jeopardize their future. Conversely, uncommitted youths—those with little or no stake in conformity—have nothing to lose and thus are freer to break the law.

Hirschi also contended that the mere involvement in conventional activities facilitates control. If idleness presents opportunities for crime, filling up a youth's day with wholesome activities—such as school and recreational pursuits—leaves little time for getting into trouble.

Finally, Hirschi (1969: 26) argued that youths who believe that they should "obey the rules of society" are less likely to violate them. The social bond of "belief" is controversial because such beliefs or "definitions" are also central to cultural deviance/differential association theory. Hirschi contended, however, that an important analytical distinction could be made: while cultural deviance theorists like Sutherland (Chapter 8) focus on beliefs that positively value crime ("definitions favorable to violation of the law"), control theorists focus on beliefs that proscribe crime. "Delinquency is not caused by beliefs that require delinquency," noted Hirschi (1969: 198), "but rather made possible by the absence of (effective) beliefs that forbid delinquency."

Hirschi's social bond theory has been subjected to numerous empirical tests—perhaps more than any other theory. Although empirical confirmation of the theory varies by such factors as a study's methodology (Agnew, 1985; Krohn, 1995), overall there is fairly consistent support for the general thesis that weak social bonds increase the risk of being involved in criminal behavior (Akers, 1997). Hirschi's claim that competing perspectives—especially "cultural deviance" theories—are not empirically viable, however, is mistaken (Akers, 1997; Krohn, 1995). A further limitation is that Hirschi's approach is largely astructural and ahistorical. Unlike Shaw and McKay (Chapter 6), he does not examine how macrosocial changes occurring in the United States affect the strength of social bonds for people located in different sectors of American society (see also Sampson and Wilson, 1995).

References

Agnew, Robert. 1985. "Social Control Theory and Delinquency: A Longitudinal Test." *Criminology* 23: 47-61.

Akers, Ronald L. 1997. *Criminological Theories: Introduction and Evaluation*, 2nd edition. Los Angeles: Roxbury.

Hirschi, Travis. 1969. *Causes of Delinquency.* Berkeley: University of California Press.

Krohn, Marvin. 1995. "Control and Deterrence Theories of Criminality." Pp. 329-347 in *Criminology: A Contemporary Handbook*, 2nd edition, edited by Joseph F. Sheley. Belmont, CA: Wadsworth.

Sampson, Robert J. and William Julius Wilson. 1995. "Toward a Theory of Race, Crime, and Urban Inequality." Pp. 36-54 in *Crime and Inequality*, edited by John Hagan and Ruth D. Peterson. Stanford, CA: Stanford University Press.

T hree fundamental perspectives on delinquency and deviant behavior dominate the current scene. According to *strain* or motivational theories, legitimate desires that conformity cannot satisfy force a person into deviance. According to *control* or bond theories, a person is free to commit delinquent acts because his ties to the conventional order have somehow been broken. According to *cultural deviance* theories, the deviant conforms to a set of standards not accepted by a larger or more powerful society. Although most current theories of crime and delinquency contain elements of at least two and occasionally all three of these perspectives, reconciliation of their assumptions is very difficult. If, as the control theorist assumes, the ties of many persons to the conventional order may be weak or virtually nonexistent, the strain theorist, in accounting for their deviance, builds into his explanation pressure that is unnecessary. If, on the other hand, it is reasonable to assume with the strain theorist that everyone is at some point strongly tied to *the* conventional system, then it is unreasonable to assume that many are not (control theories), or

that many are tied to different "conventional" systems (cultural deviance theories). . . .

Control theories assume that delinquent acts result when an individual's bond to society is weak or broken. Since these theories embrace two highly complex concepts, the *bond* of the individual to *society*, it is not surprising that they have at one time or another formed the basis of explanations of most forms of aberrant or unusual behavior. It is also not surprising that control theories have described the elements of the bond to society in many ways, and that they have focused on a variety of units as the point of control. . . .

Elements of the Bond

Attachment

In explaining conforming behavior, sociologists justly emphasize sensitivity to the opinion of others. Unfortunately, as suggested in the preceding chapter, they tend to suggest that man *is* sensitive to the opinion of others and thus exclude sensitivity from their explanations of deviant behavior. In explaining deviant behavior, psychologists, in contrast, emphasize insensitivity to the opinion of others. Unfortunately, they too tend to ignore variation, and, in addition, they tend to tie sensitivity inextricably to other variables, to make it part of a syndrome or "type," and thus seriously to reduce its value as an explanatory concept. The psychopath is characterized only in part by "deficient attachment to or affection for others, a failure to respond to the ordinary motivations founded in respect or regard for one's fellows"; he is also characterized by such things as "excessive aggressiveness," "lack of superego control," and "an infantile level of response." Unfortunately, too, the behavior that psychopathy is used to explain often becomes part of the *definition* of psychopathy. As a result, in Barbara Wootton's words: "[The psychopath] is . . . *par excellence*, and without shame or qualification, the model of the circular process by which mental abnormality is inferred from anti-social behavior while anti-social behavior is explained by mental abnormality."

The problems of diagnosis, tautology, and name-calling are avoided if the dimensions of psychopathy are treated as causally and therefore problematically interrelated, rather than as logically and therefore necessarily bound to each other. In fact, it can be argued that all of the characteristics attributed to the psychopath follow from, are effects of, his lack of attachment to others. To say that to lack attachment to others is to be free from moral restraints is to use lack of attachment to explain the guiltlessness of the psychopath, the fact that he apparently has no conscience or superego. In this view, lack of attachment to others is not merely a symptom of psychopathy, it is psychopathy; lack of conscience is just another way of saying the same thing; and the violation of norms is (or may be) a consequence.

For that matter, given that man is an animal, "impulsivity" and "aggressiveness" can also be seen as natural consequences of freedom from moral restraints. However, since the view of man as endowed with natural propensities and capacities like other animals is peculiarly unpalatable to sociologists, we need not fall back on such a view to explain the amoral man's aggressiveness. The process of becoming alienated from others often involves or is based on active interpersonal conflict. Such conflict could easily supply a reservoir of *socially derived* hostility sufficient to account for the aggressiveness of those whose attachments to others have been weakened.

Durkheim said it many years ago: "We are moral beings to the extent that we are social beings." This may be interpreted to mean that we are moral beings to the extent that we have "internalized the norms" of society. But what does it mean to say that a person has internalized the norms of society? The norms of society are by definition shared by the members of society. To violate a norm is, therefore, to act contrary to the wishes and expectations of other people. If a person does not care about the wishes and expectations of other people—that is, if he is insensitive to the opinion of others—then he is to that extent not bound by the norms. He is free to deviate.

The essence of internalization of norms, conscience, or super-ego thus lies in the attachment of the individual to others. This view has several advantages over the concept of internalization. For one, explanations of deviant behavior based on attachment do not beg the question, since the extent to which a person is attached to others can be measured independently of his deviant behavior. Furthermore, change or variation in behavior is explainable in a way that it is not when notion of internalization or superego are used. For example, the divorced man is more likely after divorce to commit a number of deviant acts, such as suicide or forgery. If we explain these acts by reference to the superego (or internal control), we are forced to say that the man "lost his conscience" when he got a divorce; and, of course, if he remarries, we have to conclude that he gets his conscience back.

This dimension of the bond to conventional society is encountered in most social control-oriented research and theory. F. Ivan Nye's "internal control" and "indirect control" refer to the same element, although we avoid the problem of explaining changes over time by locating the "conscience" in the bond to others rather than making it part of the personality. Attachment to others is just one aspect of Albert J. Reiss's "personal controls"; we avoid his problems of tautological empirical *observations* by making the relationship between attachment and delinquency problematic rather than definitional. Finally, Scott Briar and Irving Piliavin's "commitment" or "stake in conformity" subsumes attachment, as their discussion illustrates, although the terms they use are more closely associated with the next element to be discussed.

Commitment

"Of all passions, that which inclineth men least to break the laws, is fear. Nay, excepting some generous natures, it is the only thing, when there is the appearance of profit or pleasure by breaking the laws, that makes men keep them." Few would deny that men on occasion obey the rules simply from fear of the consequences. This rational component in conformity we label commitment. What does it mean to say that a person is committed to conformity? In Howard S. Becker's formulation it means the following:

First, the individual is in a position in which his decision with regard to some particular line of action has consequences for other interests and activities not necessarily [directly] related to it. Second, he has placed himself in that position by his own prior actions. A third element is present though so obvious as not to be apparent: the committed person must be aware [of other interests] and must recognize that his decision in this case will have ramifications beyond it.

The idea, then, is that the person invests time, energy, himself, in a certain line of activity—say, getting an education, building up a business, acquiring a reputation for virtue. When or whenever he considers deviant behavior, he must consider the costs of this deviant behavior, the risk he runs of losing the investment he has made in conventional labor.

If attachment to others is the sociological counterpart of the superego or conscience, commitment is the counterpart of the ego or common sense. To the person committed to conventional lines of action, risking one to ten years in prison for a ten-dollar holdup is stupidity, because to the committed person the costs and risks obviously exceed ten dollars in value. (To the psychoanalyst, such an act exhibits failure to be governed by the "reality-principle.") In the sociological control theory, it can be and is generally assumed that the decision to commit a criminal act may well be rationally determined—that the actor's decision was not irrational given the risks and costs he faces. Of course, as Becker points out, if the actor is capable of in some sense calculating the costs of a line of action, he is also capable of calculational errors: ignorance and error return, in the control theory, as possible explanations of deviant behavior.

The concept of commitment assumes that the organization of society is such that the interests of most persons would be endangered if they were to engage in criminal acts. Most people, simply by the process of living in an organized society, acquire goods, reputations, prospects that they do not want to risk losing. These accumulations are society's insurance that they will abide by the rules. Many hypotheses about the antecedents of delinquent behavior are based on this premise. For example, Arthur L. Stinchcombe's hypothesis that "high school rebellion . . . occurs when future status is not clearly related to present performance" suggests that one is committed to conformity not only by what one has but also by what one hopes to obtain. Thus "ambition" and/or "aspiration" play an important role in producing conformity. The person becomes committed to a conventional line of action, and he is therefore committed to conformity.

Most lines of action in a society are of course conventional. The clearest examples are educational and occupational careers. Actions thought to jeopardize one's chances in these areas are presumably avoided. Interestingly enough, even nonconventional commitments may operate to produce conventional conformity. We are told, at least, that boys aspiring to careers in the rackets or professional thievery are judged by their "honesty" and "reliability"—traits traditionally in demand among seekers of office boys.

Involvement

Many persons undoubtedly owe a life of virtue to a lack of opportunity to do otherwise. Time and energy are inherently limited: "Not that I would not, if I could, be both handsome and fat and well dressed, and a great athlete, and make a million a year, be a wit, a bon vivant, and a lady killer, as well as a philosopher, a philanthropist, a statesman, warrior, and African explorer, as well as a 'tone-poet' and saint. But the thing is simply impossible." The things that William James here says he would like to be or do are all, I suppose, within the realm of conventionality, but if he were to include illicit actions he would still have to eliminate some of them as simply impossible.

Involvement or engrossment in conventional activities is thus often part of a control theory. The assumption, widely shared, is that a person may be simply too busy doing conventional things to find time to engage in deviant behavior. The person involved in conventional activities is tied to appointments, deadlines, working hours, plans, and the like, so the opportunity to commit deviant acts rarely arises. To the extent that he is engrossed in conventional activities, he cannot even think about deviant acts, let alone act out his inclinations.

This line of reasoning is responsible for the stress placed on recreational facilities in many programs to reduce delinquency, for much of the concern with the high school dropout, and for the idea that boys should be drafted into the Army to keep them out of trouble. So obvious and persuasive is the idea that involvement in conventional activities is a major deterrent to delinquency that it was accepted even by Sutherland: "In the general area of juvenile delinquency it is probable that the most significant difference between juveniles who engage in delinquency and those who do not is that the latter are provided abundant opportunities of a conventional type for satisfying their recreational interests, while the former lack those opportunities or facilities."

The view that "idle hands are the devil's workshop" has received more sophisticated treatment in recent sociological writings on delinquency. David Matza and Gresham M. Sykes, for example, suggest that delinquents have the values of a leisure class, the same values ascribed by Veblen to *the* leisure class: a search for kicks, disdain of work, a desire for the big score, and acceptance of aggressive toughness as proof of masculinity. Matza and Sykes explain delinquency by reference to this system of values, but they note that adolescents at all class levels are "to some extent" members of a leisure class, that they "move in a limbo between earlier parental domination and future integration with the social structure through the bonds of work and marriage." In the end, then, the leisure of the adolescent produces a set of values, which, in turn, leads to delinquency.

Belief

Unlike the cultural deviance theory, the control theory assumes the existence of a common value system within the society or group whose norms are being violated. If the deviant is committed to a value system different from that of conventional society, there is, within the context of the theory, nothing to explain. The question is, "Why does a man violate the rules in which he believes?" It is not, "Why do men differ in their beliefs about what constitutes good and desirable conduct?" The person is assumed to have been socialized (perhaps imperfectly) into the group whose rules he is violating; deviance is not a question of one group imposing its rules on the members of another group. In other words, we not only assume the deviant *has* believed the rules, we assume he believes the rules even as he violates them.

How can a person believe it is wrong to steal at the same time he is stealing? In the strain theory, this is not a difficult problem. (In fact, as suggested in the previous chapter, the strain theory was devised specifically to deal with this question.) The motivation to deviance adduced by the strain theorist is so strong that we can well understand the deviant act even assuming the deviator believes strongly that it is wrong. However, given the control theory's assumptions about motivation, if both the deviant and the nondeviant believe the deviant act is wrong, how do we account for the fact that one commits it and the other does not?

Control theories have taken two approaches to this problem. In one approach, beliefs are treated as mere words that mean little or nothing if the other forms of control are missing. "Semantic dementia," the dissociation between rational faculties and emotional control which is said to be characteristic of the psychopath, illustrates this way of handling the problem. In short, beliefs, at least insofar as they are expressed in words, drop out of the picture; since they do not differentiate between deviants and nondeviants, they are in the same class as "language" or any other characteristic common to all members of the group. Since they represent no real obstacle to the commission of delinquent acts, nothing need be said about how they are handled by those committing such acts. The control theories that do not mention beliefs (or values), and many do not, may be assumed to take this approach to the problem.

The second approach argues that the deviant rationalizes his behavior so that he can at once violate the rule and maintain his belief in it. Donald R. Cressey has advanced this argument with respect to embezzlement, and Sykes and Matza have advanced it with respect to delinquency. In both Cressey's and Sykes and Matza's treatments, these rationalizations (Cressey calls them "verbalizations," Sykes and Matza term them "techniques of neutralization") occur prior to the commission of the deviant act. If the neutralization is successful, the person is free to commit the act(s) in question. Both in Cressey and in Sykes and Matza, the strain that prompts the effort at neutralization also provides the motive force that results in the subsequent deviant act. Their theories are thus, in this sense, strain theories. Neutralization is difficult to handle within the context of a theory that adheres closely to control theory assumptions, because in the control theory there is no special motivational force to account for the neutralization. This difficulty is especially noticeable in Matza's later treatment of this topic, where the motivational component, the "will to delinquency" appears *after* the moral vacuum has been created by the techniques of the neutralization. The question thus becomes: Why neutralize?

In attempting to solve a strain theory problem with control theory tools, the control theorist is thus led into a trap. He cannot answer the crucial question. The concept of neutralization assumes the existence of moral obstacles to the commission of deviant acts. In order plausibly to account for a deviant act, it is necessary to generate motivation to deviance that is at least equivalent in force to the resistance provided by these moral obstacles. However, if the moral obstacles are removed, neutralization and special motivation are no longer required. We therefore follow the implicit logic of control theory and remove these moral obstacles by hypothesis. Many persons do not have an attitude of respect toward the rules of society; many persons feel no moral obligation to conform regardless of personal advantage. Insofar as the values and beliefs of these persons are consistent with their feelings, and there should be a tendency toward consistency, neutralization is unnecessary; it has already occurred.

Does this merely push the question back a step and at the same time produce conflict with the assumption of a common value system? I think not. In the first place, we do not assume, as does Cressey, that neutralization occurs in order to make a specific criminal act possible. We do not assume, as do Sykes and Matza, that neutralization occurs to make many delinquent acts possible. We do not assume, in other words, that the person constructs a system of rationalizations in order to justify commission of acts he *wants* to commit. We assume, in contrast, that the beliefs that free a man to commit deviant acts are *unmotivated* in the sense that he does not construct or adopt them in order to facilitate the attainment of illicit ends. In the second place, we do not assume, as does Matza, that "delinquents concur in the conventional assessment of delinquency." We assume, in contrast, that there is *variation* in the extent to which people believe they should obey the rules of society, and, furthermore, that the less a person believes he should obey the rules, the more likely he is to violate them.

In chronological order, then, a person's beliefs in the moral validity of norms are, for no teleological reason, weakened. The probability that he will commit delinquent acts is therefore increased. When and if he commits a delinquent act, we may justifiably use the weakness of his beliefs in explaining it, but no special motivation is required to explain either the weakness of his beliefs or, perhaps, his delinquent act.

The keystone of this argument is of course the assumption that there is variation in belief in the moral validity of social rules. This assumption is amenable to direct empirical test and can thus survive at least until its first confrontation with data. For the present, we must return to the idea of a common value system with which this section was begun.

The idea of a common (or, perhaps better, a single) value system is consistent with the fact, or presumption, of variation in the strength of moral beliefs. We have not suggested that delinquency is based on beliefs counter to conventional morality; we have not suggested that delinquents do not believe delinquent acts are wrong. They may well believe these acts are wrong, but the meaning and efficacy of such beliefs are contingent upon other beliefs and, indeed, on the strength of other ties to the conventional order.

presence of, or be loyal to peers, to strike out at someone who is disliked, or simply to 'get kicks.'"

. . . There are several additional accounts of "why they do it" that are to my mind persuasive and at the same time generally compatible with control theory. But while all of these accounts may be compatible with control theory, they are by no means deducible from it. Furthermore, they rarely impute built-in, unusual motivation to the delinquent: he is attempting to satisfy the same desires, he is reacting to the same pressures as other boys (as is clear, for example, in the previous quotation from Briar and Piliavin). In other words, if included, these accounts of motivation would serve the same function in the theory that "animal impulses" traditionally served: they might add to its persuasiveness and plausibility, but they would add little else, since they do not differentiate delinquents from nondelinquents.

In the end, then, control theory remains what it has always been: a theory in which deviation is not problematic. The question "Why do they do it?" is simply not the question the theory is designed to answer. The question is, "Why don't we do it?" There is much evidence that we would if we dared.

Discussion Questions

1. Why does Hirschi say that the key question for criminologists to answer is "Why don't they do it?", as opposed to "Why do they do it?"

2. How does control theory differ from strain theory and cultural deviance theory?

3. What are the four elements of the social bond? How does each one help to control a youth from engaging in delinquency?

4. What factors in American society might cause social bonds to be weaker in inner-city neighborhoods? ✦

19

A General Theory of Crime

Michael R. Gottfredson
Travis Hirschi

Traditional sociological theories placed their primary focus on the social experiences of youths outside the family. For differential association theory, for example, most attention has been given to the role of peer groups in fostering delinquency; for strain theory, the lack of opportunities in school and in the labor market is considered as the source of crime-inducing frustration. In contrast, Gottfredson and Hirschi have redirected the attention of criminologists to the family and to what parents do, or do not do, during childhood.

In his social bond theory, Hirschi emphasized the importance of "indirect control"—how close attachment to parents allows the parents to have a "psychological presence" when youths are not under their surveillance. Gottfredson and Hirschi, however, argue that "direct control" is the key to effective parenting (see Wells and Rankin, 1988). Unless parents monitor their children closely and then take steps to punish misbehavior when it occurs—that is, unless they teach children that breaking rules has consequences—self-control will not be instilled. Instead, the child "will tend to be impulsive, insensitive, physical (as opposed to mental), risk-taking, short-sighted, and nonverbal" (Gottfredson and Hirschi, 1990: 90). As they endlessly succumb to life's temporary temptations, children burdened with low self-control will constantly engage in crime and other forms of deviance. They also will lack the persistence needed to succeed in school, in the workplace, and in social relationships. In short, they will be consigned to a wayward life replete with brushes with the law and with personal and social failure.

We should note that Gottfredson and Hirschi differentiate between "criminality," which is the propensity to offend, and "crime," which is an actual event in which a law is broken. They recognize that a propensity cannot be acted on unless the opportunity to do so exists. As a result, they see crime as a by product of people with low self-control, who have high criminogenic propensities, coming into contact with illegal opportunities. Still, given that most offenses are easy to commit and opportunities for crime are constantly available, over time people with low self-control inevitably will become deeply involved in criminal behavior. That is, self-control, not opportunities, will be the primary determinant of people's involvement in crime across their life course.

Like social bond theory, the core premise of Gottfredson and Hirschi's theory is easily identified and thus amenable to testing: the lower a person's self-control, the higher his or her involvement in criminal behavior and in acts analogous to crime. Not surprisingly, therefore, there is now a growing body of research assessing self-control theory (for just three examples, see Benson and Moore, 1992; Evans et al., 1997; Grasmick et al., 1993). In general, there is fairly consistent support for Gottfredson and Hirschi's theoretical predictions—a fact that ensures that their self-control theory will remain an important theoretical perspective in the time ahead.

The limits of self-control theory, however, should also be mentioned. Thus, in empirical tests, low self-control cannot, as Gottfredson and Hirschi predict, explain away the effects on crime of other sociological factors, especially the effects of differential association/social learning variables (see, for example, Evans et al., 1997). Perhaps more consequential, Gottfredson and Hirschi commit what Currie (1985: 185) calls the "fallacy of autonomy—the belief that what goes on inside the family can usefully be separated from the forces that affect it from the outside: the larger social context in which families are embedded for better or for worse." Thus, despite emphasizing the salience of parenting in crime causation, Gottfredson and Hirschi remain largely silent on the social forces that are transforming the American family and challenging the ability of parents to raise their children effectively.

References

Benson, Michael L. and Elizabeth Moore. 1992. "Are White-Collar and Common Offenders the Same?" *Journal of Research in Crime and Delinquency* 29: 251-272.

Currie, Elliott. 1985. *Confronting Crime: An American Challenge*. New York: Pantheon.

Evans, T. David, Francis T. Cullen, Velmer S. Burton, Jr., R. Gregory Dunaway, and Michael L. Benson. 1997. "The Social Consequences of Self-Control: Testing the General Theory of Crime." *Criminology* 35: 475-504.

Gottfredson, Michael R. and Travis Hirschi. 1990. *A General Theory of Crime*. Stanford: Stanford University Press.

Grasmick, Harold G., Charles R. Tittle, Robert J. Bursik, Jr., and Bruce K. Arneklev. 1993. "Testing the Core Empirical Implications of Gottfredson and Hirschi's General Theory of Crime." *Journal of Research in Crime and Delinquency* 30: 5-29.

Wells, L. Edward and Joseph H. Rankin. 1988. "Direct Parental Controls and Delinquency." *Criminology* 26: 263-285.

Theories of crime lead naturally to interest in the propensities of individuals committing criminal acts. These propensities are often labeled "criminality." In pure classical theory, people committing criminal acts had no special propensities. They merely followed the universal tendency to enhance their own pleasure. If they differed from noncriminals, it was with respect to their location in or comprehension of relevant sanction systems. For example, the individual cut off from the community will suffer less than others from the ostracism that follows crime; the individual unaware of the natural or legal consequences of criminal behavior cannot be controlled by these consequences to the degree that people aware of them are controlled; the atheist will not be as concerned as the believer about penalties to be exacted in a life beyond death. Classical theories on the whole, then, are today called *control theories*, theories emphasizing the prevention of crime through consequences painful to the individual.

Although, for policy purposes, classical theorists emphasized legal consequences, the importance to them of moral sanctions is so obvious that their theories might well be called underdeveloped *social control* theories. In fact, Bentham's list of the major restraining motives—motives acting to prevent mischievous acts—begins with goodwill, love of reputation, and the desire for amity (1970: 134-36). He goes on to say that fear of detection prevents crime in large part because of detection's consequences for "reputation, and the desire for amity" (p. 138). Put another way, in Bentham's view, the restraining power of legal sanctions in large part stems from their connection to social sanctions.

If crime is evidence of the weakness of social motives, it follows that criminals are less social than noncriminals and that the extent of their asociality may be determined by the nature and number of their crimes. Calculation of the extent of an individual's mischievousness is a complex affair, but in general the more mischievous or depraved the offenses, and the greater their number, the more mischievous or depraved the offender (Bentham 1970: 134-42). (Classical theorists thus had reason to be interested in the seriousness of the offense. The relevance of seriousness to current theories of crime is not so clear.)

Because classical or control theories infer that offenders are not restrained by social motives, it is common to think of them as emphasizing an asocial human nature. Actually, such theories make people only as asocial as their acts require. Pure or consistent control theories do not add criminality (i.e., personality concepts or attributes such as "aggressiveness" or "extraversion") to individuals beyond that found in their criminal acts. As a result, control theories are suspicious of images of an antisocial, psychopathic, or career offender, or of an offender whose motives to crime are somehow larger than those given in the crimes themselves. Indeed, control theories are compatible with the view that the balance of the total control structure favors conformity, even among offenders:

> For in every man, be his disposition ever so depraved, the social motives are those which . . . regulate and determine the general tenor of his life. . . . The general and standing bias of every man's nature is, therefore, towards that side to which

the force of the social motives would determine him to adhere. This being the case, the force of the social motives tends continually to put an end to that of the dissocial ones; as, in natural bodies, the force of friction tends to put an end to that which is generated by impulse. Time, then, which wears away the force of the dissocial motives, adds to that of the social. [Bentham 1970: 141]

Positivism brought with it the idea that criminals differ from noncriminals in ways more radical than this, the idea that criminals carry within themselves properties peculiarly and positively conducive to crime. [Previously], we examined the efforts of the major disciplines to identify these properties. Being friendly to both the classical and positivist traditions, we expected to end up with a list of individual properties reliably identified by competent research as useful in the description of "criminality"—such properties as aggressiveness, body build, activity level, and intelligence. We further expected that we would be able to connect these individual-level correlates of criminality directly to the classical idea of crime. As our review progressed, however, we were forced to conclude that we had overestimated the success of positivism in establishing important differences between "criminals" and "noncriminals" beyond their tendency to commit criminal acts. Stable individual differences in the tendency to commit criminal acts were clearly evident, but many or even most of the other differences between offenders and nonoffenders were not as clear or pronounced as our reading of the literature had led us to expect.

If individual differences in the tendency to commit criminal acts (within an overall tendency for crime to decline with age) are at least potentially explicable within classical theory by reference to the social location of individuals and their comprehension of how the world works, the fact remains that classical theory cannot shed much light on the positivistic finding (denied by most positivistic theories . . . . that these differences *remain reasonably stable with change in the social location of individuals and change in their knowledge of the operation of sanction systems*. This is the problem of self-control, the differential tendency of people to avoid criminal acts whatever the circumstances in which they find themselves. Since this difference among people has attracted a variety of names, we begin by arguing the merits of the concept of self-control.

Self-Control and Alternative Concepts

Our decision to ascribe stable individual differences in criminal behavior to self-control was made only after considering several alternatives, one of which (criminality) we had used before (Hirschi and Gottfredson 1986). A major consideration was consistency between the classical conception of crime and our conception of the criminal. It seemed unwise to try to integrate a choice theory of crime with a deterministic image of the offender, especially when such integration was unnecessary. In fact, the compatibility of the classical view of crime and the idea that people differ in self-control is, in our view, remarkable. As we have seen, classical theory is a theory of social or external control, a theory based on the idea that the costs of crime depend on the individual's current location in or bond to society. What classical theory lacks is an explicit idea of self-control, the idea that people also differ in the extent to which they are vulnerable to the temptations of the moment. Combining the two ideas thus merely recognizes the simultaneous existence of social and individual restraints on behavior.

An obvious alternative is the concept of criminality. The disadvantages of that concept, however, are numerous. First, it connotes causation or determinism, a positive tendency to crime that is contrary to the classical model and, in our view, contrary to the facts. Whereas self-control suggests that people differ in the extent to which they are restrained from criminal acts, criminality suggests that people differ in the extent to which they are compelled to crime. The concept of self-control is thus consistent with the observation that criminals do not require or need crime, and the concept of criminality is inconsistent with this observation. By the same token, the idea of low self-control is compatible with the observation that criminal acts require no special capabilities, needs, or motivation; they are, in this sense, available to everyone. In contrast, the idea of criminality as a special tendency suggests that criminal acts require special people for their performance and enjoyment. Finally, lack of restraint or low self-control allows almost any deviant, criminal, exciting, or dangerous act; in contrast, the idea of criminality covers only a narrow portion of the apparently diverse acts engaged in by people at one end of the dimension we are now discussing.

The concept of conscience comes closer than criminality to self-control, and is harder to distinguish from it. Unfortunately, that concept has connotations of compulsion (to conformity) not, strictly speaking, consistent with a choice model (or with the operation of conscience). It does not seem to cover the behaviors analogous to crime that appear to be controlled by natural sanctions rather than social or moral sanctions, and in the end it typically refers to how people feel about their acts rather than to the likelihood that they will or will not commit them. Thus accidents and employment instability are not usually seen as produced by failures of conscience, and writers in the conscience tradition do not typically make the connection between moral and prudent behavior. Finally, conscience is used primarily to summarize the results of learning via negative reinforcement, and even those favorably disposed to its use leave little more to say about it (see, e.g., Eysneck 1977; Wilson and Herrnstein 1985).

We are now in position to describe the nature of self-control, the individual characteristic relevant to the commission of criminal acts. We assume that the nature of this characteristic can be derived directly from the nature of criminal acts. We thus infer from the nature of crime what people who refrain from criminal acts are like before they reach the age at which crime becomes a logical possibility. We then work back further to the factors producing their restraint, back to the causes of self-control. In our view, lack of self-control does not require crime and can be counteracted by situational conditions or other properties of the individual. At the same time, we suggest that high self-control effectively reduces the possibility of crime—that is, those possessing it will be substantially less likely at all periods of life to engage in criminal acts.

The Elements of Self-Control

Criminal acts provide *immediate* gratification of desires. A major characteristic of people with low self-control is therefore a tendency to respond to tangible stimuli in the immediate environment, to have a concrete "here and now" orientation. People with high self-control, in contrast, tend to defer gratification.

Criminal acts provide easy or simple gratification of desires. They provide money without work, sex without courtship, revenge without court delays. People lacking self-control also tend to lack diligence, tenacity, or persistence in a course of action.

Criminal acts are *exciting, risky, or thrilling*. They involve stealth, danger, speed, agility, deception, or power. People lacking self-control therefore tend to be adventuresome, active, and physical. Those with high levels of self-control tend to be cautious, cognitive, and verbal.

Crimes provide *few or meager long-term benefits*. They are not equivalent to a job or a career. On the contrary, crimes interfere with long-term commitments to jobs, marriages, family, or friends. People with low self-control thus tend to have unstable marriages, friendships, and job profiles. They tend to be little interested in and unprepared for long-term occupation pursuits.

Crimes require *little skill or planning*. The cognitive requirements for most crimes are minimal. It follows that people lacking self-control need not possess or value cognitive or academic skills. The manual skills required for most crimes are minimal. It follows that people lacking self-control need not possess manual skills that require training or apprenticeship.

Crimes often result in *pain or discomfort for the victim*. Property is lost, bodies are injured, privacy is violated, trust is broken. It follows that people with low self-control tend to be self-centered, indifferent, or insensitive to the suffering and needs of others. It does not follow, however, that people with low self-control are routinely unkind or antisocial. On the contrary, they may discover the immediate and easy rewards of charm and generosity.

Recall that crime involves the pursuit of immediate pleasure. It follows that people lacking self-control will also tend to pursue immediate pleasures that are *not* criminal: they will tend to smoke, drink, use drugs, gamble, have children out of wedlock, and engage in illicit sex.

Crimes require the interaction of an offender with people or their property. It does not follow that people lacking self-control will tend to be gregarious or social. However, it does follow that, other things being equal, gregarious or social people are more likely to be involved in criminal acts.

The major benefit of many crimes is not pleasure but relief from momentary irritation. The irritation caused by a crying child is often the stimulus for physical abuse. That caused by a taunting stranger in a bar is often the stimulus for aggravated assault. It follows that people with low self-control tend to have minimal tolerance for frustration and little ability to respond to conflict through verbal rather than physical means.

Crimes involve the risk of violence and physical injury, of pain and suffering on the part of the offender. It does not follow that people with low self-control will tend to be tolerant of physical pain or to be indifferent to physical discomfort. It does follow that people tolerant of physical pain or indifferent to physical discomfort will be more likely to engage in criminal acts whatever their level of self-control.

The risk of criminal penalty for any given criminal act is small, but this depends in part on the circumstances of the offense. Thus, for example, not all joyrides by teenagers are equally likely to result in arrest. A car stolen from a neighbor and returned unharmed before he notices its absence is less likely to result in official notice than is a car stolen from a shopping center parking lot and abandoned at the convenience of the offender. Drinking alcohol stolen from parents and consumed in the family garage is less likely to receive official notice than drinking in the parking lot outside a concert hall. It follows that offenses differ in their validity as measures of self-control: those offenses with large risk of public awareness are better measures than those with little risk.

In sum, people who lack self-control will tend to be impulsive, insensitive, physical (as opposed to mental), risk-taking, short sighted, and nonverbal, and they will tend therefore to engage in criminal and analogous acts. Since these traits can be identified prior to the age of responsibility for crime, since there is considerable tendency for these traits to come together in the same people, and since the traits tend to persist through life, it seems reasonable to consider them as comprising a stable construct useful in the explanation of crime.

The Many Manifestations of Low Self-Control

Our image of the "offender" suggests that crime is not an automatic or necessary consequence of low self-control. It suggests that many noncriminal acts analogous to crime (such as accidents, smoking, and alcohol use) are also manifestations of low self-control. Our image therefore implies that no specific act, type of crime, or form of deviance is uniquely required by the absence of self-control.

Because both crime and analogous behaviors stem from low self-control (that is, both are manifestations of low self-control), they will all be engaged in at a relatively high rate by people with low self-control. Within the domain of crime, then, there will be much versatility among offenders in the criminal acts in which they engage.

Research on the versatility of deviant acts supports these predictions in the strongest possible way. The variety of manifestations of low self-control is immense. In spite of years of tireless research motivated by a belief in specialization, no credible evidence of specialization has been reported. In fact, the evidence of offender versatility is overwhelming (Hirschi 1969; Hindelang 1971; Wolfgang, Figlio, and Sellin 1972; Petersilia 1980; Hindelang, Hirschi, and Weis 1981; Rojek and Erickson 1982; Klein 1984).

By versatility we mean that offenders commit a wide variety of criminal acts, with no strong inclination to pursue a specific criminal act or a pattern of criminal acts to the exclusion of others. Most theories suggest that offenders tend to specialize, whereby such terms as robber, burglar, drug dealer, rapist, and murderer have predictive or descriptive import. In fact, some theories create offender specialization as part of their explanation of crime. For example, Cloward and Ohlin (1960) create distinctive subcultures of delinquency around particular forms of criminal behavior, identifying subcultures specializing in theft, violence, or drugs. In a related way, books are written about white-collar crime as though it were a clearly distinct specialty requiring a unique explanation. Research projects are undertaken for the study of drug use, or vandalism, or teen pregnancy (as though every study of delinquency were not a study of drug use and vandalism and teenage sexual behavior). Entire schools of criminology emerge to pursue patterning, sequencing, progression, escalation, onset, persistence, and desistance in the career of offenses or offenders. These efforts survive largely because their proponents fail to consider or acknowledge the clear evidence to the contrary. Other reasons for survival of such ideas may be found in the interest of politicians and members of the law enforcement community who see policy potential in criminal careers or "career criminals" (see, e.g., Blumstein et al. 1986).

Occasional reports of specialization seem to contradict this point, as do everyday observations of repetitive misbehavior by particular offenders. Some offenders rob the same store repeatedly over a period of years, or an offender commits several rapes over a (brief) period of time. Such offenders may be called "robbers" or "rapists." However, it should be noted that such labels are retrospective rather than predictive and that they typically ignore a large amount of delinquent or criminal behavior by the same offenders that is inconsistent with their alleged specialty. Thus, for example, the "rapist" will tend also to use drugs, to commit robberies and burglaries (often in concert with the rape), and to have a record for violent offenses other than rape.

There is a perhaps natural tendency on the part of observers (and in official accounts) to focus on the most serious crimes in a series of events, but this tendency should not be confused with a tendency on the part of the offender to specialize in one kind of crime.

Recall that one of the defining features of crime is that it is simple and easy. Some apparent specialization will therefore occur because obvious opportunities for an easy score will tend to repeat themselves. An offender who lives next to a shopping area that is approached by pedestrians will have repeat opportunities for purse snatching, and this may show in his arrest record. But even here the specific "criminal career" will tend to quickly run its course and to be followed by offenses whose content and character is likewise determined by coincidence and opportunity (which is the reason why some form of theft is always the best bet about what a person is likely to do next).

The evidence that offenders are likely to engage in noncriminal acts psychologically or theoretically equivalent to crime is, because of the relatively high rates of these "noncriminal" acts, even easier to document. Thieves are likely to smoke, drink, and skip school at considerably higher rates than nonthieves. Offenders are considerably more likely than nonoffenders to be involved in most types of accidents, including household fires, auto crashes, and unwanted pregnancies. They are also considerably more likely to die at an early age (see, e.g. Robins 1966; Eysenck 1977; Gottfredson 1984).

Good research on drug use and abuse routinely reveals that the correlates of delinquency and drug use are the same. As Akers (1984) has noted, "compared to the abstaining teenager, the drinking, smoking and drug-taking teen is much more likely to be getting into fights, stealing, hurting other people, and committing other delinquencies." Akers goes on to say, "but the variation in the order in which they take up these things leaves little basis for proposing the causation of one by the other." In our view, the relation between drug use and delinquency is not a causal question. The correlates are the same because drug use and delinquency are both manifestations of an underlying tendency to pursue short-term, immediate pleasure. This underlying tendency (i.e., lack of self-control) has many manifestations, as listed by Harrison Gough (1948):

> unconcern over the rights and privileges of others when recognizing them would interfere with personal satisfaction in any way; impulsive behavior, or apparent incongruity between the strength of the stimulus and the magnitude of the behavioral response; inability to form deep or persistent attachments to other persons or to identify in interpersonal relationships; poor judgment and planning in attaining defined goals; apparent lack of anxiety and distress over social maladjustment and unwillingness or inability to consider maladjustment qua maladjustment; a tendency to project blame onto others and to take no responsibility for failures; meaningless prevarication, often about trivial matters in situations where detection is inevitable; almost complete lack of dependability . . . and willingness to assume responsibility; and, finally, emotional poverty. [p. 362]

This combination of characteristics has been revealed in the life histories of the subjects in the famous studies by Lee Robins. Robins is one of the few researchers to focus on the varieties of deviance and the way they tend to go together in the lives of those she designates as having "antisocial personalities." In her words: "We refer to someone who fails to maintain close personal relationships with anyone else, [who] performs poorly on the job, who is involved in illegal behaviors (whether or not apprehended), who fails to support himself and his dependents without outside aid, and who is given to sudden changes of plan and loss of temper in response to what appear to others as minor frustrations" (1978: 255).

For 30 years Robins traced 524 children referred to a guidance clinic in St. Louis, Missouri, and she compared them to a control group matched on IQ, age, sex, and area of the city. She discovered that, in comparison to the control group, those people referred at an early age were more likely to be arrested as adults (for a wide variety of offences), were less likely to get married, were more likely to be divorced, were more likely to marry a spouse with a behavior problem, were less likely to have children (but if they had children were likely to leave more children), were more likely to have children with behavior problems, were more likely to be unemployed, had considerably more frequent job changes, were more likely to be on welfare, had fewer contacts with relatives, had fewer friends, were substantially less likely to attend church, were less likely to serve in the armed forces and more likely to be dishonorably discharged if they did serve, were more likely to exhibit physical evidence of excessive alcohol use, and were more likely to be hospitalized for psychiatric problems (1966: 42-73).

Note that these outcomes are consistent with four general elements of our notion of low self-control: basic stability of individual differences over a long period of time; great variability in the kinds of criminal acts engaged in; conceptual or causal equivalence of criminal and noncriminal acts; and inability to predict the specific forms of deviance engaged in, whether criminal or noncriminal. In our view, the idea of an antisocial personality defined by certain behavioral consequences is too positivistic or deterministic, suggesting that the offender must do certain things given his antisocial personality. Thus we would say only that the subjects in question are *more likely* to commit criminal acts (as the data indicate they are). We do not make commission of criminal acts part of the definition of the individual with low self-control.

Be this as it may, Robins's retrospective research shows that predictions derived from a concept of antisocial personality are highly consistent with the results of prospective longitudinal and cross-sectional research: offenders do not specialize; they tend to be involved in accidents, illness, and death at higher rates than the general population; they tend to have difficulty persisting in a job regardless of the particular characteristics of the job (no job will turn out to be a good job); they have difficulty acquiring and retaining friends; and they have difficulty meeting the demands of long-term financial commitments (such as mortgages or car payments) and the demands of parenting.

Seen in this light, the "costs" of low self-control for the individual may far exceed the costs of his criminal acts. In fact, it appears that crime is often among the least serious consequences of a lack of self-control in terms of the quality of life of those lacking it.

The Causes of Self-Control

We know better what deficiencies in self-control lead to than where they come from. One thing is, however, clear: low self-control is not produced by training, tutelage, or socialization. As a matter of fact, all of the characteristics associated with low self-control tend to show themselves in the absence of nurturance, discipline, or training. Given the classical appreciation of the causes of human behavior, the implications of this fact are straightforward: the causes of low self-control are negative rather than positive; self-control is unlikely in the absence of effort, intended or unintended, to create it. (This assumption separates the present theory from most modern theories of crime, where the offender is automatically seen as a product of possessive forces, a creature of learning, particular pressures, or specific defect. We will return to this comparison once our theory has been fully explicated.)

At this point it would be easy to construct a theory of crime causation, according to which characteristics of potential offenders lead them ineluctably to the commission of criminal acts. Our task at this point would simply be to identify the likely sources of impulsiveness, intelligence, risk-taking, and the like. But to do so would be to follow the path that has proven so unproductive in the past, the path according to which criminals commit crimes irrespective of the characteristics of the setting or situation.

We can avoid this pitfall by recalling the elements inherent in the decision to commit a criminal act. The object of the offense is clearly pleasurable, and universally so. Engaging in the act, however, entails some risk of social, legal, and/or natural sanctions. Whereas the pleasure attained by the act is direct, obvious, and immediate, the pains risked by it are not obvious, or direct, and are in any even at greater remove from it. It follows that, though there will be little variability among people in their ability to see the

pleasures of crime, there will be considerable variability in their ability to calculate potential pains. But the problem goes further than this: whereas the pleasures of crime are reasonably equally distributed over the population, this is not true for the pains. Everyone appreciates money; not everyone dreads parental anger or disappointment upon learning that the money was stolen.

So, the dimensions of self-control are, in our view, factors affecting calculation of the consequences of one's acts. The impulsive or short-sighted person fails to consider the negative or painful consequences of his acts; the insensitive person has fewer negative consequences to consider; the less intelligent person also has fewer negative consequences to consider (has less to lose).

No known social group, whether criminal or noncriminal, actively or purposefully attempts to reduce the self-control of its members. Social life is not enhanced by low self-control and its consequences. On the contrary, the exhibition of these tendencies undermines harmonious group relations and the ability to achieve collective ends. These facts explicitly deny that a tendency to crime is a product of socialization, culture, or positive learning of any sort.

The traits composing low self-control are also not conducive to the achievement of long-term individual goals. On the contrary, they impede educational and occupational achievement, destroy interpersonal relations, and undermine physical health and economic well-being. Such facts explicitly deny the notion that criminality is an alternative route to the goals otherwise obtainable through legitimate avenues. It follows that people who care about the interpersonal skill, educational and occupational achievement, and physical and economic well-being of those in their care will seek to rid them of these traits.

Two general sources of variation are immediately apparent in this scheme. The first is the variation among children in the degree to which they manifest such traits to begin with. The second is the variation among caretakers in the degree to which they recognize low self-control and its consequences and the degree to which they are willing and able to correct it. Obviously, therefore, even at this threshold level the sources of low self-control are complex.

There is good evidence that some of the traits predicting subsequent involvement in crime appear as early as they can be reliably measured, including low intelligence, high activity level, physical strength, and adventuresomeness (Glueck and Glueck 1950; West and Farrington 1973). The evidence suggests that the connection between these traits and commission of criminal acts ranges from weak to moderate. Obviously, we do not suggest that people are born criminals, inherit a gene for criminality, or anything of the sort. In fact, we explicitly deny such notions. . . . What we do suggest is that individual differences may have an impact on the prospects for effective socialization (or adequate control). Effective socialization is, however, always possible whatever the configuration of individual traits.

Other traits affecting crime appear later and seem to be largely products of ineffective or incomplete socialization. For example, differences in impulsivity and insensitivity become noticeable later in childhood when they are no longer common to all children. The ability and willingness to delay immediate gratification for some larger purpose may therefore be assumed to be a consequence of training. Much parental action is in fact geared toward suppression of impulsive behavior, toward making the child consider the long-range consequences of acts. Consistent sensitivity to the needs and feelings of others may also be assumed to be a consequence of training. Indeed, much parental behavior is directed toward teaching the child about the rights and feelings of others, and of how these rights and feelings ought to constrain the child's behavior. All of these points focus our attention on child-rearing.

Child-Rearing and Self-Control: The Family

The major "cause" of low self-control thus appears to be ineffective child-rearing. Put in positive terms, several conditions appear necessary to produce a socialized child. Perhaps the place to begin looking for these conditions is the research literature on the relation between family conditions and delinquency. This research (e.g., Glueck and Glueck 1950; McCord and McCord 1959) has examined the connection between many family factors and delinquency. It reports that discipline, supervision, and affection tend to be missing in the homes of delinquents, that the behavior of the parents is often "poor" (e.g., excessive drinking and poor supervision [Glueck and Glueck 1950: 110-11]), and that the parents of delinquents are unusually likely to have criminal records themselves. Indeed, according to Michael Rutter and Henri Giller, "of the parental characteristics associated with delinquency, criminality is the most striking and most consistent" (1984: 182).

Such information undermines the many explanations of crime that ignore the family, but in this form it does not represent much of an advance over the belief of the general public (and those who deal with offenders in the criminal justice system) that "defective upbringing" or "neglect" in the home is the primary cause of crime.

To put these standard research findings in perspective, we think it necessary to define the conditions necessary for adequate child-rearing to occur. The minimum conditions seem to be these: in order to teach the child self-control, someone must (1) monitor the child's behavior; (2) recognize deviant behavior when it occurs; and (3) punish such behavior. This seems simple and obvious enough. All that is required to activate the system is affection for *or* investment in the child. The person who cares for the child will watch his behavior, see him doing things he should not do, and correct him. The result may be a child more capable of delaying gratification, more sensitive to the interests and desires of others, more independent, more willing to accept restraints on his activity, and more unlikely to use force or violence to attain his ends.

When we seek the causes of low self-control, we ask where this system can go wrong. Obviously, parents do not prefer their children to be unsocialized in the terms described. We can therefore rule out in advance the possibility of positive socialization to unsocialized behavior (as cultural or subcultural deviance theories suggest). Still, the system can go wrong at any one of four places. First, the parents may not care for the child (in which case none of the other conditions would be met); second, the parents, even if they care, may not have the time or energy to monitor the child's behavior; third, the parents, even if they care *and* monitor, may not see anything wrong with the child's behavior; finally, even if everything else is in place, the parents may not have the inclination or the means to punish the child. So, what may appear at first glance to be nonproblematic turns out to be problematic indeed. Many things can go wrong. According to much research in crime and delinquency, in the homes of problem children many things have gone wrong: "Parents of stealers do not track ([they] do not interpret stealing . . . as 'deviant'); they do not punish; and they do not care" (Patterson 1980: 88-89; see also Glueck and Glueck 1950; McCord and McCord 1959; West and Farrington 1977).

Let us apply this scheme to some of the facts about the connection between child socialization and crime, beginning with the elements of the child-rearing model.

The Attachment of the Parent to the Child

Our model states that parental concern for the welfare or behavior of the child is a necessary condition for successful child-rearing. Because it is too often assumed that all parents are alike in their love for their children, the evidence directly on this point is not as good or extensive as it could be. However, what exists is clearly consistent with the model. Glueck and Glueck (1950: 125-28) report that, compared to the fathers of delinquents, fathers of nondelinquents were twice as likely to be warmly disposed toward their sons and one-fifth as likely to be hostile toward them. In the same sample, 28 percent of the mothers of delinquents were characterized as "indifferent or hostile" toward the child as compared to 4 percent of the mothers of nondelinquents. The evidence suggests that stepparents are especially unlikely to have feelings of affection toward their stepchildren (Burgess 1980), adding in contemporary society to the likelihood that children will be "reared" by people who do not especially care for them.

Parental Supervision

The connection between social control and self-control could not be more direct than in the case of parental supervision of the child. Such supervision presumably prevents criminal or analogous acts and at the same time trains the child to avoid them on his own. Consistent with this assumption, supervision tends to be a major predictor of delinquency, however supervision or delinquency is measured (Glueck and Glueck 1950; Hirschi 1969; West and Farrington 1977; Riley and Shaw 1985).

Our general theory in principle provides a method of separating supervision as external control from supervision as internal control. For one thing, offenses differ in the degree to which they can be prevented through monitoring; children at one age are monitored much more closely than children at other ages; girls are supervised more closely than boys. In some situations, monitoring is universal or nearly constant; in other situations monitoring for some offenses is virtually absent. In the present context, however, the concern is with the connection between supervision and self-control, a connection established by the stronger tendency of those poorly supervised when young to commit crimes as adults (McCord 1979).

Recognition of Deviant Behavior

In order for supervision to have an impact on self-control, the supervisor must perceive deviant behavior when it occurs. Remarkably, not all parents are adept at recognizing lack of self-control. Some parents allow the child to do pretty much as he pleases without interference. Extensive television-viewing is one modern example, as is the failure to require completion of homework, to prohibit smoking, to curtail the use of physical force, or to see to it that the child actually attends school. (As noted, truancy among second-graders presumably reflects on the adequacy of parental awareness of the child's misbehavior.) Again, the research is not as good as it should be, but evidence of "poor conduct standards" in the homes of delinquents is common.

Punishment of Deviant Acts

Control theories explicitly acknowledge the necessity of sanctions in preventing criminal behavior. They do not suggest that the major sanctions are legal or corporal. On the contrary, as we have seen, they suggest that disapproval by people one cares about is the most powerful of sanctions. Effective punishment by the parent or major caretaker therefore usually entails nothing more than explicit disapproval of unwanted behavior. The criticism of control theories that dwells on their alleged cruelty is therefore simply misguided or ill informed (see, e.g., Currie 1985).

Not all caretakers punish effectively. In fact, some are too harsh and some are too lenient (Glueck and Glueck 1950; McCord and McCord 1959; West and Farrington 1977; see generally Loeber and Stouthamer-Loeber 1986). Given our model, however, rewarding good behavior cannot compensate for failure to correct deviant behavior. (Recall that, in our view, deviant acts carry with them their own rewards. . . .

Given the consistency of the child-rearing model with our general theory and with the research literature, it should be possible to use it to explain other family correlates of criminal and otherwise deviant behavior.

Parental Criminality

Our theory focuses on the connection between the self-control of the parent and the subsequent self-control of the child. There is good reason to expect, and the data confirm, that people lacking self-control do not socialize their children well. According to Donald West and David Farrington, "the fact that delinquency is transmitted from one generation to the next is indisputable"(1977: 109; see also Robins 1966). Of course our theory does not allow transmission of criminality, genetic or otherwise. However, it does allow us to predict that some people are more likely than others to fail to socialize their children and that this will be a consequence of their own inadequate socialization. The extent of this connection between parent and child socialization is revealed by the fact that in the West

and Farrington study fewer than 5 percent of the families accounted for almost half of the criminal convictions in the entire sample. (In our view, this finding is more important for the theory of crime, and for public policy, than the much better-known finding of Wolfgang and his colleagues [1972] that something like 6 percent of *individual* offenders account for about half of all criminal acts.) In order to achieve such concentration of crime in a small number of families, it is necessary that the parents and the brothers and sisters of offenders also be unusually likely to commit criminal acts.

Why should the children of offenders be unusually vulnerable to crime? Recall that our theory assumes that criminality is not something the parents have to work to produce; on the contrary, it assumes that criminality is something they have to work to avoid. Consistent with this view, parents with criminal records do *not* encourage crime in their children and are in fact as disapproving of it as parents with no record of criminal involvement (West and Farrington 1977). Of course, not wanting criminal behavior in one's children and being upset when it occurs do not necessarily imply that great effort has been expended to prevent it. If criminal behavior is oriented toward short-term rewards, and if child-rearing is oriented toward long-term rewards, there is little reason to expect parents themselves lacking self-control to be particularly adept at instilling self-control in their children.

Consistent with this expectation, research consistently indicates that the supervision of delinquents in families where parents have criminal records tends to be "lax," "inadequate," or "poor." Punishment in these families also tends to be easy, short-term, and insensitive—that is, yelling and screaming, slapping and hitting, with threats that are not carried out.

Such facts do not, however, completely account for the concentration of criminality among some families. A major reason for this failure is probably that the most subtle element of child-rearing is not included in the analysis. This is the element of *recognition* of deviant behavior. According to Gerald Patterson (1980), many parents do not even recognize *criminal* behavior in their children, let alone the minor forms of deviance whose punishment is necessary for effective child-rearing. For example, when children steal outside the home, some parents discount reports that they have done so on the grounds that the charges are unproved and cannot therefore be used to justify punishment. By the same token, when children are suspended for misbehavior at school, some parents side with the child and blame the episode on prejudicial mistreatment by teachers. Obviously, parents who cannot see the misbehavior their children are in no position to correct it, even if they are inclined to do so. . . .

Reprinted from *A General Theory of Crime* by Michael R. Gottfredson and Travis Hirschi with the permission of the publishers, Stanford University Press. Copyright © 1990 by the Board of Trustees of the Leland Stanford Junior University.

Discussion Questions

1. What is low self-control? What are its main elements?

2. Give examples of acts that are "analogous" to crime? Why do Gottfredson and Hirschi believe that low self-control explains both crime and these analogous acts?

3. How does Gottfredson and Hirschi's self-control theory differ from Hirschi's earlier social bond theory?

4. What is the main reason that people have low self-control? In turn, based on Gottfredson and Hirschi's theory, what would be the best way to try to reduce crime? ◆

20

Crime and the Life Course

Robert J. Sampson
John H. Laub

Sampson and Laub were among the first criminologists to study the sources of crime across the life course. Their central thesis is that the quality of social bonds, which is the basis for the exercise of informal social control, helps to explain the onset of, persistence of, and desistance from criminal and deviant behavior. Social bonds, that is, shape why people start offending, continue offending, and change and stop offending.

Thus, like Hirschi (1969), Sampson and Laub (1993: 18) embrace the premise that "crime and deviance result when an individual's bond to society is weak or broken." They "emphasize the role of informal social controls that emerge from the role reciprocities and structure of interpersonal bonds linking members of society to one another and to wider social institutions such as work, family, and school" (p. 18). They also introduce the concept of "social capital" to refer to the resources— whether instrumental or affective—that are gained from quality social relations. As social capital increases—for example, as a marriage brings more money, family connections, support, and satisfaction—the relationship becomes more important in a person's life. This salience in turn makes the relationship more effective as a basis of informal control. Hence, a spouse's admonition to "stay out of trouble" is likely to be heeded because the emotional "capital" derived from the marriage makes the spouse's preferences matter and makes the potential cost of deviation substantial (i.e., losing a spouse's affection).

Again, Sampson and Laub propose that devising a complete causal model of crime requires studying people across their lives. They

contend that during childhood and adolescence, youngsters are subjected to "social control processes," such as direct control by and attachment to parents and ties to the school, which affect their level of delinquency. The effectiveness of this social control is influenced by larger structural factors and by individual differences. For example, parents will be less effective at social control when they are in families that move a number of times and when their children have low self-control. There is continuity in antisocial behavior as juveniles mature, but change still is possible. In adulthood, crime is stabilized by "weak attachment" to the labor force and to marriage. In contrast, offenders who secure stable employment or are fortunate to initiate a quality marriage will accumulate the social capital and be subjected to informal social controls that make change to a law-abiding life possible.

It is noteworthy that Sampson and Laub supported their theoretical model with elaborate analyses of data originally collected by Sheldon and Eleanor Glueck (see Chapter 2). Rummaging around in the basement of a Harvard University library where the Gluecks' papers were stored, they discovered the old computer cards used by the Gluecks in their research. Recall that the Gluecks compared a matched sample of 500 delinquent boys (as defined by official records) and 500 nondelinquent boys residing in high-risk Boston neighborhoods. Because these boys were followed for nearly two decades—starting in 1939–1940— Sampson and Laub could examine the sources of crime over much of the life course. Although further research is needed to confirm the findings from the Gluecks' data, initial research is supportive of Sampson and Laub's theory (see Horney et al., 1995).

References

Hirschi, Travis. 1969. *Causes of Delinquency.* Berkeley: University of California Press.

Horney, Julie, D. Wayne Osgood, and Ineke Haen Marshall. 1995. "Criminal Careers in the Short-Term: Intra-Individual Variability in Cime and Its Relation to Local Life Circumstances." *American Sociological Review* 60: 655-73.

Sampson, Robert J. and John H. Laub. 1993. *Crime in the Making: Pathways and Turning*

Points Through Life. Cambridge, MA: Harvard University Press.

Accepted wisdom holds that crime is committed disproportionately by adolescents. According to data from the United States and other industrialized countries, rates of property crime and violent crime rise rapidly in the teenage years to a peak at about ages 16 and 18, respectively (Hirschi and Gottfredson, 1983; Farrington, 1986a; Flanagan and Maguire, 1990). The overrepresentation of youth in crime has been demonstrated using multiple sources of measurement—official arrest reports (Federal Bureau of Investigation, 1990), self-reports of offending (Rowe and Tittle, 1977), and victims' reports of the ages of their offenders (Hindelang, 1981). It is thus generally accepted that, in the aggregate, age-specific crime rates peak in the late teenage years and then decline sharply across the adult life span.

The age-crime curve has had a profound impact on the organization and content of sociological studies of crime by channeling research to a focus on adolescents. As a result, sociological criminology has traditionally neglected the theoretical significance of childhood characteristics and the link between early childhood behaviors and later adult outcomes (Robins, 1966; McCord, 1979; Caspi et al., 1989; Farrington, 1989; Gottfredson and Hirschi, 1990; Loeber and LeBlanc, 1990; Sampson and Laub, 1990). Although criminal behavior does peak in the teenage years, evidence reviewed in this chapter indicates an early onset of delinquency as well as continuity of criminal behavior over the life course. By concentrating on the teenage years, sociological perspectives on crime have thus failed to address the life-span implications of childhood behavior.

At the same time, criminologists have not devoted much attention to the other end of the spectrum—desistance from crime and the transitions from criminal to noncriminal behavior in adulthood (Cusson and Pinsonneault, 1986; Shover, 1985; Garner and Piliavin, 1988). As Rutter (1988: 3) argues, we know little about "escape from the risk process" and whether predictors of desistance are unique or simply the opposite of criminogenic factors. Thus, researchers have neglected not only the early life course, but also the relevance of social transitions in young adulthood and the factors explaining desistance from crime as people age.

Finally, in all phases of the life course, criminologists have largely ignored the link between social structural context and the mediating processes of informal social control. Most researchers have examined either macro-level/structural variables (for example, social class, ethnicity, mobility) or micro-level processes (for example, parent-child interactions, discipline) in the study of crime. We believe both sets of variables are necessary to explain crime, but from the existing research we do not know precisely how structural variables and the processes of informal social control are related.

. . . [W]e confront these issues by bringing both childhood and adulthood back into the criminological picture of age and crime. To accomplish this goal, we synthesize and integrate the research literatures on crime and the life course and develop a theory of age-graded informal social control and criminal behavior. The basic thesis we develop is threefold in nature: (1) structural context mediated by informal family and school social controls explains delinquency in childhood and adolescence; (2) in turn, there is continuity in antisocial behaviors from childhood through adulthood in a variety of life domains; and (3) informal social bonds in adulthood to family and employment explain changes in criminality over the life span despite early childhood propensities. Our theoretical model thus acknowledges the importance of early childhood behaviors and individual differences in self-control (Gottfredson and Hirschi, 1990) but rejects the implication that later adult factors have little relevance (Wilson and Herrnstein, 1985; Gottfredson and Hirschi, 1990). In other words, we contend that social interaction with both juvenile *and* adult institutions of informal social control has important effects on crime and deviance. Thus, ours is a "sociogenic" model of crime and deviance that seeks to incorporate both stability and change over the life course.

We test our theoretical model through a detailed analysis of unique longitudinal data consisting of two samples of delinquent and nondelinquent boys followed from childhood and adolescence into their forties. Before describing our research strategy, we present a brief overview of the life-course perspective.

The Life-Course Perspective

The life course has been defined as "pathways through the age differentiated life span," where age differentiation "is manifested in expectations and options that impinge on decision processes and the course of events that give shape to life stages, transitions, and turning points" (Elder, 1985: 17). Similarly, Caspi, Elder, and Herbener (1990: 15) conceive of the life course as a "sequence of culturally defined age-graded roles and social transitions that are enacted over time." Age-graded transitions are embedded in social institutions and are subject to historical change (Elder, 1975, 1992).

Two central concepts underlie the analysis of life-course dynamics. A *trajectory* is a pathway or line of development over the life span, such as work life, marriage, parenthood, self-esteem, or criminal behaviors. Trajectories refer to long-term patterns of behavior and are marked by a sequence of transitions. *Transitions* are marked by life events (such as first job or first marriage) that are embedded in trajectories and evolve over shorter time spans—"changes in state that are more or less abrupt" (Elder, 1985: 31-32). Some transitions are age-graded and some are not; hence, what is often assumed to be important are the normative timing and sequencing of role transitions. For example, Hogan (1980) emphasizes the duration of time (spells) between a change in state and the ordering of events such as first job or first marriage on occupational status and earnings in adulthood. Caspi, Elder, and Herbener (1990: 25) argue that delays in social transitions (for example, being "offtime") produce conflicting obligations that enhance later difficulties (see also Rindfuss et al., 1987). As a result, life-course analyses are often characterized by a focus on the duration, timing, and ordering of major life events and their consequences for later social development.

The interlocking nature of trajectories and transitions may generate *turning points* or a change in the life course (Elder, 1985: 32). Adaptation to life events is crucial because the same event or transition followed by different adaptations can lead to different trajectories (Elder, 1985: 35). The long-term view embodied by the life-course focus on trajectories implies a strong connection between childhood events and experiences in adulthood. However, the simultaneous shorter-term view also implies that transitions or turning points can modify life trajectories—they can "redirect paths." Social institutions and triggering life events that may modify trajectories include school, work, the military, marriage, and parenthood (see Elder, 1986; Rutter et al., 1990; Sampson and Laub, 1990).

In addition to the study of patterns of change and the continuity between childhood behavior and later adulthood outcomes, the life-course framework encompasses at least three other themes: a concern with the social meanings of age throughout the life course, intergenerational transmission of social patterns, and the effects of macro-level events (such as the Great Depression or World War II) on individual life histories (Elder, 1974, 1985). As Elder (1992) notes, a major objective of the life-course perspective is to link social history and social structure to the unfolding of human lives. To address these themes individual lives are studied through time, with particular attention devoted to aging, cohort effects, historical content, and the social influence of age-graded transitions. Naturally, prospective longitudinal research designs form the heart of life-course research.

Of all the themes emphasized in life-course research, the extent of stability and change in behavior and personality attributes over time is probably the most complex. Stability versus change in behavior is also one of the most hotly debated and controversial issues in the social sciences (Brim and Kagan, 1980; Dannefer, 1984; Baltes and Nesselroade, 1984; Featherman and Lerner, 1985; Caspi and Bem, 1990). Given the pivotal role of this issue, we turn to an assessment of the research literature as it bears on stability and change in crime. As we shall see, this literature contains evidence for both continuity *and* change over the life course.

Stability of Crime and Deviance

Unlike sociological criminology, the field of developmental psychology has long been concerned with the continuity of maladaptive behaviors (Brim and Kagan, 1980; Caspi and Bem, 1990). As a result, a large portion of the longitudinal evidence on stability comes from psychologists and others who study "antisocial behavior" generally, where the legal concept of crime may or may not be a component. An example is the study of aggression in psychology (Olweus, 1979). In exploring this research tradition our purpose is to highlight the extent to which deviant childhood behaviors have important ramifications in later adult life, whether criminal or noncriminal in form.

Our point of departure is the widely reported claim that individual differences in antisocial behavior are stable across the life course (Olweus, 1979; Caspi et al., 1987; Loeber, 1982; Robins, 1966; Huesman et al., 1984; Gottfredson and Hirschi, 1990; Jessor et al., 1977, 1991). . . .

Although perhaps more comprehensive, these findings are not new. Over 50 years ago the Gluecks found that virtually all of the 510 reformatory inmates in their study of criminal careers "had experience in serious antisocial conduct" (Glueck and Glueck, 1930: 142). Their data also confirmed "the early genesis of antisocial careers" (1930: 143). In addition, the Gluecks' follow-up of 1,000 males originally studied in *Unraveling Juvenile Delinquency* (1950) revealed remarkable continuities. As they argued in *Delinquents and Non-Delinquents in Perspective*: "While the majority of boys originally included in the nondelinquent control group continued, down the years, to remain essentially law-abiding, the greatest majority of those originally included in the delinquent group continued to commit all sorts of crimes in the 17-25 age-span" (1968:170). Findings regarding behavioral or homotypic continuity are thus supported by a rich body of empirical research that spans several decades (for more extensive discussion see Robbins, 1966, 1978; West and Farrington, 1977; Gottfredson and Hirschi, 1990). In fact, much as the Gluecks had reported earlier, Robins (1978) summarized results from her studies of four male cohorts by stating that "adult antisocial behavior virtually *requires* childhood antisocial behavior" (1978:611).

In short, there is considerable evidence that antisocial behavior is relatively stable across stages of the life course. As Caspi and Moffitt (1992) conclude, robust continuities in antisocial behavior have been revealed over the past 50 years in different nations (for example, Canada, England, Finland, New Zealand, Sweden, and the United States) and with multiple methods of assessment (including official records, teacher ratings, parent reports, and peer nominations of aggressive behavior). These replications across time and space yield an impressive generalization that is rare in the social sciences.

Sociological approaches to crime have largely ignored this generalization and consequently remain vulnerable to attack for not coming to grips with the implications of behavioral stability. Not surprisingly, developmental psychologists have long seized on stability to argue for the primacy of early childhood and the irrelevance of the adult life course. But even recent social theories of crime take much the same tack, denying that adult life-course transitions can have any real effect on adult criminal behavior. In particular, Gottfredson and Hirschi (1990: 238) argue that ordinary life events (for example, jobs, getting married, becoming a parent) have little effect on criminal behavior because crime rates decline with age "whether or not these events occur." They go on to argue that the life-course assumption that such events are important neglects its own evidence on the stability of personal characteristics (1990: 237; see also Gottfredson and Hirschi, 1987). And, since crime emerges early in the life course, traditional sociological variables (such as peers, the labor market, or marriage) are again allegedly impotent (Wilson and Herrnstein, 1985). The reasoning is that since crime emerges before sociological variables appear, the latter cannot be important in modifying life trajectories.

From initial appearances it thus appears that the evidence on stability leaves little room for the relevance of sociological theories of age-graded transitions in the life course. As it turns out, however, whether one views the glass of stability as half empty or half full stems at least as much from theoretical predilections as from empirical reality. Moreover, not only are there important discontinuities in crime that need to be explained, but a reconsideration of the evidence suggests that stability itself is quite compatible with a sociological perspective on the life course.

Change and the Adult Life Course

In an important paper Dannefer (1984) sharply critiques existing models of adult development, drawn primarily from the fields of biology and psychology, for their exclusive "ontogenetic" focus and their failure to recognize the "profoundly interactive nature of self-society relations" and the "variability of social environments" (1984: 100). He further argues that "the contributions of sociological research and theory provide the basis for understanding human development as socially organized and socially produced, not only by what happens in early life, but also by the effects of social structure, social interaction, and their effects on life chances throughout the life course" (1984: 106). Is there evidence in the criminological literature to support Dannefer's general observations regarding change over the life course and the importance of social structure and interaction?

We begin to answer this question with a seeming paradox: although the studies reviewed earlier do show that antisocial behavior in children is one of the best predictors of antisocial behavior in adults, "most antisocial children do not become antisocial as adults" (Gove, 1985: 123). Robins (1978) found identical results in her review of four longitudinal studies, stating that most antisocial children do not become antisocial adults (1978: 611). A follow-up of the Cambridge-Somerville Youth study found that "a majority of adult criminals had no history as juvenile delinquents" (McCord, 1980: 158). Cline (1980: 665) states that although there is "more constancy than change. . .there is sufficient change in all the data to preclude simple conclusions concerning criminal career progressions." He concludes that there is far more heterogeneity in criminal behavior than previous work has suggested, and that many juvenile offenders do not become career offenders (Cline, 1980: 669-670). Loeber and LeBlanc make a similar point: "Against the backdrop of continuity, studies also show large within-individual changes in offending, a point understressed by Gottfredson and Hirschi" (1990: 390). . . .

In the context of personality characteristics, Caspi (1987) found that although the tendency toward explosive, under-controlled behavior in childhood was evident in adulthood, "invariant action patterns did not emerge across the age-graded life course" (1987: 1211). Similarly, using a prospective longitudinal design to study poverty, Long and Vaillant (1984) found both discontinuity and continuity across three generations of subjects. Their finding that the transmission of "underclass"or dependent life styles was not inevitable or even very likely refutes the hypothesis that the chances of escape from poverty are minimal. As they observe: "The transmission of disorganization and alienation that seems inevitable when a disadvantaged cohort is studied retrospectively appears to be the exception rather than the norm in a prospective study that locates the successes as well as the failures" (Long and Vaillant, 1984: 344; see also Vaillant, 1977).

This is an important methodological point that applies to the stability of crime. Looking *back* over the careers of adult criminals exaggerates the prevalence of stability. Looking *forward* from youth reveals the successes and failures, including adolescent delinquents who go on to be normal functioning adults. This is the paradox noted earlier: adult criminality seems to be always preceded by childhood misconduct, but most conduct-disordered children do not become antisocial or criminal adults (Robins, 1978). . . .

Rethinking Change and Stability

Taken as a whole, the foregoing review suggests that conclusions about the inevitability of antisocial continuities have been either overstated or misinterpreted. In regard to the former, long-term stability coefficients are far from perfect and leave considerable room for the emergence of discontinuities. In retrospect, criminologists should have been forewarned not to make sweeping generalizations about stability in light of the lengthy history of prediction research showing that childhood variables are quite modest prognostic devices. In a situation known as the false positive problem, prediction scales often result in the substantial overprediction of future criminality (Loeber, 1987; Farrington and Tarling, 1985). Likewise, prediction attempts often fail to identify accurately those who will become criminal even though past behavior suggests otherwise (false negatives). . . .

Based on this conceptualization of past research, our theoretical model is premised on the fact that both stability and change are present over the life course, and that we need to explain both. As Gottfredson and Hirschi (1990) note, the tendency of individuals to remain relatively stable over time on the dimension of deviance points to the early life course—especially family socialization and child rearing—as a key causal explanation of early delinquency and a stable self-control. While we agree with this conception, we are also concerned with adult behavior and how it is influenced not only by early life experiences and self-control, but also by modifying events and socialization in adulthood. Because we hypothesize that the adult life course accounts for variation in adult crime that cannot be predicted from childhood, change is a central part of our explanatory framework. . . .

Informal Social Control and Social Capital

Our theory emphasizes the importance of informal social ties and bonds to society at all ages across the life course. Hence the effects of informal social control in childhood,

adolescence, and adulthood are central to our theoretical model. Virtually all previous studies of social control in criminology have focused either on adolescents or on official (that is, formal) social control mechanisms such as arrest and imprisonment (for reviews see Gottfredson and Hirschi, 1990; Horwitz, 1990). As a result, most criminological studies have failed to examine the processes of informal social control from childhood through adulthood.

Following Elder (1975, 1985), we differentiate the life course of individuals on the basis of age and argue that the important institutions of informal and formal social control vary across the life span. For example, the dominant institutions of social control in childhood and adolescence are the family, school, peer groups, and the juvenile justice system. In the phase of young adulthood, the institutions of higher education or vocational training, work, and marriage become salient. The juvenile justice system is also replaced by the adult criminal justice system. Finally, in middle adulthood, the dominant institutions of social control are work, marriage, parenthood, investment in the community, and the criminal justice system.

Within this framework, our organizing principle derives from the central idea of social control theory (Durkheim, [1987] 1951; Reiss, 1951a; Hirschi, 1969; Janowitz, 1975; Kornhauser, 1978): crime and deviance result when an individual's bond to society is weak or broken. As Janowitz (1975) has cogently argued, many sociologists mistakenly think of social control solely in terms of social repression and State sanctions (for example, surveillance, enforced conformity, incarceration). By contrast, we adopt a more general conceptualization of social control as the capacity of a social group to regulate itself according to desired principles and values, and hence to make norms and rules effective (Janowitz, 1975: 82; Reiss, 1951a; Kornhauser, 1978). We further emphasize the role of *informal* social controls that emerge from the role reciprocities and structure of interpersonal bonds linking members of society to one another and to wider social institutions such as work, family, and school (see also Kornhauser, 1978: 24).

In applying these concepts to the longitudinal study of crime, we examine the extent to which social bonds inhibit crime and deviance early in the life course, and the consequences this has for later development. Moreover, we examine social ties to both institutions and other individuals in the adult life course, and identify the transitions within individual trajectories that relate to changes in informal social control. In this context we contend that pathways to crime *and* conformity are mediated by social bonds to key institutions of social control. Our theoretical model focuses on the transition to adulthood and, in turn, the new role demands from higher education, full-time employment, military service, and marriage. Hence, we explore the interrelationships among crime and informal social control at all ages, with particular attention devoted to the assessment of within-individual change.

We also examine social relations between individuals (for example, parent-child, teacher-student, and employer-employee) at each stage of the life course as a form of social investment or social capital (Coleman, 1988, 1990). Specifically, we posit that the social capital derived from strong social relations (or strong social bonds), whether as a child in a family, as an adolescent in school, or as an adult in a job, dictates the salience of these relations at the individual level. If these relations are characterized by interdependence (Braithwaite, 1989), they represent social and psychological resources that individuals can draw on as they move through life transitions that traverse larger trajectories. Thus, we see both social capital and informal social control as linked to social structure, and we distinguish both concepts as important in understanding changes in behavior over time.

Recognizing the importance of both stability and change in the life course, we develop three sets of thematic ideas regarding age-graded social control. The first concerns the structural and intervening sources of juvenile delinquency; the second centers on the consequences of delinquency and antisocial behavior for adult life chances; and the third focuses on the explanation of adult crime and deviance in relation to adult informal social control and social capital. Although this model was developed in the ongoing context of our analysis of the Gluecks' data and represents the best fit between our conceptual framework and available measures, we believe that our theoretical notions have wider appeal and are not solely bound by these data.

Structure and Process in Adolescent Delinquency

In explaining the origins of delinquency, criminologists have embraced either structural factors (such as poverty, broken homes) or process variables (such as attachment to parents or teachers). We believe such a separation is a mistake. [W]e join structural and process variables together into a single theoretical model. In brief, we argue that informal social controls derived from the family (for example, consistent use of discipline, monitoring, and attachment) and school (for instance, attachment to school) mediate the effects of both individual and structural background variables. For instance, previous research on families and delinquency often fails to account for social structural disadvantage and how it influences family life. As Rutter and Giller (1983: 185) have argued, socioeconomic disadvantage has potentially adverse effects on parents, such that parental difficulties are more likely to develop and good parenting is impeded. If this is true, we would then expect poverty and disadvantage to have their effects on delinquency transmitted through parenting.

The effects of family process are hypothesized to mediate structural context in other domains as well. . . . [O]ur model and data enable us to ascertain the direct and indirect effects of other key factors such as family disruption, parental criminality, household crowding, large family size, residential mobility, and mother's employment. All of these structural background factors have traditionally been associated with delinquency (for a review, see Rutter and Giller, 1983). It is our major contention, however, that these structural factors will strongly affect family and school social control mechanisms, thereby playing a largely indirect (but not unimportant) role in the explanation of early delinquency. . . . [T]he intervening processes of primary interest are family socialization (discipline, supervision, and attachment), school attachment, and the influence of delinquent siblings and friends. Overall, these two chapters provide our accounting of the causes of early delinquency and what Gottfredson and Hirschi (1990) refer to as low self-control.

The Importance of Continuity Between Childhood and Adulthood

Our second theme concerns childhood antisocial behavior (such as juvenile delinquency, conduct disorder, or violent temper tantrums) and its link to troublesome adult behaviors. As noted earlier, the theoretical importance of homotypic continuity has been largely ignored among sociological criminologists. Criminologists still focus primarily on the teenage years in their studies of offending, apparently disregarding the connections between childhood delinquency and adult crime. Reversing this tide, our main contention . . . is that antisocial and delinquent behavior in childhood—measured by both official and unofficial sources—is linked to later adult deviance and criminality in a variety of settings (for example, family violence, military offenses, "street crime," and alcohol abuse). Moreover, we argue that these outcomes occur independent of traditional sociological and psychological variables such as class background, ethnicity, and IQ.

Although some criminologists have explored the connections among conduct disorder, juvenile delinquency, and adult crime, we argue that the negative consequences of childhood misbehavior extend to a much broader spectrum of adult life, including economic dependence, educational failure, employment instability, and marital discord. . . . [W]e thus explore the adult worlds of work, educational attainment, and marriage as well as involvement in deviant behavior generally. As Hagan and Palloni (1988) argue (see also Hagan, 1989: 260), delinquent and criminal events "are linked into life trajectories of broader significance, whether those trajectories are criminal or noncriminal in form" (1988:90). Because most research by criminologists has focused either on the teenage

years or on adult behavior limited to crime, this basic idea has not been well integrated into the criminological literature.

The Significance of Change in the Life Course

Our third focus, drawing on a developmental perspective and stepping-stone approach (Lober and LeBlanc, 1990: 433-439), is concerned with changes in deviance and offending as individuals age. [O]ur thesis concerns adult behavior and how it is influenced not just by early life experiences, but also by social ties to the adult institutions of informal social control (such as family, school, and work). We argue that trajectories of both crime and conformity are significantly influenced over the life course by these adult social bonds, regardless of prior individual differences in self-control or criminal propensity.

The third major theme of our research, then, is that changes that strengthen social bonds to society in adulthood will lead to less crime and deviance. Conversely, changes in adulthood that weaken social bonds will lead to more crime and deviance. This premise allows us to explain desistance from crime as well as late onset. In addition, unlike most researchers, we emphasize the quality, strength, and interdependence of social ties more than the occurrence or timing of discrete life events (cf. Hogan, 1978; Loeber and LeBlanc, 1990: 430-432). In our view, interdependent social bonds increase social capital and investment in social relations and institutions. . . . [O]ur theoretical model rests on social ties to jobs and family as the key inhibitors to adult crime and deviance. . . .

Theory and Hypotheses

Unlike most researchers in the life-course mold, we emphasize the quality or strength of social ties more than the occurrence or timing of discrete life events (cf. Hogan, 1978; Loeber and LeBlanc, 1990: 430-432). For example, we agree with Gottfredson and Hirschi (1990: 140-141) that the structural institution of marriage per se does not increase social control. However, strong attachment to a spouse (or cohabitant) combined with close emotional ties creates a social bond or interdependence between two individuals that, all else being equal, should lead to a reduction in deviant behavior (see also Braithwaite, 1989: 90-91; Shover, 1985: 94). Similarly, employment alone does not increase social control. It is employment coupled with job stability, job commitment, and mutual ties to work (that is, employee-employer interdependence) that should increase social control and, all else being equal, lead to a reduction in criminal and deviant behavior (see also Crutchfield, 1989: 495).

The logic of our argument suggests that it is the social investment or *social capital* (Coleman, 1988) in the institutional relationship, whether it involves a family, work, or community setting, that dictates the salience of informal social control at the individual level. As Coleman (1990: 302) argues, the distinguishing feature of social capital lies in the structure of interpersonal relations and institutional linkages. Social capital is created when these relations change in ways that facilitate action. In other words, "social capital is productive, making possible the achievements of certain ends that in its absence would not be possible" (Coleman, 1988: 98). By contrast, physical capital is wholly tangible, being embodied in observable material form (1990: 304), and human capital is embodied in the skills and knowledge acquired by an individual. Social capital is even less tangible, for it is embodied in the *relations among persons* (1990: 304). A core idea, then, is that independent of the forms of physical and human capital available to individuals (for example, income, occupational skill), social capital is a central factor in facilitating effective ties that bind a person to societal institutions.

Coleman's notion of social capital can be linked with social control theory in a straightforward manner—lack of social capital is one of the primary features of weak social bonds as defined earlier (see also Coleman, 1990: 307). The theoretical task is to identify the characteristics of social relations that facilitate the social capital available to individuals, families, employers, and other social actors. According to Coleman (1990: 318-320), one of the most important factors is the closure (that is, connectedness) of networks among actors in a social system. In a system involving employers and employees, for example, relations characterized by an extensive set of obligations, expectations, and interdependent social networks are better able to facilitate social control than are jobs characterized by purely utilitarian objectives and nonoverlapping social networks. Similarly, the mere presence of a relationship (such as marriage) between adults is not sufficient to produce social capital, and hence the idea of social capital goes beyond simple structural notions of marital status.

According to this theoretical conception, adult social controls are not as direct or external as for juveniles (for example, monitoring, supervision of activities). Rather, adult social ties are important insofar as they create interdependent systems of obligation and restraint that impose significant costs for translating criminal propensities into action. It is unrealistic to expect that adults with a criminal background (or low self-control) can be wholly transformed by institutions (marriage or work), or that such institutions are even capable of imposing direct controls like surveillance. Nevertheless, we believe that adults, regardless of delinquent background, will be inhibited from committing crime to the extent that they have social capital invested in their work and family lives (see also Cook, 1975). By contrast, those subject to weak systems of interdependence (Braithwaite, 1989) and informal social control as an adult (for example, weak attachment to the labor force or noncohesive marriages) are freer to engage in deviant behavior—even if nondelinquent as a youth. This dual premise allows us to explain desistance from crime as well as late onset.

We also emphasize the reciprocal nature of social capital invested by employers and spouses. For example, employers often take chances in hiring workers, hoping that their investment will pay off. Similarly, prospective marriage partners may be aware of a potential spouse's delinquent background but may nonetheless invest their future in that person. This investment by the employer or spouse may in turn trigger a return investment in social capital by the employee or husband. The key theoretical point is that social capital and interdependence are reciprocal and are embedded in the social ties that exist between individuals and social institutions. This conception may help explain how change in delinquent behavior is initiated (for example, an employer may take a chance on a former delinquent, fostering a return investment in that job which in turn inhibits the deviant behavior of the employee.)

At first blush, our focus on change may seem at odds with the findings . . . that (1) criminal behavior is stable over time and (2) the formation of adult social bonds is negatively related to juvenile delinquency. We reconcile these facts in two ways. First, not only is continuity far from perfect, it refers to the aggregate of interindividual differences and does not capture within-individual change. In this regard, our theoretical framework implies that adult social ties can modify childhood trajectories of crime despite the general stability of between-individual differences.

Second, weak adult social bonds may also serve as a mediating and hence sequential link between early delinquency and adult criminal behavior. . . . [T]he idea of cumulative continuity suggests that delinquency tends to "mortgage" one's future by generating negative consequences for life chances (for example, arrest, official labeling, and incarceration, which in turn spark failure in school, unemployment, weak community bonds). Serious delinquency in particular may lead to the "knifing off" of opportunities (Caspi and Moffitt, 1992; Moffitt, 1991) such that participants have fewer options for a conventional life. The concept of "knifing off" appears to be especially applicable to the structurally constrained life chances of the disadvantaged urban poor (cf. Hagan, 1991).

On the other hand, the absence or infrequency of delinquency—especially encounters with the police and/or institutionalization—provides opportunities for prosocial attachments to take firm hold in adulthood. Thus, nondelinquents are not just more motivated (presumably), but also better able structurally to establish strong social ties to conventional lines of adult activity. If nothing else, incumbency in prosocial roles provides advantages in maintaining the status quo and

counteracting negative life events (for example, last hired, first fired). In this sense we emphasize the state-dependence notion (Nagin and Paternoster, 1991) that history matters—where one has been and how long one has been in that state are crucial in understanding adult developmental patterns.

Our theoretical perspective is also consistent with Gottfredson and Hirschi's (1990: 137) argument that the incidence of criminal acts is problematic and varies when self-control is held constant. That is, variations in criminal propensity reflected by early delinquency provide an incomplete explanation of adult crime because the latter's realization is dependent, among other things, on opportunity (for instance, lack of guardianship or surveillance). Ties to work and family in adulthood influence opportunities and hence the probability that criminal propensities will be translated into action. For example, all else being equal, those in stable employment and marital relations are subject to more continuity in guardianship than those is unstable employment or marital roles.

In brief, ours is a dynamic theory of social capital and informal social control that at once incorporates stability and change in criminal behavior. Change is central to our model because we propose that variations in adult crime cannot be explained by childhood behavior alone. We specifically hypothesize that the strength of adult social bonds has a direct negative effect on adult criminal behavior, controlling for childhood delinquency. At the same time our model incorporates the link between childhood delinquency and adult outcomes, implying a cumulative, developmental process whereby delinquent behavior attenuates the social and institutional bonds linking adults to society. As such, adult social bonds not only have important effects on adult crime in and of themselves, but also help to explain the probabilistic links in the chain connecting early childhood differences and later adult crime. . . .

Summary of Theoretical Model

Our theoretical framework has three major themes. The first is that structural context is mediated by informal family and school social controls, which in turn explain delinquency in childhood and adolescence. The second theme is that there is strong continuity in antisocial behavior running from childhood through adulthood across a variety of life domains. The third theme is that informal social capital in adulthood explains changes in criminal behavior over the life span, regardless of prior individual differences in criminal propensity. In our view, childhood pathways to crime and conformity over the life course are significantly influenced by adult social bonds.

Although we reject the "ontogenetic" approach dominant in developmental psychology (see Dannefer, 1984), our theoretical framework nonetheless follows a developmental strategy (see Loeber and LeBlanc, 1990; Farrington, 1986b; Patterson et al., 1989). Loeber and LeBlanc (1990: 376) define "developmental criminology" as strategies that examine within-individual changes in offending over time. Moreover, the developmental approach that we take views causality as "best represented by a developmental network of causal factors" in which dependent variables become independent variables over time (Loeber and LeBlanc, 1990: 433). Developmental criminology recognizes continuity and change over time and focuses on life transitions as a way of understanding patterns of offending. This strategy has also been referred to as a "stepping stone approach," where factors are time ordered by age and assessed with respect to outcome variables (see Farrington, 1986b).

A similar perspective can be found in interactional theory (see Thornberry, 1987 and Thornberry et al., 1991). In our theoretical framework, we draw on the key idea of interactional theory that causal influences are bidirectional or reciprocal over the life course. Interactional theory embraces a developmental approach and argues convincingly that delinquency may contribute to the weakening of social bonds and informal social control over time. In particular, Thornberry maintains that interactional theory offers an explanation for continuity in criminal trajectories over time: "The initially weak bonds lead to high delinquency involvement,

the high delinquency involvement further weakens the conventional bonds, and in combination both of these effects make it extremely difficult to reestablish bonds to conventional society at later ages. As a result, all of the factors tend to reinforce one another over time to produce an extremely high probability of continued deviance" (Thornberry et al., 1991: 30).

Thornberry's perspective is also consistent with a person-centered approach to development as described by Magnusson and Bergman (1988: 47). In our analysis of the Gluecks' qualitative data we focused explicitly on "persons" rather than "variables" by examining individual life histories over time (see Magnusson and Bergman, 1988 and 1990). This focus complemented our quantitative analyses and offered insight into the social processes of intraindividual developmental change in criminal behavior over the life course.

A summary representation of our sociogenic developmental theory as applied to the Gluecks' data is presented in Figure 20.1. In essence, this model explains probabilistic links in the chain of events from childhood to adult criminal behavior. It is our view that family and school processes of informal social control provide the key causal explanation of delinquency in childhood and adolescence. Structural background characteristics are important in terms of their effects on informal family and school processes, but these same characteristics have little direct influence on delinquency. Individual characteristics like temperament and early conduct disorder are also linked to both family and school social control processes as well as delinquency itself, but these same factors do not significantly diminish the effects of social bonding in family and school on delinquency.

The theory embodied in Figure 20.1 explicitly links delinquency and adult crime to childhood and adolescent characteristics as well as socializing influences in adulthood. Early delinquency predicts weak adult social bonds, and weak adult social bonds predict concurrent and later adult crime and deviance. The process is one in which childhood antisocial behavior and adolescent delinquency are linked to adult crime and devi-

Figure 20.1
Dynamic Theoretical Model of Crime, Deviance, and Informal Social Control Over the Life Course of 1,000 Gluecks' Men, Circa 1925–1975. (In the design, delinquent and non-delinquent males were matched on age, race/ethnicity, neighborhood SES, and IQ.)

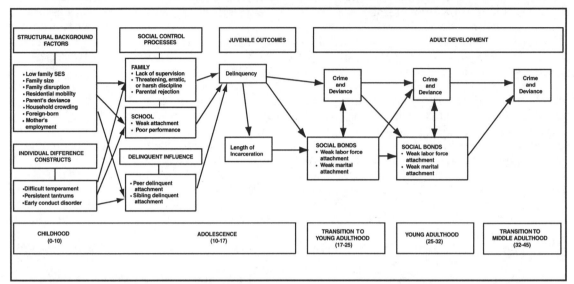

ance in part through weak social bonds. We also believe that salient life events and socialization experiences in adulthood can counteract, at least to some extent, the influence of early life experiences. For instance, late onset of criminal behavior can be accounted for by weak social bonds in adulthood, despite a background of nondelinquent behavior. Conversely, desistance from criminal behavior in adulthood can be explained by strong social bonds in adulthood, despite a background of delinquent behavior. In contrast to many life-course models, our theory emphasizes the quality or strength of social ties more than the occurrence of timing of life events (cf. Loeber and LeBlanc, 1990: 430-432). Thus, our theory provides a sociological explanation of stability and change in crime and deviance over the life course with an explicit focus on within-individual changes in offending and deviance. . . .

Discussion Questions

1. Many theorists and researchers have limited their focus to adolescents and to why juveniles become delinquent. Why would Sampson and Laub argue that it is important to study crime over the entire life course—from childhood to adulthood—rather than just examining what happens in the teenage years?

2. Why do Sampson and Laub say it is important to study not only continuity in offending but also discontinuity or change in offending?

3. Why could Sampson and Laub be categorized as "control" theorists?

4. Gottfredson and Hirschi argue that by the time childhood ends, youngsters with low self-control are trapped in a life of crime. How would Sampson and Laub respond to this contention? ✦

21

A Power-Control Theory of Gender and Delinquency

John Hagan

John Hagan's power-control theory starts with the assumption that what goes on inside the family is conditioned by what goes on outside the family. His specific focus is on how work relations affect family relations, which in turn influence gender differences in delinquency (see also, Colvin and Pauly, Chapter 34 in Part IX).

In a patriarchal family, the husband wields more power than his wife. What is the basis of this dominance? According to Hagan, gender inequality is rooted in economic inequality. When a wife is not employed but her husband is employed—especially in a position of authority where he commands other workers—a patriarchal relationship will emerge within the family. In contrast, when men and women work in similar positions—especially if both are managers of other employees—their marriages will be more egalitarian.

Hagan contends that child-rearing in patriarchal and egalitarian homes differs considerably. In essence, parents try to reproduce themselves. In patriarchal families, girls are raised in a "cult of domesticity" in which the goal is to have them to grow up to be housewives like their mothers. They are supervised carefully and develop close relationships with their mothers. On the other hand, boys are raised to be independent and to take risks—that is, to develop the traits ostensibly needed to succeed in the rugged world of work. In egalitarian families, however, the goal is to prepare both daughters and sons for the labor force. Like boys, girls are encouraged to play sports, to be assertive, and to explore new horizons. The freedoms granted them are similar to those ac-corded their brothers and far greater than those accorded girls in patriarchal homes.

These differences in family relations, Hagan theorizes, in turn explain gender differences in delinquency. In patriarchal families, boys are more involved in delinquency than girls because they experience fewer controls and develop preferences for taking risks—such as breaking the law. In egalitarian families, however, boys and girls are exposed to comparable levels of parental control and thus their risk preferences and involvement in delinquency are similar.

Although the empirical evidence on power-control theory is mixed (see, e.g., Jensen and Thompson, 1990; Singer and Levine, 1988), Hagan has conducted several empirical tests that support his perspective (see, e.g., Grasmick et al., 1996; Hagan, 1989; Hagan et al., 1990). Accordingly, there seems reason to continue to explore how power relations shape parental practices and, in turn, delinquency. Hagan's exclusive focus on control, however, seems limiting. It is not clear, for example, why husband-wife power differentials are not linked to other family processes—such as family conflict and abusive child rearing—that are known predictors of delinquency (see, e.g., Loeber and Stouthamer-Loeber, 1986).

References

Grasmick, Harold G., John Hagan, Brenda Sims Blackwell, and Bruce J. Arneklev. 1996. "Risk Preferences and Patriarchy: Extending Power-Control Theory." *Social Forces* 75: 177-199.

Hagan, John. 1989. *Structural Criminology.* New Brunswick, NJ: Rutgers University Press.

Hagan, John, A. R. Gillis, and John Simpson. 1990. "Clarifying and Extending Power-Control Theory." *American Journal of Sociology* 95: 1024-1037.

Jensen, Gary F. and Kevin Thompson. 1990. "Whats Class Got to Do with It? A Further Examination of Power-Control Theory." *American Journal of Sociology* 95:1009-1023.

Loeber, Rolf and Magda Stouthamer-Loeber. 1986. "Family Factors as Correlates and Predictors of Juvenile Conduct Problems and Delinquency." Pp. 29-149 in *Crime and Justice: An Annual Review of Research, Volume 7*, edited by Michael Tonry and Norval Morris. Chicago: University of Chicago Press.

Singer, Simon I. and Murray Levine. 1988. "Power-Control Theory, Gender, and Delinquency: A Partial Replication with Additional Evidence on the Effects of Peers." *Criminology* 26: 627-648.

Introduction

. . . Although class and gender are widely studied correlates of juvenile delinquency, little attention is given to their combined role in the explanation of delinquent behaviour. In its most general form, power-control theory asserts that the class structure of the family plays a significant role in explaining the social distribution of delinquent behaviour through the social reproduction of gender relations. "Family class structure" and "the social reproduction of gender relations" are not commonly used concepts in sociological criminology, and so we begin with some definitions.

Family class structure consists of the configurations of power between spouses that derive from the positions these spouses occupy in their work inside and outside the home. Spouses often gain power in the family through their work outside the home. So the occupational advances of women in recent decades are of particular interest to our understanding of family class structure.

The social reproduction of gender relations refers to the activities, institutions, and relationships that are involved in the maintenance and renewal of gender roles, in the family and elsewhere. These activities include the parenting involved in caring for, protecting and socializing children for the roles they will occupy as adults. According to power-control theory, family class structure shapes the social reproduction of gender relations, and in turn the social distribution of delinquency. . . .

We believe the above considerations have important implications for theory construction. The failure to consider family class structure and the social reproduction of gender relations has impeded the development of a sociological theory of crime and delinquency; this kind of omission may also help to account for a recent dormancy of sociological interest in the etiological study of crime and delinquency. One of our purposes is to reawaken this interest. . . .

The correlation of gender with criminal and delinquent behaviour is one of the few findings from the beginnings of criminological research that although questioned, never was doubted seriously. From the pioneering explorations of official crime statistics by Quetelet (1842), to the more modern tabulations by Radzinowitz (1937), Pollack (1951), Adler (1975), Simon (1975), and Smart (1977), such statistics have consistently shown that men are more criminal than women. The addition of victim (Hindelang, 1979) and self-report (Smith and Vischer, 1980) data sources to the traditional official tabulations (Steffensmeier, 1978; 1980) added to the assurance of a gender-based behavioural reality. Perhaps only age is better known for the consistency of its correlations with criminality, however measured (Hirschi and Gottfredson, 1983). The question therefore endures (Simon, 1975; Adler, 1975; Harris, 1977): can gender differences in criminal and delinquency behaviour be explained?

Feminist scholars have done the sociological study of crime and delinquency a service by refocusing attention on this important question. The effect is to suggest alternative paths that the development of the causal explanation of criminal and delinquency behaviour might usefully have taken much earlier. . . .

But feminist scholars not only bring us back to fundamental questions about the causal explanation of criminal and delinquency behaviour, they also redirect our attention to the role of the state, and especially to family structure, in the explanation of these behaviours. . . .

[F]eminist scholarship assigns renewed importance to the family and to variations in its structure. In particular, it brings attention to the role of patriarchal family relations in developing, perpetuating, and thereby reproducing gender differences in behaviour. Much of this discussion focuses on issues of power and control, concepts that are also, of course, central to the classical theories of delinquency. These concepts of power and control are central to the way we tie together our interest in class and gender. They are the conceptual cornerstones of our theory of class, gender and delinquency.

Power, Patriarchy and Delinquency

. . . Considerations of power and control nonetheless have important features in common: for example, they are both relational in content. Power theories often focus on relations of domination in the workplace, while control theories frequently focus on relations of domination in the family. We do both here. Essential to the conceptualization and measurement in both areas of theory construction is the effort to capture a relational component of social structure. In power theories of the workplace, the relational structure may be that between owner and worker, or between supervisor and supervisee. In control theories of the family, the relational structure may be that between parent and child, or between parents themselves. In both cases, however, it is a sociological concern with relational and hierarchical structure that drives the conceptualization and measurement.

Power-control theory brings together these relational concerns in a multi-level framework. In doing so, this theory highlights another concern that the power and control traditions share. This common concern is with the conditions under which actors are free to deviate from social norms. Both the presence of power and the absence of control contribute to these conditions. A particular concern of power-control theory, for example, is to identify intersections of class and family relations that provide the greatest freedom for adolescent deviation. Power-control theory assumes that the concept of patriarchy is of fundamental importance in identifying such intersections.

Curtis (1986: 171) persuasively argues that patriarchy should not be seen as a theoretical concept with a standard definition, but as a generalization about social relations that calls for sociological investigation and explication. This generalization involves the propensity of males to create hierarchical structures through which they dominate others. It is important to emphasize here that these others may be male as well as female. So the

study of patriarchy includes within it the analysis of structures through which men exercise hierarchical domination over both males and females, for example, including children of both genders in the family. Curtis goes on to point out that patriarchy is extremely widespread, including structures of the state (such as police, courts, and correctional agencies) as well as the workplace and the family. But the source of patriarchy nonetheless is assumed to be the family. Millett (1970: 33) calls the family patriarchy's "chief institution," suggesting that the family is the fundamental instrument and the foundation unit of patriarchal society, and that the family and its roles are protypical.

We are now in a position to begin sketching the outlines of a power-control theory of delinquency. We begin with the three levels of the theory, as illustrated in Figure 21.1. These include, in order of level of abstraction, *social-psychological processes* involving the adolescents whose behaviours we wish to explain, *social positions* consisting of the gender and delinquency roles in which these adolescents are located, and the class structures by which families are socially organized. Five kinds of links, described further below, bring together the social positions and social-psychological processes that are the core of power-control theory.

Figure 21.1
A Power-Control Theory of Gender and Delinquency

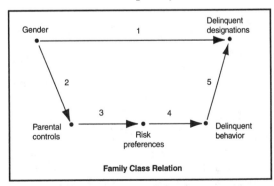

We begin with the connections between the social positions and social-psychological processes identified in Figure 21.1 Link 1 is the correlation between gender and state-defined delinquency that criminologists long have observed. We need only note here that gender and delinquency both constitute ascribed positions that are socially designated and legally identified. Our interest is in establishing the family class structures and social psychological processes that account for these social positions being joined in the correlations so consistently recorded by criminologists. Note that the interest of power-control theory is in individuals only insofar as they are located as occupants of these positions, and not, therefore, in these individuals *per se*. By virtue of the premises noted above, the question power-control theory inevitably asks is: how and why are individuals located in male adolescent positions freer to deviate in ways defined by the state as delinquent than are individuals located in female adolescent positions?

The reference to state definition above indicates that the connection between officially defined delinquency and delinquent behaviour is not assumed. Nor is a consensus assumed about what is to be called delinquent behaviour. Indeed, it is assumed that police and court practices sometimes operate to inflate the gender-delinquency correlation. As we will discuss further below, the effect of this inflation is to reinforce a sexual stratification of family and work activities, with females ascripted disproportionately for the former, and males appropriated disproportionately for the latter. Nonetheless, a sufficient consistency is hypothesized between police processing and delinquent behaviour to make the above kind of question relevant in behavioural terms.

Note also that while the above question makes no value judgements as to the "goodness" or "badness" of delinquency, it does nonetheless imply that there is a pleasurable or enjoyable aspect of delinquency. Indeed, power-control theory assumes that delinquency can be fun, if not liberating, as well as rewarding in other ways. Bordua (1961) notes that theories of delinquency too often, at least implicitly, assume that delinquency is a grim and somewhat desperate pursuit. In contrast, our assumption is that delinquency frequently is fun—and even more importantly, a kind of fun infrequently allowed to females. Said differently, delinquency may involve a spirit of liberation, the opportunity to take risks, and a chance to pursue publicly some of the pleasures that are symbolic of adult male status outside the family. One reason why delinquency is fun, then, is because it anticipates a range of activities, some criminal and some more conventional, that are more open to men than women. The interests of power-control theory are in how a sense of this sexually stratified world of licit and illicit adult pleasures, and restrictions of access to them, are communicated and reproduced across generations through gender relations.

Link 2 takes the first step in addressing such issues by explicating a connection between gender positions and the parental control of children. This link first calls attention to the proposition that parental controls are imposed selectively: that is, daughters are controlled more extensively than sons. Conceptually we represent this by noting that parents are characteristically the instruments of familial controls, while children are the objects; but most significantly, *daughters* are disproportionately the objects of this socially structured domination. So the instrument-object relationship established between parents and children is applied more selectively and extensively to daughters than sons. Beyond this, within patriarchal family structures mothers are particularly likely to be placed in the primary position of implementing this instrument-object relationship: that is, mothers more than fathers are assigned responsibility for perpetuating this instrument-object relationship.

Of course, control can be established through ties of affiliation as through subordination. Indeed, it might well be argued that a lot of affiliation and a little subordination is the most effective basis of social domination. Again, however, power-control theory predicts that ties of affiliation selectively and more extensively will be applied to daughters than sons. We will refer to these affiliative ties as relational controls, as contrasted with more instrumental kinds of controls involving supervision and surveillance. However, it is again the sexual asymmetry that is of greatest importance here, with power-control theory predicting that the larger burden of these controls is imposed on daughters rather than sons. Furthermore, it is mothers more than fathers that the patriarchal family holds responsible for the everyday imposition of these controls, again, on daughters more than sons.

Links 3, 4 and 5 in our theoretical framework lead us to a consideration of the consequences of this sexual stratification of social control. In link 3 the focus is on the risk preferences of adolescents. Risk-taking can be regarded as an expression of freedom, an expression that power-control theory predicts will be allowed selectively and more extensively to males than females. Delinquency can be regarded as an adolescent form of risk-taking (hence links 4 and 5) that we have argued can carry with it an element of pleasure, excitement, and therefore fun. The interest of power-control theory is in how a taste for such risk-taking is channeled along sexually stratified lines.

Link 3 in our theoretical framework predicts that gender differences in risk preferences will be observed and that they are mediated by the structures of parental control introduced above. That is, parents control their daughters more than their sons, and in so doing they diminish the preferences of daughters to take risks. The logical links in this theory therefore predict that daughters will be more risk-averse than sons, and that therefore daughters will be less delinquent in their behaviour than sons. In an important sense, then, what a power-control theory of delinquency is saying is that the higher likelihood of delinquency among boys than girls, and ultimately the higher likelihood of crime among men than women, is an expression of gender differences in risk preferences, which in turn are a product of the different patterns of parental control imposed on daughters compared to sons. In a still more ultimate sense, however, power-control theory goes beyond this to locate the source of such gender differences in a patriarchal connection between the family and the world of work outside it. We turn next to an explication of this connection between work and family.

Class, State and Household

We have made recurring references to the role of the patriarchal family in reproducing the five links presented in Figure 21.1 as the core of power-control theory. In this section we will argue that the patriarchal family is one distinct type of family class structure. Power-control theory predicts that the links identified in Figure 21.1 are strongest within this family class relation, and therefore that this type of family structure plays a central role in accounting for a strong connection between gender and crime. Because patriarchal family structures historically have played such a prominent role in the development of industrial capitalist societies, the effects of this family structure may be seen throughout our society, even within families that seek to reduce or eliminate patriarchy. We live, in short, in a patriarchal society. Nonetheless, if power-control theory is correct, it should be possible to identify variations in the effects of patriarchy across family class structures. The second part of this volume includes several tests of our theory. First, however, we consider the historical roots of the patriarchal family structure to which we attach so much importance, and the place of this family structure in the theory we propose.

Power-control theory focuses on the social organization of gender relations. It is concerned with the ways in which gender relations are established, maintained, perpetuated, or in other words, reproduced. The social reproduction of gender relations occurs across generations, and so adolescence provides a crucial context in which to address such issues. Meanwhile, societies vary in the social organization and reproduction of their gender relations, and so it is highly significant that our development of power-control theory occurs within an industrial capitalist society. Indeed, the question we must initially confront is: what is it about the macrolevel development of industrial capitalist societies that accounts for the way in which they reproduce gender relations?

Weber (1947) answers this question by noting that an important juncture in the development of modern capitalism involved the separation of the workplace from the home.

Two distinct spheres, which Weber regarded as crucial to the rationalization of an industrial capitalist economy, resulted from this separation: the first was populated by women and focused on domestic labour and consumption, and the second was populated by men and centered around labour power and direct production. Weber referred to these respectively as the consumption and production spheres.

The differentiation of the production and consumption spheres is significant for the social reproduction of gender relations. The reproduction of gender relations occurs in both spheres. The state (through police, courts, and correctional agencies) assumes responsibility for reproductive functions in the production sphere, while the family assumes responsibility for such functions in the consumption sphere. These reproductive functions are inversely related and sexually stratified.

The inverse relationship derives from the fact that as the reproductive activities of the family and kinship groups decline, the reproductive activities of state agencies increase. So, for example, we have elsewhere (Hagan et al., 1979) tested the thesis that as informal social controls of family and kinship groups decrease, contact with state agencies such as the police increases. This inverse relationship between state and family based systems of social control is discussed by Donald Black (1976) and Andrew Scull (1977), among recent sociologists interested in issues of social control. The important point here is that this differentiation of state and family reproductive functions, and the inverse relationship between them, also has its source in the separation of the workplace from the home that accompanied the emergence of Western capitalist societies. So the separation of the workplace from the home brought a change in production relations that in turn resulted in changes in reproductive relations, both of which had profound implications for gender relations. Among the most significant of the new gender relations was an intensification of the sexual stratification of reproductive functions.

The sexual stratification of reproductive functions in the production and consumption spheres inheres in the fact that while females disproportionately are the instruments and objects of the informal social control activities of the family, males disproportionately are the instruments and objects of formal social control agencies of the state, such as the police. The overall effect of the sexual stratification of these functions is to perpetuate a gender division in the production and consumption spheres, with females restricted to the home-based consumption sphere, and males appropriated to the production sphere; where, among other things, males are more liable to police contact.

The reproductive structures of both the production and consumption spheres are patriarchal in form. However, the family is the primary source of patriarchal relations, and as a result in following chapters we give greater attention to the reproductive activities of the family than the state. Our attention turns now to the role of the patriarchal family in reproducing the separation of the production and consumption spheres, and to recent evidence of change in these arrangements.

The new family that emerged from the separation of work and home assumed responsibility for reproducing the gender division of the production and consumption spheres (Vogel, 1983). This family was patriarchal in form and created a "cult of domesticity" around women (Welter, 1966). Today, however, Coser (1985) notes that there is a declining division of the consumption and production spheres which is reflected in the increased participation of women in the labour force. Coser goes on to note that as women have joined the labour force, they have gained new power in the family, particularly in the upper classes. The result is considerable variation in family class structure. . . . For the moment, we consider a highly abridged version of this model of family class structure, noting that these structures vary between two extreme family class relations that form real-life counterparts to two ideal-type families.

The first of these ideal types is largely a residue from an earlier period in which the consumption and production spheres were more strictly divided by gender. To reflect this legacy, we will call this the patriarchal family.

Of the family class relations we identify . . . the one that should most closely correspond to the ideal-type patriarchal family consists of a husband who is employed outside the home in a position with authority over others, and a wife who is not employed outside the home. Power-control theory predicts that patriarchal families will tend to reproduce daughters who focus their futures around domestic labour and consumption, as contrasted with sons who are prepared for participation in direct production. We say more about how this happens below. Here we simply repeat that Weber regarded this process of social reproduction, and implicitly the social reproduction of gender relations, as crucial to the rationalization of industrial capitalism.

At the other extreme is an ideal type we call the egalitarian family, in which the consumption and production spheres are undivided by gender. Of the family class relations we identify in the following chapter, the one that should most closely correspond to the ideal-type egalitarian family includes a mother and father who both are employed in positions with authority over others outside the home. Power-control theory predicts that egalitarian families tend to socially reproduce daughters who are prepared along with sons to join the production sphere. Such families are therefore a part of an overlapping of the consumption and production spheres, which a post-industrial society no longer so clearly keeps apart; such families are a part as well as a product of changing economic relations.

So the patriarchal family perpetuates a gender division in the consumption and production spheres, whereas the egalitarian family facilitates an overlapping of these spheres. The question is how this occurs. How does this happen and what are its consequences? Power-control theory answers these questions by joining a class analysis of the family with an analysis of the division of parental social control labour discussed above. The link is that parents socially reproduce their own power relationships through the control of their children. The key process involves the instrument-object relationship described under link 2 of Figure 21.1, which is assumed to be at its extreme in the patriar-

chal family. Here fathers and especially mothers (i.e., as instruments of social control) are expected to control their daughters more than their sons (i.e., as objects of social control). In regard to mothers, we should emphasize that our point is not that they are, in any ultimate causal sense, more important than fathers in the control of daughters, but rather that mothers in patriarchal families are assigned a key instrumental role that involves them more in the day-to-day control of their children, especially their daughters. This imbalanced instrument-object relationship is a product of a division in domestic social control labour and it is a distinguishing feature of the control of daughters in patriarchal families. This instrument-object relationship is a key part of the way in which patriarchal families socially reproduce a gender division in the spheres of consumption and production.

Alternatively, a reduction of this relationship enables egalitarian families to reproduce an overlap of the production and consumption spheres. This does not mean that in these families fathers are as involved as mothers in the parental control of children; indeed, evidence mounts that this is not the case (e.g., Huber, 1976). What it does mean is that parents in egalitarian families will redistribute their control efforts so that daughters are subjected to controls more like those imposed on sons. In other words, in egalitarian families, as mothers gain power relative to husbands, daughters gain freedom relative to sons. In terms of the social reproduction of gender relations, the presence of the imbalanced instrument-object relationship helps perpetuate patriarchy, and its absence facilitates equality.

Our final task at this stage is to link this discussion of ideal-type families and the instrument-object relationship with predicted gender differences in common delinquent behaviour. This final intervening connection involves the attitudes toward risk-taking involved in the discussion of links 3 and 4 in Figure 21.1. At one extreme, the patriarchal family and its acute instrument-object relationship between parents and daughters engenders a lower preference for risk-taking among daughters. Risk-taking is the antithesis of the passivity that distinguishes the "cult of domesticity." So, in patriarchal families, daughters are taught by their parents to be risk-averse. Alternatively, in egalitarian families, daughters and sons alike are encouraged to be more open to risk-taking. In part, this accommodation of risk is an anticipation of its role in the entrepreneurial and other activities associated with the production sphere, for which daughters and sons are similarly prepared in egalitarian families.

Control theories often regard delinquency as a form of risk-taking (Thrasher, 1927; Hirschi, 1969), sometimes as an unanticipated consequence of a rewarded willingness to take risks. The result is a correspondence in delinquent and entrepreneurial orientations that is reflected in Veblen's frequently quoted observation that "the ideal pecuniary man is like the ideal delinquent in his unscrupulous conversion of goods and persons to his own ends, and in a callous disregard of (i.e., freedom from) the feelings and wishes of others or the remoter effects of his actions" (1967: 237). Power-control theory does not regard this parallel as simple irony, but as an unintended consequence of a patriarchal social structure that is valued for its capacity to foster entrepreneurial, risk-taking orientations. With this in mind, power-control theory predicts that patriarchal families will be characterized by large gender differences in common delinquent behaviour, while egalitarian families will be characterized by smaller gender differences in delinquency. In egalitarian families, daughters become more like sons in their involvement in such forms of risk-taking as delinquency. . . .

Alternatively, there is another range of delinquent behaviour that is distinguished both by its frequency in Western capitalist societies and, most importantly, by its relevance to the power-control theory we wish to develop and test. The theory we wish to consider assumes that the presence of power and the absence of control both exercise their influence through cognitive processes in which actors evaluate courses of action. In particular, a key intervening process in power-control theory involves choices made by actors among behaviours based on their risk preferences and assessments. For actors to be influenced by such processes of risk assessment, the behaviours involved must be products of calculation. Our premise is that this is likely to be truer of minor forms of theft, vandalism and physical aggression (measurement of these behaviours is described in greater detail in the following chapter) than it will be of more serious forms of criminal and delinquent behaviour, particularly the crimes of violence emphasized in indices of "serious" crime and delinquency. In short, ours is a theory of common delinquent behaviour. . . .

Discussion Questions

1. What is the difference between a patriarchal and an egalitarian family? How might these families raise boys and girls differently?

2. What makes power-control theory a "control" theory? How does it differ from other control theories, such as Gottfredson and Hirschi's perspective?

3. In light of the Women's Movement, how have sex roles changed over the past two decades? What effect would power-control theory predict that these changes in sex roles would have on the involvement of girls in delinquency?

4. Many American youths are now growing up in a family headed by a single parent. What would power-control theory predict would be the effect on delinquency of being raised in a single-parent family? ✦

Part VI

Integrated Theories of Crime

Several major theories of crime have been examined up to this point, including biological, psychological, and sociological theories. Most of these theories were at the "micro" level, attempting to explain the criminal behavior of individuals; some were at the "macro" level, attempting to explain crime rates in social groups. Included in our examination were the three major theories in contemporary criminology: learning, strain/anomie, and control theories. We typically concluded our review of each theory by stating that it had *some* empirical support. In particular, certain of the variables identified by the theory were able to explain *some* of the variation in crime. Given this conclusion, it is natural to ask about the possibility of integrating these theories so that we might explain more of the variation in crime. It is to this topic that we now turn: integrated theories of crime.

The most comprehensive discussion of integrated theories is provided in an edited volume by Messner et al. (1989). Messner et al. begin their volume by stating that "to integrate theories is to formulate relationships among them" (1989:1). Integrated theories, then, do more than simply list variables from different theories. They attempt to describe the relationships between these variables. Several strategies for integration have been described (Akers, 1997; Hirschi, 1979; Mess-

ner et al., 1989; Tittle, 1995). The most commonly employed strategy is the "end-to-end" strategy, in which theorists describe the temporal ordering between variables, "so that the dependent variables of some theories constitute the independent variables of others." A theorist, for example, might argue that high levels of strain lead individuals to form or join delinquent subcultures, which in turn lead to crime.

Integrated theories actually have a long history in criminology. Lombroso, for example, proposed what is essentially an integrated theory of crime in his later work, arguing that a full explanation of crime required that we take account of biological, psychological, social, and other variables (e.g., the climate). Several integrated theories have already been presented in this volume. Recent work in biology and psychology tends to integrate theories across different disciplines ("interdisciplinary integration"), combining variables from biological, psychological, and sociological theories. Such theories typically focus on individual traits conducive to crime and/or on the processes by which individuals learn to engage in crime. These theories, however, recognize that biological factors of both a genetic and nongenetic origin affect the development of individual traits and impact the learning process (i.e., they affect what can be learned, the rate of learning, the predisposition to learn certain things). Likewise, these theories recognize that the social environment, especially the early family environment, provides the context for learning and also influences the development of individual traits and their impact on crime. Biological factors, for example, are most likely to result in traits conducive to crime in disrupted family environments. These theories often have less to say about the social environment beyond the family or they discount the importance of the larger social environment (e.g., see Wilson and Herrnstein, Chapter 4 in Part I).

We have also had several examples of integrated theory within the discipline of sociology. The theories employed by the founding members of the Chicago School (see Chapter 6), such as Shaw and McKay, often combined elements from strain, learning, and control theories. Cohen's theory (Chapter 14) was a deliberate effort to combine strain and differential association/cultural deviance theories. Cohen, in particular, used strain theory to help explain the origin of deviant subcultures. He then argued that deviant subcultures condition the impact of strain on crime. That is, strained individuals are less likely to engage in crime if they do not form or join a deviant subculture like a delinquent gang. Cloward and Ohlin (see Chapter 15) also combined strain and differential association/culture conflict theory. The specifics of their argument differ from those of Cohen, but like Cohen they draw on strain theory to help explain the origin of deviant subcultures and they argue that strain is unlikely to result in a sustained pattern of crime unless individuals have access to deviant subcultures.

Many additional examples of integrated theory can be given (e.g., Bernard, 1990; Catalano and Hawkins, 1996; Colvin and Pauly in Chapter 34; Gold, 1964; Hagan in Chapter 21, Part V; Johnson, 1979; Pearson and Weiner, 1985; Tittle, 1995). Most integrations are at the micro-level: theorists integrate two or more theories which seek to explain individual deviance. A few theorists, however, have attempted to integrate macro-level theories (see Messner et al., 1989). Macro-level theories attempt to explain crime rates in groups, most commonly in

terms of cultural and structural properties of these groups. Messner and Rosenfeld's institutional anomie theory (Chapter 16) can be viewed as an integrated macro-theory: they integrate Merton's macro-level emphasis on the cultural system (the cultural system emphasizes the unrestrained pursuit of money by everyone) with structural arguments that are compatible with social disorganization theory (the dominance of the economy weakens the ability of other institutions to effectively socialize people and sanction deviance). There have also been some attempts to integrate macro-level and micro-level theories (see Messner et al., 1989). Theorists describe the ways in which macro-level variables ultimately impact the criminal behavior of individuals. In doing so, they better describe how such variables affect crime rates, for crime rates are based on individual criminal behavior.

In sum, there have been efforts at theoretical integration throughout the history of criminology—with such efforts becoming especially common in recent years. It is important to note, however, that not everyone agrees that integration is a good strategy. The most common objection is that the theories being integrated are often based on opposing assumptions (because theories were often developed in opposition to one another; see Hirschi, 1989). Therefore, integration is impossible without fundamentally altering the theories that are being combined.

For example, strain theory assumes that the motivation to crime (the frustration and anger that individuals experience) is variable. Such variation explains the variation in crime. Control theories, however, assume that the motivation to crime is largely constant. That is, everyone experiences more or less the same amount of motivation for crime (greed, anger, etc.). Variation in crime is explained by variation in social restraints or controls. People high in social control do not act on their motivations for crime, while people low in social control often do. Given these opposing assumptions, how does one integrate strain and control theory in a way that preserves the integrity of both? Likewise, differential association theory assumes that our society is characterized by cultural conflict, with some individuals being exposed to definitions that are conducive to crime. Social control theory, however, assumes that our society is largely conventional. It denies that people engage in crime because of procriminal definitions. At most, ineffective socialization results in amoral individuals: those who believe that crime is neither good nor bad. Once more, theoretical integration seems impossible without substantially altering at least one of the theories involved. Given this situation, theorists such as Hirschi (1979; 1989) have questioned the strategy of integration and have instead suggested that we focus on the development of individual theories. Hirschi contends that the potential of most crime theories is far from tapped (see Messner et al., 1989, for an excellent discussion of these issues).

The first selection in Chapter 22 in this section, from Elliott et al. (1979), provides an end-to-end integration of the three leading theories of crime: strain, social control, and differential association/social learning theory. It is among the most popular of the integrated theories in contemporary research and it was the guiding force behind the National Youth Survey, one of the best surveys on juvenile delinquency ever conducted (see Elliott et al., 1985; 1989). Elliott et al. describe two major pathways to delinquency: (1) low social control increases the likelihood of association with delinquent peers, which increases the likelihood of delinquency; and (2) individuals high in social control experience strain, which reduces their level of control, which increases their likelihood of association with delinquent peers and thereby delinquency. Elliott et al. (1985; 1989) found much support for slightly modified versions of this integrated theory. Elliott et al.'s model has been criticized by Hirschi (1979; 1989), who argues that it violates certain of the core assumptions of control theory. Elliott et al. (1985), however, feel that these violations are justified and that certain core elements from control theory have been retained (also see the discussion of Elliott et al.'s theory in Tittle, 1995).

Thornberry's (1987) interactional theory of delinquency combines control and learning theories (see Chapter 23 in this Part). Like Elliott et al.'s theory, the integration consists largely of an end-to-end integration of micro-level variables, although Thornberry does describe how certain macro-level variables may affect the micro-level variables in his theory. What most distinguishes Thornberry's theory, however, is the attention he devotes to developmental processes and reciprocal effects. He describes how the variables in his theory change in importance over the life course, and he uses his theory to explain career patterns in crime (e.g., why some people desist from crime at adulthood and others do not). Further, he recognizes that the causal ordering between the variables in his theory is more complex than is commonly portrayed. Most theorists simply argue that one variable, like family attachment, causes another, like school commitment. Thornberry, however, argues that most variables have reciprocal causal effects on one another (e.g., family attachment has a causal effect on school commitment and school commitment has a causal effect on family attachment). Delinquency itself is involved in this pattern of reciprocal causation. Tentative data provide some support for key parts of Thornberry's interactional theory, suggesting that certain variables do have reciprocal causal efforts on one another and that the importance of certain variables changes over time—although much more research is needed in this later area (see Thornberry, 1996 for a review).

While both Elliott et al. and Thornberry employ the "end-to-end" strategy of integration (or a variation of it that recognizes reciprocal effects), others have employed alternative strategies. One such strategy is exemplified by Akers (1985; 1989; 1997). He notes that his social learning theory is more general than other micro-level theories in sociology. He then argues that the concepts from these theories can be rephrased using the language of social learning theory ("conceptual integration"). Hirschi's bond of commitment, for example, essentially refers to "negative punishment" (we refrain from doing something because we fear that we will lose our current rewards). Further, social learning theory can be used to make predictions about the relationships between these concepts and their effect on deviance. Akers does acknowledge that, in certain cases, these predictions differ from those of the original theories. Control and social learning theories, for example, make different predictions about the effect of attachment on crime (control theorists argue that attachments to all others reduce crime, while learning theorists argue that only attachments to conventional others reduce crime). Such differences can and have been empirically examined (e.g., Conger, 1976). Akers, then, argues that several micro-level theories can be subsumed (with some modification) under his more general social learning theory. (He also argues that social learning theory can be the vehicle for integrating macro- and micro-level theories, since it can explain the mechanisms by which macro-level variables ultimately affect the individual.)

Another strategy for integration is illustrated by the Cullen selection (see Chapter 24). Cullen (1994) does not present an end-to-end integration of variables nor does he attempt to subsume several theories under a more general theory. Rather, Cullen points to a common theme that is implicit or explicit in several different theories; namely, the idea that social support has a bearing on one's criminal behavior. He then draws on these theories to construct a new theory that more explicitly and more fully describes the relationship between social support and crime. Among other things, this theory argues that social support has a direct causal effect on crime; that it has a causal effect on other variables which influence crime, like social control; and that it conditions the effect of other variables on crime (e.g., strain is most likely to lead to crime when social support is low). In a sense, Cullen has developed a new theory of crime, but this new theory pulls together and extends certain arguments from several divergent theories. Cullen, then, achieves integration by highlighting and elaborating on a common theme in several different crime theories (see Braithwaite, in Chapter 30 in Part VIII, for a similar approach to integration). Cullen's theory is compatible with much existing data, and has received tentative support in a preliminary empirical test (Wright, 1995; Wright and Cullen, 1996).

The three selections in this section present moderately complex theories of crime, but we suspect that they will pale in comparison to future attempts at integration. Such efforts will likely involve variables from different disciplines and from different levels of analysis, will recognize the complex relationships that exist between these variables (i.e., the reciprocal effects described by Thornberry as well as the conditional effects described by Cullen [1984] and others), and will pay explicit attention to developmental issues (e.g., whether variables change in importance over the life course, how we can explain different patterns in crime over the life course). Further, the issue of whether different theories are necessary for different groups (e.g., gender, race, and class groups; chronic versus sporadic offenders) and for different categories of crime will be a central concern. At the same time, it is also quite certain that many criminologists will heed Hirschi's advice and work on the refinement of individual theories. Such work, of course, will ultimately contribute to theoretical integration since an integrated model obviously reflects the strength of its component parts.

References

Akers, Ronald L. 1985. *Deviant Behavior: A Social Learning Approach*. Belmont, CA: Wadsworth.

———. 1989. "A Social Behaviorist's Perspective on Integration of Theories of Crime and Deviance." Pp. 23-36 in *Theoretical Integration in the Study of Deviance and Crime: Problems and Prospects*, edited by Steven F. Messner, Marvin D. Krohn, and Allen E. Liska. Albany: State University of New York Press.

———. 1997. *Criminological Theories: Introduction and Evaluation*, 2nd edition. Los Angeles: Roxbury.

Bernard, Thomas J. 1990. "Angry Aggression Among the 'Truly Disadvantaged.'" *Criminology* 28: 73-96.

Catalano, Richard F. and J. David Hawkins. 1996. "The Social Development Model: A Theory of Antisocial Behavior." Pp. 149-197 in *Delinquency and Crime: Current Theories*, edited by J. David Hawkins. Cambridge: Cambridge University Press.

Conger, Rand D. 1976. "Social Control and Social Learning Models of Delinquent Behavior: A Synthesis." *Criminology* 14: 17-40.

Cullen, Francis T. 1994. "Social Support as an Organizing Concept for Criminology: Presidential Address to the Academy of Criminal Justice Sciences." *Justice Quarterly* 11: 527-559.

Elliott, Delbert S., Suzanne S. Ageton, and Rachelle J. Canter. 1979, "An Integrated Theoretical Perspective on Delinquent Behavior." *Journal of Research in Crime and Delinquency* 16: 3-27.

Elliott, Delbert S., David Huizinga, and Suzanne S. Ageton. 1985. *Explaining Delinquency and Drug Use*. Beverly Hills, CA: Sage.

Elliott, Delbert S., David Huizinga, and Scott Menard. 1989. *Multiple Problem Youth: Delinquency, Substance Use, and Mental Health Problems*. New York: Springer-Verlag.

Gold, Martin. 1963. *Status Forces in Delinquent Boys*. Ann Arbor: Institute for Social Research, University of Michigan.

Hirschi, Travis. 1979. "Separate and Unequal Is Better." *Journal of Research in Crime and Delinquency* 16: 34-38.

——. 1989. "Exploring Alternatives to Integrated Theory." Pp. 37-49 in *Theoretical Integration in the Study of Deviance and Crime: Problems and Prospects*, edited by Steven F. Messner, Marvin D. Krohn, and Allen E. Liska. Albany: State University of New York Press.

Johnson, Richard E. 1979. *Juvenile Delinquency and Its Origins*. Cambridge: Cambridge University Press.

Messner, Steven F., Marvin D. Krohn, and Allen E. Liska, eds. 1989. *Theoretical Integration in the Study of Deviance and Crime: Problems and Prospects*. Albany: State University of New York Press.

Pearson, Frank S. and Neil Alan Weiner. 1985. "Toward an Integration of Criminological Theories." *Journal of Criminal Law and Criminology* 76: 116-150.

Thornberry, Terence P. 1987. "Toward an Interactional Theory of Delinquency." *Criminology* 25: 863-891.

——. 1996. "Empirical Support for Interactional Theory: A Review of the Literature." Pp. 198-235 in *Delinquency and Crime: Current Theories*, edited by J. David Hawkins. Cambridge: Cambridge University Press.

Tittle, Charles R. 1995. *Control Balance: Toward a General Theory of Deviance*. Boulder, CO: Westview.

Wright, John Paul. 1995. "Parental Support and Juvenile Delinquency: A Test of Social Support Theory." Unpublished Ph.D. dissertation, University of Cincinnati.

Wright, John Paul and Francis T. Cullen. 1996. "Parental Support and Delinquent Behavior: The Limits of Control Theory?" Paper presented at the annual meeting of the American Society of Criminology. ✦

22

An Integrated Theoretical Perspective on Delinquent Behavior

Delbert S. Elliott
Suzanne S. Ageton
Rachelle J. Canter

Elliott et al.'s integrated theory combines the three leading theories of crime: strain, social control, and social learning theories. It should be noted, however, that Elliott et al. revise the classic strain theories of Merton, Cohen, and Cloward and Ohlin (see Part IV). Elliott et al. argue that adolescents may pursue a variety of goals and that goal achievement is not simply a function of social class. These revisions allow strain theory to explain middle-class as well as lower-class delinquency. Middle-class adolescents may have as much trouble achieving their goals as lower-class adolescents, perhaps because their aspirations are higher or perhaps because they are pursuing goals whose achievement is a function of factors like athletic ability or physical appearance. Elliott et al. also propose measuring social control in terms of integration and commitment, arguing that such measures create fewer difficulties and are more clearcut than the four elements of the social bond listed by Hirschi (attachment, commitment, involvement, belief—see Chapter 18 in Part V).

The integrated theory of Elliott et al. argues that there are two primary pathways to delinquency. In the first, individuals low in social control get involved with delinquent peers, which increases their likelihood of engaging in a sustained pattern of delinquency. In the second, individuals high in social control have certain experiences which weaken their level of control, with the failure to achieve conventional goals (i.e., strain) being one such experience. Such individuals may then become involved with delinquent peers and turn to delinquency. One's exposure and commitment to delinquent peer groups is the central variable in the integrated theory, although Elliott et al. argue that strain and low social control may have small direct effects on delinquency.

Elliott et al. tested slightly modified versions of their integrated theory in Explaining Delinquency and Drug Use *(1985) and* Multiple Problem Youth *(1989). They found that association with delinquent peers was the best predictor of delinquency (other than prior delinquency). Further, low social control increased the likelihood of association with delinquent peers. Social control also conditioned the effect of delinquent peers on delinquency, such that association with delinquent peers had a much stronger effect on delinquency when social control was low. Strain increased the likelihood that individuals would be low in social control. These results provide support for the integrated theory. However, neither the strain nor social control measures had a direct effect on delinquency. Partly as a result of such support, Elliott et al.'s theory is among the most popular of current integrated theories (although see Tittle, 1995: 95-97 for a recent overview and critique of the theory).

References

Elliott, Delbert S., David Huizinga, and Suzanne S. Ageton. 1985. *Explaining Delinquency and Drug Use.* Beverly Hills, CA: Sage.

Elliott, Delbert S., David Huizinga, and Scott Menard. 1989. *Multiple Problem Youth.* New York: Springer-Verlag.

Tittle, Charles R. 1995. *Control Balance: Toward a General Theory of Deviance.* Boulder, CO: Westview.

. . . Our concern here is to return to consideration of the etiology of delinquent and criminal behavior and to propose a new integrated theoretical formulation as a guide to research and understanding. The focus is on the offender and those social processes and features of social contexts which both generate and maintain delinquent patterns of behavior. More specifically, our objective is to provide a conceptual framework in which traditional strain, social-learning, and social control perspectives are integrated into a single explanatory paradigm which avoids the class bias inherent in traditional perspectives and which accounts for multiple etiologies of (multiple causal paths to) sustained patterns of delinquent behavior. . . .

Previous Theories: Strain and Control

The Anomie/Strain Perspective

The term *anomie* was coined by the French sociologist Emile Durkheim (1897/1938, 1951), who argued that, under certain social conditions, traditional societal norms and rules lose their authority over behavior, resulting in a state of normlessness, which Durkheim called anomie. During periods of rapid social change, traditional norms may be viewed as no longer applicable to behavior, leaving people free to pursue any ends by any means (anomie).

Merton (1957) was the first to elaborate Durkheim's concept of anomie. The basic premise of all theoretical statements in this tradition is that delinquent behavior is a result of socially induced pressures to delinquency, rather than pathological impulses of individuals. This general body of theory is thus referred to as strain theory, since it assumes that man is basically a conforming being who violates normative expectations only as a result of external social pressures or socially induced stress. While different theories specify different social processes and organizational structures which generate particular forms of deviance, virtually all concur with Merton's view that the structure of contemporary American society has generated anomie in specific social institutions, and that deviance is, in part, a response to or result of this condition. Strain theory has become the most influential and widely used

contemporary formulation in the sociology of delinquent behavior.

A specific application of strain theory to delinquency has been proposed by Cloward and Ohlin (1960) and, more recently, by Elliott and Voss (1974). Cloward and Ohlin's work is of particular interest to us because their formulation, like that proposed here, represents an attempt to integrate and extend current theoretical positions. Although their theory has been viewed primarily as an extension of the earlier work of Durkheim and Merton, it is equally an extension of the differential association perspective and the prior work of Sutherland (1947). Indeed, much of its significance lies in the fact that it successfully integrated these two traditional perspectives on the etiology of delinquent behavior. Cloward and Ohlin maintain that limited opportunity for achieving conventional goals is the motivational stimulus for delinquent behavior. The specific form and pattern of delinquent behavior are acquired through normal learning processes within delinquent groups. Experiences of limited or blocked opportunities (a result of structural limitations on success) thus lead to alienation (perceived anomie) and an active seeking out of alternative groups and settings in which particular patterns of delinquent behavior are acquired and reinforced (social learning).

Following Merton, Cloward and Ohlin have conceptualized the condition leading to anomie in terms of differential opportunities for achieving socially valued goals. Differential access to opportunity creates strain: this is postulated to occur primarily among disadvantaged, low-SES youths, resulting in the concentration of delinquent subcultures in low-SES neighborhoods. It important to note, however, that Cloward and Ohlin have changed the level of explanation from the macrosociological level which characterized Durkheim's work to an individual level. It is the *perception* of limited access to conventional goals that motivates the *individual* to explore deviant means. This change in level of explanation was essential for the integration of strain and learning perspectives.

Elliott and Voss's more recent work (1974) has attempted to deal with the class-bound assumptions inherent in strain theory. Their formulation extends Cloward and Ohlin's classic statement in the following three ways: (1) The focus on limited opportunities was extended to a wider range of conventional goals. (2) The goal-means disjunction was modified to be logically independent of social class. (3) The role of social learning in the development of delinquent behavior was further emphasized. Elliott and Voss have proposed a sequential, or developmental, model of delinquency: (1) Limited opportunities or failure to achieve conventional goals serves to (2) attenuate one's initial commitment to the normative order and (3) results in a particular form of alienation (normlessness), which serves as a "permitter" for delinquency, and (4) exposure to delinquent groups, which provide learning and rewards for delinquent behavior for those whose bonds have undergone the attenuation process.

From this perspective, aspiration-opportunity disjunctions provide motivation for delinquent behavior. As compared with Merton and Cloward and Ohlin, Elliott and Voss view *both* goals and opportunities as variables. They postulate that middle-class youths are just as likely to aspire beyond their means as are low-SES youths. While the absolute levels of aspirations and opportunities may vary by class, the discrepancies between personal goals and opportunities for realizing these goals need not vary systematically by class. Given Durkheim's (1897/ 1951:254) view that poverty restrains aspirations, Elliott and Voss have postulated that aspiration-opportunity disjunctions would be at least as great, if not greater, among middle-class youths. In any case, the motivational stimulus for delinquent behavior in the form of aspiration-opportunity discrepancies or goal failure is viewed as logically independent of social class.

Normlessness, the expectation that one must employ illegitimate means to achieve socially valued goals (Seeman, 1959), is postulated to result from perceived aspiration-opportunity disjunctions. When a person cannot reach his or her goals by conventional means, deviant or illegitimate means become rational and functional alternatives. When the source of failure or blockage is perceived as external—resulting from institutional practices and policies—the individual has some justification for withdrawing his or her moral commitment to these conventional norms. In this manner, a sense of injustice mitigates ties to conventional norms and generates normlessness.

Once at this point in the developmental sequence, the relative presence or absence of specific delinquent learning and performance structures accounts for the likelihood of one's behavior. The time-ordering of the exposure to delinquency variable is not explicit. It may predate failure or it may be the result of seeking a social context in which one can achieve some success. While the exposure may result in the acquisition of delinquent behavior patterns, actual delinquent behavior (performance) will not result until one's attachment to the social order is neutralized through real or anticipated failure, and the delinquent behavior has been reinforced.

The results of research relative to this set of propositions have been generally encouraging. Using a predictive design which allowed for establishing the correct temporal sequences, Elliott and Voss (1974) found that this set of variables did, in fact, account for 31 percent of the variance in self-reported delinquency frequency scores and 21 percent of the variance in self-reported delinquency gain scores across time. Brennan and Huizinga's (1975) path-analytical work on a sample of 730 youths also supports this theoretical model. They concluded that the most powerful predictors of delinquent behavior were youth perceptions of limited opportunity, negative labeling, peer group pressures for delinquency, and normlessness. They were able to explain 31 percent of the variance in self-reported delinquency scores on the basis of these variables. Jessor et al. (1968) also found good support for a similar set of predictor variables on a general measure of self-reported deviant behavior.

While considerable empirical support for an integrated strain-learning approach to delinquency has been amassed, most of the variance in delinquency remains unexplained. If the power of this theoretical formulation is to be improved, some basic modification is required. One avenue is suggested by the weak predictive power of the aspiration-opportunity discrepancy variables. In both the Elliott and Voss and the Brennan and Huizinga studies, for example, anticipated failure to achieve occupational or educational goals was not predictively associated with changes in levels of delinquency. Limited academic success at school and failure in one's relationship with parents were predictive, but only weakly. To some extent, the low strength of these predictors might be anticipated, since they are the initial variables in the causal sequence and are tied to delinquency only through a set of other conditional variables. On the other hand, the strong emphasis placed on these specific variables in strain theories seems questionable, given the available data. It might be argued that the difficulty lies in the operationalization or measurement of the relevant goal-opportunity disjunctions. However, we are inclined to reject this position because previous findings as to this postulated relationship have been generally weak and inconclusive (Spergel, 1967; Short, 1964, 1965; Elliott, 1962; Short, Rivera, and Tennyson, 1965; Jessor et al., 1968; Hirschi, 1969; Liska, 1971; and Brennan, 1974). Furthermore, there is substantial evidence in the above-mentioned studies that many adolescents engaging in significant amounts of delinquent behavior experience no discrepancies between aspirations and perceived opportunities. The lack of consistent support for this relationship suggests that failure or anticipated failure constitutes only one possible path to an involvement in delinquency.

The Control Perspective

The different assumptions of strain and control theories are significant. Strain formulations assume a positively socialized individual who violates conventional norms only when his or her attachment and commitment are attenuated. Norm violation occurs only after the individual perceives that opportunities for socially valued goals are blocked. Strain theory focuses on this attenuation process. Control theories, on the other hand, treat the socialization process and commitment to conventional norms and val-

ues as problematic. Persons differ with respect to their commitment to and integration into the conventional social order. As Reiss (1951:196) put it:

> Delinquency results when there is a relative absence of internalized norms and rules governing behavior in conformity with the norms of the social system to which legal penalties are attached, a breakdown in previously established controls, and/or a relative absence of or conflict in social rules or techniques for enforcing such behavior in the social groups or institutions of which the person is a member. Hence, delinquency may be seen as a functional consequence of the type of relationship established among the personal and social controls.

From a control perspective, delinquency is viewed as a consequence of (1) lack of internalized normative controls, (2) breakdown in previously established controls, and/or (3) conflict or inconsistency in rules or social controls. Strain formulations of delinquency appear to be focusing on those variables and processes which account for the second condition identified by Reiss (1951)—attenuation or breakdown in previously established controls. On the other hand, most control theorists direct their attention to the first and third conditions, exploring such variables as inadequate socialization (failure to internalize conventional norms) and integration into conventional groups or institutions which provide strong external or social controls on behavior. From our perspective, these need not be viewed as contradictory explanations. On the contrary, they may be viewed as alternative processes, depending on the outcome of one's early socialization experience.

For example, Hirschi (1969) has argued that high aspirations involve a commitment to conventional lines of action that functions as a positive control or bond to the social order. Strain theories, on the other hand, view high aspirations (in the face of limited opportunities) as a source of attenuation of attachment to the conventional order. Recognizing this difference, Hirschi suggested that examination of this relationship would constitute a crucial test of the two theories. Empirically, the evidence is inconsistent and far from conclusive. One possible interpretation is that both hypotheses are correct and are part of different etiological sequences leading to delinquent behavior.

Empirical studies using the control perspective have focused almost exclusively on the static relation of weak internal and external controls to delinquency without considering the longer developmental processes. These processes may involve an initially strong commitment to and integration into society which becomes attenuated over time, with the attenuation eventually resulting in delinquency. The source of this difficulty may lie in the infrequent use of longitudinal designs. Without a repeated-measure design, youths with strong bonds which subsequently become attenuated may be indistinguishable from those who never developed strong bonds.

An Integrated Strain-Control Perspective

Our proposed integrated theoretical paradigm begins with the assumption that different youths have different early socialization experiences, which result in variable degrees of commitment to and integration into conventional social groups. The effect of failure to achieve conventional goals on subsequent delinquency is related to the strength of one's initial bonds. Limited opportunities to achieve conventional goals constitute a source of strain and thus a motivational stimulus for delinquency only if one is committed to these goals. In contrast, limited opportunities to achieve such goals should have little or no impact on those with weak ties and commitments to the conventional social order.

Limited opportunities to achieve conventional goals are not the only experiences which weaken or break initially strong ties to the social order. Labeling theorists have argued that the experience of being apprehended and publicly labeled a delinquent initiates social processes which limit one's access to conventional social roles and statuses, isolating one from participation in these activities and relationships and forcing one to assume a delinquent role (Becker, 1963;

Schur, 1971, 1973; Kitsuse, 1962; Rubington and Weinberg, 1968; Ageton and Elliott, 1974; and Goldman, 1963). It has also been argued that the effects of social disorganization or crisis in the home (divorce, parental strife and discord, death of a parent) and/or community (high rates of mobility, economic depression, unemployment) attenuate or break one's ties to society (Thomas and Znaniecki, 1927; Shaw, 1931; Savitz, 1970; Monahan, 1957; Toby, 1957; Glueck and Glueck, 1970; Andry, 1962; and Rosen, 1970).

In sum, we postulate that limited opportunities, failure to achieve valued goals, negative labeling experiences, and social disorganization at home and in the community are all experiences which may attenuate one's ties to the conventional social order and may thus be causal factors in the developmental sequence leading to delinquent behavior for those whose early socialization experiences produced strong bonds to society. For those whose attachments to the conventional social order are already weak, such factors may further weaken ties to society, but are not necessary factors in the etiological sequence leading to delinquency.

Our basic conceptual framework comes from control theory, with a slightly different emphasis placed on participation in and commitment to delinquent groups. Further, it identifies a set of attenuating/bonding experiences which weaken or strengthen ties to the conventional social order over time. Our focus is on experiences and social contexts which are relevant to adolescents.

A diagram of our proposed theoretical scheme is shown in Figure 22.1. The arrows in Figure 22.1 indicate the direction and sequence of the hypothesized relationships. While the time order designated in Figure 22.1 is unidirectional, the actual relationships between initial socialization, bonding/attenuation processes, normative orientations of groups, and behavior are often reciprocal and reinforcing. We have also presented the variables in dichotomized form to simplify the model and the discussion of its major elements.

Figure 22.1
Integrated Strain-Control Paradigm

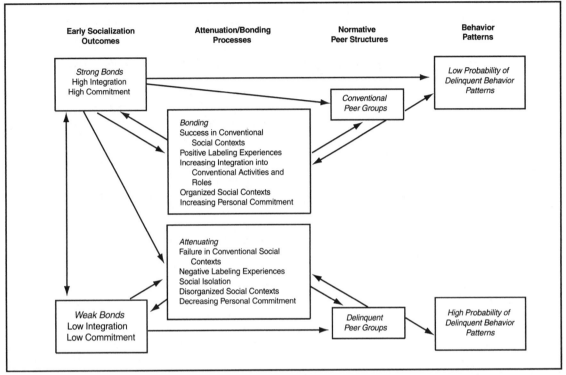

Bonds

Control theorists disagree about sources of control, but then, all accept the central proposition that delinquent behavior is a direct result of weak ties to the conventional normative order. In operationalizing control theory, major emphasis has been placed on the bond(s) which tie a person to society. Hirschi (1969) conceptualized four elements of this bond. First, *attachment* implies a moral link to other people and encompasses such concepts as conscience, superego, and internalization of norms. *Commitment*, the second factor, is the rational element in the bond. Hirschi views commitment to conformity as an investment in conventional lines of action, such as an educational or occupational career. Other theorists have tied the concept of commitment to such notions as "stake in conformity" (Goode, 1960) and "side bets" (Becker, 1960). *Involvement* is the time and energy dimension of the bond for Hirschi. Given the limits of time and energy,

involvement in conventional activities acts as a social constraint on delinquent behavior. The final bond, *belief*, refers to one's acceptance of the moral validity of social rules and norms. According to Hirschi, this psychological element of the bond is effective as long as a person accepts the validity of the rules. If one denies or depreciates the validity of the rules, one source of control is neutralized.

Other control theorists, such as Reiss (1951), Nye (1958), and Reckless (1967), use a more general classification of bonds as internal (personal) and external (social) controls. Hirschi's dimensions are not easily placed into these two general categories, although Hirschi identifies attachment as an internal and involvement as an external element of the bond (1969:19). We believe that distinguishing internal controls, whose locus is within the person (beliefs, commitment, attitudes, perceptions), from external controls, whose locus is in the surrounding social and physical milieu, poses fewer difficulties and produces greater conceptual clarity than is found in Hirschi's four concepts.

The external, or social, bond we have defined as *integration*. By this, we refer to involvement in and attachment to conventional groups and institutions, such as the family, school, peer networks, and so on. Those persons who occupy and are actively involved in conventional social roles are, by this definition, highly integrated. Group controls exist in the form of sanctioning networks (the formal and informal rules and regulations by which the behavior of social role occupants or group members is regulated). This conceptualization of integration is akin to Hirschi's concepts of involvement and commitment.

The internal, or personal, bond is defined as *commitment*. Commitment involves personal attachment to conventional roles, groups, and institutions. At another level, it reflects the extent to which one feels morally bound by the social norms and rules and the degree to which one internalizes or adopts those norms as directives for action. Our notion of commitment is akin to Hirschi's concepts of attachment and belief.

Integration and commitment together constitute the bonds which tie an individual to the prevailing social order. High levels of integration and commitment imply strong bonds and general insulation from delinquent behavior. Conversely, low social integration and commitment presuppose weak bonds and a susceptibility to delinquent behavior. All gradations of integration and commitment are possible.

Building Social Control: The Bonding/Attenuation Processes

The inclusion of the bonding/attenuation process in the model suggests that, throughout adolescence, youths are involved in experiences and processes which attenuate or reinforce their childhood bonds to the conventional social order. Adolescence is a critical life period, both psychologically and socially. As youths make the transition from childhood to adulthood, the level of involvement in the immediate family declines and they move into new and more complex social settings at school and in the community. For one who developed strong childhood bonds, such

factors as (1) success experiences at school and in the larger community, (2) positive labeling in these new settings. and (3) a continuous, stable, harmonious home life constitute positive reinforcements of initially strong bonds and continuing insulation from delinquency. For some, the transition is not as smooth, and failure, negative labeling, isolation, and rejection occur in these new social settings: these, in turn, may create difficulties in the youth's relationship with his family. The net effect of these new experiences may be a weakening of one's integration into and commitment to these social groups and institutions and an increasing likelihood of involvement in delinquent behavior. Finally, for those who never developed strong bonds during childhood, bonding/attenuation experiences will either strengthen the weak bonds, thus reducing the likelihood of delinquency, or further attenuate them, thus maintaining or increasing the probability of delinquent behavior.

We do not propose that this specific set of variables exhausts the possible experiences or conditions which might attenuate or reinforce one's bonds to society during adolescence. Rather, we have purposely selected those conditions and experiences which prior theory and research have suggested as critical variables to illustrate the major dimensions of the paradigm.

Delinquent Learning and Performance Structures

A major criticism of control theory has been that weak bonds and the implied absence of restraints cannot alone account for the specific form or content of the behavior which results. They may account for a state of "drift," as described by Matza (1964), but they do not explain why some youths in this state turn to delinquency, drug use, and various unconventional subcultures, while others maintain an essentially conforming pattern of behavior; nor can they account for emerging patterns of delinquency which may be unique to particular ages or birth cohorts. We therefore postulate that access to and involvement in delinquent learning and performance structures is a necessary (but not sufficient) variable in the etiology of delinquent behavior. Following Sutherland (1947), we maintain that delinquent behavior, like conforming behavior, presupposes a pattern of social relationships through which motives, rationalizations, techniques, and rewards can be learned and maintained (Burgess and Akers, 1966; Akers, 1977; Bandura, 1969, 1973; and Mischel, 1968). Delinquent behavior is thus viewed as behavior which has social meaning and must be supported and rewarded by social groups if it is to persist.

By the time children enter adolescence, virtually all have been sufficiently exposed to criminal forms of behavior to have "learned" or acquired some potential for such acts. The more critical issue for any theory of delinquency is why and how this universal potential is transformed into delinquent acts for some youths and not others. For most learning theorists, a distinction is made between learning and performance and the latter is directly tied to reinforcements (Rotter, 1954; Bandura and Walters, 1963; Mischel, 1968; and Bandura, 1969). As Mischel (1968:159-160) put it:

> It is useful to distinguish between the learning and acquisition of behaviors and their performance. A person does not perform all the behaviors he has learned; there are discrepancies between what he has learned or knows and can do, and what he actually does in particular situations. Individuals, of course, learn a multitude of potentially antisocial or deviant, as well as prosocial, behaviors. For example, most adolescent boys know how to throw rocks, wield knives, and break windows. But even among boys who have acquired these skills to the same degree there are striking individual differences in the extent to which they perform them. . . .
>
> According to the present social learning formulation, learning or acquisition of novel responses is regulated by sensory and cognitive processes; learning may be facilitated by reinforcement but does not depend on it (e.g., Bandura and Walters, 1963; Hebb, 1966). Direct and vicarious reinforcement are, however, important determinants of response selection in performance.

The delinquent peer group thus provides a positive social setting that is essential for the performance and maintenance of delinquent patterns of behavior over time. Those committed to conventional goals, although they may have been exposed to and learned some delinquent behaviors, should patterns of such behavior unless (1) their ties to the conventional social order are neutralized through some attenuating experiences and (2) they are participating in a social context in which delinquent behavior is rewarded. In social learning terms, they may have acquired or learned delinquent behavior patterns, but the actual performance and maintenance of such behavior are contingent on attenuation of their commitment to conventional norms and their participation in a social context supportive of delinquent acts. Alternatively, for those with weak ties and commitments to the conventional social order, there is no reason for a delay between acquisition and performance of delinquent acts.

In the causal sequence described by strain theory, the individual holds conventional goals but is unable to attain them by conventional means. If attachment to the goals is strong enough, it may support delinquent behavior without participation in delinquent groups, for attaining these goals may provide sufficient reinforcement to maintain the behavior. Therefore, our model shows one direct route to delinquent behavior from attenuating experiences, without mediating group support for delinquency. We view this as the atypical case, however, and postulate that it is difficult to sustain this causal sequence for extended periods of time.

Involvement in a delinquent group is a necessary condition for sustained patterns of delinquency among persons who do not subscribe to conventional goals (the weakly socialized person described by control theory). Individual patterns of delinquency (without group support) are more viable for those committed to conventional goals because there are generally shared expectations and social supports for achievement of those goals. For youths with weak bonds, involvement in a delinquent peer group serves this support function. Cohen (1966) has observed that delinquency often involves a desire for recognition and social acceptance, and, therefore, requires group visibility and support. Maintenance of delinquent behavior patterns should require some exposure to and participation in groups supporting delinquent activities. Though not a necessary condition for delinquent behavior among those with initially strong bonds, contact with delinquent groups should, nevertheless, increase the likelihood of sustained delinquent behavior.

Delineation of the delinquent peer group as a necessary condition for maintenance of delinquent behavior patterns represents an extension of previous statements of control theory, for example, Hirschi (1969:230) concludes:

> The theory underestimated the importance of delinquent friends; it overestimated the significance of involvement in conventional activities. Both of these miscalculations appear to stem from the same source, the assumption of "natural motivation" to delinquency. If such natural motivation could legitimately be assumed, delinquent friends would be unnecessary, and involvement in conventional activities would curtail the commission of delinquent acts.

It is one thing to be a social isolate with weak bonds to conventional peer groups and another to be highly committed to and integrated into a delinquent peer group. Both persons may be characterized as having weak bonds to the social order, with few conventional restraints on their behavior; but those committed to and participating in delinquent peer groups have some incentive and social support for specifically delinquent forms of behavior. We agree with Hirschi's (1969) and Hepburn's (1976) argument that those with a large stake in conformity (strong bonds) are relatively immune to delinquent peer group influence. However, we postulate that, in addition to weak bonding and an absence of restraints, some positive motivation is necessary for sustained involvement in delinquent behavior. In the absence of positive motivation, we would not predict significant involvement in delinquency across time even for those with weak bonds, for there is no apparent mechanism for maintaining such behavior (Brennan, Huizinga, and Elliott, 1978). It may be that some exploratory, "primary" forms of delinquency (Lemert, 1951) may occur without group support, or that this constitutes a pathological path to delinquency, but the maintenance of delinquent behavior patterns usually requires some exposure to and participation in groups supporting delinquent activity.

In sum, we postulate that bonding to conventional groups and institutions insulates one from involvement in delinquent patterns of behavior and that bonding to deviant groups or subcultures facilitates and sustains delinquent behavior. When examining the influence of social bonds, it is critical that the normative orientation of particular groups be taken into account. This focus on the normative orientations of groups is the central theme in subcultural theories of delinquency (Cohen, 1955, Cloward and Ohlin, 1960; and Miller, 1958) and constitutes an important qualification to a simple interpretation of the relationship between social bonds and delinquency.

This position has an empirical as well as a theoretical base. Severy (1973) and Elliott and Voss (1974) found exposure and commitment to delinquent groups to be the strongest predictors of subsequent increases in delinquent behavior. Both investigations found that the predictive effect of exposure alone was not particularly strong, but exposure plus high commitment to the delinquent group was a very powerful predictor of delinquency (i.e., there was a substantial interaction effect for these two independent variables). Participation in a delinquent peer group thus had an independent effect on delinquent behavior, in addition to the effect associated with strength of conventional bonds. Akers (1977), Conger (1976), and Linden and Hackler (1973) have reported data which suggest that strong peer bonds are associated with *both* delinquent and conforming behavior patterns, depending on the normative orientation of peers. Finally, data from the Chicago Gang Study (Rivera and Short, 1967a, 1967b; Short and Strodtbeck, 1965; and Tennyson, 1967) indicate that highly delinquent gang boys are more closely bonded to their class communities (subculture) than are less delinquent, nongang boys.

Delinquent Behavior

Delinquent behavior is viewed as a special subclass of deviant behavior. While deviance includes all violations of all prevailing norms, delinquent behavior includes only violations of statutory proscriptive norms, or, as they are usually called, laws. Thus, delinquent behavior takes on special meaning because (1) there is generally broad community consensus for these norms, (2) virtually all persons are aware that these specific proscriptions are enforced by official sanctions, and (3) the risk of detection and punishment influences the performance of delinquent acts.

We are not concerned here with the isolated delinquent act. Our focus is on sustained patterns of delinquent behavior, whether the person involved is socially or self-defined as a delinquent or nondelinquent person. Although our definition of delinquency subsumes one characteristic of a delinquent role (sustained patterns of delinquent behavior), it is our view that continuing involvement in delinquency may not necessarily involve the enactment of a delinquent role (Becker, 1963). There is empirical evidence that many embezzlers, auto thieves, check forgers, shoplifters, and persons involved in violent assaults against persons (including rape) do not view themselves as criminal or delinquent (Cressey, 1971; Gibbons, 1977; Lemert, 1951, 1953; Cameron, 1964; Robin, 1974; Gauthier, 1959; and Gebhard et al., 1965). Furthermore, many adolescents involved in sustained patterns of delinquent behavior are never apprehended and publicly labeled as delinquent persons, and have neither a public nor a self-definition as a delinquent or criminal person (Sykes and Matza, 1957; Reiss, 1962; Cameron, 1964; Hirschi, 1969; Kelly, 1977; and Jensen, 1972). Thus, our conceptualization of delinquency focuses on sustained patterns of illegal behavior and is logically independent of the concept of delinquent role.

Multiple Etiological Paths to Delinquency

There are two dominant etiological paths to delinquency in the paradigm shown in Figure 22.1. The first involves an integration of traditional control theory and social-learning theory. Weak integration into and commitment to the social order, absence of conventional restraints on behavior, and high vulnerability to the influence of delinquent peer groups during adolescence characterize the socialization experiences related to the first path. Depending on the presence and accessibility of conventional and delinquent peer groups, some weakly bonded youths turn to delinquency while others maintain an essentially conforming pattern of behavior or a legal, but unconventional, lifestyle.

The crucial element in this path is the delinquent peer group. Weakly bonded youths may not hold conventional aspirations (as for academic success), but then do share in more general aspirations for friendship and acceptance, as well as status and material rewards, which may be offered through participation in a group. Given an absence of conventional restraints and access to delinquent groups, the reasons for involvement are not unlike those for involvement in more conventional peer groups during adolescence.

The second path represents an integration of traditional strain and social learning perspectives. Youths who follow this path develop strong bonds to the conventional social order through their socialization experiences. The crucial element in this sequence is the attenuation, or weakening, of these bonds. Attenuating experiences during adolescence involve personal failure to achieve conventional goals and/or threats to the stability and cohesion of one's conventional social groups. Once one's bonds are effectively weakened, like those who never developed strong bonds, one is free to explore alternative means for goal achievement and to participate in delinquent or unconventional groups.

In most instances, this path also involves participation in peer groups which tolerate or encourage delinquent forms of behavior. It is our view that truly individual adaptations to this situation are unlikely to survive long enough to generate detectable patterns of delinquent behavior. However, two possible subtypes deserve mention. The diagram of this integrated paradigm shows a direct causal path from initially strong bonds and subsequent attenuation experiences to delinquent behavior patterns. Under some circumstances, participation in groups providing reinforcements for delinquent acts is unnecessary. Attenuating experiences are sufficient to motivate repeated acts of delinquency, which are attempts to regain conventional rewards through unconventional means. This pattern involves the classic strain model, in which the person retains a strong commitment to conventional goals and values and uses illegal means as a temporary expedient. The attenuation process is only partial, and these youths retain some commitment to and integration into conventional groups. We anticipate such patterns to be of relatively short duration and to involve highly instrumental forms of delinquent behavior. Patterns of theft may characterize this etiological path.

A second subtype corresponds to that described generally by Simon and Gagnon (1976) in their article on the anomie of affluence. This path involves those whose commitments to conventional goals are attenuated by a decreasing gratification derived from goal achievement. Unlike the previously described subtype, which involved failure to achieve conventional success goals because of limited means or abilities, this type has ability and a ready access to legitimate means and is successful by conventional standards. The failure to derive personal gratification from "success" results in an attenuation of the commitment to these success goals and sets in motion a search for alternative goals whose attainment will provide a greater measure of personal gratification. This path to delinquency clearly requires participation in social groups in which delinquent behavior patterns can be learned and reinforced. This pattern of delinquency is characterized by a search for new experiences, which frequently involves illegal forms of behavior, such as illicit drug use and sex-related offenses.

At a more tentative level, we postulate that the two major paths (1) typically involve different forms of personal alienation and (2) result in different self-images and social labels. Conceptually, alienation plays a slightly different role within strain and control perspectives. From a control perspective, alienation, in the form of powerlessness, societal estrangement, and social isolation, directly reflects a weak personal commitment to conventional groups and norms. For strain theory, however, alienation represents a crucial intervening variable linking failure to delinquency. It is evidence of the attenuation of one's commitment bond or, in Hirschi's (1969) terms, the neutralization of "moral obstacles" to delinquency. In the form of alienation described by Cloward and Ohlin (1960), the neutralization is achieved through a blaming process in which failure is attributed to others or to general societal injustice. These same elements are present in Sykes and Matza's (1957) techniques of neutralization. Cartwright et al. (1966) and Cartwright (1971) identify four types of alienation which provide this direct encouragement, justification, or permission for delinquency: normlessness, futility, lack of trust, and perceived indifference. If we assume some relationship between the two causal paths and social class, there is some indirect empirical support for the hypothesis that the form of alienation is tied to the strength of one's initial commitment bond. Brennan and Huizinga (1975) have reported that normlessness was the dominant form of alienation among middle-class delinquent youths, while powerlessness and societal estrangement were the predominant forms of alienation among low-SES delinquent youths. We thus postulate that the form of alienation defines the particular causal path involved.

We also hypothesize that those with initially strong bonds are less likely to view themselves as delinquent, even when they are involved in sustained patterns of delinquent behavior. Such persons are more likely to come from advantaged backgrounds and to have prosocial self-images. Consequently, they are likely to view their delinquent acts as temporary expedients, retaining at least a partial commitment to conventional goals. The probability of apprehension and public labeling by the police and courts is also much lower for such youths. In contrast, those who never developed strong bonds to the social order are more vulnerable to labeling processes and thus more likely to be viewed as delinquents by themselves and by others (Jensen, 1972). This may account, in part, for the persistent view among law enforcement officials and the general public that most delinquents are poor and/or nonwhite, in spite of the compelling evidence that the incidence of delinquent behavior is unrelated to these variables.

Summary and Discussion

We have postulated two primary paths, or sets of conditions, which lead youths into delinquent behavior. The first (and probably most frequent) sequence involves (1) weak bonds to conventional society and (2) exposure and commitment to groups involved in delinquent activity; the second involves (1) strong bonds to conventional society, (2) conditions and experiences which attenuate those bonds, and, in most instances, (3) exposure and commitment to groups involved in delinquency.

Two types of bonds or controls were specified—integration (internal) and commitment (external). Integration includes such variables as occupancy of conventional social roles; participation in conventional activities, organizations, and institutions; and the presence of effective sanctioning networks in one's immediate social contexts. Commitment includes such variables as perceived legitimacy of conventional norms, normlessness, social isolation, societal estrangement, powerlessness, attachment to parents and peers, belief in conventional goals and values, and tolerance for deviance.

We also discussed some specific experiences or conditions frequently encountered during adolescence, which reinforce or attenuate one's bonds. Variables identified here include failure-success experiences; positive or negative labeling; and social crisis and disorganization in the home, school, and community. Under these conditions of stress, even those with initially strong bonds to society have an increasing likelihood of involvement in delinquent behavior. In addition, delinquent learning and performance structures are a necessary variable in both etiological sequences for the majority of adolescent offenders.

We believe the synthesis of traditional strain, social control, and social-learning perspectives into a single paradigm has several advantages over a conceptualization which treats each theory as separate and independent. First, the provision for multiple etiological paths to delinquency in a single paradigm presents a more comprehensive view. The integration of strain and control perspectives assumes that these two paths are independent and additive and that their integration will account for more variance in sustained patterns of delinquent behavior than either can explain independently. Independent tests of these traditional perspectives in the past have often failed to include the variables necessary to test alternative explanations, and even when such variables were available, the alternative explanations were assumed to be competitive and were thus evaluated with respect to the relative strengths of the two competing hypotheses (Hirschi, 1969; and Eve, 1977). Such an approach misses the possibility that both hypotheses are correct and are accounting for different portions of the variance in delinquency. We have also suggested that different patterns of delinquency may be tied to alternative etiological paths; for example, we postulated that one of the strain paths (limited means/goal failure) should produce forms of delinquency which are considered very instrumental by conventional values. The alternative strain path (attenuated commitment to conventional goals) should result in less instrumental forms of delinquency, since it characteristically involves a search for new experiences (e.g., drug use) rather than attempts to achieve conventional goals.

Second, we believe that our integrated paradigm is consistent with previous empirical findings and offers some insight into contradictory findings. Previous research using the social control perspective has established a relationship between the strength of one's bonds and social class, with low-SES and minority youths characterized by weaker bonds (Nye, 1958; Gold, 1963; McKinley, 1964, and Hirschi, 1969). In contrast, the attenuated commitment strain path has been associated with affluence and the limited means-strain path seems most relevant to working-class youths. The combined effect seems consistent with the observed class distribution of self-reported delinquent behavior. Our assumption that weakly bonded youths run the greatest risk of official processing (because of greater surveillance in their neighborhoods, more traditional forms of delinquent behavior, and limited resources with which to avoid processing in the justice system) would account for the observed class distribution of official measures of delinquency.

The integrated paradigm also offers an explanation for the contradictory findings on aspirations and delinquency. It may also account for the generally weak results of tests of the labeling hypothesis, since we view labeling as an attenuating process, which thus should affect youths with prior commitment to the conventional order most directly. Such a view is consistent with the findings of Short and Strodtbeck (1965), Gould (1969), and Ageton and Elliott (1974) that the impact of negative labeling experiences is greater for middleclass youths, and that, for most youths who are apprehended and processed officially (primarily weakly bonded youths), the effects of official labeling are very weak (Fisher, 1972; Foster, Dinitz, and Reckless, 1972; Jensen, 1972; Ageton and Elliott, 1974; Bernstein, Kelly, and Doyle, 1977; and Thomas, 1977).

This integrated conceptual framework may, at present, appear too all-inclusive. However, it is our view that a broad range of variables must be considered before a truly parsimonious set can be identified. Clearly, a satisfactory explanation of delinquent behavior requires multiple variables and a broader conceptualization than has been used to date. This conceptual framework provides the broader perspective, and additional research using this paradigm should result in a more precise set of variables.

Discussion Questions

1. Describe how the version of strain theory employed by Elliott et al. is similar to and different from the classic strain theories of Merton, Cohen, and Cloward and Ohlin (see Part IV).

2. Certain theorists have argued that it is impossible to develop truly integrated theories since the theories being integrated are often based on opposing assumptions. Describe the opposing assumptions between strain, learning, and/or control theories. Which of these assumptions does Elliott et al.'s integrated theory violate? Do you feel the goal of integration is worthwhile, given this necessity for violating certain theoretical assumptions?

3. Elliott et al. argue that individuals with strong social bonds may experience an attenuation of these bonds for several reasons. What are these reasons?

4. The central variable in Elliott et al.'s integrated theory is association with delinquent peers: strain and control variables are said to affect delinquency largely through their effect on this variable. Why do Elliott et al. assign such a central role to this variable (conversely, why do they claim that strain and social control variables will only have small direct effects on delinquency)? ✦

23

Toward an Interactional Theory of Delinquency

Terence P. Thornberry

Thornberry's interactional theory of delinquency shares certain elements in common with Elliott et al.'s integrated theory. In particular, Thornberry argues that low social control (or weak social bonds) leads to delinquency by increasing the likelihood of association with delinquent peers. This is the primary path to delinquency in Elliott et al.'s theory. Unlike Elliott et al., however, Thornberry draws on Hirschi's conceptualization of the elements of the social bond (although each bond is defined quite broadly). And he does not incorporate strain theory into his model (strain theory was at the low point of its popularity at the time his theory was developed; it has since experienced a resurgence in interest—see Part IV). What most distinguishes Thornberry's theory, however, is its emphasis on reciprocal effects and the developmental process.

Thornberry argues that there is good reason to believe that many of the variables in his model have reciprocal effects on one another. So, while one might argue that association with delinquent peers increases the likelihood of delinquency, it is also reasonable to argue that delinquency increases the likelihood of association with delinquent peers. Such reciprocal effects are quite important, for they suggest that many youths get involved in an "amplifying causal structure" that leads to greater and greater involvement in delinquency. Thornberry also argues that the causes of delinquency change over the life course of the individual. For example, the importance of parental attachment diminishes as the adolescent ages, while new variables—like commitment to conventional activities (job, college, military)—enter the model. Most models of delinquency focus on mid-adolescence and do not consider such developmental trends. The consideration of such trends allows Thornberry to better explain patterns in delinquency over the life course—like the fact that most offenders desist from delinquency in late adolescence. While Thornberry's integrated theory is phrased primarily at the micro-level, he does discuss the role of structural variables like social class and gender. He argues that such variables are important because they affect one's initial level of social control and exposure to delinquent peers, values, and behaviors.

Only a few studies have examined reciprocal relationships and developmental patterns of the type described by Thornberry (see Thornberry, 1996 for a summary). These studies find support for some of the reciprocal relationships in Thornberry's model, particularly reciprocal relationships between the learning variables (delinquent values and peers) and delinquency. These studies also suggest that certain of the causes of delinquency may vary in importance over the life course, although it is too early to draw any firm conclusions in this area. In sum, the core arguments of Thornberry's theory have some support and the data certainly suggest that theories of crime need to consider both reciprocal effects and developmental issues.

Reference

Thornberry, Terrence P. 1996. "Empirical Support for Interactional Theory." Pp. 198-235 in *Delinquency and Crime: Current Theories*, edited by J. David Hawkins. Cambridge: Cambridge University Press.

A variety of sociological theories have been developed to explain the onset and maintenance of delinquent behavior. Currently, three are of primary importance: social control theory (Hirschi, 1969), social learning theory (Akers, 1977), and integrated models that combine them into a broader body of explanatory principals (Elliott, Ageton, and

Canter, 1979; Elliott, Huizinga, and Ageton, 1985).

Control theory argues that delinquency emerges whenever the social and cultural constraints over human conduct are substantially attenuated. As Hirschi states in his classic presentation (1969), control theory assumes that we would all be deviant if only we dared. Learning theory, on the other hand, posits that there is no natural impulse toward delinquency. Indeed, delinquent behavior must be learned through the same processes and mechanisms as conforming behavior. Because of these different starting points, control and learning models give causal priority to somewhat different concepts, and integrated models capitalize on these complementary approaches. Muting the assumptive differences, integrated theories meld together propositions from these (and sometimes other theories—for example, strain) to explain delinquent behavior.

Although these approaches have substantially informed our understanding of the causes of delinquency, they and other contemporary theories suffer from three fundamental limitations. First, they rely on unidirectional rather than reciprocal causal structures. By and large, current theories ignore reciprocal effects in which delinquent behavior is viewed as part of a more general social nexus, affected by, but also affecting, other social factors. Second, current theories tend to be nondevelopmental, specifying causal models for only a narrow age range, usually midadolescence. As a result, they fail to capitalize on developmental patterns to explain the initiation, maintenance, and desistence of delinquency. Finally, contemporary theories tend to assume uniform causal effects throughout the social structure. By ignoring the person's structural position, they fail to provide an understanding of the sources of initial variation in both delinquency and its presumed causes. In combination, these three limitations have led to theories that are narrowly conceived and which provide incomplete and, at times, misleading models of the causes of delinquency.

The present article develops an interactional theory of delinquency that addresses and attempts to respond to each of these limitations. The model proposed here pays particular attention to the first issue, recursive versus reciprocal causal structures, since the development of dynamic models is seen as essential to represent accurately the interactional settings in which delinquency develops.

Origins and Assumptions

The basic premise of the model proposed here is that human behavior occurs in social interaction and can therefore best be explained by models that focus on interactive processes. Rather than viewing adolescents as propelled along a unidirectional pathway to one or another outcome—that is, delinquency or conformity—it argues that adolescents interact with other people and institutions and that behavioral outcomes are formed by that interactive process. For example, the delinquent behavior of an adolescent is formed in part by how he and his parents *interact* over time, not simply by the child's perceived, and presumably invariant, *level* of attachment to parents. Moreover, since it is an interactive system, the behaviors of others—for example, parents and school officials—are influenced both by each other and by the adolescent, including his or her delinquent behavior. If this view is correct, then interactional effects have to be modeled explicitly if we are to understand the social and psychological processes involved with initiation into delinquency, the maintenance of such behavior, and its eventual reduction.

Interactional theory develops from the same intellectual tradition as the theories mentioned above, especially the Durkheimian tradition of social control. It asserts that the fundamental cause of delinquency lies in the weakening of social constraints over the conduct of the individual. Unlike classical control theory, however, it does not assume that the attenuation of controls leads directly to delinquency. The weakening of controls simply allows for a much wider array of behavior, including continued conventional action, failure as indicated by school dropout and sporadic employment histories, alcoholism, mental illness, delinquent and criminal careers, or some combination of these outcomes. For the freedom resulting from weakened bonds to be channeled into delinquency, especially serious prolonged delinquency, requires an interactive setting in which delinquency is learned, performed, and reinforced. This view is similar to Cullen's structuring perspective which draws attention to the indeterminancy of deviant behavior. "It can thus be argued that there is an *indeterminate* and not a determinate or etiologically specific relationship between motivational variables on the one hand and any particular form of deviant behavior on the other hand" (Cullen, 1984: 5).

Although heavily influenced by control and learning theories, and to a lesser extent by strain and culture conflict theories, this is not an effort at theoretical integration as that term is usually used (Elliott, 1985). Rather, this paper is guided by what we have elsewhere called theoretical elaboration (Thornberry, 1987). In this instance, a basic control theory is extended, or elaborated upon, using available theoretical perspectives and empirical findings to provide a more accurate model of the causes of delinquency. In the process of elaboration, there is no requirement to resolve disputes among other theories—for example, their different assumptions about the origins of deviance (Thornberry, 1987: 15-18); all that is required is that the propositions of the model developed here be consistent with one another and with the assumptions about deviance stated above.

Organization

The presentation of the interactional model begins by identifying the central concepts to be included in the model. Next, the underlying theoretical structure of the proposed model is examined and the rationale for moving from unidirectional to reciprocal causal models is developed. The reciprocal model is then extended to include a developmental perspective, examining the theoretical saliency of different variables at different developmental stages. Finally, the influence of the person's position in the social structure is explored. Although in some senses the last issue is logically prior to the others, since it is concerned with sources of initial variation in the causal variables, it is discussed last so that the reciprocal relationships among the concepts—the heart of an interactional perspective—can be more fully developed.

Theoretical Concepts

Given these basic premises, an interactional model must respond to two overriding issues. First, how are traditional social constraints over behavior weakened and, second, once weakened, how is the resulting freedom channeled into delinquent patterns? To address these issues, the present article presents an initial version of an interactional model, focusing on the interrelationships among six concepts: attachment to parents, commitment to school, belief in conventional values, associations with delinquent peers, adopting delinquent values, and engaging in delinquent behavior. These concepts form the core of the theoretical model since they are central to social psychological theories of delinquency and since they have been shown in numerous studies to be strongly related to subsequent delinquent behavior (see Elliott et al., 1985, Chs. 1-3, for an excellent review of this literature).

The first three derive from Hirschi's version of control theory (1969) and represent the primary mechanisms by which adolescents are bonded to conventional middle-class society. When those elements of the bond are weakened, behavioral freedom increases considerably. For that freedom to lead to delinquent behavior, however, interactive settings that reinforce delinquency are required. In the model, those settings are represented by two concepts associations with delinquent peers and the formation of delinquent values which derive primarily from social learning theory.

For the purpose of explicating the overall theoretical perspective, each of these concepts is defined quite broadly. Attachment to parents includes the affective relationship between parent and child, communication patterns, parenting skills such as monitoring and discipline, parent-child conflict, and the like. Commitment to school refers to the stake in conformity the adolescent has developed and includes such factors as success in school, perceived importance of education, attachment to teachers, and involvement in school activities. Belief in conventional values represents the granting of legitimacy to such middle-class values as education, personal industry, financial success, deferral of gratification, and the like.

Three delinquency variables are included in the model. Association with delinquent peers includes the level of attachment to peers, the delinquent behavior and values of peers, and their reinforcing reactions to the adolescent's own delinquent or conforming behavior. It is a continuous measure that can vary from groups that are heavily delinquent to those that are almost entirely nondelinquent. Delinquent values refer to the granting of legitimacy to delinquent activities as acceptable modes of behavior as well as a general willingness to violate the law to achieve other ends.

Delinquent behavior, the primary outcome variable, refers to acts that place the youth at risk for adjudication; it ranges from status offenses to serious violent activities. Since the present model is an interactional one, interested not only in explaining delinquency but in explaining the effects of delinquency on

other variables, particular attention is paid to prolonged involvement in serious delinquency. . . .

Model Specification

A causal model allowing for reciprocal relationships among the six concepts of interest—attachment to parents, commitment to school, belief in conventional values, association with delinquent peers, delinquent values, and delinquent behavior—is presented in Figure 23.1. This model refers to the period of early adolescence, from about ages 11 to 13, when delinquent careers are beginning, but prior to the period at which delinquency reaches its apex in terms of seriousness and frequency. In the following sections the model is extended to later ages.

The specification of causal effects begins by examining the three concepts that form the heart of social learning theories of delinquency—delinquent peers, delinquent values, and delinquent behavior. For now we focus on the reciprocal nature of the relationships, ignoring until later variations in the strength of the relationships.

Traditional social learning theory specifies a causal order among these variables in which delinquent associations affect delin-

Figure 23.1
A Reciprocal Model of Delinquent Involvement at Early Adolescence[a]

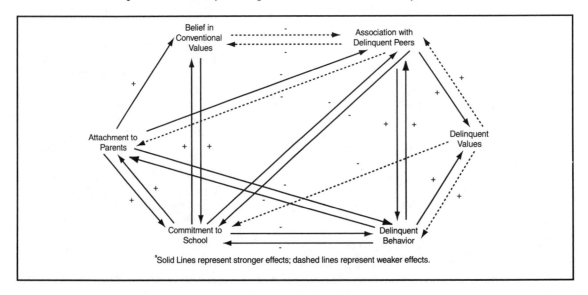

[a]Solid Lines represent stronger effects; dashed lines represent weaker effects.

quent values and, in turn, both produce delinquent behavior (Akers, Krohn, Lanza-Kaduce, and Radosevich, 1979; Matsueda, 1982). Yet, for each of the dyadic relationships involving these variables, other theoretical perspectives and much empirical evidence suggest the appropriateness of reversing this causal order. For example, social learning theory proposes that associating with delinquents, or more precisely, people who hold and reinforce delinquent values, increases the chances of delinquent behavior (Akers, 1977). Yet, as far back as the work of the Gluecks (1950) this specification has been challenged. Arguing that "birds of a feather flock together," the Gluecks propose that youths who are delinquent seek out and associate with others who share those tendencies. From this perspective, rather than being a cause of delinquency, associations are the result of delinquents seeking out and associating with like-minded peers.

An attempt to resolve the somewhat tedious argument over the temporal priority of associations and behavior is less productive theoretically than capitalizing on the interactive nature of human behavior and treating the relationship as it probably is a reciprocal one. People often take on the behavioral repertoire of their associates but, at the same time, they often seek out associates who share their behavioral interests. Individuals clearly behave this way in conventional settings, and there is no reason to assume that deviant activities, such as delinquency, are substantially different in this regard.

Similar arguments can be made for the other two relationships among the delinquency variables. Most recent theories of delinquency, following the lead of social learning theory, posit that delinquent associations lead to the formation of delinquent values. Subcultural theories, however, especially those that derive from a cultural deviance perspective (Miller, 1958) suggest that values precede the formation of peer groups. Indeed, it is the socialization of adolescents into the "lower-class culture" and its particular value system that leads them to associate with delinquent peers in the first place. This specification can also be derived from a social control perspective as demonstrated in

Weis and Sederstrom's social development model (1981) and Burkett and Warren's social selection model (1987).

Finally, the link between delinquent values and delinquent behavior restates, in many ways, the basic social psychological question of the relationship between attitudes and behavior. Do attitudes form behavior patterns or does behavior lead to attitude formation? Social psychological research, especially in cognitive psychology and balance models (for example, Festinger, 1957; Brehm and Cohen, 1962) points to the reciprocal nature of this relationship. It suggests that people indeed behave in a manner consistent with their attitudes, but also that behavior is one of the most persuasive forces in the formation and maintenance of attitudes.

Such a view of the relationship between delinquent values and behavior is consistent with Hindelang's findings:

> This general pattern of results indicates that one can "predict" a respondent's self approval [of illegal behaviors] from knowledge of that respondent's involvement/non-involvement [in delinquency] with fewer errors than vice-versa. (1974: 382)

It is also consistent with recent deterrence research which demonstrates that the "experiential effect," in which behavior affects attitudes, is much stronger than the deterrent effect, in which attitudes affect behavior (Paternoster, Saltzman, Chiricos, and Waldo 1983).

Although each of these relationships appears to be reciprocal, the predicted strengths of the associations are not of equal strength during the early adolescent period (see Figure 23.1). Beliefs that delinquent conduct is acceptable and positively valued may be emerging, but such beliefs are not fully articulated for 11- to 13-year-olds. Because of their emerging quality, they are viewed as more effect than cause, produced by delinquent behavior and associations with delinquent peers. As these values emerge, however, they have feedback effects, albeit relatively weak ones at these ages, on behavior and associations. That is, as the values become more fully articulated and delinquency becomes positively valued, it increases the likelihood of such behavior and further reinforces associations with like-minded peers.

Summary: When attention is focused on the interrelationships among associations with delinquent peers, delinquent values, and delinquent behavior, it appears that they are, in fact, reciprocally related. The world of human behavior is far more complex than a simple recursive one in which a temporal order can be imposed on interactional variables of this nature. Interactional theory sees these three concepts as embedded in a causal loop, each reinforcing the others over time. Regardless of where the individual enters the loop, the following obtains: delinquency increases associations with delinquent peers and delinquent values; delinquent values increase delinquent behavior and associations with delinquent peers; and associations with delinquent peers increases delinquent behavior and delinquent values. The question now concerns the identification of factors that lead some youth, but not others, into this spiral of increasing delinquency.

Social Control Effects

As indicated at the outset of this essay, the premise of interactional theory is that the fundamental cause of delinquency is the attenuation of social controls over the person's conduct. Whenever bonds to the conventional world are substantially weakened, the individual is freed from moral constraints and is at risk for a wide array of deviant activities, including delinquency. The primary mechanisms that bind adolescents to the conventional world are attachment to parents, commitment to school, and belief in conventional values, and their role in the model can now be examined.

During the early adolescent years, the family is the most salient arena for social interaction and involvement and, because of this, attachment to parents has a stronger influence on other aspects of the youth's life at this stage than it does at later stages of development. With this in mind, attachment to parents is predicted to affect four other variables. Since youths who are attached to their parents are sensitive to their wishes (Hirschi,

1969: 16-19) and, since parents are almost universally supportive of the conventional world, these children are likely to be strongly committed to school and to espouse conventional values. In addition, youths who are attached to their parents, again because of their sensitivity to parental wishes, are unlikely to associate with delinquent peers or to engage in delinquent behavior.

In brief, parental influence is seen as central to controlling the behavior of youths at these relatively early ages. Parents who have a strong affective bond with their children, who communicate with them, who exercise appropriate parenting skills, and so forth, are likely to lead their children towards conventional actions and beliefs and away from delinquent friends and actions.

On the other hand, attachment to parents is not seen as an immutable trait, impervious to the effects of other variables. Indeed, associating with delinquent peers, not being committed to school, and engaging in delinquent behavior are so contradictory to parental expectations that they tend to diminish the level of attachment between parent and child. Adolescents who fail at school, who associate with delinquent peers, and who engage in delinquent conduct are, as a consequence, likely to jeopardize their affective bond with their parents, precisely because these behaviors suggest that the "person does not care about the wishes and expectations of other people. . ." (Hirschi, 1969: 18), in this instance, his or her parents.

Turning next to belief in conventional values, this concept is involved in two different causal loops. First, it strongly affects commitment to school and in turn is affected by commitment to school. In essence, this loop posits a behavioral and attitudinal consistency in the conventional realm. Second, a weaker loop is posited between belief in conventional values and associations with delinquent peers. Youths who do not grant legitimacy to conventional values are more apt to associate with delinquent friends who share those views, and those friendships are likely to attenuate further their beliefs in conventional values. This reciprocal specification is supported by Burkett and Warren's findings concerning religious beliefs and peer associations (1987). Finally, youths who believe in conventional values are seen as somewhat less likely to engage in delinquent behavior.

Although belief in conventional values plays some role in the genesis of delinquency, its impact is not particularly strong. For example, it is not affected by delinquent behavior, nor is it related to delinquent values. This is primarily because belief in conventional values appears to be quite invariant, regardless of class of origin or delinquency status, for example, most people strongly assert conventional values (Short and Strodtbeck, 1965: Ch. 3). Nevertheless, these beliefs do exert some influence in the model, especially with respect to reinforcing commitment to school.

Finally, the impact of commitment to school is considered. This variable is involved in reciprocal loops with both of the other bonding variables. Youngsters who are attached to their parents are likely to be committed to and succeed in school, and that success is likely to reinforce the close ties to their parents. Similarly, youths who believe in conventional values are likely to be committed to school, the primary arena in which they can act in accordance with those values, and, in turn, success in that arena is likely to reinforce the beliefs.

In addition to its relationships with the other control variables, commitment to school also has direct effects on two of the delinquency variables. Students who are committed to succeeding in school are unlikely to associate with delinquents or to engage in substantial amounts of serious repetitive delinquent behavior. These youths have built up a stake in conformity and should be unwilling to jeopardize that investment by either engaging in delinquent behavior or by associating with those who do.

Low commitment to school is not seen as leading directly to the formation of delinquent values, however. Its primary effect on delinquent values is indirect, via associations with delinquent peers and delinquent behavior (Conger, 1980: 137). While school failure may lead to a reduced commitment to conventional values, it does not follow that it directly increases the acceptance of values that support delinquency.

Commitment to school, on the other hand, is affected by each of the delinquent variables in the model. Youths who accept values that are consistent with delinquent behavior, who associate with other delinquents, and who engage in delinquent behavior are simply unlikely candidates to maintain an active commitment to school and the conventional world that school symbolizes.

Summary: Attachment to parents, commitment to school, and belief in conventional values reduce delinquency by cementing the person to conventional institutions and people. When these elements of the bond to conventional society are strong, delinquency is unlikely, but when they are weak the individual is placed at much greater risk for delinquency. When viewed from an interactional perspective, two additional qualities of these concepts become increasingly evident.

First, attachment to parents, commitment to school, and belief in conventional values are not static attributes of the person, invariant over time. These concepts interact with one another during the developmental process. For some youths the levels of attachment, commitment, and belief increase as these elements reinforce one another, while for other youths the interlocking nature of these relationships suggests a greater and greater attenuation of the bond will develop over time.

Second, the bonding variables appear to be reciprocally linked to delinquency, exerting a causal impact on associations with delinquent peers and delinquent behavior; they also are causally effected by these variables. As the youth engages in more and more delinquent conduct and increasingly associates with delinquent peers, the level of his bond to the conventional world is further weakened. Thus, while the weakening of the bond to conventional society may be an initial cause of delinquency, delinquency eventually becomes its own indirect cause precisely because of its ability to weaken further the person's bonds to family, school, and conventional beliefs. The implications of this amplifying causal structure is examined below. First, however, the available support for reciprocal models is reviewed and the basic model is extended to later developmental stages. . . .

Developmental Extensions

The previous section developed a strategy for addressing one of the three major limitations of delinquency theories mentioned in the introduction—namely, their unidirectional causal structure. A second limitation is the nondevelopmental posture of most theories which tend to provide a cross-sectional picture of the factors associated with delinquency at one age, but which do not provide a rationale for understanding how delinquent behavior develops over time. The present section offers a developmental extension of the basic model.

Middle Adolescence

First, a model for middle adolescence, when the youths are approximately 15 or 16 years of age is presented. This period represents the highest rates of involvement in delinquency and is the reference period, either implicitly or explicitly, for most theories of delinquent involvement. Since the models for the early and middle adolescent periods have essentially the same structure and causal relationships (Figure 23.1), discussion focuses on the differences between them and does not repeat the rationale for individual causal effects.

Perhaps the most important difference concerns attachment to parents which is involved in relatively few strong relationships. By this point in the life cycle, the most salient variables involved in the production of delinquency are likely to be external to the home, associated with the youth's activities in school and peer networks. This specification is consistent with empirical results for subjects in this age range (Johnson, 1979: 105; and Schoenberg, 1975, quoted in Johnson). Indeed, Johnson concludes that "an adolescent's public life has as much or more to do with his or her deviance or conformity than do 'under-the-roof' experiences" (1979: 116).

This is not to say that attachment to parents is irrelevant; such attachments are involved in enhancing commitment to school and belief in conventional values, and in preventing associations with delinquent peers. It is just that the overall strength of parental effects are weaker than at earlier ages when the salience of the family as a locus of interaction and control was greater.

The second major change concerns the increased importance of delinquent values as a causal factor. It is still embedded in the causal loop with the other two delinquency variables, but now it is as much cause as effect. Recall that at the younger ages delinquent values were seen as emerging, produced by associations with delinquent peers and delinquent behavior. Given their emergent nature, they were not seen as primary causes of other variables. At midadolescence, however, when delinquency is at its apex, these values are more fully articulated and have stronger effects on other variables. First, delinquent values are seen as major reinforcers of both delinquent associations and delinquent behavior. In general, espousing values supportive of delinquency tends to increase the potency of this causal loop. Second, since delinquent values are antithetical to the conventional settings of school and family, youths who espouse them are less likely to be committed to school and attached to parents. Consistent with the reduced saliency of family at these ages, the feedback effect to school is seen as stronger than the feedback effect to parents.

By and large, the other concepts in the model play the same role at these ages as they do at the earlier ones. Thus, the major change from early to middle adolescence concerns the changing saliency of some of the theoretical concepts. The family declines in relative importance while the adolescent's own world of school and peers takes on increasing significance. While these changes occur, the overall structure of the theory remains constant. These interactive variables are still seen as mutually reinforcing over time.

Later Adolescence

Finally, the causes of delinquency during the transition from adolescence to adulthood, about ages 18 to 20, can be examined. At these ages one should more properly speak of crime than delinquency, but for consistency we will continue to use the term delinquency in the causal diagrams and employ the terms delinquency and crime interchangeably in the text.

Two new variables are added to the model to reflect the changing life circumstances at this stage of development. The more important of these is commitment to conventional activities which includes employment, attending college, and military service. Along with the transition to the world of work, there is a parallel transition from the family of origin to one's own family. Although this transition does not peak until the early 20s, for many people its influence is beginning at this stage. Included in this concept are marriage, plans for marriage, and plans for childrearing. These new variables largely replace attachment to parents and commitment to school in the theoretical scheme; they represent the major sources of bonds to conventional society for young adults.

Both attachment to parents and commitment to school remain in the model but take on the cast of exogenous variables. Attachment to parents has only a minor effect on commitment to school, and commitment to school is proposed to affect only commitment to conventional activities and, more weakly, delinquent behavior.

The other three variables considered in the previous models—association with delinquent peers, delinquent values, and delinquent behavior—are still hypothesized to be embedded in an amplifying causal loop. As indicated above, this loop is most likely to occur among adolescents who, at earlier ages, were freed from the controlling influence of parents and school. Moreover, via the feedback paths delinquent peers, delinquent values, and delinquent behavior further alienate the youth from parents and diminish commitment to school. Once this spiral begins, the probability of sustained delinquency increases.

This situation, if it continued uninterrupted, would yield higher and higher rates of crime as the subjects matured. Such an outcome is inconsistent with the desistence that has been observed during this age period (Wolfgang, Thornberry, and Figlio, 1987). Rates of delinquency and crime begin to subside by the late teenage years, a phenomenon often attributed to "maturational reform."

Such an explanation, however, is tautological since it claims that crime stops when adolescents get older, because they get older. It is also uninformative since the concept of maturational reform is theoretically undefined.

A developmental approach, however, offers an explanation for desistence. As the developmental process unfolds, life circumstances change, developmental milestones are met (or, for some missed), new social roles are created, and new networks of attachments and commitments emerge. The effects of these changes enter the processual model to explain new and often dramatically different behavioral patterns. In the present model, these changes are represented by commitment to conventional activity and commitment to family.

Commitment to conventional activity is influenced by a number of variables, including earlier attachment to parents, commitment to school, and belief in conventional values. And once the transition to the world of work is made, tremendous opportunities are afforded for new and different effects in the delinquency model. Becoming committed to conventional activities—work, college, military service, and so on—reduces the likelihood of delinquent behavior and associations with delinquent peers because it builds up a stake in conformity that is antithetical to delinquency.

Moreover, since the delinquency variables are still embedded in a causal loop, the effect of commitment to conventional activities tends to resonate throughout the system. But, because of the increased saliency of a new variable, commitment to conventional activities, the reinforcing loop is now set in motion to *reduce* rather than increase delinquent and criminal involvement.

The variable of commitment to family has similar, albeit weaker, effects since the transition to the family is only beginning at these ages. Nevertheless, commitment to family is proposed to reduce both delinquent associations and delinquent values and to increase commitment to conventional activity. In general, as the individual takes on the responsibilities of family, the bond to conventional society increases, placing additional constraints on behavior and precluding further delinquency.

These changes do not occur in all cases, however, nor should they be expected to since many delinquents continue on to careers in adult crime. In the Philadelphia cohort of 1945, 51% of the juvenile delinquents were also adult offenders, and the more serious and prolonged the delinquent careers were, the greater the odds of an adult career (Wolfgang et al., 1987: Ch. 4).

The continuation of criminal careers can also be explained by the nature of the reciprocal effects included in this model. In general, extensive involvement in delinquency at earlier ages feeds back upon and weakens attachment to parents and commitment to school (see Figure 23.1). These variables, as well as involvement in delinquency itself, weaken later commitment to family and to conventional activities (Figure 23.1). Thus, these new variables, commitment to conventional activities and to family, are affected by the person's situation at earlier stages and do not "automatically" alter the probability of continued criminal involvement. If the initial bonds are extremely weak, the chances of new bonding variables being established to break the cycle towards criminal careers are low and it is likely that criminal behavior will continue. . . .

Structural Effects

Structural variables, including race, class, sex, and community of residence, refer to the person's location in the structure of social roles and statuses. The manner in which they are incorporated in the interactional model is illustrated here by examining only one of them, social class of origin.

Although social class is often measured continuously, a categorical approach is more consistent with the present model and with most theories of delinquency that incorporate class as a major explanatory variable—for example, strain and social disorganization theories. For our purposes, the most important categories are the lower class, the working lower class, and the middle class.

The lower class is composed of those who are chronically or sporadically unemployed, receive welfare, and subsist at or below the poverty level. They are similar to Johnson's "underclass" (1979). The working lower class is composed of those with more stable work patterns, training for semiskilled jobs, and incomes that allow for some economic stability. For these families, however, the hold on even a marginal level of occupational and economic security is always tenuous. Finally, the middle class refers to all families above these lower levels. Middle-class families have achieved some degree of economic success and stability and can reasonably expect to remain at that level or improve their standing over time.

The manner in which the social class of origin affects the interactional variables and the behavioral trajectories can be demonstrated by comparing the life expectancies of children from lower- and middle-class families. As compared to children from a middle-class background, children from a lower-class background are more apt to have (1) disrupted family processes and environments (Conger, McCarty, Wang, Lahey, and Kroop, 1984; Wahler, 1980); (2) poorer preparation for school (Cloward and Ohlin, 1960); (3) belief structures influenced by the traditions of the American lower class (Miller, 1958; Anderson, 1976); and (4) greater exposure to neighborhoods with high rates of crime (Shaw and McKay, 1942; Braithwaite, 1981). The direction of all these effects is such that we would expect children from lower-class families to be *initially* less bonded to conventional society and more exposed to delinquent values, friends, and behaviors.

As one moves towards the working lower class, both the likelihood and the potency of the factors just listed decrease. As a result, the initial values of the interactional variables improve but, because of the tenuous nature of economic and social stability for these families, both the bonding variables and the delinquency variables are still apt to lead to considerable amounts of delinquent conduct. Finally, youths from middle-class families, given their greater stability and economic security, are likely to start with a stronger family structure, greater stakes in conformity, and higher chances of success, and all of these factors are likely to reduce the likelihood of initial delinquent involvement.

In brief, the initial values of the interactional variables are systematically related to the social class of origin. Moreover, since these variables are reciprocally related, it follows logically that social class is systematically related to the behavioral trajectories described above. Youngsters from the lowest classes have the highest probability of moving forward on a trajectory of increasing delinquency. Starting from a position of low bonding to conventional institutions and a high delinquency environment, the reciprocal nature of the interrelationships leads inexorably towards extremely high rates of delinquent and criminal involvement. Such a view is consistent with prevalence data which show that by age 18, 50%, and by age 30, 70% of low SES minority males have an official police record (Wolfgang et al., 1987).

On the other hand, the expected trajectory of middle-class youths suggests that they will move toward an essentially conforming lifestyle, in which their stakes in conformity increase and more and more preclude serious and prolonged involvement in delinquency. Finally, because the initial values of the interactional variables are mixed and indecisive for children from lower-working-class homes, their behavioral trajectories are much more volatile and the outcome much less certain.

Summary: Interactional theory asserts that both the initial values of the process variables and their development over time are systematically related to the social class of origin. Moreover, parallel arguments can be made for other structural variables, especially those associated with class, such as race, ethnicity, and the social disorganization of the neighborhood. Like class of origin, these variables are systematically related to variables such as commitment to school and involvement in delinquent behavior, and therefore, as a group, these structural variables set the stage on which the reciprocal effects develop across the life cycle.

Discussion Questions

1. Give three examples of reciprocal causal effects from Thornberry's model. What does Thornberry mean by an "amplifying causal structure" or a "spiral of increasing delinquency"?

2. Describe how Thornberry's model changes from early to late adolescence (what variables decrease or increase in importance, what new variables enter the model).

3. Why are some adolescents able to desist from delinquency in early adulthood, while others continue to engage in crime?

4. Why does Thornberry state that lower-class children "have the highest probability of moving forward on a trajectory of increasing delinquency"? ✦

24

Social Support and Crime

Francis T. Cullen

This selection by Cullen illustrates a rather different approach to theoretical integration. Unlike Elliott et al. and Thornberry, Cullen does not select concepts from different theories and then describe the relationships between them. Rather, he points to a common theme that is implicitly or explicitly treated in several theories, ranging from the early theories of the Chicago school (see Part II) to the recent theoretical work of feminist and peacemaking criminologists. The theme is that social support is implicated in crime. Cullen draws on these different theories in an effort to elaborate on that theme. In doing so, he presents 13 propositions regarding social support. Among other things, he argues that social support has a direct effect on crime; that it influences other variables which affect crime, like the level of social control; that it conditions the impact of certain variables on crime (e.g., strain is more likely to lead to crime when social support is low); and that it plays a critical role in the prevention of crime and the rehabilitation of offenders. Cullen applies the concept of social support to both micro-level and macro-level questions (e.g., why the United States has such a high crime rate), and also uses it to shed light on developmental issues (e.g., the desistence from crime in early adulthood).

The concept of social support represents an important addition to criminology. Even though numerous theories make implicit or explicit reference to social support, Cullen is the first to draw explicit attention to the central role this concept may play in crime. In doing so, he introduces a new variable into mainstream criminology. Support is related to, but distinct from, concepts such as social control and social disorganization. Second, the concept of social support moves us toward a rather different approach to reducing crime. Current policies focus largely on the control of crime, often through very punitive policies. Cullen's theory of social support, however, suggests a more humanitarian approach.

Cullen's theory is compatible with much data on crime (as described in his article; see also Cullen and Wright, 1997). Preliminary empirical tests also provide some evidence in favor of the theory. In one study based on a sample of 1,775 adolescents and their parents interviewed for the National Survey of Families and Households, Wright (1995) found that structural factors, such as poverty and broken homes, increase delinquency mainly by diminishing the amount of support that parents are able to supply their children. In another study based on the National Longitudinal Survey of Youth, Wright and Cullen (1996) reported that social support reduces delinquent involvement both directly and in combination with parental control (that is, when parents both support and control their children).

References

Cullen, Francis T. and John Paul Wright. 1997. "Liberating the Anomie-Strain Paradigm: Implications from Social-Support Theory." Pp. 187-206 in *The Future of Anomie Theory*, edited by Nikos Passas and Robert Agnew. Boston: Northeastern University Press.

Wright, John Paul. 1995. *Parental Support and Juvenile Delinquency: A Test of Social Support Theory*. Unpublished Ph.D. dissertation, University of Cincinnati.

Wright, John Paul and Francis T. Cullen. 1996. "Parental Support and Delinquent Behavior: The Limits of Control Theory?" Paper presented at the annual meeting of the American Society of Criminology, Chicago.

... My intention is to argue that notions of social support appear in diverse criminological writings. . . .

What is lacking, however, is an attempt to integrate these diverse insights on social support into a coherent criminological paradigm. In the sociology of mental illness, for example, considerable progress has been made in this direction (Lin, Dean, and Ensel

1986; Vaux 1988). But in criminology the insights linking social support to crime remain disparate, and are not systematized so far as to direct theoretical and empirical investigation. Indeed, I can offer one (nonetheless significant) indicator of the latency of this concept: virtually no introductory or theoretical textbook lists "social support" in its index. . . .

My goal, then, is to argue that social support, if approached systematically, can be an important organizing concept for criminology. In the pages ahead, I will discuss propositions that might form the parameters, in a preliminary way, for a criminological paradigm, which draws on existing knowledge to illuminate new research vistas.

What Is Social Support?

. . . Lin (1986:18) defines social support as "the perceived or actual instrumental and/or expressive provisions supplied by the community, social networks, and confiding partners." Dissection of this definition reveals three major dimensions of support. The first is the distinction between the objective delivery and the perception of support. Taking perceptions into account is important because it leads to the insight that people do not receive support in a mechanical way but interpret, appraise, and anticipate it in the context of social situations (see Matsueda 1992).

Second, although different typologies exist, social support is usually divided into two broad rubrics: instrumental and expressive. According to Lin (1986:20), "the instrumental dimension involves the use of the relationship as a means to a goal, such as seeking a job, getting a loan, or finding someone to babysit." Vaux (1988:21) suggests that "instrumental functions may be served through the provision of goods or money (material aid or financial assistance) and through providing information, making suggestions, and clarifying issues (advice and guidance)."

The expressive dimension, again according to Lin (1986:20), "involves the use of the relationship as an end as well as a means. It is the activity of sharing sentiments, ventilating frustrations, reaching an understanding on issues and problems, and affirming one's own as well as the other's worth and dignity."

Vaux (1988:21) notes that the "affective functions" of support "include meeting the needs for love and affection, esteem and identity, and belonging and companionship. These needs are met respectively through emotional support, feedback and social reinforcement, and socializing."

Third, Lin's definition indicates that support occurs on different social levels. Micro-level support can be delivered by a confiding individual, such as a spouse or a best friend. But social support also can be viewed as a property of social networks and of communities and larger ecological units in which individuals are enmeshed.

A fourth dimension, not discussed by Lin, must be added: whether the support is delivered by a formal agency or through informal relations (Vaux 1988). Informal social support would occur through social relationships with others who lack any official status relative to the individual. Formal social support might be provided by schools, governmental assistance programs, and—perhaps most interesting to us—the criminal justice system.

The Ecology of Social Support

In the past decade, scholars have shown a renewed interest in studying the social ecology of crime, as did Shaw and McKay (1942) (Bursik and Grasmick 1993a; Byrne and Sampson 1986; Reiss and Tonry 1986). This research has shown that crime rates vary across nations and, within a single nation, across communities. It is noteworthy, if unsurprising, that the United States has higher rates of serious crime, especially violent offenses, than other Western industrialized nations (Adler 1983; Archer and Gartner 1984; Currie 1985; Messner and Rosenfeld 1994; also see Lynch 1995). This finding prompts my first proposition:

1. America has higher rates of serious crime than other industrialized nations because it is a less supportive society.

I am not claiming that Americans, as individuals, are ungenerous in giving their money to charity or their time to voluntary organizations; quite the opposite appears to be the case (Wuthnow 1991). Even so, I assert that American society is not *organized*, structurally or culturally, to be socially supportive. This conclusion receives confirmation from several sources, which makes interrelated or complementary points.

First, Braithwaite (1989:100) observes that societies differ in their "communitarian" quality—that is, in the extent to which "individuals are densely enmeshed in interdependencies which have the special qualities of *mutual help and trust*" (emphasis added). With a mobile, heterogenous, urban population, the United States is low in communitarianism. Accordingly the structural basis for creating and sustaining supportive social relations is weak.

Second, numerous commentators—often referred to as communitarians—have documented the corrosive effects of America's culture of excessive individualism (Bellah et al. 1985, 1991; Coles 1993; Etzioni 1993; Reich 1988; Wuthnow 1991). In the influential *Habits of the Heart*, Bellah et al. (1985) decry in particular "utilitarian individualism"—the dominance of individual self-interest in the pursuit of desired, usually material ends (also see Messner and Rosenfeld 1994). "We have committed," says Bellah et al. (1985:285), "what to the republican founders of our nation was the cardinal sin: we have put our own good, as individuals, as groups, as a nation, above the common good." Building a "good society," in which concern for community and mutuality of support dominate, awaits a fundamental "transformation of American culture" (Bellah et al. 1985:275-96, 1991).

Wuthnow (1991) notes that even compassion is "bounded" by the culture of individualism. Compassionate behavior is managed by being segmented into limited roles (e.g., a few hours of volunteer work). If pursued so extensively that it interferes with a person's self-interest, such behavior is regarded as an unhealthy obsession (1991:191-220). As a result, while "some of the work—the work that can be divided up into limited commitments—is accomplished, much of it remains to be done" (1991:220). . . .

In short, Wuthnow suggests that the demand for support in America exceeds the supply. This observation leads to a corollary to the first proposition: *The more a society is deficient in the support needed, the higher its crime rate will be.*

Third, Currie (1985, 1989, 1993) makes perhaps the most compelling case that support is low in America and is linked inextricably to the country's high violent crime rate. As Currie points out, America's past and recent economic development has disrupted the traditional "private cushions" provided by networks of social support. Unlike other Western nations, however, America's welfare state has been stingy, if not mean-spirited, in the support it offers to the casualties of the social dislocation and wide inequalities bred by this development (also see Block et al. 1987). The cost of undermining the delivery of support, argues Currie, is an inordinately high rate of violent crime. . . .

Currie also challenges attempts to relate America's high crime rate to a weakness in control. Because other Western nations are more socially integrated, the argument goes, they are better able to exercise informal controls over their citizens (Adler 1983; Bayley 1976). Although this view may have merit, it overlooks the role of support in reducing crime. Japan offers an instructive example. Currie (1985:46) notes that previous analyses have neglected "the ways in which Japanese society is more *supportive* than ours, not simply more 'controlling'" (author's emphasis). In particular, he points both to Japan's "private mechanisms of social obligation" and to Japan's efforts to limit inequality and to provide lifetime job security to most workers (also see Beirne and Messerschmidt 1991:608-609).

As I will discuss again later, the broader point here is that criminologists often confound the effects of informal control with those of social support. These concepts are not necessarily rivals in explaining criminal behavior; in reality, support and control may be mutually reinforcing in reducing crime. Still the distinction between the two is important both for achieving theoretical precision and because their policy implications can differ dramatically. . . .

The social ecology of support and crime varies not only across but also within nations

(Currie 1985). Thus I offer a second proposition:

2. The less social support there is in a community, the higher the crime rate will be.

This thesis is buttressed by several pieces of evidence. Admittedly, quantitative research on communities and crime has not systematically explored the relationship of social support to crime (Bursik and Grasmick 1993a; Byrne and Sampson 1986; Reiss and Tonry 1986; but see Zuravin 1989). Nonetheless, variables employed in various studies may be viewed as operationalizing the concept of support.

First, there is evidence that governmental assistance to the poor tends to lessen violent crime across ecological units (DeFronzo 1983; Messner 1986; see Rosenfeld 1986). Thus, contrary to conservatives' claims that welfare corrodes individual initiative and fosters irresponsibility, including lawlessness (Murray 1984; but see Block et al. 1987; Ellwood 1988), it appears that state support buffers against criminogenic forces (also see Currie 1985, 1989, 1993).

Second, research reveals that crime rates are higher in communities characterized by family disruption, weak friendship networks, and low participation in local voluntary organizations (Sampson 1986a, 1986b; Sampson and Groves 1989). Sampson interprets these findings as an indication that such communities are unable to exert informal social control over their residents (also see Bursik and Grasmick 1993b). Although this perspective may have merit, it is unclear why these variables are measures of control and not of support. It is telling that the mental illness literature uses neighborhood interaction and participation in voluntary organizations to assess "community and network support" (Lin, Dumin, and Woelfel 1986). Further, high rates of family disruption may operationalize not only adults' ability to exert surveillance over youths but also the availability to youths of both adult support networks and the opportunity to develop intimate relations. In short, existing ecological studies can be interpreted as containing measures of social support and, in turn, as showing that support reduces rates of criminal involvement. . . .

Quantitative and ethnographic research on the "underclass" or the "truly disadvantaged" also is relevant to the social ecology of crime and support. This research documents the powerful social forces—deindustrialization, joblessness, persisting racial segregation, migration to the suburbs—that have created socially and economically isolated inner-city enclaves (Devine and Wright 1993; Jencks and Peterson 1991; Lemann 1991; Massey and Denton 1993; Sullivan 1989; Wilson 1987). This trend, which has been described as a continuing process of social and cultural "disinvestment" in these neighborhoods, has enormous social consequences (Hagan 1993a; Short 1990, 1991).

The literature essentially documents the erosion of community social institutions and of their ability to provide social support. Wilson (1987:144) notes, for example, that the departure of many middle-class families from inner-city neighborhoods reduced the "social buffer" or human capital needed to "absorb the shock or cushion the effect of uneven economic growth and periodic recessions." Similarly, in his review of Anderson's (1990) *Street Wise*, an ethnography of the Philadelphia neighborhood of "Northton," Hagan (1993a:329) shows how "structural and cultural disinvestment" has frayed the supportive relations between adults and youths that previously protected youths against crime. . . .

In short, my thesis is that both across nations and across communities, crime rates vary inversely with the level of social support. The social ecologists of crime have largely overlooked this possibility, but (as I hope I have revealed) their work contains evidence favoring the social support thesis and offers important clues for future investigation. In the next section I explore ways in which the presence or absence of support is implicated in individuals' involvement in crime.

Support and Crime

Since the inception of American criminology, interest in the criminogenic effects of family life has ebbed and flowed (Wilkinson 1974). Over the past decade, attention has increased once again, in part because of the

American family's beleaguered status (Sykes and Cullen 1992) and in part because of the emergence of salient criminological findings showing that the pathway to serious adult criminality begins in childhood (Loeber and Le Blanc 1990; Nagin and Farrington 1992; Nagin and Paternoster 1991; Sampson and Laub 1993).

This renewed interest has prompted not only numerous empirical studies on family correlates of crime (Loeber and Southamer-Loeber 1986; Wells and Rankin 1991) but also widely read theoretical frameworks. Although these theories differ fundamentally, they emphasize the criminogenic role that the family plays by the way it exercises or instills *control* (Colvin and Pauly 1983; Gottfredson and Hirschi 1990; Hagan 1989; Regoli and Hewitt 1994; Wilson and Herrnstein 1985). These perspectives are earning a measure of empirical confirmation (see, for example, Akers 1994; Burton et al. 1994; Grasmick et al. 1993; Hagan 1989; Hagan, Gillis, and Simpson 1990; Messner and Krohn 1990); thus I will not argue against their value. At the same time, as a result of criminologists' emphasis on control, virtually no theoretical attention has been paid to how family-related social support, or its absence, is involved in crime causation. Accordingly I offer my third proposition:

3. *The more support a family provides, the less likely it is that a person will engage in crime.*

We have considerable evidence that parental expressive support diminishes children's risk of criminal involvement. . . .

The firmest empirical evidence, however, can be drawn from Loeber and Southamer-Loeber's (1986) comprehensive meta-analysis of family correlates of delinquency: factors indicating a lack of parental support clearly increase delinquent involvement. (Also see Feldman's [1993:196] discussion of "positive parenting.") Loeber and Stouthamer-Loeber conclude that delinquency is related inversely to "child-parent involvement, such as the amount of intimate communication, confiding, sharing of activities, and seeking help" (1986:42). Similarly, their analysis indicates that measures of parental rejection of children, such as "rejection, not warm, lack

of love, lack of affection, less affectionate," were "consistently related to delinquency and aggression" (1986:54; also see Sampson and Laub 1993:119). These "support" elements, moreover, were among the most powerful family factors related to delinquency; their effects exceeded those of parental criminality, marital discord, parental absence, parental health, and family size (1993:120-23). . . .

In contrast to expressive support, criminological research contains few empirical studies on the impact of instrumental family support on crime (see, for example, Loeber and Stouthamer-Loeber 1986). It is premature to conclude that instrumental support is as salient as expressive support, and possibly these forms of support vary in their effects across the life cycle. In any case, the literature contains some clues as to the importance of instrumental family support. Thus, if we revisit Glueck and Glueck (1950:129-30), we discover that delinquents were more likely than nondelinquents to have parents who "had not given any thought to the boys' futures." Further, as noted above, family-based networks are an important source of entry into the job market; this, in turn, can undermine continued involvement in crime (Sullivan 1989; also see Curtis 1989: 155).

Finally, any discussion of families and crime must be careful to avoid what Currie (1985:185) calls the "fallacy of autonomy— the belief that what goes on inside the family can usefully be separated from the forces that affect it from the outside: the larger social context in which families are embedded for better or for worse." Indeed, large social forces have transformed many American families in ways that often have reduced their capacity to support children (see, for example, Hewlett 1991; Wilson 1987). For example, adolescents today are much less likely than in the past to eat evening meals with parents or to spend time at home (Felson 1994:104; Messner and Rosenfeld 1994:103); the potential time that parents have to spend with children is declining (Hewlett 1991:90-92); and "less than 5 percent of all families have another adult (e.g., grandparent) living in the home, compared to 50 percent two generations ago. This reduces the backup support that might otherwise be available to working parents" (Panel on High-Risk Youth 1993:56).

Most disconcerting, however, is the concentration of forces that have ripped apart families of the underclass, or the "truly disadvantaged" (Devine and Wright 1993; Wilson 1987), and have made inner-city youths vulnerable to crime, drugs, and an array of unhealthy behaviors (Currie 1985, 1993; Panel on High-Risk Youth 1993). The Panel on High-Risk Youth states,

> Perhaps the most serious risk facing adolescents in high-risk settings is isolation from the nurturance, safety, and guidance that comes from sustained relationships with adults. Parents are the best source of support, but for many adolescents, parents are not positively involved in their lives. In some cases, parents are absent or abusive. In many more cases, parents strive to be good parents, but lack the capacity or opportunity to be so. (1993:213)

Accordingly I offer this as a corollary to my third proposition: *The more support is given to families, the less crime will occur.* As Rivara and Farrington (forthcoming) observe, "increased social support to families can take the form of information (e.g., parenting programs), emotional support (e.g., home visitors), provision of material needs (e.g., food stamps, housing) or instrumental help (e.g., day care)." They also note that the "most successful interventions appear to be those which offer more than one type of social support service, thereby affecting a number of risk factors for the development of delinquency and violence" (forthcoming; also see Farrington 1994). Echoing this theme, Currie (1989:18-19, 1993:310-17) argues persuasively that the government should institute a "genuinely supportive national family policy," including, for example, child care, family leaves, and special programs for families at risk for mistreating children.

Currie's (1985, 1989, 1993) analyses and the above discussion on changing levels of support within the American family lead to a second corollary: *Changes in levels of support for and by families have contributed since the 1960s to increases in crime and to the concentration of serious violence in high-risk inner-*

city neighborhoods. This statement contradicts the thinking of Murray (1984), who blames the "generous revolution" of the Great Society programs for eroding individual responsibility and for fostering criminal and other deviant behaviors (see Lemann 1991; Lupo 1994).

Beyond the family, Krohn (1986) contends that social networks may provide a "web of conformity" (also see Sampson and Laub 1993). Krohn emphasizes how dimensions of networks operate to control behavior; scholars in the sociology of mental illness study how these characteristics of networks are an important source of social support (Lin et al. 1986; Vaux 1988). In short, the web of conformity involves not only constraints but also supports (Sullivan 1989; also see Zuravin 1989). This point leads to my fourth proposition:

4. The more social support in a person's social network, the less crime will occur.

Social support theorists have examined most extensively how supports mitigate the effects of strain or "stress." The relationships are complex, but social supports can prevent stresses from arising or can lessen negative consequences if stresses should emerge (House 1981; Vaux 1988). These findings are important in light of the recent revitalization of strain theory, particularly empirical research linking strain to criminal behavior (Agnew 1985a, 1989; Agnew and White 1992; Burton and Cullen 1992; Farnworth and Leiber 1989; McCarthy and Hagan 1992; Vaux and Ruggiero 1983). . . .

The remaining issue, largely ignored by strain theorists (Cullen 1984), is how people respond to this range of stressful conditions. Building on the social support literature (e.g., Vaux 1988), Agnew (1992) suggests that the ability to cope with criminogenic strains is contingent on access to supports. "Adolescents with conventional social support," he observes, "should be better able to respond to objective strains in a nondelinquent manner" (1992:72). This contention suggests my fifth proposition:

5. Social support lessens the effects of exposure to criminogenic strains.

In their important reassessment of Glueck and Glueck's longitudinal data, Sampson and

Laub (1993) study not only sources of the stability of crime across the life course but also the "turning points" at which offenders depart from the criminal "pathway." Their analysis shows that during adulthood, job stability and attachments to spouse contribute to desistance from crime. They interpret these findings as indicating that "adult social bonds" provide offenders with social capital which subjects them to "informal social controls" (1993:140-43). "Adult social ties," they observe, "create interdependent systems of obligation and restraint that impose significant costs for translating criminal propensities into action" (1993:141).

I will not take issue with the control theory set forth by Sampson and Laub, but I observe that their *Crime in the Making* also contains insights on the salience of adult *social supports*. Thus Sampson and Laub (1993:141) take note of the "social capital invested by employers and spouses," not simply that invested by offenders. With regard to marriage, for example, life histories on offenders in Glueck and Glueck's sample reveal that this investment took the form of wives' providing "material and emotional *support*" (Sampson and Laub 1993:205, 220, emphasis added; also see Vaux 1988:173). Two points follow from this observation.

First, marital and employment "social supports" may reduce crime by increasing social capital and thus expanding the basis for informal social controls. Second, these social supports may exert independent (main) effects on crime not by facilitating control but by reducing other sources of crime (e.g., lessening emotional difficulties, relieving strains, transforming deviant identities). More broadly, I offer my sixth proposition:

6. *Across the life cycle, social support increases the likelihood that offenders will turn away from a criminal pathway.*

I do not mean to confine this proposition to the role of adult social supports in crime desistance. In particular, accounts of at-risk youths suggest that supports can trigger their turning away from crime (see also Dubow and Reid 1994). Such supports may involve a youth's special informal relationship with an adult (e.g., teacher, coach), participation in a mentorship program (Kuznik 1994; Panel on

High-Risk Youth 1993:213-14), or placement in a community program (Curtis 1989:154-60).

Commentary on impoverished juveniles at risk for crime also frequently emphasizes the sense of isolation felt by these youths. The Panel on High-Risk (1993:217), for example, notes that "young people from high-risk settings" often "confront the emotional pain and feelings of hopelessness that can interfere with positive development." Echoing this theme, Curtis (1989:158) observes that inner-city minority youths think "the cards are stacked hopelessly against them. These youths believe that fate will not permit them to 'make it' in any legitimate form."

This isolation might be viewed as a detachment from social bonds that lessens control and increases criminal involvement, but another process also may be operating. These youths may perceive that they will always lack the instrumental and expressive supports needed to change the circumstances in which they are enmeshed. This possibility leads to my seventh proposition:

7. *Anticipation of a lack of social support increases criminal involvement.*

Thus far I have concentrated on how *receiving* support diminished criminality, but it also seems important to consider how *giving* support affects involvement in crime. The logic of writings from the peacemaking/humanist and feminist perspectives suggests that providing support should reduce criminal propensities (McDermott 1994). Pepinsky (1988), in fact, regards crime as the opposite of "responsiveness" to others. Further, in *The Call of Service*, Coles (1993) tells how the experience of supporting others can transform selves, inculcate idealism, foster moral purpose, and create long-standing interconnections—all of which would seem anti-criminogenic.

I know of no systematic empirical investigation of the link between giving support and crime, but some insights can be gleaned from the research. Sampson and Laub (1993:219-20), for example, note that the offenders in their study were likely to desist from crime when they were devoted to their spouses and children, and were "financially responsible not only to their spouses, but also to parents and siblings if the need arose." That is, as offenders assumed a role as providers of expressive and instrumental support, their involvement in crime ceased. . . .

Lynne Goodstein (personal communication, January 2, 1994) offers another pertinent insight: "Women's traditional responsibility for the delivery of social support and nurturance to others (children, elders, partners) and the dramatically lower crime rates for women is an interesting association." Although this association is open to differing interpretations, it suggests that the experience of providing support creates sentiments (e.g., compassion), identities, role expectations, and problem-solving skills that are generally incompatible with the "seductions of crime" (Katz 1988; also see Gilligan, Ward, and Taylor 1988).

In any event, these various considerations lead to my eighth proposition:

8. Giving social support lessens involvement in crime.

Finally, Albert Cohen (personal communication, January 29, 1994) has alerted me to the need to consider the broader concept of "differential social support." To this point, I have largely explored the role of supports in making conformity possible. Cohen, however, observes

> that social support is equally important to non-conformity, to crime. Indeed, the burden of much of the literature on causation is that associations, the situation of company, provide much of the support that makes it possible to break the law, more effectively to thwart the justice process and reduce the "hurtfulness" and other consequences of punishment.

Indeed, insights on support for crime are evident in the literature on peers and co-offending (Reiss 1988), on the acquisition and performance of criminal roles (Cloward 1959; Steffensmeier 1983), and on the organizational conditions that make corporate crime possible (Hills 1987; Sutherland 1949). Differential social support also might operate in situational contexts. As shown by Richard Felson (1982: Felson and Tedeschi 1993), "third parties" to interpersonal conflict can support the escalation of violence or can mediate tensions and diminish subsequent aggression. These observations lead to my ninth proposition:

9. Crime is less likely when social support for conformity exceeds social support for crime.

In a related vein, Ronald Akers (personal communication, January 1994) has cautioned that social supports are likely to be most effective when they are linked to "conformity-inducing outcomes." The *source* of the support may be particularly important. For instance, support from conformist sources may not only address criminal risk factors (e.g., strain) but also provide an opportunity for prosocial modeling (Andrews and Bonta 1994:202-205). Conversely, support from criminal friends (e.g., comfort in the face of a stressful life event) may be counteracted if these associations also expose youths to criminogenic influences.

On this point, the research on the effects of marriage provides relevant data. Although the findings are not fully consistent (Sampson and Laub 1993), we find some evidence that marriage—conceptualized here as a social support—reduces crime only if spouses are not themselves deviant or criminal (Farrington, Ohlin, and Wilson, 1986:56; West 1982:100-104). Thus I offer this corollary to Proposition 9: *Social support from conformist sources is most likely to reduce criminal involvement.*

Support and Control

As stated earlier, recent advances in criminological theory have been dominated by attempts to link control with crime. I have tried to show that these perspectives overlook social support and potentially confound the effects of control and with the effects of support. Now I wish to make a different, but related, argument, which is set forth in my tenth proposition:

10. Social support often is a precondition for effective social control.

The criminological literature contains numerous illustrations of this proposition. Braithwaite's (1989) influential theory of "reintegrative shaming," however, is perhaps the most noteworthy example (also see Braithwaite and Muford 1994; Makkai and Braithwaite 1994). In brief, Braithwaite contends that legal violations often evoke formal and informal attempts at "shaming," which he defines as "all processes of expressing disapproval which have the intention or effect of invoking remorse in the person being shamed and/or condemnation by others who become aware of the shaming" (1989:9). Braithwaite observes, however, that shaming takes two general forms. Disintegrative shaming is criminogenic; as labeling theory would predict, it stigmatizes, excludes, and ensures the exposure of offenders to criminogenic conditions. Reintegrative shaming, in contrast, achieves conformity. After the act is condemned, attempts are made "to reintegrate the offender back into the community of law-abiding or respectable citizens through words or gestures of forgiveness or ceremonies to decertify the offender as deviant" (1989:100-101). Even if repeated efforts are required, the goal is to avoid exclusion and thus to embed the offender in conventional, accepting relationships (Braithwaite and Muford 1994).

In the language of the social support paradigm, Braithwaite is asserting that control can be effective only in the context of support (see Sherman 1992). Further, the very likelihood that reintegrative shaming will be used depends on the extent to which the larger society is supportive, or, as Braithwaite puts it, "communitarian." Not surprisingly, shaming in the United States tends to be disintegrative (also see Benson 1990).

A related insight can be gained from the correctional literature. It appears that family support of offenders during and after incarceration improves chances of successful completion of parole supervision (Farrington et al. 1986:147; Wright and Wright 1992:54). In short, control with support is more effective than control by itself.

The family socialization literature also offers useful information. Wilson and Herrnstein (1985:237-40) argue that "restrictive" parenting is important in detecting and discouraging rule transgressions and thus in teaching that behavior has consequences. But restrictiveness is most effective when coupled with parental warmth. "A warm parent," they state, "is approving and supportive of the child, frequently employs praise as a reinforcement for good behavior, and explains the reasons for rules" (1985:237). In this case, warmth (support) empowers restrictiveness (control): when children care about their parents, obedience is rewarding and disobedience is unrewarding (1985: 239). . . .

Good Criminology and the Good Society

Over the past decade, an increasing number of voices have joined in a national conversation about the requirements for what Robert Bellah and his colleagues call the "Good Society" (Bellah et al. 1991; also see Bellah et al. 1985; Coles 1993; Etzioni 1993; Reich 1988; Wuthnow 1991). Fundamental to this ongoing conversation is a critique of the excessive individualism in the United States, which too often degenerates into a politics justifying either the crass pursuit of rights or materialistic self-aggrandizement. In this context, there is a lack of attention to the public good, service to others, and an appreciation for our need for connectedness. Accordingly there is a call to revitalize our common bonds and to build a society supportive of all its citizens.

I realize the risk in linking one's criminology to a larger social agenda: regardless of how crime is affected, attempts to build a Good Society certainly should stand or fall on their own merits (Felson 1994:12-13). Still, it is equally misguided to assume that criminological ideas have no consequences (Bohm 1993; Lilly et al. 1989). A criminology that emphasizes the need for social supports thus may have the potential to make a difference.

Indeed, if the social supports paradigm proves to be "Good Criminology," it will provide empirical grounds for suggesting that an important key to solving the crime problem is the construction of a supportive social order—the Good Society. Accordingly this paradigm may present an opportunity to challenge the current hegemony of punitive policy in criminal justice. It may prompt us to consider that the cost of a nonsupportive society, exacerbated by mean-spirited or neglectful public policies, is a disgraceful level of crime and violence (Currie 1985). And, hopefully, it may provide the basis for criminal justice and public policies which help to create a society that is more supportive and hence safer for its citizens.

Discussion Questions

1. What is social support (describe the major types of support in your response)? What types of questions would you ask someone to measure the social support they receive? How does social support differ from social control?

2. Why does the United States provide less social support than many other industrialized nations? Why do some communities and families provide less social support than others?

3. Describe the different ways in which low social support might contribute to crime. Consider social support as a direct cause of crime, and as an indirect cause (which influences other variables which cause crime), and as a conditioning variable (which influences the effect of other variables on crime).

4. Describe how the concept of social support is related to any two of the other theories discussed in this volume (e.g., do these theories make implicit or explicit reference to social support; would a more explicit consideration of social support strengthen these theories—for example, by shedding additional light on the causes of the independent variables in these theories or on the factors that influence the effects of these variables on crime). ✦

Part VII

Rational Choice and Routine Activities Theories

Rational Choice Theory

Most of the theories presented in the previous chapters focus on the factors that *constrain* individuals to engage in crime—factors like individual traits, disorganized communities, association with delinquent peers, and strain. The impression one gets from reading these chapters is that crime is largely the result of forces beyond an individual's control. Individuals do not freely chose to engage in crime, but rather their criminal behavior is determined by a variety of individual and social factors. This "deterministic" view of crime has dominated crime theory since the late 1800s. It stands in contrast to the "classical school," which dominated crime theory during the late 1700s and much of the 1800s.

According to the classical school, individuals freely choose to engage in crime based on a rational consideration of the costs and benefits associated with crime (see Vold and Bernard, 1986, for an overview). That is, individuals engage in crime when they believe that crime maximizes their net benefits (i.e., their benefits minus costs). This fundamental idea has been revived and extended in the work of several economists and criminolo-

gists, and it now once again occupies a central place in crime theory.

This idea, in particular, is at the core of Gary Becker's (1968) classic article on "Crime and Punishment: An Economic Approach" (see Chapter 25 in this Part). Becker argues that individuals deliberately choose to engage in crime because they believe that in their particular case the benefits of crime outweigh the costs. The number of offenses committed by a person is a function of their probability of being caught and convicted for an offense, the severity of punishment, and other factors related to the benefits and costs of crime—like the income available to the person through legal activities. Becker's approach to crime has been elaborated and refined in recent years by other economists and by those criminologists who have developed the "rational choice" perspective on crime.

The "rational choice" perspective on crime was developed by Ronald Clarke and Derek Cornish in the mid 1980s (Clarke and Cornish, 1985; Cornish and Clarke, 1986), and it has come to have a major impact on crime theory and research (see Chapter 26 in this Part). The central assumption of this perspective is that "offenders seek to benefit themselves by their criminal behavior; that this involves the making of decisions and of choices, however rudimentary on occasion these processes might be; and that these processes exhibit a measure of rationality, albeit constrained by limits of time and ability and the availability of relevant information" (Cornish and Clarke, 1986:1). It is important to emphasize that rational choice theorists do not claim that offenders are perfectly rational. It is not claimed, for example, that offenders carefully plan all crimes, systematically collecting information on the expected benefits and costs of the crime and carefully weighing benefits against costs. Rather, the core assumption of rational choice theory is that offenders typically give some consideration to costs and benefits when contemplating crime—even though this consideration may be hurried and based on incomplete or inaccurate information. Further, it should be emphasized that the benefits of crime include both monetary and nonmonetary factors (e.g., the "thrill" associated with vandalism). Likewise, the costs of crime include both formal and informal sanctions (e.g., the disapproval of parents) and "moral costs"— such as the guilt one may experience from breaking the law. (In these senses, the rational choice approach is broader than Becker's early economic model of crime; see Clarke and Felson, 1993:5.) Cornish and Clarke state that while the rational choice approach may be more relevant to certain types of crime, like income-generating crimes, it has some relevance to "pathologically motivated" and "impulsively executed" crimes.

The rational choice perspective, then, appears to stand in marked contrast to the theories we have examined so far. While these theories focus on the factors that constrain individuals to crime, the rational choice perspective argues that individuals frequently choose to engage in crime based on a consideration of costs and benefits. Certain theorists, however, have argued that the rational choice perspective is not really that different from existing crime theories (e.g., Akers, 1990). While rational choice theorists focus on choice, they devote much attention to the factors that constrain choice. These factors include variables from the leading crime theories, such as individual traits, attitudes toward crime, and the extent to which individuals have been reinforced and punished for crime (see the selection by Cornish and Clarke in Chapter 26). Further, the leading crime theories do not deny that individuals choose to engage in crime. They simply focus on those factors that constrain individual choice. These factors typically have to do with the benefits and costs of crime. This is most obviously the case with respect to social learning theories (see the Bandura and Akers selections in this volume). These theories explicitly focus on the expected reinforcements (benefits) and punishments (costs) associated with crime. Akers (1990), in fact, has argued that rational choice theory is easily subsumed by his social learning theory.

Rational choice theory, then, is not as different from the leading crime theories as it might first appear. The theory, in fact, may be viewed as a form of integrated theory because it draws on the leading crime theories in order to more fully specify the costs and benefits associated with crime (see Figure 1 in the Cornish and Clarke selection). At the same time, rational choice theory has advanced our understanding of crime in several ways. Rational choice theorists argue that a complete explanation of crime must distinguish between "criminal involvement" and "criminal events." Criminal involvement deals with the decision to become involved in crime (as well as to continue in crime and to desist from crime). Criminal events deal with the decision to commit specific criminal acts. Most crime theories focus on the decision to become involved in crime, but do not deal with the factors influencing the decision to commit a particular crime. These factors often have to do with the immediate circumstances and situation of the individual. Rational choice theory has directed much attention to these circumstances and situations, and has thereby supplemented the approach of the leading crime theories. Rational choice theorists also argue that it is necessary to adopt a "crime-specific focus" when examining crime. That is, we should focus on particular types of crime, like residential burglaries committed in middle-class suburbs, rather than examining all crimes together. This is because the costs and benefits associated with different types of crime may differ, particularly at the situational level. So, while the rational choice perspective may not be that different from the leading crime theories, it has moved us beyond these theories in certain ways (see Cornish, 1993).

Does the evidence support economic and rational choice theories of crime? Initially, economic theories of crime were tested by examining the impact of the certainty and severity of official punishments on crime. That is, is crime deterred as the certainty and severity of punishment increases? Data suggest that increasing the certainty and severity of punishment has, at best, only a small to moderate impact on crime, with certainty more important than severity (see Akers, 1997 for an overview). Interviews with criminal offenders explain why this might be so. Offenders frequently report that their crimes were not carefully planned and they were not very concerned about the possibility of official sanctions. They often believe that they will not be caught and that, if caught, the sanctions will not be severe (e.g., Tunnel, 1992). More recent studies, however, focus on a broader range of factors, including the reinforcements individuals receive from crime and the likelihood that individuals will experience informal sanctions and "moral costs" for engaging in crime. Such studies provide more support for economic and rational choice theories (although, as Akers [1997] points out, the results of these studies also support control and learning theories of crime). Finally, recent studies shed interesting light into the immediate circumstances and situations associated with crime. These studies suggest that while many crimes involve little planning, some consideration is frequently given to the costs and benefits of the crime. Burglars, for example, often target unoccupied homes that can be easily entered with little risk of being seen by others (see Birkbeck and LaFree, 1993; Clarke and Felson, 1993; Cornish and Clarke, 1986; Meier and Miethe, 1993).

Routine Activities Theory

Rational choice/economic models argue that individuals choose to engage in crime. But as Felson (1986:119) has stated, "people make choices, but they cannot choose the choices available to them." Some people are more likely than others to confront situations where the benefits of crime are high and the costs are low. The routine activities approach deals with the factors that influence the range of choices available to individuals.

According to this theoretical approach, three elements are necessary for a crime to occur: *motivated offenders* must come in contact with *suitable targets* in the absence of *capable guardians.* The routine activities approach takes the supply of motivated offenders as given, and explains variation in crime by variations in the supply of suitable targets (e.g., expensive, lightweight merchandise) and capable guardians (e.g., neighbors, property owners, police). Suitable targets have to do with the benefits of crime, while capable guardians have to do with the costs. According to the theory, the supply of suitable targets and the presence of capable guardians are a function of our "routine activities" (our family, work, leisure, consumption and other activities).

For example, Cohen and Felson point to a major change in routine activities in the post-World War II United States: people are more likely to spend time away from home. As a result, motivated offenders are more likely to encounter suitable targets in the absence of capable guardians. Homes are left unprotected during the day and frequently at night, and individuals are more often in public locations, where they may fall prey to motivated offenders. Cohen and Felson discuss additional changes in routine activities during this time period, and such changes are used to explain increases in the crime rate through their effect on suitable targets and capable guardians (also see Clarke and Felson, 1993). As Clarke and Felson (1993) point out, the routine activities approach is quite different from most crime theories. While most theories focus on the factors that motivate offenders to become involved in crime, the routine activities approach takes the supply of motivated offenders as given and focuses on the opportunities for crime.

The data are generally supportive of routine activities theory, as evidenced in the selection by Cohen as Felson. (There are some problems with the tests that have been conducted, however, and not all tests are supportive [for overviews, see Akers, 1997; Birkbeck and LaFree, 1993; Meier and Miethe, 1993].) Nevertheless, the routine activities perspective points to certain of the factors which influence the choices available to potential offenders, and thereby helps us better understand the context in which potential offenders make decisions regarding crime.

In closing, it should be noted that the economic, rational choice, and routine activities approaches are directly relevant to issues of crime control; in fact, the rational choice perspective was developed in an effort to provide more guidance to crime prevention efforts. These approaches, in particular, suggest that we control crime by raising its costs and reducing its benefits. This approach is most often implemented by increasing the official sanctions for crime, but some rather creative alternatives to this common strategy have been tried—often with much success (e.g., Clarke, 1992; Clarke and Felson, 1993).

References

Akers, Ronald. 1990. "Rational Choice, Deterrence, and Social Learning in Criminology: The Path Not Taken." *Journal of Criminal Law and Criminology* 81:653-676.

——. 1997. *Criminological Theories: Introduction and Evaluation*, 2nd edition. Los Angeles: Roxbury.

Becker, Gary S. 1968. "Crime and Punishment: An Economic Approach." *Journal of Political Economy* 76:169-217.

Birkbeck, Christopher and Gary LaFree. 1993. "The Situational Analysis of Crime and Deviance." *Annual Review of Sociology* 19:113-137.

Clarke, Ronald V. and Derek B. Cornish. 1985. "Modeling Offenders' Decisions: A Framework for Research and Policy." Pp. 147-85 in *Crime and Justice: An Annual Review of Research, Volume 6*, edited by Michael Tonry and Norval Morris. Chicago: University of Chicago Press.

Clarke, Ronald V. and Marcus Felson. 1993, eds. *Advances in Criminological Theory, Volume 5: Routine Activity and Rational Choice*. New Brunswick, NJ: Transaction.

Cohen, Lawrence E. and Marcus Felson. 1979. "Social Change and Crime Rate Trends: A Routine Activity Approach." *American Sociological Review* 44:588-607.

Cornish, Derek. 1993. "Theories of Action in Criminology: Learning Theory and Rational Choice Approaches," Pp. 351-382 in *Advances in Criminological Theory, Volume 5: Routine Activity and Rational Choice*, edited by Ronald V. Clarke and Marcus Felson. New Brunswick, NJ: Transaction.

Cornish, Derek B. and Ronald V. Clarke. 1986. *The Reasoning Criminal*. New York: Springer-Verlag.

Felson, Marcus. 1986. "Linking Criminal Choices, Routine Activities, Informal Control, and Criminal Outcomes." Pp. 119-28 in *The Reasoning Criminal*, edited by Derek B. Cornish and Ronald V. Clarke. New York: Springer-Verlag.

Meier, Robert F. and Terance D. Miethe. 1993. "Understanding Theories of Criminal Victimization." Pp. 459-499 in *Crime and Justice, Volume 17*, edited by Michael Tonry. Chicago: University of Chicago Press.

Tunnel, Kenneth D. 1992. *Choosing Crime*. Chicago: Nelson-Hall.

Vold, George B. and Thomas J. Bernard. 1986. *Theoretical Crimonology*, 3rd edition. New York: Oxford University Press. ✦

25

Crime and Punishment: An Economic Approach

Gary S. Becker

This classic article, written in 1968, had a major impact on subsequent theory and research. Becker argues that economic models of choice can be used to explain criminal behavior. Such models assume that people are rational, investing their time and resources in ways that maximize their benefits and minimize their costs. Given this assumption, one can in theory predict a person's level of crime by calculating their expected benefits and costs from crime. So, for example, we would predict that the number of offenses committed will decrease as the certainty and severity of punishment increase. (As Becker notes, changes in the certainty of punishment should be more important for people who prefer risk, like gamblers, while changes in the severity of punishment should be more important for people who do not like to take risks.)

Becker's article stimulated additional research on crime by economists, with such research attempting to better model the costs and benefits of crime (see DiIulio, 1996; Ehrlich, 1996; Freeman, 1996; Heineke, 1978; Witte, 1983). It also helped stimulate much research on deterrence. That is, does an increase in the certainty and severity of punishment reduce crime? As noted in the introduction to this section, such research shows modest deterrent effects at best.

Finally, Becker's work contributed to the development of rational choice theory in criminology (see Clarke and Cornish, 1985). Rational choice theorists, like economists, view crime as a function of its costs and benefits. Rational choice theorists, however, have not devoted as much attention to the development of mathematical equations representing the major benefits and costs of crime. Perhaps as a result, rational choice theorists have been able to consider a fuller range of benefits and costs and to take greater account of individual differences in the criminal decision-making process (see Clarke and Felson, 1993:5).

References

Clarke, Ronald V. and Derek B. Cornish. 1985. "Modeling Offenders' Decisions: A Framework for Policy and Research." Pp. 147-85 in *Crime and Justice, Volume 6*, edited by Michael Tonry and Norval Morris. Chicago: University of Chicago Press.

Clarke, Ronald V. and Marcus Felson, eds. 1993. *Advances in Criminological Theory, Volume 5: Routine Activity and Rational Choice*. New Brunswick, NJ: Transaction.

DiIulio, John J. Jr. 1996. "Help Wanted: Economists, Crime and Public Policy." *Journal of Economic Perspectives* 10:3-24.

Ehrlich, Isaac. 1996. "Crime, Punishment, and the Market for Offenses." *Journal of Economic Perspectives* 10:43-67.

Freeman, Richard B. 1996. "Why Do So Many Young American Men Commit Crimes and What Might We Do About It?" *Journal of Economic Perspectives* 10:25-42.

Heineke, J. M. 1978. *Economic Models of Criminal Behavior*. Amsterdam: North-Holland Publishing Company.

Witte, Ann Dryden. 1983. "Crime Causation: Economic Theories." Pp. 316-322 in the *Encyclopedia of Crime and Justice*, edited by Sanford H. Kadish. New York: Free Press.

... Theories about the determinants of the number of offenses differ greatly from emphasis on skull types and biological inheritance to family upbringing and disenchantment with society. Practically all the diverse theories agree, however, that when other variables are held constant, an increase in a person's probability of conviction or punishment if convicted would generally decrease, perhaps substantially, perhaps negligibly, the number of offenses he commits. In addition, a common generalization by persons with judicial experience is that a change in the probability has a greater effect on the number of offenses than a change in the punishment, although, as far as I can tell, none of the prominent theories shed any light on this relation.

The approach taken here follows the economists' usual analysis of choice and assumes that a person commits an offense if the expected utility to him exceeds the utility he could get by using his time and other resources at other activities. Some persons become "criminals," therefore, not because their basic motivation differs from that of other persons, but because their benefits and costs differ. I cannot pause to discuss the many general implications of this approach, except to remark that criminal behavior becomes part of a much more general theory and does not require ad hoc concepts of differential association, anomie, and the like, nor does it assume perfect knowledge, lightening-fast calculation, or any caricatures of economic theory.

This approach implies that there is a function relating the number of offenses by any person to his probability of conviction, to his punishment if convicted, and to other variables, such as the income available to him in legal and other illegal activities, the frequency of nuisance arrests, and his willingness to commit an illegal act. This can be represented as

$$O_j = O_j(p_j, f_j, u_j),$$

Where O_j is the number of offenses he would commit during a particular period, p_j his probability of conviction per offense, f_j his punishment per offense, and u_j a portmanteau variable representing all these other influences.

Since only convicted offenders are punished, in effect there is "price discrimination" and uncertainty: if convicted, he pays f_j per convicted offense, while otherwise he does not. An increase in either p_j or f_j would reduce the utility expected from an offense and thus would tend to reduce the number of offenses because either the probability of "paying" the higher "price" or the "price" itself would increase. That is,

$$O_{f_i} = \frac{\partial O_i}{\partial p_i} < O$$

and

$$O_{f_i} = \frac{\partial O_i}{\partial f_i} < O$$

which are the generally accepted restrictions mentioned above. The effect of changes in some components of u_j could also be anticipated. For example, a rise in the income available in legal activities or an increase in law-abidingness due, say, to "education" would reduce the incentive to enter illegal activities and thus would reduce the number of offenses. Or a shift in the form of the punishment, say, from a fine to imprisonment, would tend to reduce the number of offenses, at least temporarily, because they cannot be committed while in prison.

This approach also has an interesting interpretation of the presumed greater response to a change in the probability than in the punishment. An increase in p_j "compensated" by an equal percentage reduction in f_j would not change the expected income from an offense but could change the expected utility, because the amount of risk would change. It is easily shown that an increase in p_j would reduce the expected utility, and thus the number of offenses, more than an equal percentage increase in f_j if j has preference for risk; the increase in f_j would have the greater effect if he has aversion to risk; and they would have the same effect if he is risk neutral. The widespread generalization that offenders are more deterred by the probability of conviction than by the punishment when convicted turns out to imply in the expected-utility approach that offenders are risk preferrers, at least in the relevant region of punishments.

The total number of offenses is the sum of all the O_j and would depend on the set of p_j, f_j, and u_j. Although these variables are likely to differ significantly between persons because of differences in intelligence, age, education, previous offense history, wealth, family upbringing, etc., for simplicity I now consider only their average values, p, f, and u, and write the market offense function as

$$O = O(p, f, u).$$

This function is assumed to have the same kinds of properties as the individual functions, in particular, to be negatively related to p and f and to be more responsive to the former than the latter if, and only if, offenders on balance have risk preference. Smigel (1965) and Ehrlich (1967) estimate functions like (14) for seven felonies reported by the Federal Bureau of Investigation using state data as the basic unit of observation. They find that the relations are quite stable, as evidenced by high correlation coefficients; that there are significant negative effects on O of p and f, and that usually the effect of p exceeds that of f, indicating preference for risk in the region of observation. . . .

Reprinted from Gary Becker, "Crime and Punishment: An Economic Approach" in *JPE* 76. Copyright © 1968 by the University of Chicago Press. Reprinted by permission of the University of Chicago Press.

Discussion Questions

1. Drawing on Becker's theory, describe the major factors that might be expected to affect a person's decision to engage in crime.

2. What strategies might Becker recommend for controlling crime?

3. How does Becker explain the fact that "offenders are more deterred by the probability of conviction than by the punishment when convicted"? ✦

26

Crime as a Rational Choice

Derek B. Cornish
Ronald V. Clarke

The rational choice perspective draws heavily on classical theory and economic theories of crime, and argues that "crimes are broadly the result of rational choices based on analyses of anticipated costs and benefits" (Cornish and Clarke, 1985: vi). Individuals, then, choose to engage in crime in an effort to maximize their benefits and minimize their costs. This choice process occurs in two major stages.

First, individuals decide whether they are willing to become involved in crime to satisfy their needs (the "initial involvement model"). Individuals may consider a range of different ways of satisfying their needs—some criminal and some not. Whether they decide to engage in crime is heavily influenced by their previous learning and experience, including their moral code, view of themselves, personal and vicarious experiences of crime, and the degree to which they can plan and exercise foresight (Clarke and Cornish, 1985:166). Their previous learning and experience, in turn, are heavily influenced by a range of background factors, including individual traits, their upbringing, and their social and demographic characteristics (e.g., sex, class). Most of the factors said to influence this decision to become involved in crime are drawn from the leading crime theories, discussed in previous sections.

Second, once individuals decide they are ready to engage in crime, they must decide to commit a particular offense (the "criminal event model"). This decision is heavily influenced by the immediate situation of the individual. The individual may have a desperate need for money or may be out with friends who suggest engaging in crime. The individual then selects a target for the offense (e.g., a home to burglarize) based on a consideration of costs and benefits (e.g., is the home occupied, is it easily accessible, is there reason to believe that it contains valuable items). The factors that individuals consider may differ dramatically from one type of crime to another, which is why rational choice theorists argue that "crime-specific" models must be employed. That is, different models of decision making are necessary for different types of crime. The leading crime theories have paid little attention to those factors that influence the decision to commit a particular criminal offense, and one of the leading contributions of rational choice theory has been to focus attention on this area. Research in this area has also contributed to the development of crime control strategies (see Clarke, 1992).

References

Akers, Ronald L. 1990. "Rational Choice, Deterrence, and Social Learning Theory in Criminology: The Path Not Taken." *Journal of Criminal Law and Criminology* 81:653-676.

Clarke, Ronald V. 1992. *Situational Crime Prevention.* New York: Harrow and Heston.

Clarke, Ronald V. and Derek B. Cornish. 1985. "Modeling Offenders' Decisions: A Framework for Research and Policy." Pp. 147-85 in *Crime and Justice: An Annual Review of Research, Volume 6* edited by Michael Tonry and Norval Morris. Chicago: University of Chicago Press.

. . . The synthesis we had suggested—a rational choice perspective on criminal behavior—was intended to locate criminological findings within a framework particularly suitable for thinking about policy-relevant research. Its starting point was an assumption that offenders seek to benefit themselves by their criminal behavior; that this involves the making of decisions and of choices, however rudimentary on occasion these processes might be; and that these processes exhibit a measure of rationality, albeit constrained by limits of time and ability and the availability of relevant information. It was recognized that this conception of crime seemed to fit some forms of offending better than others. However, even in the case of offenses that seemed to be pathologically motivated or impulsively executed, it was felt that rational components were also often present and that the identification and description of these might have lessons for crime-control policy.

Second, a crime-specific focus was adopted, not only because different crimes may meet different needs, but also because the situational context of decision making and the information being handled will vary greatly among offenses. To ignore these differences might well be to reduce significantly one's ability to identify fruitful points for intervention (similar arguments have been applied to other forms of "deviant" behavior, such as gambling: cf. Cornish, 1978). A crime-specific focus is likely to involve rather finer distinctions than those commonly made in criminology. For example, it may not be sufficient to divide burglary simply into its residential and commercial forms. It may also be necessary to distinguish between burglaries committed in middle-class suburbs, in public housing, and in wealthy residential enclaves. Empirical studies suggest that the kinds of individuals involved in these different forms of residential burglary, their motivations, and their methods all vary considerably (cf. Clarke and Hope, 1984, for a review). Similar cases could be made for distinguishing between different forms of robbery, rape, shoplifting, and car theft to take some obvious cases. (In lay thinking, of course, such distinctions are also often made, as between mugging and other forms of robbery, for example.) A corollary of this requirement is that the explanatory focus of the theory is on crimes, rather than on offenders. Such a focus, we believe, provides a counterweight to theoretical and policy preoccupations with the offender.

Third, it was argued that a decision-making approach to crime requires that a fundamental distinction be made between criminal involvement and criminal events. Criminal involvement refers to the processes through which individuals choose to become initially involved in particular forms of crime, to continue, and to desist. The decision processes in these different stages of involvement will be influenced in each case by a different set of factors and will need to be separately mod-

eled. In the same way, the decision processes involved in the commission of a specific crime (i.e., the criminal event) will utilize their own special categories of information. Involvement decisions are characteristically multistage, extend over substantial periods of time, and will draw upon a large range of information, not all of which will be directly related to the crimes themselves. Event decisions, on the other hand, are frequently shorter processes, utilizing more circumscribed information largely relating to immediate circumstances and situations.

The above points can be illustrated by consideration of some flow diagrams that the editors previously developed (Clarke and Cornish, 1985) to model one specific form of crime, namely, burglary in a middle-class residential suburb. Figure 26.1, which represents the processes of initial involvement in this form of crime, has two decision points. The first (Box 7) is the individual's recognition of his or her "readiness" to commit the specific offense in order to satisfy certain needs for money, goods, or excitement. The preceding boxes indicate the wide range of factors that bring the individual to this condition. Box 1, in particular, encompasses the various historical (and contemporaneous) background factors with which traditional criminology has been preoccupied; these have been seen to determine the values, attitudes, and personality traits that dispose the individual to crime. In a rational choice context, however, these factors are reinterpreted as influencing the decisions and judgments that lead to involvement. The second decision (Box 8) actually to commit this form of burglary is the outcome of some chance event, such as an urgent need for cash, which demands action.

Figure 26.2, which is much simpler, depicts the further sequence of decision making that leads to the burglar selecting a particular house. The range of variables influencing this decision sequence is much narrower and reflects the influence of situational factors related to opportunity, effort, and proximal risks. In most cases this decision sequence takes place quite quickly. Figure 26.3 sketches the classes of variables, relating to changes in the individual's degree of profes-

Figure 26.1
Initial Involvement Model (example: burglary in a middle-class suburb)

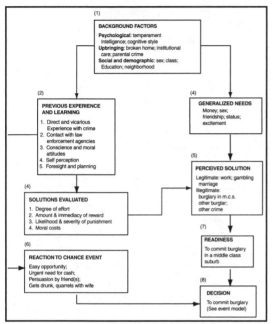

Source: From *Crime and Justice*, vol. 6. M. Tonry and N Morris (eds.), University of Chicago Press, 1985. By permission

Figure 26.2
Event Model (example: burglary in a middle-class suburb)

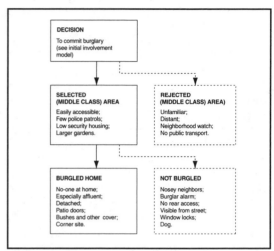

Source: From *Crime and Justice*, vol. 6. M. Tonry and N Morris (eds.), University of Chicago Press, 1985. By permission

sionalism, peer group, life-style, and values, that influence the constantly reevaluated decision to continue with this form of burglary.

Figure 26.4 illustrates, with hypothetical data, similar reevaluations that may lead to desistance. In this case, two classes of vari-

Figure 26.3
Continuing Involvement Model (example: burglary in a middle-class suburb)

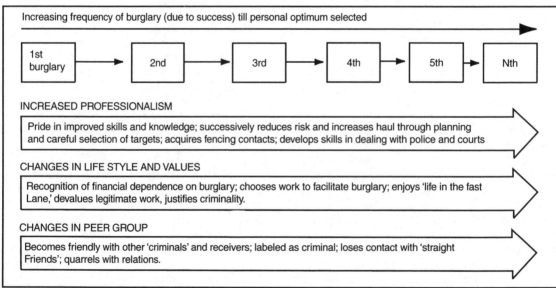

Source: From *Crime and Justice*, vol. 6. M. Tonry and N Morris (eds.), University of Chicago Press, 1985. By permission

Figure 26.4
Desistance Model (example: burglary in a middle-class suburb)

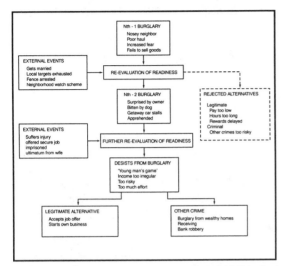

Source: From *Crime and Justice*, vol. 6. M. Tonry and N Morris (eds.), University of Chicago Press, 1985. By permission

ables are seen to have a cumulative effect: life-events (such as marriage), and those more directly related to the criminal events themselves.

These, then, are the main features of the framework that was developed out of our review of recent work in a variety of disciplines that have an interest in crime. It differs from most existing formal theories of criminal behavior, however, in a number of respects. It is true that, like many other criminological theories, the rational choice perspective is intended to provide a framework for understanding all forms of crime. Unlike other approaches, however, which attempt to impose a conceptual unity upon divergent criminal behaviors (by subsuming them under more general concepts such as delinquency, deviance, rule breaking, short-run hedonism, criminality, etc.), our rational choice formulation sees these differences as crucial to the tasks of explanation and control. Unlike existing theories, which tend to concentrate on factors disposing individuals to criminal behavior (the initial involvement model), the rational choice approach, in addition, em-

phasizes subsequent decisions in the offender's career. Again, whereas most existing theories tend to accord little influence to situational variables, the rational choice approach explicitly recognizes their importance in relation to the criminal event and, furthermore, incorporates similar influences on decisions relating to involvement in crime. In consequence, this perspective also recognizes, as do economic and behaviorist theories, the importance of incentives— that is, of rewards and punishments—and hence the role of learning in the criminal career. Finally, the leitmotif encapsulated in the notion of a "reasoning" offender implies the essentially nonpathological and commonplace nature of much criminal activity. . . .

Discussion Questions

1. Does the rational choice perspective assume that offenders carefully plan all crimes?

2. Cornish and Clarke argue that we must employ a "crime-specific focus" when attempting to describe the costs and benefits offenders consider in planning their crimes. Pick two different crimes and describe how the benefits and costs that offenders may consider might differ for these crimes.

3. In discussing "criminal involvement," Cornish and Clarke distinguish between the decisions to become involved in crime, continue in crime, and desist from crime. They state that each of these decisions is influenced by different sets of factors. Describe the factors that might be relevant for each of these decisions.

4. Akers (1990) has argued that rational choice theory can be subsumed under his social learning theory (see Chapter 10 in Part III). Do you agree? ✦

27

Routine Activity Theory

Lawrence E. Cohen
Marcus Felson

The routine activities approach is based on two rather simple ideas. First, it argues that in order for a crime to occur, motivated offenders must converge with suitable targets in the absence of capable guardians. Second, it argues that the probability of this occurring is influenced by our "routine activities"—including our work, family, leisure, and consumption activities. So, for example, if we spend more time in public places—such as in bars and on the street—we increase the likelihood that we will come into contact with motivated offenders in the absence of capable guardians. As a consequence, we are more likely to be victimized.

In this selection, Cohen and Felson demonstrate that these simple ideas can be used to help explain the increase in crime experienced in the United States after World War II. They show much creativity in applying these ideas, and they make a powerful case for the routine activity approach. The routine activities approach has also been used to explain geographic differences in crime rates and differences in the amount of crime experienced by sociodemographic groups (e.g., why young African American males have a high rate of crime victimization). As was indicated in the introduction to this section, the data are generally supportive of the theory, although not all studies support the theory (see Akers, 1997; Birkbeck and LaFree, 1993; Felson, 1994; Meier and Miethe, 1993, for overviews).

The routine activities approach is valuable because it complements traditional crime theories in a fundamental way. These theories typically focus on the factors that motivate or dispose individuals to engage in crime (that is, they focus on the production of motivated offenders). The routine activities approach usually takes the supply of motivated offenders for granted (which has been one criticism of the approach), and instead focuses on the opportunities for crime. (Miethe and Meier, 1994, developed an integrated theory that attempts to explain both offender motivation and the opportunities for crime.)

References

Akers, Ronald L. 1997. *Criminological Theories: Introduction and Evaluation*, 2nd edition. Los Angeles: Roxbury.

Birkbeck, Christopher and Gary LaFree. 1993. "The Situational Analysis of Crime and Deviance." *Annual Review of Sociology* 19:113-37.

Felson, Marcus. 1994. *Crime and Everyday Life*. Thousand Oaks, CA: Pine Forge Press.

Meier, Robert F. and Terance D. Miethe. 1993. "Understanding Theories of Criminal Victimization." Pp. 459-99 in *Crime and Justice, Volume 17*, edited by Michael Tonry. Chicago: University of Chicago Press.

Miethe, Terance D. and Robert F, Meier. 1994. *Crime and Its Social Context*. Albany, NY: State University of New York Press.

. . . We argue that structural changes in routine activity patterns can influence crime rates by affecting the convergence in space and time of the three minimal elements of direct-contact predatory violations: (1) motivated offenders, (2) suitable targets, and (3) the absence of capable guardians against a violation. We further argue that the lack of any one of these elements is sufficient to prevent the successful completion of a direct-contact predatory crime, and that the convergence in time and space of suitable targets and the absence of capable guardians may even lead to large increases in crime rates without necessarily requiring any increase in the structural conditions that motivate individuals to engage in crime. That is, if the proportion of motivated offenders or even suitable targets were to remain stable in a community, changes in routine activities could nonetheless alter the likelihood of their convergence in space and time, thereby creating more opportunities for crimes to occur. Control therefore becomes critical. If controls through routine activities were to decrease, illegal predatory activities could then be likely to increase. . . .

Unlike many criminological inquiries, we do not examine why individuals or groups are inclined criminally, but rather we take criminal inclination as given and examine the manner in which the spatio-temporal organization of social activities helps people to translate their criminal inclinations into action. Criminal violations are treated here as routine activities which share many attributes of, and are interdependent with, other routine activities. . . .

The Minimal Elements of Direct-Contact Predatory Violations

As we previously stated, despite their great diversity, direct-contact predatory violations share some important requirements which facilitate analysis of their structure. Each successfully completed violation minimally requires an *offender* with both criminal inclinations and the ability to carry out those inclinations, a person or object providing a *suitable target* for the offender, and *absence of guardians* capable of preventing violations. We emphasize that the lack of any one of these elements normally is sufficient to prevent such violations from occurring. Though guardianship is implicit in everyday life, it usually is marked by the absence of violations, hence it is easy to overlook. While police action is analyzed widely, guardianship by ordinary citizens of one another and property as they go about routine activities may be one of the most neglected elements in sociological research on crime, especially since it links seemingly unrelated social roles and relationships to the occurrence or absence of illegal acts.

The conjunction of these minimal elements can be used to assess how social structure may affect the tempo of each type of violation. That is, the probability that a violation will occur at any specific time and place might be taken as a function of the convergence of likely offenders and suitable targets in the absence of capable guardians. Through consideration of how trends and fluctuations in social conditions affect the frequency of this convergence of criminogenic circum-

stances, an explanation of temporal trends in crime rates can be constructed. . . .

The Ecological Nature of Illegal Acts

Since illegal activities must feed upon other activities, the spatial and temporal structure of routine legal activities should play an important role in determining the location, type and quantity of illegal acts occurring in a given community or society. Moreover, one can analyze how the structure of community organization as well as the level of technology in a society provide the circumstances under which crime can thrive. For example, technology and organization affect the capacity of persons with criminal inclinations to overcome their targets, as well as affecting the ability of guardians to contend with potential offenders by using whatever protective tools, weapons and skills they have at their disposal. Many technological advances designed for legitimate purposes—including the automobile, small power tools, hunting weapons, highways, telephones, etc.—may enable offenders to carry out their own work more effectively or may assist people in protecting their own or someone else's person or property.

Not only do routine legitimate activities often provide the wherewithal to commit offenses or to guard against others who do so, but they also provide offenders with suitable targets. Target suitability is likely to reflect such things as value (i.e., the material or symbolic desirability of a personal or property target for offenders), physical visibility, access, and the inertia of a target against illegal treatment by offenders (including the weight, size, and attached or locked features of property inhibiting its illegal removal and the physical capacity of personal victims to resist attackers with or without weapons). Routine production activities probably affect the suitability of consumer goods for illegal removal by determining their value and weight. Daily activities may affect the location of property and personal targets in visible and accessible places at particular times. These activities also may cause people to have on hand objects that can be used as weapons for criminal acts or self-protection or to be preoccupied with tasks which reduce their capacity to discourage or resist offenders.

While little is known about conditions that affect the convergence of potential offenders, targets and guardians, this is a potentially rich source of propositions about crime rates. For example, daily work activities separate many people from those they trust and the property they value. Routine activities also bring together at various times of day or night persons of different background, sometimes in the presence of facilities, tools or weapons which influence the commission or avoidance of illegal acts. Hence, the timing of work, schooling and leisure may be of central importance for explaining crime rates. . . .

Microlevel Assumptions of the Routine Activity Approach

The theoretical approach taken here specifies that crime rate trends in the post-World War II United States are related to patterns of what we have called routine activities. We define these as any recurrent and prevalent activities which provide for basic population and individual needs, whatever their biological or cultural origins. Thus routine activities would include formalized work, as well as the provision of standard food, shelter, sexual outlet, leisure, social interaction, learning and childrearing. These activities may go well beyond the minimal levels needed to prevent a population's extinction, so long as their prevalence and recurrence makes them a part of everyday life.

Routine activities may occur (1) at home, (2) in jobs away from home, and (3) in other activities away from home. The latter may involve primarily household members or others. We shall argue that, since World War II, the United States has experienced a major shift of routine activities away from the first category into the remaining ones, especially those nonhousehold activities involving nonhousehold members. In particular, we shall argue that this shift in the structure of routine activities increases the probability that motivated offenders will converge in space and time with suitable targets in the absence of capable guardians, hence contributing to significant increases in the points in the direct-

contact predatory crime rates over these years.

If the routine activity approach is valid, then we should expect to find evidence for a number of empirical relationships regarding the nature and distribution of predatory violations. For example, we would expect routine activities performed within or near the home and among family or other primary groups to entail lower risk of criminal victimization because they enhance guardianship capabilities. We should also expect that routine daily activities affect the location of property and personal targets in visible and accessible places at particular times, thereby influencing their risk of victimization. Furthermore, by determining their size and weight and in some cases their value, routine production activities should affect the suitability of consumer goods for illegal removal. Finally, if the routine activity approach is useful for explaining the paradox presented earlier, we should find that the circulation of people and property, the size and weight of consumer items etc., will parallel changes in crime rate trends for the post-World War II United States.

The veracity of the routine activity approach can be assessed by analyses of both microlevel and macrolevel interdependencies of human activities. While consistency at the former level may appear noncontroversial, or even obvious, one nonetheless needs to show that the approach does not contradict existing data before proceeding to investigate the latter level.

Empirical Assessment

Circumstances and Location of Offenses

The routine activity approach specifies that household and family activities entail lower risk of criminal victimization than nonhousehold-nonfamily activities, despite the problems in measuring the former.

National estimates from large-scale government victimization surveys in 1973 and 1974 support this generalization (see methodological information in Hindelang et al., 1976: Appendix 6). Table 27.1 presents several incident-victimization rates per 100,000 population ages 12 and older. Clearly, the rates in Panels A and B are far lower at or near home than elsewhere and far lower among relatives than others. The data indicate that risk of victimization varies directly with social distance between offender and victim. Panel C of this table indicates, furthermore, that risk of lone victimization far exceeds the risk of victimization for groups. These relationships are strengthened by considering time budget evidence that, on the average, Americans spend 16.26 hours per day at home, 1.38 hours on streets, in parks, etc., and 6.36 hours in other places (Szalai, 1972:795). Panel D of Table 27.1 presents our estimates of victimization per billion person-hours spent in such locations. For example, personal larceny rates (with contact) are 350 times higher at the hands of strangers in streets than at the hands of nonstrangers at home. Separate computations from 1973 victimization data (USDJ, 1976: Table 48) indicate that there were two motor vehicle thefts per million vehicle-hours parked at or near home, 55 per million vehicle-hours in streets, parks, playgrounds, school grounds or parking lots, and 12 per million vehicle-hours elsewhere. While the direction of these relationships is not surprising, their magnitudes should be noted. It appears that risk of criminal victimization varies dramatically among the circumstances and locations in which people place themselves and their property.

Target Suitability

Another assumption of the routine activity approach is that target suitability influences the occurrence of direct-contact predatory violations. Though we lack data to disaggregate all major components of target suitability (i.e., value, visibility, accessibility and inertia), together they imply that expensive and movable durables, such as vehicles and electronic appliances, have the highest risk of illegal removal.

As a specific case in point, we compared the 1975 composition of stolen property reported in the Uniform Crime Report (FBI, 1976: Tables 26-7) with national data on personal consumer expenditures for goods (CEA, 1976: Tables 13-16) and to appliance industry estimates of the value of shipments the same year (*Merchandising Week*, 1976).

We calculated that $26.44 in motor vehicles and parts were stolen for each $100 of these goods consumed in 1975, while $6.81 worth of electronic appliances were stolen per $100 consumed. Though these estimates are subject to error in citizen and police estimation, what is important here is their size relative to other rates. For example, only 8¢ worth of nondurables and 12¢ worth of furniture and nonelectronic household durables were stolen per $100 of each category consumed, the motor vehicle risk being, respectively, 330 and 220 times as great. Though we lack data on the "stocks" of goods subject to risk, these "flow" data clearly support our assumption that vehicles and electronic appliances are greatly overrepresented in thefts.

The 1976 Buying Guide issue of *Consumer Reports* (1975) indicates why electronic appliances are an excellent retail value for a thief. For example, a Panasonic car tape player is worth $30 per lb., and a Phillips phonograph cartridge is valued at over $5,000 per lb., while large appliances such as refrigerators and washing machines are only worth $1 to $3 per lb. Not surprisingly, burglary data for the District of Columbia in 1969 (Scarr, 1972: Table 9) indicate that home entertainment items alone constituted nearly four times as many stolen items as clothing, food, drugs, liquor, and tobacco combined and nearly eight times as many stolen items as office supplies and equipment. In addition, 69% of national thefts classified in 1975 (FBI, 1976: Tables 1, 26) involve automobiles, their parts or accessories, and thefts from automobiles or thefts of bicycles. Yet radio and television sets plus electronic components and accessories totaled only 0.10% of the total truckload tonnage terminated in 1973 by intercity motor carriers, while passenger cars, motor vehicle parts and accessories, motorcycles, bicycles, and their parts, totaled only 5.5% of the 410 million truckload tons terminated (ICC, 1974). Clearly, portable and movable durables are reported stolen in great disproportion to their share of the value and weight of goods circulating in the United States.

Family Activities and Crime Rates

One would expect that persons living in single-adult households and those employed outside the home are less obligated to confine their time to family activities within households. From a routine activity perspective, these persons and their households should have higher rates of predatory criminal victimization. We also expect that adolescents and young adults who are perhaps more likely to engage in peer group activities rather than family activities will have higher rates of criminal victimization. Finally, married persons should have lower rates than others. . . . We note that victimization rates appear to be related inversely to age and are lower for persons in "less active" statuses (e.g., keeping house, unable to work, retired) and persons in intact marriages. A notable exception is . . . where persons unable to work appear more likely to be victimized by rape, robbery and personal larceny with contact than are other "inactive persons." Unemployed persons also have unusually high rates of victimization. However, these rates are consistent with the routine activity approach offered here: the high rates of victimization suffered by the unemployed may reflect their residential proximity to high concentrations of potential offenders as well as their age and racial composition, while handicapped persons have high risk of personal victimization because they are less able to resist motivated offenders. Nonetheless, persons who keep house have noticeably lower rates of victimization than those who are employed, unemployed, in school or in the armed forces. . . .

Burglary and robbery victimization rates are about twice as high for persons living in single-adult households as for other persons in each age group examined. Other victimization data (USDJ, 1976: Table 21) indicate that, while household victimization rates tend to vary directly with household size, larger households have lower rates per person. For example, the total household victimization rates (including burglary, household larceny, and motor vehicle theft) per 1,000 households were 168 for single-person households and 326 for households containing six or more persons. Hence, six people distributed over six single-person households experience an average of 1,008 household victimizations, more than three times as many as one six-person household. Moreover, age of household head has a strong relationship to a household's victimization rate for these crimes. For households headed by persons under 20, the motor vehicle theft rate is nine times as high, and the burglary and household larceny rates four times as high as those for households headed by persons 65 and over (USDJ, 1976: Table 9).

While the data presented in this section were not collected originally for the purpose of testing the routine activity approach, our efforts to rework them for these purposes have proven fruitful. The routine activity approach is consistent with the data examined and, in addition, helps to accommodate within a rather simple and coherent analytical framework certain findings which, though not necessarily new, might otherwise be attributed only "descriptive" significance. In the next section, we examine macrosocial trends as they relate to trends in crime rates.

Changing Trends in Routine Activity Structure and Parallel Trends in Crime Rates

The main thesis presented here is that the dramatic increase in the reported crime rates in the U.S. since 1960 is linked to changes in the routine activity structure of American society and to a corresponding increase in target suitability and decrease in guardian presence. If such a thesis has validity, then we should be able to identify these social trends and show how they relate to predatory criminal victimization rates.

Trends in Human Activity Patterns

The decade 1960-1970 experienced noteworthy trends in the activities of the American population. For example, the percent of the population consisting of female college students increased 118% (USBC, 1975: Table 225). Married female labor force participant rates increased 31% (USBC, 1975: Table 563), while the percent of the population living as primary individuals increased by 34% (USBC, 1975: Table 51; see also Kobrin,

1976). We gain some further insight into changing routine activity patterns by comparing hourly data for 1960 and 1971 on households *unattended* by persons ages 14 or over when U.S. census interviewers first called. . . . These data suggest that the proportion of households unattended at 8 A.M. increased by almost half between 1960 and 1971. One also finds increases in rates of out-of-town travel, which provides greater opportunity for both daytime and nighttime burglary of residences. Between 1960 and 1970, there was a 72% increase in state and national park visits per capita (USBC, 1975), an 144% increase in the percent of plant workers eligible for three weeks vacation (BLS, 1975: Table 116), and an 184% increase in overseas travellers per 100,000 population (USBC, 1975: Table 366). The National Travel Survey, conducted as part of the U.S. Census Bureau's Census of Transportation, confirms the general trends, tallying an 81% increase in the number of vacations taken by Americans from 1967 to 1972, a five-year period (USBC, 1973a: Introduction).

The dispersion of activities away from households appears to be a major recent social change. Although this decade also experienced an important 31% increase in the percent of the population ages 15-24, age structure change was only one of many social trends occurring during the period, especially trends in the circulation of people and property in American society.

The importance of the changing activity structure is underscored by taking a brief look at demographic changes between the years 1970 and 1975, a period of continuing crime rate increments. Most of the recent changes in age structure relevant to crime rates already had occurred by 1970; indeed, the proportion of the population ages 15-24 increased by only 6% between 1970 and 1975, compared with a 15% increase during the five years 1965 to 1970. On the other hand, major changes in the structure of routine activities continued during these years. For example, in only five years, the estimated proportion of the population consisting of husband-present, married women in the labor force households increased by 11%, while the estimated number of non-husband-wife house-

holds per 100,000 population increased from 9,150 to 11,420, a 25% increase (USBC. 1976: Tables 50, 276, USBC, 1970-1975). At the same time, the percent of population enrolled in higher education increased 16% between 1970 and 1975.

Related Property Trends and Their Relation to Human Activity Patterns

Many of the activity trends mentioned above normally involve significant investments in durable goods. For example, the dispersion of population across relatively more households (especially non-husband-wife households) enlarges the market for durable goods such as television sets and automobiles. Women participating in the labor force and both men and women enrolled in college provide a market for automobiles. Both work and travel often involve the purchase of major movable or portable durables and their use away from home.

Considerable data are available which indicate that sales of consumer goods changed dramatically between 1960 and 1970 (as did their size and weight), hence providing more suitable property available for theft. For example, during this decade, constant-dollar personal consumer expenditures in the United States for motor vehicles and parts increased by 71%, while constant-dollar expenditures for other durables increased by 105% (calculated from CEA, 1976: Table B-16). In addition, electronic household appliances and small household shipments increased from 56.2 to 119.7 million units (*Electrical Merchandising Week*, 1964; *Merchandising Week*, 1973). During the same decade, appliance imports increased in value by 681% (USBC, 1975: Table 1368).

This same period appears to have spawned a revolution in small durable product design which further feeds the opportunity for crime to occur. Relevant data from the 1960 and 1970 Sears catalogs on the weight of many consumer durable goods were examined. Sears is the nation's largest retailer and its policy of purchasing and relabeling standard manufactured goods makes its catalogs a good source of data on widely merchandised consumer goods. The lightest television listed for sale in 1960 weighed 38 lbs., compared with 15 lbs. for 1970. Thus, the lightest televisions were 2 ½ times as heavy in 1960 as 1970. Similar trends are observed for dozens of other goods listed in the Sears catalog. Data from *Consumer Reports Buying Guide*, published in December of 1959 and 1969, show similar changes for radios, record players, slide projectors, tape recorders, televisions, toasters and many other goods. Hence, major declines in weight between 1960 and 1970 were quite significant for these and other goods, which suggests that the consumer goods market may be producing many more targets suitable for theft. In general, one finds rapid growth in property suitable for illegal removal and in household and individual exposure to attack during the years 1960-1975.

Related Trends in Business Establishments

Of course, as households and individuals increased their ownership of small durables, businesses also increased the value of the merchandise which they transport and sell as well as the money involved in these transactions. Yet the Census of Business conducted in 1958, 1963, 1967, and 1972 indicate that the number of wholesale, retail, service, and public warehouse establishments (including establishments owned by large organizations) was a nearly constant ratio of one for every 16 persons in the United States. Since more goods and money were distributed over a relatively fixed number of business establishments, the tempo of business activity per establishment apparently was increasing. At the same time, the percent of the population employed as sales clerks or salesmen in retail trade declined from 1.48% to 1.27%. between 1960 and 1970, a 14.7% decline (USBC, 1975: Table 589).

Though both business and personal property increased, the changing pace of activities appears to have exposed the latter to greater relative risk of attack, whether at home or elsewhere, due to the dispersion of goods among many more households, while concentrating goods in business establishments. However, merchandise in retail establishments with heavy volume and few employees to guard it probably is exposed to ma-

jor increments in risk of illegal removal than is most other business property.

Composition of Crime Trends

If these changes in the circulation of people and property are in fact related to crime trends, the *composition* of the latter should reflect this. We expect relatively greater increases in personal and household victimization as compared with most business victimizations, while shoplifting should increase more rapidly than other types of thefts from businesses. We expect personal offenses at the hands of strangers to manifest greater increases than such offenses at the hands of nonstrangers. Finally, residential burglary rates should increase more in daytime than nighttime.

The available time series on the composition of offenses confirm these expectations. For example, Table 27.1 shows that commercial burglaries declined from 60% to 36% of the total, while daytime residential burglaries increased from 16% to 33%. Unlike the other crimes against business, shoplifting increased its share. Though we lack trend data on the circumstances of other violent offenses, murder data confirm our expectations. Between 1963 and 1975, felon-type murders increased from 17% to 32% of the total. Compared with a 47% increase in the rate of relative killings in this period, we calculated a 294% increase in the murder rate at the hands of known or suspected felon types.

Thus the trends in the composition of recorded crime rates appear to be highly consistent with the activity structure trends noted earlier. In the next section we apply the routine activity approach in order to model crime rate trends and social change in the post-World War II United States.

The Relationship of the Household Activity Ratio to Five Annual Official Index Crime Rates in the United States, 1947-1974

In this section, we test the hypothesis that aggregate official crime rate trends in the United States vary directly over time with the dispersion of activities away from family and

Table 27.1
Offense Analysis Trends for Robbery, Burglary, Larceny and Murder; United States, 1960–1975

A. ROBBERIES[a]	1960	1965	1970	
Highway Robbery	52.6	57.0	59.8	
Residential Robbery	8.0	10.1	13.1	
Commercial Robbery	39.4	32.9	27.1	
Totals	100.0	100.0	100.0	
B. BURGLARIES	1960	1965	1970	1975
Residential	15.6	24.5	31.7	33.2
Residential Nightime	24.4	25.2	25.8	30.5
Commercial	60.0	50.2	42.5	36.3
Total	100.0	99.9	100.0	100.0
C. LARCENIES	1960	1965	1970	1975
Shoplifting	6.0	7.8	9.2	11.3
other	94.0	92.2	90.8	88.7
Total	100.0	100.0	100.0	100.0
D. MURDERS	1963	1965	1970	1975
Relative Killings	31.0	31.0	23.3	22.4
Romance, Arguments[b]	51.0	48.0	47.9	45.2
Felon Types[c]	17.0	21.0	28.8	32.4
Totals	100.0	100.0	100.0	100.0

Source: Offense Ananlysis from UCR, various years.
[a] Excluding miscellaneous robberies. The 1975 distribution distribution ommited due to apparent instability of post–1970 data.
[b] Includes romantic triangles, lovers' quarrels and arguments.
[c] Includes both known and suspected felon acts.

household. The limitations of annual time series data do not allow construction of direct measures of changes in hourly activity patterns, or quantities, qualities and movements of exact stocks of household durable goods, but the Current Population Survey does provide related time series on labor force and household structure. From these data, we calculate annually (beginning in 1947) a household activity ratio by adding the number of married, husband-present female labor force participants (source: BLS, 1975: Table 5) to the number of non-husband-wife households (source: USBC, 1947-1976), dividing this sum by the total number of households in the U.S. (source: USBC, 1947-1976). This calculation provides an estimate of the proportion of American households in year t expected to be most highly exposed to risk of personal and property victimization due to the dispersion of their activities away from family and household and/or their likelihood of owning extra sets of durables subject to high risk of attack. Hence, the household activity ratio should vary directly with official index crime rates.

Our empirical goal in this section is to test this relationship, with controls for those variables which other researchers have linked empirically to crime rate trends in the United States. Since various researchers have found such trends to increase with the proportion of the population in teen and young adult years (Fox, 1976; Land and Felson, 1976; Sagi and Wellford, 1968; Weliford, 1973), we include the population ages 15-24 per 100,000 resident population in year t as our first control variable (source: USBC, various years). Others (e.g., Brenner, 1976a; 1976b) have found unemployment rates to vary directly with official crime rates over time, although this relationship elsewhere has been shown to be empirically questionable (see Mansfield et al., 1974: 463; Cohen and Felson, 1979). Thus, as our second, control variable, we take the standard annual unemployment rate (per 100 persons ages 16 and over) as a measure of the business cycle (source: BLS, 1975).

Four of the five crime rates that we utilize here (forcible rape, aggravated assault, robbery and burglary) are taken from FBI estimates of offenses per 100,000 U.S. population (as revised and reported in OMB, 1973). . . . For our homicide indicator we employ the homicide mortality rate taken from the vital statistics data collected by the Bureau of the Census (various years). . . .

Findings

Our time-series analysis for the years 1947-1974 consistently revealed positive and statistically significant relationships between the household activity ratio and each official crime rate change. . . .

Discussion

In our judgment many conventional theories of crime (the adequacy of which usually is evaluated by cross-sectional data, or no data at all) have difficulty accounting for the annual changes in crime rate trends in the post-World War II United States. These theories may prove useful in explaining crime trends during other periods, within specific communities, or in particular subgroups of the population. Longitudinal aggregate data for the United States, however, indicate that the trends for many of the presumed causal variables in these theoretical structures are in a direction opposite to those hypothesized to be the causes of crime. For example, during the decade 1960-1970, the percent of the population below the low-income level declined 44% and the unemployment rate declined 186%. Central city population as a share of the whole population declined slightly, while the percent of foreign stock declined 0.1%, etc. (see USBC, 1975: 654, 19, 39).

On the other hand, the convergence in time and space of three elements (motivated offenders, suitable targets, and the absence of capable guardians) appears useful for understanding crime rate trends. The lack of any of these elements is sufficient to prevent the occurrence of a successful direct-contact predatory crime. The convergence in time and space of suitable targets and the absence of capable guardians can lead to large increases in crime rates without any increase or change in the structural conditions that motivate individuals to engage in crime. Presumably, had the social indicators of the variables hypothesized to be the causes of crime in conventional theories changed in the direction of favoring increased crime in the post-World War II United States, the increases in crime rates likely would have been even more staggering than those which were observed. In any event, it is our belief that criminologists have underemphasized the importance of the convergence of suitable targets and the absence of capable guardians in explaining recent increases in the crime rate. Furthermore, the effects of the convergence in time and space of these elements may be multiplicative rather than additive. That is, their convergence by a fixed percentage may produce increases in crime rates far greater than that fixed percentage, demonstrating how some relatively modest social trends can contribute to some relatively large changes in crime rate trends. . . .

Without denying the importance of factors motivating offenders to engage in crime, we have focused specific attention upon violations themselves and the prerequisites for their occurrence. However, the routine activity approach might in the future be applied to the analysis of offenders and their inclinations as well. For example, the structure of primary group activity may affect the likelihood that cultural transmission or social control of criminal inclinations will occur, while the structure of the community may affect the tempo of criminogenic peer group activity. We also may expect that circumstances favorable for carrying out violations contribute to criminal inclinations in the long run by rewarding these inclinations.

We further suggest that the routine activity framework may prove useful in explaining why the criminal justice system, the community and the family have appeared so ineffective in exerting social control since 1960. Substantial increases in the opportunity to carry out predatory violations may have undermined society's mechanisms for social control. For example, it may be difficult for institutions seeking to increase the certainty, celerity and severity of punishment to compete with structural changes resulting in vast increases in the certainty, celerity and value of rewards to be gained from illegal predatory acts.

It is ironic that the very factors which increase the opportunity to enjoy the benefits of life also may increase the opportunity for predatory violations. For example, automobiles provide freedom of movement to offenders as well as average citizens and offer vulnerable targets for theft. College enrollment, female labor force participation, urbanization, suburbanization, vacations, and new electronic durables provide various opportunities to escape the confines of the household while they increase the risk of predatory victimization. Indeed, the opportunity for predatory crime appears to be enmeshed in the opportunity structure for legitimate activities to such an extent that it might be very difficult to root out substantial amounts of crime without modifying much of our way of life. Rather than assuming that predatory crime is simply an indicator of social breakdown, one might take it as a by product of freedom and prosperity as they manifest themselves in the routine activities of everyday life.

Reprinted from Lawrence E. Cohen and Marcus Felson, "Social Change and Crime Rate Trends: A Routine Activity Approach" in *American Sociological Review*, Vol. 44, 588-608. Copyright © 1979 by the American Sociological Association. Reprinted by permission of the American Sociological Association.

Discussion Questions

1. According to the routine activity approach, it is possible to experience large increases in the crime rate *without* any increase in the supply of motivated offenders. How can this be?

2. What do Cohen and Felson mean by "suitable targets" and "the absence of capable guardians"? Describe how targets and guardianship have changed in the United States since World War II.

3. Describe the "routine activities" in which you engage. How might these activities increase or decrease your chance of criminal victimization?

4. Young people and males have higher rates of criminal victimization. How might the routine activities approach explain this? ✦

Part VIII

Labeling, Interaction, and Crime: Societal Reaction and the Creation of Criminals

Nearly all criminological theories use the *offender* as the starting point of their analysis. Vigorous debates subsequently ensue over whether the key cause of crime is found inside or outside the offender, and, in either case, there is the additional debate over which specific individual difference or which social experience trumps the others as the preeminent criminogenic factor. Still, these differences aside, there is consensus that the search for crime's etiology must begin by studying the people who break the law.

The distinctiveness of the "labeling" or "societal reaction" perspective, however, lies in its rejection of using the offender as the lynchpin of criminological analysis. Labeling theory proposes that we focus our attention not on the behavior of offenders but on the *behavior of those who label, react to, and otherwise seek to control offenders*. Labeling theory argues that it is these efforts at social control that ultimately trigger the processes that trap individuals in a criminal career. Labeling or societal reaction thus has ironic and unanticipated effects; it creates the very thing it is intended to stop—it produces a self-fulfilling prophecy.

Creating Criminals: Secondary Deviance

Many early criminologists recognized that placing people in prisons—or "houses of corruption" as Shaw (1966 [1930]) called them—could deepen involvement in crime. These insights on the effects of "labeling," however, were largely voiced in passing and were not integrated into the scholar's theory of criminal behavior. Frank Tannenbaum's (1938: 19-21) discussion of the "dramatization of evil" stands out as a noteworthy exception to this tendency to treat the effects of labeling as a subsidiary concern. For this reason, the roots of labeling theory are often traced to his work.

In *Crime and the Community*, Tannenbaum endorsed the view of the Chicago school that crime was not a manifestation of individual differences but learned as part of an "educational process" in the community. Youths were surrounded by criminal influences, including gangs and older offenders. Even so, a "decisive step in the education of the criminal" is being arrested and having his or her delinquent status held up for public scrutiny—that is, having one's evil "dramatized" (1938: 71). In his most famous passage,

Tannenbaum asserted that "the process of making the criminal, therefore, is a process of tagging, defining, identifying, segregating, describing, emphasizing, making conscious and self-conscious; it becomes a way of stimulating, suggesting, emphasizing, and evoking the very traits that are complained of" (p. 20).

In setting forth this thesis, Tannenbaum anticipated many of the key ideas elaborated by later labeling theorists. He noted, for example, that once arrested and labeled a criminal, a youth is forced "into companionship with other children similarly defined," the result of which is that the youth is exposed to criminal "mores" and "has a new set of experiences that lead directly to a criminal career" (p. 20). Youngsters also begin to think differently about themselves. "In this entirely new world," observed Tannenbaum, "he is made conscious of himself as a different human being than he was before his arrest. He becomes classified as a thief, perhaps, and the entire world about him has suddenly become a different place for him and will remain different for the rest of his life" (p. 19). In the end, by labeling a juvenile with the official status of a delinquent, "the person becomes the thing he is described as being" (p. 20). The best policy in dealing with juveniles is "a refusal to dramatize the evil. The less said about it the better" (p. 20).

The idea that reacting to wayward conduct only makes it worse was conceptualized even more clearly by Edwin Lemert (Chapter 28 in this Part). Writing in 1951, he introduced the concepts of "primary" and "secondary" deviance (see also Lemert, 1972). For Lemert, primary deviations occur for a wide range of reasons, some individual and some situational. These deviations are seen by individuals as peripheral to their identity and to the conventional social roles they typically perform on a daily basis. The inconsistency of deviating but not seeing this conduct as a reflection on one's identity creates tension that is "rationalized or otherwise dealt with as functions of a socially accepted role" (Lemert, 1951: 75). One might drink a great deal, but still see oneself as a college student, not a "drunk."

Secondary deviance occurs when the individual no longer dissociates from their devia-

tion. Instead, the person's "life and identity are organized around the facts of deviance" (Lemert, 1972: 63). But what causes this qualitative shift from primary to secondary deviance? Lemert argued that the key factor prompting a person's life to coalesce around deviance is the "reactions of others." Typically, a gradual process unfolds in which a cycle of deviation and negative reactions from others is repeated and amplified. Continued deviations call forth increasingly stigmatizing reactions from others. In the course of this interaction, the person eventually accepts his or her "deviant social status" and makes "efforts at adjustment based on the associated role" (1951: 77). They see themselves as deviant, and make life choices that are constrained by and reaffirm their deviant status. "When a person begins to employ his deviant behavior or a role based upon it as a means of defense, attack, or adjustment to the overt and covert problems created by the consequent societal reaction to him," stated Lemert (1951:76), "his deviation is secondary."

Thus, Lemert and Tannenbaum both proposed that when wayward people experience stigmatizing societal reactions, their world is transformed into one in which their criminal (or deviant) status defines their social existence and self-conception. The result is a deepening, not a reduction, of their criminality. Neither Lemert's nor Tannenbaum's insights, however, gained the sustained attention of their contemporaries. It was not until the mid-1960s, with the writings of Howard Becker (1963), Kai Erikson (1966), John Kitsuse (1964), Edwin Schur (1969), and others, that an identifiable school of criminology emerged that self-consciously referred to itself as "labeling" or "societal reaction" theory. In fact, it was at this time that the earlier works of Lemert and Tannenbaum were resurrected and redefined as falling within the tradition of labeling theory.

The Rise and Fall of Labeling Theory

Extending the work of Lemert and Tannenbaum, a group of scholars in the 1960s and early 1970s argued that societal reaction, not the offender, should be the centerpiece of criminological analysis. They focused on three issues that, in one way or another, challenged the assumptions traditionally held in the discipline.

First, criminologists usually define crime as "behavior that violates a criminal law." For labeling theorists, however, this definition takes the existing laws as a given rather than treating them as a social reality that has been "constructed." A systematic analysis of "societal reactions" questions existing reality and asks why certain behaviors are labeled as crime and others are not. It also asks why definitions of these behaviors can change over time.

Take, for example, the sexual assault of women that occurs on a date. Until recently, these assaults were not seen or treated as a "rape." This label was largely reserved for those victimizations in which a woman was raped by a stranger and visibly injured in the process of resisting the assault—the signs that a "real rape" had taken place (Estrich, 1987). The lengthy struggle of women's rights groups, however, challenged what should be considered a rape. The invention and growing acceptance of the concept of "date rape" redefined sexual assaults committed in intimate relationships. Coercion, not whether the victim and offender knew one another, was trumpeted as the criterion that should distinguish when the crime of rape has been committed. A new reality thus was constructed in which the legal category of rape took on expanded meaning and encompassed a wider range of victimizations.

Second, once labels or categories of crime have been invented, not everyone who "breaks the law" is detected and designated a "criminal." Being a "criminal," therefore, does not depend only on a person's actions but on how others react to that person. Various factors—legal and extralegal—affect whether a label is attached and, as a result, the person's public reputation is qualitatively altered.

Commenting on the concept of deviance—in words that just as well could be applied to the concept of crime—Howard Becker (1963) captured the thrust of the labeling theory argument that deviance is socially constructed rather than an invariant, objective reality. He began by noting that the traditional "socio-logical view I have just discussed defines deviance as the infraction of some agreed-upon rule." But "such an assumption seems to me to ignore the central fact about deviance: it is created by society." More specifically, "*social groups create deviance by making the rules whose infraction constitutes deviance*, and by applying those rules to particular people and labeling them as outsiders." In Becker's view, then, "deviance is *not* a quality of the act the person commits, but rather a consequence of the application by others of rules and sanctions to the 'offender.'" Labeling or societal reaction thus creates deviants. "The deviant is one to whom the label has successfully been applied; deviant behavior is behavior that people so label" (all quotes from Becker, 1963: 8-9; emphasis in original).

While these concerns illuminated the need to study the creation and application of labels, the third focus of labeling theory was on the *consequences* of being labeled and treated as a criminal. As noted, in a rejection of offender-based explanations of crime, labeling theorists argued that reacting to people as "criminals" initiated processes that had the self-fulfilling prophecy of making the person become a criminal—someone more deeply entrenched in a criminal career. They noted that once a person bore the label of a "criminal," it became a "master status"—the most salient public feature of that person. Being a "criminal" thus serves as the focal point of virtually every interaction, a defining designation that cannot be escaped.

Drawing on the sociological theory of symbolic interactionism, labeling theorists argued that a person's identity or self-conception is shaped by the messages other people deliver as to "who the person is." Although the process is not rigidly deterministic—identities can be resisted and can be manipulated (e.g., by putting "one's best foot forward")—the constant appraisal that a person is a "criminal" eventually takes its toll. Over time, those who have been labeled come to embrace the idea that they are, in fact, "criminals." This identity in turn makes choosing crime more likely, as people act consistently with their public and now privately held identity.

Labeling not only transforms a person's identity but also his or her social relationships. Although not often phrased this way, in essence scholars saw labeling as triggering the very conditions that competing theories linked to crime. Thus, once stigmatized as a "criminal," the person loses conventional social relationships (social bond theory), is forced to associate mainly with other criminals—whether in prison or on the streets (social learning theory), and as an "ex-offender" is denied opportunities for employment (strain theory). Engulfed by these criminogenic conditions, the labeled person is constrained to pursue a life in crime.

As the 1960s progressed, labeling theory's popularity grew to the point where it rivaled, if not surpassed, that of more traditional theoretical perspectives (Cole, 1975). As Hagan (1973) notes, part of labeling theory's appeal was that it was "interesting." Criminologists are attracted to ideas, says Hagan, that reverse a "conventionally assumed causal sequence" (1973: 456), which is precisely what labeling theory attempts. Thus, common sense would dictate that arresting, trying, imprisoning, and rehabilitating offenders would make crime less likely; after all, the manifest function of processing offenders through the criminal justice system is to reduce their recidivism and to make society safer. The unique twist to labeling theory was the claim that these very efforts to prevent crime actually cause crime.

But labeling theory was appealing for another reason: the theory, if correct, contained a stinging critique of state power as exercised by the criminal justice system. Recall that during the 1960s and early 1970s, the United States was greeted with revelation after revelation of the government abusing its power— from Civil Rights demonstrators being beaten, to inmates being gunned down at Attica, to students being shot at Kent State, to Viet Nam, to Watergate, and on and on. As trust in the state plummeted—especially on university campuses—a theory that blamed the government for causing more harm than good struck a chord of truth. Labeling theory, of course, did precisely this in arguing that the criminal justice system stigmatized offenders and ultimately trapped them in a criminal career. The obvious policy implication was to reduce state intervention into the lives of offenders (Schur, 1973). Most important, juveniles were to be diverted from the system altogether, and virtually all offenders were to be kept out of prison.

The long-term viability of labeling theory as a comprehensive explanation of crime, however, was undermined by its apparent empirical weakness (see, especially, Gove, 1980; compare with Cullen and Cullen, 1978). In its most extreme and interesting form, labeling theory proposed that societal reaction, especially by the criminal justice system, was the key factor in—indeed, a necessary and sufficient condition for—offenders becoming stabilized in a criminal career. But this claim is obviously false, as early critics realized (see, e.g., Mankoff, 1971). As life-course research reveals, stability of crime and deviance often emerges early in life before formal interventions have taken place (Moffitt, Chapter 5; Sampson and Laub, Chapter 20).

On a broader level, labeling theory wishes to pretend that being raised in criminogenic conditions for 10, 15, or 20 years is largely inconsequential. The effects of these day-in and day-out experiences—such as having a dysfunctional family life, associating with delinquent friends, and failing at school—are said to pale in comparison to the effects, albeit over a more limited time, of being arrested and perhaps jailed. This assertion is not credible and cannot be sustained empirically.

Contemporary Labeling Theories

Chastened by withering critiques of labeling theory, criminologists moved on to other theoretical frameworks. Whereas they had once embraced the theory without any evidence of its validity (Hagan, 1973), criminologists now rejected labeling theory on the grounds that the perspective "had no empirical support." More recently, however, a revisionist position has emerged which suggests that it may be premature to dismiss societal reaction as irrelevant to crime causation (Paternoster and Iovanni, 1989). Although the evidence is not consistent (Akers, 1997), several quality longitudinal studies have shown that contact with the criminal justice system increases recidivism (Farrington, 1977; Hagan and Palloni, 1990; Palamara et al., 1986; Sampson and Laub, 1993). Further, two theoretical developments have emerged that may help to revitalize interest in studying the effects of societal reaction: Ross Matsueda's focus on informal reactions and John Brathwaite's focus on reintegrative shaming.

Within criminology, labeling theory had usually been interpreted as contending that the application of *formal* criminal sanctions was the key societal reaction that fostered career criminality. This position made sense, since criminal sanctions involved a person's official and public designation as a "criminal" and could involve a lengthy stay behind bars. Less attention was paid, however, to the potential role played by *informal* sanctions— that is, the societal reactions of parents, friends, neighbors, and the like. There is at least beginning evidence that, under some circumstances, informal societal reactions can worsen wayward conduct (see, e.g., Triplett and Jarjoura, 1994; Ward and Tittle, 1993; see also, Wells and Rankin, 1988).

Ross Matsueda (1992 [Chapter 29 in this Part]) provides the most sophisticated theoretical statement of the potential criminogenic effects of informal labeling. Drawing on symbolic interactionism, Matsueda argues that a key proximate cause of delinquent behavior is the "reflected appraisals of others"—that is, a youth's perception that other people—especially those "significant" to the youngster (e.g., parents)—view him or her as a "delinquent." In part, this reflected appraisal is influenced by the youth's own behavior: juveniles who engage in delinquency are more likely to believe that others see them as "troublemakers." Reflected appraisals also are influenced, however, by the "actual appraisals of others." Thus, when youngsters are appraised or labeled as a delinquent (e.g., by their parents), they perceive that others see them as wayward and act upon this conception of themselves. In short, labeling creates a delinquent "self," which in turn prompts illegal conduct. It is noteworthy that Matsueda has marshaled evidence supporting this causal sequence (Bartusch and Matsueda, 1996; Matsueda, 1992; see also Heimer and Matsueda, 1994).

Another avenue for the revitalization of labeling theory starts with the observation that the effects of societal reaction are contingent on a range of factors. Traditional statements of labeling theory assumed that societal reaction virtually always increases crime and deviance. This thesis, however, is clearly false. Research from corrections, for example, shows that while punitive interventions have no effect or increase recidivism, rehabilitation programs reduce future criminality (Andrews and Bonta, 1994). Similarly, Sherman (1993: 445) observes that "legal punishment either reduces, increases, or has no effect on future crimes, depending on the type of offenders, offenses, social settings, and levels of analysis." Sherman proposes that in the face of criminal penalties, "defiance" and greater crime are likely to result when offenders are poorly bonded to society and define the sanctions against them as stigmatizing and unfair. In contrast, recidivism is less likely when offenders have close ties to conventional society (e.g., employed) and see the sanctions against them as deserved and fairly applied.

John Braithwaite (1989 [Chapter 30]) has developed the most noteworthy attempt to specify when societal reaction, whether formal or informal, results in more or less criminality. "The first step to productive theorizing about crime is to think about the contention that labeling offenders makes things worse. The contention," observes Braithwaite (1989: 12), "is both right and wrong." When a criminal act is detected, attempts usually are made to "shame" the person, a concept used to encompass "all social processes of expressing disapproval which have the intention or effect of invoking remorse in the person being shamed and/or condemnation by others who become aware of the shaming" (p. 100). Whether such shaming "makes things worse," however, depends on the *quality* of the societal reaction.

In his central proposition, Braithwaite argues, consistent with labeling theory, that *stigmatizing* shaming increases crime. In this instance, "no effort is made to reconcile the offender with the community" (p. 101). Instead, the offender is made into an outcast and is cut off from conventional relationships. As a result, the offender joins criminal subcultures, where his or her criminality is reinforced and opportunities to commit illegal acts are plentiful.

Unlike labeling theory, however, Braithwaite recognizes that another form of societal reaction exists: *reintegrative* shaming, a process in which shaming "is followed by efforts to reintegrate the offender back into the community of law-abiding or respectable citizens through words or gestures of forgiveness or ceremonies to decertify the offender as deviant" (1992: 100-101). This type of shaming sends a message to the individual and to the larger community that the offender's behavior is wrong and should not be repeated. At the same time, the reintegrative aspect of the reaction communicates that the offender as a person is not beyond redemption. Accepting the repentant offender back into the community reinforces the offender's conventional social bonds and keeps him or her from seeking out the company of other criminals. The result is that reintegrative shaming strengthens prosocial influences in the offender's life and thus reduces recidivism.

At this point, it is unlikely that labeling theory—even in its most sophisticated forms, such as Matsueda's and Braithwaite's perspectives—will provide a complete explanation of criminal behavior. Frequently, it would seem, societal reaction is the result, rather than the cause, of law-breaking. A large omission in labeling theory is that it places little focus on the early years of life during which the conduct problems that underlie much stable serious criminality first emerge. Labeling theorists also often pay insufficient attention to how, independent of societal reaction, structural inequality and the concentration of disadvantage in inner-city communities might affect behavior. Nonetheless, scholars working in this tradition have identified a factor—stigmatizing, rejecting, nasty societal reactions—that rarely makes matters better and more often serves only to solidify an offender's commitment to a criminal career. It would be unwise, therefore, for criminologists to assume that "labeling has no effects," and more prudent for them to continue to specify the conditions under which societal reaction pushes offenders into, rather than out of, a life in crime.

References

Akers, Ronald L. 1997. *Criminological Theories: Introduction and Evaluation*, 2nd edition. Los Angeles: Roxbury.

Andrews, D. A. and James Bonta. 1994. *The Psychology of Criminal Conduct.* Cincinnati: Anderson.

Bartusch, Dawn Jeglum and Ross L. Matsueda. 1996. "Gender, Reflected Appraisals, and Labeling: A Cross-Group Test of an Interactionist Theory of Delinquency." *Social Forces* 75: 145-177.

Becker, Howard S. 1963. *Outsiders: Studies in the Sociology of Deviance.* New York: The Free Press.

Braithwaite, John. 1989. *Crime, Shame and Reintegration.* Cambridge, UK: Cambridge University Press.

Cole, Stephen. 1975. "The Growth of Scientific Knowledge: Theories of Deviance as a Case Study." Pp. 175-220 in *The Idea of Social Structure: Papers in Honor of Robert K. Merton*, edited by Lewis A. Coser. New York: Harcourt Brace Jovanovich

Cullen, Francis T. and John B. Cullen. 1978. "Labeling Theory and the Empty Castle Phenomenon." *Western Sociological Review* 9: 28-38.

Erikson, Kai T. 1966. *Wayward Puritans: A Study in the Sociology of Deviance.* New York: John Wiley.

Estrich, Susan. 1987. *Real Rape.* Cambridge, MA: Harvard University Press.

Farrington, David P. 1977. "The Effects of Public Labeling." *British Journal of Criminology* 17: 112-125.

Gove, Walter R., ed. 1980. *The Labelling of Deviance*, 2nd edition. Beverly Hills, CA: Sage.

Hagan, John. 1973. "Labelling and Deviance: A Case Study in the 'Sociology of the Interesting.'" *Social Problems* 20:447-458.

Hagan, John and Alberto Palloni. 1990. "The Social Reproduction of a Criminal Class in Working-Class London, Circa 1950-1980." *American Journal of Sociology* 96: 265-299.

Heimer, Karen and Ross L. Matsueda. 1994. "Role-Taking, Role Commitment, and Delinquency: A Theory of Differential Social Control." *American Sociological Review* 59: 365-390.

Kitsuse, John I. 1964. "Societal Reaction to Deviant Behavior: Problems of Theory and Method." Pp. 87-102 in *The Other Side*, edited by Howard S. Becker. New York: The Free Press.

Lemert, Edwin M. 1951. *Social Pathology: A Systematic Approach to the Theory of Sociopathic Behavior*. New York: McGraw-Hill.

——. 1972. *Human Deviance, Social Problems, and Social Control*, 2nd edition. Englewood Cliffs, NJ: Prentice-Hall.

Mankoff, Milton. 1971. "Societal Reaction and Career Deviance: A Critical Analysis." *Sociological Quarterly* 12: 204-218.

Matsueda, Ross L. 1992. "Reflected Appraisals, Parental Labeling, and Delinquency: Specifying a Symbolic Interactionist Theory." *American Journal of Sociology* 6: 1577-1611.

Palamara, Frances, Francis T. Cullen, and Joanne C. Gersten. 1979. "The Effect of Police and Mental Health Intervention on Juvenile Deviance: Specifying Contingencies in the Impact of Formal Reaction." *Journal of Health and Social Behavior* 27: 90-105.

Paternoster, Raymond and LeeAnn Iovanni. 1989. "The Labeling Perspective and Delinquency: An Elaboration of the Theory and an Assessment of the Evidence." *Justice Quarterly* 6:359-394.

Sampson, Robert J. and John H. Laub. 1993. *Crime in the Making: Pathways and Turning Points Through Life*. Cambridge, MA: Harvard University Press.

Schur, Edwin M. 1973. *Radical Non-Intervention: Rethinking the Delinquency Problem*. Englewood Cliffs, NJ: Prentice-Hall.

Schur, Edwin M. 1969. "Reactions to Deviance: A Critical Assessment." *American Journal of Sociology* 75: 309-322.

Shaw, Clifford R. 1966 [originally published in 1930]. *The Jack-Roller: A Delinquent Boy's Own Story*. Chicago: University of Chicago Press.

Sherman, Lawrence W. 1993. "Defiance, Deterrence, and Irrelevance: A Theory of the Criminal Sanction." *Journal of Research in Crime and Delinquency* 30: 445-473.

Tannenbaum, Frank. 1938. *Crime and the Community*. New York: Columbia University Press.

Triplett, Ruth A. and G. Roger Jarjoura. 1994. "Theoretical and Empirical Specification of a Model of Informal Labeling." *Journal of Quantitative Criminology* 10: 241-276.

Ward, David A. and Charles R. Tittle. "Deterrence or Labeling: The Effects of Informal Sanctions." *Deviant Behavior* 14: 43-64.

Wells, L. Edward and Joseph H. Rankin. 1988. "Direct Parental Controls and Delinquency." *Criminology* 263-285. ✦

28

Primary and Secondary Deviance

Edwin M. Lemert

Although Lemert's Social Pathology *was over 450 pages long, it was his short discussion of primary and secondary deviance that, ironically, proved to be the lasting contribution of this volume. Not surprisingly, then, Lemert eventually addressed these concepts in considerably more detail in a later work,* Human Deviance, Social Problems, and Social Control *(1972). In the process, Lemert both advanced and criticized labeling theory.*

Lemert realized that in cruder versions of labeling theory, people were portrayed as innocent victims who, unfairly labeled by others, are driven in a very deterministic way into a life in crime. For Lemert, however, becoming firmly rooted in crime or deviance was not a random occurrence in which the labeled person played no role. Instead, Lemert envisioned an interactionist process in which individuals deviated, were sanctioned by others, made choices that further embedded them in deviance, experienced more reactions from others, and eventually came to accept and act consistently with their public designation as a "deviant."

*In Lemert's (1972: 62) framework, primary deviance "is polygenic, arising out of a variety of social, cultural, psychological, and physiological factors." This kind of waywardness "has only marginal implications for the status and psychic structure of the person concerned" (p. 62). Deviations have more profound impacts on people's lives, however, when they inspire societal reactions. As people are stigmatized, punished, segregated, and controlled, the "general effect is to differentiate the symbolic and interactional environment to which the person responds, so that early or adult sociali-*zation is categorically changed" (p. 63). They now come to be defined differently, which in turn affects their identity or conceptions of themselves and narrows their ability to choose conventional over wayward paths. Their "life and identity are organized around the facts of deviance," a reality that makes continued deviation likely (p. 63). Lemert calls their deviance "secondary," because this conduct is not generated by the original causes of primary deviance but rather falls into a "special class of socially defined responses which people make to problems created by the societal reaction to their deviance" (p. 63).*

The distinction between primary and secondary deviance is conceptually appealing, but Lemert's assertion that they have different causes is problematic. Like other labeling theory arguments, a key issue is whether societal reaction is in fact required to create offenders who are deeply embedded—both psychologically and behaviorally—in a criminal lifestyle. Current criminological theory and research would suggest that stable involvement in crime is rooted more fully in individual differences and in family, school, and community life (see, e.g., Gottfredson and Hirschi, Chapter 19; Moffitt, Chapter 5; Sampson and Laub, Chapter 20). Still, societal reaction is not inconsequential. While it may not be the main source of persistent criminality, societal reaction can reinforce a criminal lifestyle and make desistance from crime more difficult.

References

Lemert, Edwin M. 1972. *Human Deviance, Social Problems, and Social Control,* 2nd edition. Englewood Cliffs, NJ: Prentice-Hall.

Types of Deviation

. . . There has been an embarrassingly large number of theories, often without any relationship to a general theory, advanced to account for various specific pathologies in human behavior. For certain types of pathology, such as alcoholism, crime, or stuttering, there are almost as many theories as there are writers on these subjects. This has been occasioned in no small way by the preoccupation with the origins of pathological behavior and by the fallacy of confusing *original* causes with *effective* causes. All such theories have elements of truth, and the divergent viewpoints they contain can be reconciled with the general theory here if it is granted that original causes or antecedents of deviant behaviors are many and diversified. This holds especially for the psychological process leading to similar pathological behavior, but it also holds for the situational concomitants of the intitial aberrant conduct. A person may come to use excessive alcohol not only for a wide variety of subjective reasons but also because of diversified situational influences, such as the death of a loved one, business failure, or participating in some sort of organized group activity calling for heavy drinking of liquor. Whatever the original reasons for violating the norms of the community, they are important only for certain research purposes, such as assessing the extent of the "social problem" at a given time or determining the requirements for a rational program of social control. From a narrower sociological viewpoint the deviations are not significant until they are organized subjectively and transformed into active roles and become the social criteria for assigning status. The deviant individuals must react symbolically to their own behavior aberrations and fix them in their sociopsychological patterns. The deviations remain primary deviations or symptomatic and situational as long as they are rationalized or otherwise dealt with as functions of a socially acceptable role. Under such conditions normal and pathological behaviors remain strange and somewhat tensional bedfellows in the same person. Undeniably a vast amount of such segmental and partially integrated pathological behavior exists in our society and has impressed many writers in the field of social pathology.

Just how far and for how long a person may go in dissociating his sociopathic tendencies so that they are merely troublesome adjuncts of normally conceived roles is not known. Perhaps it depends upon the number of alternative definitions of the same overt behavior that he can develop; perhaps certain physiological factors (limits) are also involved. However, if the deviant acts are repetitive and have a high visibility, and if there is a severe societal reaction, which, through a process of identification is incorporated as part of the "me" of the individual, the probability is greatly increased that the integration of existing roles will be disrupted and that reorganization based upon a new role or roles will occur. (The "me" in this context is simply the subjective aspect of the societal reaction.) Reorganization may be the adoption of another normal role in which the tendencies previously defined as "pathological" are given a more acceptable social expression. The other general possibility is the assumption of a deviant role, if such exists; or, more rarely, the person may organize an aberrant sect or group in which he creates a special role of his own. *When a person begins to employ his deviant behavior or a role based upon it as a means of defense, attack, or adjustment to the overt and covert problems created by the consequent societal reaction to him, his deviation is secondary.* Objective evidences of this change will be found in the symbolic appurtenances of the new role, in clothes, speech, posture, and mannerisms, which in some cases heighten social visibility, and which in some cases serve as symbolic cues to professionalization.

Role Conceptions of the Individual Must Be Reinforced by Reactions of Others

It is seldom that one deviant act will provoke a sufficiently strong societal reaction to bring about secondary deviation, unless in the process of introjection the individual imputes or projects meanings into the social situation which are not present. In this case anticipatory fears are involved. For example, in a culture where a child is taught sharp distinctions between "good" women and "bad" women, a single act of questionable morality might conceivably have a profound meaning for the girl so indulging. However, in the absence of reactions by the person's family, neighbors, or the larger community, reinforcing the tentative "bad-girl" self-definition, it is questionable whether a transition to secondary deviation would take place. It is also doubtful whether a temporary exposure to a severe punitive reaction by the community will lead a person to identify himself with a pathological role, unless, as we have said, the experience is highly traumatic. Most frequently there is a progressive reciprocal relationship between the deviation of the individual and the societal reaction, with a compounding of the societal reaction out of the minute accretions in the deviant behavior, until a point is reached where ingrouping and outgrouping between society and the deviant is manifest. At this point a stigmatizing of the deviant occurs in the form of name calling, labeling, or stereotyping.

The sequence of interaction leading to secondary deviation is roughly as follows: (1) primary deviation; (2) social penalties; (3) further primary deviation; (4) stronger penalties and rejections; (5) further deviation, perhaps with hostilities and resentment beginning to focus upon those doing the penalizing; (6) crisis reached in the tolerance quotient, expressed in formal action by the community stigmatizing of the deviant; (7) strengthening of the deviant conduct as a reaction to the stigmatizing and penalties; (8) ultimate acceptance of deviant social status and efforts at adjustment on the basis of the associated role.

As an illustration of this sequence the behavior of an errant schoolboy can be cited. For one reason or another, let us say excessive energy, the schoolboy engages in a classroom prank. He is penalized for it by the teacher. Later, due to clumsiness, he creates another disturbance and again he is reprimanded. Then, as sometimes happens, the boy is blamed for something he did not do. When the teacher uses the tag "bad boy" or "mischief maker" or other invidious terms, hostility and resentment are excited in the boy, and he may feel that he is blocked in playing the role expected of him. Thereafter, there may be a strong temptation to assume his role in the class as defined by the teacher, particularly when he discovers that there are rewards as well as penalties deriving from such a role. There is, of course, no implication here that such boys go on to become delinquents or criminals, for the mischief-maker role may later become integrated with or retrospectively rationalized as part of a role more acceptable to school authorities. If such a boy continues this unacceptable role

and becomes delinquent, the process must be accounted for in the light of the general theory of this volume. There must be a spreading corroboration of a sociopathic self-conception and societal reinforcement at each step in the process.

The most significant personality changes are manifest when societal definitions and their subjective counterpart become generalized. When this happens, the range of major role choices becomes narrowed to one general class. This was very obvious in the case of a young girl who was the daughter of a paroled convict and who was attending a small Middle Western college. She continually argued with herself and with the author, in whom she had confided, that in reality she belonged on the "other side of the railroad tracks" and that her life could be enormously simplified by acquiescing in this verdict and living accordingly. While in her case there was a tendency to dramatize her conflicts, nevertheless there was enough societal reinforcement of her self-conception by the treatment she received in her relationship with her father and on dates with college boys to lend it a painful reality. Once these boys took her home to the shoddy dwelling in a slum area where she lived with her father, who was often in a drunken condition, they abruptly stopped seeing her again or else became sexually presumptive. . . .

Discussion Questions

1. What is the difference between primary and secondary deviance?

2. What is meant by the concept of a "societal reaction"? How do the reactions of others affect someone who is being defined as a deviant? Why does this lead, in Lemert's words, to "secondary deviance"?

3. What are the policy implications of Lemert's theory? For example, what would be the best way to respond to youths who are caught committing delinquent acts? ✦

29

Reflected Appraisals, Parental Labeling, and Delinquency

Ross L. Matsueda

Matsueda consciously roots his theory of delinquency in the larger sociological perspective of symbolic interactionism. This perspective contends that all individuals have a "self"—a conception of who one is—that is instrumental in directing behavior. The self arises in the process of socialization as individuals "take the role of the other" and receive messages or "appraisals" of who they are. These appraisals are perceived, more or less accurately, and reflected upon by the person. In this sense, the self is "formed as an object from the standpoint of others" (Matsueda, 1992: 1581). This self-conception can be stable, which accounts for why an individual's behavior can be stable across time and situation. Even so, the self is an ongoing accomplishment, which can be transformed if a person confronts either altered appraisals from others or new social situations.

Existing theories of crime largely ignore the potential role of the "self" in the etiology of unlawful behavior. Matsueda's contribution is in showing that self-conceptions may well be implicated in directing youths into delinquency. He pays special attention to "reflected appraisals," which he defines as a person's view of how other people see him or her. "Those who see themselves (from the standpoint of others) as persons who engage in delinquent behavior in certain situations," observes Matsueda (1992: 1582), "are more likely to engage in delinquency."

Matsueda does not deny that engaging in delinquent behavior can affect self-conceptions.

Even so, he places special emphasis on how youths are "appraised" or labeled by "significant others," such as parents. Recall that the self is an "object" that is formed by individuals reflecting on how others see them. Hence, if parents send messages to their child that he or she is a "troublemaker" or a "delinquent," these appraisals are reflected upon, shape the self, and make delinquent action more likely. Reflected appraisals thus are the link between parental labeling and delinquency. Using data from the National Youth Survey, Matsueda (1992) has confirmed this causal sequence (see also, Bartusch and Matsueda, 1996).

The use of survey data on individual respondents, however, assesses only part of Matsueda's perspective. As a symbolic interactionist theory, an important issue is how youths in the process of group interaction come to the point of breaking the law. Each youth in a group brings a self-conception to the interaction, but an individual youth's behavior is not shaped only by his or her personal sense of "self." Instead, a dynamic process ensues in which individual participants announce who they are and initiate actions that are reacted to by others and, in turn, that they then reflect upon. From this ongoing "conversation of gestures," a line of action emerges, which may or may not be delinquent.

Thus, in the course of social transactions, "the important mechanism by which interactants influence each other is role-taking, which consists of projecting oneself into the role of other persons and appraising, from their standpoint, the situation, oneself in the situation, and possible lines of action" (1992: 1580). In situations where misconduct is possible, argues Matsueda (1992: 1580), individuals "take each others' roles through verbal and nonverbal communication, fitting their lines of action together into joint delinquent behavior." The forthcoming challenge for criminologists is to use this perspective to guide qualitative research so as to illuminate the situational dynamics of delinquency.

References

Bartusch, Dawn Jeglum and Ross L. Matsueda. 1996. "Gender, Reflected Appraisals, and Labeling: A Cross-Group Test of an Interactionist Theory of Delinquency." *Social Forces* 75: 145-177.

Matsueda, Ross L. 1992. "Reflected Appraisals, Parental Labeling, and Delinquency: Specifying a Symbolic Interactionist Theory." *American Journal of Sociology* 6: 1577-1611.

An important question in the study of social control involves the mechanisms by which informal groups control the behavior of members. Much research on informal controls and delinquent behavior has examined relationships between parental socialization, self-concepts, and delinquency. As Wells and Rankin (1983) put it, self-concepts should be an important mediating factor in delinquency, intervening between parental socialization and delinquent behavior. Accordingly, researchers have produced a voluminous literature that investigates the relationship between self-concepts and delinquency. The results of that research have been disappointing. When conceptualized as global self-esteem or self-rejection, self-concepts appear to have modest or inconsistent effects on delinquent behavior. These results suggest the need for considering alternative conceptualizations of the self and its role in the process of social control.

In this article I will draw on the writings of George Herbert Mead (1934) and the school of symbolic interactionism to conceptualize the self as being rooted in social interaction, comprising multiple dimensions, and providing a crucial link between self-control and social control. I will draw on theories of labeling and reference groups to specify the broader determinants of the self and argue that delinquency is in part determined by one's appraisals of self from the standpoint of others. . . .

Self-Control as Social Control: A Conception of Self Based on Mead

The perspective of symbolic interactionism presupposes that social order is the product of an ongoing process of social interaction and communication. Of central importance is the process by which shared meanings, behavioral expectations, and re-flected appraisals are built up in interaction and applied to behavior. These shared meanings attach to positions in society and thus link individual conduct to the organization of groups and to social structure. Social structure—the patterned regularities in society—is an ongoing process, built up by social interactions; moreover, social structure in turn constrains the form and direction of these interactions by structuring communication patterns, interests, and opportunities (Stryker 1980). The specific mechanism linking interaction and social structure is role-taking.

Role-Taking and Delinquency

To analyze interaction, symbolic interactionists define the unit of analysis as the transaction, which consists of an interaction between two or more individuals. Within transactions, the important mechanism by which interactants influence each other is role-taking, which consists of projecting oneself into the role of other persons and appraising, from their standpoint, the situation, oneself in the situation, and possible lines of action. With regard to delinquency, individuals confronted with delinquent behavior as a possible line of action take each other's roles through verbal and nonverbal communication, fitting their lines of action together into joint delinquent behavior (Mead 1934; Blumer 1969).

The transaction is built up through this dynamic process of reciprocal role-taking: one person initiates action—say, an unlawful act—a second takes the role of the other and responds, then the first person reacts to the response, and so on, until the jointly developed goal is reached, a new goal is substituted, or the transaction simply fades. Through reciprocal role-taking, or a conversation of gestures, consensus over situational goals and the appropriate means for attaining those goals is constructed, individual lines of action are coordinated, and there is concerted action toward achieving the goal (Blumer 1969). Thus, the initiated delinquent act of one youth might elicit a negative response from another youth, causing the group to search for another, more suitable alternative. Whether or not a goal is achieved using unlawful means is determined by each individual's contribution to the direction of the transaction; those contributions, in turn, are determined by the individual's prior life experience or biography (Hewitt 1988).

Early in the socialization process, individuals engage in a serial process of taking the role of specific significant others who are present in the interaction. Later in the socialization process, individuals learn to take the role of the entire group or "generalized other," which includes the norms, rules, and expectations governing various positions and roles of a group, community, or society. Here, individuals learn to relate the activities and expectations of their roles to the activities and expectations of other roles within an organized system (Mead 1934, pp. 152-64). This form of taking the role of an organized and abstract group appears in more institutionalized settings and constitutes the most effective form of social control, since the organized institutions and norms enter individual behavior.

Role-taking also provides a framework for an interactionist theory of cognition. Cognitive processes arise in problematic situations, in which a line of action (impulse) is temporarily blocked by physical objects in the situation, by verbal responses of others, or by subjective reactions such as repugnance, shame, and fear (Shibutani 1961). The blocked impulse is transformed into a self-image (the self as an object or the "me"), consisting of alternative lines of action, anticipated reactions of others, and, most significantly, a view of self from the standpoint of others. The line of action is then reacted to by another impulse (the "I"), which either reacts positively and follows the line of action into overt behavior or reacts negatively, blocking the impulse to act and eliciting another self-image. This cognitive process continues until the problem is solved or the transaction ends. Thus, cognition is identical, in form and content, to role-taking between interactants, except that it occurs in the mind in an imaginative rehearsal between the "I" and the "me" (Mead 1934).

Moreover, similar situations will call out similar "me's"—the self formed as an object from the standpoint of others. Therefore, a stable self arises because the self-images ("me's") called up in a situation, to which the "I" will react, will resemble previous "I's" and "me's" from similar past situations. This stable set of self-images is multidimensional, containing an organized set of stable meanings about oneself from the standpoint of others. Mead (1934, p. 142) termed this self "multiple personality" to emphasize that it is a reflection of the organized social process; McCall and Simmons (1978) and Stryker (1980) conceptualized it as "role-identities" to emphasize that it corresponds to the many social roles one plays; and Kinch (1963) conceived it as "reflected appraisals" to emphasize that it is a reflection of appraisals made by significant others. With regard to delinquency, the important element of the self formed as an object is the specific meaning or content of the self with respect to delinquency. Those who see themselves (from the standpoint of others) as persons who engage in delinquent behavior in certain situations are more likely to engage in delinquency. Thus, if the self as a delinquent is an important dimension of the self for individuals, such that it endures across situations, it should predict individuals' delinquent behavior.

Most behavior, particularly in highly institutionalized and routinized transactions, occurs in nonproblematic situations and results from nonreflective habitual behavior, based on the way in which previous problematic situations were resolved. When a problematic situation is repeatedly encountered, it becomes less problematic, as one learns to resolve it proficiently. Eventually, the situation becomes nonproblematic and the behavior habitual. This implies that over time, delinquent behavior will become increasingly stable, so long as one encounters similar situations. Of course, behavior will not be completely stable because situations are in part selected through cognitive processes and the response of the "I" is not completely determined by the "me."

The process by which role-taking can lead to delinquent behavior is illustrated by four classic studies of delinquency. Briar and Piliavin (1965) found that boys freed from commitments to conventional lines of action are often incited into delinquency by "situationally induced motives," which are verbal motives presented by other boys. Free from considering the reactions of conventional others, these boys can take the role of each other, present delinquent motives, and jointly adopt a delinquent line of action. Short and Strodtbeck (1965) noted that one's decision to join a gang fight often revolves around the risk of losing status within the gang. Gang members would take the role of the group, consider the group's negative reactions, and join in on the action for fear of losing status. Cohen (1955) argued that adolescent groups engage in a tentative probing conversation of gestures—a process best characterized as one of trial and error—and collectively innovate a new status hierarchy, a delinquent subculture. Finally, Gibbons (1971) claimed that as a result of group interactions, novel shades of norms and values emerge to influence the direction of joint behavior (Short 1974). Such processes, consistent with Smelser's (1963) "value added" and Turner's (1964) "emergent norm" approaches to collective behavior, show how a group controls the behavior of its members within a situation.

This discussion of role-taking implies four major features for a theory of the self and delinquent behavior. First, the self consists of an individual's perception of how others view him or her, and thus, is rooted in symbolic interaction. Second, the self as an object arises partly endogenously within situations, and partly exogenously from prior situational selves being carried over from previous experience. This results because self-images ("me's") called up in a situation will resemble previous "me's," while the "I" will respond in novel ways arising from the immediate situation. Thus, we can speak of a set of patterned selves that is somewhat stable over time but varies across individuals. Third, the self as an object is a *process* determined by the self at a previous point in time and by prior behavior (resolutions of problematic situations). Fourth, delinquent behavior will result in part from the formation of habits and in part from stable perceptions of oneself from the standpoint of others. Through the latter process, delinquency is controlled by one's reference groups.

Role-Taking, Reference Groups, and Delinquency

Role-taking usually entails taking the role of members of one's reference group, which is a group that serves as a source of one's values, perspectives, and self-comparisons. Reference groups consist of individual significant others, such as parents, friends, and teachers, but also organized groups (generalized others) such as classmates, gangs, and families. In mass societies, members have multiple reference groups; which significant other or reference group is invoked *within a given situation* depends on many factors, the most important of which is the relevance of the group to the perceived problematic situation at hand. Moreover, those persons we care about, from whom we gain personal status, and who have helped form our self-image in the past, are most likely to be selected, since we want to maintain a favorable self-image in their eyes.

More broadly, an adolescent's multiple reference groups are determined by a complex set of individual variables, such as propinquity (Festinger 1954) and his or her perception that the group will provide a positive self-image (Hyman and Singer 1968). These individual determinants are structured by communication channels, which in turn are patterned by the larger social structure (Hewitt 1988, p. 125). I would expect that communication channels will be influenced by structural variables such as social class, family structure, residential area, and neighborhood structure, as well as individual characteristics such as age, race, sex, and cognitive ability. Thus, social structure should affect delinquency by structuring communication channels and reference groups, which in turn influence self-control—engaging in self-conscious reflective behavior. Therefore, self-control is social control because social structure enters behavior through role-taking, and because the self is constructed in a social process (Blumer 1969). We might term this "differential social control," since the direction of control—whether toward delinquency or toward conformity—differs by the problematic situation, the reference group, and the prior views of self by the individual (Glaser 1979).

Reflected Appraisals of Self and Delinquent Behavior

The foregoing discussion implies a specific conception of the self as a mechanism of social control. While the self as an object arises in problematic situations, we can also conceive of a self, in the form of consistent "me's," that is relatively stable across situations. Such a self, specified by Cooley (1922) as a "looking-glass self," and by Mead (1934) as the "self as an object," is a process consisting of three components: how others actually see one (others' actual appraisals); how one perceives the way others see one (reflected appraisals); and how one sees oneself (self-appraisals). Thus, one's self is in part a "reflected appraisal" of how significant others appraise one (Kinch 1963; Felson 1985). . . .

An interactionist conception of self as social control, however, does not imply a one-to-one correspondence between reflected appraisals and actual appraisals (Hewitt 1988, p. 129). Clearly, reflected appraisals are the result of *selective perception* of actual appraisals, which depends on the particular problematic situations that give rise to the reflected appraisals. Thus, reflected appraisals should be only partially a function of actual appraisals. . . .

Long ago, Kinch (1963) derived a theoretical model of reflected appraisals and behaviour from symbolic interactionism, which posits a long causal chain (see the top section of fig. 29.1). According to the model, initial behavior determines others' actual appraisals of a person, which in turn, lead to the person's reflected appraisals of self; reflected appraisals then determine self-appraisals, which in turn, lead to behavior. The model implies that, in the causal sequence explaining behavior, each antecedent variable in the model is entirely mediated by each subsequent variable. In light of the theoretical discussion above, I can derive a more plausible model of reflected appraisals and behavior.

The revised model, diagrammed in the bottom section of Figure 29.1, follows Kinch by specifying that actual appraisals by others affect behavior only by affecting one's reflected appraisals of self. The alternative hypothesis, which contradicts symbolic interactionism, posits that actual appraisals influence behavior directly, regardless of reflected appraisals (indicated by a broken line in the bottom section of Fig. 29.1). This could result if significant others are particularly proficient at appraising one and, therefore, predicting one's behavior or if other elements of the self besides reflected appraisals mediate actual appraisals. Moreover, the model diverges from Kinch's model in three ways. First, it deletes self-appraisals from the

Figure 29.1
Alternative Models of Reflected Appraisals

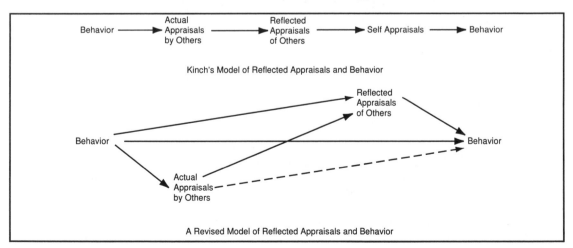

Behavior ⟶ Actual Appraisals by Others ⟶ Reflected Appraisals of Others ⟶ Self Appraisals ⟶ Behavior

Kinch's Model of Reflected Appraisals and Behavior

A Revised Model of Reflected Appraisals and Behavior

model, stipulating reflected appraisals of self as the key variable for explaining behavior. Second, it allows behavior to have a direct effect on subsequent behavior. This is consistent with our theoretical framework, which posits that institutionalized behavior, corresponding to Mead's (1934) nonreflective behavior and Dewey's (1922) habitual behavior, occurs in nonproblematic situations and is determined not by role-taking but by prior behavior. Third, it allows behavior to have a direct effect on reflected appraisals, since those appraisals are formed in part from previous behavioral solutions to problematic situations. Symbolic interactionism would predict that reflected appraisals are determined more by actual appraisals of others than by past behavior.

This last model can explain the relationships between parental appraisals, reflected appraisals, and delinquent behavior. It allows me to test three restrictions specified by Kinch (1963): (1) prior delinquency has no direct effect on later delinquency; (2) prior behavior has no direct effect on reflected appraisals; and (3) actual appraisals have no direct effect on future delinquency. To link these social psychological mechanisms to broader determinants of delinquency, I turn to labeling theory.

The Parental Context of Control: Labeling and Reflected Appraisals

Most etiological statements of labeling theory, particularly Tannenbaum's (1938) concept of the dramatization of evil, Lemert's (1951) concept of secondary deviance, and Mead's ([1918] 1964) concept of the hostile attitude of punitive justice, are rooted in the perspective of symbolic interactionism. Therefore, we can draw on labeling theory to specify the broader social determinants of the reflected appraisal process (see Elliott, Ageton, and Canter 1979; Farrell and Swigert 1988).

Focusing primarily on the negative consequences of labeling an individual as "deviant" or "delinquent," labeling theory argues that initial acts of delinquency are relatively harmless instances of primary deviance. From the standpoint of the child, such acts

are defined as "play" or "mischief"; however, from the standpoint of the larger community, they are viewed as "evil" or as a "law violation." The community's response, which initially includes reactions of parents, teachers, and peers, and later encompasses reactions of the juvenile justice system, is to label the child as "bad" or "evil." The label, in turn, influences the self-image of the child, who comes to view him or herself as bad or delinquent, which in turn increases the likelihood of future deviance. Eventually, this spiraling labeling process can leave the youth in the hands of juvenile justice officials—cut off from conventional society, stigmatized by parents and teachers, and left with a delinquent self-image. Thus, a self-fulfilling prophecy is set up: through this process of deviance amplification, or secondary deviance, an otherwise conforming child may eventually respond to the initial labeling of harmless acts by confirming the delinquent label (Tannenbaum 1938). Mead (1964) argued that the hostile response of the criminal justice system, under the justification of deterrence or retribution, could operate to exacerbate rather than ameliorate the crime problem, perhaps creating a stable criminal class (Hagan and Palloni 1990).

A hallmark of labeling theory is the proposition that deviant labels are not randomly distributed across the social structure, but are instead more likely to apply to the powerless, the disadvantaged, and the poor. Because of existing stereotypes—which portray criminals as members of lower classes, minorities, urban dwellers, and young adults—individuals who belong to such groups are more likely than others to be labeled delinquent (Simmons 1965; Farrell and Swigert 1978, 1988). Because these stereotypes are widespread in society, they are likely to be used not only by members of the juvenile justice system, but also by parents, teachers, and peers. While actual deviant behavior increases the likelihood of being labeled a deviant, delinquency is not a necessary condition for being labeled. The "falsely accused" are persons who refrain from deviance but get labeled anyway (Becker 1963). Moreover, the powerless, having fewer cultural and material resources at their disposal, may be more likely to accept deviant labels. Again, the result is a self-fulfilling prophecy: members of disadvantaged groups are labeled delinquent, which alters their self-conceptions and causes them to deviate, thus fulfilling the prophecy of their initial label. Finally, labels are not restricted to deviance. One can be labeled a conformist or a success at conventional activity, which should increase the likelihood of conventional behavior, while decreasing the likelihood of deviance.

Empirical research on labeling theory has produced equivocal results. While some research has found official labeling to have trivial effects on self-image (Gibbs 1974), especially when prior self-reported delinquency is controlled (Hepburn 1977), other research has found official labels to have effects for some youth (whites and nonserious delinquents) but not others (Ageton and Elliott 1974). In summarizing this research, Jensen (1980) concluded that official labeling may have a greater impact on delinquent self-images and attitudes among those less heavily involved in delinquency. Research on the effect of official labeling on subsequent delinquent behavior has found positive effects on delinquency (Meade 1974), but when prior levels of self-reported delinquency are controlled, the results have been inconsistent (Thomas and Bishop 1984; Ray and Downs 1986). Recently, Hagan and Palloni (1990) found evidence that official labeling of parents and sons interacts to produce greater self-reported delinquency. They conclude that labeling leads to an intergenerational reproduction of a criminal class, which supports the ideas of Mead, Tannenbaum, and Lemert. While this research literature has led some researchers to dismiss labeling theory (Hirschi 1980), others have concluded that attention should focus more on the consequences of informal rather than official labels (Paternoster and Iovanni 1989). Menard and Morse (1984) found support for the latter proposition: perceived informal social labels had substantial effects on delinquency and helped mediate the effect of IQ on delinquency.

Labeling theory can help specify the relationships between background characteristics, the informal labeling process, and delinquency. First, youths who have engaged in delinquent behavior should be more likely to be labeled delinquent by their parents. Second, insofar as parents act on conventional stereotypes of deviance, their appraisals of their children as either deviant or conforming may be influenced by structural conditions that reflect disadvantages. Urban, minority, lower-class, older adolescent youths may be more likely to be labeled by their parents as deviant and less likely labeled as conforming, in part because they engage in more objective deviance. Indeed, parents could act on stereotypes to such an extent that those parents of disadvantaged children are more likely to label their children deviant, regardless of their children's behavior. This would constitute strong evidence for a labeling perspective since the parents share the disadvantages of their children but nevertheless still act on conventional stereotypes. Third, parental appraisals of youths as deviant or conforming will influence their further delinquency, primarily by influencing youths' reflected appraisals of self as deviant or conforming. . . .

Reprinted from Ross L. Matsueda, "Reflected Appraisals, Parental Labeling, and Delinquency" in the *American Journal of Sociology* 6. Copyright © 1992 by the University of Chicago Press. Reprinted by permission of the University of Chicago Press.

Discussion Questions

1. How is the self formed? Why are "reflected appraisals" important? How does the self affect the way in which people behave?

2. According to Matsueda, what is the main reason that juveniles commit delinquent acts?

3. Does Matsueda believe that youths must be labeled by the criminal justice system to become involved in delinquency? Why not?

4. Why would Matsueda's perspective be classified as a "labeling theory"? ✦

30

Crime, Shame, and Reintegration

John Braithwaite

Braithwaite's central thesis is that crime is higher when shaming is stigmatizing and lower when shaming is reintegrative. This thesis explains both why some societies have higher rates of crime than others and why some individuals are more likely to offend that others.

At the macro-level, Braithwaite starts with assumptions that mirror social disorganization theory: societies marked by urbanization and residential mobility are less "communitarian" and less likely to have interdependency between its citizens. When societies lack communitarianism—that is, when individuals are not "densely enmeshed in interdependencies which have the special qualities of mutuality and trust" (1989: 100)—they will engage in shaming that is stigmatizing. As large numbers of people are stigmatized, they come together to develop ongoing criminal subcultural groups that provide learning environments for crime and "illegitimate opportunities to indulge tastes." At any given time, stigmatized individuals have incentives to participate in these ongoing subcultural groups because they are excluded from conventional society. Furthermore, the process of stigmatization has a feedback effect that erodes communitarianism. The end result is a society—such as the United States—that has a high crime rate.

On the micro-level, stigmatizing shaming has its greatest negative effects on individuals with few social bonds to conventional society—especially young, unmarried, unemployed males. Lacking interdependencies that might blunt stigma and foster reintegration, these rejected individuals have their social bonds further attenuated. As controls weaken, they join criminal subcultural groups in which antisocial values are reinforced and illegitimate opportunities are made available. In short, stigmatizing shaming evokes the conditions that control theory and differential association theory link to crime. The result is the continued, if not heightened, involvement of the individual offender in criminal activities.

Unlike labeling theorists, Braithwaite does not suggest that nonintervention is the most effective criminal justice policy. In fact, shaming is necessary for social control: the offender and the larger community benefit from a public ceremony in which the criminal act—but not the criminal—is defined as immoral. This moralizing is also done informally by those in the offenders' social networks. The key issue is what follows shaming: reintegration or stigmatization. Reintegration is essential because shamed individuals are at a turning point in their lives—a time when they can reattach to conventional society or deepen their commitment to crime. When quality social relations exist, they provide the means through which offenders are given the forgiveness and support needed to become a member of the community.

Within the United States, "restorative justice" programs most closely mirror Braithwaite's admonition to meld shaming with reintegration. In these programs, the goal is to "restore" both the victim, who has been harmed, and the offender, who has done the harming. Victims are likely to receive both restitution and, after conveying to the offender in a face-to-face encounter the pains they have experienced, a public apology. Repentant offenders potentially are granted a measure of forgiveness by victims and are reaccepted by family and community.

Such attempts at shaming and reintegration present an appealing alternative to stigmatizing criminal justice sanctions (see Braithwaite and Mugford, 1994; Makkai and Braithwaite, 1991). It remains to be demonstrated, however, that these interventions have the capacity to alter the life course of persistent offenders. The critical issue, it would seem, is not the public ceremony in which shaming occurs but the quality of the reintegration that follows. Unless these efforts at reintegration are prolonged and target for change the known predictors of recidivism, the reform of offenders is unlikely (see Andrews and Bonta, 1994).

References

Andrews, D. A. and James Bonta. 1994. *The Psychology of Criminal Conduct*. Cincinnati: Anderson.

Braithwaite, John. 1989. *Crime, Shame and Reintegration*. Cambridge, UK: Cambridge University Press.

Braithwaite, John and Stephen Mugford. 1994. "Conditions of Successful Reintegration Ceremonies: Dealing with Juvenile Offenders." *British Journal of Sociology* 34: 139-171.

Makkai, Tony and John Braithwaite. 1994. "Reintegrative Shaming and Compliance with Regulatory Standards." *Criminology* 32: 361-386.

The theory in this book suggests that the key to crime control is cultural commitments to shaming in ways that I call reintegrative. Societies with low crime rates are those that shame potently and judiciously; individuals who resort to crime are those insulated from shame over their wrongdoing. However, shame can be applied injudiciously and counterproductively; the theory seeks to specify the types of shaming which cause rather than prevent crime. . . .

The first step to productive theorizing about crime is to think about the contention that labeling offenders makes things worse. The contention is both right and wrong. The theory of reintegrative shaming is an attempt to specify when it is right and when wrong. The distinction is between shaming that leads to stigmatization—to outcasting, to confirmation of a deviant master status—versus shaming that is reintegrative, that shames while maintaining bonds of respect or love, that sharply terminates disapproval with forgiveness, instead of amplifying deviance by progressively casting the deviant out. Reintegrative shaming controls crime; stigmatization pushes offenders toward criminal subcultures. . . .

The theory of reintegrative shaming posits that the consequence of stigmatization is attraction to criminal subcultures. Subcultures supply the outcast offender with the opportunity to reject her rejectors, thereby maintaining a form of self-respect. In contrast, the consequence of reintegrative shaming is that criminal subcultures appear less attractive to the offender. Shaming is the most potent weapon of social control unless it shades into stigmatization. Formal criminal punishment is an ineffective weapon of social control party because it is a degradation ceremony with maximum prospects for stigmatization.

The nub of the theory of reintegrative shaming is therefore about the effectiveness of reintegrative shaming and the counterproductivity of stigmatization in controlling crime. In addition, the theory posits a number of conditions that make for effective shaming. Individuals are more susceptible to shaming when they are enmeshed in multiple relationships of interdependency; societies shame more effectively when they are communitarian. Variables like urbanization and residential mobility predict communitarianism, while variables like age and gender predict individual interdependency. A schematic summary of these aspects of the theory is presented in Figure 30.1 (page [289]).

Some of the ways that the theory of reintegrative shaming builds on earlier theories should now be clear. Interdependency is the stuff of control theory; stigmatization comes from labeling theory; subculture formation is accounted for in opportunity theory terms; subcultural influences are naturally in the realm of subcultural theory; and the whole theory can be understood in integrative cognitive social learning theory terms such as are provided by differential association. . . .

Preventing Crime

We have seen that the micro process of shaming an individual has consequences far beyond the life of that individual. The social process of gossip links a micro incident into a macro pattern. A shaming incident reinforces cultural patterns which underwrite further cultural products like a moralistic children's story, a television program, a schoolteacher's homily. The latter modalities of public (societal) shaming exert pressure for further private (individual) shaming.

The reasons why reintegrative shaming works in preventing crime might be summarized as follows:

1. The deterrence literature suggests that specific deterrence associated with detection

for criminal offending works primarily through fear of shame in the eyes of intimates rather than fear of formal punishment.

2. Shame not only specifically deters the shamed offender, it also generally deters many others who also wish to avoid shame and who participate in or become aware of the incident of shaming.

3. Both the specific and general deterrent effects of shame will be greater for persons who remain strongly attached in relationships of interdependency and affection because such persons will accrue greater interpersonal costs from shame. This is one reason why reintegrative shaming makes for more effective social control than stigmatization.

4. A second reason for the superiority of reintegrative shaming over stigmatization is that the latter can be counterproductive by breaking attachments to those who might shame future criminality and by increasing the attractiveness of groups that provide social support for crime.

5. However, most compliance with the law is not achieved through either specific or general deterrence. Most of us comply with the law most of the time, not because we rationally weigh our fear of the consequences of detection against the benefits of the crime, but because to commit the crime is simply unthinkable to us. Shaming is the social process which leads to the cognition that a particular type of crime is unthinkable. Cultures where the social process of shaming is muted are cultures where citizens often do not internalize abhorrence for crime.

6. A third reason for the superiority of the reintegrative shaming over stigmatization is that a combination of shame at and repentance by the offender is a more powerful affirmation of the criminal law than one-sided moralizing. A shaming ceremony followed later by a forgiveness and repentance ceremony more potently builds commitment to the law than a shaming ceremony alone. Nothing has greater symbolic force in community-wide conscience-building than repentance.

7. Because shaming is a participatory form of social control, compared with formal sanctioning which is more professionalized than

participatory, shaming builds consciences through citizens being instruments as well as targets of social control. Participation in expressions of abhorrence toward the criminal acts of others is part of what makes crime an abhorrent choice for ourselves to make.

8. Once consciences have been formed by cultural processes of shaming and repentance, pangs of conscience become the most effective punishment for crime because whereas conscience delivers a timely anxiety response to every involvement in crime, other negative reinforcers, including shame, are delivered unreliably or with delay.

9. Shaming is therefore both the social process which builds consciences, and the most important backstop to be used when consciences fail to deliver conformity. Formal punishment is another backstop, but a less effective one than reintegrative shaming.

10. Gossip within wider circles of acquaintances and shaming of offenders not even known to those who gossip are important for building consciences because so many crimes will not occur in the direct experience of limited groups like families. Societal incidents of shaming remind parents and teachers of the need to moralize with their children across the whole curriculum of crimes.

11. Public shaming puts pressure on parents, teachers and others to ensure that they engage in private shaming which is sufficiently systematic, and public shaming increasingly takes over the role of private shaming once children move away from the influence of the family and school. The latter is one reason why public shaming by courts of law has a more important role to play with strictly adult offenses like crimes against the environment than with predominantly juvenile offenses like vandalism.

12. Public shaming generalizes familiar principles to unfamiliar or new contexts. It integrates new categories of wrongdoing, which may arise from technological change into pre-existing moral frameworks. Public shaming transforms the loss of life in a battle at My Lai into a "war crime" and a "massacre", and through our distant involvement in the incident of shaming, the moral category of illegal killing acquires some expanded meanings.

13. Cultures with heavy emphasis on reintegrative shaming establish a smoother transition between socialization practices in the family and socialization in the wider society. Within the family, as the child grows, social control shifts from external to internal controls; punishment-oriented cultures set this process more starkly in reverse in the public domain than do shame-oriented cultures. To the extent that crime control can be made to work by continuing to catalyze internal controls it will be more effective; this is precisely why families are more effective agents of social control than police forces.

14. Gossip and other modalities of shaming can be especially effective when the targets of shame are not directly confronted with the shame, but are directly confronted with gestures of forgiveness or reintegration. Citizens who have learnt the culture do not have to be shamed to their faces to know that they are the subject of gossip, but they may need to be directly offered gestures of acceptance before they can be confident that they are again part of the community of law abiding citizens. In other words, shaming which is excessively confrontational renders the achievement of reintegration a tall order. There is thus something to be said for hypocrisy: our friends are likely to recover from a suspicion that we have stabbed them in the back, but stabbing them in the front can be divisive!

15. The effectiveness of shaming is often enhanced by shame being directed not only at the individual offender but also at her family, or her company if she is a corporate criminal. When a collectivity as well as an individual is shamed, collectivities are put on notice as to their responsibility to exercise informal control over their members, and the moralizing impact of shaming is multiplied. For reasons which will be elaborated in the next chapter, a shamed family or company will often transmit the shame to the individual offender in a manner which is as regenerative as possible. From the standpoint of the offender, the strategy of rejecting her rejectors may resuscitate her own self-esteem, but her loved ones or colleagues will soon let her know that sinking deeper into the deviant role will only exacerbate the shame they are suffering on her behalf.

The Theory of Reintegrative Shaming

Figure 30.1 provides a schematic summary of the theory. In the first part of this chapter clear definitions are attempted for the key concepts in Figure 30.1. The cluster of six variables around interdependency at the top left of Figure 30.1 are characteristics of individuals; the three at the top right are characteristics of societies; while high levels of crime and shaming are variables which apply to both individuals and societies. The theory as summarized in Figure 30.1 thus gives an account both of why some kinds of individuals and some kinds of societies exhibit more crime.

We could get a more parsimonious theory by collapsing the similar constructs of interdependency (an individual-level variable) and communitarianism (a societal variable) into a single construct, but then we would no longer have a framework to predict both which individuals and which societies will have more crime. On the desirability of being able to do this I can only agree with Cressey:

> A theory explaining social behavior in general, or any specific kind of social behavior, should have two distinct but consistent aspects. First, there must be a statement that explains the statistical distribution of the behavior in time and space (epidemiology), and from which predictive statements about unknown statistical distributions can be derived. Second, there must be a statement that identifies, at least by implication, the process by which individuals come to exhibit the behavior in question, and from which can be derived predictive statements about the behavior of individuals. (Cressey, 1960:47)

Key Concepts

Interdependency is a condition of individuals. It means the extent to which individuals participate in networks wherein they are dependent on others to achieve valued ends and others are dependent on them. We could describe an individual as in a state of interde-

Figure 30.1
Summary of the Theory of Reintegrative Shaming

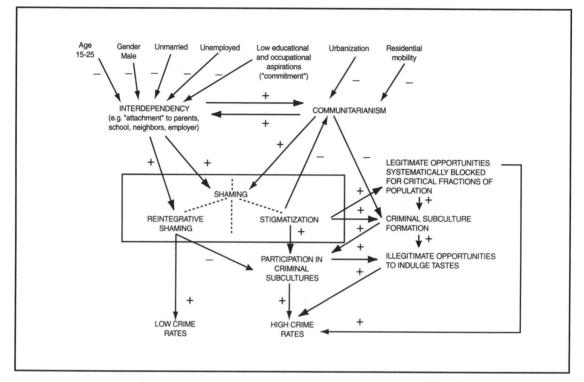

pendency even if the individuals who are dependent on him are different from the individuals on whom he is dependent. Interdependency is approximately equivalent to the social bonding, attachment and commitment of control theory.

Communitarianism is a condition of societies. In communitarian societies individuals are densely enmeshed in interdependencies which have the special qualities of mutual help and trust. The interdependencies have symbolic significance in the culture of group loyalties which take precedence over individual interests. The interdependencies also have symbolic significance as attachments which invoke personal obligation to others in a community of concern, rather than simply interdependencies of convenience as between a bank and a small depositor. A communitarian culture rejects any pejorative connotation of dependency as threatening individual autonomy. Communitarian cultures resist interpretations of dependency as weakness and emphasize the need for mutuality of

obligation in interdependency (to be both dependent and dependable). The Japanese are said to be socialized not only to *amaeru* (to be succored by others) but also to *amayakasu* (to be nurturing to others) (Wagatsuma and Rosett, 1986).

Shaming means all social processes of expressing disapproval which have the intention or effect of invoking remorse in the person being shamed and/or condemnation by others who become aware of the shaming. When associated with appropriate symbols, formal punishment often shames. But societies vary enormously in the extent to which formal punishment is associated with shaming or in the extent to which the social meaning of punishment is no more than to inflict pain to tip reward—cost calculations in favor of certain outcomes. Shaming, unlike purely deterrent punishment, sets out to moralize with the offender to communicate reasons for the evil of her actions. Most shaming is neither associated with formal punishment nor perpetrated by the state, though both shaming by the state and shaming with punishment are important types of shaming. Most shaming is by individuals within interdependent communities of concern.

Reintegrative shaming is shaming which is followed by efforts to reintegrate the offender back into the community of law-abiding or respectable citizens through words or gestures of forgiveness or ceremonies to decertify the offender as deviant. Shaming and reintegration do not occur simultaneously but sequentially, with reintegration occurring before deviance becomes a master status. It is shaming which labels the act as evil while striving to preserve the identity of the offender as essentially good. It is directed at signifying evil deeds rather than evil persons in the Christian tradition of "hate the sin and love the sinner." Specific disapproval is expressed within relationships characterized by general social approval; shaming criminal behavior is complemented by ongoing social rewarding of alternative behavior patterns. Reintregrative shaming is not necessarily weak; it can be cruel, even vicious. It is not distinguished from stigmatization by its potency, but by (a) a finite rather than open-ended duration which is terminated by forgiveness; and by (b) efforts to maintain bonds of love or respect throughout the finite period of suffering shame.

Stigmatization is disintegrative shaming in which no effort is made to reconcile the offender with the community. The offender is outcast, her deviance is allowed to become a master status, degradation ceremonies are not followed by ceremonies to decertify deviance.

Criminal subcultures are sets of rationalizations and conduct norms which cluster together to support criminal behavior. The clustering is usually facilitated by subcultural groups which provide systematic social support for crime in any of a number of ways—supplying members with criminal opportunities, criminal values, attitudes which weaken conventional values of law-abidingness, or techniques of neutralizing conventional values.

Short Summary of the Theory

The following might serve as the briefest possible summary of the theory. A variety of life circumstances increase the chances that individuals will be in situations of greater interpendency, the most important being age (under 15 and over 25), being married, female, employed, and having high employment and educational aspirations. Interdependent persons are more susceptible to shaming. More importantly, societies in which individuals are subject to extensive interdependencies are more likely to be communitarian, and shaming is much more widespread and potent in communitarian societies. Urbanization and high residential mobility are societal characteristics which undermine communitarianism.

The shaming produced by interdependency and communitarianism can be either of two types—shaming that becomes stigmatization or shaming that is followed by reintegration. The shaming engendered is more likely to become reintegrative in societies that are communitarian. In societies where shaming does become reintegrative, low crime rates are the result because disapproval is dispensed without eliciting a rejection of the disapprovers, so that the potentialities for future disapproval are not dismantled. Moreover, reintegrative shaming is superior even to stigmatization for conscience-building. . . .

Shaming that is stigmatizing, in contrast, makes criminal subcultures more attractive because these are in some sense subcultures which reject the rejectors. Thus, when shaming is allowed to become stigmatization for want of reintegrative gestures or ceremonies which decertify deviance, the deviant is both attracted to criminal subcultures and cut off from other interdependencies (with family, neighbors, church, etc.). Participation in subcultural groups supplies criminal role models, training in techniques of crime and techniques of neutralizing crime (or other forms of social support) that make choices to engage in crime more attractive. Thus, to the extent that shaming is of the stigmatizing rather than the reintegrative sort, and that criminal subcultures are widespread and accessible in the society, higher crime rates will be the result. While societies characterized by high levels of stigmatization will have higher crime rates than societies characterized by reintegrative shaming, the former will have higher or lower crime rates than societies with little shaming at all depending largely on the availability of criminal subcultures.

Yet a high level of stigmatization in the society is one of the very factors that encourages criminal subculture formation by creating populations of outcasts with no stake in conformity, no chance of self-esteem within the terms of conventional society—individuals in search of an alternative culture that allows them self-esteem. A communitarian culture, on the other hand, nurtures deviants within a network of attachments to conventional society, thus inhibiting the widespread outcasting that is the stuff of subculture formation.

For clarity of exposition the two types of shaming have been presented as a stark dichotomy. In reality, for any society some deviants are dealt with in ways that are more stigmatic while others receive more reintegrative shaming. Indeed, a single deviant will be responded to more stigmatically by some, more reintegratively by others. To the extent that the greater weight of shaming tends to stigmatization, the crime-producing processes on the right of Figure 30.1 are more likely to be triggered; to the extent that the balance of shaming tips toward reintegration, informal processes of crime control are more likely to prevail over these crime-producing processes.

The other major societal variable which fosters criminal subculture formation is systematic blockage of legitimate opportunities for critical fractions of the population. If black slum dwellers are systematically denied economic opportunities because of the stigma of their race and neighborhood, then criminal subcultures will form in these outcast neighborhoods. It can be seen that stigmatization (as opposed to social integration) as a cultural disposition may contribute to the systematic blockage of these economic opportunities; but cultural variables like stigmatization will be of rather minor importance compared with structural economic variables in determining opportunities. I have argued that the blockages in this part of the theory are not restricted to closed opportunities to climb out of poverty; systematically blocked opportunities for ever greater wealth accumulation by the most affluent of corporations often lead to corporate criminal subculture formation. . . .

Criminal subcultures are the main mechanism for constituting illegitimate opportunity structures—knowledge on how to offend, social support for offending or communication of rationalizations for offending, criminal role models, subcultural groups which assist with the avoidance of detection and which organize collective criminal enterprises. However, illegitimate opportunities are greater in some societies than others for a variety of further reasons which are not incorporated within the theory. While the effects of legitimate and illegitimate opportunities on crime are mostly mediated by participation in criminal subcultures, the blockage of legitimate opportunities combined with the availability of illegitimate opportunities can independently increase crime. Whether illegitimate opportunities to engage in crime are supplied by participation in criminal subcultures or otherwise, they must be opportunities that appeal to the tastes of tempted individuals for them to result in crime.

This summary is crudely simple because it ignores what goes on within the shaming box in Figure 30.1. That is, it ignores the treatment . . . of the social processes that combine individual acts of shaming into cultural processes of shaming which are more or less integrative: gossip, media coverage of shaming incidents, children's stories, etc. In turn, the summary has neglected how these macro processes of shaming feed back to ensure that micro practices of shaming cover the curriculum of crimes. . . .

Shunting the Colliding Locomotives of Criminological Theory

This sharp contrast with the inability of the existing dominant theories to explain much of what we know about crime is achieved, ironically, through the addition of just one element—the partitioning of shaming—as a shunt to connect these diverging theoretical tracks. Through putting the old theoretical ingredients together in a new way, we can do better at accounting for the facts than can any of these traditions separately. Moreover, we can do better compared with adding together their separate (contradictory!) elements as partial explanations within an atheoretical multi-factor model.

The top left of Figure 30.1 incorporates the key variables of control theory; the far right—opportunity theory; the middle and bottom right—subcultural theory; the bottom, particularly the bottom left—learning theory; the right side of the middle box—labeling theory. With one crucial exception (reintegrative shaming), there is therefore no originality in the elements of this theory, simply originality of synthesis.

Through the effect of interdependency in reducing crime, we can capture the explanatory successes of control theory in accounting for primary deviance. Through shunting stigmatization away from other forms of shaming (as that sort of shaming which triggers subcultural participation) we proffer a more promising approach to the explanation of secondary deviance in labeling and subcultural theory terms. We achieve a more specified theory of differential association with

conventional others versus others who share a subculture. Conceived another way, it is a theory of differential shaming. Most shaming is by conventional others on the anti-criminal side of a tipping point. When stigmatization produces secondary deviance, it is because the balance of shame has tipped; for those who share the subculture there is sufficient approval for crime . . . to outweigh the shaming of conventional society.

Discussion Questions

1. What is the difference between shaming that is stigmatizing and shaming that is reintegrative?

2. In the United States, what kind of shaming is most common? Can you provide some examples?

3. Why does stigmatizing shaming cause crime? How does this relate to labeling theory?

4. If you were going to develop a reintegrative shaming program for juvenile delinquents, what would it involve? ✦

Part IX

Critical Criminology: Power, Inequality, and Crime

In the quarter century following World War II, notes James Patterson (1996, p. vii), Americans had "great expectations" about "the capacity of the United States to create a better world abroad and a happier society at home." These expectations reached a feverish pitch in the 1960s. With an economic boom under way and unprecedented support for broadening equal rights, President Lyndon Johnson called for the creation of a "great society"—a call that at the time did not seem naive. Scarcely a decade later, however, much of this optimism had turned to despair. Equal economic opportunity for all now seemed beyond reach, and racial cleavages—despite gains in formal legal rights for minorities—seemed to widen, as urban riots and white resistance to integration made clear. Viet Nam, Kent State, Attica, and Watergate—together these events and many others revealed the abuse of state power in the pursuit of questionable, if not illegal, goals. The assassinations of John and Robert Kennedy and of Martin Luther King, Jr., leaders who preached hope and peace, were perhaps the most vivid and enduring reminders that achieving true social justice remained an American dream.

What lessons were to be drawn from the failure to achieve the "great expectations" for American society? For a generation of criminologists who grew up in these tumultuous times and whose campus days were spent in protest marches, their social world had been transformed. Their utopian belief in a just society and faith in the "system" had been replaced by the sobering realization that inequality was deeply entrenched and that those in power wished to reinforce, not change, the status quo. Once all the rhetoric about America being the "land of opportunity" had been dispelled, they learned that fundamental reform would require unmasking and challenging the structures of power and the forces that undergirded them.

Equipped with this vision, criminologists in the late 1960s and early 1970s found "traditional" theories of crime—such as those covered in the previous parts of this volume—intellectually sterile, if not unthinkingly dangerous. These theories seemed blind to the central reality of American society: its pervasive economic and racial inequality. Traditional perspectives largely ignored and thus left unchallenged the powerful interests that benefited from this inequality. As a result, crime was detached from the very structural forces that sustained the mean streets of inner-city neighborhoods and, it might be added, that gave rise to rapacious corporations.

In contrast, this generation of criminologists called for a "new criminology" that would take a "critical" stance toward society and, intellectually, toward the assumptions and content of traditional criminology (Krisberg, 1975; Taylor et al., 1973). The category of "critical criminology"—sometimes also called conflict, radical, or Marxian criminology—encompasses diverse lines of inquiry (see Bohm, 1982; Milovanovic, 1992; Thomas and O'Maolchatha, 1989). At the risk of missing the richness of theorizing within this approach, however, it is possible to identify several themes that make a theoretical work distinctively "critical" in its focus.

Central Themes of Critical Criminology

First, the concepts of inequality and power are integral to any understanding of crime and its control. Building on the work of Karl Marx, critical criminologists note that capitalism enriches some and impoverishes many, thus inevitably producing a wide economic gap between the social classes. Pursuing their own interests, the affluent use their money to ensure that government policies do not threaten their position of advantage. As a result, the state—including the criminal law and the criminal justice system—operates to legitimate and protect social arrangements that benefit those profiting from capitalism.

Second, "crime" is a political, not a value-free, concept. Traditional criminology accepts that crime is behavior that violates the law. Critical criminology, however, recognizes that what is and is not outlawed reflects the power structure in society. In general, the injurious acts of the poor and powerless are defined as crime, but the injurious acts of the rich and powerful—such as corporations selling defective products or the affluent allowing disadvantaged children to go without health care—are not brought within the reach of the criminal law. Only by rejecting state definitions of crime and replacing them with a new standard—such as defining crime as the violation of human rights—can criminologists oppose, rather than reinforce, existing inequalities. "What is certain is that the legalistic definitions cannot be justified as long as they make the activity of criminologists subservient to the state," comment Schwendinger and Schwendinger (1975, p. 138). "In the process of redefining crime, criminologists will redefine themselves, no longer to be the defenders of order but rather the guardians of human rights."

Third, as a defender of the existing social order, the criminal justice system ultimately serves the interests of the capitalist class. The system is largely set up to process poor and minority offenders—most of whom could find no meaningful place in the labor market—while ignoring the illegalities of rich and corporate offenders. As Reiman (1984) puts it, the system is designed so that "the rich get richer and the poor get prison." In enforcing order, moreover, criminal justice officials are not beyond breaking the law themselves, such as through police brutality and receiving pay-offs in vice operations (Henderson and Simon, 1994). On a broader level, to protect its interests, the capitalist state will use its power to commit, largely with impunity, crimes against its own dissident citizens (e.g., illegal wiretapping against protesters), not to mention sponsoring covert actions to undermine other governments (Barak, 1991).

Fourth, capitalism is the root cause of criminal behavior (see Greenberg, 1993). Under capitalism, the human needs of the poor are ignored. Instead, they face demoralizing living conditions that foster crime by stunting healthy development (Currie, 1985) and/or by making crime a rational response (Gordon, 1973). More noteworthy, capitalism creates a fertile environment for crimes by corporations (Pearce, 1976). Pressures for profits, combined with lax state regulation and the infrequent application of criminal penalties, induce business enterprises to pursue profits through illegal methods. The consequences are not only huge economic losses but also violence that may well surpass that exacted by street crimes. Thus, by selling dangerously defective products, polluting the environment, and exposing workers to job hazards and toxic agents, corporations exact an enormous toll in illnesses, injuries, and deaths (see Cullen et al., 1987; Hills, 1987).

Fifth, the solution to crime is the creation of a more equitable society. Equipped with this knowledge, critical criminologists should unmask the ways in which capitalist-based exploitation creates crime and victimization. Equally important, they should not be armchair criminologists but rather should work to foster greater social justice. In particular, they should support humane policies aimed at preventing harm from occurring (see Maguire, 1988) and, more broadly, they should engage in political activity advocating a fairer distribution of wealth and power in society. For many critical criminologists, the goal of this reform effort is a socialist economy combined with a democratic political system sensitive to the needs of all citizens.

These broad principles inform much of the scholarship done under the broad name of critical criminology. Again, however, the intellectual richness of this perspective has resulted in many specific theoretical contributions—indeed, so many that it is beyond the scope of this volume to capture them all (see Greenberg, 1993a; Lynch and Groves, 1986). Our main focus is on those works that have been particularly influential in addressing the question, why does crime occur? We should note that critical criminologists are often criticized for studying how powerful interests shape the content of law and the operation of the criminal justice system (see, e.g., Chambliss and Seidman, 1982; Quinney, 1974; Turk, 1966) instead of providing specific insights into the etiology of criminal behavior. In contrast, the strength of traditional criminology is precisely its sustained concern with explaining involvement in crime and in subjecting theories to empirical tests. Critical criminology's viability as an alternative to traditional perspectives thus depends on advancing explanations of criminality that are both theoretically persuasive and backed up by the data.

Capitalism and Crime

Most critical criminologists' thinking is influenced, at least in a general way, by the work of Karl Marx. Marx believed that in a capitalist system, the bourgeoisie—those who owned the means of production—inevitably exploited the proletariat—workers who did not own the means of production. Capitalism thus resulted in the immiseration and demoralization of the working class, a state that would only be alleviated when workers shed their false consciousness that existing economic arrangements were legitimate, realized their joint interests, and revolted to create a socialist system.

For our purposes, it is noteworthy that Marx, despite sporadic writings on criminality and law, did not spell out systematically the connection between capitalism and crime (Greenberg, 1993a; Taylor et al., 1973). It remained for Willem Bonger, a Dutch criminologist, to author in 1916 what is now considered the first classic attempt to use Marx to explain crime, *Criminality and Economic Conditions* (see Chapter 31 in this Part).

Following Marxs dim view of the social consequences of capitalism, Bonger offered the central thesis that the capitalist mode of production breeds crime. Bonger believed that the key proximate cause of criminality is the mental state of egoism, whereas the social sentiment of altruism fosters prosocial conduct. Egoism is rooted in economic relations; after all, the basis of capitalism is ruthless competition and the exploitation of others in the pursuit of individual profits. The larger social good is not considered and thus altruism is not encouraged. In the proletariat, especially among those most impoverished, brutish living conditions, efforts by the bourgeoisie to incite materialistic desires, and the lack of moral training intensify egoistic impulses. Not surprisingly, criminal behavior is widespread in this class.

Anticipating the work of Edwin Sutherland on white-collar crime, Bonger also recognized that capitalism creates crime among the bourgeoisie. Crimes such as bank fraud, selling adulterated products, and large-scale swindles are at times committed by businesses that are economically imperiled. But many offenses are engaged in by those whose businesses are flourishing. These illegalities are a product of a "bourgeois environment" that inculcates, even in children, the moral principle that honesty is to be valued only so long as it does not interfere with one's advantage (Bonger, 1969 [1916], p. 136). Furthermore, bourgeois crimes are made attractive because "the opportunity to commit these offenses undetected is enormous" (p. 138). This "unlimited opportunity to deceive the public" is made possible by capitalism; indeed, these "bourgeois crimes . . . can be committed only under an economic system of the kind that ours is" (p. 140). Bourgeois economic criminals, moreover, have little to fear from the criminal law. As Bonger (1969: p. 142) noted, "the penalties prescribed for these crimes are relatively light as compared with those for ordinary crimes," and the "number of punishable acts is very limited as compared with those which really deserve punishment." In short, "it is these crimes which show clearly the class character of the penal law" (p. 142).

As might be anticipated, Bonger believed that under socialism—where the means of production were owned by the community—egoism would be discouraged and children would be morally educated to value altruism. Although sympathetic to his general theory, Taylor et al. (1973) take issue with Bonger's emphasis on the control of egoism as the key to reducing crime. In many ways, Bonger's theory moves away from Karl Marx and toward Emile Durkheim, the early anomie theorist who advocated the restraint of desires through moral education. This theoretical shift risks clouding Marx's fundamental focus on the misery caused by persisting inequality and on the need for working people to struggle against their exploitation. "Criminal man is consistently depicted [by Bonger] not so much as a man produced by a matrix of unequal social relationships, nor indeed as a man attempting to resolve those inequalities of wealth, power and life-chances," note Taylor et al. (1974: p. 235); "rather, criminal man is viewed as being in need of social control. . . . Socialism is preferable to capitalism, most of all, because it will control the baser instincts of man."

In contrast, the centrality of the proletariat's struggle against oppression by the capitalist class is vivid in Richard Quinney's *Class, State, and Crime* (Chapter 32 in this Part), an important book written a half century after Bonger's *Criminality and Economic Conditions*. "The contradictions of developing capitalism," maintained Quinney (1980, p. 59), "heighten the level of class struggle and thereby increase (1) the need to dominate by the capitalist class and (2) the need to accommodate and resist by the classes exploited by capitalism, particularly the working class." In an effort to secure their advantage, the capitalist class commits economic crimes, denies people basic human rights, and uses the state to protect its interests and to repress the poor. For the working class, crime is best understood as a response to their harsh, inequitable living conditions. Their illegalities "range from unconscious reactions to exploitation, to conscious acts of survival within the capitalist system, to politically conscious acts of rebellion" (p. 65).

Similar to Bonger, Quinney notes that the "only lasting solution to the crisis of capitalism is socialism" (p. 67). In the 2nd edition of *Class, State, and Crime*, Quinney (1980) turned away from a strict Marxian theory of crime to recognize the importance of religion in human life. In his view, capitalism not only was beset by materialistic contradictions but also by a spiritual crisis—a "sacred void." Socialism thus must become spiritual, merging the secular and sacred to create a "prophetic socialist faith . . . a religious socialist culture" (p. ix). "The socialist struggle," commented Quinney, "requires a religious consciousness as much as a class consciousness . . . the religious goal transcends concrete societies. The prophetic expectation speaks finally to that which is infinite and eternal" (p. 68).

Quinney's embrace of the spiritual and its transformative powers, at the expense of the crass materialism of Marxism, is seen again in his subsequent efforts to lay the foundation for a "peacemaking criminology" (Pepinsky and Quinney, 1991). Quinney (1991) suggests that as individuals we are on a spiritual journey, which involves transcending one's egocentric self to understand the suffering in ourselves and in the world. Inner peace and peacemaking actions are intertwined and reinforcing. Without such peace, crime is inevitable. "Crime is suffering," Quinney reminds us, and "the ending of crime is possible only with the ending of suffering" (p. 11). But advancing peace and diminishing suffering require social justice; "this is the biblical command" (p. 11). The goal of a peacemaking criminology is thus to seek "to end suffering and thereby eliminate crime. . . . Without peace within us and in our actions, there can be no peace in our results. Peace is the way" (pp. 11-12).

Today, many critical scholars are embracing Quinney's prescription to make peace. For them, criminologists should use their knowledge and lives to create social justice. They reject, in particular, traditional "get tough" criminal justice responses to crime, which they argue attempt fruitlessly to fight violence with violence, suffering with more suffering. Instead, they favor programs such as "restorative justice" that seek to mediate conflict, to address the real needs of victims, and to reintegrate offenders into a community that can instruct them in the ways of peace.

Pathways to Crime

Critical criminologists such as Quinney propose that capitalism is the root cause of criminal behavior. Their analyses, however, often are couched in general terms, with bourgeois crime attributed to the need for the capitalist class to maintain its dominance and working-class crime attributed to the dehumanizing and demoralizing conditions of life under capitalism. Although useful in sensitizing scholars to processes involved in producing crime, these analyses do not detail the specific factors under capitalism that foster criminal conduct. The theoretical statements of David Greenberg, of Mark Colvin and John Pauly, and of John Hagan are a useful corrective to this tendency to leave out the details in explaining what causes wayward behavior (see Chapters 33, 34, and 35 in this Part).

Greenberg (1993b [1977]) situates delinquency within the historically specific structural conditions in which today's youths find themselves. In previous eras, youths were more likely to work at an early age. As capitalism has developed into its more advanced stage, however, the economic system is unable to provide full-time jobs for teenagers. Instead, adulthood is delayed as youths are consigned to schools, whose main function is "to keep juveniles out of the labor market" and to create "a docile, disciplined and stratified labor force" (1993: p. 351).

The prolongation of adolescence exposes many youngsters to intense criminogenic pressures. Acceptance from other youths requires the ability to participate in peer-group activities focused on consumption and leisure activities. But many youths lack the financial resources to purchase clothes, cars, concert tickets, and the like—largely because they are excluded from the job market. "Adolescent theft," observes Greenberg, "occurs in response to the disjunction between the desire to participate in social activities with peers and the absence of legitimate sources of funds to finance this participation" (p. 339). These youths also must endure a school environment that restrains their autonomy and, for those who are unpopular or unsuccessful academically, that subjects them to degradation. In response to their frustration, these adolescents often strike back at authority through nonutilitarian delinquent acts, such as vandalizing school property. Finally, Greenberg notes the importance of "masculine status anxiety," which confronts males concerned about their ability to gain employment and to assume the traditional responsibilities of the male role. Violence, including that against women, can occur in effort to reaffirm their masculinity and potency in the face of this anxiety.

It is noteworthy that Greenberg's perspective embraces a key assumption of the strain theories discussed in Part IV: crime is often a way of adapting to the strains youths experience. Much like Agnew's general strain theory (Chapter 17), he details different types of strain. Informed by a critical perspective, however, Greenberg shows how criminogenic strains may well be rooted not in the mere blockage of the American dream but in the structural conditions of the nation's "oligopoly-capitalist economy" (p. 351). In short, he reminds us that the everyday frustrations and anxieties that drive youths into crime cannot be understood apart from the larger macro-level forces that circumscribe their lives at this particular point in history.

Colvin and Pauly (1983 [Chapter 34]) propose another pathway through which an inequitable class structure produces delinquency: the family. Similar to Hagan's power-control theory (Chapter 21), Colvin and Pauly argue that parents' class position in the labor market affects how they exercise control over their children. How parents are disciplined in the workplace, they contend, affects how they discipline their own children.

Colvin and Pauly are most concerned with those who are employed in the secondary labor market (in "dead-end jobs"), because these workers are controlled through coercive sanctions (e.g., yelling at or firing of workers). Importing this style of control into the family, these parents tend to discipline their children coercively, attempting to enforce conformity through erratic, harsh punishment rather than through, for example, parent-child discussions aimed at developing internalized self-control. Such coercive discipline, however, proves counterproductive, alienating children and weakening bonds to parents. As problem behavior surfaces in school, the children are placed in strict or coercive class settings (e.g., special classes), further weakening their bond to society. They also are likely to associate with other alienated peers and to participate in delinquent subcultures. In short, they are on a pathway of deepening involvement in delinquency.

Finally, John Hagan (1994 [Chapter 35]) focuses on the importance of community as the intervening link between structural inequality and embeddedness in crime. The defining feature of today's postindustrial capitalist society, observes Hagan, is the increasing "capital disinvestment" in inner-city minority neighborhoods. A combination of enduring racial segregation, the persisting economic gap between whites and African Americans, and the residential concentration of the "truly disadvantaged" has resulted in distressed communities that are largely left to fend for themselves. Youths growing up in these areas do not have the "social capital"— the dense social networks and quality interpersonal relationships—that provides the learning experiences, contacts, and opportunities needed for advancement in school and in the workplace. They also lack the "cultural capital"—the dress, language, attitudes, knowledge of the arts, and so on—that facilitates mobility in conventional social institutions.

As a result, youths are largely cut off from employment in the core labor market—jobs that provide living wages, benefits, advancement, and the like. They are likely to "drift into cultural adaptations that bring short-term status and material benefits, but whose longer-term consequences include diminished life chances" (p. 93). Hagan observes that criminal subcultural adaptations can be seen as a form of "recapitalization" in which youths "use what resources are available, albeit usually illicit, to reach attainable goals" (p. 98). The creation of drug markets is one example of recapitalization in inner-city communities.

Hagan is one of a number of criminologists who, informed by a critical view of capitalism, warn that crime—especially violence— is the cost of enduring inequality whose worst manifestation is socially isolated and economically impoverished minority communities (see also, Blau and Blau, 1982; Currie, 1985; Hagan and Peterson, 1995; Sampson, 1997; Short, 1997). Although not Marxist in their orientation, they nonetheless argue that the concentration of violence in inner-city neighborhoods cannot be understood apart from the race-linked inequality generated by postcapitalist industrial America. And, although not calling for a socialist revolution, they are clear in arguing that no lasting solution to the crime problem can occur without the concerted investment of public and private sector resources, or "capital," in these neighborhoods.

References

Barak, Gregg, ed. 1991. *Crimes by the Capitalist State: An Introduction to State Criminality.* Albany: State University of New York Press.

Blau, Judith R. and Peter M. Blau. 1982. "The Cost of Inequality: Metropolitan Structure and Violent Crime." *American Sociological Review* 47: 114-129.

Bohm, Robert M. 1982. "Radical Criminology." *Criminology* 19: 565-589.

Bonger, Willem. 1969 [originally published in 1916]. *Criminality and Economic Conditions*, abridged edition, edited by Austin T. Turk. Bloomington: Indiana University Press.

Chambliss, William and Robert Seidman. 1982. *Law, Order, and Power*, 2nd edition. Reading, MA: Addison-Wesley.

Colvin, Mark and John Pauly. 1983. "A Critique of Criminology: Toward an Integrated Structural-Marxist Theory of Delinquency Production." *American Journal of Sociology* 89: 513-551.

Cullen, Francis T., William J. Maakestad, and Gray Cavender. 1987. *Corporate Crime Under Attack: The Ford Pinto Case and Beyond.* Cincinnati: Anderson.

Currie, Elliott. 1985. *Confronting Crime: An American Challenge.* New York: Pantheon.

Gordon, David M. 1973. "Capitalism, Class, and Crime in America." *Crime and Delinquency* 19: 163-186.

Greenberg, David F., ed. 1993a. *Crime and Capitalism: Readings in Marxist Criminology*, expanded and updated edition. Philadelphia: Temple University Press.

———. 1993b [originally published in 1977]. "Delinquency and the Age Structure in Society." Pp. 334-356 in *Crime and Capitalism: Readings in Marxist Criminology*, expanded and updated edition, edited by David F. Greenberg. Philadelphia: Temple University Press.

Hagan, John. 1994. *Crime and Disrepute.* Thousand Oaks, CA: Pine Forge Press.

Hagan, John and Ruth D. Peterson, eds. 1995. *Crime and Inequality.* Stanford, CA: Stanford University Press.

Henderson, Joel H. and David R. Simon. 1994. *Crimes of the Criminal Justice System.* Cincinnati: Anderson.

Hills, Stuart L., ed. 1987. *Corporate Violence: Injury and Death for Profit.* Totowa, NJ: Rowman and Littlefield.

Krisberg, Barry. 1975. *Crime and Privilege: Toward a New Criminology.* Englewood Cliffs, NJ: Prentice-Hall.

Lynch, Michael J. and W. Byron Groves. 1986. *A Primer in Radical Criminology.* New York: Harrow and Heston.

Maguire, Brendan. 1988. "The Applied Dimension of Radical Criminology: A Survey of Prominent Radical Criminologists." *Sociological Spectrum* 8: 133-151.

Milovanovic. Dragan. 1982. "Review Essay: Contemporary Directions in Critical Criminology." *Humanity and Society* 6: 303-313.

Patterson, James T. 1996. *Grand Expectations: The United States, 1945-1974.* New York: Oxford University Press.

Pearce, Frank. 1976. *Crimes of the Powerful: Marxism, Crime and Deviance.* London, UK: Pluto Press.

Pepinsky, Harold E. and Richard Quinney, eds. 1991. *Criminology as Peacemaking.* Bloomington: Indiana University Press.

Quinney, Richard. 1974. *Critique of Legal Order: Crime Control in Capitalist Society.* Boston: Little, Brown.

———. 1980. *Class, State, and Crime.* 2nd edition. New York: Longman.

———. 1991. "The Way of Peace: On Crime, Suffering, and Service." Pp. 3-13 in *Criminology as Peacemaking*, edited by Harold E. Pepinsky and Richard Quinney. Bloomington: University of Indiana Press.

Reiman, Jeffrey H. 1984. *The Rich Get Richer and the Poor Get Prison: Ideology, Class, and Criminal Justice*, 2nd edition. New York: John Wiley.

Sampson, Robert J. 1997. "The Embeddedness of Child and Adolescent Development: A Community-Level Perspective on Urban Violence." Pp. 31-77 in *Violence and Childhood in the Inner City*, edited by Joan McCord. Cambridge, UK: Cambridge University Press.

Schwendinger, Herman and Julia Schwendinger. 1975. "Defenders of Order or Guardians of Human Rights?" Pp. 113-146 in *Critical Criminology*, edited by Ian Taylor, Paul Walton, and Jock Young. London, UK: Routledge and Kegan Paul.

Short, James F. 1997. *Poverty, Ethnicity, and Violent Crime.* Boulder, CO: Westview.

Taylor, Ian, Paul Walton, and Jock Young. 1973. *The New Criminology: For a Social Theory of Deviance.* London, UK: Routledge and Kegan Paul.

Thomas, Jim and Aogan O'Maolchatha. 1989. "Reassessing the Critical Metaphor: An Optimistic Revisionist View." *Justice Quarterly* 6: 143-172.

Turk, Austin T. 1966. "Conflict and Criminality." *American Sociological Review* 31: 338-352. ✦

31

Criminality and Economic Conditions

Willem Bonger

For Bonger, crime is a form of egoism—a rejection of the social instinct of altruism and of placing one's own interests above those of other people. Understanding crime, therefore, depends on answering the question, "Why does a man act egoistically?" (Bonger, 1969 [1916], p. 26).

Writing in 1916, Bonger took pains to dismiss the answer of his contemporary Lombroso (see Chapter 1) and the members of his Italian or positivist school of criminology, who saw criminals' egoism as a "manifestation of atavism, that is, that some individuals present anew traits of character belonging to their very remote ancestors" (Bonger 1969 [1916]: p. 26). This explanation could not account, said Bonger, for evidence of altruism in earlier, supposedly less civilized times or for bourgeois crimes in the present. Referring to the lawlessness of the rich, Bonger noted that "even the Italian school is forced to admit that the stigmata found elsewhere cannot be pointed out in these individuals. Furthermore," continued Bonger, "in this case we can hardly speak of atavism. It may be that our ancestors were great offenders, but it is not probable that they ever were guilty of swindles of this kind" (p. 142).

Instead, Bonger contended that egoism was a product of the social environment and, in particular, was linked intimately to the "mode of production." In his view, capitalism breeds egoism because it is, by its very nature, an economic system in which individual self-interest is pursued regardless of its consequences on others. The bourgeoisie—those who own the means of production—thus use unscrupulous means, illegal if necessary, to protect and advance their economic advantage. In search of

profits, they also exploit the proletariat, paying them as little as possible for their labor and feeling no reciprocity or sense of obligation toward them. Instead, the bourgeoisie see workers as mere instruments to serve their interests—people whose human needs and material well-being are of scant concern.

For the proletariat, capitalism causes egoism and thus crime to flourish. Their exploitive, rather than reciprocal, relationships with the bourgeoisie dull their altruistic sentiments. Brutish living conditions also serve to demoralize the proletariat, especially those in the "lower proletariat . . . who do not succeed, for any reason, in selling their labor" (p. 52). In these harsh circumstances, the moral training necessary for the development of altruism is undermined as youths are prematurely sent to work, are denied education, are raised in families and housing conditions detrimental to their healthy development, and are exposed to criminal influences on the street.

In the end, observed Bonger, "we have a right to say that the part played by economic conditions in criminality is preponderant, even decisive" (p. 197). Still, room for optimism remained. If crime "were principally the consequence of innate human qualities (atavism, for example)," as Lombroso might claim, "the pessimistic conclusion that crime is a phenomenon inseparably bound up with the social life would be well founded" (p. 197). But because "crime is the consequence of economic and social conditions," contended Bonger, "we can combat it by changing those circumstances" (p. 197). The answer is to replace capitalism by socialism, by a society in which "the means of production are held in common" (p. 198). According to Bonger, "such a society will not only remove the causes which now make men egoistic, but will awaken, on the contrary, a strong feeling of altruism" (p. 200). With the economic basis of crime thus eliminated, only crimes committed by "pathological individuals" would continue to exist (p. 200).

Bonger's criminology can be criticized for its rather crude economic determinism, its simple psychology of crime that tied crime only to the sentiments of egoism versus altruism, and its utopian view of socialism. Even so, Bonger's theory has value in showing that a capitalist economy has consequences, simultaneously *creating demoralizing conditions that impede the healthy development of the poor and creating strong incentives for the rich to break the law.*

Reference

Bonger, Willem. 1969 [originally published in 1916]. *Criminality and Economic Conditions*, abridged edition, edited by Austin T. Turk. Bloomington: Indiana University Press.

. . . To find the causes of crime we must . . . first solve the question: "Why does an individual do acts injurious to the interests of those with whom he forms a social unit?", or in other words; "Why does a man act egoistically?"

Capitalism, Egoism, and Crime

. . . As we have seen in the preceding pages, it is certain that man is born with social instincts, which, when influenced by a favorable environment can exert a force great enough to prevent egoistic thoughts from leading to egoistic acts. And since crime constitutes a part of the egoistic acts, it is of importance, for the etiology of *crime in general*, to inquire whether the present method of production and its social consequences are an obstacle to the development of the social instincts, and in what measure. We shall try in the following pages to show the influence of the economic system and of these consequences upon the social instincts of man.

After what we have just said it is almost superfluous to remark that the egotistic tendency does not *by itself* make a man criminal. For this something else is necessary. It is possible for the environment to create a great egoist, but this does not imply that the egoist will necessarily become criminal. For example, a man who is enriched by the exploitation of children may nevertheless remain all his life an honest man from the legal point of view. He does not think of stealing, because he has a surer and more lucrative means of getting wealth, although he lacks the moral sense which would prevent him from committing a crime if the thought of it occurred to him. We shall show that, as a consequence

of the present environment, man has become very egoistic and hence more *capable of crime*, than if the environment had developed the germs of altruism.

The present economic system is based upon exchange. As we saw at the end of the preceding section such a mode of production cannot fail to have an egoistic character. A society based upon exchange isolates the individuals by weakening the bond that unites them. When it is a question of exchange the two parties interested think only of their own advantage even to the detriment of the other party. In the second place the possibility of exchange arouses in a man the thought of the possibility of converting the surplus of his labor into things which increase his well-being in place of giving the benefit of it to those who are deprived of the necessaries of life. Hence the possibility of exchange gives birth to cupidity.

The exchange called simple circulation of commodities is practiced by all men as consumers, and by the workers besides as vendors of their labor power. However, the influence of this simple calculation of commodities is weak compared with that exercised by capitalistic exchange. It is only the exchange of the surplus of labor, by the producer, for other commodities, and hence is for him a secondary matter. As a result he does not exchange with a view to profit (though he tries to make as advantageous a trade as possible), but to get things which he cannot produce himself.

Capitalistic exchange, on the other hand, has another aim—that of making a profit. A merchant, for example, does not buy goods for his own use, but to sell them with advantage. He will, then, always try, on the one hand, to buy the best commodities as cheaply as possible, by depreciating them as much as he can; on the other hand, to make the purchaser pay as high a price as possible, by exaggerating the value of his wares. *By the nature of the mode of production itself* the merchant is therefore forced to make war upon two sides, must maintain his own interests against the interests of those with whom he does business. If he does not injure too greatly the interests of those from whom he buys, and those to whom he sells, it is for the simple reason that these would otherwise do business with those of his competitors who do not find their interest in fleecing their customers. Wherever competition is eliminated for whatever cause the tactics of the merchant are shown in their true light; he thinks only of his own advantage even to the detriment of those with whom he does business. "No commerce without trickery" is a proverbial expression (among consumers), and with the ancients Mercury, the god of commerce, was also the god of thieves. This is true, that the merchant and the thief are alike in taking account *exclusively* of their own interest to the detriment of those with whom they have to do. . . .

As we have seen above the merchant capitalist makes war in two directions; his interests are against those of the man who sells to him, and of the man who buys from him. This is also true of the industrial capitalist. He buys raw materials and sells what he produces. But to arrive at his product he must buy labor, and this purchase is "sui generis."

Deprived as he is of the means of production the working-man sells his labor only in order not to die of hunger. The capitalist takes advantage of this necessitous condition of the worker and exploits him. We have already indicated that capitalism has this trait in common with the earlier methods of production. Little by little one class of men has become accustomed to think that the others are destined to amass wealth for them and to be subservient to them in every way. Slavery, like the wage system, demoralizes the servant as well as the master. With the master it develops cupidity and the imperious character which sees in a fellow man only a being fit to satisfy his desires. It is true that the capitalist has not the power over the proletarian that the master has over his slave; he has neither the right of service nor the power of life and death, yet it is none the less true that he has another weapon against the proletarian, a weapon whose effect is no less terrible, namely enforced idleness. The fact that the supply of manual labor always greatly exceeds the demand puts this weapon into the hands of every capitalist. It is not only the capitalists who carry on any business that are subjected

to this influence, but also all who are salaried in their service.

Capitalism exercises in still a third manner an egoistic influence upon the capitalistic "entrepreneur." Each branch has more producers than are necessary. The interests of the capitalists are, then, opposed not only to those of the men from whom they buy or to whom they sell, but also to those of their fellow producers. It is indeed claimed that competition has the effect simply of making the product better and cheaper, but this is looking at the question from only one point of view. The fact which alone affects criminality is that competition forces the participants, under penalty of succumbing, to be as egoistic as possible. Even the producers who have the means of applying all the technical improvements to perfect their product and make it cheaper, are obliged to have recourse to gross deceits in advertising, etc., in order to injure their competitors. Rejoicing at the evil which befalls another, envy at his good fortune, these forms of egoism are the inevitable consequence of competition.

Following the same classification that we employed in the preceding chapter we come now to that part of the bourgeoisie which, without having any occupation, consumes what has been made by others. Not to feel obliged to contribute to the material well-being of humanity in proportion to one's ability must necessarily have a demoralizing influence. A parasite, one who lives without working, does not feel bound by any moral tie to his fellows, but regards them simply as things, instruments meant to serve and amuse him. Their example is a source of demoralization for those about them, and excites the envy of those who see this easy life without the power of enjoying it themselves, and awakes in them the desire to exchange their painful existence for this "dolce far niente.". . .

The Proletariat

To be thorough we begin by making mention of one of the consequences of the economic position of the proletariat, of which we have already treated briefly, namely the dependence in which persons of this class find themselves in consequence of their lacking the means of production, a state which has a prejudicial influence upon character. The oppressed resort to means by which they would otherwise scorn. As we have seen above, the basis of the social feelings is reciprocity. As soon as this is trodden under foot by the ruling class the social sentiments of the oppressed become weak towards them.

We come now (following the order adopted in the first chapter of Part II) first to the consequences of the labor of the young. The paid labor of the young has a bad influence in several ways. First, it forces them, while they are still very young, to think only of their own interests; then, brought into contact with persons who are rough and indifferent to their well-being, they follow these only too quickly, because of their imitative tendencies, in their bad habits, grossness of speech, etc. Finally, the paid labor of the young makes them more or less independent at an age where they have the greatest need of guidance. Even if the statistical proof of the influence of the labor of children and young people upon criminality were totally wanting, no one could deny that influence. Child labor is entirely a capitalistic phenomenon being found especially in the great manufacturing countries like England and Germany. And then one of the most salient facts of criminality is the amount of juvenile crime, which is so enormous that England, followed by other countries, has established a special system to combat this form of criminality. Certainly this increase of juvenile crime is chiefly due to the influence of bad domestic conditions (wage-labor of married women, etc.), but the labor of the young people themselves also plays its part.

It has rightly been said that work has a strong moral influence. But it is also true that immoderate labor has the contrary effect. It brutalizes a man, makes him incapable of elevated sentiments, kills as Key says (in "das Jahr-hundert des Kindes"), the man in the beast, while moderate labor ennobles the beast in the man.

The housing conditions of the proletariat have also a significance as regards criminality, and for the special group of sexual offenses their importance is very great. We shall speak of this more fully when we treat especially of these offenses, and will, for the moment, note simply their general consequences.

The disorder and squalor of the home communicate themselves to the inmates; the lack of room obliges the children to live, during a great part of the day, on the streets, with the result that they are brought into contact with all sorts of demoralizing companions. Finally, the living together of a great number of uneducated persons in one small dwelling is the cause of constant quarrels and fights. The situation of those who are merely nightlodgers is especially unfortunate, as we have already seen. . . .

As has already been said at the beginning of those observations as to the influence of the economic life upon the development of social feelings on the part of the proletariat, the egoistic side of the human character is developed by the fact that the individual is dependent, that he lives in a subordinate position, and that he feels himself poor and deprived of everything. However, in so far as the proletarian sells his labor he is guaranteed against famine, however miserable his condition, and conscious of the utility of his role in society, he feels himself, notwithstanding his poverty, a man who, except for his employer, is independent of all men. But if work is not to be found, or if the proletarian, sick and infirm, is not able to work, it goes without saying that the resulting unemployment is very demoralizing. The lack of steady work, the horrors of the penury into which he and his fall, and the long train of evils which result from both, kill the social feelings in a man, for, as we have seen above, these feelings depend upon reciprocity. Let one familiarize himself with the thought of the condition of the man who lives in the greatest poverty, *i.e.* the man who is abandoned by all, and he will understand how egoistic must be the feelings of such.

From the position in which the proletarians find themselves it follow that, towards each other, it is rather the altruistic than the egoistic feelings that develop; living less isolated than the bourgeois, they see the misfortune that strikes their neighbor, and have felt the same themselves, and above all, their economic interests are not opposed. Forced idleness—at present chronic, and acute in times of panic—modifies these conditions at times; it makes competitors of the workers, who take the bread out of each other's mouths.

The proletarian is never sure of his existence: like the sword of Damocles unemployment is constantly hanging over his head. Upon this subject Engels says:

"But far more demoralizing than poverty in its influence upon the English working man is the insecurity of his position, the necessity of living upon wages from hand to mouth, that in short which makes a proletarian of him. The smaller peasants in Germany are usually poor, and often suffer want, but they are less at the mercy of accident, they have at least something secure. The proletarian, who has nothing but his two hands, who consumes today what he earned yesterday, who is subject to every chance, and has not the slightest guarantee for being able to earn the barest necessities of life, whom every crisis, every whim of his employer may deprive of bread, this proletarian is placed in the most revolting, inhuman position conceivable for a human being" (Engels, "Condition of the Working Class in England," p. 76).

This uncertainty of existence is one of the reasons which explain why, in relatively prosperous times the workingman often spends his wages as soon as he receives them, for he knows that the economies possible to him are so small that he could never be saved from misery in case of unemployment.

Finally we must speak of ignorance and lack of training on the part of the proletariat, as a factor of criminality. . . .

The first reason why ignorance and the lack of general culture must be ranked among the general factors of crime is this: the person who, in our present society, where the great majority of parents care very little for the education of their children, does not go to school, is deprived of the moral ideas (honesty, etc.) which are taught there, and ordinarily passes his time in idleness and vagabondange.

The second reason which makes ignorance a factor of crime, is that generally an ignorant man is, more than others, a man moved by the impulse of the moment, who allows himself to be governed by his passions, and is induced to commit acts which

he would not have committed if his intellectual equipment had been different.

In the third place, it is for the following reasons that ignorance and the lack of training fall within the etiology of crime. The mind of the man whose psychic qualities, whether in the domain of the arts, or the sciences, have been developed, has become less susceptible to evil ideas. His intellectual condition constitutes thus a bridle which can restrain evil thoughts from realizing themselves; for real art and true science strengthen the social instincts. . . .

The Lower Proletariat

In the preceding pages I have already spoken of the influence exercised by bad material surroundings upon a man's character; I have pointed out the moral consequences of bad housing conditions, and also that he becomes embittered and malicious through lack of the necessaries of life. All this applies to the proletariat in general, but much more strongly still to those who do not succeed, for any reason, in selling their labor, that is the lower proletariat.

If the dwellings of the working-class are bad, those of the lower proletariat are more pitiable still. There are, through sickness or lack of work, periods of dire poverty in the life of almost every worker—for the lower proletariat these periods are without intermission. Its poverty is chronic. And when the poverty makes itself felt for a long time together, the intellectual faculties become blunted to such a point that there remains of the man only the brute, struggling for existence.

Although the material and intellectual poverty of the lower proletariat is much greater than that of the proletariat, the difference between them is only quantitative. In one connection, however, there is also a qualitative difference, a very important one, namely that the working-man is a useful being without whom society could not exist. However oppressed he may be, he is a man who has a feeling of self-respect. It is different with the member of the lower proletariat. He is not useful, but a detriment. He produces nothing, and tries to live upon what others make; he is merely tolerated. He who has lived long in poverty loses all feeling of self-respect, and lends himself to anything whatever that will suffice to prolong his existence.

In short, poverty (taken in the sense of absolute want), kills the social sentiments in man, destroys in fact all relations between men. He who is abandoned by all can no longer have any feeling for those who have left him to his fate. . . .

Conclusions

What are the conclusions to be drawn from what has gone before? When we sum up the results that we have obtained it becomes plain that economic conditions occupy a much more important place in the etiology of crime than most authors have given them.

First we have seen that the present economic system and its consequences weaken the social feelings. The basis of the economic system of our day being exchange, the economic interests of men are necessarily found to be in opposition. This is a trait that capitalism has in common with other modes of production. But its principal characteristic is that the means of production are in the hands of a few, and most men are altogether deprived of them. Consequently, persons who do not possess the means of production are forced to sell their labor to those who do, and these, in consequence of their economic preponderance, force them to make the exchange for the mere necessaries of life, and to work as much as their strength permits.

This state of things especially stifles men's social instincts; it develops, on the part of those with power, the spirit of domination, and of insensibility to the ills of others, while it awakens jealousy and servility on the part of those who depend upon them. Further the contrary interests of those who have property, and the idle and luxurious life of some of them, also contribute to the weakening of the social instincts.

The material condition, and consequently the intellectual condition, of the proletariat are also a reason why the moral plane of that class is not so high. The work of children brings them into contact with persons to associate with whom is fatal to their morals. Long working hours and monotonous labor

brutalize those who are forced into them; bad housing conditions contribute also to debase the moral sense, as do the uncertainty of existence, and finally absolute poverty, the frequent consequence of sickness and unemployment. Ignorance and lack of training of any kind also contribute their quota. Most demoralizing of all is the status of the lower proletariat.

The economic position of woman contributes also to the weakening of the social instincts.

The present organization of the family has great importance as regards criminality. It charges the legitimate parents with the care of the education of the child; the community concerns itself with the matter very little. It follows that a great number of children are brought up by persons who are totally incapable of doing it properly. As regards the children of the proletariat, there can be no question of the education properly so-called, on account of the lack of means and the forced absence of one or both of the parents. The school tends to remedy this state of things, but the results do not go far enough. The harmful consequences of the present organization of the family make themselves felt especially in the case of the children of the lower proletariat, orphans, and illegitimate children. For these the community does but little, though their need of adequate help is the greatest.

Prostitution, alcoholism, and militarism, which result, in the last analysis, from the present social order, are phenomena that have demoralizing consequences.

As to the different kinds of crime, we have shown that the very important group of economic criminality finds its origin on the one side in the absolute poverty and the cupidity brought about by the present economic environment, and on the other in the moral abandonment and bad education of the children of the poorer classes. Then, professional criminals are principally recruited from the class of occasional criminals, who, finding themselves rejected everywhere after their liberation, fall lower and lower. The last group of economic crimes (fraudulent bankruptcy, etc.) is so intimately connected with our present mode of production, that it would not be possible to commit it under another.

The relation between sexual crimes and economic conditions is less direct; nevertheless these also give evidence of the decisive influence of these conditions. We have called attention to the four following points.

First, there is a direct connection between the crime of adultery and the present organization of society, which requires that the legal dissolution of a marriage should be impossible or very difficult.

Second, sexual crimes upon adults are committed especially by unmarried men; and since the number of marriages depends in its turn upon the economic situation, the connection is clear; and those who commit these crimes are further almost exclusively illiterate, coarse, raised in an environment almost without sexual morality, and regard the sexual life from the wholly animal side.

Third, the causes of sexual crime upon children are partly the same as those of which we have been speaking, with the addition of prostitution.

Fourth, alcoholism greatly encourages sexual assaults.

As to the relation between crimes of vengeance and the present constitution of society, we have noted that it produces conflicts without number; statistics have shown that those who commit them are almost without exception poor and uncivilized, and that alcoholism is among the most important causes of these crimes.

Infanticide is caused in part by poverty, and in part by the opprobrium incurred by the unmarried mother (an opprobrium resulting from the social utility of marriage).

Political criminality comes solely from the economic system and its consequences.

Finally, economic and social conditions are also important factors in the etiology of degeneracy, which is in its turn a cause of crime.

Upon the basis of what has gone before, we have a right to say that the part played by economic conditions in criminality is preponderant, even decisive.

This conclusion is of the highest importance for the prevention of crime. If it were principally the consequence of innate human qualities (atavism, for example), the pessimistic conclusion that crime is a phenomenon inseparably bound up with the social life would be well founded. But the facts show that it is rather the optimistic conclusion that we must draw, that where crime is the consequence of economic and social conditions, we can combat it by changing those conditions. . . .

Discussion Questions

1. Willem Bonger and Cesare Lombroso were both writing in the same general time period. How do their theories of crime differ?

2. How does capitalism cause egoism and thus crime?

3. If Bonger were observing the United States today, what would he have to say about the nation's crime problem?

4. For Bonger, what is the solution to reducing crime? ✦

32

Class, State, and Crime

Richard Quinney

As with other critical theorists, Quinney (1980) begins with the Marxian thesis that capitalism is characterized by the struggle between the capitalist class and the working class. Capitalists face the continuing problem of how to maintain their advantage, especially since they seek to continue to accumulate profits while convincing workers that the system is fair to everyone.

As Quinney notes, "one of the contradictions of capitalism" is that the rich must violate the law "in order to secure the existing system" (p. 57). These crimes of "domination and repression" fall into three categories: "crimes of economic domination," such as price-fixing and environmental pollution; "crimes of government," such as political corruption and assassinating foreign officials; and "crimes of control," such as police brutality and the violation of citizens' civil liberties. The capitalist elite also commits "social injuries," acts not outlawed by the state but that involve "the denial of basic human rights," including "sexism, racism, and economic exploitation" (p. 59).

The crimes of the working class are also created by capitalism. Although both are employed as a "means of survival," people make either of two criminal responses to their dehumanizing condition: "accommodation" or "resistance." Crimes of accommodation encompass traditional property and violent offenses. Often directed at members of their own class, these acts are "an expression of false consciousness, an individualistic reaction to the forces of capitalist production" (p. 60). Crimes of resistance, however, are more of an expression of political consciousness, such as when alienated workers sabotage factory machinery. When such consciousness reaches the stage of political action, revolt is possible in which crimes are not only directed "against the system but are also an attempt to overthrow it" (p. 66).

Quinney's analysis is coherent and reminds us of how the inequalities generated by capitalism shape crime in the United States (see Currie, 1985, 1997). Still, Quinney's theorizing often remains on a general level that does not move much beyond the thesis that "capitalism causes crime." The precise processes through which macro-economic forces expose youths to criminogenic influences are not specified (e.g., by creating dysfunctional families or delinquent subcultures). Further, as is common in other Marxist perspectives, Quinney does not explore why some capitalist societies, such as Japan, have low rates of crime (but see Currie, 1997). Finally, the proposal that socialism is the solution to crime does not seem plausible in light of the dominance of capitalism in today's global economy.

References

Currie, Elliott. 1985. *Confronting Crime: An American Challenge.* New York: Pantheon.

——. 1997. "Market, Crime and Community: Toward a Mid-Range Theory of Post-Industrial Violence." *Theoretical Criminology* 1: 147-172.

Quinney, Richard. 1980. *Class, State, and Crime,* 2nd edition. New York: Longman.

. . . A class society arises when the system of production is owned by one segment of the society to the exclusion of another. All production requires ownership of some kind; but in some systems of production ownership is private rather than social or collective. In these economies social relations are dependent on relations of domination and subjection. Marxist economists thus observe: "Relations of domination and subjection are based on private ownership of the means of production and express the exploitation of man by man under the slave-owning, fedual and capitalist systems. Relations of friendly co-operation and mutual assistance between working people free of exploitation are typical of socialist society. They are based on the public ownership of the means of production, which cut out exploitation."

Social life in capitalist society, which includes crime, therefore, is related to the economic conditions of production and the struggle between classes produced by these conditions. In other words, in capitalist society the behavior of any group or any individual is part of the conflict that characterizes class relatins, a conflict produced by the capitalist system of production. The life of one class is seen in relation to that of the other.

. . . For the capitalist system to operate and survive, the capitalist class must exploit the labor (appropriate the *surplus labor*) of the working class.

. . . The capitalist class survives by appropriating the labor of the working class, and the working class as an exploited class exists as long as labor is required in the productive process: each class depends on the other for its character and existence.

The amount of labor appropriated, the techniques of labor exploitation, the conditions of working-class life, and the level of working-class consciousness have all been an integral part of the historical development of capitalism. In like manner, the degree of antagonism and conflict between classes has varied at different stages in the development. Nevertheless, it is the basic contradiction between classes, generalized as class conflict, that typifies the development of capitalism. Class conflict permeates the whole of capitalist development, represented in the contradiction between those who own property and those who do not, and by those who oppress and those who are oppressed. All past history that involves the development of capitalism is the history of class struggle.

Domination and Repression

. . . Historically the capitalist state is a product of a political economy that depends on a division of classes. With the development of an economy based on the exploitation of one class by another, a political form was needed that would perpetuate that order. With the development of capitalism, with class divisions and class struggle, the state became necessary. A new stage of development, Frederick Engels observes, called for the creation of the state.

. . . The state thus arose to protect and promote the interests of the dominant class, the class that owns and controls the means of production. The state exists as a device for controlling the exploited class, the class that labors, for the benefit of the ruling class. Modern civilization, as epitomized in capitalist societies, is founded on the exploitation of once class by another. Moreover, the capitalist state is oppressive not only because it supports the interests of the dominant class but also because it is responsible for the design of the whole system within which the capitalist ruling class dominates and the working class is dominated. The capitalist system of production and exploitation is secured and reproduced by the capitalist state.

The coercive force of the state, embodied in law and legal repression, is the traditional means of maintaining the social and economic order. Contrary to conventional wisdom, law, instead of representing the community custom, is an instrument of the state that serves the interests of the developing capitalist class. Law emerged with the rise of capitalism. As human labor became a commodity, human relations in general began to be the object of the commodity form. Human beings became subject to juridic regulation; the capitalist mode of production called forth its equivalent mode of regulation and control, the legal system. And criminal law developed as the most appropriate form of control for capitalist society. Criminal law and legal repression continue to serve the interests of the capitalist class and the perpetuation of the capitalist system.

. . . Although the capitalist state creates and manages the institutions of control (employing physical force *and* manipulation of consciousness), the basic contradictions of the capitalist order are such that this control is not absolute and, in the long run, is subject to defeat. Because of the contradictions of capitalism, the capitalist state is more weak than strong. Eventually the capitalist state loses its legitimacy and no longer is able to perpetuate the ideology that capital accumulation for capitalists (at the expense of workers) is good for the nation or for human interests. The ability of the capitalist economic order to exist according to its own interests is eventually weakened. The problem becomes especially acute in periods of economic crisis, periods that are unavoidable under capitalism.

In the course of reproducing the capitalist system crimes are committed. One of the contradictions of capitalism is that some of its laws must be violated in order to secure the existing system. The contradictions of capitalism produce their own sources of crime. Not only are these contradictions heightened during times of crisis, making for an increase in crimes of domination, but the nature of these crimes changes with the further development of capitalism.

The crimes of domination most characteristic of capitalist domination are those crimes that occur in the course of securing the existing economic order. These *crimes of economic domination* include the crimes committed by corporations, ranging from price fixing to pollution of the environment in order to protect and further capital accumulation. Also included are the economic crimes of individual businessmen and professionals. In addition, the crimes of the capitalist class and the capitalist state are joined in organized crime. The more conventional criminal operations of organized crime are linked to the state in the present stage of capitalist development. The operations of organized crime and the criminal operations of the state are united in the attempt to assure the survival of the capitalist system.

Then there are the *crimes of government* committed by the elected and appointed officials of the capitalist state. The Watergate crimes, carried out to perpetuate a particular governmental administration, are the most publicized instances of these crimes. There are also those offenses committed by the government against persons and groups who would seemingly threaten national security. Included here are the crimes of warfare and the political assassination of foreign and domestic leaders.

Crimes of domination also occur in the course of state control. These are the *crimes of control*. They include the felonies and misdemeanors that law-enforcement agents, especially the police, carry out in the name of the law, usually against persons accused of other violations. Violence and brutality have become a recognized part of police work. In addition to these crimes of control, there are crimes of a more subtle nature in which agents of the law violate the civil liberties of citizens, as in the various forms of surveillance, the use of provocateurs, and the illegal denial of due process.

Finally, many *social injuries* committed by the capitalist class and the capitalist state are not usually defined as criminal in the legal codes of the state. These systematic actions, involving the denial of basic human rights (resulting in sexism, racism, and economic exploitation), are an integral part of capitalism and are important to its survival. . . .

Accommodation and Resistance

The contradictions of developing capitalism heighten the level of class struggle and thereby increase (1) the need to dominate by the capitalist class and (2) the need to accommodate and resist by the classes exploited by capitalism, particularly the working class. Most of the behavior in response to domination, including actions of the oppressed defined as criminal by the capitalist class, is a product of the capitalist system of production. In the course of capitalist appropriation of labor, for the accumulation of capital, conditions are established that call for behaviors that may be defined as criminal by the capitalist state. These behaviors become eligible for crime control when they disturb or threaten in some way the capitalist order. . . .

Hence, the class that does not own or control the means of production must adapt to the conditions of capitalism. Accommodation and resistance to the conditions of capitalism are basic to the class struggle. The argument here is that action by people who do not own and control the means of production, those who are exploited and oppressed, is largely an accommodation or resistance to the conditions produced by capitalist production. Thus, criminality among the oppressed classes is action (conscious or otherwise) in relation to the capitalist order of exploitation and oppression. Crime, with its many historical variations, is an integral part of class struggle in the development of capitalism.

Following Marx and Engels' limited and brief discussion, criminals outside the capitalist class are usually viewed as being among the lumpen proletariat. Accordingly, criminals of the oppressed classes are regarded as unproductive workers; they are parasitical in that they do not contribute to the production of goods, and they create a livelihood out of commodities produced by the working class. Much criminal activity in the course of accommodation is an expression of false consciousness, an invidualistic reaction to the forces of capitalist production.

Many crimes of accommodation are of this lumpen nature. Nevertheless, these actions occur within the context of capitalist oppression, stemming from the existing system of production. Much criminal behavior is of a parasitical nature, including burglary, robbery, drug dealing, and hustling of various sorts. These are *predatory crimes*. The behavior, although pursued out of the need to survive, is a reproduction of the capitalist system. The crimes are nevertheless antagonistic to the capitalist order. Most police activity is directed against these crimes.

In addition to predatory crimes there are *personal crimes*, which are usually directed against members of the same class. These are the conventional criminal acts of murder, assault, and rape. They are pursued by those who are already brutalized by the conditions of capitalism. These actions occur in immediate situations that are themselves the result of more basic accommodations to capitalism.

Aside from these lumpen crimes, actions are carried out, largely by the working class, that are in resistance to the capitalist system. These actions, sometimes directed against the work situation, are direct reflections of the alienation of labor—a struggle, conscious or unconscious, against the exploitation of the life and activity of the worker. For example, workers may engage in concrete political actions against their employers:

> On the assembly lines of the American automobile industry, this revolt extends as far as clandestine acts of sabotage against a product (the automobile body)

which appears to the worker as the detestable materialization of the social uselessness and individual absurdity of his toil. Along the same lines is the less extreme and more complex example of miners fighting with admirable perseverance against the closing of the mines where they are exploited under inferior human and economic conditions—but who, individually, have no difficulty in recognizing that even if the coal they produced were not so bad and so expensive, their job, under the prevailing conditions, would still be abominable (Gorz, *Strategy for Labor*, pp. 57-58).

These defensive actions by workers are likely to become even more politically motivated and organized in the future. For built into the capitalist economy is the contradiction that increased economic growth necessitates the kind of labor that further alienates workers from their needs. Further economic expansion can bring with it only an increase in crimes of resistance. For the purpose of class struggle, leading to socialist revolution, a Marxist analysis of crime gives attention to *crimes of resistance*, committed primarily by members of the working class.

. . . For the unemployed, as well as for those who are always uncertain about their employment, this life condition has its personal and social consequences. Basic human needs are thwarted when the life-giving activity of work is lost or curtailed. This form of alienation gives rise to a multiplicity of psychosocial maladjustments and psychic disorders. In addition, unemployment means the loss of personal and family income. Choices, opportunities, and even life maintenance are jeopardized. For many people, the appropriate reaction consists not only of mental disturbance but also of outright acts of personal and social destruction.

Although the statistical evidence can never show conclusively the relation between unemployment and crime, largely because such statistics are politically constructed in the beginning to obscure the failings of a capitalist economy, there is sufficient observation to recognize the obvious fact that unemployment produces criminality. Crimes of economic gain increase whenever the jobless seek ways to maintain themselves and their families. Crimes of violence rise when the problems of life are futher exacerbated by the loss of life-supporting activity. Anger and frustration at a world that punishes rather than supports produce their own forms of destruction. Permanent unemployment—and the acceptance of that condition—can result in a form of life where criminality is an appropriate and consistent response.

Hence, crime under capitalism has become a response to the conditions of life. Nearly all crimes among the working class in capitalist society are actually a means of *survival*, an attempt to exist in a society where survival is not assured by other, collective means. Crime is inevitable under capitalist conditions.

Yet, understanding crime as a reaction to capitalist conditions, whether as acts of frustration or means of survival, is only one side of the picture. The other side involves the problematics of the consciousness of *criminality* in capitalist society. The history of the working class is in large part one of rebellion against the conditions of capitalist production, as well as against the conditions of life resulting from work under capitalism.

. . . With an emerging consciousness that the state represses those who attempt to tip the scales in favor of the working class, working class people engage in actions against the state and the capitalist class. This is crime that is politically conscious.

Crimes of accommodation and resistance thus range from unconscious reactions to exploitation, to conscious acts of survival within the capitalist system, to politically conscious acts of rebellion. These criminal actions, moreover, not only cover the range of meaning but actually evolve or progress from *unconscious reaction* to *political rebellion*. Finally, the crimes may eventually reach the ultimate stage of conscious political action—revolt. In revolt, criminal actions are not only against the system but are also an attempt to overthrow it. . . .

Crime in Capitalist Society

An understanding of crime, as developed here, begins with an analysis of the political economy of capitalism. The class struggle endemic to capitalism is characterized by a dialectic between domination and accommodation. Those who own and control the means of production, the capitalist class, attempt to secure the existing order through various forms of domination, especially crime control by the capitalist state. Those who do not own and control the means of production, especially the working class, accommodate to and resist the capitalist domination in various ways.

Crime is related to this process. Crime control and criminality (consisting of the crimes of domination and the crimes of accommodation) are understood in terms of the conditions resulting from the capitalist appropriation of labor. Variations in the nature and amount of crime occur in the course of developing capitalism. Each stage in the development of capitalism is characterized by a particular pattern of crime. The meaning and changing meanings of crime are found in the development of capitalism.

What can be expected in the further development of capitalism? The contradictions and related crises of a capitalist political economy are now a permanent feature of advanced capitalism. Further economic development along capitalist lines will solve none of the internal contradictions of the capitalist mode of production. The capitalist state must therefore increasingly utilize its resources—its various control and repressive mechanisms—to maintain the capitalist order. The dialectic between oppression by the capitalist class and the daily struggle of survival by the oppressed will continue—and at a quickened pace.

The only lasting solution to the crisis of capitalism is socialism. Under late, advanced capitalism, socialism will be achieved in the struggle of all people who are oppressed by the capitalist mode of production, namely, the workers and all elements of the surplus population. An alliance of the oppressed must take place. Given the objective conditions of a crisis in advanced capitalism, and the conditions for an alliance of the oppressed, a mass socialist movement can be formed, cutting across all divisions in the working class.

The objective of our analysis is to promote a further questioning of the capitalist system, leading to a deeper understanding of the consequences of capitalist development. The *essential meaning* of crime in the development of capitalism is the need for a socialist society. And as the preceding discussion indicates, in moving toward the socialist alternative, our study of crime is necessarily based on a social and moral analysis of capitalist society. Crime is essentially a product of the material and spiritual contradictions of capitalism. Crime can be a force in development when it becomes a part of the class struggle, increasing political consciousness. But we must continue to concentrate on the capitalist system itself. Our understanding is furthered as we critically investigate the nature, sources, and consequences of the development of capitalism.

As we engage in this work we realize the prophetic goal of socialism. The socialist struggle requires a religious consciousness as much as a class consciousness. The transition of socialism is both political and religious. And, ultimately, the religious goal transcends concrete societies. The prophetic expectation speaks finally to that which is infinite and eternal.

Discussion Questions

1. False consciousness is when workers accept existing arrangements as fair and do not recognize that they share a common interest in overthrowing the capitalist class. Why, then, is an intraclass crime, where one poor person victimizes another, a form of false consciousness?

2. Explain how crimes by corporations are a form of economic domination.

3. Quinney is critical of virtually all features of capitalism. Do you believe that there is anything about capitalism that might make crime less likely?

4. How would Quinney explain the high rates of homicide in America's inner cities? In turn, how might you use Quinney's perspective to develop programs for reducing inner-city violence? ✦

33

Delinquency and the Age Structure of Society

David F. Greenberg

Greenberg (1993 [1977]) starts his analysis with the empirical observation that youths are disproportionately involved in crime. He attributes their high rates of crime to teenagers' exposure to intense criminal motivations and to weak controls. These sources of crime are rooted in the unique "structural position of juveniles in American society" (p. 337). In turn, as adolescents mature into young adults and their structural position changes, they are likely to desist from crime.

Greenberg notes that youths in capitalist America are largely excluded from meaningful participation in the labor market for most of their teenage years. This lack of work places them at risk of experiencing three sources of strain that predispose them to delinquency.

First, achieving status or being "popular" with other youths requires the ability to participate in peer-group activities that are largely centered around leisure and consumption. Money is needed to purchase the goods and services that facilitate integration with peers (e.g., cars, alcohol, clothes, concert tickets). Their exclusion from jobs, however, means that teenagers are "less and less capable of financing an increasingly costly social life" (p. 339). Much theft, proposes Greenberg, results from the "disjunction between the desire to participate in social activities with peers and the absence of legitimate sources of funds to finance this participation" (p. 339).

Second, because the capitalist system has no need for their labor, youths are shunted into schools whose main purpose is to occupy their time and to prepare them to be obedient workers. In this stifling environment, their auton-

omy is constantly thwarted. Especially for youths who are not popular or receive poor grades, school is frustrating and humiliating. Their hostility toward school is manifested in delinquent acts that often represent a lashing out at the world that has rejected them.

Third, Greenberg suggests that males may experience the added burden of "masculine status anxiety" precipitated by their worry over their "anticipated or actual inability to fulfill traditional sex role expectations concerning work and support of family" (p. 347). To reaffirm their masculinity, these youths may manifest an exaggerated toughness and be quick to resort to violence, including using physical means to dominate women.

While youths are exposed to criminogenic motivations, they also risk paying few costs for their indiscretions. Because juveniles are seen as less responsible and their delinquencies as part of growing up, their law breaking is treated leniently by parents, school officials, and the courts. This lack of control encourages their criminality. In contrast, older youths tend to desist from crime partially due to the stiffer legal punishments accorded their illegal conduct. As young adulthood approaches, they also face fewer frustrations as they complete their schooling and establish "stakes in conformity" by securing jobs and getting married (pp. 348-349).

Greenberg's analysis can be challenged on two grounds. First, Hirschi and Gottfredson (1983) propose that the high rate of crime among juveniles is an "invariant" empirical fact that occurs across societies and thus is not unique to contemporary capitalist America (but see Greenberg, 1985). Second, Greenberg implies that youths who are employed and have money are less likely to be delinquent. Research indicates, however, that adolescents who work have higher involvement in crime (Cullen et al. in press; Williams et al., 1996; Wright et al., 1997). In fact, from a critical criminological perspective such a finding might be anticipated (Cullen et al., in press). Working mainly to satisfy materialistic desires fostered by advertising that targets the "youth market," juveniles are employed primarily as cheap labor in the secondary labor market (e.g., fast-food jobs). Their jobs often interfere with school performance, are stressful, lack *close adult supervision, and foster associations with older, more delinquent youths (see Bonger, 1969 [1916]: p. 47). It is noteworthy that compared to other Western nations, school-aged youths in the United States have much higher rates of labor market participation.*

References

Bonger, Willem. 1969 [1916]. *Criminality and Economic Conditions,* abridged edition, edited by Austin T. Turk. Bloomington: Indiana University Press.

Cullen, Francis T., Nicolas Williams, and John Paul Wright. in press. "Work Conditions and Juvenile Delinquency: Is Youth Employment Criminogenic?" *Criminal Justice Policy Review.*

Greenberg, David F. 1985. "Age, Crime, and Social Explanation." *American Journal of Sociology* 91: 1-21.

———. 1993 [originally published in 1977]. "Delinquency and the Age Structure in Society." Pp. 334-356 in *Crime and Capitalism: Readings in Marxist Criminology,* expanded and updated edition, edited by David F. Greenberg. Philadelphia: Temple University Press.

Hirschi, Travis and Michael R. Gottfredson. 1983. "Age and the Explanation of Crime." *American Journal of Sociology* 89: 552-584.

Williams, Nicolas, Francis T. Cullen, and John Paul Wright. 1996. "Labor Market Participation and Youth Crime: The Neglect of 'Working' in Delinquency Research." *Social Pathology* 2: 195-217.

Wright, John Paul, Francis T. Cullen, and Nicolas Williams. 1997. "Working While in School and Delinquent Involvement: Implications for Social Policy." *Crime and Delinquency* 43: 203-221.

An extraordinary amount of crime in American society is the accomplishment of young people. In recent years, more than half of those arrested for the seven FBI index offenses have been age 18 or under. . . .

The increasingly disproportionate involvement of juveniles in major crime categories is not readily explained by current sociological theories of delinquency, but it can be readily understood as a consequence of the historically changing position of juveniles in industrial societies. This changing position has its origin, at least in Europe and the United States, in the long-term tendencies of a capitalist economic system. . . .

That is the approach I will take. I will present an analysis of the position of juveniles in American society and elaborate the implications of that position for juvenile involvement in crime. The explanation of high levels of juvenile involvement in crime will have two major components. The first, a theory of motivation, locates sources of motivation toward criminal involvement in the structural position of juveniles in American society. The second, derived from control theory, suggests that the willingness to act on the basis of criminal motivation is distributed unequally among age groups because the cost of being apprehended are different for persons of different ages. Although some of the theoretical ideas (e.g. control theory) on which I will be drawing have already appeared in the delinquency literature, each by itself is inadequate as a full theory of delinquency. When put together with some new ideas, however, a very plausible account of age and other systematic sources of variation in delinquent involvement emerges.

Anomie and the Juvenile Labor Market

. . . The potential explanatory power of anomie theory, is, however, not exhausted by Cloward and Ohlin's formulation, because delinquency can be a response to a discrepancy between aspirations and expectations for the attainment of goals other than occupational ones. Most people have a multiplicity of goals, and only some of them are occupational. As the salience of different life goals can vary with stages of the life-cycle, our understanding of delinquency may be advanced more by examining those goals given a high priority by adolescents than by considering the importance attached to different goals in American culture generally.

The transition from childhood to adolescence is marked by a heightened sensitivity to the expectations of peers and a reduced concern with fulfilling parental expectations (Blos, 1941; Bowerman and Kinch, 1959; Tuma and Livsen, 1960; Conger, 1973: 286-92). Popularity with peers becomes highly valued, and exclusion from the most popular cliques leads to acute psychological distress.

Adolescent peer groups and orientation to the expectations of peers are found in many societies (Eisenstadt, 1956; Bloch and Neiderhoffer, 1958); but the natural tendency of those who share common experiences and problems to prefer one another's company is accentuated in American society by the importance that parents and school attach to popularity and to developing social skills assumed to be necessary for later occupational success (Mussen et al., 1969). In addition, the exclusion of young people from adult work and leisure activity forces adolescents into virtually exclusive association with one another, cutting them off from alternative sources of validation for the self (as well as reducing the degree of adult supervision). A long-run trend toward increased age segregation created by changing patterns of work and education has increased the vulnerability of teenagers to the expectations and evaluations of their peers (Panel on Youth, 1974).

This dependence on peers for approval is not itself criminogenic. In many tribal societies, age-homogenous bands of youths are functionally integrated into the economic and social life of the tribe and are not considered deviant (Mead, 1939; Eisenstadt, 1956: 56-92). In America, too, many teenage clubs and cliques are not delinquent. Participation in teenage social life, however, requires resources. In addition to personal assets and skills (having an attractive appearance and "good personality," being a skilled conversationalist, being able to memorize song lyrics and learn dance steps, and in some circles, being able to fight), money is needed for buying clothes, cosmetics, cigarettes, alcoholic beverages, narcotics, phonograph records, transistor radios, gasoline for cars and motorcycles, tickets to films and concerts, meals in restaurants, and for gambling. The progressive detachment of teenage social life from that of the family and the emergence of advertising directed toward a teenage market (this being a creation of post-war affluence and the "baby boom") have increased the importance of these goods to teenagers and hence have inflated the costs of their social activities.

When parents are unable or unwilling to subsidize their children's social life at the level required by local convention, when children want to prevent their parents from learning of their expenditures, or when they are reluctant to incur the obligations created by taking money from their parents, alternative sources of funds must be sought. Full or part-time employment once constituted such an alternative, but the long-run, persistent decline in teenage employment and labor force participation has progressively eliminated this alternative. During the period from 1870 to 1920, many states passed laws restricting child labor and establishing compulsory education. Therefore, despite a quadrupling of the "gainfully employed" population from 1870 to 1930, the number of gainfully employed workers in the 10- to 15-year-old age bracket *declined*. The Great Depression resulted in a further contradiction of the teenage labor force and increased the school-leaving age (Panel on Youth, 1974: 36-38). In 1940 the U.S. government finally stopped counting all persons over the age of 10 as part of the labor force (Tomson and Fiedler, 1975)! . . .

This process has left teenagers less and less capable of financing an increasingly costly social life whose importance is enhanced as the age segregation of society grows. Adolescent theft then occurs as a response to the disjunction between the desire to participate in social activities with peers and the absence of legitimate sources of funds needed to finance this participation. . . .

Where parents subsidize their children adequately, the incentive to steal is obviously reduced. Because the cost of social life can increase with class position, a strong correlation between social class membership and involvement in theft is not necessarily predicted. Insofar as self-reporting studies suggest that the correlation between participation in nonviolent forms of property acquisition and parental socioeconomic status is not very high, this may be a strong point for my theory. By contrast, the theories of Cohen, Miller, and Cloward and Ohlin all clash with the self-reporting studies. . . .

As teenagers get older, their vulnerability to the expectations of peers is reduced by institutional involvements that provide alternative sources of self-esteem; moreover, opportunities for acquiring money legitimately expand. Both processes reduce the motivation to engage in acquisitive forms of delinquent behavior. Consequently, involvement in theft should fall off rapidly with age, and it does.

Delinquency and the School

To explain juvenile theft in terms of structural obstacles to legitimate sources of money at a time when peer-oriented leisure activities require it is implicitly to assume that money and goods are stolen because they are useful. Acts of vandalism, thefts in which stolen objects are abandoned or destroyed, and interpersonal violence not necessary to accomplish a theft cannot be explained in this way. These are the activities that led Albert Cohen to maintain that much delinquency is "malicious" and "non-utilitarian" (1955: 25) and to argue that the content of the delinquent subculture arose in the lower class male's reaction to failure in schools run according to middle class standards. . . .

I believe that two features of the school experience, its denial of student autonomy, and its subjection of some students to the embarrassment of public degradation, are especially important in causing "non-utilitarian" delinquency.

In all spheres of life outside the school, and particularly within the family, children more or less steadily acquire larger measures of personal autonomy as they mature. Over time, the "democratization" of the family has reduced the age at which given levels of autonomy are acquired. The gradual extension of freedom that normally takes place in the family (not without struggle!) is not accompanied by parallel deregulation at school. Authoritarian styles of teaching, and rules concerning such matters as smoking, hair styles, manner of dress, going to the bathroom, and attendance, come into conflict with expectations students derive from the relaxation of controls in the family. The delegitimation of hierarchical authority

structures brought about by the radical movements of the 1960s has sharpened student awareness of this contradiction.

The symbolic significance attached to autonomy exacerbates the inherently onerous burden of school restrictions. Parents and other adults invest age-specific rights and expectations with moral significance by disapproving "childish" behavior and by using privileges to reward behavior they label "mature." Because of this association, the deprivation of autonomy is experienced as "being treated like a baby," that is, as a member of a disvalued age-status.

All students are exposed to these restrictions, and to some degree, all probably resent them. For students who are at least moderately successful at their schoolwork, who excel at sports, participate in extracurricular school activities, or are members of popular cliques, this resentment is likely to be more than compensated for by rewards associated with school attendance. These students tend to conform to school regulations most of the time, rarely collide with school officials, and are unlikely to feel overtly hostile to school or teachers. Students who are unpopular, and whose academic record, whether from inability or disinterest, is poor, receive no comparable compensation. For them, school can only be a frustrating experience: it brings no current gratification and no promise of future payoff. Why then should they put up with these restrictions? These students often get into trouble, and feel intense hostility to the school. . . .

Only a few decades ago, few working class youths—or school failures with middle class family backgrounds—would have been exposed to a contradiction between their expectations of autonomy and the school's attempts to control them, because a high proportion of students, especially working class students, left school at an early age. However, compulsory school attendance, low wages and high unemployment rates for teenagers, along with increased education requirements for entry-level jobs, have greatly reduced dropout rates. Thus in 1920, 16.8% of the 17-year-old population were high school graduates; and in 1956, 62.3% (Toby, 1967). In consequence, a greater proportion of students, especially those who benefit least from school, is exposed to this contradiction.

Common psychological responses to the irritation of the school's denial of autonomy range from affective disengagement ("tuning out" the teacher) to smouldering resentment, and at the behavioral level responses range from truancy to self-assertion through the flouting of rules. Such activities as getting drunk, using drugs, joy-riding, truanting, and adopting eccentric styles of dress, apart from any intrinsic gratification these activities may provide, can be seen as forms of what Gouldner has called "conflictual validation of the self" (1970: 221-22). By helping students establish independence from authority (school, parents, etc.), these activities contribute to self-regard. Their attraction lies in their being forbidden. . . .

As a status system, the school makes further contributions to the causation of delinquency. Almost by definition, status systems embody invidious distinctions. Where standards of evaluation are shared, and position is believed to reflect personal merit, occupants of lower statuses are likely to suffer blows to their self-esteem (Cohen, 1955: 112-13; Sennett and Cobb, 1972). . . .

Students, especially failing students, and those with lower class or minority origins, are accorded no comparable degree of respect. As they lack the appropriate institutional affiliations, their moral commitment to the dominant institutions of society is suspect. In this sense, they are social strangers; we don't quite know what we can expect from them. They are, moreover, relatively powerless. In consequence, they are exposed to evaluations from which adults are ordinarily shielded. School personnel continuously communicate their evaluations of students through grades, honor rolls, track positions, privileges, and praise for academic achievement and proper deportment. On occasion, the negative evaluation of students conveyed by the school's ranking systems is supplemented by explicit criticism and denunciation on the part of teachers who act as if the academic performance of failing students could be elevated by telling them they are stupid, or lazy, or both. Only the most extreme

failures in the adult world are subjected to degradation ceremonies of this kind. . . .

The impact of school degradation ceremonies is not limited to their effect on students' self-esteem. When a student is humiliated by a teacher the student's attempt to present a favorable self to schoolmates is undercut. Even students whose prior psychological disengagement from the value system of the school leaves their self-esteem untouched by a teacher's disparagement may react with anger at being embarrassed before peers. It is the situation of being in the company of others whose approval is needed for self-esteem that makes it difficult for teenagers to ignore humiliation that older individuals, with alternative sources of self-esteem, could readily ignore.

Visible displays of independence from, or rejections of, authority can be understood as attempts to re-establish moral character in the face of affronts. This can be accomplished by direct attacks on teachers or school, or through daring illegal performances elsewhere. These responses may or may not reflect anger at treatment perceived to be unjust, may or may not defend the student against threats to self-esteem, may or may not reflect a repudiation of conventional conduct norms. What is crucial is that these activities *demonstrate* retaliation for injury and the rejection of official values to an audience of peers whose own resentment of constituted authority causes it to be appreciative of rebels whom it would not necessarily dare to imitate. Secret delinquency and acts that entailed no risk would not serve this function. . . .

The similarity between the subculture of delinquency and that of the leisurely affluent, noted by Matza and Sykes (1961), makes sense in view of the position of the delinquent vis à vis the school. Like the factory, the school frequently requires monotonous and meaningless work. Regimentation is the rule. Expressions of originality and spontaneity are not only discouraged, but may be punished. Sociability among students is prohibited by the discipline of the classroom. Students who reap no present rewards from their schoolwork or who anticipate only the most limited occupational returns as a compensation for their adherence to the onerousness of school discipline are free to cultivate the self-expressive traits which the school fails to reward, because they will lose nothing that is important to them by doing so. As Downes (1966) points out, they may come to regard adults who work as defeated and lifeless because of their subordination to a routine that necessitates self-suppression, and hence try to avoid work because of the cost in self-alienation. . . .

The similarity between delinquent and non-criminal recreational risk-taking warns us that the pursuit of status through risk-taking does not *necessarily* arise from problems in self-esteem. Once a status system rewarding delinquent activity exists, students may act with reference to it in order to *increase* prestige in the group, not only to prevent prestige from falling. Thus teachers may be provoked (Werthman, 1967), gang rivals taunted, and daring thefts and assaults perpetrated, even in the absence of humiliation.

When students drop out or graduate from high school, they enter a world that, while sometimes inhospitable, does not restrict their autonomy and assault their dignity in the same way the school does. The need to engage in crime to establish a sense of an autonomous self and to preserve moral character through risk-taking is thus reduced. In addition, the sympathetic audience of other students of the same age is taken away. Thus school-leaving eliminates major sources of motivation toward delinquency. Indeed, American studies indicate that the self-esteem of dropouts rises after they leave school (Bachman et al., 1972) and that dropping out produces an immediate decline in delinquency involvement (Mukherjee, 1971; Elliot and Voss, 1974). In England, when the school-leaving age was raised by one year, the peak age for delinquency rose simultaneously by one year (McClean and Wood, 1969). These findings are especially ironic, in that nineteenth-century reformers touted the extension of public schooling as a way of reducing delinquency; and present-day delinquency prevention programs have involved campaigns to keep delinquents in school.

Masculine Status Anxiety and Delinquency

Many observers have remarked on the disproportionate involvement of males in delinquency, and the exaggerated masculine posturing that characterizes their involvement, particularly where violence offenses are concerned. . . .

Males who are not in doubt about their identity as males may nevertheless feel anxiety in connection with anticipated or actual inability to fulfill traditional sex role expectations concerning work and support of family. This masculine *status* anxiety can be generated by a father who is present but ineffectual, and by living in a neighborhood where, for social-structural reasons, many men are unemployed—regardless of whether one's own father is present in the household.

Men who experience such anxiety because they are prevented from fulfilling conventional male role expectations may attempt to alleviate the anxiety by exaggerating those traditionally male traits that *can* be expressed. Attempts to dominate women (including rape) and patterns of interpersonal violence can be seen in these terms. In other words, crime can be a response to masculine status anxiety no less than to anxiety over male identity; it can provide a sense of potency that is expected and desired but not achieved in other spheres of life.

In this interpretation, a compulsive concern with toughness and masculinity arises not from a hermetically sealed lower-class subculture "with an integrity of its own" nor from the psychodynamics of a female-headed household (Miller, 1958), but as a response to a contradiction between structural economic-political constraints on male status attainment and the cultural expectations for men that permeate American society. The role of the subculture Miller describes is to make available the behavioral adaptations that previous generations have developed in response to this contradiction. . . .

One would expect masculine status anxiety to appear with greatest intensity and to decline most slowly in those segments of the population in which adult male unemployment is exceptionally high. This conforms to the general pattern of arrests for violent offenses such as homicide, forcible rape and assaults—offenses often unconnected with the pursuit of material gain, and hence most plausibly interpreted as a response to masculine status anxiety. Rates of arrest for these offenses peak in the immediate post-high school age brackets (several years later than for the property offenses) and the decline is slower than for property offenses. Moreover, blacks are overrepresented in violence offense arrests to a much greater degree than in arrests for property offenses.

Costs of Delinquency

So far, some possible sources of age-linked variation in motivation to participate in criminal activity have been identified, but this is only half the story, for one may wish to engage in some form of behavior but nevertheless decide not to do so because its potential costs are deemed unacceptably high. Costs can be a consequence of delinquency, and must be taken into account. Control theorists have begun to do so (Briar and Piliavin, 1965; Hirschi, 1969; Piliavin et al. 1969).

In early adolescence the potential costs of all but the most serious forms of delinquency are relatively slight. Parents and teachers are generally willing to write off a certain mount of misbehavior as "childish mischief," while enormous caseloads have forced juvenile courts in large cities to adopt a policy that comes very close to what Schur (1973) has called "radical nonintervention." Given the slight risk of apprehension for any single delinquent act, the prevalence of motivations to violate the law, and the low cost of lesser violations, we should expect minor infractions to be common among juveniles, and the self-reporting studies generally suggest that they are. As teenagers get older, the potential costs of apprehension increase: victims may be more prone to file a complaint, and police to make an arrest. Juvenile court judges are more likely to take a serious view of an older offender, especially one with a prior record. Older offenders risk prosecution in criminal court, where penalties tend to be harsher, and where an official record will have more serious consequences for later job opportunities. . . .

Just as the costs of crime are escalating, new opportunities in the form of jobs, marriage, or enlistment in the armed forces create stakes in conformity and, as Matza points out (1964: 55), may also relieve problems of masculine status anxiety. Toward the end of high school, when student concern about the future increases, the anticipation of new opportunities is manifested in desistance from delinquency and avoidance of those who do not similarly desist. Consistent with this interpretation is the fact that in both England and the United States, the peak year for delinquent involvement is the year *before* school-leaving.

Those whose opportunities for lucrative employment are limited by obstacles associated with racial and/or class membership, however, will have far less reason to desist from illegal activity than those whose careers are not similarly blocked. The jobs available to young members of the lower strata of the working class tend to be limited, tedious, and low paying. Marriage may appear less appealing to young men whose limited prospects promise inability to fulfill traditional male expectations as breadwinner. Even an army career may be precluded by an arrest record, low intelligence test scores, physical disability, or illiteracy. Thus the legitimate opportunity structure, even if relatively useless for understanding entrance into delinquency, may still be helpful in understanding patterns of desistance.

The same may be said of the illegal opportunity structure. Those few delinquents who are recruited into organized crime or professional theft face larger rewards and less risk of serious penalty than those not so recruited, and their personal relationships with partners may be more satisfying. They should be less likely to desist from crime, but their offense patterns can be expected to change. . . .

Delinquency and the Social Construction of the Juvenile

Among the structural sources of adolescent crime identified here, the exclusion of juveniles from the world of adult work plays a crucial role. It is this exclusion that simultaneously exaggerates teenagers' dependence on peers for approval and eliminates the possibility of their obtaining funds to support their intensive, leisure-time social activities. The disrespectful treatment students receive in school depends on their low social status, which in turn reflects their lack of employment and income. In late adolescence and early adulthood, their fear that this lack of employment will persist into adulthood evokes anxiety over achievement of traditional male gender role expectations, especially among males in the lower levels of the working class, thus contributing to a high level of violence. . . .

The exclusion of teenagers from serious work is not characteristic of all societies. Peasant and tribal societies could not afford to keep their young idle as long as we do. In such societies, juvenile crime rates were low. Under feudalism, too, children participated in farming and handicraft production as part of the family unit beginning at a very early age.

In depriving masses of serfs and tenant farmers of access to the means of production (land), European capitalism in its early stages of development generated a great deal of crime, but in a manner that cut across age boundaries. Little of the literature on crime in Elizabethan and Tudor England singles out juveniles as a special category.

The industrial revolution in the first half of the nineteenth century similarly brought with it a great deal of misery, but its effect on crime was not restricted to juveniles. Children of the working class in that period held jobs at an early age and in some sectors of the economy were given preference. Only middle and upper class children were exempt from the need to work, and they were supervised much more closely than they are nowadays. As far as can be judged, juvenile crime in that period was a much smaller fraction of the total than at present, and was more confined to the lower classes than it is now.

In modern capitalist societies, children of all classes share, for a limited period, a common relationship to the means of production (namely exclusion) which is distinct from that of most adults, and they respond to their common structural position in fairly similar ways. Although there are class differences in the extent and nature of delinquency, especially violent delinquency, they are less pronounced than for adults, for whom occupational differentiation is much sharper.

The deteriorating position of juveniles in the labor market in recent years has been ascribed to a variety of causes, among them the inclusion of juveniles under minimum wage laws; changes in the structure of the economy (less farm employment); teenage preference for part-time work (to permit longer periods of education), which makes teenage labor less attractive to employers; and the explosion in the teenage labor supply, created by the baby boom, at a time when women were entering the labor market in substantial numbers (Kalacheck, 1973). Whatever contribution these circumstances may have made to shifting teenage employment patterns in the short run, the exclusion of juveniles from the labor market has been going on for more than a century, and may more plausibly be explained in terms of the failure of the oligopoly-capitalist economy to generate sufficient demand for labor than to these recent developments (Carson, 1972; Bowers, 1975).

In both the United States and England, the prolongation of education has historically been associated with the contraction of the labor market, casting doubt on the view that more education is something that the general population has wanted for its own sake. Had this been true, the school-leaving age would have jumped upward in periods of prosperity, when a larger proportion of the population could afford more education, not during depressions. Moreover, the functionalist argument that increased education is necessary as technology becomes more complex would apply at best to a small minority of students, and rests on the dubious assumption that full-time schooling is pedagogically superior to alternative modes of organizing the education of adolescents.

The present social organization of education, which I have argued contributes to delinquency, has also been plausibly attributed to the functional requirement of a capitalist economy for a docile, disciplined and stratified labor force, as well as to the need to keep juveniles out of the labor market. Thus the high and increasing level of juvenile crime we are seeing in present-day United States and in other Western countries originates in the structural position of juveniles in an advanced capitalist economy. . . .

Discussion

For decades, criminologists have proposed such reforms as eliminating poverty and racial discrimination to solve the crime problem (see, Silberman, 1978, for the latest of this genre). None of them seriously addresses how the serious obstacles to achieving this task are to be overcome within the framework of a capitalist society. To suppose that the writing of an article or a book calling for an end to poverty and racism will actually contribute to ending poverty and racism is to betray a whimsical bit of utopianism. Marxist theorists tend to see these problems as largely produced by a class society, and insoluble within it. Efforts to tack these problems may certainly be worthwhile, but not because they can be expected to achieve full success.

My analysis of delinquency suggests that most proposed "solutions" to the delinquency problem would have limited impact. Thoroughly integrating teenagers into the labor force, on at least a part-time basis, would go far toward reducing delinquency. But the jobs for adolescents are not there; and the drastic restructuring of education that would be required is hardly to be expected in the foreseeable future.

If young people had a good understanding of the structural sources of their frustration and oppression, their response might well be different. Instead of individualistic and predatory adaptations, we might see collective, politicized, and non-predatory challenges to their exclusion. It seems unlikely that such a radical transformation in consciousness would develop spontaneously, but in the context of a mass socialist movement, it could well occur. . . .

Discussion Questions

1. How does involvement in crime vary by age? Do youths have high or low rates of criminal involvement?

2. Recall the discussion of strain theory in Part IV. Why might Greenberg's theory be see as a "strain" theory?

3. Why is Greenberg a "critical criminologist"? How does he believe that capitalism is at the ultimate cause of the high rate of crime among youths in American society?

4. Recall the time when you might have been employed in high school. How might this experience have made a youth less likely to break the law? More likely to break the law? ✦

34

An Integrated Structural-Marxist Theory of Delinquency

Mark Colvin
John Pauly

Colvin and Pauly (1983: 513) define their approach as "structural-Marxist insofar as its analytical starting point is the objective structure of social relations grounded in the process of material production under capitalism." They observe that the United States is characterized by a capitalist class and a working class. These classes, however, are not homogeneous but are divided into "class fractions." Of special concern are the three fractions of the working class: fraction I, which consists of workers in the secondary labor market (i.e., low-skill, "dead-end" jobs); fraction II, which consists of unionized workers in industries such as automobile manufacturing and mining; and fraction III, which consists of workers who are involved in jobs that require independent initiative such as wage-earning craft workers and salaried professionals.

According to Colvin and Pauly, the capitalist class has an interest in securing the conformity of its employees in the workplace. The workers in each class fraction, however, are subjected by employers to different types of control in their jobs. Fraction II workers are controlled largely by offers of material rewards (e.g., pay, benefits), while fraction III workers comply with the mandates of authority because doing so brings more job autonomy, decision-making powers, and thus status among fellow employees. Fraction I workers, however, are subjected to coercive control. Mired in jobs

that offer low pay, no security, and little hope of advancement, their conformity is secured mainly through "threatened or actual dismissal from the job" (p. 532). This coercion creates for the worker an alienated, rather than a positive, bond to the employer.

The innovative theoretical contribution of Colvin and Pauly is their contention that how parents are disciplined at work affects how parents discipline their own children at home. "Through the process of parental control over children, a parent's bond to the authority of the workplace is reproduced in the child's initial bond to parental authority" (p. 535). Most criminogenic, then, are the child-rearing styles of fraction I workers, who use coercive means—especially harsh and erratic punishment—to enforce their children's conformity. The result is an alienating bond to the parent. In turn, these youngsters are likely to reproduce their alienated bonds with teachers. They are at-risk for poorer school performance and of being placed in lower-level educational tracks that stress discipline and conformity over autonomy and intellectual creativity. These school experiences deepen the youth's alienation and help to drive them into delinquent peer groups comprised of youths also experiencing alienated bonds to society. The end of this causal pathway is persistent involvement in delinquent behavior.

There is considerable evidence that inconsistent, coercive, excessively harsh parenting is an important cause of delinquency (see Loeber and Stouthamer-Loeber, 1986). Even so, research has yet to confirm Colvin and Pauly's central thesis that parental disciplinary practices are mainly a product of how parents are controlled in the workplace (Messner and Krohn, 1990; Paternoster and Tittle, 1990). It is equally plausible, for example, that parenting styles are learned not in the workplace but during one's own upbringing. The role of nonworking parents, typically mothers, in child rearing also is not made clear. If not from work, what is the origin of their parenting styles? Colvin and Pauly's theory would benefit as well from more attention to gender issues. For example, how does the state's attempt to control mothers on welfare affect the child-rearing practices of these women? How do power differences between men and women in the home *affect the way discipline is carried out? Does Colvin and Pauly's theory operate the same way for girls and boys? (see Hagan, Chapter 21; Simpson and Elis, 1994).*

References

Colvin, Mark and John Pauly. 1983. "A Critique of Criminology: Toward an Integrated Structural-Marxist Theory of Delinquency Production." *American Journal of Sociology* 89: 513-551.

Loeber, Rolf and Magda Stouthamer-Loeber. 1986. "Family Factors as Correlates and Predictors of Juvenile Conduct Problems and Delinquency." Pp. 29-149 in *Crime and Justice: An Annual Review of Research, Volume 7*, edited by Michael Tonry and Norval Morris. Chicago: University of Chicago Press.

Messner, Steven F. and Marvin D. Krohn. "Class, Compliance Structures, and Delinquency: Assessing Integrated Structural-Marxist Theory." *American Journal of Sociology* 96: 300-328.

Paternoster, Raymond, and Charles R. Tittle. 1990. "Parental Work Control and Delinquency: A Theoretical and Empirical Critique." Pp. 39-65 in *Advances in Criminological Theory, Volume 2*, edited by William S. Laufer and Freda Adler. New Brunswick, NJ: Transaction.

Simpson, Sally S. and Lori Elis. 1994. "Is Gender Subordinate to Class? An Empirical Assessment of Colvin and Pauly's Structural Marxist Theory of Delinquency." *Journal of Criminal Law and Criminology* 85: 453-480.

...We attempt in this paper to present a comprehensive theoretical approach to understanding the social production of serious patterned delinquent behavior. . . . Our approach can be considered "structural-Marxist" insofar as its analytical starting point is the objective structure of social relations grounded in the process of material production under capitalism (Appelbaum 1979; Blackburn 1972; Burris 1979; Gimenez 1982; Godelier 1972). . . .

We focus first on social control structures at workplaces and then on those within families, schools, and peer groups. We see these various structures of control as interconnected in a process of social reproduction, contoured by class and production relations of capitalism. . . .

An Integrated Structural-Marxist Approach

The process of socialization described by integrated theorists can be placed within a context of larger structural relations that define these processes. Structural-Marxists have attempted to connect relations of production theoretically with those relations necessary to reproduce a social formation. It is within this theoretical framework that the latent social production of delinquency is best understood.

In a Marxist paradigm, the fundamental structural relations are those that are entered into at the point of material production. All other human relationships rest on those relationships that revolve around the provision of the physical means of life. Thus Marxists consider the mode of production and reproduction to be the essential starting point of any social analysis, because human existence depends first on the biological survival of the species and thus on the meeting of human needs for which material resources must be expropriated from nature. The relationships among human actors that arise from these essential productive tasks set limits on other, nonproductive social relations, without necessarily determining in any mechanistic sense their form and content. Entering into these necessary productive relationships not only produces the means for physical subsistence but also produces and reproduces the practical intercourse between human beings, that is, produces and reproduces the structured relations through which human actors interact in the essential tasks of material production (Marx and Engels 1967, pp. 6-7).

Individuals do not enter into these relations arbitrarily or simply as a product of their will but encounter them as a given product of the historic development of productive forces. Individuals must interact with these relations (and change them) within the structural limits set by the relations. . . .

These relations of production also define the class structure at any point in history. Structural Marxism conceptualizes classes in

326 Part IX ♦ *Critical Criminology*

social structural rather than interpersonal terms: classes are integral, not external, to social structure; they are defined by the social relations of production, specifically by relations to the means of production. Classes can be distinguished by their ownership and control of the means of production and of its end products. This differs from defining classes from the point of view of attributes of individuals, for example, life chances, education, income, or occupational prestige, though these may be related to the structural definition of class. As such, classes exist in relation to each other only vis-à-vis the means of production. And as such, the activities of class members, of ruling or subordinate classes or class fractions, are determined by (1) the structure of the mode of production and the patterns of its development; and (2) the relations of that class or fraction with other classes or fractions, which are often antagonistic relations because of structural contradictions characterizing the mode of production. . . .

Since petty commodity production continually gives way to capitalist incursions, the expansionary dynamic of capitalism renders the latter the dominant mode of production in the modern United States. Yet, even the capitalist mode of production has not generated two monolithic classes at this point in history. Both the capitalist class and the working class are composed of class fractions that have evolved with the development of capitalism.

Fractions of the capitalist class have emerged through the struggle between capitalists for market shares, which has resulted in an uneven expansion of capital and the corresponding rise of sectors within the capitalist economy (Edwards 1979; O'Connor 1973; Oster 1979; Tolbert, Horan, and Beck 1980). Some capitalists have been able to capture greater market shares and monopolize certain industries, such as mining, transportation, utilities, communications, and some manufacturing industries (e.g., auto, steel, electronics, and petroleum). . . .

It is primarily in the monopoly sector of capital that top managerial and supervisory positions have been established to provide the more sophisticated control networks

within organizations to deal with complicated market arrangements that may have international scope. . . .

The other major fraction of the capitalist class is composed of competitive-sector capitalists. These capitalists are less protected than the monopoly sector from market fluctuations; they are concentrated in wholesale, retail, and service industries and in a few manufacturing industries, such as lumber, textiles, and apparel. . . .

Edwards (1979) presents the most comprehensive analysis to date of the major fractions of the working class. Fraction I is composed of workers who labor in more competitive industries and who, in Edwards's terminology, are involved in a "secondary labor market," which operates largely by the law of supply and demand for labor in setting the price of labor power. Thus, fraction I is most affected by, and includes a huge proportion of, the floating and stagnant surplus populations which compete for fraction I jobs. These include low-skill jobs in small, nonunion manufacturing; southern textile jobs; service jobs; lower-level clerical and sales jobs; and agricultural wage-labor. These jobs are "typically dead-end jobs, with few prospects for advancement and little reward for seniority in the form of either higher pay or a better job" (Edwards 1979, p. 167). Employers forcefully resist organizing efforts by workers. There is a large turnover of employees in fraction I, which undermines labor-organizing efforts and also reflects the predominant control mechanism for worker discipline—threatened or actual dismissal from the job.

Edwards defines the control mechanism used to discipline fraction I workers as "simple control," which, in our view, corresponds to Etzioni's (1970) "coercive compliance structure." This compliance structure rests predominantly on "coercive power," which Etzioni (1970, p. 104) defines as involving "the application or the threat of application of physical sanctions" that include "the controlling through force the satisfaction of needs." Dismissal from the job definitely involves the forced removal from the means for satisfying basic needs and thus is a coercive mechanism of power. Coercive power tends to create an "alienative involvement," or intense negative orientation (Etzioni 1970, p. 106) on the part of the worker toward the employer and the organization. This workplace control structure conditions the worker's ideological orientation or bond to authority at the workplace. In this case an alienated or negative bond is created by the more coercive simple control used with fraction I workers.

Fraction II is composed of organized workers who, through earlier struggles, gained wage and benefit concessions, job protection, and the establishment of industry-wide unions. The auto, steel, and rubber industries; machine manufacture; and mining offer the best examples of fraction II workers. According to Edwards, capitalists and their managers were forced to shift from simple control to more sophisticated technical control in response to organized worker resistance to the arbitrary and coercive discipline of simple control. Technical control is machine paced and impersonal and relies on the worker calculating his or her material self-interest for pay raises and job security based on seniority with the firm. Edwards identifies fraction II workers as being involved in a "subordinate primary labor market" that relies very little on external pressure from a floating surplus population, which is usually protected in this fraction by more generous, union-connected unemployment benefits. Job performance is usually routine and boring and holds little intrinsic interest for the worker. The main control is the calculation of extrinsic rewards of material security through movement up a union pay ladder; this process produces a firm-specific "internal labor market" (Edwards 1979, p. 172). This form of control, which defines fraction II, is consonant with Etzioni's (1970, p. 109) "utilitarian compliance structure" composed of "renumerative power," involving the manipulation of material rewards. A "calculative involvement" of intermediate intensity on the part of the worker is produced in this type of control structure. It is a precarious ideological bond, depending on continual remuneration and advancement up the pay ladder and producing little loyalty on the part of the worker.

Fraction III is defined by its involvement in an "independent primary labor market" composed of jobs that are likely "to require independent initiative or self-pacing" (Edwards 1979, p. 174), including: (1) middle-layer workers, such as technical staff, foremen, personal secretaries, and middle-level supervisors; (2) wage-earning craft workers, such as electricians, carpenters, plumbers, and machinists, who are usually members of craft guilds; and (3) salaried professional workers, such as corporation accountants, corporation research scientists and engineers, corporate and state lawyers, social workers, and school teachers. The bulk of state workers are included in fraction III. This fraction, just as other working-class fractions, spans both blue-collar and white-collar occupations. The jobs in fraction III are ruled by more universal standards of professional or craft guild conduct. This differs from the machine-paced and firm-specific standards of the "subordinate primary labor market" of fraction II. . . .

In any event, the work tasks of most fraction III workers preclude the use of pure technical control, since the work tasks cannot be easily routinized, requiring instead a certain degree of flexible response and initiative on the part of the worker. . . .

Bureaucratic control involves an elaborate manipulation of symbols and statuses that elicits ideological commitments to the organization. The bureaucratic control structure "fosters occupational consciousness; that is, [it] provides the basis for job-holders to define their own identities in terms of their particular occupation" (Edwards 1979, p. 177). Thus, fraction III jobs hold more intrinsic meaning for these workers. While pay scales are commensurate with increases in job status, it is primarily the possibility of job status increase that compels worker compliance. In fact, many fraction III workers are paid less than unionized fraction II workers.

"Bureaucratic control" corresponds to Etzioni's "normative compliance structure" that includes "normative power," which "rests on the allocation and manipulation of symbolic rewards" (Etzioni 1970, p. 104) and elicits a "moral involvement," designating "a positive orientation of high intensity" on the part of the worker toward authority and the organization (Etzioni 1970, p. 107). . . .

Family Control Structures and Delinquency

Melvin Kohn (1977) argues that a parent who experiences greater external control at work comes to "understand" the importance (for physical and financial survival) of conformity to external authority. The stress on conformity to external authority is then (consciously or unconsciously) impressed on children during child-rearing activities in the family. In contrast, parents who experience a lower degree of external control and exercise greater decision-making power at work come to view "internalized self-control," initiative, and creativity as valued attributes that are impressed on their children.

Both orientations for parental values spring from the parents' ideological bonds produced in differential work experiences. An underlying message to the child in both instances is an ideological statement about the world: control of life circumstances and the determinants of one's behavior spring from either external compulsion or internal motivation. The child, in his or her everyday interactions with parents, learns that one acts toward authority either out of fear or calculation of external consequences or out of a sense of internalized respect or commitment. Through the process of parental control over children, a parent's bond to the authority of the workplace is reproduced in the child's initial bond to parental authority. . . .

The child participates in a family control structure that contains certain rewards and punishments for specific types of behavior and perceived motives. The more coercive this structure of control, the more negative are the bonds produced in the child. The degree of coerciveness of family control structures is influenced by material resources available to parents as reinforcements and by the ideological bond of the parent, which influences the types of child behavior that will be rewarded or punished. Both material resources and parental bonds are associated with workplace control structures.

As with the parents' social control experiences at work, an initial ideological orientation toward conformity to external authority, based on fear or calculation of external consequences, or toward internalized "self-direction" is produced in the child, depending on the coerciveness of the control structure within the family. This family control structure is shaped by the stability and level of parents' association with control structures at work.

Thus we postulate that parents from fraction I of the working class, typified by more coercive workplace controls and more sporadic associations with specific workplaces, tend to enforce an uneven and erratic family control structure that swings unpredictably between being lax and being highly punitive. (see Rubin's [1976] discussion of "settled living" versus "hard living" life-styles within the working class.) We expect more alienated initial bonds to be produced in children who experience such arbitrary, inconsistent, and coercive family control structures. Parents from fraction II of the working class, characterized by more steady and long-term association with a utilitarian compliance structure at work, tend to enforce a more utilitarian compliance structure in the family that produces calculative bonds of intermediate intensity in their children, who can dependably predict external consequences for behavior. Parents in more "self-directing" workplace situations—such as fraction III workers, semiautonomous wage earners, top managers, and owners of the means of production—tend to enforce a more normative family compliance structure in which positive initial bonds of high intensity are produced in children. . . .

Regarding delinquency, significant positive associations between more physical and punitive parental disciplining practices and delinquency and between erratic parental disciplining practices and delinquency have been reported in studies using both official and self-reported delinquency measures (Glueck and Glueck 1950; Hirschi 1969; McCord, McCord, and Zola 1959; Nye 1958; West and Farrington 1973). Hirschi (1969) reports that juveniles' positive bonds to parents are inversely related to self-reported delinquency; later studies (see Johnson 1979) suggest, however, that the influence of parental bonding on delinquency is at best indirect. These studies suggest that the coerciveness of family control structures, conditioned by parents' work experiences, contributes at least indirectly to the production of delinquency.

School Control Structures and Delinquency

The next important process in the generational reproduction of labor power, necessary for capitalist production relations, is formal schooling. . . .

When entering school, the child, with initial bonds produced in a family control structure, confronts a new structure of control. The school, like parents' workplaces, contains gradations of control (within various "tracks") that are exercised over students. A child with negative initial bonds is likely to be placed in a control structure at school that parallels the coercive family control structure that produced the child's negative bond. This process operates both by deliberate design and through subtle mechanisms. . . .

Thus, parents' bonds engendered by workplace control structures are reproduced in the child through family controls: the child's initial ideological orientation toward authority is most likely to be reinforced in school control structures by mechanisms which render the child suitable for eventual placement in a workplace control structure similar to that of the parent. Thus, inequality and the class structure are subtly reproduced.

Some research suggests that school control structures and related variables are associated with delinquency. . . .

Peer Associations, Structures of Control, and Delinquency

Peer associations mediate the relationship between delinquency and the other control structures we have discussed. The structured experiences associated with parents' workplaces, families, and schools form the necessary conditions and delinquent peer associations create the sufficient conditions for patterned delinquent behavior.

Peer groups form largely around juveniles' interactions at and around school and reflect the patterns of association structured by school tracking systems and by the differential distribution of opportunities among neighborhoods. Structures of control over adolescents, who are marginal to workplace control structures and who are increasingly moving away from the influence of family control structures, are shaped by a combination of school, neighborhood, and peer group relationships (Greenberg 1977).

Our theory assumes that juveniles with similar bonds (due to similar experiences in schools, neighborhoods, and families) will be in greater contact with each other and will be drawn to each other on the basis of shared values and experiences. Specifically, students in higher educational tracks, in which positive bonds are reinforced, tend to form peer associations that contain more normative compliance structures that continue the production of positive bonds and thus insulate these juveniles from delinquent involvement. Students in intermediate tracks, which are more conducive to calculative involvement, are likely to form peer relations oriented around the pursuit of extrinsic rewards. The possible contradiction between rewards in school and those associated with peer relationships places these juveniles under greater strain. Such a situation can attenuate their bonds and lead to occasional involvement in less serious types of instrumental delinquency. Students in lower educational tracks, which tend to produce more alienated bonds, would be most open to associating with similarly negatively bonded peers who are likely to reinforce tendencies toward serious, patterned delinquency (Elliott et al. 1979). . . .

Peer groups which reinforce patterned delinquent behavior and those which reinforce conventional behavior are characterized by distinct structures of internal control that affect individual bonds and reinforce specific types of behavior. The internal structures of control within peer groups spring from control structures within the school and from differential opportunity structures in the social and economic environment of neighborhoods. Depending on the interaction between specific internal structures of control within delinquent groups and specific external structures of opportunity in the surrounding environment, the delinquent peer groups will produce either instrumental or violent patterned delinquent behavior.

Summary

Our theory focuses on the structures of control in several locations in the production and social reproduction processes. Our discussion of structures of control incorporates insights about micro-level processes from learning, strain, control, labeling, and integrated theories in criminology. We suggest that structures of control have parallel patterns associated with work, families, schools, and peer groups, and that those patterns form the mechanisms for the reproduction of the class structure. Expanding on insights about macro-level processes from conflict and radical criminology, we construct a structural-Marxist approach that views delinquency as a latent outcome of the social reproduction process in capitalism.

The structures of control tend to produce differential ideological bonds, depending on the individual's particular path through the control structures. We see ideological bonds as malleable, but they are usually sustained in the socialization process by somewhat similar experiences in control structures that individuals encounter along the path of socialization. The direction of socialization is initiated by the parents' location in workplace control structures, which are shaped by the historical interaction between competition among capitalists and the level of class struggle. These workplace control structures affect the structures of control within families. Children's initial bonds are shaped by family control relations and tend to set the child up for, or preclude placement in, specific control structures at school. School control structures create differential experiences of reward and punishment and reinforce or attenuate initial bonds. The juvenile is then open for recruitment to a variety of peer group experiences that are also shaped by structures of control among peers, which interact with differential opportunity structures in the surrounding community to produce specific patterns of peer group behavior. If patterned delinquent peer groups are available in the immediate social environment, a juvenile's structurally induced bond will open him up to, or insulate him from, entry into such peer relations. Entry into this type of peer association continues the pattern of reinforcement toward more sustained delinquent behavior.

Figure 34.1 presents a general path model of delinquency production focusing on the individual's structurally conditioned experiences as he moves toward becoming a more serious, patterned delinquent. From our integrated structural-Marxist approach, we predict the following empirical relationships (numbered as in the figure).

Parents' *class position* (defined by ownership and control over the means and ends of production) is (*1*) negatively associated with parents' experience or coerciveness in *workplace control structures*, which (*2*) is positively associated with more alienated bonds in parents.

Alienated parental bonds (*3*) contribute to the development of more coercive *family control structures*, which (*4*) are positively related to more alienated initial bonds in juveniles.

Juveniles with alienated initial bonds (*5*) have a greater probability of being placed in more coercive *school control structures*, which (*6* and *7*) reinforce the juveniles' alienated bonds.

Juveniles' reinforced alienated bonds lead to (*8* and *9*) greater association with alienated peers, who form *peer group control structures* which, in interaction with (*10, 11,* and *12*) class-related, community, and neighborhood distributions of opportunities, create qualitatively different paths of delinquent development (*13* and *14*).

In the first path (leading from line *13*), the experience of coerciveness in peer group control relations mutually interacts (*15* and *16*) with juveniles' alienated bonds to (*17* and *18*) propel these juveniles into serious, patterned, *violent delinquent behavior*.

In the second path (leading from line *14*), the experience of remuneration from illegitimate sources (*19* and *20*) creates an alternative utilitarian control structure which mutually interacts (*21* and *22*) with newly formed calculative bonds to propel these juveniles (*23* and *24*) into serious, patterned, *instrumental delinquent behavior*. . . .

Figure 34.1
General Path Model of Patterned Delinquency

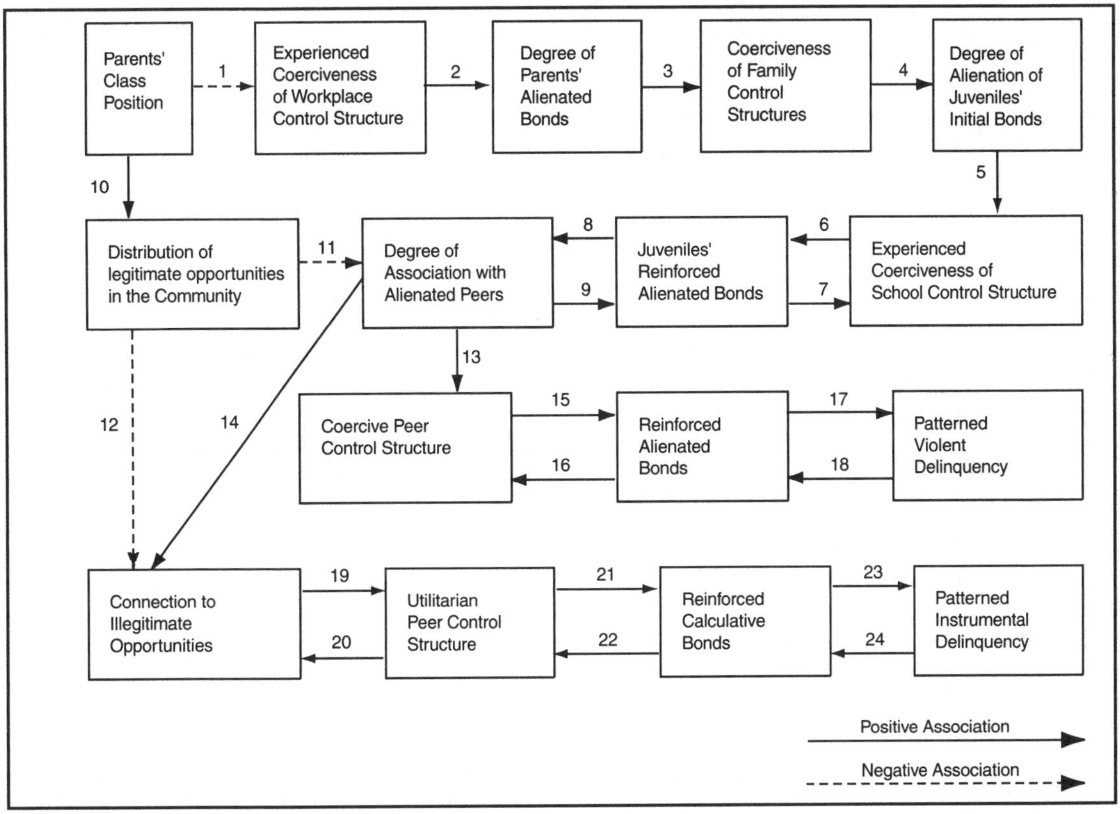

Reprinted from Mark Colvin and John Pauly, "An Integrated Structural-Marxist Theory of Delinquency" in the *American Journal of Sociology* 89. Copyright ©1983 by the University of Chicago Press. Reprinted by permission.

Discussion Questions

1. Karl Marx originally conceived of capitalist society as divided into two classes: the bourgeoisie and the proletariat. How does Colvin and Pauly's conceptualization of class in the United States overlap with and differ from Marx's view?

2. Many critical criminologists argue that capitalism causes crime. According to Colvin and Pauly, how does this occur?

In particular, how are family, school, and peer group relations influenced by class position and in turn contribute to a youth's involvement in delinquency?

3. Recall John Hagan's power-control theory (Chapter 21). How does Colvin and Pauly's structural-Marxist theory differ from Hagan's perspective? How is it similar?

4. Short of calling for a socialist system, what kinds of policies would Colvin and Pauly's theory suggest might help to reduce delinquency? For example, what interventions might be used with families? With schools? ✦

35

Social Capital and Crime

John Hagan

"A *new sociology of crime and disrepute," observes John Hagan (1994: p. 98), "focuses attention on the criminal costs of social inequality." Over the past 25 years, inequality has increased in the United States. The impact of this inequality has been unevenly distributed and has most affected the lives of those residing in distressed inner-city minority communities. Persisting racial segregation, the loss of decent-paying manufacturing jobs, the residential concentration of the poorest citizens, and government cutbacks in support—all these have combined to cause a large-scale "capital disinvestment" in these communities. The result is high rates of crime.*

Hagan contends that there are different forms of "capital." Economists previously have focused on physical capital (the means of production) and on human capital ("the skills and knowledge acquired by individuals through education and training") (p. 67). Borrowing from the work of Coleman (1990), Hagan notes that there is also social capital. This concept is perhaps best understood as the quality of the social relationships that exist between people in families, interpersonal networks, and neighborhoods that make it possible to achieve individual and group goals. Quality relationships are the conduit through which human capital is transmitted from parent to child, through which social support is provided, through which "contacts" for jobs are acquired, and so on.

As noted, Hagan argues that inner-city communities, increasingly socially isolated and economically distressed, have suffered a depletion of social capital. Youths in these communities lack the density of quality social relationships in their families and neighborhood net-

works that facilitate access to jobs in the core labor market. In response to their restricted opportunities, they develop subcultural adaptations supportive of crime. Hagan refers to this process as "recapitalization, an effort to reorganize what resources are available, even if illicit, to reach attainable goals" (p. 70). A prime example of recapitalization is the creation of drug markets, which furnish participants with the "material symbols of wealth and success in the neighborhood" (p. 96). Such involvement in crime, however, undermines long-term life outcomes. Prison, violence on the streets, and exclusion from the core labor market await those embedded in a criminal life-course.

The concept of social capital is, at times, hard to grasp. It seems more sensitizing than precise, and it seems to encompass a wide range of relational processes. For Hagan's perspective to develop, the theory will have to define more systematically the components of social capital and how each is implicated in the origins of criminal behavior. Causal models will need to be specified and tested with data that truly capture the essential features of social capital. Still, Hagan's social capital approach is rich with theoretical possibilities. Most importantly, it allows for the integration of the macro-level and micro-level by identifying the conduit—social capital—through which structural conditions such as inequality affect the life choices, including those to commit crime, that individuals make each day.

References

Coleman, James S. 1990. *Foundations of Social Theory*. Cambridge, MA: Belknap/Harvard University Press.

Hagan, John. 1994. *Crime and Disrepute*. Thousand Oaks, CA: Pine Forge Press.

Social and Cultural Capital

Forms of Capital

. . . The forms of capital require an introduction. The concept of *physical capital* is familiar as referring to tools, machinery, and other productive equipment. Physical capital is a foundation of economic relations. However, economists have added to this the further idea of *human capital*, which refers to the skills and knowledge acquired by individuals through education and training (Schultz, 1961; Becker, 1964). The capital that is embodied in humans is somewhat less tangible than that embodied in tools or machinery, but both involve the creation of resources or power through a transformative process, so that "just as physical capital is created by making changes in materials so as to form tools and facilitate production, human capital is created by changing persons so as to give them skills and capabilities that make them able to act in new ways" (Coleman, 1990: 304). Human capital is most often created through education and training.

Social Capital

The creation of *social capital* involves analogous processes that are no less real and probably even more important, even though the product is less tangible than human or physical capital. The creation of social capital involves the creation of capabilities through socially structured relations between individuals in groups. Coleman (1990:305) uses Figure 35.1 to illustrate how the social capital of the family is used by parents to create the skills and capabilities that become the human capital of their children. The nodes represented by the capital letters in this figure constitute human capital, while the connecting lines or links constitute social capital. Coleman reasons that for parents B and C to further the cognitive development of child A, there must be capital in the nodes *and* the links of the diagram. That is, the human capital of parents B and C must be passed on to child A through the social capital represented in the social structure of the connecting links between A and B, or between A and C, and for overall maximum effect between A, B, and C. Coleman (1988; 1990) refers to the last of these possibilities as the *closure of social networks*, and this can more generally refer, for example, to not only the functioning of intact nuclear and extended families but also to well-integrated neighborhoods, communities, and even nation states. Social groups are expected to make their maximum contributions to the

development of the various forms of capital when they have this characteristic of closure.

Figure 35.1
Three-Person Structure: Human Capital in Nodes and Social Capital in Relations

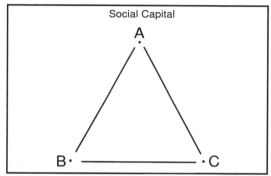

Source: Coleman, 1990:305

Cultural Capital

Meanwhile, groups and individuals must also adapt themselves to existing and continuing accumulations of capital that characterize the settings that they inherit and inhabit. Adaptations to these circumstances are expressed through various formations of *cultural capital*. When social capital is abundant in the community and family, these cultural adaptations may easily include the accumulation of the credentials of higher education and even involvements in high culture, for example, including participation in the arts and their supporting institutions, such as museums, the symphony, and the theater. In these community and family settings, social capital is used to successfully endow children with forms of cultural capital that significantly enhance their later life chances (see DiMaggio, 1982; 1987; DiMaggio and Mohr, 1985).

However, in less-advantaged community and family settings without such abundant social and cultural capital, parents are less able to endow or transmit such opportunities to their children. Survival itself is often a struggle, and children and families must adapt to the diminished circumstances and opportunities they encounter. So while many parents who are well situated within secure and supportive social networks may be destined or driven by their capital positions and connected inclinations to endow their children with forms of social and cultural capital that make success in school and later life quite likely, the children of less advantageously positioned and less-driven and controlling parents may more often drift or be driven into and along less-promising paths of social and cultural adaptation and capital formation (Hagan, 1991b). . . .

It is important to again emphasize that disadvantaging social and economic processes at the societal and community levels can make divergent and oppositional adaptations and formations of social and cultural capital common in particular settings. These settings typically have sites of what we will call *capital disinvestment*. Processes of capital disinvestment are destructive of conventional forms of social and cultural capital, and they often produce subcultural adaptations, which are in effect a form of *recapitalization*, an effort to reorganize what resources are available, even if illicit, to reach attainable goals. As noted earlier, disinvestment processes often are rationalized by dubious economic and political perspectives that causally connect social inequality with economic efficiency. Processes of capital disinvestment and recapitalization occupy a central place in the analytic framework for a new sociology of crime and disrepute. . . .

Three disinvestment processes that discourage societal and community level formations of conventional social capital involve *residential segregation, race-linked inequality*, and *concentrations of poverty*. . . .

The New Ethnographies of Poverty and Crime

A number of recent ethnographies document the significance of the process of capital disinvestment and adaptations to limitations of social and cultural capital we have described. These studies characteristically operate on two levels: as studies of communities, and as studies of the life course experiences of individuals. They also typically consider both the behavioral activities of individuals and the effects of responses of authorities to these individuals. These points will become apparent as we review examples of this research.

First, however, it is important to emphasize that the new ethnographies of poverty and crime all give attention to the role of drugs and to what otherwise were referred to in earlier chapters as ethnic vice industries and deviance service centers. This is important because while the processes of capital disinvestment we have described stress the consequences of the diversion and withdrawal of economic and social resources from disadvantaged communities, often in these same communities there is a process of recapitalization that involves the development of deviance service industries.

This process is partly indigenous to communities and partly a product of the actions of external authorities. The key to deviance service industries is that illegal markets emerge whenever desired substances and services—such as narcotic drugs, prostitution, and gambling—are made illegal. Authorities with responsibility for the enforcement of such laws, whether they wish to or not, have the power to regulate the development and operation of these markets, and members of communities that are denied access and involvement to legal markets often pursue these illegal opportunities. For example, we noted in earlier chapters the succession of ethnic groups that have participated in such markets as a mobility mechanism during this century in the United States. . . .

When deviant services provided by minority group members are concentrated on a majority group clientele, they can provide an external source of financial capital and serve a redistributive function for the minority community. Organization and provision of these services can also recapitalize the financial and even social lives of the individual entrepreneurs involved. In this sense, these activities are adaptive reflections of the accumulations of new forms of social and cultural capital. However, when these services are concentrated internally, and when they run into interference from external authorities and otherwise disrupt and endanger the lives of individuals and the host community, they become disruptive of social and cultural capital, both for the individuals and the communities involved. . . .

Echoes of this story reverberate throughout the recent ethnographic studies that we now discuss as examples of the processes of capital disinvestment and racapitalization that are central aspects of crime in urban America.

Three New York City Neighborhoods

In an ethnography provocatively titled *Getting Paid*, Mercer Sullivan (1989) and his collaborators interviewed members of cliques about their life histories in New York City neighborhoods: an African-American public housing project, a Hispanic neighborhood adjacent to a declining industrial area, and a white working class community. The latter predominantly white neighborhood serves as an essential reference point because it did not experience the loss of core sector jobs and more general capital disinvestment that occurred in the comparison minority communities. Various forms of social capital remained intact. The community retained viable legitimate labor market networks that offered opportunities for obtaining jobs through personal contact. There were still unionized core sector jobs in which adults had some security. Two-parent households were also more viable, and family and community controls were more stable. These are all indications of the kind of closure of social networks that Coleman identifies as a key source of social capital. This had important implications for the life course experiences and prospects of the youth of this neighborhood. For example, when youths in this neighborhood got into trouble with the law, they were more likely to be reintegrated into their families and community, and they were less likely to be permanently marginalized from labor market opportunities. The closure of social networks provided protective social capital.

Access to labor market opportunities is crucial. In the white working class neighborhood, Sullivan found personalized job referral networks that led adolescents to adult employment opportunities, with jobs circulating through friendship, family, and neighborhood-based connections that linked local residents to desirable blue-collar jobs throughout the metropolitan labor market.

Conditions were much different in the Hispanic- and African-American communities studied. Here the consequences of capital disinvestment became strikingly apparent. Sullivan links this process to changes in the world economy we have discussed, including the transition to a post-industrial economy in which lower wage and insecure jobs in the information and service sectors only partly and inadequately have replaced the loss of higher wage and more secure jobs in the manufacturing and industrial sectors. He notes that our cities in effect have exported jobs and unemployment in a set of intranational and international realignments that we are only beginning to understand (see also Revenga, 1992).

A result is that the Hispanic- and African-American neighborhoods Sullivan studied were physically isolated from core sector employment. Many of the parents in these neighborhoods had no jobs, while those parents who were employed tended to work in government jobs that recruited by bureaucratic means rather than through personal contact. That is, these parents had little of the social capital that derives from the closure of social networks and embeddedness in employment networks that can provide others with referrals and leads to jobs. Sullivan found that "without family connections even to low-paying jobs, these youths had to rely on more impersonal methods" (80). In contrast, for white youths, "social ties between residents and local employers reinforced physical proximity to produce a much greater supply of . . . jobs" (104).

These patterns are reflective of a process of capital disinvestment that has corroded the social and cultural capital of these communities and that is associated with a recapitalization of community life around underground economic activities that include drugs and crime. We come, then, to the provocative title of Sullivan's book, which plays on the ghetto jargon of "getting paid" or "getting over" to describe the illegal economic strategies that include the muggings, robberies, and other forms of theft and drug-related crime common to American city life.

Sullivan's point is that these are not intergenerationally transmitted expressions of cultural preferences, but rather cultural adaptations to restricted opportunities for the redistribution of wealth. Put another way, these youth have substituted investments in subcultures of youth crime and delinquency for involvements in a dominant culture that provides little structural or cultural investment in their futures. Their subcultural adaptations represent investments for short-term economic gains. Drawing on the classic analysis of Paul Willis (1977) in *Learning to Labour*, Sullivan argues that this participation in youth crime temporarily achieves a "penetration of their condition." However, he then turns his eye to the life course consequences of these involvements and notes that

> Over time, this penetration becomes a limitation, binding them back into [the social] structure as they age out of youth crime and accept . . . low wage, unstable jobs. . . . Alternatively, some will die; others will spend much of their lives in prisons or mental hospitals. (250)

For these youths, problems connected to youth crime are prolonged into adulthood.

It is important to emphasize the role of the police, courts, and prisons in the development of these youthful criminal careers. Sullivan found in the more stable white neighborhood that parents, using their well-developed social networks and resulting social capital, "sought to manipulate the system—and were often successful in doing so—by means of money and personal connections" (196). In contrast, in both of the minority neighborhoods youths began to move further away from home to commit violent economic crimes and encountered more serious sanctions when they did so. These crimes produced short-term gains, but they also separated minority youths from the legal labor market, stigmatizing and further damaging their social and cultural capital in terms of later job prospects. Of the minority youths Sullivan studied, he writes that "their participation in regular acts of income-producing crime and the resulting involvement with the criminal justice system in turn kept them out of school and forced them to abandon their earlier occupational goals" (64). Court appearances and resulting confinements re-

moved these youths from whatever possibility for closure of job referral networks school might provide and paced them within prison and community-based crime networks that further isolated these youths from legitimate employment. . . .

The New Quantitative Studies of Crime, Class, and Community

The new ethnographies of poverty and crime provide a picture of distressed communities in which capital disinvestment processes have made economic prospects bleak, and in which crime has become a short-term adaptive form of recapitalization for youth whose longer term life chances are further jeopardized by these involvements. A new tradition of quantitative research provides further support for this view of crime in urban America, by focusing on crime at the level of communities, as well as on the development of crime in the lives of individuals over the life course. These studies often further articulate the ways in which community level processes of capital disinvestment affect social networks in the community and the social capital of families and their capacities to assist the formation of human and cultural capital for their children.

Community Effects

Community-level studies done in a number of U.S. cities persuasively link street crime in America to the capital disinvestment processes of residential segregation, racial inequality, and the concentration of poverty emphasized in our earlier discussion and in the new ethnographies of poverty and crime. For example, recent studies in large U.S. cities reveal high levels of homicide victimization for African Americans in tracts with high concentrations of poor families. The same studies show low levels of homicide victimization for both blacks and whites in higher socioeconomic areas (Lowry et al., 1988; Centerwall, 1984; Munford et al., 1976). Since poor black communities are much more distressed economically than poor white communities, and since it is only in higher socioeconomic communities that it is possible to establish real similarity of black and white life conditions, these studies imply that racial differences in homicide rates have their origins in socioeconomic experiences (Short, 1994). . . .

In an important recent review of the literature that contains many community-level studies, Land et al. (1990) located a cluster of these kinds of factors (including median income, percent of families below the poverty line, an index of income inequality, percent of black population, and percent of single-parent families) that had a clear causal influence on homicide rates. However, these factors could not be fully decomposed into more specific causal effects. These factors are probably too closely intertwined to be specifically distinguished. One implication is that capital disinvestment processes operate in a more general and interconnected way.

Still, it is important to try to determine more about how capital disinvestment processes might exercise their community- as well as individual-level effects, and important advances are being made along these lines. Much of this work is tied together by an underlying concern with the effects of changing labor markets on youths attempting to make the transition to adulthood in racially segregated and impoverished communities. . . .

Resulting Disorganization and Aggression

Blau and Blau (1982; see also Messner and Rosenfeld, 1993; Messner, 1989) describe the conspicuous connection between race and lack of access to stable and rewarding jobs as resulting in "prevalent disorganization" and as sparking "diffuse aggression," while Sampson and Wilson (1994; see also Bursik and Grasmick, 1993a) conceptualize related concentrations of poverty as producing a "dislocation" and "disorganization" of social control. These theoretical frameworks share with other contemporary sociological approaches a common concern with linking economic and political processes of change to the dislocations they produce in community settings. . . .

The structure of community and social organization also involves informal social networks and formal institutions that guide and monitor leisure-time youth activities (Bursik and Grasmick, 1993a). Consequences of the loss of this kind of closure in neighborhood social networks are found in the prevalence of unsupervised teenage peer-groups in a community, with large resulting effects on rates of robbery and violence by strangers (Sampson and Groves, 1989). Alternatively, with closely coordinated supervision, gangs in some instances have been connected to external sources of funding from community programs that have successfully reduced gang activity and fear of crime (see Bursik and Grasmick, 1993b; Erlanger, 1979).

Many of these kinds of findings can be synthesized in terms of the concepts of social and cultural capital that we introduced earlier and have used throughout much of this chapter. In conventional circumstance, intact families, informal social networks, and more formal institutions in a community are sources of a closure of social networks and resulting social capital that can be converted into cultural capital to improve the life chances of youth as they become adults. However, in distressed communities these structures and processes are often disrupted and jeopardized. Youths have less access to well-articulated social networks and therefore less hope of finding the stable core sector jobs that will allow them to successfully traverse the gap from adolescence to adulthood: in large part because the economy is not providing them, but also because their communities and families do not have the social networks and capital to help them prepare themselves for such jobs or to find them when they are available.

Capital Disinvestment and Embeddedness in the Criminal Economy of Drugs

As we saw in the ethnographic studies considered earlier, during the same approximate period of capital disinvestment when access to legitimate job networks linked to core sector jobs declined in many distressed minority communities, networks of contacts into the world of drugs and drug-related crime proliferated, paving the way for many youths to become embedded in the criminal economy. Fagan (1993) finds in field studies with over a thousand participants in the Washington Heights and Central Harlem neighborhoods of New York City that this criminal economy employs large numbers of individuals in support roles (for example, lookouts and renting storefronts or apartments) as well as drug sales and in a greatly expanded sex trade. This activity can assume an important role in the neighborhood economy, with white-collar as well as blue-collar customers bringing cash into the community, and at least some of the funds being redistributed within the neighborhood. This criminal economy is a contemporary institutionalized link to the deviance service centers and ethnic vice industries of America's past.

However, today's illegal drug industry is also much more competitive, violent, and unstable than in the past. Where drug distribution was once centralized through relatively circumscribed networks of heroin and later cocaine users who retailed drugs on the street, the more recent experience with crack has involved a less regulated market with violent competition for territory and market share (Williams, 1989). As well, while entry-level roles and the market for drugs more generally have increased, the redistribution of profits has declined. This contrasts with an earlier period when marijuana sales predominated. Drug income now is less often invested in local businesses, and profits more often are concentrated among individuals elsewhere in the city and outside the country (see also Ianni, 1974).

Yet, low-level participation in the drug economy, despite its poor career prospects and declining returns to the community, is still a cultural adaptation with compelling short-term capital attractions. In the absence of better sources of employment, drug selling is a primary route to gaining material symbols of wealth and success in the neighborhood. The drug industry also offers the hope, however illusory, of self-determination and economic independence, as contrasted with the petty humiliations and daily harassment faced in secondary service sector jobs (Fagan, 1993).

This is likely why 1 in 6 African-American males born in 1967 in Washington, D.C., is estimated to have been arrested for drug selling between 1985 and 1987, with rates of actual participation in drug selling presumably being much higher (Reuter et al., 1990:46). Street-level sellers are estimated to have incomes ranging from $15,000 to $100,000 annually (Williams, 1989). A Boston study concludes that disadvantaged youths during the economic boom of the mid-1980s would have had to take sharp reductions in income to move from drug selling to legal jobs (Freeman, 1991). Drug selling is simply more profitable per hour invested than legitimate employment (Reuter et al., 1990). So the illegal drug industry is an important source of social and economic capital for individuals. Unfortunately, this capital is quickly depleted, with excess earnings dispersed through loosely articulated family and social networks, consumption of drugs, and conspicuous spending. And we have seen that imprisonment and unemployment further jeopardize the capital position of youths involved in drug selling.

Capital disinvestment processes and changes in the illegal drug industry also have influenced the lives of many minority women. The increasing number of female-headed households and families has placed new demands on minority women to generate income. The disappearance through deaths and imprisonment of numbers of young adult males may also have relaxed barriers to female participation in street-level drug selling. And the emergence of crack escalated the demand for drugs. These factors have increased the participation of minority women in drug use and sales and also in prostitution (Fagan, 1993).

The ethnic vice industries and deviance service centers that surround drugs and drug-related crime pose great policy dilemmas in the New York City neighborhoods that Fagan studied. As exploitative and corrosive of the community and individuals as these activities may be in the long term, their short-term benefits are often difficult for neighborhood residents to resist.

First, since neighborhood residents benefit from the redistributive aspects of drug selling, this undercuts their efforts at formal and informal social control. Residents may be less willing to disrupt drug selling since some directly benefit, and especially when economic alternatives do not compete well or the risks are not acute or immediate. As suppliers of a commodity to others in the city, funds flow into the neighborhood and are recirculated to some extent before accumulating to individuals. What will happen if this circulation is interrupted? Unless risk increase from drug selling or living in its milieu, it is unreasonable to ask people to act against their economic well-being. (Fagan, 1993)

In the end, these are the kinds of dilemmas that continuing social inequality and capital disinvestment provoke.

The New Sociology of Crime, Inequality, and Disrepute

A new sociology of crime and disrepute focuses attention on the criminal costs of social inequality. It does so against the backdrop of a common belief that social inequality encourages individual initiative and is therefore economically efficient. This belief is challenged by the last half-century of economic development in the advanced capitalist nations, when declining social inequality accompanied economic expansion, and increases in social inequality were joined with reduced economic growth. Meanwhile, increased social inequality and reduced economic growth are both associated with increases in crime, especially in America's low-income minority communities.

Structural changes have brought increasing inequality into the American economy and into the lives of individuals who live in its most distressed communities. Three interconnected processes of capital disinvestment—residential segregation, racial inequality, and the concentration of poverty—have intensified the crime problems of these communities. These disinvestment processes are encouraged by the unsubstantiated belief that efforts to increase social equality are wasteful and that they diminish economic efficiency. Meanwhile, capital disinvestment impairs the closure of social networks and the formation of social and cultural capital in distressed communities and families, and it indirectly encourages subcultural adaptations. These adaptations are in effect forms of recapi-

talization, that is, they represent efforts to reorganize what resources are available, albeit usually illicit, to reach attainable goals.

Often these efforts at recapitalization occur through involvement in ethnic vice industries and the formation of deviance service centers, the sometimes free enterprise zones of crime. One of the most enduring of these illicit industries involves illegal drugs. This illicit enterprise has sometimes provided an external source of financial capital that serves a redistributive function in distressed ethnic communities and that has recapitalized the economic and social lives of the individuals involved. However, the more recent American experience, especially with crack, is more violent, exploitative, and disruptive than past experiences with drugs. Furthermore, as consumption of such drugs has become more concentrated within minority communities, drug sales have brought in and redistributed reduced amounts of money from outside these communities, and have encountered mounting interference from external authorities. The results are increasingly disruptive and dangerous to the communities and individuals involved. These points are confirmed by a growing number of ethnographic and quantitative studies. . . .

Discussion Questions

1. What are the different forms of capital? In particular, what is social capital?

2. Why is social capital less likely to exist in inner-city neighborhoods? How is this related to capitalism and to race-linked inequality in American society?

3. If a youth has social capital, why would he or she be unlikely to become deeply embedded in crime? Conversely, why might the lack of social capital make a criminal life course more likely?

4. What does Hagan mean by the concept of "recapitalization"? How does this relate to the emergence of drug markets in inner-city neighborhoods? ✦

Part X

Feminist Theories: Gender, Power, and Crime

For much of its history, criminology as a discipline focused almost exclusively on crimes committed by men. Most empirical studies used data only on male offenders, and theories were constructed to explain why boys and men broke the law (Belknap, 1996; Leonard, 1982; Simon, 1975; Smart, 1977). Part of the neglect of females stemmed from the disproportionate involvement of males in crime, especially serious offenses, and from the overwhelming maleness of the prison population. Women's criminality thus was seen as tangential to the crime problem—as not really worth investigating and as having no implications for the understanding of males' illegality. A more salient reason for the failure to consider gender in criminological analyses, however, was that, as was the case in other academic disciplines, criminologists were nearly all men: males were studying and writing about males.

Equally disquieting, on those infrequent occasions when female criminals received scholarly attention, the resulting analyses were decidedly sexist. Although exceptions existed (Steffensmeier and Clark, 1980), prominent scholars often viewed female criminality as a departure from "natural" female behavior—that is, maternal, passive, and gentle. What would cause such "odd," "unfemale" behavior? Female lawbreakers, it was thought, could only have contravened their feminine nature because of a pathological defect in their biological makeup or within their psyche (Klein, 1973; Smart, 1977). The traditional female role thus was seen as normal; any departure, such as crime, was seen as abnormal. In this perspective, social factors, especially gender-based inequality, were accorded little or no causal importance in the behavior of women—or, for that matter, in the behavior of men.

Starting in the 1970s and continuing to this day, such male-centered, asocial theorizing has been challenged as sexist and as theoretically impoverished. A revisionist approach, which elevated gender to the center of theoretical analysis, was fueled in important ways by the emergence of the Women's Movement and its fight for equality between the sexes. This movement had two noteworthy effects. First, as educational and occupational opportunities broadened, increasing numbers of women entered the field of criminology, bringing with them fresh insights rooted in personal histories unlike those of male criminologists. Second, the Women's Movement focused attention on the social situation of women vis-à-vis men, including such crucial issues as gender-based differences in socialization and inequalities in power. For many criminologists—especially female scholars—the idea that gender was not implicated in crime and criminal justice now seemed incongruous.

The rejection of male-centered traditional criminology has resulted in the emergence of the competing paradigm of "feminist criminology." In this approach, sex is not simply another variable added to a multivariate empirical analysis (usually as a "control" variable). Rather, gender relations become central to understanding human behavior, including crime. There is a special focus on how crime is related to gender-based inequality between males and females. Finally, to a greater or lesser extent, feminist analyses—similar to critical criminology—are oriented to the production of knowledge so as to unmask and change the structural relationships in society that result in the discrimination against and the oppression of women (see Daly and Chesney-Lind, 1988 [Chapter 37 in this Part]; see Daly and Chesney-Lind, 1988 [Chapter 37 in this Part]; see also Ollenburger and Moore, 1998).

Within feminist criminology, however, there is a diversity of thinking, as well as a dynamism that leads to continuing theoretical developments (for an analysis of recent contributions, see Daly, 1997). Over the past two decades, the most poignant split has been between "liberal feminists," who focus on the salience of sex-role socialization and equality of opportunities, and feminists who take a more "critical" or "radical" approach, emphasizing structural inequality in power between men and women. These latter theorists see male and female crime as fundamentally linked to patriarchy—a deeply entrenched system in which males exert dominance through their power (financial and, if necessary, physical) and through a hegemonic culture that defines male ways of doing things as "normal" and male control of women as legitimate. In general, liberal feminist views had the most powerful influence in the earlier days of feminist criminological scholarship, while more radical approaches currently direct most theory and research within the feminist paradigm.

Liberation and Crime

As the Women's Movement grew in strength and swept across the nation, it was tempting to conclude that substantial equality between men and women was within reach. Although gender socialization and inequalities ultimately would prove difficult to transform, significant social changes did occur. Almost on a daily basis, it seemed, women were breaking one social or occupational barrier after another. Witnessing these changes in progress, it became almost inevitable to ask, how will this refashioning of the experiences of women affect their criminality? For those with a sociological imagination who saw male crime as rooted in their social experiences, the answer seemed clear. If girls were raised like boys and if in their life course they had the same opportunities as boys, then it seemed logical that their behavior—including their criminal conduct—would become more like that of boys. In short, women's liberation ultimately would result in "equality of the wanted list."

These ideas informed Rita Simon's (1975) important contribution, *Women and Crime*. "If one assumes that the changes in women's roles, in their perceptions of self, and in their desire for expanded horizons that began in the latter part of the sixties will not be abated," observed Simon (1975: p. 1), "then we would expect that one of the major byproducts of the women's movement will be a high proportion of women who pursue careers in crime." Simon contended that females' entry into the job market would prove particularly consequential because it would give them access to opportunities for "financial and white-collar crimes," such as "fraud, embezzlement, larceny, and forgery" (p. 2). She rejected the idea, however, that women's participation in violent crimes would increase. Arguing that women committed violent crimes largely because of the "frustration, the subservience, and the dependency that have characterized the traditional female role," Simon reasoned that occupational advancement would reduce these "feelings of being victimized and exploited" and thus would blunt "their motivation to kill" (p. 2).

This liberation thesis was stated even more boldly and eloquently by Freda Adler in her classic book, *Sisters in Crime*, which carried the revealing subtitle *The Rise of the New Female Criminal* (1975 [Chapter 36 in this Part]). Adler proclaimed that women were not only committing more crimes but also were engaging in traditionally male offenses. She noted that between 1960 and 1972, female arrests increased 168 percent for burglary, 277 percent for robbery, 280 percent for embezzlement, and over 300 percent for larceny (1975: p. 16). She linked these ostensible dramatic shifts in female criminality to the transformation of gender roles that were then occurring in American society. "Women are no long indentured to the kitchens, baby carriages, or bedrooms of America," observed Adler. "Allowed their freedom for the first time, women—by the tens of thousands—have chosen to desert those kitchens and plunge exuberantly into the formerly all-male quarter of the working world" (p. 12). But there was also a "shady aspect of liberation": the rise of new female criminals. "In the same way that women are demanding equal opportunity in fields of legitimate endeavor," concluded Adler, "a similar number of determined women are forcing their way into the world of major crimes" (p. 13).

The work by Adler and Simon was critically important in bringing gender into criminological discourse and in prompting sustained research on women's criminality. Still, their versions of the liberation thesis have been subjected to much critical scrutiny. Many criminologists, including later feminist scholars, have rejected this thesis (see, e.g., Belknap, 1996; Daly and Chesney-Lind, Chapter 37 in this Part). Although several concerns have been voiced, three criticisms of the liberation thesis seem most important to review.

First, the empirical predictions of the thesis have not proven correct. Writing in 1978, Darrell Steffensmeier showed that since 1960, female patterns of crime actually were more stable than changing. Most women were not "new female criminals" but rather remained nonviolent, petty property offenders. Female crime did rise during the 1960s, but so did male crime. Further, citing the large percentage jump in female law breaking was misleading, largely because the low number of female violent crimes in 1960 meant that even modest numerical increases would produce enormous percentage increases. In fact, the largest growth in women's criminality was in larceny-theft, a crime category which includes the traditionally "female" offense of shoplifting. Now, two decades later, female crime patterns still have not experienced dramatic changes. Steffensmeier and Allan (1995) note that this may be because gender roles have not equalized as much as Adler had anticipated. Although women have made gains occupationally, "the traditional gender roles of wife-mother and sex object have remained remarkably stable" (1995: p. 96).

Second, the liberation thesis implied (if not stated directly in places) that females' labor market participation and achievement of equality across a range of social opportunities would foster criminality. The data showed, however, that gender equality's "dark side" was not to create offenders. Instead, crime was more common among those who did *not* achieve equality—among women who were trapped in economically marginal positions (Giordano et al., 1981; Wolfe et al., 1984). True equality, therefore, might well reduce, rather than increase, women's criminal involvement.

Third and relatedly, the liberation thesis's focus on gender socialization and occupational opportunities did not consider the structural roots of the inequality between men and women. To be sure, as liberal feminists, scholars such as Adler and Simon were critical of the barriers that they and other women faced. More radical feminists, however, contended that the analyses of liberation theorists did not get to the core of the problem: that patriarchy—a system of men's dominance of women—underlay how women were socialized, why women experienced discrimination in the workplace, and why women were consigned—often alone and with children—to marginal economic positions. A feminist theory of crime, they claimed, thus must move beyond discussions of liberation to illuminate how power affects the crime and victimization of women.

Patriarchy and Crime

Radical feminism, which places patriarchy at the center of its analysis, has had a widespread influence on criminological scholarship (see Belknap, 1996; Simpson, 1989). Within criminal justice, for example, it has spawned research on gender inequities in sentencing and on how the law is used to reaffirm traditional, subordinate female roles and to control women's sexuality (e.g., the "double-standard" in the juvenile justice system of institutionalizing "promiscuous" girls but not boys) (Chesney-Lind and Shelden, 1997; Daly and Tonry, 1997). This perspective also illuminated the importance of investigating the victimization of women by men. Studies showed how male violence against women—such as nonstranger rape and the battering of intimates—was traditionally subject to virtually no sanctions by the state. Such violence was thus conceptualized as a means by which men dominate women and, in doing so, reproduce the existing patriarchal system (Daly and Chesney-Lind, 1988 [Chapter 37 in this Part]).

In rejecting male-centered criminology, radical feminism also argued that there would be a need to develop gender-specific theories. Because they neglected gender and ignored the role of patriarchy as the underlying social context for behavior, traditional theories were incapable of explicating the gendered experiences that were central to a full understanding of female (and male) criminality. Chesney-Lind (1989: p. 23), for example, observes that "girls are frequently the recipients of violence and sexual abuse." Patriarchy is conducive to such abuse because females in general are objectified as "sexual property." "In a society that idealizes inequality in male/female relationships and venerates youth in women, girls are easily defined as sexually attractive by older men" (p. 24). Escape from this abuse, however, is not easy. Girls who run away often are returned to their homes by the state—a practice that ignores the girls' genuine fears of continued victimization and serves to confirm parental, patriarchal authority. The only option thus for many abused girls is to seek refuge in the "streets," where they must commit crimes to survive. But patriarchy shapes their experience and victimization here as well. "It is no accident that [these] girls. . . get involved in criminal activities that exploit their sexual object status," comments Chesney-Lind. "American society has defined as desirable youthful, physically perfect women. This means that girls on the streets, who have little else of value to trade, are encouraged to use this 'resource' " (p. 24). It is noteworthy that considerations of sexual abuse, its relation to patriarchy, and its etiological role in crime have been virtually absent in the major theories of crime authored by males.

The case for gender-specific theories, however, has raised a debate over whether traditional, nonfeminist perspectives can identify factors that have similar effects for both sexes. Daly and Chesney-Lind (1988: p. 514 [Chapter 37]) call this the "generalizability problem: Do theories of men's behavior apply to women?" There is a growing body of evidence showing that the theoretical variables which predict male criminality also predict female criminality (see, e.g., Smith, 1979; Steffensmeier and Allan, 1995). Thus, Andrews and Bonta (1994: p. 68) report the results of a meta-analysis of 372 studies that examined by gender the effects of six factors (antisocial attitudes/associates, antisocial temperament/misconduct/personality, parental/family factors, personal education/vocational achievement, personal distress/psychopathology, and lower-class origin). They note that these factors have the same rank-order and very similar effects on the incidence of crime for both males and females.

These results do not mean that gender-specific theories are of questionable value. It would be foolish to argue that men and women have no unique experiences, especially when gender is studied in light of men's and women's age, class, and racial position (see Messerschmidt, 1993 [Chapter 38 in this Part]; Simpson, 1991; Simpson and Elis, 1995). Still, it would be equally mistaken to dismiss the potential of more traditional theories to illuminate why females, as well as men, go into crime. Further and perhaps more important, a worthy theoretical task would entail "gendering" traditional theories—linking up known predictors of crime (e.g., associating with delinquent peers) with the larger structural (patriarchal?) conditions that shape exposure and reaction to these causal factors (see Daly and Chesney-Lind 1988 [Chapter 37]).

Recently, for example, Broidy and Agnew (1997) have applied "general strain theory" to the explanation of gender differences in crime (see Agnew, Chapter 17). Based on a detailed review of the existing theoretical and empirical literature, they conclude that general strain theory has utility in explaining male and female crime (see also Mazerolle, in press). Still, gender shapes most of the causal factors central to this theory. Thus, Broidy and Agnew (1997: 295) contend that men and women experience different types of strain, do not interpret strains the same way, vary in their emotional reactions to strain, and "differ in their propensity to react to strain/anger with crime." Equally noteworthy, they argue that gender inequality is integrally involved in the criminogenic strains that women experience. "Women's oppression in various social arenas," contend Broidy and Agnew, "may play an important role in the generation of strain, and ultimately in criminal behavior" (p. 298). Admittedly, these insights are not developed into a full-blown feminist theory, but they do provide a useful starting point for exploring whether an integrated feminist-strain theory can advance our understanding of female criminality.

Masculinities and Crime: Doing Gender

In *Masculinities and Crime*, James Messerschmidt (1993 [Chapter 38]) challenges both traditional and feminist criminological theories of criminal conduct. Traditional theories may be male-centered, but they do not examine how "being male" is related to crime. Men might be strained, lack control, and differentially associate with peers, but how their gender is implicated in their behavior is not analyzed. Feminists have brought gender to the center of criminological analysis, but their vision of men tends to be stereotypical and unidimensional. In particular, when the lens of patri-

archy is employed, males are conceptualized as dominant. This approach, however, ignores the considerable variations among men, especially in how they seek to affirm their masculinity.

To Messerschmidt, criminality and masculinity are intertwined. He argues that in social situations, men are constantly confronted with the task of establishing their manliness. When legitimate means of demonstrating masculinity are denied, crime becomes a resource to accomplish this task. Criminal behavior thus is best seen as a way of "doing gender."

Messerschmidt recognizes that males "do gender" largely within the confines of "hegemonic masculinity"—the prevailing idealized cultural conception which defines "masculinity" as involving the dominance of women, heterosexuality, the pursuit of sexual gratification, independence, and so on (1993: p. 82). Still, this general masculinity is specified by the intersection of age, class, and race. Different "masculinities"—tied to structural locations—thus emerge and have varying impacts on the rate and content of criminal behavior. For example, middle-class, white boys often engage in petty delinquency to show their masculinity, but they also have access to conventional ways to "do gender," such as through success in school and, later, in the labor market. In contrast, lower-class, minority boys, who face structural barriers and dismal futures, are more likely to seek to demonstrate their masculinity through repeated robberies and acts of violence. As Messerschmidt notes, the pursuit of these different masculinities both reflects and serves to reproduce the existing class, racial, and gender inequalities in society.

Messerschmidt's focus on masculinities and on "crime as doing gender" is an important contribution that is prompting scholarly investigations (see, e.g., Jefferson and Carlen, 1996). The empirical adequacy of this perspective, however, remains to be demonstrated. For example, how would a masculinities approach explain the onset in early childhood of conduct problems that later develop into delinquency? But perhaps the largest theoretical task for Messerschmidt to address is how his perspective relates to female crime. As Heimer (1994: p. 861) queries, "If crime by males represents attempts to display masculinity, what is the meaning of crime by females? Does it also represent attempts to claim masculinity? If so, doesn't this imply that female offenders are too masculine?" We suspect that Messerschmidt would not wish to proceed down this path, which seems close to the liberation thesis that radical feminists have soundly rejected. Instead, his next project might well be to see how "femininities" are structured by the intersection of age, class, and race and in turn shape involvement in crime.

References

Adler, Freda. 1975. *Sisters in Crime: The Rise of the New Female Criminal*. New York: McGraw-Hill.

Andrews, D. A. and James Bonta. 1994. *The Psychology of Criminal Conduct*. Cincinnati: Anderson.

Belknap, Joanne. 1996. *The Invisible Woman: Gender, Crime, and Justice*. Belmont, CA: Wadsworth.

Broidy, Lisa and Robert Agnew. 1997. "Gender and Crime: A General Strain Theory Perspective." *Journal of Research in Crime and Delinquency* 34: 275-306.

Chesney-Lind, Meda. 1989. "Girls' Crime and Woman's Place: Toward a Feminist Model of Female Delinquency." *Crime and Delinquency* 35: 5-29.

Chesney-Lind, Meda and Randall G. Shelden. 1998. *Girls, Delinquency, and Juvenile Justice*, 2nd edition. Belmont, CA: Wadsworth.

Daly, Kathleen. 1997. "Different Ways of Conceptualizing Sex/Gender in Feminist Theory and Their Implications for Criminology." *Theoretical Criminology* 1: 25-51.

Daly, Kathleen and Meda Chesney-Lind. 1988. "Feminism and Criminology." *Justice Quarterly* 5: 497-535.

Daly, Kathleen and Michael Tonry. 1997. "Gender, Race, and Sentencing." Pp. 201-252 in *Crime and Justice: A Review of Research, Volume 22*, edited by Michael Tonry. Chicago: University of Chicago Press.

Giordano, Peggy C., Sandra Kerbel, and Sandra Dudley. 1981. "The Economics of Female Criminality: An Analysis of Police Blotters, 1890–1976." Pp. 65-82 in *Women and Crime in America*, edited by Lee H. Bowker. New York: Macmillan.

Heimer, Karen. 1994. "Review of *Masculinities and Crime*." *Contemporary Sociology* 23: 860-861.

Jefferson, Tony and Pat Carlen, eds. 1996. "Masculinities, Social Relations and Crime." *British Journal of Criminology*, Special edition, 36:337-444.

Klein, Dorie. 1973. "The Etiology of Female Crime: A Review of the Literature." *Issues in Criminology* 8: 3-30.

Leonard, Eileen B. 1982. *Women, Crime, and Society: A Critique of Criminology Theory*. New York: Longman.

Mazerolle, Paul. In press. "Gender, General Strain, and Delinquency: An Empirical Examination." *Journal of Research in Crime and Delinquency*.

Messerschmidt, James W. 1993. *Masculinities and Crime: Critique and Reconceptualization of Theory*. Lantham, MD: Rowman and Littlefield.

Ollenburger, Jane C. and Helen A. Moore. 1998. *A Sociology of Women: The Intersection of Patriarchy, Capitalism, and Colonization*. Upper Saddle River, NJ: Prentice Hall.

Simon, Rita James. 1975. *Women and Crime*. Lexington, MA: Lexington Books.

Simpson, Sally S. 1989. "Feminist Theory, Crime, and Justice." *Criminology* 27: 605-631.

——. 1991. "Caste, Class, and Violent Crime: Explaining Difference in Female Offending." *Criminology* 29: 115-135.

Simpson, Sally S. and Lori Elis. 1995. "Doing Gender: Sorting Out the Caste and Crime Conundrum." *Criminology* 33: 47-81.

Smart, Carol. 1977. *Women, Crime and Criminology: A Feminist Critique*. London, UK: Routledge and Kegan Paul.

Smith, Douglas A. 1979. "Sex and Deviance: An Assessment of Major Sociological Variables." *Sociological Quarterly* 20: 183-195.

Steffensmeier, Darrell. 1978. "Crime and the Contemporary Woman: An Analysis of Changing Levels of Female Property Crime, 1960–75." *Social Forces* 57: 566-584.

Steffensmeier, Darrell and Emilie Allan. 1995. "Criminal Behavior: Gender and Age." Pp. 83-113 in *Criminology: A Contemporary Handbook*, 2nd edition, edited by Joseph F. Sheley. Belmont, CA: Wadsworth.

Steffensmeier, Darrell and Robert E. Clark. 1980. "Sociocultural Vs. Biological/Sexist Explanations of Sex Differences in Crime: A Survey of American Criminology Textbooks, 1918–1965." *The American Sociologist* 15: 246-255.

Wolfe, Nancy T., Francis T. Cullen, and John B. Cullen. 1984. "Describing the Female Offender: A Note on the Demographics of Arrests." *Journal of Criminal Justice* 12: 483-492. ✦

36

Sisters in Crime

Freda Adler

In 1938, Clifford Shaw of the Chicago school of criminology published Brothers in Crime, a work whose title revealed his central focus on male crime. Nearly four decades later, Freda Adler (1975) signified a break with this perspective by naming her book Sisters in Crime. Indeed, her scholarship helped to ensure that no future generation of criminologists would ignore gender in the study of criminal behavior.

Adler's most provocative claim was that the movement to achieve equality between the sexes would result in increasing female crime, especially in domains previously dominated by men. As noted previously, this liberation thesis underestimated the tenacity of existing gender roles and inequality. Gender differences in socialization and opportunities were not swept away and, in many ways, boys and girls continued to be raised in different social worlds. Accordingly, the "new female criminals" that Adler saw gathering on the horizon did not, at least in large numbers, materialize (see, however, Alarid et al., 1996).

This does not mean, however, that Adler's sensitivity to how gender-based social experiences influence crime was misplaced. Steffensmeier and Allan (1995: p. 88-91), for example, explain female crime as a product of such factors as: gender norms, especially the "two powerful focal concerns" of "female beauty and sexual virtue" and "nurturant role obligations"; gender differences in moral development; gender differences in supervision; and gender differences in access to criminal opportunities. Similarly, Hagan's (Chapter 21) power-control theory argues that power structures in the home affect crime largely by influencing how boys and girls are socialized and controlled by parents.

It also may be premature to dismiss the possibility that long-term changes in gender roles will influence the criminal participation of women. A strong liberation thesis may be untenable, but it is not farfetched to theorize that the incremental transformation of gender roles—a transformation that affects the social experiences of women across class and racial boundaries—might be implicated in the amount and content of women's criminality. In terms of social change, Adler's Sisters in Crime is still a "young" book. It will be interesting to revisit her ideas a half century from now to see if she has proven more prophetic than we now imagine.

Finally, a special feature of Sisters in Crime as Adler's insightful challenge to previous attempts to pathologize female offenders. Instead, she illuminated the way in which social experiences shape the life-choices, including the choice of crime, that women make. She develops the case that the major barriers to females' participation in crime are not biological but social. While later criminologists, especially radical feminists, may find the specifics of Adler's liberation thesis problematic, she still deserves much credit for ushering in a feminist paradigm that shifted attention away from the supposed abnormalities of individual female offenders and toward an appreciation of the social circumstances in which women are enmeshed.

References

Adler, Freda. 1975. *Sisters in Crime: The Rise of the New Female Criminal.* New York: McGraw-Hill.

Alarid, Leanne Fiftal, James W. Marquart, Velmer S. Burton, Jr., Francis T. Cullen, and Steven J. Cuvelier. 1996. "Female Crime Roles in Serious Offenses: A Study of Adult Felons." *Justice Quarterly* 13: 431-454.

Shaw, Clifford R., with the assistance of Henry D. McKay and James F. McDonald. 1938. *Brothers in Crime.* Chicago: University of Chicago Press.

Steffensmeier, Darrell and Emilie Allan. 1995. "Criminal Behavior: Gender and Age." Pp. 83-113 in *Criminology: A Contemporary Handbook*, 2nd edition, edited by Joseph F. Sheley. Belmont, CA: Wadsworth.

Women are no longer indentured to the kitchens, baby carriages, or bedrooms of

America. The skein of myths about women is unraveling, the chains have been pried loose, and there will be no turning back to the days when women found it necessary to justify their existence by producing babies or cleaning houses. Allowed their freedom for the first time, women—by the tens of thousands—have chosen to desert those kitchens, and plunge exuberantly into the formerly all-male quarters of the working world. . . .

In the same way that women are demanding equal opportunity in fields of legitimate endeavor, a similar number of determined women are forcing their way into the world of major crimes. . . .

It is this segment of women who are pushing into—and succeeding at—crimes which were formerly committed by males only. Females like Marge are now being found not only robbing banks single-handedly, but also committing assorted armed robberies, muggings, loan-sharking operations, extortion, murders, and a wide variety of other aggressive, violence-oriented crimes which previously involved only men. . . .

By every indicator available, female criminals appear to be surpassing males in the rate of increase for almost every major crime. Although males continue to commit the greater absolute number of offenses, it is the women who are committing those same crimes at yearly rates of increase now running as high as six and seven times greater than those for males. . . .

In summary, what we have described is a gradual but accelerating social revolution in which women are closing many of the gaps, social and criminal, that have separated them from men. The closer they get, the more alike they look and act. This is not to suggest that there are no inherent differences. Differences do exist and will be elaborated later in this book, but it seems clear that those differences are not of prime importance in understanding female criminality. The simplest and most accurate way to grasp the essence of women's changing patterns is to discard dated notions of femininity. That is a role that fewer and fewer women are willing to play. In the final analysis, women criminals are human beings who have basic needs and abilities and opportunities. Over the years these needs have not changed, nor will they. But women's abilities and opportunities have multiplied, resulting in a kaleidoscope of changing patterns whose final configuration will be fateful for all of us. . . .

Social Differences

Whatever equality may have existed between Adam and Eve before the Fall, there was a clear distinction in their social roles afterward. Adam was thenceforth required to till the soil and earn his bread by the sweat of his brow; Eve was condemned to painful childbirth and total submission to her husband. In one august decree, her reproductive role and social role were established and fixed. To be a woman, then as now, meant not just to be a distinctive blend of physiological and psychological characteristics. It meant and means that one is perceived differently, treated differently, responded to differently, and the subject of different expectations. Given the varying social forces that weigh unequally on the sexes in creatures as culture-dependent as humans, it seems clear that the resulting differences in behavior owe more to wide disparities in social-role than to the narrow differences in physical and psychological makeup.

The answer to the nursery-rhyme question, "what are little girls made of?" is revealing at several different levels. The list of ingredients—"sugar and spice and everything nice"—contains both a biological theory and a social demand. We are told, first of all, that little girls are good because of their inherent structure, and secondly, that they had better be good if they hope to enjoy the status of femininity and avoid the social disapproval which accompanies deviancy. Little boys, too, are under social pressure, but of a different kind. They are made of "snakes and snails and puppy-dog tails"—a combination designed to contrast mischievously and dynamically with the inert and saccharine constitution of their female counterparts. They, too, are saddled with social and presumed biological imperatives which compress the wide-ranging human potential for variation into the narrow confines of social-role expectation. There is hardly any important individual or social area—play, personal hygiene, manners, discipline, dependency, dress, activity, career, sexual activity, aggressiveness, etc.—which has not been polarized and institutionalized as a sex-role difference. While it is true that men have tended to stigmatize women as a group, deviation from social standards is even worse—e.g., the "effeminate" man and the "masculine" woman.

Traditionally, the little girl and later the woman are confined to a low-level of noise, dirt, disorder, and physical aggression. They must be obedient, dependent, modest about their bodies, and avoid sex play as well as rough and tumble competition. But life is not all no-no's: for her pains she is allowed to turn more readily to others for gratification, to cry when hurt, to be spontaneously affectionate, and to achieve less in school and work. Whatever the natural inclination of the sexes may be, society does not depend on spontaneous acquisition of the profile it considers desirable: besides identification with the parent of the same sex, which is probably the single most important determinant of behavior, it selects out from the random range of childhood activities those certain ones which will be accentuated or discarded. The shaping process includes toys—mechanical and problem-solving for boys, and soft and non-challenging for girls—social structuring, individual rewards and punishments, and the satisfactions apparently inherent in conforming to role expectations. The development of aggressive and dependent traits, both of which are considered to be sex-related, is a case in point. One research study found that while aggressive boys become aggressive men and dependent girls become dependent women, the reverse was true for dependent boys and aggressive girls: as they approach maturity, they reverse themselves and also become aggressive men and dependent women, respectively. Similarly, there is a greater overlap of sex-role personality traits when the sibling in a two-child family is of the opposite sex, and this effect is greater with the younger siblings than with the older ones. Clearly, learning and social pressure are influential in effecting sex-role expectations. Extending the argument that social roles are related to biological processes only indi-

rectly, presumably a technology which permitted father to nurture the child could result in a complete social-role reversal. In a pithy and accurate observation, Simone de Beauvoir summed up the consensus of current thinking when she said, "One is not born, but rather becomes, a woman."

In the interests of clarity, I have spoken separately of the major physical, psychological, and social characteristics which distinguish women from men, although obviously each molds the final form of the other, both clinically and theoretically. Investigations of animal behavior demonstrate, for example, that rat pups who are psychologically stimulated develop larger and presumably smarter brains than those exposed to sensory isolations; a litter born to a low-status African wild dog is less likely to survive than one born to a high-status female because the pups are less well fed and less protected by the pack; the male offspring of low-status baboon females, regardless of their innate characteristics, are less likely to become dominant than those born to high-status females because the latter spend more time in physical proximity to the inner circle of dominant males and learn dominance behavior; and the ovulatory cycle of a dove is retarded when a glass partition is placed between her and the rest of the flock, and it is stopped altogether if she is isolated in a room, unless there is a mirror. The interdependency between biological drive and learning is described in Konrad Lorenz's formulation of the concept of "instinct-training interlocking behavior": he describes this as a blend of instinctive and learned components, with instinct guaranteeing the readiness for certain kinds of learning and behavior to occur but experience shaping its final form.

In summary, females are smaller and meeker than men, they are less stable physiologically, they produce fewer androgenic hormones, and they have been socially shaped toward passivity, dependency, and conformity. Men are bigger, stronger, more aggressive, achievement-oriented, and more willing to break rules and take risks. This profile of the "normal" male and the "normal" female is consistent with the traditional differences which, until the last few decades, have prevailed for their criminal counterparts. However, the increasing "masculinization" of female social and criminal behavior forces us to reexamine the basis for her previous feminine limitations. A common-sense approach, and one followed by even such uncommon men as Freud and Adler, would suggest that what is natural to the female could be inferred from a factual description of the way the majority of females think and feel and act. Understandably, this is what has been done, and just as understandably it has been wrong. . . .

Female Passivity: Genetic Fact or Cultural Myth?

In the past, aggression was thought to be chiefly a biologically controlled trait. As a matter of their birth and ongoing internal chemistry, males were assumed to be "naturally aggressive"—hence the explanation of their historic roles as soldiers, hard-boiled businessmen, and merciless criminals. Women, on the other hand, were thought to be innately timid, passive, and conforming. Their general failure to be anything but mothers and housewives was offered as proof of their inability to be aggressive.

Of all the differences between the sexes, only four—size, strength, aggression, and dominance—have been implicated in any way with the overrepresentation of males in the criminal system.

The first two are biological givens; the other two are largely, if not entirely, socially learned. Let us examine them separately. In non-technological societies and in earlier periods in industrial societies, physical strength was often the final arbiter of social interaction, but even so, it was not the only one. In man as well as in the apes, psychological factors including social manipulation, ruses, and group alliances were often decisive for leadership and effective action. In animals as well as men, the battle did not always go to the strong nor the race to the swift. But even if it did, this edge has been diminished by the technology of modern weapons. The deadliness of a gun is not necessarily less dangerous in the hands of a woman—although some have claimed that her lack of aggressiveness

makes her a very unlikely and ineffective gunslinger. This is an interesting assumption because it is a common stereotype and is grounded in studies of male hormonal influences on lower animals, which gives it a ring of biological authenticity. There is much truth in this, but it is only a partial truth which, when stretched beyond its limits, conveys a falsehood. The truth is that in lower animals males are characteristically more aggressive, and this aggression is so directly linked to male hormones that if the male is castrated or injected with estrogen (the female hormone) he will stop fighting. Likewise, the prenatal administration of testosterone to pregnant monkeys results in pseudohermaphroditic female offspring who even three years after birth are more aggressive than normal females. However, it would be misleading to formulate the equation androgen = aggression or estrogen = nonaggression for all but the simplest and least socially developed species. Furthermore, it cannot be claimed that aggression is the exclusive prerogative of males. Mature female chimpanzees regularly drive off lower status males and any female mammal's defense of her cubs is as fierce as it is legendary.

But relevant as this is in establishing that aggression can co-exist with estrogen and can be unrelated to male hormones in mammals, the evidence for hormonal-behavioral detachment is even more compelling in subhuman primates and men. It is not possible to understand the behavior of social animals outside the context of a social situation. For example, an electric shock applied to an animal in a dominant position vis-à-vis another will result in an attack; the same stimulus applied to the same animal who is in a subdominant position vis-à-vis another will result in cringing, submissive behavior. Likewise, the response of anger vs. fear or fight vs. flight depends less on the release of specific chemicals than on whether we perceive the threatening stimulus, in relation to ourselves, to be smaller or larger. The human capacity for abstraction and symbol formulation extends the range of "size" to include factors only remotely related to actual mass, so that characteristics such as wealth, lineage, social connections, skill, and intelligence may be perceived as "big" and accorded dominance. In the evolutionary progression toward higher mammals, there is a decreasing dependency between hormones and behavior, and in humans we find an almost complete cultural "override" of innate drives and tendencies. Thus, while status and dominance appear to be constants throughout the order of social primates, culture defines which characteristics will be labeled as dominant. Likewise, the distinctive sex-appropriate behaviors so rigidly controlled by hormones in lower animals have yielded to a rich variety of gender roles in human societies.

In *Sex and Temperament in Three Primitive Societies*, Margaret Mead described three revealing cultural variations. In one tribe, both sexes acted in the mild, parental, responsive manner we expect of women; in a second, both sexes acted in the fierce initiating fashion we expect of men; in a third, the men were chatty, wore curls, and went shopping in the manner of our stereotype of women, while the women were their unadorned, managerial, energetic partners. She concluded that sex roles were "mere variations of human temperament, to which the members of either or both sexes may, with more or less success in the case of different individuals, be educated to approximate." She also concluded that regardless of what social role the male plays, it is always the lead.

Regardless of what his characteristic behavior may be and even when it is imitative of "feminine behavior," it is considered high status when he adopts it. While historically and universally it is indeed a man's world, it does not follow that modern industrial man is innately more dominant than modern woman. It could be argued that the equalizing effects of a technological civilization like ours is without historical parallel and that the universal dominance of men may have resulted more from the institutionalization of man's superior strength than from any innate feminine submissiveness.

Western history is replete with examples of women who have risen above their cultural stereotype to become leaders of vigor and acclaim. Nor has their reign or tenure in office been particularly noteworthy for its tranquillity, peacefulness, or lack of aggressive adventures, all characteristics of their countrywomen in the social role of housewife. These women have, in fact, displayed a remarkable talent for ruthless and highly aggressive leadership. For instance, few world leaders have ever been so renowned for their tyrannical, belligerent rule as the English queens. One can still be stirred by the picture of Elizabeth I attired with her gold crown and shining breastplate, mounted on a white stallion, and moving like an avenging angel through her army of twenty thousand men at Tilbury . . .; Cleopatra of ancient Egypt, a biological woman's woman by any standards, was known for her shrewd political manipulations and insatiable appetite for military conquests; Maria Theresa was the founder of the modern Austrian state; the Russian Empress Catherine, who mothered a dozen children during her reign, still found time to annex ever-widening territories and seek new armies to defeat. In the present day, it is noteworthy that the two major countries with female rulers have both been at war within the last few years: Indira Gandhi of India and Golda Meir of Israel have shown no timidity—each, in wars across her border, has wielded political and military might as effectively as any man. Of course, such women as these who have risen to national leadership possess extraordinary characteristics which distinguish them from the mass of women— and the mass of men, for that matter. The very capacity and drive for ascension through a male world involved a selection process which would have discouraged weaker women. Notwithstanding their small numbers, the resoluteness, and fortitude of such women challenge the myth of innate female passivity. On a broader scope, and one which encompassed more ordinary women, was the female incursion into criminal areas, previously considered male, during World War II. In law-enforcing as well as law-breaking, it would appear that social position and social-role expectations are more important than sex in determining behavior.

During the early 1940s, the mobilization of males from the civil to the military sector resulted in the necessity for a large number of women to fill positions previously held by men. And fill them they did, in a way not altogether anticipated. It had been known and expected that lesser men often rise to the stature of a role thrust on them by circumstance. It should not have been surprising, therefore, that "lesser men" who happen to be women would do the same thing. What was most portentous, however, about this vocational shift was not that women could assume men's jobs, but that in doing so they could also presume to men's social roles. One need not look to psychological theories to explain the enthusiasm with which women embraced men's esteemed positions. Their own, as housewife and playmate, had been eroding for years and a desperately labor-short male establishment had further devalued it in the interests of national defense, as something akin to indolence, if not disloyalty. "Rosie the Riveter," symbol of the women working for the war, was proclaimed a heroine in song and style by a grateful country. As the residence of female status shifted from the home to the office or factory, a trip that men had made long before, the American woman accommodated so congenially to the change that few people at the time challenged her credentials to perform. However, many were concerned that she was not just commuting to her new-found roles but might settle down to stay. In unprecedented numbers women crossed the sex-role line in their jobs and in their crimes during the war years, 1940 to 1945. In that period, the crimes committed by women almost doubled in number and even began to assume the same patterns as male crime. The trend peaked in 1945 and declined rapidly after the war with the return of men to their jobs, but it could never be the same. Women were now urged to act more like women by a male establishment which wanted to return to the position it had temporarily (it hoped) vacated. But in social evolution as in biological evolution, there is no easy road back, especially since in a very profound sense the women could not go home again. Labor-saving household appliances and the denigration of the domestic work ethic they conveyed rendered her old position untenable. In addition, there was a shift in the male attitude. Men were seeing women as worthy rivals and feeling considerably less charitable and more competitive toward

them. Furthermore, in a world grown too full of people, even the once sacrosanct status of motherhood was beginning to bear unhappy resemblances to overproductive pollution. With zero population as a national goal and household drudgery an accepted epithet, where was the woman to go? The road back was blocked, and while the road forward was not completely open it was now more accessible than ever before.

The pressure was all for discarding the separate-but-equal provisions of the old social contract and opting for a chance to compete in the same field and under the same conditions as men. Unfortunately, the men were not as ready for this change as the women. Psychoanalysts, long accustomed to the futile penis envy of women, were now talking about breast envy and womb envy, an example of male jealousy toward women almost unheard of in Freud's day.

While women proceeded to widen their social and criminal roles, many men, especially middle- and lower-class men, who had the least ground to yield in the status hierarchy, resisted in every way they could. . . .

Gender Equality and Crime

The old ways do indeed die hard, not only because we need our stereotypes and our subdominants, but also because cognitive systems tend to become security blankets to which we cling most tenaciously just when we are most threatened. It is perhaps for these reasons that the coming of age of the Western woman was not forecast by the behavioral scientists who should have known, but instead it caught us unawares and overtook our comfortable prejudices with a *fait accompli*. While most were predicting that it was impossible and many were arguing that it wasn't happening, it had already occurred. It is tempting to think no deeper than an apparent fact, and it must be admitted that the "facts" of female inferiority were apparent to all who could read the figures that supported them. It did not seem productive to search out the reasons behind the figures. They were self-evident because they confirmed what we already knew about the natural superiority of men. If it were otherwise, we surely would have been told by this time. But, indeed, we were being told new "facts" in compelling ways by new figures which were challenging old theories.

In the countless indices which measure female output of degrees and income and factory production, and in the Uniform Crime Reports which tabulate her legal transgressions, these rising figures were intruding not only on our beliefs but on the mores which supported them. At first, the rising crime rates were greeted as an apparition, a mirage; at first, they were dismissed as an aberration which would correct itself by statistical adjustments; at last, they were recognized as ancient female strengths which had always been latent and were just now, at this sociotechnological juncture of history, realizing their potential. Everything we know about the history of woman and everything we see about her current behavior tells us that her past limitations as a worker and lawbreaker have been largely, if not entirely, the result of her physical weakness and the cultural institutions which derived from that fact. Save only her inferiority in size and strength, her differences from men are just *that*, differences. Some confer an advantage, others a disadvantage, depending on the particular culture. In our own, given her education, aspirations (these, too, have been liberated), freedom from unwanted pregnancies, healthy assertiveness, and access to labor-saving devices, including guns, she shares the same fortunate or unfortunate criminogenic qualities as men.

I have not contended here that women are equal *to* men, simply that they are potentially the equal of men. There are many differences which we have described and no doubt more will be discovered, but all evidence points to two complementary conclusions: First, the small natural differences between the sexes have been polarized and institutionalized in special ways by different cultures to produce a gender disparity which reveals more about emotional needs of the society than about the innate possibilities of the individual. And second, when size and strength between the sexes are discounted by technology, as they have been within the ranks of men, social expectations and social roles, including the criminal roles, tend increasingly to merge.

There was a time early in the history of the physical sciences, before the concepts of mass and gravity were formulated, when the weight of an object was thought to reside within the physical boundaries of the object. Because weight is palpable and measurable, it was a conclusion which met the requirements of common sense and common experience. But the limitation of common sense is that it owes too much allegiance to the past to permit conceptual breakthroughs to the future. It is a better follower than leader. As physicists later discovered, the weight of an object is not inherent within it but rather the measure of an outside gravitational pull acting upon it. In an analogous manner, scientific thinking about human behavior has evolved in the same centrifugal direction. From the predecessors of Lombroso to the followers of Freud and into modern times, the search for the causes of female criminality have focused on her biology with scant heed to her sociology. We have only recently recognized that the clothes of social-role expectations not only make the man, they also form the woman.

Even if it is established that humans have innate biological drives, and even if it were confirmed that females have a different biogrammar (i.e., a behavioral repertoire of signals) from males, the social forces which impinge on her from without would still be decisive for her conformist as well as her deviant behavior. In the profoundest evolutionary sense, the social factors which sustain and suspend us also create our destiny, and biology must follow where society leads.

Discussion Questions

1. How do you think that the Women's Movement and the corresponding changes that were occurring in American society affected Adler's ideas on female crime as she wrote *Sisters in Crime*?

2. What is the liberation thesis? How does this related to Adler's views about the "rise of a new female criminal"?

3. Why did Adler argue that biology is not the main cause of female behavior, including female criminality?

4. Think back to your own childhood and teenage years. How might the socialization practices that you witnessed while you were growing up be related to why the criminal behaviors of males and females differ? ✦

37

Feminism and Criminology

Kathleen Daly
Meda Chesney-Lind

As two of the leading feminist criminologists, Kathleen Daly and Meda Chesney-Lind (1988) attempt in this essay to outline the contours of a feminist criminology (see also Simpson, 1989). Students wishing an update on developments in this area would do well to consult a recent article by Daly (1997; see also Chesney-Lind and Shelden, 1998).

Daly and Chesney-Lind note that a feminist approach represents a fundamental departure from traditional criminology. Although the richness of perspectives makes defining "feminism" a daunting, if not impossible, task, they argue that feminist analyses tend to share a set of unifying principles. Thus, gender is not seen as naturally rooted in biology but rather as "a complex social, historical, and cultural product." Gender relations are central to social life, especially since they "are based on an organizing principle of men's superiority and social and political-economic dominance over women." Daly and Chesney-Lind also recognize that feminism reveals that much seemingly neutral knowledge actually "reflects men's views of the natural and social world." To rectify this situation, "women should be at the center of intellectual inquiry, not peripheral, invisible, or appendages to men" (1988: 504).

In explaining the relationship of gender to criminal behavior, Daly and Chesney-Lind observe that criminologists' inquiries have tended to focus on two issues: the "generalizability problem," which asks whether "theories of men's crime apply to women," and the "gender-ratio problem," which asks why women are "less likely than men to be involved in crime" (pp. 514-515). Although factors identified by traditional theories might be implicated in (or "generalizable" to) female criminality, Daly and Chesney-Lind argue that this conclusion, taken by itself, begs important questions and does not obviate the importance of gender in crime causation. It does not tell us, for example, why women seem to be exposed less to the criminogenic influences identified by traditional theories, thus accounting for their lower involvement in crime. Might this have something to do with gender relations? (See Simpson and Elis, 1995.)

Further, even if empirically relevant, these male-centered theories certainly do not exhaust all that might be known about the nature of female offending. In fact, Daly and Chesney-Lind call for research that moves beyond statistical assessments of the generalizability and gender-ratio problems. Much like the life histories that the members of the Chicago school collected on male offenders, additional qualitative investigations are needed, especially by those with a gendered perspective, to detail the social context that shapes the lives of female offenders.

Daly and Chesney-Lind also highlight the special role that feminist criminology has played in studying men's violence toward women, especially rape and intimate violence. They note how "radical feminists" see violence against women as "the result and linchpin of patriarchal systems, in which women's bodies and minds are subject to men's dominion" (p. 521).

Finally, Daly and Chesney-Lind observe how feminist scholars have focused attention on a range of criminal justice issues, such as gender equality in the sanctioning of men and women and the role of the state in controlling pornography, prostitution, rape, and intimate violence (e.g., wife battering) (see also Daly and Tonry, 1997).

References

Chesney-Lind, Meda and Randall G. Shelden. 1998. *Girls, Delinquency, and Juvenile Justice*, 2nd edition. Belmont, CA: Wadsworth.

Daly, Kathleen. 1997. "Different Ways of Conceptualizing Sex/Gender in Feminist Theory and Their Implications for Criminology." *Theoretical Criminology* 1: 25-51.

Daly, Kathleen and Meda Chesney-Lind. 1988. "Feminism and Criminology." *Justice Quarterly* 5: 497-535.

Daly, Kathleen and Michael Tonry. 1997. "Gender, Race, and Sentencing." Pp. 201-252 in *Crime and Justice: A Review of Research, Volume 22*, edited by Michael Tonry. Chicago: University of Chicago Press.

Simpson, Sally S. 1989. "Feminist Theory, Crime, and Justice." *Criminology* 27: 605-631.

Simpson, Sally S. and Lori Elis. 1995. "Doing Gender: Sorting Out the Caste and Crime Conundrum." *Criminology* 33: 47-81.

. . . Working toward a reinvention of theory is a major task for feminists today. Although tutored in "male-stream" theory and methods, we work within and against these structures of knowledge to ask new questions, to put old problems in a fresh light, and to challenge the cherished wisdom of our disciplines. Such rethinking comes in many varieties, but these five elements of feminist thought distinguish it from other types of social and political thought:

> Gender is not a natural fact but a complex social, historical, and cultural product; it is related to, but not simply derived from, biological sex difference and reproductive capacities.

> Gender and gender relations order social life and social institutions in fundamental ways.

> Gender relations and constructs of masculinity and femininity are not symmetrical but are based on an organizing principle of men's superiority and social and political-economic dominance over women.

> Systems of knowledge reflect men's views of the natural and social world; the production of knowledge is gendered.

> Women should be at the center of intellectual inquiry, not peripheral, invisible, or appendages to men.

These elements take different spins, depending on how a scholar conceptualizes gender, the causes of gender inequality, and the means of social change. Generally, however, a feminist analysis draws from feminist theories or research, problematizes gender, and considers the implications of findings for empowering women or for change in gender relations. Finally, we note that scholars may think of themselves as feminists in their personal lives, but they may not draw on feminist theory or regard themselves as feminist scholars. For personal or professional reasons (or both), they may shy away from being marked as a particular kind of scholar. . . .

Tracing Developments: The Awakening to the 1980s

In the late 1960s, Bertrand (1969) and Heidensohn (1968), respectively a Canadian and a British female criminologist, drew attention to the omission of women from general theories of crime. Although they were not the first to do so, their work signaled an awakening of criminology from its androcentric slumber. Several years earlier Walter Reckless had observed in the 3rd edition of *The Crime Problem* (1961: 78),

> If the criminologist, before propounding or accepting any theory of crime or delinquency, would pause to ask whether that theory applied to women, he would probably discard it because of its inapplicability to women.

Then, as today, the problem identified by Bertrand, Heidensohn, and Reckless has two dimensions. First, it is uncertain whether general theories of crime can be applied to women's (or girls') wrongdoing. Second, the class-, race-, and age-based structure of crime forms the core of criminological theory, but the gender-based structure is ignored. Although related, these dimensions pose different questions for criminology. The first is whether theories generated to describe men's (or boys') offending can apply to women or girls (the *generalizability problem*). The second is why females commit less crime than males (the *gender ratio problem*). Both questions now occupy a central role in research on gender and crime, which we shall address below. . . .

Approaches to Building Theories of Gender and Crime

Theories of gender and crime can be built in several ways, and we see criminologists taking three tacks. Some are focusing on what we have called the generalizability problem, while others are interested in what we have termed the gender ratio problem. Still others want to bracket both problems, regarding each as premature for an accurate understanding of gender and crime.

The Generalizability Problem

Do theories of men's crime apply to women? Can the logic of such theories be modified to include women? In addressing the generalizability problem, scholars have tested theories derived from all-male samples to see if they apply to girls or women (e.g., Cernkovich and Giordano 1979; Datesman and Scarpitti 1975; Figueira-McDonough and Selo 1980; Giordano 1978; Warren 1982; Zietz 1981). Others have borrowed elements from existing theories (e.g., Moyer 1985 on conflict theory) or have recast the logic of a theory altogether (e.g., Schur 1984 on labeling). According to Smith and Paternoster's (1987) review of the large body of studies taking this approach, the available evidence is limited, mixed, and inconclusive. More studies likely will confirm a consistent, logical answer to the question "Do theories of men's crime apply to women?" The answer is "yes and no": the truth lies in this equivocation.

The Gender Ratio Problem

The gender ratio problem poses the following questions: Why are women less likely than men to be involved in crime? Conversely, why are men more crime-prone than women? What explains gender differences in rates of arrest and in variable types of criminal activity? In contrast to the gender composition of generalizability scholars, almost all gender ratio scholars seem to be men. Their approach is to develop new theoretical formulations by drawing primarily from statistical evidence, secondary sources, elements of existing theory (e.g., social control, conflict, Marxist), and at times from feminist theory. Box (1983), Gove (1985), Hagan, Simpson, and Gillis (1987), Harris (1977), Messerschmidt (1986), Steffensmeier (1983), and Wilson and Herrnstein (1985) have offered ideas on this issue. Heidensohn (1985) is one of few female criminologists to take this route.

Juxtaposing the Generalizability and Gender Ratio Problems

Much of the confusion and debate that surround the building of theories of gender and crime can be resolved when scholars realize that they are on different tracks in addressing the generalizability and gender ratio problems. Members of each camp seem to be unaware of the other's aims or assumptions; but when the two are juxtaposed, their logic and their limitations are revealed. Analogous developments have taken place in building theories of gender and the labor market; thus we sketch some of that literature to clarify problems in developing theories of gender and crime.

A model of occupational status attainment, outlined by Blau and Duncan (1967) and using an all-male sample, was applied subsequently to samples of women. This research suggested that the same variables predicted occupational status for men and for women (see Sokoloff's 1980 review); the implication was that the processes of intergenerational occupational mobility were the same for men and women. Those taking a more structural approach to the labor market soon raised this question, however: how was it that the "same" processes produced such distinctive distributions of men and women in the paid occupational structure (job segregation) and caused such marked differences in men's and women's wages? That query inspired a rethinking of the structural and organizational contexts of men's and women's work (paid and unpaid), which now commands the attention of many sociologists and economists.

The gender and labor market literature today is several steps ahead of that for gender and crime, but similarities at different stages are clear. Generalizability scholars are not concerned with gender differences in rates of arrest or in arrests for particular crimes (or in rates and types of delinquent acts). Instead they want to know whether the same processes (or variables) describe intragender variability in crime and delinquency. Setting aside the mixed research findings, they (like status attainment theorists) confront a vexing question. Even if (for the sake of argument) the same processes or variables explain intragender variability in crime and delinquency or in its detection, why do such similar processes produce a distinctive gender-based structure to crime or delinquency? Moreover, what does it mean to develop a gender-neutral theory of crime, as some scholars now advocate, when neither the social order nor the structure of crime is gender-neutral?

Smith and Paternoster (1987) propose developing a gender-neutral theory of crime because gender-specific theories of the past (meaning theories of female criminality) held sexist and stereotypic assumptions of female behavior. (Note that theories of male crime are assumed to be universal and are not construed as gender-specific.) When Smith and Paternoster then consider the gender ratio problem, they suggest that the volume of criminal deviance may reflect *"differential exposure* to factors that precipitate deviant behavior among both males and females" (1987:156). Their surmise begs the question of how gender relations structure "differential exposure" and "factors," and seemingly denies the existence of gender relations.

Like structural analysts of gender and the labor market, gender ratio criminologists take the position that patterns of men's and women's crime are sufficiently different to warrant new theoretical formulations. Focusing on intergender variability in rates of arrest or in arrests for particular crimes, general theorists offer these starting points: the power relations both between and among men and women, the control and commodification of female sexuality, sources of informal social control, and the greater enforcement of conformity in girls' and women's lives. In contrast to generalizability scholars, gender ratio scholars assume that different (or gender-specific) variables predict intergender variability in crime or delinquency.

In the wake of arguments developed by gender ratio scholars, those who pursue the generalizability problem may begin to rethink concepts or variables, or they may abandon their enterprise as too limiting. That change may require some time, however, because the contributions of the gender ratio scholars to date are also limited or provisional. Although they acknowledge that crime (like the occupational order) is gendered, many display only a primitive understanding of what this fact means, and all face problems of slim evidence (save statistical distributions) from which to develop sound propositions about female crime or gender differences in crime.

Bracketing the Two Problems

Many feminist criminologists tend for the present to bracket the generalizability and the gender ratio problems. They are skeptical of previous representations of girls' or women's lives and want a better understanding of their social worlds. Moreover, they are unimpressed with theoretical arguments derived from questionable evidence and having little sensitivity to women's (or men's) realities. Like criminologists of the past (from the 1930s to the 1960s), they seek to understand crime at close range, whether through biographical case studies, autobiographical accounts, participant observation, or interviews (e.g., Alder 1986; Bell 1987; Campbell 1984; Carlen 1983, 1985; Carlen and Worrall 1987; Chesney-Lind and Rodriguez 1983; Delacoste and Alexander 1987; Miller 1986; Rosenbaum 1981). For this group of scholars, the quality and the depth of evidence are insufficient to address the generalizability or gender ratio problems. Perhaps more important, the ways in which questions are framed and results are interpreted by many (though not all) of those pursuing the generalizability or gender ratio problems remain tied to masculinist perspectives, ignoring the insights from feminist scholarship.

Observations

Because the building of theories of gender and crime is recent, and because a focus on women or on gender difference is viewed as a marginal problem for the field, we think it imprudent to judge some efforts more harshly than others. We may find, for example, that different explanations for intra- and intergender variability are necessary, or that a more careful examination of patterns of girls' or women's crime may improve our understanding of boys' or men's criminal deviance, among other possibilities. At this stage of theory building, all approaches must be explored fully. In advocating this position we are aware that some varieties of theory building and some methodological approaches are thought to be more elegant (or, as our male colleagues like to say, more powerful). Specifically, global or grand theoretical arguments and high-tech statistical analyses are valued more highly by the profession. Thus we examine the approaches taken by criminologists in this intellectual context. Our concern is that scholars begin to see that the dimensions of a major criminological problem—the place of men and of women in theories of crime—cannot be separated from a problem for the sociology of knowledge—the place of men and of women in constructing theory and conducting research. Harris (1977:15) alluded to this problem when he said:

> Dominant typifications about what kinds of actors "do" criminal behavior—typifications which have served dominant male interests and have been held by both sexes—have played a crucial dual role in . . . keeping sociologists from seeing the sex variable in criminal deviance and . . . keeping men in crime and women out of it.

If the words "criminal behavior," "criminal deviance," and "crime" are replaced with "criminology" in this statement, we can extend Harris's insight with the following observations.

Preferable modes of theory building are gender-linked. Male scholars, for example, have moved rather boldly into theoretical work on the gender ratio problem in both juvenile (e.g., Hagan et al. 1987) and adult arenas (e.g., Messerschmidt 1986). Meanwhile female scholars have displayed more tentativeness and a discomfort with making global claims. In a related vein, it is clear that preferred modes of data collection are also gender-linked. Although both male and female criminologists are required to display their statistical talents, the women's empirical approaches in understanding crime today are more likely than the men's to involve observations and interviews. They are more interested in providing texture, social context, and case histories; in short, in presenting accurate portraits of how adolescent and adult women become involved in crime. This gender difference is not related to "math anxiety" but rather to a felt need to comprehend women's crime on its own terms, just as criminologists of the past did for men's crime.

As increasing numbers of women (and feminists) enter criminology, they face dilemmas if they wish to understand men's, women's, or gender differences in crime or delinquency. A safe course of action—intellectually and professionally—is to focus on the generalizability problem and to use a domesticated feminism to modify previous theory. Something may be learned by taking this tack (i.e., intragender variability), but there remains an issue, not yet pursued vigorously: whether theoretical concepts are inscribed so deeply by masculinist experiences that this approach will prove too restrictive, or at least misleading.

Our final observation is more speculative. It is inspired by Heidensohn's (1985) remarks on studies of adolescent boys' gangs, both the classics and more recent efforts. She suggests that the men conducting these studies were "college boys . . . fascinated with the corner boys" (1985:141). These researchers "vicariously identified" with the boys, romanticizing their delinquency in heroic terms. We think that this sense of affinity has eluded female criminologists thus far in their analyses of girls' or women's crime. An example will illustrate this point.

Miller (1986:189) reports at the close of her book on street hustlers that "the details of these women's lives would run together in my mind and make me angry, generally upset, and depressed." Angered at the lives these women had led as children and at the daily brutality in their current lives, she saw little hope for the women's or their children's futures. As empathetic as Miller was in describing women's illicit work, her story contains few heroines; the initial excitement of criminal activity turns into self-destruction and pain. How strongly her impressions differ from men's ethnographies of juvenile males, who are described as "cool cats" or as "rogue males [engaging in] untrammelled masculinity" (Heidensohn 1985:125-44). Heidensohn terms this genre the "delinquent machismo tradition in criminology" (1985:141), in which the boys' deviance, and to some degree their violence, are viewed as normal and admirable. By contrast, it is far more difficult for female criminologists to find much to celebrate in girls' or women's crime.

As suggested earlier, all three approaches to reformulating theories of gender and crime have merit. Nevertheless we think that the most pressing need today is to bracket the generability and the gender ratio problems, to get our hands dirty, and to plunge more deeply into the social worlds of girls and women. The same holds true for boys and men, whose patterns of crime have changed since the 1950s and 1960s, when ethnographies of delinquency flourished in criminology. Recent changes in youth gangs highlight the need for this work (Hagedorn 1988; Huff 1988; Moore 1978). Our concern is that explicitly feminist approaches to women's crime or to the gender patterns of crime will not be noticed, will be trivialized merely as case studies, or will be written off as not theoretical enough. That sort of dismissal would be unfortunate but perhaps not surprising, in view of the professional norms governing the discipline and their masculinist bias.

Controlling Men's Violence Toward Women

The victimization (and survivorship) of women is a large and growing part of criminology and is of central interest to feminists in and outside criminology. The relatively high feminist visibility in this area may lead criminologists to regard it as the only relevant site for feminist inquiry in criminology. Not so; the more one reads the literature on victimization—the physical and sexual abuse of children, women, and men—the more difficult it becomes to separate victimization from offending, especially in the case of

women (Browne 1987; Chesney-Lind forthcoming; Chesney-Lind and Rodriguez 1983; McCormack, Janus, and Burgess 1986; Silbert and Pines 1981).

In research on physical abuse and sexual violence by men against women, these major themes and findings are seen:

Rape and violence—especially between intimates—are far more prevalent than imagined previously.

Police, court officials, juries, and members of the general public do not take victims of rape or violence seriously, especially when victim-offender relations involve intimates or acquaintances.

Myths about rape and intimate violence are prevalent.

They appear in the work of criminologists, in criminal justice practices, and in the minds of members of the general public.

Whereas female victims feel stigma and shame, male offenders often do not view their behavior as wrong.

Strategies for change include empowering women via speakouts, marches, shelters and centers, and legal advocacy; and changing men's behavior via counseling, presumptive arrest for domestic violence, and more active prosecution and tougher sanctions for rape.

Although feminists of all types agree that men's rape and battery of women require urgent attention, scholars and activists have different views on the causes and the malleability of men's sexual and physical aggression. Pornography (and its links to men's sexual violence) and prostitution (and its links to pornography) are prominent in the dissensus. We turn to these debates and their implications for criminal justice policy.

Causes of Men's Violence Toward Women

Radical feminists tend to construct men's nature as rapacious, violent, and oriented toward the control of women (see, e.g., Brownmiller 1975; Dworkin 1987; MacKinnon 1982, 1983, 1987; Rich 1980). Both rape and intimate violence are the result and the linchpin of patriarchal systems, in which women's bodies and minds are subject to men's dominion. Marxist and socialist feminists (e.g., Hooks 1984; Klein 1982; Messerschmidt 1986; Schwendinger and Schwendinger 1983) differ from radical feminists on one key point: they believe that men's nature cannot be described in universalistic (or biologically based) terms but is a product of history and culture, and is related to other systems of domination such as classism, racism, and imperialism. In contrast, liberal feminists offer no theory of causes, but like Marxist and socialist feminists they envision the possibility that men's socially structured violent nature can change. What role, then, should the state play in controlling men's violence and protecting women from such violence? Feminist responses are contradictory and the dilemmas are profound.

Questioning the Role of the State

Pornography. Differences among feminists over the causes of men's violence and the state's role in controlling it are nowhere so clear as in the pornography issue. Part of the debate concerns the effect of pornography on increasing or causing men's sexual violence toward women. Research ethics preclude an answer, but clinical evidence to date shows that pornography with violent content increases aggression, whereas pornography without violent content diminishes aggression (see Baron and Strauss 1987: 468). Such evidence hardly settles the matter either for anti-pornography or for anticensorship feminists. At issue are different views of men's sexuality and the causes of men's violence, with radical feminists initiating the antipornography movement. Also at issue is whether state officials can be trusted to render the judgments that antipornography activists seek via the proposed civil remedy (Waring 1986). Finally, anticensorship feminists see greater harm for women and sexual minorities in efforts to suppress the many forms of commercialized pornography.

Prostitution. Debates among and between feminists and sex-trade workers (Bell 1987; Delacoste and Alexander 1987) reveal differences in how women view sexuality and sexual power, as well as problems in relying on a male-dominated state to protect women.

These differences are often submerged in a coalition of civil liberties groups, women's groups, and sex-trade workers' organizations who reject state regulation *or* criminalization of prostitution. In advocating the decriminalization of prostitution and a range of issues associated with prostitutes' right to work, the concerned groups achieve a short-term solution: women can make a living and are not singled out as criminals in a commercial activity that men control, use, and profit from. Nevertheless, the institution of prostitution remains intact, and with it this feminist dilemma: will support for some women's right to work perpetuate an institution that ultimately objectifies women and exploits them sexually, may foster violence against women, and may harm female prostitutes? Today, however, as in the past, the state's stance on vigorous enforcement of prostitution and other related ordinances depends on how prostitution harms men via sexually transmitted diseases, rather than on the institution's impact on women (Alexander 1987; Bland 1985; Daly 1988; Walkowitz 1980).

In juxtaposing prostitution and pornography, one sees the contradictions and dilemmas for feminists who campaign for redress against men's violence toward women (often by seeking an expanded role for the state in protecting women) while simultaneously advocating women's economic and sexual freedom. Similar dilemmas arise in controlling intimate violence.

Intimate Violence and Rape. State criminal laws for the arrest and prosecution of spouse (or intimate) abuse and rape have changed significantly in a short period of time (see reviews by Bienen 1980; Lerman 1980). Civil remedies such as the temporary restraining order to protect battered women are more readily available than in the past. These legal changes are a symbolic victory for many feminists, who see in them the state's accomoodation to their demands for protection against men's violence. Yet the effect of new laws and programs on changing police and court practices seems far less impressive. Officials' resistance and organizational inertia are common themes; program success can be short-lived (Berk, Loseke,

Berk, and Rauma 1980; Berk, Rauma, Loseke, and Berk 1982; Crites 1987; Grau, Fagan, and Wexler 1984; Quarm and Schwartz 1984; Spencer 1987). Some scholars think legal reforms may serve a deterrent and educative function over the long term, and thus that it may be unreasonable to expect immediate change in men's violence or in the state's response (Osborne 1984).

Gender Equality in the Criminal Justice System

In the early days of second-wave feminism, calls for legal equality with men were apparent everywhere, and the early feminist critics of criminal law and justice practices reflected this ethos. Today feminist legal scholars are more skeptical of a legal equality model because the very structure of law continues to assume that men's lives are the norm, such that women's legal claims are construed as "special treatment." Alternatives to thinking about equality and difference have been proposed in view of women's social and economic subordinate status and gender differences in paid employment, sexuality, and parenthood; see, e.g., *International Journal of the Sociology of Law* 1986; MacKinnon 1987; Rhode 1987; Vogel Forthcoming; *Wisconsin Women's Law Journal* 1987. Feminist dissensus over what should be done partly reflects different perspectives on gender, but increasingly one finds that strategies for change reflect lessons learned from engaging in the legal process. As feminists have moved to change the law, so too has the law changed feminism.

Questioning Equality Doctrine and the Equal Treatment Model

Feminist analyses of criminal justice practices reflect a similar shift by moving away from a liberal feminist conceptualization of gender discrimination as a problem of equal treatment. This recent change is more pronounced in British than in American criminology (related, no doubt, to the preponderance of statistical approaches in the United States). It is seen in studies and literature reviews by Allen (1987), Chesney-Lind (1986, 1987), Daly (1987a, 1987b, forthcoming), Ea-

ton (1983, 1985, 1986, 1987), Heidensohn (1986, 1987), Smart (1985), and Worrall (1987). Unlike previous statistical studies of gender-based disparities in court outcomes (for reviews see Nagel and Hagan 1983; Parisi 1982), more recent qualitative studies of legal processes analyze the interplay of gender, sexual and familial ideology, and social control in courtroom discourse and decision-making at both the juvenile and the adult levels. This work addresses how gender relations structure decisions in the legal process, rather than whether men and women are treated "the same" in a statistical sense. Eaton (1986: 15) sums up the limitations of analyzing sentencing as an equal treatment problem in this way: "The [discrimination] debate is conducted within the terms of legal rhetoric—'justice' and 'equality' mean 'equal treatment,' existing inequalities are to be ignored or discounted." Thus, just as feminist legal scholars are critiquing equality doctrine, feminist criminologists now are questioning how research on discrimination in the courts is conducted. . . .

The limitations of current equality doctrine are also apparent for changing the prison (or jail) conditions of incarcerated women. Litigation based on equal protection arguments can improve conditions for women to some degree (e.g., training, educational, or work release programs), but such legal arguments are poorly suited to the specific health needs of women and to their relationships with children (Leonard 1983; Resnik and Shaw 1980). Indirectly they may also make it easier to build new familities for female offenders than to consider alternatives to incarceration. Historical studies of the emergence of women's prisons in the United States suggest that separate spheres notions, which were applied to penal philosophy, may have offered somewhat better conditions of confinement for women (notably white, not black women; see Rafter 1985) than an equality-with-men model (Freedman 1981; SchWeber 1982). Therefore equality defined as equal treatment of men and women, especially when men's experiences and behavior are taken as the norm, forestalls more fundamental change and in some instances may worsen women's circumstances.

Conclusion

We are encouraged by the burst of research attention that has been given to women and to gender differences in crime, to the response to delinquency and crime in the juvenile and criminal justice systems, and to women's victimization. Yet with the possible exception of women's victimization, criminology has not felt the full impact of feminism except in its most rudementary liberal feminist form. In this vein we underscore a point made several times in the essay: feminist inquiry is relevant and should be applied to *all* facets of crime, deviance, and social control. A focus on gender and gender difference is not simply a focus on women or on what some scholars term "women's issues" in a narrow sense. It is and should be a far more encompassing enterprise, raising questions about how gender organizes the discipline of criminology, the social institutions that fall within its scope, and the behavior of men and women.

We are surprised by those who continue to say that a focus on gender is unimportant for theories of crime because there are "so few women criminals." We have also been told that discussions of women's crime are "entertaining," meaning that they are a trivial footnote to more general and important problems. Still the fact remains: of whatever age, race, or class and of whatever nation, men are more likely to be involved in crime, and in its most serious forms. Without resorting to essential arguments about women's nature, we see in this pattern some cause for hope. A large price is paid for structures of male domination and for the very qualities that drive men to be successful, to control others, and to wield uncompromising power. Most theories of crime suggest the "normalcy" of crime in the light of social processes and structures, but have barely examined the significance of patriarchal structures for relations among men and for the forms and expressions of masculinity. Gender differences in crime suggest that crime may not be so normal after all. Such differences challenge us to see that in the lives of women, men have a great deal more to learn.

Discussion Questions

1. What is a feminist theory? How does it differ from other explanations of human behavior, including crime?

2. What are the generalizability and gender-ratio problems?

3. How would a feminist criminologist explain male violence against women? How would this be related to patriarchy?

4. Why might a feminist perspective argue that the elimination of patriarchy might lead to much lower crime rates in society? ✦

38

Masculinities and Crime

James W. Messerschmidt

Although sympathetic to radical feminism, James Messerschmidt observes that feminist analyses do not take seriously the study of masculinity. The tendency to attribute male behavior to patriarchy is reductionistic: it places all men in a single category—one in which "women are good, men are bad, plain and simple. And it is this essential badness that leads to patriarchy and violence against women" (1993: 43). But men are not all the same. In particular, gender intersects with race and class to create different "masculinities" or conceptions of what it means to be male. Understanding male behavior thus entails understanding the historical and structural conditions that construct the masculinities that structure male social action, including crime.

Messerschmidt makes the important insight that "crime by men is not simply an extension of the 'male sex role' " or, for that matter, of some male trait (1993: 85). In any social situation that males enter, they are faced with the ongoing task of showing that they are manly, of "accomplishing" their masculinity. Precisely what this entails differs by age-class-racial position in society. The meaning of masculinity varies by structural location, and in turn these meanings are "reproduced" or reconfirmed as men in these locations act to reaffirm their manly identities in the ways available to them.

In this framework, crime is seen as a resource for "doing gender"—that is, it is a way of showing that one is masculine. Messerschmidt argues that crime is most likely to occur when legitimate means of demonstrating masculinity are stifled. It is noteworthy that class and racial inequality restrict the conventional avenues for doing gender, such as success in school and in the labor market. In response to their emas-

culation and humiliation in these settings, juveniles and later adults develop "opposition masculinities," which involve the rejection of conventional ways of doing gender. Instead, criminal acts—from vandalism to violence— become vivid ways of showing their manliness. The end result, however, is that these criminal displays of masculinity only serve to restrict life chances and thus to reproduce existing structural inequalities.

Messerschmidt does not offer a class-biased theory. He recognizes that middle-class youths and adults also break the law, whether it is through juvenile mischief, displays of drunkenness, sexual harassment in the workplace, or white-collar crime. Still, in most ways, he sees more affluent white males as having access to and using "accommodating masculinities" that allow them to do gender in ways that accrue advantage and reinforce their gender, class, and racial dominance.

Finally, Messerschmidt recognizes that, in one way or another, all males act to do gender within the confines of the dominant conception of masculinity which teaches that heterosexual men are superior to women. Messerschmidt calls this "hegemonic masculinity," which is "defined through work in the paid-labor market, the subordination of women, heterosexism, and the driven uncontrollable sexuality of men" (1993: 82). "Refined further," he observes, "hegemonic masculinity emphasizes practices toward authority, control, competitive individualism, independence, aggressiveness, and the capacity for violence" (p. 82). As men do masculinity within these cultural scripts, they also reinforce their dominance over females in society.

Messerschmidt's theory can be questioned on a number of grounds: females are omitted from the analysis; his menu listing the ways in which men can demonstrate masculinity seems narrow, ignoring, for example, being a good father, participating in voluntary organizations, talking about sports, and so on; conformity among disadvantaged groups is not easily explained; and his motivational theory—the need to do masculinity—may overexplain many criminal acts that are committed simply because they are fun or gratifying (cf. Gottfredson and Hirschi, Chapter 19). Still, for any male who has given a "high five" after scoring a basket, who has grunted with one's fellows, who has exchanged sexist jokes with "the guys," or who has performed risky acts to show he is not "chicken," the idea that masculinity is intimately involved in male behavior—including crime—has enormous intuitive appeal.

Reference

Messerschmidt, James W. 1993. *Masculinities and Crime: Critique and Reconceptualization of Theory*. Lanham, MD: Rowman and Littlefield.

. . . Criminological theory—although traditionally written by men and primarily about boys and men—has been alarmingly gender-blind. That is, gendered men and boys have never been the object of the criminological enterprise. Feminism has challenged the overall "malestream" nature of criminology by highlighting the repeated omission and/or misrepresentation of women in criminological enquiry. The result of this critique is twofold: (1) it has increased attention to women in criminological theory and research but (2) when criminology addresses gender it speaks exclusively of women, with little or no attention directed to the impact of gender on men. Although some consideration has focused on masculinity and crime, this relationship has been examined through an essentialist, antiquated, and fallacious sex-role theory.

[I previously] demonstrated that radical feminism is not a viable alternative theory. A feminism that insists upon alleged natural differences between women and men, and goes on to explain crime committed by men in terms of that essentialism, not only homogenizes men (as does sex-role theory) but also proves itself inadequate to explaining crime committed by men. Although radical feminism is applauded for moving sexuality and gender power to the forefront of feminist thought, we are compelled to reject all forms of essentialism and reductionism. . . .

To structure a comprehensive feminist theory of gendered crime, we must bring men into the framework. However, we should do this not by treating men as the normal subjects, but by articulating the gendered con-

tent of men's behavior and of crime. This approach requires a different theoretical lens—one that focuses on a sociology of masculinity—to comprehend why men are involved disproportionately in crime and why they commit different types of crime. In what follows, I build on the critique . . . by employing the insights of Giddens (1976; 1981), Connell (1987), West and Zimmerman (1987), Festermaker, West, and Zimmerman (1991), Goffman (1979), and others to present new theoretical tools for comprehending crime committed by men.

At least two significant theoretical undertakings are suggested from the criticisms outlined [previously]. First, it is essential to make the relevant theoretical links among class, gender, and race without surrendering to some type of separate systems approach (e.g., capitalism plus patriarchy). Second, it is critical to construct a theory of crime that recognizes that illegal behavior, like legal behavior, personifies synchronously both social practice and social structure. Indeed, social structures do not exist autonomously from humans; rather, they arise and endure through social practice. Social structures originate, are reproduced, and change through social practice. In short, we can only speak of *structured action*: social structures can be understood only as constituting practice; social structures, in turn, permit and preclude social action. . . .

To understand why men engage in more and different types of crimes than women and in differing amounts and forms among themselves, we need an adequate account of social action. We can begin by recognizing that in society all individuals engage in purposive behavior and monitor their own action reflexively. That is, we comprehend our actions and we modify them according to (among other things) our interpretation of other people's responses. Social action is creative, inventive, and novel, but it never occurs separately from, or external to, social structures. Social structures are constituted by social action and, in turn, provide resources and power from which individuals construct "strategies of action" (Swidler, 1986: 227). Social structures organize the way individuals think about their circumstances and generate methods for dealing with them.

Gendered Social Action and Crime

. . . Masculinity is accomplished, it is not something done to men or something settled beforehand. And masculinity is never static, never a finished product. Rather, men construct masculinities in specific social situations (although not in circumstances of their own choosing); in so doing, men reproduce (and sometimes change) social structures. As Giddens (1976: 138) forcefully argues, "every act which contributes to the reproduction of a structure is also an act of production, a novel enterprise, and as such may initiate change by altering that structure at the same time as it reproduces it."

. . . Hegemonic masculinity is the idealized form of masculinity in a given historical setting. It is culturally honored, glorified, and extolled, and this "exaltation stabilizes a structure of dominance and oppression in the gender order as a whole" (Connell, 1990: 94). In contemporary Western industrialized societies, hegemonic masculinity is defined through work in the paid-labor market, the subordination of women, heterosexism, and the driven and uncontrollable sexuality of men. Refined still further, hegemonic masculinity emphasizes practices toward authority, control, competitive individualism, independence, aggressiveness, and the capacity for violence (Connell, 1990, 1992; Segal, 1990). Because "most men benefit from the subordination of women, and hegemonic masculinity is the cultural expression of this ascendancy," most men engage in practices that attempt to sustain hegemonic masculinity (Connell, 1987: 185). Indeed, most men help maintain hegemonic masculinity (and consequently the subordination of women) by means of the practices that reflect their particular positions in society. . . .

When men enter a setting, they undertake social practices that demonstrate they are "manly." The only way others can judge their "essential nature" as men is through their behavior and appearance. Thus, men use the resources at their disposal to communicate gender to others. For many men, crime may serve as a suitable *resource* for "doing gender"—for separating them from all that is feminine. Because types of criminality are possible only when particular social conditions present themselves, when other masculine resources are unavailable, particular types of crime can provide an alternative resource for accomplishing gender and, therefore, affirming a particular type of masculinity. For, although men are always doing masculinity, the significance of gender accomplishment is socially situated and, thus, an intermittent matter. That is, certain occasions present themselves as more intimidating for showing and affirming masculinity. As Coleman (1990: 196) states, "Such an occasion is where a man's "masculinity" risks being called into question." The taken-for-granted "essential nature" of a man or boy can be questioned, undermined, and threatened in certain contexts, those situations where he lacks resources for masculine accomplishment.

In such predicaments, sex category is particularly salient; it is, as David Morgan (1992: 47) puts it, "more or less explicitly put on the line," and doing masculinity necessitates extra effort, generating a distinct type of masculinity. Under such conditions, performance as a member of one's sex category is subjected to extra evaluation and crime is more likely to result. Crime, therefore, may be invoked as a practice through which masculinities (and men and women) are differentiated from one another. Moreover, crime is a resource that may be summoned when men lack other resources to accomplish gender. . . .

Crime by men is not simply an extension of the "male sex role." Rather, crime by men is a form of social practice invoked as a resource, when other resources are unavailable, for accomplishing masculinity. By analyzing masculinities, then, we can begin to understand the socially constructed differences among men and thus explain why men engage in different forms of crime. . . .

Social Structures, Masculinities, and Crime in Youth Groups

I explore the way social action is linked to structured possibilities/constraints, identifying in particular how the class, race, and gendered relations in society constrain and enable the social activity of young men in the school and the youth group, and how this structured action relates to youth crime.

"Boys will be boys" differently, depending upon their position in social structures and, therefore, upon their access to power and resources. Social structures situate young men in a common relation to other young men and in such a way that they share structural space. Collectively, young men experience their daily world from a particular position in society and differentially construct the cultural ideals of hegemonic masculinity. Thus, within the school and youth group there are patterned ways in which masculinity is represented and which depend upon structures of labor and power in class and race relations. Young men situationally accomplish public forms of masculinity in response to their socially structured circumstances; indeed, varieties of youth crime serve as a suitable resource for doing masculinity when other resources are unavailable. These forms of youth crime, as with other resources, are determined by social structures. . . .

In what follows, I attempt to identify certain of the chief class and race junctures in the social construction of youthful public masculinities and crimes—in particular, the important relationship between youth crime and school. The focus is on how some young men come to define their masculinity against the school and, in the process, choose forms of youth crime as resources for accomplishing gender and for constructing what I call *opposition masculinities*. I begin with white, middle-class boys.

White, Middle-Class Boys

Given the success of the middle-class Saints and Socs in school [two youth groups studied by other researchers], it is this very success that provides a particular resource for constructing a specific form of masculinity. In this type of masculinity, the penchant for a career is fundamental: a "calculative attitude is taken towards one's own life" and the crucial themes are "rationality and responsibility rather than pride and aggressiveness"

(Connell, 1989: 296-297). Throughout their childhood development, white, middle-class boys are geared toward the ambiance and civility of the school. Within the school environment, for these boys, masculinity is normally accomplished through participation in sports and academic success. This participation in (or at least avid support for) sport creates an environment for the construction of a masculinity that celebrates toughness and endurance, incessantly advocates competitiveness and shame of losing, and "connects a sense of maleness with a taste for violence and confrontation" (Kessler, Ashenden, Connell, Dowsett, 1985: 39). Yet, in addition to creating this specific type of masculinity, sport is so revered and glorified within the school that it subordinates other types of masculinity, such as the sort constructed by the "brains" who participate in nonviolent games like debate (p. 39).

Over and above sport, white, middle-class masculinity in the school is typically achieved through a reasonable level of academic success. As Tolson (1977: 34-36) argues, the middle-class family supports this trajectory: "books in the home and parental help with homework provide a continuous emotional context for academic achievement"; moreover, middle-class families also tend to emphasize the importance of obtaining the appropriate qualifications for "respectable careers" that guarantee the "security" of a "profession." As Heward (1988: 8) experienced in an English boarding school, white, middle-class parents "planned their sons' futures carefully and then pursued their plans very actively, with the aim of placing them in suitable occupations and careers." For the white middle class, then, manliness is about having a secure income from a "respectable" professional occupation. Thus, there is an important link between school and family in middle-class life, and both transmit class-specific notions of hegemonic masculinity to white, middle-class boys—a particular type of work in the paid-labor market, competitiveness, personal ambition and achievement, and responsibility.

Accommodating and Opposition Masculinities

Nonetheless, hegemonic masculinity also involves practices characterizing dominance, control, and independence. . . . Such masculine ideals are, however, the very qualities that schooling discourages. Although white, middle-class youth generally exercise greater authority and control in school than do youth from other class and race backgrounds, research on secondary schooling reveals that adaptation to the social order of the school requires that all students, regardless of their class and race, submit to rock-hard authority relations in which students are actually penalized for creativity, autonomy, and independence (Bowles and Gintis, 1976; Greenberg, 1977; Messerschmidt, 1979). In other words, white, middle-class boys, like other boys, experience a school life that is circumscribed by institutionalized authoritarian routine.

In spite of this constraint, within the school most white, middle-class boys conform, since proper credentials are necessary to attaining careers. As Greenberg (1977: 201) notes, students "who believe that their future chances depend on school success are likely to conform if they resent the school's attempt to regulate their lives." Within the social setting of the school, then, white, middle-class boys accomplish gender by conforming to school rules and regulations and by dominating student organizations, reflecting a wholehearted obligation to the school and its overall enterprise. White, middle-class boys "accept" school values and therefore the school exercises a prominent and influential restraint on these youth, at least within its own boundaries (Tolson, 1977: 39).

Because masculinity is a behavioral response to the particular conditions and situations in which we participate, white, middle-class boys thus do masculinity within the school in a specific way that reflects their position in the class and race divisions of labor and power. Their white, middle-class position both constrains and enables certain forms of gendered social action, and these boys monitor their action in accord with those constraints and opportunities, thus reproducing simultaneously class, race, and gender relations. Moreover, this particular masculinity is sustained as a type of collective product in a particular social setting—white middle-class schools.

However, because the school is "emasculating" in the fashion discussed earlier, white, middle-class boys who join a youth group act outside the school in ways that help restore those hegemonic masculine ideals discouraged in school. In this process of "doing gender," these boys simultaneously construct age-specific forms of criminality. Youth crime, within the social context of the youth group outside the school, serves as a resource for masculine realization and facilitates (as do such other practices as school athletics) "dominance bonding" among privileged young men (Messner, 1989: 79).

Successful "pranks," "mischief," vandalism, minor thefts, and drinking outside the school validate a boy's "essential nature." Such behaviors reflect an age-specific attempt to reestablish a public masculine identity somewhat diminished in the school, behaviors that are purposely chosen and manipulated for their ability to impress other boys. Moreover, outside the confines of the school, white, middle-lass boys' masculinity is still held accountable, not to school officials, but to other white, middle-class boys. These behavioral forms help a white, middle-class boy to carve out a valued masculine identity by exhibiting those hegemonic masculine ideals the school denies—independence, dominance, daring, and control—to resolve the problem of accountability outside the school, and to establish for himself and others his "essential nature" as a "male." Indeed, most accounts of these forms of youth crime miss the significance of gender: it is young men who are overwhelmingly the perpetrators of these acts (Chesney-Lind and Shelden, 1992: 7-18). Accomplishing gender by engaging in vandalism, "pranks," and "mischief" (as an age-specific resource) incontrovertibly provides a public masculine resolution to the spectacle of self-discipline and emotional restraint in the school.

Thus we see that white, middle-class, youth masculinity is accomplished differently in separate and dissimilar social situations. For white, middle-class boys, the problem is to produce configurations of masculine behavior that can be seen by others as normative. Yet, as the social setting changes, from inside the school to outside in the youth group, so does the conceptualization of what is normative masculine behavior.

Through class appeal for educational credentials, white, middle-class boys are drawn into different masculine construction within the school: they develop an *accommodating masculinity*—a controlled, cooperative, rational gender strategy of action for institutional success. The white, middle-class boy's agenda within the school, then, is simply to become the accomplice to the institutional order, thereby reaping the privileges it offers—access to higher education and a professional career (Connell, 1989: 295-297). In other words, as white, middle-class boys accomplish gender in the school setting, they simultaneously reproduce class and race relations through the same ongoing practices.

Being a man is about developing the essential credentials to obtain a suitable middle-class occupation. However, because the school both creates and undermines hegemonic masculinity, within the company of peers outside the school some white, middle-class boys draw primarily on nonviolent forms of youth crime, thus constructing an *opposition masculinity*—a masculinity based on the very hegemonic masculine ideals the school discourages. In short, white, middle-class boys are forming different types of masculinity that can be assessed and approved in both social settings (inside and outside school) as normal and natural. Through this specific type of youth crime in the peer group, middle-class masculinities are differentiated from one another.

The case of white, middle-class youth demonstrates how we maintain different gendered identities that may be emphasized or avoided, depending upon the social setting. White, middle-class boys construct their gendered actions in relation to how such actions might be interpreted by others (that is, their accountability) in the particular social context in which they occur. White, middle-class boys are doing masculinity differently

because the setting and the available resources change.

School Success, Masculinity, and Youth Crime

Social control theorists argue that youth who develop close bonds to the school are the least likely to engage in youth crime (Hirschi, 1969; Wiatrowski, Griswold, and Roberts, 1981). Yet the considerable amount of youth crime committed by the Saints and the Socs (who were the school "wheels" and high academic achievers) outside the school justifies reasonable concern regarding this argument. Nevertheless, middle-class schools, like schools in other social settings, develop a status system based on academic success. Research has consistently shown that students who fail academically (for whatever reason) and/or who occupy the lowest status positions in school, exhibit the highest rates of youth crime. (see Messerschmidt, 1979 for a review of this research.) Consequently, for white, middle-class boys who are not successful at schoolwork and who do not participate in school sports or extracurricular activities, the school is a frustrating masculine experience as a result of which they are likely to search out other masculine-validating resources.

This view was demonstrated in one study of an upper-middle-class, white neighborhood, described by the authors as an "environmental paradise" that "harbors mansions and millionaires as well as deer and raccoons" (Muchlbauer and Dodder, 1983: 35). The particular neighborhood youth group which called itself "the losers," was composed primarily of boys who did not do well in school and who demonstrated little athletic interest or ability. "The losers" spent considerable time "hanging out" together at the town square, but were not at all fond of interpersonal violence and controlling turf. Rather, they engaged chiefly in acts of vandalism—such as breaking streetlamps, making graffiti, destroying traffic signs, and doing donuts on the lawns of the more affluent members of the community—as well as organizing drinking parties at public beaches and parks. Indeed, the only serious violence committed by "the losers" was the firebombing of the personal automobiles of two representatives of "emasculating" authority: the chief of police and the vice-principal of the school. Thus, the specific types of youth crime engaged in by "the losers" served as a resource for masculine construction when other types of class-specific resources were unappealing and/or unattractive (e.g., academic success).

Although this opposition masculinity outside the school is clearly not the only version of white, middle-class youth masculinity, nor perhaps the most common version, it differs considerably from that of white, working-class youth, especially because of its reduced emphasis on the public display of interpersonal aggression/violence. It follows that we must consider more closely how this type of youthful, white, middle-class, masculine construction and its attendant youth crime differs from that of youthful, white, working-class men.

White, Working-Class Boys

As exemplified by the Roughnecks and the Eses [youth groups studied by other researchers], white, working-class boys engage in such acts as vandalism, truancy, and drinking because, as demonstrated more precisely below, they also experience school authority as an "emasculating" power. Not surprisingly, many of these boys also turn to this age-specific resource for "doing gender" outside the school. And yet, they define their masculinity against the school in a different way than do white middle-class boys, a way that nevertheless leads to an in-school opposition masculinity as well.

"The Lads' and the 'Ear'oles"

Paul Willis's (1977) classic study *Learning to Labour* demonstrates how a group of white, working-class British boys ("the lads") reject both schoolwork and the "ear'oles" (earholes, or other young men who conform to the school rules) because "the lads" perceive office jobs and "bookwork" as "sissy stuff." The lads come to school armed with traditional notions of white, working-class masculinity: the idea that "real men" choose manual, not mental labor. Because of this

particular gendered strategy, schooling is deemed irrelevant to their working-class future and "emasculating" to their conception of masculinity. In other words, schooling is unmanly in a different and broader way for these boys than for the white, middle-class boys discussed above. Accordingly, the lads evolve into an unstructured, counterschool group that carves out a specific masculine space within the school, its overwhelming rules, and unnerving authority.

In resisting the school, the lads construct behavior patterns that set them apart from both the ear'oles and also the school. Because the ear'oles are enthusiastic about schooling and support its rules, they are a major conformist target for the lads. One such practice for opposing the school and the ear'oles is "having a laff," that is, devising techniques to circumvent the controlled environment of the school. . . .

Another activity that distinguished the lads from the ear'oles is fighting. The lads exhibited "a positive joy in fighting, in causing fights through intimidation, in talking about fighting and about the tactics of the whole fight situation" (p. 34). Constructing masculinity around physical aggression, the lads—eschewing academic achievement—draw on an available resource that allows them to distance and differentiate themselves from the nonviolent ear'oles. As Willis (p. 34) points out, "Violence and the judgement of violence is the most basic axis of the 'lads' ascendance over the conformists, almost in the way that knowledge is for teachers." The lads reject and feel superior to the ear'oles; moreover, they construct such practices as having a laff and fighting to demonstrate their perceived masculine eminence.

In this way, then, the lads accomplish gender in a specific relational way by opposing both the school and its conformists. Whereas white, middle-class boys are more likely to oppose school outside its boundaries but conform within school, the social setting for the lads is different. *They are the opposition both inside and outside the school.* Understandably, there is no accommodating masculinity here. Because schooling is conceived as unnecessary to their future while simultaneously encompassing effeminate endeavors, the lads earn symbolic space from the school by engaging in different forms of "pranks" and "mischief" within the school itself. Such behaviors help transcend the "sissyish" quality of the school day while simultaneously distancing the lads from the conformists.

But the lads also draw on forms of physical intimidation and violence to differentiate themselves from the ear'oles and the girls. For the lads, the fight "is the moment when you are fully tested"; it is "disastrous for your informal standing and masculine reputation if you refuse to fight or perform very amateurishly" (p. 35). In fact, physical aggressiveness seems to be an institutionalized feature of the lads' group. As Willis (p. 36) notes, "the physicality of all interactions, the mock pushing and fighting, the showing off in front of girls, the demonstrations of superiority and put-downs of the conformists, all borrow from the grammar of the real fight situation." These activities provide the fodder with which to accomplish their gender and to establish (for the lads) their "essential male nature." They are designed with an eye to gender accountability and resultingly construct inequality among boys by attempting to place the ear'oles masculinity beneath their own within the public context of the school. The lads are constructing an opposition masculinity as a collective practice; notwithstanding, this specific type is significantly different from the white, middle-class in school accommodating masculinity and gains meaning in relation to the masculinity of the ear'oles.

Outside the School

It is not only conformists to the school whom white, working-class youth, like the lads, attempt to subordinate in the process of doing gender. In Western industrialized societies, what have become known as hate crimes—racist and anti-gay violence—are disproportionately committed by groups of white, working-class boys, crimes that can also be understood in the way discussed above (Beirne and Messerschmidt, 1991: 562-563; Comstock, 1991: 72-92).

For some white, working-class boys, their public masculinity is constructed through

hostility to, and rejection of, all aspects of groups that may be considered inferior in a racist and heterosexist society. For example, the ear'oles are considered inferior and subordinate to the lads because of their conformity to, and seeming enjoyment of, effeminate schooling projects. But other groups outside the school are also viewed as inferior by many white, working-class boys. Willis (1977: 48) found that different skin color was enough for the lads to justify an attack on, or intimidation of, racial minorities. Indeed, the meaning of being a "white man" has always hinged on the existence of, for example, a subordinated "black man." Thus, a specific *racial gender* is constructed through the identical practice of racist violence; a social practice that bolsters, within the specific setting of white, working-class youth groups, one's masculine "whiteness" and, therefore, constitutes race and gender simultaneously. White, working-class, youthful masculinity acquires meaning in this particular context through racist violence.

Moreover, for some white, working-class youth, homosexuality is simply unnatural and effeminate sex, and many turn this ideology into physical violence. As one white, working-class youth put it, "My friends and I go 'fag-hunting' around the neighborhood. They should all be killed" (Weissman, 1992: 173). Gay bashing serves as a resource for constructing masculinity in a specific way: physical violence against gay men in front of other young, white, working-class men reaffirms one's commitment to what is for them natural and masculine sex—heterosexuality. In other words, the victim of gay bashing serves, "both physically and symbolically, as a vehicle for the sexual status needs of the offenders in the course of recreational violence" (Harry, 1992: 15). Accordingly, gender is accomplished and normative heterosexuality is reproduced.

White, working-class boys such as the lads construct public masculinities outside the school in other ways as well. As with the Roughnecks and the Eses, the lads also occasionally participate in various forms of theft. Because they want to take part in the youth culture (go to pubs, wear the "right" clothes, date, and so on) shortage of cash becomes "the single biggest pressure, perhaps at any rate after school, in their lives" (Willis, 1977: 39). Through contacts with family and friends, many of the lads acquired part-time, after-school, and summer jobs; in fact, Willis found that it is not uncommon for these youths to work over ten hours a week during the school year. Consequently, "this ability to 'make out' in the 'real world' . . . and to deal with adults nearly on their own terms" is seen by the lads as evidence of their "essential nature" as "males"—a practice that reproduces this specific type of white, working-class masculinity (p. 39). In addition, because of their access to paid employment, the lads' involvement in theft is irregular rather than systematic, providing a little extra pocket money when needed. . . .

In this specific context, then, intermittent theft is a resource that helps construct an "out-of-school," autonomous, independent, and daring opposition masculinity. And with part-time work available as a masculine resource, outside the school these white, working-class youths only sporadically turn to theft as a resource to accomplish gender. Thus, theft not only provides these youth with a resource for doing masculinity in the specific social setting of the group, it also helps construct a gendered line of action in which future gender accountability may be at risk. That is, it contributes to the wherewithal for adequate masculine participation in the youth culture.

Yet while the part-time workplace and youth group are initially seen as superior to the school—a milieu where masculinity as they know it is accepted—these working-class boys eventually find themselves locked into dead-end jobs, making less money than those who did not participate in the group and who conformed to the school. In this way, Willis's books show how white "working-class kids get working-class jobs." The initial context, and ultimate result, of the lads' opposition masculinity in the school was an orientation toward manual labor. Through their specific construction of masculinity, the lads themselves (and, similarly, the Hamilton Park boys) thus reproduced class, race, and gender relations as the structures constituted in those relations constrain and enable their collective social action.

Lower-Working-Class, Racial-Minority Boys

Consider now how this white, working-class opposition masculinity (and the white, middle-class masculinity discussed earlier) differs from youth masculinity of lower-working-class racial minorities who engage in youth crime. Because these youth have no access to paid labor (as have the lads and Hamilton Park boys) and their parents are unable to subsidize their youth culture needs (as are the parents of white, middle-class boys), the youth gang in lower-working-class, racial-minority communities takes on a new and significant meaning inasmuch as it is here where resources are available with which to sustain a masculine identity. For many of these youths (although far from all), life is neither the workplace nor the school; it is the street. . . .

For many lower-working-class, racial-minority boys, the street group has become both a collective solution to their prohibitions and a life-style that sometimes takes the form of street crime. For these youths, then, street crime becomes a "field of possibilities" for transcending class and race domination and an important resource for accomplishing gender.

Opposition in School

Most white, middle-class boys envision a future in mental labor and members of the white, working-class (such as Willis's lads and Sullivan's Hamilton Park youths) realistically anticipate manual-labor positions. Consequently, these youths have resources (and a future) for masculine construction that are unavailable to lower-working-class, racial-minority boys. For marginalized, racial-minority boys, no such occupational future can be realistically anticipated and, accordingly, hegemonic masculinity is severely threatened. Under such conditions, life inside school takes on a significantly different meaning. . . .

Because the school is seen simply as another institutional impediment to a future in hegemonic masculine ways and because they lack the resources of white, middle-class and working-class boys, these young men are more likely to turn to those hegemonic masculine ideals that remain available, such as physical violence.

Physical violence within the school is a resource employed for masculine construction. In situations where class and race structural disadvantage are severe, one's taken-for-granted "essential nature" is more likely to be undermined and threatened; therefore, gender is held more accountable. In short, at the level of personal practice, this translates into a display of physical violence as a specific type of in-school, opposition masculinity. . . .

Thus, for lower-working-class, racial-minority boys in the process of opposing the school, doing masculinity necessitates extra effort; consequently, they are more likely than other boys to accomplish gender within the school by constructing a physically violent opposition masculinity. And in doing so, they turn to available hegemonic masculine ideals with which to construct such masculinity. This physical violence in the school is one practice that differentiates lower-working-class opposition masculinity from the other types discussed earlier.

Opposition Outside School

In addition to opposition within the school, because the school has less significance to these youths than to young men in other social classes, the street group also takes on a distinct and significant meaning in which opposition masculinity outside the school is likewise quite different from that of other youths. Marginalized, racial-minority boys are disproportionately involved in such serious property crimes as robbery and in such publicly displayed forms of group violence as "turf wars" (Steffensmeier and Allen, 1981; Elliott and Huizinga, 1983; Tracy, Wolfgang, and Figlio, 1991). The roots of this violent street crime are found in the disconcerting nature of the school and in the social conditions of poverty, racism, negated future, and power accorded men. Because of these social conditions and their attendant possibilities/constraints, young ghetto men are the most likely to commit certain types of street

crime and thus to construct a different type of opposition masculinity outside the school. . . .

Sullivan and others (Zimring and Zuehl, 1986: Conklin, 1972) have reported that most robberies are committed by a group of young street men. Within this collective setting, robbery is a means of getting money when other resources are unavailable, and is particularly attractive for young boys on the street. Robbery provides a public ceremony of domination and humiliation of others. Because young street boys are denied access to the labor market and are relegated to a social situation (the street group) where gender accountability is augmented, they are more often involved in crimes that entail actual or possible confrontation with others. As such, robbery provides an available resource with which to accomplish gender and, therefore, to construct a specific type of public masculinity—what Katz (1988: 225-236) terms "hardmen," or men who court danger and who, through force of will, subject others to it.

"Doing stickup" is doing masculinity by manufacturing "*an angle of moral superiority* over the intended victim" and, thereby, succeeding "in making a fool of his victim" (pp. 169, 174). . . .

The robbery setting provides the ideal opportunity to construct an "essential" toughness and "maleness"; it provides a means with which to construct that certain type of masculinity—hardman. Within the social context that ghetto and barrio boys find themselves, then, robbery is a rational practice for "doing gender" and for getting money. . . .

Marginalized, racial minority boys—as with white, middle- and working-class boys—produce specific configurations of behavior that can be seen by others within the same immediate social situation as "essentially male." As we have seen, these different masculinities emerge from practices that encompass different resources and that are simultaneously based on different collective trajectories. In this way, then, class and race relations structure the age-specific form of resources used to construct specific opposition masculinities. Young, middle-class, working-class, and lower-working-class men produce unique types of masculinity (situationally accomplished by drawing on different forms of youth crime) by acknowledging an already determined future and inhabiting distinct locations within the social structural divisions of labor and power. Collectively, young men experience their everyday world from a specific position in society and so they construct differently the cultural ideals of hegemonic masculinity.

Opposition masculinities, then, are based on a specific relation to school generated by the interaction of school authority with class, race, and gender dynamics. For white, middle-class boys, a nonviolent opposition masculinity occurs primarily outside school; for white, working-class and lower-working-class, racial-minority boys, specific types of opposition masculinities prevail both inside and outside school. Yet for each group of boys, a sense of masculinity is shaped by their specific relation to the school and by their specific position in the divisions of labor and power. . . .

Reprinted from James W. Messerschmidt, "Masculinities and Crime" in *Masculinities and Crime: Critique and Reconceptualization.* Copyright ©1993 by Rowman and Littlefield Publishers. Reprinted by permission of Rowman and Littlefield Publishers.

Discussion Questions

1. How does the concept of "masculinities" help to revise views of men held by both feminists and traditional criminologists?

2. Why do youths in different class-race locations in society engage in different amounts and types of crime?

3. Why is crime a matter of "doing gender"? Are there other ways to "do gender"?

4. Think back to your days in high school. Can you give any examples of how masculinity was involved in some delinquent act that you witnessed? ✦